TRANSFORMATIONS
in AMERICAN
LEGAL HISTORY

TRANSFORMATIONS in AMERICAN LEGAL HISTORY

Essays in Honor of Professor Morton J. Horwitz

EDITORS:

Daniel W. Hamilton

Alfred L. Brophy

HARVARD LAW SCHOOL
Distributed by
HARVARD UNIVERSITY PRESS
Cambridge, Massachusetts and London, England 2009

Published by
Harvard Law School
1563 Massachusetts Avenue
Cambridge, MA 02138
617-495-3100 (Phone)
http://www.law.harvard.edu

ISBN 978-0-674033-46-7

Publication of this work was made possible by a generous grant from Dean Elena Kagan and Harvard Law School.

Library of Congress Cataloging-in-Publication Data

Transformations in American legal history : essays in honor of professor Morton J. Horwitz / Daniel W. Hamilton and Alfred L. Brophy.
p. cm.
Includes bibliographical references and index.
ISBN 978-0-674-03346-7
1. Law--United States--History. 2. Law--United States--Philosophy--History. 3. Horwitz, Morton J., 1938- I. Horwitz, Morton J., 1938- II. Hamilton, Daniel W. III. Brophy, Alfred L.
KF352.T73 2009
349.73--dc22

2008046136

Contents

Foreword

It's generally agreed that Morton Horwitz's two-volume magnum opus, *The Transformation of American Law,* marked a giant step in the transformation of American legal history scholarship. In setting forth an entirely new understanding of the relationship between law and economic change, Morty's work has sparked countless articles and books responding to his arguments—as if for every page he writes, other scholars have to write ten more. I think it's safe to say that no one in my lifetime has had the impact on legal history that Morty has had—has caused people to think more deeply about how the law has operated and what its causes and consequences have been in our nation's past. Nor has anyone been so successful in getting legal scholars generally to understand legal history as central to their discussions and debates.

What's less well known is that, for all his eminence as a legal historian, this is far from the only realm in which Morty's contributions have been both lasting and profound. Along with transforming legal history scholarship, Morty has transformed the lives of countless law students and younger colleagues, many of whom now enjoy great success in their own academic careers. He's not only an extraordinary scholar but also an extraordinary teacher and mentor. And this other part of Morty's life is what I want to highlight in my contribution to this festschrift. Because on this score, I can speak from personal experience. In fact, I have a story to tell.

Back in the fall of 1983, I was a Harvard Law 1L—as driven, excited, anxious, and determined as any 1L today. I was privileged to be a student in Morty's legendary torts class, which quickly became for me—and for my classmates—the quintessential law school experience. (We fondly referred to him as "Mort the Tort.") As a teacher, Morty was a marvel, a master of hiding the ball. He gave us the maddening—and exhilarating—sense that if we just worked harder, reasoned more acutely, we would find The Solution. And I don't mean the solution to any particular case but to the entire class—if not The Law itself. It's no exaggeration to say that we were pretty obsessed.

Then came grades. And the grade that I received in torts was, shall we say, disappointing. A B-minus actually. Not the grade I'd hoped for or expected. Nor could I say that the grades in my other courses were much better.

I still remember how I felt that day, that sense of real failure, of asking myself where I had gone wrong and wondering what it meant. Then, to my great surprise, I received a note in my student mailbox, a summons from the professor himself, asking that I come see him. I think I will remember that conversation until the day I die. I believed then—and believe now—that it changed my life, that without this meeting, my law school experience and my whole career would have taken an entirely different turn. What he said to me was this: "You are not a B-minus student. You are an A-plus student. We have to figure out what you did wrong and how to change it." I cannot tell you the impact those words had on me. While I don't recall his specific advice, I remember as if it were yesterday the effect of what he said. I thought: "I know I can do better because he just told me so." And so I did.

More than twenty years later, I am still deeply grateful for Morty's helping hand—not only because he inspired me to live up to my potential but also because he taught me what a professor can be. Today, when I teach my own classes, I remember Morty's example, and on occasion I make a point of writing the sort of note that he wrote me to one of my own students. In this way, they too are beneficiaries of Morty's legacy.

The pivotal role Morty played in my own career is entirely in keeping with the role he has played for scores of other students and younger scholars, including a number of rising stars in the academy. Morty single-handedly raised the profile of legal history among American historians, inspiring a generation of scholars—many of them former students—to follow in his footsteps. My colleague Kenneth Mack, one outstanding protégé, recently described his time in Morty's 1990 legal history class as "the most impressive pedagogical and intellectual experience of my entire education." Ken credits Morty's work, and this class in particular, with deeply influencing his own scholarship, noting that his seminal article on rethinking civil rights lawyering took its intellectual structure from what he began to learn there.

Like Ken Mack, I continue to marvel at Morty's rare ability to hold a classroom spellbound—a skill he's honed with thousands of students over the course of more than three decades. Among the words recent students have used to describe him are "the best," "incredible," "brilliantly insightful," "enthusiastic," "wonderful," "engaging," "kind," "funny," "fantastic," "caring." "Morty is God," wrote one. "A golden god," wrote another. "Mort is the strict liability equivalent of a deity who should have a statue in Langdell," claimed a third. (I don't know exactly what this last one means, but it sure sounds impressive.) Morty's popularity as a teacher led to a recent National Public Radio report on a Warren Court class he taught at Harvard College—a report that featured Morty serenading his students with a tune popularized by Frank Sinatra that asks, "What is America to me?" Students spoke of their surprise that the class could be serious, interesting, and fun, all at the same time—a fact that, of course, comes as no surprise to those of us who know Morty.

One of the most impressive things about Morty is that, eminent as he is, he has never lost his taste for spirited debate, wholeheartedly embracing the questions and challenges that come his way. Assistant professor Jed Shugerman, one of this law school's wonderful young faculty members, told me recently how nervous he was at the prospect of meeting with Morty during his Harvard Law School job interviews a few years back. His own work had taken aim at some of the assumptions in the senior professor's work. What a surprise when he was greeted with a broad grin, an enthusiastic handshake, and warm assurances. Morty even had a name for Jed and other young Turks taking on his premises: "You are part of a new school of legal history—a chaos theory school of legal history" is how he described it. The meeting that had caused such anxiety became a fruitful exchange. "He was organizing us into a helpful category," Jed happily recalled to me. "Now that he'd become upper management, he was helping the new kids unionize!"

As a scholar, teacher, and mentor, Morty is one of a kind. Even as he has transformed the field of legal history, he has transformed my life—and those of countless others—in the course of his remarkable career. His vision, talents, and insights continue to bear fruit, and I am truly thankful for his countless gifts, both in the past and to come.

Elena Kagan
Dean and Charles Hamilton Houston Professor of Law
Harvard Law School

Preface

Over the past three decades, Morton Horwitz has transformed the study of American legal history. He came to the field in the early 1970s with a PhD in government (he was a student of Louis Hartz), a Harvard law degree, and a clerkship on the D.C. circuit. Professor Horwitz brought an interest in understanding the functions that law served in society, as did many of the young Harvard Law faculty in those days, when part of the country was breaking free from the old order—from the era of Jim Crow and the stability of postwar America.

When Morty began his study of legal history, it was a field dominated by antiquarian interests and by hagiography. It is entirely understandable that one of his first publications was a review of a work of hagiography of Justice Story.[1] Like historians working in other fields, Morty sought to break free of the consensus view of American history that had dominated in the complacent 1950s. Whereas those working before him had seen Americans all working in the same direction, toward the same goals—like manifest destiny—Morty saw division and asked who benefited from law, and how did they do so. Morty asked, as colleagues like Duncan Kennedy and Roberto Unger did in their fields, what ideological purposes scholarship served. He found that it served to make law and the distribution of power that it supported look neutral and natural. Such studies are commonplace now, but in the early 1970s, they were not so common, and thus they brought fresh insight. Reading Morty's work from that period suggests how the field sizzled as he laid bare the ways that judges remade law to promote economic growth—all the while talking as though what they were doing was foreordained by the common law.

There was excitement as Morty and other faculty at Harvard and around the country remade legal thought, as they exposed the rules that the keepers of power keep their power by (to paraphrase Ralph Ellison's *Invisible Man*), and as they remade legal education at the same time. Morty, for example, was a supporter of clinical legal education as well as the importation of insights from the social sciences into law.

So Morty came to the field with a sense of the possibilities, to use legal history as a field for testing theories about the evolution of law. His first book, *The Transformation of American Legal History, 1780–1860,* appeared in 1977. It paralleled the development of law and economics in its illustration of the multiple ways that judges remade the law to promote economic growth. And while Morty and the then new field of law and economics shared a sense of how the common law evolved, they draw very different lessons from that understanding. Morty's was a project of describing the connections of law to the powerful—and then hoping that such knowledge might lead to a change. He wrote in the wake of the 1960s movement of putting power into the hands of the people and of the national disgust at Watergate. There were real possibilities then, and Morty joined with lots of scholars and activists in seeking out those possibilities. *Transformation* set the framework for debate about the nature of most of American legal history for several decades. Even work that was outside the time period of *Transformation* often deployed its concepts (such as the idea that judges employed an "instrumental conception" of the common law).

In the years after his landmark book, our country and our legal thought moved, for reasons big and small, in different directions. And as our country and our judges steered to the right in the 1980s, Morty's work evolved into intellectual history, analyzing the way intellectuals harnessed legal thought in the century after the Civil War. In his second groundbreaking book, *The Transformation of American Legal History, 1870–1960,* published in 1992, Morty detailed the possibilities of Progressive-era reform and the New Deal, as well as some of the origins of the 1950s sense that law is neutral, a conception that he himself helped to change in the 1970s and beyond. In more recent years, Morty has published other important books, including *The Warren Court and the Pursuit of Justice* and a coedited volume on legal realism, in addition to the foreword to the *Harvard Law Review* and articles and reviews too numerous to mention. He is finishing up a magisterial volume on the Warren Court for the Oliver Wendell Holmes Devise History of the Supreme Court and talking of returning to the Civil War era as well.

It is not just, then, that two of Morty's books are called the *Transformation of American Law.* Morty has transformed the study of American legal history. So when some of us began talking about a festschrift, we knew immediately what it must be called. Because Morty's work is so vibrant and he is so energetic and generous, he seems perpetually young. That is, perhaps, one of the great virtues of spending a life in the academy—you are around students who are exploring ideas for the first time and, thus, you stay young as well.

And as we started to assemble a list of contributors, we realized that a great many legal historians are students of Morty's in one sense or another, and so the list of potential contributors might very well include almost everyone working in legal history—his proponents, his opponents, and all of us who are engaged in the legal and historical debates that Horwitz helped start. Because Morty is so expansive in his intellectual range and so inclusive in discussion with everyone in the field, even those who disagree with him, we needed to establish somewhat arbitrary boundaries for inviting contributions.

We sent out invitations in late 2004 to Morty's colleagues who teach legal history at Harvard Law School, his PhD students (in the history departments at

Harvard and Brandeis and the History of American Civilization Program at Harvard), his SJD students at Harvard Law School, and his AB and JD students at Harvard who went on to take the PhD elsewhere. Already that list was long, and we were gratified with the response. In keeping with Morty's wide-ranging interests and the legendary freedom he accords students to work in areas that interest them, we asked contributors to write something for this volume that relates to their interests (rather than limiting it to responses to Morty's work). As a result, we have essays across an extraordinary spectrum of time and subjects, from the origins of judicial review in colonial America to property rights during the Civil War, to Israeli law in the late twentieth century. Some of the work engages with themes in the first volume of *Transformation,* like Kent's thought and the role of utility in antebellum legislation. Others take off from themes in the second volume of *Transformation,* including legal realism, legal pluralism, and law and technology. Still others take off from Morty's current interest in the Warren Court and Israeli legal history. Finally, others consider the future of legal history.

The papers here illustrate how broad legal history is as a field—and how it is, like law and economics, becoming itself a mode of analysis. For legal history is not just a field; it is a method. And so we have historical studies of civil, criminal, constitutional, and administrative law, quantitative and qualitative studies on topics from moral philosophy to law and economics to law and psychology, and everything in between. Women, minorities, and even conservative white men are all subjects of study. Religious and business leaders, as well as social reformers—the reformer and the conservative alike are within this burgeoning field.

And so as we completed the editing of this festschrift, it became apparent that, indeed, it is impossible to limit the essays to our teacher and friend to a single volume. Hence, we have another volume in the works that will have contributions from Morty's colleagues and his "students," more broadly construed. We are looking forward to that volume, and to many more years of learning from Morty in person and through his work.

NOTE

1. Morton J. Horwitz, "The Conservative Tradition in the Writing of American Legal History," *American Journal of Legal History* 17 (1973): 274–94.

Acknowledgements

When one is compiling a volume celebrating the scholarly life, the writing, and the teaching of a beloved teacher, the community of people to be thanked is even larger than it is for the average book. Of course, we are all bound together by our affection for Morton Horwitz. His scholarship has taught us all so much, and in person he is always warm and inclusive. With his characteristic generosity and openness, Morty has helped shape the scholarship of everyone who contributed to this volume. And, though this is perhaps not so evident in our writing, he has helped shape our teaching as well. There are students all over the country who hear every semester echoes of Morty's lectures and Socratic dialogues in our teaching.

We are particularly thankful for Morty and Pnina Lahav's encouragement of this project and the September 2008 conference in his honor. Dean Elena Kagan of Harvard Law School provided an extraordinarily generous grant that allowed for the publication of this volume, as well as the conference. We are all grateful for both her and the Harvard Law School's support of this project.

Sara Davis at Harvard University Press has been enormously helpful. Sonia Fulop and David Follmer of Lyceum Books have been terrific to work with and have expertly guided this project. The Illinois Legal History Project at the University of Illinois College of Law and the *Harvard Civil Rights–Civil Liberties Law Review* have provided important support and were co-sponsors of the Harvard Law School conference in honor of Morton Horwitz.

We are of course grateful to the authors of the excellent contributions to this volume. All the contributors have provided encouragement and support throughout. Their scholarship and intellectual energy are perhaps the best tribute to the work and career of Morton Horwitz. His scholarship and teaching have provided an important model for us all as we have worked to continue Morty's transformation of American legal history

DWH and ALB

1

Debating the Transformation of American Law: James Kent, Joseph Story, and the Legacy of the Revolution

DANIEL J. HULSEBOSCH

MOST HISTORIANS WOULD SETTLE FOR ONE LANDMARK BOOK. MORTON Horwitz has published two already. The two volumes of *The Transformation of American Law* exist, however, in uneasy relation.[1] To risk the reductionism that Professor Horwitz has always avoided, *Transformation I* was framed within historical materialism and strove to debunk the celebratory narratives of early American legal history. *Transformation II*, on the other hand, mapped onto an intellectual history that takes ideology seriously, and not only as an expression of Gramscian hegemony that dominant interests had to take seriously, too.[2] An interesting counterfactual question is how *Transformation I* would differ if Professor Horwitz had written it in the spirit of *Transformation II*. What would the antebellum judiciary look like if its doctrines were viewed as something other than the expression of a legal profession that, in exchange for a monopoly on commercial dispute resolution, dedicated itself to the expansion of capitalist markets? If we took the legal reasoning of judges in the early Republic as seriously as Professor Horwitz took those of the "old" and "new" conservatives of the late nineteenth century, how would we characterize their decisions?[3] The revision would not alter the outlines of Professor Horwitz's compelling argument about the economic consequences of doctrinal change. But it would at least complicate and humanize a judiciary that, in *Transformation I*, appears largely unitary and nameless.

It might also return early American legal culture to its transatlantic and post-

The author is grateful for comments received at a summer faculty workshop at New York University School of Law, June 2007, and for the support of the School of Law's D'Agostino/Greenberg Research Fund.

Revolutionary context. Professor Horwitz demonstrated that the "Commonwealth" historians who preceded him and examined some of the same issues, such as Oscar and Mary Handlin, Louis Hartz, and Willard Hurst, did not account for the distributional consequences of legal change.[4] Yet both the Commonwealth historians and Professor Horwitz treated the reshaping of American law as a national phenomenon of the early nineteenth century while also describing a model of publicly subsidized economic development that could be applied to other places or times—and even revived in the United States a century later to help legitimize the New Deal. A step toward mediating the tension between exceptionalism and universalism in these narratives is to explore how the experience and memory of the Revolution affected legal reasoning into the nineteenth century.

Most early American lawyers saw history playing out on a stage larger than the nation, but not marching across the entire globe. For decades they wrestled with the meaning, for law, of the Revolution. Internally, the British Empire had left them with a fragmented and pluralist legal order; the reconstitution of authority on the basis of popular sovereignty restructured but did not eliminate that fragmentation. Externally, they still derived most of their legal learning from Europe, especially England. The American constitutions did not specify how the legal systems in the new Union would operate. Their structure, personnel, and doctrine were left primarily to the legal professionals themselves. They had to solve problems of institutional design such as, Which structures worked best? What were the appropriate sources of law? And what literary forms should be used to teach and communicate law?

Seeing early American judges as actors in a fluid, pluralist, and transatlantic legal culture throws a different light on the central theme of *Transformation I*. There, judicial decisions appear to flow from courts that, for the most part, agreed on their primary task: transforming law to subsidize economic development at the expense of agrarian producers. Professor Horwitz acknowledges that a few judges remained committed to agrarian values and dissented from the transformative consensus. Because of the deterministic premise of *Transformation I*, he treats these dissenters as voices from a fading world rather than as worthy opponents of modernization. It is correct, at least, not to treat them with nostalgia, because some of the dissenters objected less to economic transformation than to the reasoning process by which their brethren fostered it. In other words, even judges who supported commercial development disagreed about the limits that legal reasoning placed on those means. Instead of marching in lockstep, early American judges were arranged in constellations defined by region, education, training, and political ideology.[5] Some constellations contained internal disagreement, too. The doctrinal changes that Professor Horwitz characterized as a single transformation reflected a variety of attempts, by many judges, to manage legal diversity among the states and, by some of them, to integrate the Union into the Atlantic world.

This essay does not attempt to chart all the constellations of judges in the early United States.[6] Instead, it explores disagreements between two of its most influential judges, Chancellor James Kent of New York and Justice Joseph Story of the U.S. Supreme Court, to illuminate how even judges committed to the same project—commercial union and international respect—disagreed about such fundamental questions of law as the extent of the federal commerce power, the reach of federal court jurisdiction, and the discretion of criminal juries. These disagreements reflected different understandings of the sources and methods of legal reasoning, as well as diverging assessments of the role of state, local, and popular institutions in American constitutionalism. Both were seeking to define who would administer legal change as the states evolved from a patchwork of British colonies into a federal union.

These historical questions push beyond, or in different directions from, Professor Horwitz's monumental research agenda in *Transformation I*. They reopen the problem of law's role in developing not just the American economy but also its political economy. They also encourage us to view the early United States as a collection of postcolonial provinces rather than as a young nation on an inevitable path toward modernization. From this perspective, the root of all these questions was how early American lawyers and judges made sense of the Revolution's effect on law.

KENT AND STORY IN THE NARRATIVE OF TRANSFORMATION

Chancellor Kent and Justice Story are among the few judges identified by name in *Transformation I* and usually appear as instrumentalist decision makers.[7] The treatment of Kent and Story reveals the strengths and weaknesses of the argument that the judiciary used law to subsidize economic growth: each lines up on both sides of the transformation scorecard, favoring traditional notions of property or contract in some areas, and dynamic conceptions in others. For example, Professor Horwitz views Kent and Story as instrumentalists when they initiated the treatise tradition to generate national commercial law.[8] They were also instrumentalist when permitting tenants to remove fixtures that they had built on their landlords' property, thus providing an incentive for improvement. Kent, on the other hand, was a traditionalist when criticizing the statutory trend allowing a good-faith possessor to recoup the value of his improvements when ousted by the holder of a superior title.[9] On the basis of an 1822 chancery decision, Kent is held up as a lonely defender of the just price theory of consideration in contract law. On the next page, Professor Horwitz highlights *Seixas v. Woods*, a New York case decided two decades earlier, as evidence of the rise of the contrary doctrine of caveat emptor.[10] But Kent wrote one of the seriatim opinions for the majority in *Seixas*. To defend caveat emptor, Kent observed that "the only writer of authority, that calls this doctrine into question, is professor *Woodeson*, in his *Vinerian Lectures*, and he does not cite any judicial decision as the basis of his opinion."[11] Kent believed that caveat emptor was endorsed by overwhelming authority and, therefore, uncontroversial. However, in a hard case of a land sale by a dissolute father, which were the facts in the 1822 case, he refused to enforce an unfair bargain. For Kent, the difference between the two cases turned on something other than the just price theory or economic transformation.[12]

At times in *Transformation I,* Story and Kent appear as transitional figures. One example is their defense of state-chartered monopolies as a means of encouraging investment in public works, a compromise that subsidized development but also hampered competition. This compromise is best memorialized in Justice Story's dissenting opinion in the *Charles River Bridge Case,*[13] in which Chief Justice Roger Taney's majority opinion represented the more dynamic approach to property rights.[14] Another instance is their support of the will theory of contract, in which subjective agreement between contracting parties trumped calculations of equitable exchange. Professor Horwitz argues that early in the century, judges like Kent and Story used the will theory to defeat the just price theory of consideration. Soon, however, they were overtaken by supporters of an objective theory of contract, who rejected the will theory in favor of standardized interpretation of contract terms to facilitate interstate commerce.[15]

Additional evidence of their transitional status comes from their early support of the just compensation principle, which Professor Horwitz argues vaulted a new private conception of property above a traditional public one. However, Kent and Story also awarded consequential damages in eminent domain proceedings, while other instrumentalist judges denied them in an effort to reduce the cost of improvements undertaken by private transportation corporations.[16] Compensation was a liberal principle; some judges believed that awards should not be too liberal. Again, Kent and Story shared a transitional approach to riparian rights, moving crabwise away from natural use and prior appropriation rules toward a reasonable use standard.[17] In these transitional situations, the truly instrumentalist judges were not these elite jurists but instead a group of mostly forgotten state judges who were openly consequentialist.[18] Finally, Professor Horwitz sometimes portrays Kent as simply confused.[19]

Despite the spread of their decisions across the spectrum of transformation, Professor Horwitz is right to treat Kent and Story as partners in the project of economic development. In meetings, correspondence, and mutual citations, they communicated their shared view that the United States ought to have a national commercial law. When President Madison appointed thirty-two-year-old Joseph Story (his third choice) to the Supreme Court in 1811, the forty-eight-year-old James Kent had been on New York's supreme court for thirteen years, and its chief justice for seven years. Three years later Kent became New York's chancellor, the highest judicial officer in the state.[20] The relationship, however, was one of equality and mutual admiration—though never quite friendship. By 1820, Story was praising the New Yorker as "another Hardwicke," the great eighteenth-century English chancellor.[21] This was a tribute to Kent's almost single-handed creation of American equity jurisprudence, which covered a significant amount of commercial law. When he became New York's chancellor in 1814, he published the first regular equity reports in the Union. Story relied heavily on these reports when deciding equity cases on circuit in Massachusetts, which had no chancery court. There, federal equity law was largely Kent's equity law. Kent, in turn, complimented Story, probably the most learned American admiralty judge in the nineteenth century, for writing admiralty decisions like those of John Scott, later Lord Stowell, who was the chief judge of the High Admiralty Court in Britain.[22]

These transatlantic comparisons were full of meaning. Hardwicke and Stowell were, along with Lord Mansfield, the most influential judges in England since the Glorious Revolution. A signal reason for their influence was that their decisions were published and circulated widely across the Atlantic. Kent and Story emulated these judges while also seeking to improve their methods. Kent, for example, remade the judicial opinion into its modern form, carefully sifting through authorities to discover the guiding principles of decision, ranging over the arguments for and against applying those principles to the plaintiff's case, and then concluding with a clear judgment.[23] He also helped shape the doctrinal treatise as a genre. His four-volume *Commentaries on American Law* (1826–30) went through fourteen editions and found its way onto almost every American lawyer's bookshelf in the nineteenth century. Story, in turn, was perhaps the most creative judge of his time and published ten treatises that stretched from constitutional law to promissory notes. For thirty years his hands were all over the publication process of the *United States Reports*, and he drafted congressional legislation specifying the Court's own jurisdiction.[24] Both believed that lawyers and judges played an indispensable role in American constitutionalism, not least as guardians of constitutional interpretation through judicial review, an institution they promoted on the bench and in their books.[25] Both opposed the reduction of suffrage requirements at their respective state constitutional conventions in 1820 and 1821.[26] Both also drew on the law of nations and the Continental civil law to place American law in a cosmopolitan framework.[27] The point of all this writing was not only to resolve individual disputes. It was also to solidify and broadcast principles of American law within and beyond their jurisdictions.

For Professor Horwitz, these projects were all of a piece—a Weberian piece. The new treatises helped transform a static body of law that safeguarded traditional uses of land and protected individuals from commercial exploitation into a modern instrument of capitalism. Their writers sought to "creat[e] uniformity" to help merchants gauge commercial expectations and to "suppress all the centrifugal legal tendencies before they could even be conceived."[28]

Again, much of this account is true. Kent and Story had similar training, admired and learned from each other, and agreed on many principles. They and like-minded judges embraced commerce. In the sociology of the Scottish Enlightenment, which both had learned from British books, commerce was the primary index of civilization.[29] Buying and selling was central to commerce, and they designed doctrines to foster such exchange within and across the states. But commerce was a means to two related ends: political union within the United States, and reintegration of the Union into the Atlantic world.[30]

Broad agreement on political ends, and on the role of private law as a means to attain those ends, did not mean that they agreed about the reach of Congress's commerce power, the extent of federal admiralty jurisdiction, and the law-finding power of criminal juries. These were not just marginal differences. Instead, they revealed fundamental disagreement about the nature of legal reasoning, which in turn depended on their understandings of English legal materials, the relationship between jurisdictions in a pluralist Union, and the degree to which a legal culture should respect popular decision making.

These questions had puzzled Anglo-American legal culture for generations. The failure of the British Empire to resolve them had contributed to the American Revolution. Although the state and federal constitutions provided new blueprints, they did not settle all jurisdictional relationships or interpretive rules. Debates about locating precise boundaries, which began during the ratification of the federal Constitution, only established a modus vivendi (soon called "constitutional law") for interpreting them.[31]

Beneath the enduring problem of competing jurisdictions lay a deeper question that was genuinely new because it was a consequence of the Revolution: What was the appropriate historical context for construing the American constitutions that structured the state and federal legal environments? The constitutions did not answer this question. Despite occasional calls from legal nativists for the indigenization of authority to reflect the popular sovereignty on which the constitutions rested, most lawyers and judges assumed that legal authority would remain transatlantic, especially English. That, at least, is how they behaved. Their educational routines and resources, for example, changed little for at least three decades after the Revolution.[32]

The imperial legacy was, however, various. Story was more eclectic in his use of legal resources, which also made him seem, to Kent, more instrumentalist. He treated the Revolution as a legal as well as political revolution, one that gave talented jurists an opportunity to curate constitutional ideas from whatever time or place suited their understanding of the best interpretation. Kent, on the other hand, believed that most baseline questions had to be answered against the background of English law as understood in the late eighteenth century and as confirmed or changed by the experience of the Revolution. In assessing that experience, he was more willing to refer to the practices of the other institutions and levels of government.

Both Kent and Story were seeking ways to mark out a realm of law separate from the new and dynamic republican politics. They experimented with new and old techniques of legal thinking and expression to develop a mode of reasoning that captured their felt sense that law was not just politics. As in politics, there was disagreement; in contrast with partisan politics, they aspired toward civility, articulation, and persuasion. The medium was part of the message: each tried to persuade the other without criticizing him strongly in print. Frank assessments were kept private.

The clashes between Kent and Story about congressional power, federal court jurisdiction, and the criminal jury are not well known now, and they were not well publicized then. Kent and Story, however, were aware of them. They exchanged their interpretations, respectfully disagreed, and tried to explain why one was right and the other wrong. They also carried their debates into their publications, so that the canon of nineteenth-century law was written intertextually. In his *Commentaries,* Kent criticized some of Story's decisions, and Story answered in his *Commentaries on the Constitution* (1833). Kent then amended his text in later editions to respond to Story's reading of his work.[33] A central issue in the dialogue was the meaning and practice of the rule of law in a new constitutional system based on popular sovereignty.

THE BOUNDARIES OF FEDERALISM: CONCURRENT VERSUS EXCLUSIVE COMMERCE POWER

At first glance, it seems remarkable that Kent and Story disagreed at all about Congress's power to regulate commerce. In their respective *Commentaries*, each emphasized the importance of the federal power to regulate international and interstate commerce. Story described the power as "exclusive"; Kent wrote that it was "plenary and absolute within its acknowledged limits."[34] They disagreed, however, about how much power the states retained to regulate activity within their borders that affected or overlapped with interstate commerce.

Kent, who authored the key opinions in the New York State cases that evolved into *Gibbons v. Ogden*,[35] embraced the flexible standard that the states and Congress had "concurrent" power over activity that might be characterized for some purposes as internal commerce and for others as interstate commerce. Even when praising and citing Kent, Story drew on dicta in *Gibbons* to formulate a more categorical interpretation of exclusive federal power and endorsed the dormant commerce clause. Their different interpretations influenced other judges when they measured state laws against federal commercial statutes (now called the doctrine of preemption) and when they considered whether or not to embrace the dormant commerce power.[36]

Gibbons involved the conflict between a New York State grant of a ferry monopoly on the Hudson River and the Federal Coastal Licensing Act of 1793. In 1824, the Supreme Court held that the state law conflicted with the federal statute. In addition, Chief Justice John Marshall declared in dicta that the federal power to regulate commerce was exclusive.[37] It was conceivable, therefore, that state statutes might transgress federal power even when not preempted by a specific congressional statute. On the other hand, Marshall also admitted that "the line cannot be drawn with sufficient distinctness between the municipal powers of the one, and the commercial powers of the other."[38]

When New Jersey competitors had challenged the monopoly in New York's courts a decade earlier, the state supreme court upheld the charter in *Livingston v. Van Ingen*. Kent, who wrote an opinion in the case, dismissed the claim that the state statute conflicted with the federal commerce power because he saw no conflict with any congressional statute. He invoked the distinction between internal and external regulation, which the North American colonists had used to oppose parliamentary legislation before the Revolution, and defined the commerce clause as relating "to external not to internal commerce and it is confined to the *regulation* of that commerce." He argued that this power was "not . . . susceptible of precise definition" and had to be interpreted flexibly. "It may be difficult to draw an exact line between those regulations which relate to external and those which relate to internal commerce," Kent wrote, "for every regulation of the one will, directly or indirectly, affect the other. To avoid doubts, embarrassment and contention on this complicated question, the general rule of interpretation . . . is extremely salutary. It removes all difficulty, by its simplicity and certainty." Kent's "general rule of interpretation" gave deference to federal power *when* it was exercised. He denied that the power operated independently of legislation. "The states are under no other restrictions than those expressly specified in the constitution," he added, "and such regulations as the national government may, by treaty, and by laws, from time to time, prescribe. Subject to these restrictions, I contend, that the states are at liberty to make their own commercial regulations."[39]

When the Livingston-Fulton ferry group sought to enforce its monopoly with an injunction from Kent's equity court a few years later, the competitors raised the new claim that the charter conflicted with the federal Coastal Licensing Act. Kent dismissed that defense too, concluding that the federal statute was not "incompatible with an exclusive right . . . to navigate steamboats upon the waters of this State" and "never meant to determine the right of property, or the use or enjoyment of it, under the laws of the States." At the least, the "clear manifestation of some constitutional law, or some judicial decision of the supreme power of the Union, acting upon those [state] laws" was necessary before the state courts could "retire from the support and defense of them."[40]

Kent was of course a *state* judge and thus more sympathetic to state regulation than some federal judges. More than jurisdictional loyalty, however, was at work. Kent's reasoning demonstrates that his vision of federalism was more subtle and flexible than Story's. Both agreed that congressional legislation could trump state legislation, but Kent knew that the states and localities undertook most commercial regulation in America, and he supported that regulation. His use of the familiar language of colonial discourse—internal versus external regulation—signaled that he viewed the Constitution as a compromise designed to settle, or work out, the tensions that had split the old empire rather than replace them with a new analytic understanding of interstate commerce.

Related to both this political realism and historical perspective was Kent's adherence to a form of constitutional behaviorism or respect for experiential construction that has lately been cataloged as one mode of "popular constitutionalism." This meant simply that legislative practice helped flesh out the meaning of constitutional powers. "There were members in that legislature [i.e., the state legislature that granted the steamboat monopoly], as well as in all the other departments of the government," Kent recalled,

> who had been deeply concerned in the study of the constitution of the United States, and who were masters of all the critical discussions which had attended the interesting progress of its adoption. Several of them had been members of the state convention, and this was particularly the case with the exalted character, who at that time was chief magistrate of this state, (Mr. Jay,) and who was distinguished, as well in the council of revision, as elsewhere, for the scrupulous care and profound attention with which he examined every question of a constitutional nature.[41]

In addition, New York's judges and governor sat on the Council of Revision, which reviewed all state legislation to see if it conformed to the state or federal constitution, or whether it reflected wise policy.[42] The council—again including John Jay—had reviewed the monopoly grant and not seen a conflict with federal law. This process served as additional evidence that the statute was permissible under any conventional interpretation of the commerce power.[43]

When the Supreme Court reversed the New York courts in *Gibbons* and held that the steamboat monopoly conflicted with the federal licensing statute, Kent accepted the high court's doctrine: a federal statute regulating interstate commerce trumped a state statute regulating the same activity. But the account of the case in his *Commentaries* suggests that he still did not see a conflict between the two statutes. "The only great point on which the Supreme Court of the United States and the courts of New York have differed," Kent concluded, "is in the construction and effect given to a coasting license." They did not disagree "in any general view of the powers of Congress." Finally, Kent maintained that "the Supreme Court expressly waived any inquiry or decision on the point, whether the exercise of the power assumed by the steamboat laws would have been illegal, provided there was no existing regulation of Congress that came in collision with them."[44] Kent still believed that there was no dormant commerce clause. The federal power was large—but only when exercised.[45]

Kent included a lecture entitled "Of the Concurrent Jurisdiction of the State Governments" in his *Commentaries* and cited Story's concurrence in a militia regulation case for the principle that the powers granted to Congress are concurrent with similar state powers, except when the Constitution declares them to be exclusive. Kent then elaborated his understanding of this principle of concurrent powers that were bounded by Congress's preemptive right to regulate exclusively: "The powers granted to Congress were never exclusive of similar powers existing in the states, unless where the Constitution has expressly in terms given an exclusive power to Congress, or the exercise of a like power was prohibited to the states, or there was a direct repugnancy or incompatibility in the exercise of it by the states. This is the same description of the nature of the powers as that given by the Federalist."[46]

Kent never cited or discussed *Gibbons* in this lecture. Instead, he again quoted his own opinion in *Livingston*. " 'Our safe rule of construction and action,' as it was there observed, 'was this, that if any given power was originally vested in this state, if it had not been exclusively ceded to Congress, or if the exercise of it had not been prohibited to the states, we might then go on in the exercise of the power until it came practically in collision with the exercise of some congressional power.' "[47] In his discussion of concurrent powers, Kent presented *Livingston* as correct in principle and did not refer to the dormant commerce clause.

In his own *Commentaries on the Constitution*, Story lauded Kent's analysis of *Gibbons* and the commerce power in the *Commentaries on American Law* as "very able and candid." He added that "I gladly avail myself of this, as well as of all other occasions, to recommend his [i.e., Kent's] learned labours to those, who seek to study the law, or the constitution, with a liberal and enlightened spirit."[48] However, Story's description of the commerce power differed markedly. Whereas Kent wrote of overlapping powers of commercial regulation and the uncertain line between internal and external activity, Story declared simply that the federal power was exclusive. "The reasoning, by which the power given to congress to regulate commerce is maintained to be exclusive, has not been of late seriously controverted," Story wrote, "and it seems to have the cheerful acquiescence of the learned tribunals of a particular state, one of whose acts brought it first under judicial examination," citing Kent's discussion in his *Commentaries*.[49] According to Story, the states had no power to touch the regulation of interstate commerce. They did have the power to regulate "things having connexion with commerce" pursuant to their police powers, such as through health, safety, inspection, ferry, and turnpike laws. But there was a bright line between "police" and interstate commerce: "They are not so much regulations of commerce, as of police; and may truly be said to belong, if at all to commerce, to that which is purely internal."[50]

Story, therefore, marginalized evidence of concurrent state power. The Supreme Court case of *Wilson v. Blackbird Creek Marsh Co.* in 1829 raised the question of whether a state could dam a navigable river within its borders.[51] The court held that it could. Story treated the state power to regulate internal navigable waters as an exception to the rule of exclusivity, and not a violation of the dormant commerce clause.[52] For Kent, on the other hand, *Wilson* was the exception that disproved the rule: when tested, there was no dormant power.[53]

Story held on to the exclusive-and-dormant-power conception of the commerce clause through the next decade. In a case upholding a New York statute that required a ship captain to post bonds for immigrant passengers, Story dissented, finding that a "state cannot make a regulation of commerce, to enforce its health laws, because it is a means withdrawn from its authority. . . . If the power to regulate commerce be exclusive in congress, then there is no difference between an express and an implied prohibition upon the states."[54] The Supreme Court marked out a compromise position by maintaining that the states had concurrent power to regulate at least some sorts of commercial activity—those deemed "local"—with interstate consequences, while Congress retained exclusive control over "national" commerce.[55] Which was which remained unclear—and still does.[56]

In sum, Kent and Story both celebrated commerce as a means of uniting the states and tying them to the larger world. They also endorsed the federal power to regulate commerce. They disagreed, however, about how to interpret this power. Included in this area of disagreement were both the controversial dormant commerce power and the relative inclination to find federal preemption.

FEDERAL ADMIRALTY JURISDICTION: THE BOUNDARIES OF JURYLESS CENTRAL COURTS

Both Kent and Story championed the exclusive admiralty jurisdiction of the federal courts and the international body of law they applied. Admiralty law was at the core of the law of nations, with both wartime and peacetime branches. The former covered privateering; the latter covered civil causes relating to shipping, including in some nations maritime insurance contracts. Early modern England, however, excluded maritime insurance contracts from the admiralty courts. Kent and Story disagreed about whether such cases should be excluded from the federal admiralty courts, too. Once again, their disagreement turned on different historical contexts for interpreting the Constitution.

Justice Story joined the Supreme Court just as the War of 1812 broke out with Britain. The spike in federal prize litigation, combined with his fascination with the origins and extent of admiralty jurisprudence, led Story to become an avid student of prize and maritime law. He also had an antiquarian streak and enjoyed perusing medieval yearbooks and statutes. From these older sources, he learned that English admiralty courts used to have greater subject matter jurisdiction, including over maritime contracts not directly relating to sea voyages. Some of this jurisdiction had been lost as recently as the seventeenth century; it had been taken by common-law judges rather than by statute. Story concluded that admiralty jurisdiction, at least dating from statutes under Richard II in the fourteenth century until Sir Edward Coke restricted the jurisdiction of non-common-law courts in the seventeenth century, had covered contracts made on land that were executed on the sea, including insurance contracts. Maritime subject matter jurisdiction remained capacious in continental Europe. It had also been larger in colonial North America than in England.

In *DeLovio v. Boit*,[57] Story marshaled English legal history, Continental maritime law, and the jurisdiction of colonial vice-admiralty courts to hold that federal admiralty jurisdiction permitted federal courts to hear those insurance cases concurrently with state courts. The advantage of federal admiralty jurisdiction to at least some insurance companies was that it operated without juries. Federal judges, rather than juries, determined the facts and calculated damages. The case also fit into Story's program to expand admiralty jurisdiction in general, including his failed attempt to reach criminal cases.[58] After reviewing piles of medieval and early modern reports, statutes, and commentaries from England, the colonies, and Europe, Story concluded that Anglo-American admiralty courts had once had jurisdiction over maritime contracts and, for convenience at least, should again. Crucially, he declared that contemporary English doctrine denying this jurisdiction to the admiralty courts was no bar. "Whatever may in England be the binding authority of the common law decisions upon this subject," Story concluded, "in the United States we are at liberty to re-examine the doctrines, and to construe the jurisdiction of the admiralty upon enlarged and liberal principles."[59] The upshot was that he thought it constitutional and politically wise to extend federal admiralty jurisdiction to such contracts. But it would be concurrent rather than exclusive jurisdiction. "There can be no possible question," he added in a footnote at the end of his opinion, "that the courts of common law have acquired a concurrent jurisdiction, though, upon the principles of the ancient common law, it is not easy to trace a legitimate origin to it."[60] In sum, Story grudgingly accepted concurrent subject matter jurisdiction and then expanded it to increase the power of the federal courts.

Professor Horwitz interprets Story's decision in *DeLovio* as a boon to insurance companies, which feared jury determinations of verdicts and damages, although he notes that, in practice, the retention of concurrent state court jurisdiction limited the decision's impact.[61] He also links the decision with other attempts to expand federal jurisdiction, such as the famous 1842 case of *Swift v. Tyson*,[62] in which Story held for the Supreme Court that federal courts could refer to the "general commercial law" rather than state law when hearing commercial cases under diversity jurisdiction.[63]

Professor Horwitz does not note that some judges sympathetic to Story's expansive claims criticized *DeLovio* on legal rather than political or economic grounds. Kent, for example, did not oppose broad federal court jurisdiction. On the contrary, he welcomed federal participation in developing common-law doctrine. Where the federal courts had jurisdiction, he wrote in his *Commentaries*, "the common law, under the correction of the Constitution and statute law of the United States, would seem to be a necessary and a safe guide, in all cases, civil and criminal, arising under the exercise of that jurisdiction, and not specially provided for by statute." The common law provided a safe "guide" to decision making and was not a license for "dangerous discretion," nor did it permit judges to "roam at large in the trackless field of their imaginations."[64] The Judiciary Act of 1789 directed federal courts to apply the law of the states where they sat. In the fifth edition of his *Commentaries*, Kent cited Story's decision in *Swift v. Tyson* as a salutary rule: the act "only extended to the statutes and permanent local usages of a state," not to "contracts, or other instruments of a commercial nature."[65]

However, Kent had long thought that Story's opinion in *DeLovio* exhibited poor reasoning in two respects. First, it conflicted with the Court's own interpretation of the meaning of "exclusive jurisdiction" in Article III's grant of the judicial power in the federal Constitution. Second, it dismissed two hundred years of common-law development, which by the time of the American Revolution had restricted admiralty court jurisdiction within England, if not in the colonies.

Kent devoted several pages to criticizing Story's reasoning in *DeLovio* in the first edition of his *Commentaries*. He buffered his criticism of any judge with respect, a technique he learned from reading the decisions of English judges.[66] Kent therefore praised the Massachusetts Circuit Court's "great ability and research," and his published criticism (which never mentioned Story by name) was muted. He also recapitulated the court's reasoning and historical references, as if to allow the reader to come to her own conclusion. On the merits, Kent noted that Article III of the Constitution extends the judicial power to "*all cases* of admiralty and maritime jurisdiction."[67] Story's opinion, however, stated that federal admiralty jurisdiction over maritime contracts would be concurrent with, rather than exclusive of, the jurisdiction of state courts. Kent, on the other hand, believed that "all cases" meant just that: all cases classified as admiralty had to be tried in federal court.

If Story was right, all maritime contracts "must be tried in the admiralty by a single judge, to the exclusion of the trial by jury, and the state courts would be devested, at one stroke, of a vast field of commercial jurisdiction."[68] It was not within Congress's power to enlarge admiralty jurisdiction beyond "what was understood and intended when the constitution was adopted, because it would be depriving the suitor of the right of trial by jury, which is secured to him by the constitution in suits at common law" in the "saving to suitors" clause.[69] Similarly, Kent objected to the trend toward prosecuting violations of federal navigation and impost laws in admiralty court, where there were no juries. He conceded that the colonial vice-admiralty courts had prosecuted such cases. He also reminded his readers that this jurisdiction was a source of protest on the eve of the Revolution.[70] All these gambits contradicted the "active practice under the English jurisprudence when the constitution was made." Instead, they followed practices prior to the time that "admiralty had been invaded and partly subdued by the bold and free spirit of the courts of common law, armed with the protecting genius and masculine vigour of the trial by jury."[71] English legal history and colonial resistance had left Kent suspicious of expansive admiralty jurisdiction.

Finally, the New York Supreme Court had always heard maritime contract cases. Kent wrote many opinions in those cases, devoted over two hundred pages to the subject in his *Commentaries*, and took extensive notes on the leading Continental treatise on maritime insurance law.[72] He was confident that, in this area as in others, expert opinions like his own would operate as persuasive authority in all the states courts. Here, at least, federal jurisdiction was unnecessary.

Kent's analysis of *DeLovio* nettled Story. In his *Commentaries on the Constitution*, Story defended his interpretation and suggested that Kent's reasoning was itself "founded in a mistake." Prize jurisdiction in the federal courts was exclusive because in England it was vested exclusively in the English admiralty courts. "But," Story added, "in cases, where the jurisdiction of the courts of common law and the admiralty are concurrent, (as in cases of possessory suits, mariners, wages, and marine torts,) there is nothing in the constitution, necessarily leading to the conclusion, that the jurisdiction was intended to be exclusive; and there is as little ground, upon general reasoning, to contend for it."[73] It was true that state and federal courts had concurrent jurisdiction already over possessory, marine tort, and mariners' wage suits. The difference in *DeLovio* was that common-law courts by the eighteenth century had *exclusive* jurisdiction over marine contracts, including insurance contracts. Story challenged contemporary English doctrine on that exclusivity while at the same time accepting the contemporary distinction between prize cases (exclusive) and, say, mariners' wage cases (concurrent).

Kent pointed out in the third edition of his *Commentaries*, published three years after Story's treatise on the Constitution, that Story's logic conflicted with the Supreme Court's opinion—Story's opinion—in *Martin v. Hunter's Lessee* in 1816.[74] Responding directly to Story's charge that he had been "mistaken," Kent reminded the reader that Story had interpreted "all cases" in Article III as an imperative that gave the federal courts exclusive jurisdiction; it was concurrent only when the phrase "all cases" was omitted.[75] Kent agreed with Story's opinion in *Hunter* that state courts could exercise concurrent jurisdiction "only . . . in those cases where, previous to the constitution, state tribunals possessed jurisdiction independent of national authority."[76] The issue joined on the question of where marine insurance contracts fell in the distribution of jurisdiction between the two courts: was it exclusively in the common-law courts (Kent's interpretation, following contemporary English law), exclusively in admiralty courts (English medieval practice), or concurrent (Story's interpretation in *DeLovio*)? For Story, the interpretation of Article III depended on a combination of the best comparative legal wisdom as he understood it and "public convenience."[77] For Kent, English jurisdictional law in the eighteenth century was the correct context for interpreting Article III.

Story's use of history was the second failure of legal reasoning in *DeLovio*. Kent praised Story's understanding of the historical conflict between the common-law and admiralty courts, and he was persuaded by Story's "exposition of the ancient cases" that "Lord Coke was mistaken, in his attempt to confine the ancient jurisdiction [i.e., territorial jurisdiction] of the admiralty to the high seas, and to exclude it from the narrow tide waters, and from ports and havens."[78] Neither would Kent have disagreed with the general proposition that American courts could reevaluate English precedent in light of local needs and circumstances. Kent was less persuaded by the argument that medieval admiralty courts had subject matter jurisdiction over all maritime questions. The key disagreement, however, was whether, as Story claimed, "public convenience," "the enlightened reason of the civil law," and "the customs and usages of the maritime nations" were enough to sustain his interpretation of the Constitution.[79] His historical investigation demonstrated only that admiralty jurisdiction had changed over time. It could not answer the question of whether the Supreme Court should interpret the Constitution according to medieval or early modern understandings of maritime jurisdiction—or by some other standard.

For Kent, the baseline for interpreting the historical meaning of key constitutional terms lay in late eighteenth-century England. He had no desire to return to medieval English law. If Story accepted the medieval bounds of admiralty jurisdiction, he would also have to accept other incidents of that era and forgo later improvements. On the flyleaf in his personal copy of the report containing *DeLovio*, Kent asked:

> But Quere: did not the Constitution of US. mean by *admiralty & maritime jurisdiction*, that which was *then settled* as such in the English Jurisprudence. Did they mean to go back to the *Gothic Ages* for the Jurisdiction then existing? When the Constitution says *Trial by Jury* shall be preserved, & their verdicts not re-examined than according to the rules of the com. law, did they mean the com. law before *Lord Coke's* day when no new Trial could be awarded, & the Jury were carried from County to County in Carts? When the Constitution said Cases in *Equity* should be included in the judicial Power, did it not mean Equity as improved & settled *since* the time of Lord Coke? Why should one paragraph of the Constitution be construed by old usage & another by the new? To embrace *Policies* [i.e., insurance policies] in admiralty & maritime Jurisdiction, deprives the Insurer of *Trial by Jury*, & is trying to recover conquered ground.[80]

If Story wanted the extensive admiralty court jurisdiction of the era before Coke, he would have to do without recent innovations like the new trial, by which a judge could overturn a civil jury verdict and command a new trial under stern instructions. Losing the new trial was, of course, a stiff price that neither Story nor Kent would have paid.[81] Kent's point was that American judges could not rummage through English legal history to find their preferred institutions and rules. They had discretion, but not the freedom that Story claimed.

In his first edition, Kent implied that the Supreme Court might overturn *DeLovio* just as it had Story's contemporaneous circuit court decision claiming non-statutory jurisdiction over maritime crimes.[82] Kent recorded in later editions that some federal courts had embraced *DeLovio* while others had rejected it. In his fifth edition, published in 1844, Kent pleaded that it was "high time" for the Supreme Court to resolve the circuit split. It finally did so after the Civil War, when it embraced Story's construction.[83]

Perhaps this sharp disagreement is why Story considered the third volume of the *Commentaries*, which surveyed commercial, law, to be superior to the first two volumes, most of which covered jurisdiction and status categories. Whether it was because the subject matter was "commercial & general Law, which have been your favorite Studies, or whether that you are grown more anxious for public favour, I know not," Story wrote to Kent upon receiving the third volume, "but I cannot but think, that the present volume has more of your self thrown into it; in learning; in spirit; in judicial sagacity, than either of the former volumes, excellent as they were."[84] Eight years later, when Story received Kent's gift of the third edition of his *Commentaries*, he further marked out the terms of respectful disagreement:

> Even where you have come across some of my own views, I see the diligence, with which you have examined the topics, & the vast force, as well as the unsullied candour, with which you point out your own opinions. If I am not quite convinced, that my own notions in these cases are erroneous, I perceive, that there is very strong reasons for maintaining the opposite opinions. Nay; I rejoice at the difference, because it makes me feel the full value of an independent search into the great elements of judicial truth. Your work must forever remain the true Standard for all future American Text Writers.[85]

Kent never accepted Story's willingness to resort to "public convenience" when interpreting the Constitution. That was too instrumental. For his part, Story might never have shaken his early and modest estimation of Kent. "On the whole, if he be not a very great man," Story concluded in 1807, "I am satisfied that he is not humble in his acquirements."[86] It was as if Story believed that his description of another New York lawyer, reputedly the best litigator in the state, fit Kent too: "He wants specific greatness, original and striking energy, and a bold superiority to the mere reasoning of authorities. He would apply settled principles with great precision, but it may be doubtful if he could create elementary ones."[87]

These evaluations revealed more about Story's self-conception than about their putative subjects: a great judge knew when to set aside old principles and make new ones. His creative powers reached their height whenever he got near a jury.

THE LAW-FINDING DISCRETION OF CRIMINAL JURIES: MARKING THE BOUNDARIES OF JUDICIAL POWER

The jury offers a good example of how Kent and Story shared general principles but differed about how to derive and apply them. Both sought to curb the power of civil juries. They did so by developing a clear law-fact distinction, delivering strong instructions, and granting post-verdict remedies. Both also agreed that U.S. judges should interpret the constitutional rights to jury trials in the Sixth and Seventh Amendments against the backdrop of English practice. They disagreed, however, on the historical boundaries of that practice.

In 1812, Story argued that the common-law jury guaranteed in the Seventh Amendment ought to be defined by the historical meaning of jury in England. The case involved a civil suit brought by the federal government against a Massachusetts merchant who was accused of violating the Embargo Act, which forbade exports to Britain. The trial jury held for the defendant. The U.S. district attorney wanted to retry the case on appeal because Massachusetts law permitted the retrial of facts on appeal. The question was whether congressional statutes that gave the federal courts appellate jurisdiction in admiralty and equity cases also gave them appellate jurisdiction in common-law cases, or whether that review was still limited to writs of error. Story construed the statutes to mean the latter because the guarantee of the jury trial was to be interpreted against English common law rather than Massachusetts law. "Beyond all question," Story held, "the common law here alluded to [i.e., in the Seventh Amendment] is not the common law of any individual state, (for it probably differs in all), but it is the common law of England, the grand reservoir of all our jurisprudence. It cannot be necessary for me to expound the grounds of this opinion, because they must be obvious to every person acquainted with the history of the law."[88] The point was to prevent a new trial of the peculiar New England variety, at the losing party's demand rather than at the judge's discretion, and force Story's circuit court to sit through another jury trial. Story used the English jury as the measuring stick to mitigate the problem of procedural diversity among the states. The answer had not been "obvious" during the ratification period. Indeed, the question had bred an early discussion about legal federalism.[89] And to which era of "the history of law" was Story referring? The Supreme Court now assumes that his "historical test" referred to the late eighteenth century, but his reasoning left this unclear.[90] Story's ambiguity on this point was the gist of Kent's criticism of *DeLovio*.

Elsewhere Story engaged in a more controversial historical interpretation of the jury. In *United States v. Battiste*,[91] a circuit court case in1835, Story instructed jurors in a criminal case that even under a general plea of not guilty, they could only determine facts, not law. Story conceded that every general issue mixed fact and law, but he maintained that the definition of law was for the judge, and fact for the jury. He therefore admitted that the jury had the practical power of nullification ("the physical power to disregard the law, as laid down to them by the Court") while questioning the constitutionality of that power. "I hold it the most sacred constitutional right of every party accused of crime, that the jury should respond as to the facts, and the Court as to the law," he instructed the jury. "It is the duty of the Court to instruct the jury as to the law; and it is the duty of the jury to follow the law, as laid down by the Court."[92] Story also included this charge in his published opinion.

The instruction cut against a venerable strand of common-law thought, especially prominent during the Revolutionary era, that a jury was the voice of the community and, in particular, that juries had the power to interpret criminal statutes under the general issue.[93] Although a jury's power to interpret civil law was less clear historically, and its practical power to do so was in decline, the law-finding prerogative of criminal juries was upheld in several, though not all, of the American states.[94]

The different understandings of Kent and Story reflected that regional diversity. Story's opinion shocked Kent. "I was quite confounded," he noted in his copy of the Massachusetts Circuit Court reports,

> when I read the monstrous heretical doctrine in the charge to a Jury at pa. 243. My judicial opinion against such a Doctrine is to be seen in *Croswell's Case* in *3 Johnson's* Cases, in the Appendix. If the Jury have nothing to do with *the law* on the plea of not guilty on Trials in capital cases, if whether the accused did the Act traiterously or feloniously, Be not a proper question for the Jury, then I think the boasted Trial by Jury evaporates in Smoke, & our English & American Ancestors were in gross Error in asserting with such vehemence the right to *Trial by Jury* as the Safety & Glory of the common law. *Actus non facil rerum nisi meus sit rea*, & whether the mind be or be not in fault is a question that a jury can decide better & safer than a learned & technical Judge. When the law says that the Jury may lawfully take on themselves the whole Issue, it means that they may do it *rightfully* & *morally rightfully*, for it would be monstrous, & destructive of all Principles & Integrity, for the law to tell the Jury that they may *lawfully* judge both law & fact in criminal Cases, on the Plea of not guilty, & yet that if they do it, they *break the moral law*. Such a solecism & inconsistency cannot be well founded. The Doctrine that the Jury have a *right* in *every Cause* to judge of law & fact [under] the general Issue in criminal Cases, has had the Sanction of ages & the higher legislative declaratory Authority.[95]

Again, Kent and Story both sought to restrict the power of the civil jury. But Kent defended an interpretation of the criminal jury's power that had played a role in the Revolution and persisted into the partisan seditious libel trials in the early Republic, including the famous *Croswell* case, in which a jury refused to convict a Federalist editor of libeling President Jefferson.[96] Kent continued to see the criminal jury as a bulwark against oppressive government. It is also possible that he held the criminal jury in esteem because he wanted to contrast it to the more flexible civil jury, whose power had been curtailed in both England and the United States. It was almost as if inroads against the civil jury had to be compensated for by a stern defense of the criminal jury. In addition, criminal law never interested Kent the way civil law did. He barely discussed criminal law in his *Commentaries*. Criminal law remained state or local law, and within it the jury retained much power. The criminal jury was powerful in England, too, at the end of the eighteenth century, which was Kent's historical baseline. Innovations there and in the states came from legislatures rather than the bench.

Story, on the other hand, sat on a federal court and dealt with a limited number of federal crimes. In particular, he supported the cessation and criminalization of the slave trade. The statute at issue in *Battiste* made it a capital crime to carry slaves on the high seas.[97] The U.S. attorney charged a crew member of a vessel that had transported slaves along the African coast from one Portuguese colony in Africa to another, rather than across the Atlantic. Although Story supported criminalization of the trade, he did not believe that Congress intended to penalize the intra-imperial transportation of slavery as severely as it did the international slave trade. The key was the intent of the defendant: was it to "impress" on someone or "continue" the condition of slavery in the future, which would require "some title or interest in or power over" slaves? Or "merely" to transport them? "It seems to me impossible to believe," he instructed the jury, "that congress could have intended to punish capitally, as a piracy, such an act as the mere transportation of slaves from one port to another of the same country. It would confound all moral distinctions in regard to crimes. It would punish an act involving not the slightest moral turpitude, in the same manner, as it would punish the hardened atrocity, inhumanity, and horrible iniquities attending the slave trade on the coast of Africa."[98] In addition, he informed the jury that there was a federal noncapital statute that penalized the "mere transportation" of slaves on the seas. In essence, Story directed the jury to find the defendant not guilty and signaled to the prosecutor that he should charge the defendant under the noncapital statute. That is what happened. The jury found the defendant not guilty, and apparently after being charged under the other statute, he pleaded guilty to a noncapital offense.

In *Battiste*, Story attempted to reconceptualize a classic instance of jury nullification as something more ambiguous: judge-instructed acquittal paired with judge-directed recharging. He put heavy hands on the two discretionary end points of the criminal process: the prosecutor's charge and the jury's verdict. If not heresy, as Kent charged, it was definitely heterodox.

CONCLUSION

Both Chancellor Kent and Justice Story favored a strong central government, fostered commerce through legal doctrine, and sought to contribute to a transatlantic legal culture. They disagreed, however, about such fundamental questions as the extent of the federal commerce power, the reach of federal admiralty jurisdiction, and the discretion of the criminal jury. These disagreements do not disprove Professor Horwitz's claim in *Transformation* I that American lawyers used law to assist economic development so much as illuminate the variety of institutional forms and modes of legal reasoning that were in play in the early Republic. There were changes, but they were not inevitable, and there was no single transformation—much like the legal world of the late nineteenth century that Professor Horwitz analyzed in *Transformation II.*

Disagreements between these two like-minded jurists reflected different approaches to interpreting the English legal legacy as well as their different roles in the constitutional system. Their visions of the rule of law in a pluralistic republic kept diverging throughout their acquaintance. From the beginning, Chancellor Kent was a state judge and a more devoted student of contemporary English law. He came of age during the Revolution and Constitution-making period, gained office through Federalist patronage, and idolized his friend Alexander Hamilton, whom he saw as a consummate lawyer and the ablest proponent of an independent judiciary. He never accepted partisan politics as an unqualified good, but late in life he fit comfortably within the Whig Party. Story, on the other hand, began his life as a Republican, albeit a New England Republican, but by the end of his life was deeply suspicious of representative government.[99] In those later years, he too began to invoke Hamilton, but it was a different and more extremist Hamilton than Kent's old friend.

Kent witnessed Story's trajectory and took notes on it. In the winter of 1835, Story visited Kent's office in New York City, as he often did when visiting New York. On this day Story was melancholy and anxious about the nation's future. He began by telling Kent that he was planning to write one treatise a year for a dozen years. So far, he had completed three. The point, evidently, was to rein in state judges, whom he did not trust because they were increasingly elected rather than appointed on the basis of merit. Under President Jackson, Story told Kent, all government was infected by partisan elections. He had come to appreciate the skepticism that Aristotle, Cicero, and Burke had about democracy. "In a French Translation of Aristotle on Politics," Kent noted in his copy of Story's *Commentaries on the Constitutions*, Story had "found that *Aristotle* treated of representative Government of the People, & said it could not do & never could do, because the People never could be brought for any length of time to choose the most wise & virtuous men to govern them. Whoever reads Cicero *De Republica* would see the Evils of democracy as they are & always will be." Finally, Story invoked

Hamilton as "the greatest & wisest man of this Country." He, like the others in Story's pantheon, was skeptical of elected governments. "He saw fifty Years ahead, & what he saw then is *fact now*."[100]

What Hamilton saw, according to Story, was the hopelessness of representative government. Story reported to Kent that

> all sensible men at Washington in private Conversation admit that the Government is deplorably weak, factious & corrupt. That every thing is sinking down into despotism under the disguise of a democratic Government. He [i.e., Story] says the Sup. Court is sinking, & so is the Judicial in every State. We began with first rate men for judicial Trusts, & we have now got down to the third rate. In 25 years there will not be a Judge in the US. who will not be made elective, & for short Periods, & on slender Salaries. Our Constitutions were all framed for Man *as he should be*, not for Man *as he is* & *ever will be*. . . . Indeed the case of this Country & the cause of popular representative Government are conducive to Liberty & Justice & Wisdom, is as Hamilton suspected & rather believed it to be, a mere *ignii fatuis* or dream of the Imagination.[101]

Story started as a Republican and became a reactionary. Kent, who had opposed populist politics his entire life, took Jacksonian democracy in stride. He also enjoyed political struggle, while Story saw it as evidence of decay. They had long disagreed about the virtue of local political and legal institutions. By 1835, they also disagreed about the viability of representative government. Although Kent did not trust all local juries, state judges, and legislators, his experience in New York taught him to trust at least *some* of them.

These differences were about more than the jurisdictional boundaries of three central institutions of the constitutional system. Beneath them lay a disagreement about the nature of legal reasoning and the means of distinguishing law from politics—themes that are central to all of Professor Horwitz's work. Both judges were cosmopolitan when they celebrated the best English judges, the law of nations, and Continental civil law. When it came to marking the baselines of American constitutionalism, however, Kent focused on the experience of the American founding generation: the words they used, the imperial and revolutionary context of those words, and the definitions available in contemporary English common law. Story, on the other hand, was attracted to elementary principles wherever and whenever they could be found. The legal eclecticism that marked their shared project of developing a national commercial law extended for Story into basic legal and constitutional reasoning. For him, independence was an opportunity to remake legal culture rather than just an historical event that marked its boundaries. In their letters and treatises, Kent and Story continued till they died in the 1840s to debate the legal transformation wrought by the Revolution. Not least because they embedded their arguments in the canon of American legal literature, that debate lives on today.

NOTES

1. Morton J. Horwitz, *The Transformation of American Law, 1780–1860* (Cambridge, Mass.: Harvard University Press, 1977); Morton J. Horwitz, *The Transformation of American Law, 1870–1960: The Crisis of Legal Orthodoxy* (New York: Oxford University Press, 1992). See also Eben Moglen, "The Transformation of Morton Horwitz," *Columbia Law Review* 93 (1993): 1042–60. (arguing that "the richness and complexity of his arguments [in *Transformation II*] so far exceeds that of the his first volume as to justify his faith in the newer styles of discourse").

2. See, e.g., Horwitz, *Transformation II,* 10. See also Robert Gordon, "Critical Legal Histories," *Stanford Law Review* 36 (1984): 57–125.

3. Professor Horwitz discusses the conflict between "old" and "new" conservatism in his analysis of corporate theory in *Transformation II,* 65–107.

4. See Oscar Handlin and Mary Flug Handlin, *Commonwealth: A Study of the Role of Government in the American Economy, Massachusetts, 1774–1861* (Cambridge, Mass.: Belknap Press of Harvard University Press, 1969); Louis Hartz, *Economic Policy and Democratic Thought: Pennsylvania* (Cambridge, Mass.: Harvard University Press, 1948); J. Willard Hurst, *Law and the Conditions of Freedom in the Nineteenth-Century United States* (Madison: University of Wisconsin Press, 1956).

5. For regional differences in early nineteenth-century American law, see Alfred L. Brophy, "Reason and Sentiment: The Moral Worlds and Modes of Reasoning of Antebellum Jurists," *Boston University Law Review* 80 (1999): 1161–213; Peter Karsten, *Heart versus Head: Judge-Made Law in Nineteenth-Century America* (Chapel Hill: University of North Carolina Press, 1996); Renée L. Lerner, "American Judges, English Judges, and the Power to Comment on Evidence" (unpublished manuscript, 2007).

6. For a preliminary sketch, see Daniel J. Hulsebosch, "Writs to Rights: The Transformation of the Anglo-American Common Law in the Age of Revolution" (unpublished manuscript, 2005).

7. Other judges who appear a few times each are Chief Justices Isaac Parker and Lemuel Shaw of Massachusetts, Chief Justice Roger Taney of the Supreme Court, and Lord Mansfield and Sir William Blackstone of England.

8. Horwitz, *Transformation I,* 144, 257–58.

9. Ibid., 55–56, 61–62, 132.

10. Horwitz, *Transformation II,* 179–80.

11. *Seixas v. Woods,* 2 Cai. R. 48, 55 (N.Y. Sup. Ct. 1804) (Kent, J.).

12. Compare *Seixas* with *Seymour v. Delancey,* 6 Johns. Ch. 222, 232, 233, 234 (N.Y. Ch. 1822), rev'd, 3 Cow. 445 (N.Y. Ct. Err. 1824) (reversing, 14–10). New York's High Court of Errors, with fourteen state senators voting to reverse, reversed Kent's equitable decree two years later.

13. *Charles River Bridge v. Warren Bridge,* 36 U.S. (11 Pet.) 420 (1837).

14. Horwitz, *Transformation I,* 117–18, 123–28, 138–39. Kent sympathized with Story's position in *Charles River Bridge*: "though the Constitution . . . does not reach such state laws, they remain, nevertheless, to be in most cases strongly condemned, as being contrary to right and justice." James Kent, *Commentaries on American Law,* 4th ed. (1840), 1:*456 n. (b).

15. Horwitz, *Transformation I,* 183–85, 196–201.

16. Ibid., 73.

17. Ibid., 39, 43.

18. See, e.g., *Carson v. Blazer,* 2 Binn. 475 (Pa. 1810), which altered the legal meaning of

"navigable," thereby taking property rights away from riparian holders without compensation and giving them to canal companies. See also Daniel J. Hulsebosch, "Writs to Rights: 'Navigability' and the Transformation of the Common Law in the Nineteenth Century," *Cardozo Law Review* 23 (2002): 1090–92.

19. Kent's treatment of riparian rights and the doctrine of ancient lights could justify that conclusion. Horwitz, *Transformation I,* 43, 281 n. 63; Hulsebosch, "Writs to Rights," 1084–85.

20. For Story's biography, see R. Kent Newmyer, *Supreme Court Justice Joseph Story: Statesman of the Old Republic* (Chapel Hill: University of North Carolina Press, 1985). For Kent, see John T. Horton, *James Kent: A Study in Conservatism, 1763–1847* (New York: D. Appleton-Century, 1939).

21. Johnson to James Kent, Nov. 16, 1816; Moss Kent to James Kent, Feb. 1, 1817 (reporting that Story called Kent "another *Hartwick*" [sic]), James Kent Papers, Library of Congress (microfilm, New York University School of Law).

22. James Kent, back flyleaf notes to volume 1 of Charles Sumner's *Reports of Cases Argued and Determined in the Circuit Court of the United States for the First Circuit* (Boston: Hilliard, Gray, 1836) (complimenting a Story opinion that was "full of the classical Taste of Lord Stowell"), James Kent Library, Rare Book Collection, Columbia Law School, New York.

23. See Daniel J. Hulsebosch, "Crafting Authority: James Kent and the Development of American Law" (unpublished manuscript, 2008).

24. Story's involvement in the reporting process is evident in his correspondence with Henry Wheaton, who was the Court's reporter from 1816 to 1827. See Henry Wheaton Papers, Pierpont Morgan Library. For his legislative drafting, see "The Project of Extending Admiralty Jurisdiction over the Lakes and Rivers of the United States," *Western Law Journal* 2 (1845): 563–67; *Jackson v. The Magnolia,* 61 U.S. (20 How.) 296, 342 (1857) (Campbell, J., dissenting) (stating that Justice Story "has the reputation of being the author of the act"). See also Joseph Story, *Life and Letters of Joseph Story,* ed. William W. Story (1851), 1:293–303, 315, 437.

25. Kent wrote an early and influential defense of judicial review in the 1790s, exercised it while on the bench, and argued that it was the defining feature of American constitutionalism in his *Commentaries*. James Kent, *An Introductory Lecture to a Course of Law Lectures, delivered November 17, 1794* (1794), 9–12; Kent, *Commentaries,* 1st ed. (1826), 1:22–26. Story also exercised judicial review, and in his *Commentaries on the Constitution* his chapter on judicial review was entitled "Who Is Final Judge or Interpreter in Constitutional Controversies." Joseph Story, *Commentaries on the Constitution* (1833), 1:344. Neither ever held that a federal statute was unconstitutional.

26. See Merrill D. Peterson, ed., *Democracy, Liberty and Property: The State Constitutional Conventions of the 1820's* (Indianapolis, Ind.: Bobbs-Merrill, 1966), 77–91, 190–97.

27. Both cited civilian sources often, especially in private law cases, although the depth of their learning is in doubt. See Alan Watson, "Chancellor Kent's Use of Foreign Law," in *The Reception of Continental Ideas in the Common Law World, 1820–1920,* ed. Mathias Riemann, 45–62 (Berlin: Duncker & Humblot, 1993); Alan Watson, *Joseph Story and the Comity of Errors: A Case Study in Conflict of Laws* (Athens: University of Georgia Press, 1992).

28. Horwitz, *Transformation I,* 249.

29. Kent's general library, for example, contains central works of the Scottish Enlightenment, including those by David Hume, Lord Kames, William Robertson, and Adam Smith. James Kent Library, Rare Book and Manuscripts Library, Columbia University, New York. On the stadial

theory in law, see Peter Stein, *Legal Evolution: The Story of an Idea* (New York: Cambridge University Press, 1980), 23–50.

30. On this theme in early American law, see Daniel J. Hulsebosch, *Constituting Empire: New York and the Transformation of Constitutionalism in the Atlantic World, 1664–1830* (Chapel Hill: University of North Carolina Press, 2005), 274–302; Daniel J. Hulsebosch, "A Discrete and Cosmopolitan Minority: The Loyalists, the Atlantic World, and the Origins of Judicial Review," *Chicago-Kent Law Review* 81 (2006): 825–66. Kent's dedication to this project pervades his *Commentaries*. For example, in a striking departure from the model of William Blackstone's *Commentaries on the Laws of England* (1765–69), Kent devoted a quarter of his work to personal property and commercial law (five times more than Blackstone), placed it before the law of real property, and stated that the learning surrounding the former "overshadows" that of the latter. Kent, *Commentaries*, 1st ed., 1:278. See also Joseph Dorfman, "Chancellor Kent and the Developing American Economy," *Columbia Law Review* 61 (1961): 1290–317. For his part, five of Story's ten treatises were on commercial law topics.

31. Hulsebosch, *Constituting Empire,* 237–58.

32. See Steve Sheppard, ed., *The History of Legal Education in the United States: Commentaries and Primary Sources,* 2 vols. (Pasadena, Calif.: Salem Press, 1999).

33. Professor Horwitz long ago observed that "I cannot emphasize enough how valuable I have found working with consecutive editions of treatises," especially Kent's *Commentaries*. Morton J. Horwitz, "Sources of American Legal History: Treatise Literature," *Law Library Journal* 49 (1976): 460–61.

34. Story, *Commentaries on the Constitution*, vol. 1, sec. 1063; Kent, *Commentaries,* 1st ed. (1826), 1:409–10.

35. 22 U.S. (9 Wheat.) 1 (1824).

36. For recent analysis of the history of dormant commerce clause jurisprudence, see Norman R. Williams, "*Gibbons*," *New York University Law Review* 79 (2004): 1398–499.

37. *Gibbons,* 22 U.S. at 227, 236 (reasoning that the commerce power "must be exclusive; it can reside but in one potentate; and hence this power carries with it the whole subject, leaving nothing for the State to act upon").

38. Id. at 238.

39. *Livingston v. Van Ingen,* 9 Johns. 507, 578 (N.Y. Sup. Ct. 1812) (Kent, C. J.).

40. *Ogden v. Gibbons,* 4 Johns. Ch. 150, 156–57, 158–59 (N.Y. Ch. 1819).

41. *Livingston,* 9 Johns. at 573. See also *Ogden,* 4 Johns. Ch. at 158–59 (observing that the charters were granted after the federal statute "and it must have struck every one, at the time, to have been perfectly idle to pass such laws . . . if a coasting license . . . was sufficient to interpose and annihilate the force and authority of those laws"). On political construction of the Constitution, see Keith E. Whittington, *Constitutional Construction: Divided Powers and Constitutional Meaning* (Cambridge, Mass.: Harvard University Press, 2001); Larry D. Kramer, *The People Themselves: Popular Constitutionalism and Judicial Review* (New York: Oxford University Press, 2004).

42. See Alfred B. Street, *The Council of Revision of the State of New York: Its History, a History of the Courts with Which Its Members Were Connected; Biographical Sketches of Its Members; and Its Votes* (Albany, N.Y.: W. Gould, 1859).

43. *Livingston,* 9 Johns. at 573 (Kent, C. J.). See also id. at 564 (Thompson, J); id. at 507 (arguments of T. A. Emmett for the holders of the monopoly charter).

44. Kent, *Commentaries,* 1st ed., 1:411.

45. See ibid., 1:406. Kent added in his second edition, published after the decision in *Wilson v. Blackbird Creek Marsh Co.*, that "the state legislation in [*Wilson*] was not considered as repugnant to the power in Congress in its *dormant* state to regulate commerce." Kent, *Commentaries,* 2d ed. (1832), 1:439. This statement of principle replaced two paragraphs in the first edition that defended *Livingston* directly. Kent, *Commentaries,* 1st ed. (1826), 1:411–13.

46. Kent, *Commentaries,* 1st ed. (1826), 1:365–66. His examples of exclusive powers included those to control forts, coin money, naturalize immigrants, and create admiralty jurisdiction.

47. Ibid., 1:367 (quoting *Livingston v. Van Ingen*; footnote omitted).

48. Story, *Commentaries on the Constitution,* vol. 2, sec. 1067, n. 40.

49. Ibid., sec. 1067.

50. Ibid., sec. 1068

51. 27 U.S. (2 Pet.) 245 (1829).

52. Story, *Commentaries on the Constitution,* vol. 2, sec. 1069.

53. Kent, *Commentaries,* 2d ed. (1832), 1:439.

54. See *Mayor of New York v. Miln,* 36 U.S. (11 Pet.) 102, 153, 156–57 (1837) (upholding New York City's alien registration ordinance) (Story, J., dissenting).

55. *Cooley v. Bd. of Wardens,* 53 U.S. (12 How.) 299 (1851) (upholding state pilotage law as local rather than national).

56. The local-national distinction gave way to new formulations in the twentieth century turning on direct versus indirect effects and, more recently, the degree of discrimination against interstate commerce. For recent analysis, see Norman R. Williams, "Why Congress May Not 'Overrule' the Dormant Commerce Clause," *UCLA Law Review* 53 (2005): 153–238.

57. 2 Gall. Rep. 398, 7 Fed. Cas. 418 (C.C.D. Mass. 1815). See also *Hale v. Washington Ins. Co.,* 2 Story 176, 11 Fed. Cas. 189 (C.C. Mass. 1842) (Story, J.) (stating belief that Chief Justice John Marshall and Justice Bushrod Washington agreed with Story's interpretation).

58. See *United States v. Coolidge,* 14 U.S. (1 Wheat.) 415 (1816); *United States v. Bevans,* 16 U.S. (3 Wheat.) 336 (1818).

59. 7 Fed. Cas. at 441.

60. Id. at 444 n. 48.

61. Cf. William A. Fletcher, "The General Common Law and Section 34 of the Judiciary Act of 1789," *Harvard Law Review* 97 (1984): 1562–75 (arguing that state and federal courts drew on the same sources in marine insurance cases and coordinated their decisions).

62. 41 U.S. (16 Pet.) 1 (1842).

63. Horwitz, *Transformation I,* 250–52.

64. Kent, *Commentaries,* 1st ed. (1826), 1:320–21.

65. Kent, *Commentaries,* 5th ed. (1844), 1:*341. Kent made clear in the last edition he prepared that he also agreed with the specific commercial doctrine that Story applied in *Swift*: a holder in due course could enforce commercial paper against the maker even if the paper had originally been obtained by fraud if the holder took it as security for a preexisting debt. Kent had endorsed that rule as a judge, but it had been cast in doubt after he left the bench. Kent, *Commentaries,* 6th ed. (1848), 3:*81 n. (b).

66. "The great Civility & profound Respect with which they treat each other's opinions is proof of the polished Manner & high Cultivation of the English Jurists." James Kent, back flyleaf

notes to volume 2 of John Schoales and Thomas Lefroy's *Reports of Cases Argued and Determined in the High Court of Chancery, in Ireland, during the Time of Lord Redesdale* (1806), James Kent Library, Rare Book Collection, Columbia Law School, New York.

67. Kent, *Commentaries,* 1st ed. (1826), 1:351.

68. Ibid., 1:346–47.

69. Ibid., 1:347.

70. Ibid., 1:351.

71. Ibid., 1:352.

72. Ibid., 3:93–306; Charles E. Shields III, "Chancellor Kent's Abridgment of Emerigon's Maritime Insurance," *Penn State Law Review 108*(2004): 1123–247. See also Fletcher, "The General Common Law," 1566–68 (noting that "the marine insurance law developed in New York was particularly influential").

73. Story, *Commentaries on the Constitution,* vol. 3, sec. 1666 n. 3.

74. 14 U.S. (1 Wheat.) 304 (1816).

75. Kent, *Commentaries,* 3d ed. (1836), 1:*377 n. (c) (citing *Martin*).

76. Kent, *Commentaries,* 1st ed. (1826), 1:372. However, in the third edition Kent wrote that he was "happy to be taught . . . that the state courts have all the concurrent cognizance, which they had originally in 1787 over maritime contracts, and that this concurrent jurisdiction does not depend . . . on the pleasure of congress." Kent, *Commentaries,* 3d ed. (1836), 1:*377 n. (c).

77. 7 Fed. Cas. at 441.

78. Kent, *Commentaries,* 1st ed. (1826), 1:344.

79. Ibid., 1:345–46.

80. Kent, back flyleaf notes to volume 2 of John Gallison's, *Reports of Cases Argued and Determined in the Circuit Court of the United States for the First Circuit* (1817), James Kent Library, Rare Book Collection, Columbia Law School, New York.

81. On the development of the new trial in the United States, see Renée B. Lettow, "New Trial for Verdict against Law: Judge-Jury Relations in Early Nineteenth-Century America," *Notre Dame Law Review* 71 (1996): 505–53; William E. Nelson, *The Americanization of the Common Law: The Impact of Legal Change on Massachusetts Society, 1760–1830* (Cambridge, Mass.: Harvard University Press, 1975), 165–71.

82. Kent, *Commentaries,* 1st ed. (1826), 1:346. Kent was referring to *United States v. Coolidge,* 14 U.S. 415 (1816), in which the Supreme Court praised Justice Story's "learned and elaborate opinion" on circuit but rejected it, citing *United States v. Hudson and Goodwin,* 11 U.S. 32 (1812), for the proposition that the federal courts had no jurisdiction over common-law crimes. *Coolidge,* 14 U.S. at 416.

83. Kent, *Commentaries,* 5th ed. (1844), 1:*371 n. (a).; *New England Mut. Ins. Co. v. Dunham,* 78 U.S. (11 Wall.) 1 (1871).

84. Joseph Story to James Kent, Nov. 25, 1828, fragment pasted into back flyleaf of volume 3 of the first edition of Kent's *Commentaries,* James Kent Library, Rare Book Collection, Columbia Law School, New York.

85. Joseph Story to James Kent, Aug. 13, 1836, pasted to back flyleaf of volume 1 of the third edition of Kent's *Commentaries,* James Kent Library, Rare Book Collection, Columbia Law School, New York.

86. Joseph Story to Samuel P. P. Fay, May 18, 1807, in *Life and Letters of Joseph Story,* 1:145.

87. Joseph Story to Samuel P. P. Fay, June 21, 1807, in *Life and Letters of Joseph Story,* 1:156.

88. *United States v. Wonson,* 28 Fed. Cas. 745 (C.C.D. Mass. 1812).

89. On the ratification debates over the meaning of the jury and federal appellate jurisdiction, see Hulsebosch, *Constituting Empire,* 243–46.

90. See, e.g., *Gasperini v. Center for the Humanities,* 518 U.S. 415, 452 (U.S. 1996) (citing *Wonson*).

91. 2 Sumn. 240, 24 Fed. Cas. 1042 (C.C.D. Mass., 1835).

92. 24 Fed. Cas. at 1043.

93. See Mark DeWolfe Howe, "Juries as Judges of Criminal Law," *Harvard Law Review* 52 (1939): 582–616.

94. Cf. Stanton D. Krauss, "An Inquiry into the Right of Criminal Juries to Determine the Law in Colonial America," *Journal of Criminal Law & Criminology* 89 (1998): 111–215. On the decline of civil juries, see James Oldham, *Trial by Jury: The Seventh Amendment and Anglo-American Special Juries* (New York: New York University Press, 2006), 25–44.

95. Kent, flyleaf note pasted to volume 2 of Charles Sumner's *Reports of Cases Argued and Determined in the Circuit Court of the United States for the First Circuit* (1837), James Kent Library, Rare Book Collection, Columbia Law School, New York.

96. *People v. Croswell,* 3 Johns. Cas. 337 (N.Y. 1804).

97. The statute declared that any U.S. citizen owning or on an American ship who "shall land from any such ship or vessel, and on any foreign shore, seize any negro or mulatto, not held to service or labor by the laws of either of the states or territories [of the United States], with intent to make such negro or mulatto a slave; or shall decoy, or forcibly bring or carry, or shall receive such negro or mulatto, on board of any such ship or vessel, with intent as aforesaid, such citizen or person shall be adjudged a pirate, and on conviction thereof, &c. shall suffer death." *Battiste,* 24 Fed. Cas. at 1044.

98. Id. at 1045.

99. See Newmyer, *Joseph Story,* 389–92.

100. Kent, notes, March 18, 1835, pasted into the back flyleaf of volume 1 of Joseph Story's *Commentaries on the Constitution,* James Kent Library, Rare Book Collection, Columbia Law School, New York.

101. Ibid.

2

Colonial Constitutionalism and Constitutional Law

MARY SARAH BILDER

THE TRANSFORMATION OF CONSTITUTIONAL LAW—THE SHIFT FROM A colonial constitutional culture to an explicit written constitution—is apparent yet elusive. Thirty years ago, Morton Horwitz's pathbreaking *The Transformation of American Law, 1780–1860* insisted on a transformation in "private law (tort, contract, property, commercial law)" from the colonial period.[1] Horwitz's focus on private law diminished interest in the development of early American constitutionalism. As Stanley Katz wrote in 1984, "Constitutional history is certainly not dead, but it is not flourishing and its significance for colonial history is not altogether obvious."[2] Twenty years later, constitutional history and, in particular, colonial constitutional history have once again begun to flourish. Interest in colonial constitutionalism appears in recent work by Lauren Benton, Alexander Haskell, Daniel Hulsebosch, Alison LaCroix, David Konig, Bernadette Meyler, Bill Offut, Ellen Pearson, Carla Pestana, Claire Priest, Richard Ross, George Van Cleve, Craig Yirush, and myself, among others.[3] Yet there remain significant questions about the transformation of colonial constitutionalism to American Constitutional law. This essay argues that this larger transformation was less the result of the admittedly important invention of a written constitution than of three less apparent transformations.

Constitutionalism is rampant with transformations: the well-discussed shift from the "little *c*" to "big *C*" constitution,[4] the creation of Constitutional law as "a new substantive legal genre,"[5] and the invention of judicial review.[6] Since Sir

My thanks to Alfred Brophy, Paul Halliday, Bernie Meyler, Catherine Patterson, Sharon O'Connor, and participants at the American Society for Legal History (2006) and at the Cornell Law School's Law and Humanities Colloquium (2007) for comments; to David Warrington and Whitney Bagnall for manuscript assistance; to Natasha Hsieh and Andrew Golden for assistance in checking footnotes; and to Morton Horwitz and Dan Hulsebosch, with whom I first read Joseph Smith.

Henry Maine penned his famous transformation of law—from status to contract—legal historians have been enamored of transformations.[7] For Maine, as for the legally trained who followed him, transformations that can be summed up in a phrase—a holding—have been particularly appealing. Daniel Hulsebosch offers a fine example of such a succinct transformation in his argument of a shift from a preconstitutional focus on jurisdiction to a constitutional focus on jurisprudence.[8]

American constitutionalism has been enamored of one particular transformation: the shift from the organic, unwritten British constitution to the defined and enumerated written American Constitution. This appealing orthographical shift, however, is our own creation. The word "constitution"—in the small *c* sense—often appeared in the pre-1776 period with a capital *C*. Bolingbroke's oft-quoted description appeared as: "By *Constitution* We mean . . . that Assemblage of Laws, Institutions, and Customs, derived from certain fix'd Principles of Reason . . . that compose the general System, according to which the Community hath agreed to be governed."[9] Conversely, writers continued to refer to the written federal Constitution with a small *c* into the early nineteenth century.[10] Indeed, *The Federalist Papers* originally appeared with "constitution" consistently spelled with a small *c*.[11] In modernizing the spelling of "Constitution," reprints of constitutional-era texts actually alter our understandings of those texts.[12]

Another seemingly apparent transformation is the rise of Constitutional law, what Hulsebosch has perceptively referred to as the "shift from common-law constitutionalism" to the "genre of constitutional law."[13] Hulsebosch points to Chief Justice John Jay's 1794 reference in *Chisholm v. Georgia* to the "free course of Constitutional law and Government" as a statement that "readers" would understand.[14] But precisely when and what did readers understand? In late eighteenth- and early nineteenth-century constitutional works, Constitutional law (where the phrase is a proper noun) can be hard to distinguish from constitutional law (where "constitutional" is an adjective describing a type of law).[15] The phrase curiously does not seem to appear again in the printed Supreme Court reports until the arguments of counsel in *Ogden v. Saunders* in 1827.[16] By the 1840s, publication of St. George Tucker's lectures marks more widespread use of the phrase.[17] Yet only in 1862 does Joel Parker adopt the single title *Constitutional Law* for a pamphlet.[18] Only after the Civil War do treatises entitled simply "Constitutional Law" begin to appear.[19] The recognition of a distinct body of law arising from the Constitution and conforming to certain interpretive traditions appears to postdate by some years the Constitution itself.

This difficulty in identifying the transformation occurs with constitutionalism. Used by late nineteenth-century political scientists, constitutionalism became influential when Andrew McLaughlin and Charles McIlwain concluded that it lay at the heart of liberal democracy.[20] In 1932, McLaughlin's *The Foundations of American Constitutionalism* traced "certain essential principles" of limited government—covenants, representation, social compact, judicial review, and federalism—in the pre-Revolutionary period.[21] In 1940, McIlwain's *Constitutionalism: Ancient and Modern* looked back further and declared that "in all its successive phases, constitutionalism has one essential quality: it is a legal limitation on government."[22] In England, the "essential principles . . . were no less constitutional" because they were "unwritten."[23] Others sought greater precision respecting the type of limitation. Robert Schuyler suggested that the word "unconstitutional" underwent a shift from meaning "the act in question was contrary to established usage and convention" to signifying that "it was illegal or void."[24] Walton H. Hamilton's definition emphasized written-ness: "'Constitutionalism' is the name given to the trust which men repose in the power of words engrossed on parchment to keep a government in order."[25] Constitutionalism itself thus fluctuates between a narrative of continuity in legal limitations on government and a narrative of discontinuity in the specific written form of limitations.

How do we talk about the continuities and discontinuities created as the world in which British constitutionalism involved legal limitations not written in one document gave way to an American constitutionalism in which a single written document was the limitation? The sense of an abrupt transformation in the 1780s is reinforced because no word describes the constitutional state of affairs before the Revolution. Reserving constitutionalism for the period of written constitutions overemphasizes the post-1776 or perhaps even post-1787 American construction of constitutionalism. Focusing on common law, the ancient constitution, and the British constitution overemphasizes the English (as opposed to colonial) construction of constitutionalism.[26]

Considering the transformation of colonial constitutional law to postcolonial constitutional law solves these problems. Harold Hazeltine, John Reid, and Jonathan Bush have described the relationship between American colonial law and England and Great Britain as a constitutional law.[27] As Eliga Gould and other Atlantic historians have demonstrated, situating American colonial constitutionalism within the context of the empire allows for a periodization in which the Revolution and the Constitution mark neither beginning nor ending points.[28] The term "colonial constitutional law" traditionally describes the law that governed other colonies within the British Empire.[29] The legal opinions of Crown law officers on colonial questions were called *Cases and Opinions on Constitutional Law*; American colonial opinions were included in an earlier collection of similar materials.[30] The term is not wholly anachronistic. Eighteenth-century contemporaries perceived a distinct constitution of the colonies. Thomas Pownall referred to the "constitution of the colonies" and their "constitutional dependence" on Britain.[31] James Abercromby discussed the "different Constitutions of the Colonies."[32] Pre-Revolutionary Pennsylvanians characterized people as "Friends to our present Constitution."[33] Stephen Hopkins referred to Rhode Island judges as "under a peculiar constitution."[34] We might thus consider colonial constitutional law.

This essay reconsiders the transformation to Constitutions, Constitutionalism, and Constitutional law. In arguing for a "historicist interpretation of constitutional law," H. Jefferson Powell writes, "Constitutional law is thoroughly historical, dependent throughout on the contingencies of time and political circumstances, and . . . a coherent tradition of argument."[35] As a coherent tradition, the transformation of constitutional law does not map neatly onto the 1776–90 period. A first essential transformation in constitutionalism occurred long before 1776 when seventeenth-century colonists created a new conception of the written and published charter as the location of authority and liberties. A second essential transformation occurred only after 1790 when appeals in judicial cases began to be publicly reported in print, thereby creating a stable and analyzable body of law. A third essential transformation occurred in 1787—but with implications not immediately appreciated. Privy Council review of colonial legislation ended and no similar review took its place, thus leaving the judiciary the sole arbiter of constitutional law. These three transformations created modern American constitutionalism—a law two centuries in the making.

PATENTS TO CHARTERS

The shift from charter to constitution is central to American constitutional scholarship. The early reliance on charters is often cited as creating a culture that would favor written constitutions, either because of the written nature of the charter's liberties or because of the habit of defending charters against the Crown.[36] As recent scholarship demonstrates, however, English boroughs had a long, robust history of dealing with and defending charters and chartered liberties.[37] Nevertheless, English law does not produce a culture favoring written constitutions—indeed, arguably the contrary. In part, a written constitution may be the product of the necessity of declaring independence. If the English boroughs had attempted to declare independence, perhaps they too would have founded their authority solely on a written document. The American colonists nonetheless were extremely taken with written documents as sources of and limitations on government.

Admittedly, prior to 1776, colonists dealt with charters; after 1776, they wrote constitutions. Yet this verbal transformation may not signify the immediate transformation that we assume. Within the larger British Empire, this same semantic shift occurred over two centuries. Charters governed the early seventeenth-century Canadian settlements for Nova Scotia (1621),[38] Avalon (Newfoundland) (1623), and Ruperts Bay (the Hudson's Bay Company) (1670).[39] Charters remained relevant even as Americans turned toward constitutions. New South Wales's Charter of Justice (1787) established court jurisdictions prior to settlement governance.[40] The East India Company continued to govern India pursuant to a charter into the nineteenth century.[41] By the mid-nineteenth century, however, the empire began to shift toward constitutions. Unlike American documents, these took the form of either a letters patent[42] or a parliamentary act such as the British North America Act (1867), often referred to as the Constitution Act, and the Commonwealth of Australia Constitution Act (1900).[43] The latter was a British statute passed by Parliament after colonial convention, ratified, and approved by Parliament with amendments.[44] Rhetorically the empire moved from charter to constitution—but substantively, the shift in authority was more transitional and subtle. The word "constitution" continues to carry a different meaning than it does for Americans.[45]

The shift from charters to constitutions on the American side may also be misleading. A more crucial shift occurred a century earlier when the colonists developed a conception of the charter as opposed to a patent. Colonists did not initially refer to what we think of as a charter as a charter; rather they called it a patent, short for "letters patent." The leading scholar on the Connecticut charter, Albert Bates, concluded that the words "charter" and "patent" were used interchangeably."[46] This conclusion seems true with respect to English charters. Those in corporate towns referred to their incorporating letters patent as letters patent and charters.[47] Among trading companies, a similar use of the word "charter" seems to have been common. The published charter of the Worshipful Company of Shipwrights (c. 1612) included numerous self-references to charter.[48] Historians have made their own distinctions. Historians have conventionally used "patent" to refer to a document with less authority (for example, the Peirce Patent or the Plymouth Patent) and reserved "charter" for the document that appears to be the genealogical ancestor of a state constitution. But this distinction is modern.

What was the historic difference between a patent and a charter? Throughout the medieval period, although both were issued under the Great Seal, charters were grants in perpetuity, in Latin, attested to by witnesses, addressed to a particular group of officials and nobility, and recorded in the Charter Rolls. "Letters patent" referred to a more general type of document, so called because they were literally open letters as opposed to letters close and were addressed "to all whom these presents come." After 1516, grants creating rights in perpetuity under seal—charters—were created by letters patent and copied into the patent rolls.[49] Yet "patent" retained a separate meaning as a more temporary grant of privileges, a point reinforced by the debate over monopolies and the Statute of Monopolies (1623).[50] Some commentators suggest that the charter/patent distinction continued in the color of the wax seal used: green for charters, yellow (or red) for temporary patents.[51]

Neither charters nor patents were designed as physical documents to facilitate precise public knowledge. The documents were written on multiple sheepskin parchments, with a depiction of the king, an ornate border, and rows of tiny writing not organized in paragraphs. "Publishing" the charter in the sense of enabling the community to learn of its provisions had been a problem since the thirteenth century, when in theory Henry III had ordered the Great Charter of John read aloud.[52] Relatively few English patents or charters were published in print before the seventeenth century.

Colonists in the early decades of the seventeenth century used the word "patent" over "charter." In Virginia, "patent" appears where we would expect the word "charter."[53] The *Orders and Constitutions* (1619–20) listed books to be held by the secretary. The first book was to include copies of the "Kings Letters Patents to the Companie"; the third book was to include "Patents, Charters, and Indentures" granted by the company.[54] While the company itself gave a "greate Charter or commission of privileges, orders, and laws" delegating its authority to the local political corporation in 1618, it continually referred to the document from the Crown as a "patent."[55] The distinction is particularly noticeable in the 1620s when the Crown attempted to call in the Virginia charter. The Crown described the document as a charter; the settlers responded by talking about the letters patent.[56] Moreover, the Virginia Company made no effort to publish these documents in print.[57]

A similar preference for the word "patent" appears in Massachusetts Bay. One of the few references to a charter appears in the Form of Government adopted by the company in April 1629. The company declared that "his Majesty's said charter" had given "power and authority" sufficient to "settle and establish an absolute government."[58] Yet the famous vote transferring the government of the company to Massachusetts Bay referred only to the "Patent."[59] John Winthrop later wrote with respect to the clause: "For it being the manner for such as procured Patents for Virginia, Bermudas and the Weste Indies, to keep the chiefe Government in the hands of the Company residinge in England . . . this clause is inserted in this and all other Patents."[60] Throughout the 1630s, the word "patent" repeatedly appeared. In *New Englands Prospect* in 1634, William Wood discussed "our Patent for the Massachusetts Bay."[61] In 1641, Emmanuel Downing wrote to Hugh Peter about the quo warranto action, noting it had been brought "against our Patentees, thinking to damme our patent."[62] As in Virginia, no publication of the charter or patent appeared. John Cotton's *An Abstract; or,* The Lawes of New England in 1641, Nathaniel Ward's manuscript version of the *Body of Liberties* in 1641, and the *Laws and Liberties* of 1648 did not contain references to a charter. Perhaps governing authorities operating outside the authority conveyed had little to gain from publication.[63] Charter as both word and substantive document lacked positive political resonance—the colonists had patents.

Public declarations of the political connotation of the word "charter" as an important document providing authority occur with the Maryland proprietary. Unlike the Massachusetts Bay and Virginia "charters," the 1632 letters patent given to Lord Baltimore was in Latin, although without the elaborate greetings of the medieval charters. It described itself as "hanc presentem Chartam nostrum"—"this our present Charter."[64] (Note the unusual *ch* spelling of the Latin word for charter.) Contemporaries referred to it as a charter. In 1635, *A Relation of Maryland* included the "Charter to the Lord *Baltemore*, translated into English."[65] Although a few English trading company charters had been printed, the Maryland charter appears to have been the first printed colonial charter.[66] In 1637, Lord Baltimore referred to the document as a charter.[67] A proprietor given expansive powers under the charter may have gained from a publicly available document.

With the English Revolution, the political meanings of "charter" and "patent" begin to separate. On one hand, in Massachusetts, John Winthrop clings to patent. In his "Discourse on Arbitrary Government" of 1644, he focused on the legal authority conveyed by the "foundation" of the government under the "patent."[68] Winthrop closely read the clauses to establish a "Regulated" government.[69] The Committee of Deputies in response argued that they found no "suche distinction in the Patent."[70] Yet elsewhere that same year, the word "charter" seems to be growing in appeal. Parliament gave Rhode Island a "free Charter of Civil Incorporation and Government." (Historians interestingly call it a patent.) By 1649, Plymouth leader Edward Winslow called the Plymouth patent "their Charter."[71] In 1654, a Barbados "charter" was published. The growing appeal of the word "charter" to convey authority was evident in the fact that the document was not a charter but Articles of Agreement (1651) between Crown commissioners and Lord Willoughby of Parnham.[72] Conversely, by the 1650s, a pamphlet attacking Baltimore's grant refused to call it a charter, referring throughout to "the illegality of his patent."[73]

The return of royal power did not dampen the growing preference for charters. Like the letters patent for Massachusetts and the one for Virginia, the 1662 and 1663 Connecticut and Rhode Island documents did not call themselves charters. Indeed, in England, John Winthrop described the Connecticut document as a patent while conducting negotiations.[74] Yet colonists had no doubt they had gained charters. In 1662, the General Assembly read the "Patent or Charter" and thereafter referred to it continually as a charter.[75] Rhode Island law provided for the transfer at the governor's death of "the Charter, with his Majesty's letters, and such other papers as concern the colony."[76] By 1665, Massachusetts Bay residents similarly began to refer to the 1629 document as a charter.[77] The 1663 charter for Carolina and the 1681 charter to William Penn followed earlier proprietary charters explicitly describing themselves as charters. Indeed, the charter to William Penn for Pennsylvania apparently has a green seal, as sometimes has been suggested to signify charter.[78] This transformation from patent to charter may explain why the letters patent from the Crown to Virginia in 1676, which declared itself to be a letters patent, is rarely referred to as a charter, despite John Burk's titling the document such in his publication.[79]

By choosing "charter" over "patent," the mid-seventeenth-century colonists absorbed into their documents the connotation of an ancient grant of liberties, customs, and self-governance. Catherine Patterson notes that in English boroughs, the charter had "an almost sacred quality in the minds of most citizens."[80] Sacredness was hard to establish in a recently granted document, never mind one often replaced and possibly revoked. Indeed, the changing orthography of "Magna Carta" reinforced this association between a charter and ancient liberties and authority.[81] By the mid-seventeenth century, the majority of political treatises preferred the *ch* spelling—"Magna Charta"—with its visual insistence on charter. Henry Care's *English Liberties; or, The Free-Born Subjects Inheritance* of 1682 is the most notable of these works.[82] By 1689, Gershom Bulkeley referred to "ancient Charter-privileges" of the decidedly un-ancient Connecticut charter.[83]

Ironically, by the 1680s, charters had become vulnerable to writs of quo warranto, legal proceedings to revoke a charter. The Crown, for the "first time in centuries, fought quo warrantos all the way to final judgment."[84] Most shocking for colonists was the revocation of London's perceived ancient charter in 1681–83. In England, after 1680, the controversy produced multiple print publications of London's charter and books on the quo warranto proceedings—many of which traveled across the Atlantic to interested observers. The title pages of these charter publications emphasized the importance of their appearance in print "verbatim" with explanations for the public.[85]

Although these publications had not prevented loss of London's charter, colonists perceived the publication as a method for declaration of lawful and local authority. Colonial charters soon began to appear in print, Carolina in 1682 and 1684, and Pennsylvania in 1687. In 1689, Samuel Green even produced a posthumous printing of the 1629 Massachusetts charter, which was legally revoked in 1684. The publication attempted to create and legitimize local authority after the loss of the charter and the ascension of William of Orange.[86]

In these new printed charters, colonial authority was literally written large. The 1691 Massachusetts charter appeared in print in 1692. On the title page, CHARTER and NEW-ENGLAND loomed in substantial typeface, dwarfing the far smaller acknowledgement "Granted by their Majesties King William and Queen Mary."[87] By the eighteenth century, colonial statute collections that began with the charter visually insisted that legal authority arose from the charter.[88] Printing the charters distanced them from Crown prerogative and converted them to matters of right. Thus in 1721, Jeremiah Dummer wrote *A Defence of the New-England Charters* to explain the "Right which the Charter Governments have to those Privileges."[89] This perception that the charters represented independent colonial authority rather than royal grants grew even greater by the 1760s. In 1764, John Dickinson thus wrote of Pennsylvania's colonial constitution, "Let any impartial person reflect how contradictory some of these privileges are to the most ancient principles of the English constitution, and how directly opposite other of them are to the settled prerogatives of the crown."[90] The printed charters had become the property of the colonists, not the Crown.

Charters thus embodied colonial constitutions. The 1765 *Laws of Maryland* aimed to include matters "relative to the Constitution" of the province, central of which was the charter, demarcated on the title page in large letters.[91] In 1774 and 1775, the Continental Congress framed its responses to British actions in Massachusetts as violations and subversions of the charter.[92] The South Carolina constitution of March 1776 condemned material alterations in the "chartered constitution of government." By 1776, Thomas Paine explained that "the articles or charter of government" should precede the choice of men to execute the government.[93] He proposed a "CONTINENTAL CHARTER, or Charter of the United Colonies; (answering to what is called the Magna Charta of England)" for the new nation.[94] The Declaration of Independence echoed this repositioning of the charter as a colonial right. It condemned the king for "taking away *our* charters."[95]

The new Americans would write documents that they would come to refer to as constitutions because they literally constituted new forms of government. Gradually "constitution" became the name of such documents.[96] Indeed, James Madison initially described the Articles of Confederation as a "federal Constitution" in his 1787 notes of the Constitutional Convention.[97] These written documents were based on the colonial conception of a charter, in which public authority, not Crown authority, was declared and defined. Thus Rhode Island and Connecticut initially were completely comfortable with retaining colonial charters once the references to the Crown had been struck.[98] As late as 1819, James Madison could write, "It could not but happen, and was foreseen at the birth of the Constitution, that difficulties and differences of opinion might occasionally arise in expounding terms and phrases necessarily used in such a charter."[99] The Constitution was a type of charter—a particular type that the colonists had been attempting to claim for years.

Rather than a dramatic step from charter to Constitution that bifurcates the colonial period from the constitutional one, the adoption of the term "constitution" was perhaps initially a less dramatic step.[100] The technical replacement of the people for the Crown as the ultimate source of governmental authority was significant but did not mean that constitutional understandings based on practice under the colonial charters vanished. The modes of legal practice in the chartered world continued to prove relevant for legal practice in a Constitutional world. Relocating this transformation in the late seventeenth century in the growing belief in a publicly available printed charter as the source and limit of governmental authority would suggest a constitutional tradition that crosses over the founding period rather than commencing in it.

PRINTED CASES TO THE PRINTED REPORTS

If the transformation from patent to charter suggests that the American constitutional tradition stretches back with historical and legal continuity to the late seventeenth century, a transformation involving colonial appeals to the Privy Council stretches this tradition into the nineteenth century. Because the decisions in these appeals were not reported in print, they have not been seen as creating a body of colonial constitutional law.

Yet Americans after the Revolution did not uniformly embrace printed and published reports. No cases from the Supreme Court appeared in a reported volume until 1798, an official court reporter was not appointed until 1817, and only in 1834 did the Court conclude that the copyright in the opinions rested with the public.[101] Although unreported in print, the decisions in Privy Council appeals were known to elite colonial and English lawyers. If a body of colonial constitutional law existed, then law in the early national period likely related to it either by continuing or rejecting substantive boundaries and interpretive conventions.

For Americans, appeals to the Privy Council are part of an obscure and less well-understood historical jurisdiction. In much of the former British Empire, however, appeals to the Privy Council, or more accurately, the Judicial Committee of the Privy Council, remain a significant and contested aspect of British constitutionalism. The Judicial Committee, created in its present form in 1833, continues to operate as "the court of final appeal for the UK overseas territories and Crown dependencies, and for those Commonwealth countries that have retained the appeal to Her Majesty in Council or, in the case of Republics, to the Judicial Committee."[102] Until 1949 Canada fell within this jurisdiction; until 1986, Australia; and until 2004, New Zealand.[103] Over twenty-five various territories, states, republics, and islands remain under the controversial jurisdiction. The membership of the committee is comprised of the former and present Lord Chancellors, certain Privy Counselors with judicial experience, various overseas members (senior judges and former judges from countries where there is a right of appeal), and Lords of Appeal. In 2007, ninety-three overseas appeals were entered.[104] The committee remains important in areas such as the death penalty.[105] In 2004, the committee concluded that Jamaica's mandatory death penalty in cases of murder was "inhuman."[106] But it has been commercial litigants who have been one of the major forces in favor of retention, approving of the committee's perceived expertise and uniformity.[107]

Until the mid-nineteenth century, Privy Council judgments were not reported.[108] At Macquarie University, Bruce Kercher has published unreported Privy Council appeals on the Web.[109] He explains that "we were taught at law school in the early 70s that Australian law nearly always followed that of England. Now a number of us have found that to be quite wrong."[110] A similar problem occurred with respect to the colonial American appeals. George Chalmers pointed out that Blackstone's *Commentaries* "were barren on such legal topics, as relate to our colonies." Blackstone was unable to "obtain materials," as appeals from the colonies "lay to the king in his council" rather than in his bench. If appeals had been to the bench, "there would there have been many reports laid before the public" and Blackstone could have drawn on these reports. However, there "have been scarcely any reports of cases, which were decided, on such appeals, and were accessible to research."[111]

The perception that constitutional law must begin with the Supreme Court is the product of this fact that colonial constitutional law prior to the Revolution did not appear in print. In fact, what understanding we have of the appeals has been the product of print publication. One appeal in 1728, *Winthrop v. Lechmere*, has received the most attention because of the mid-nineteenth-century publication of the Connecticut governor's papers with extensive discussion of the appeal. In *Winthrop*, the Privy Council addressed whether Connecticut's intestacy law requiring partible inheritance (real property to be divided among children) was permissible. The Privy Council declared the statute "null and void." The appeal has often been seen as a precedent for judicial review. As a result, however, the appeal is idiosyncratic. Two later appeals from Massachusetts and Connecticut both upheld partible inheritance. Similarly, an English solicitor who handled an extensive number of the colonial appeals noted that the "null and void" language "was never done in any one Case, before or since, to my Knowledge."[112] It was due in part to the defendant's apparently terrible defense and to the fact that Connecticut laws were not subject to prior review. In other colonies, with the exception of Rhode Island, appeals involved laws that had been previously reviewed by the council.[113]

The colonial appeals to the Privy Council demarcate a body of colonial constitutional law. Extant appeals briefs—often referred to as Printed Cases—can help describe the boundaries and interpretive traditions of colonial constitutional law. Four large collections contain briefs collected by English barristers and judges, in particular, George Lee and Charles Yorke, who argued before the committee and later served on the committee.[114] The Columbia collection is believed to be that of William Samuel Johnson of Connecticut, who traveled to England between 1767 and 1771 and collected Printed Cases in a variety of English appeals. Briefs also survive for the New England intestate cases *Phillips v. Savage* and *Winthrop v. Lechmere*. Additional briefs likely survive, particularly in the papers of the English solicitors, barristers, and judges and among family papers of those involved in the appeals.

Colonial appeals were repeatedly structured by the constitutional requirement in charters and instructions that colonial law not be repugnant to the laws of England.[115] The centrality of this requirement is made clear in a brief in the Massachusetts *Phillips* appeal in 1734. *Phillips* raised the same intestate issue as had been raised in *Winthrop*. After *Winthrop*, Rhode Island had repealed its partible intestate law, Connecticut had stopped deciding intestate cases while attempting to figure out how to reverse the appeal, and Massachusetts worried about its own statute.[116] The appeal argued that partible inheritance was repugnant to the laws of England. The colonial assembly had the power under the charter only to make laws "as are not repugnant or contrary to the Laws of England," and the laws subverted "the established Rules and Principles of Law" relating to descents of real estates. To emphasize the importance of repugnancy as the constitutional standard, the lawyer underlined on the brief the quoted charter sentence relating to repugnancy.[117]

With repugnancy as a constitutional standard, decisions with respect to one colony might have bearing on another colony. In the same brief in the *Phillips* appeal, the second argument was that "the Point in Question hath already received a Determination by his Majesty's Order in Council on the Appeal in Winthrop, which is conceived to be a Case in Point."[118] To the English counsel arguing the case, other appeals—in this instance *Winthrop*—held some relevant value. Moreover, after the committee decided *Phillips* in favor of the colony's intestate act under the theory that partible inheritance was an ancient colony custom, a second appeal was brought from Connecticut, and a similar result followed.[119] The Connecticut agent made reference to the "Precedent" of the *Winthrop* case in noting that it was likely to be alterable.[120]

Colonial legal observers perceived a body of colonial constitutional law. While in England, Johnson attended hearings of the Privy Council Committee, the House of Lords, and other courts. His handwritten notes, with one or two exceptions, are only on the briefs from the colonies.[121] Some comments related to the appeal practice. In *Freebody v. Brenton*, Johnson made a note that it was better to introduce colonial acts in writing under seal, as the judges had refused in one appeal to hear read to them "several Laws of Rho[d]e Island out of the Printed Colony Law Book."[122] Almost always, Johnson included the outcome: "reversed" or "affirmed." Sometimes, Johnson wrote more extensive comments explaining the reasons for the decision. Two examples involving Caribbean appeals indicate that colonial constitutionalism appears to have been characterized by a flexible or at least contextual interpretation of repugnancy and that the boundaries of substantive law were not our familiar private/public law divide.

The contextual nature of repugnancy appears in an appeal from Grenada. The issue was whether a Roman Catholic mother would lose guardianship of her child after the father's death (a possibility under English law). Grenada had been recently brought within the empire after the Treaty of Paris of 1763. The Privy Council Committee reversed the lower judgment barring her guardianship. The mother and her new husband won. In analyzing the appeal, Joseph Smith applied a rigid theoretical theory of the extension of English law to the plantations and concluded that the "Committee demonstrated little understanding of the question posed" and that the reversal was on "untenable and patently nonlegalistic grounds."[123] Rather than betraying that the committee misunderstood applicable law, the comment reveals the degree to which the appeals were decided under a constitutional jurisprudence that differed from common law. The brief had argued that the laws in England against Catholics should not be executed with rigor in "the new ceded governments" where "they were allowed the free Exercise of their

Religion . . . so far as is not repugnant to the Laws of Great Britain."[124] Johnson's interest in the appeal likely stemmed from the question of whether colonial laws and practices in favor of Roman Catholics were repugnant to the laws of England. Johnson interpreted the appeal to support non-repugnancy. He concluded, "The Laws agst Roman Catholicks are not executed with that rigour in England that the Mother should be deprived of the Guardianship of her Child, much less should they be so in the ceded Islands where it would be contrary to Justice and to all sound Policy. Even a Jewiss has been permitted to be Guardian in England, a fortiori a Roman Catholic."[125] "Justice" and "sound Policy" mattered. Free exercise of religion for Roman Catholics appeared not repugnant in the colonies.

What Smith bemoaned as the "patently nonlegalistic" decision in appeals may have significance for understanding the way in which early constitutional cases were argued and decided. While colonial appeals often raised questions of technical interpretation and careful construction, they also provided a forum in which claims about the colonies' place in the empire and the relationship of law to society was openly invited. From the colonial perspective, colonial constitutional law was a body of law in which law, policy, and justice intertwined. Bruce Kercher in a recent article on judicial interpretation of repugnancy in Australia points out that "colonial judges were in a very different position from their counterparts in England, on whom they were supposed to model themselves." He concludes that Australian judges "did not take these repugnancy provisions to mean just a conflict of one particular rule with another, but took a much broader, constitutional approach."[126] Did early Supreme Court justices model their interpretation on the English common-law bench or on the Privy Council that had overseen the validity of colonial law?

Free exercise of religion is a familiar area of modern constitutional law. However, a Virginia appeal in 1766, *Corbin v. Lomax*, reflects the differing dimensions of colonial constitutionalism. Nothing about the appeal seems constitutional to our notion of constitutional jurisprudence. Among other issues, it involved whether an Elizabethan statute, the Statute against Fraudulent Conveyances (1585), applied in Virginia. As a technical matter, the case involved the validity of a fee tail in a situation involving a conveyance after marriage without monetary consideration. The committee affirmed the colony's judgment.[127] Johnson explained succinctly, "Stat. of 27 Eliz. doth not extend to Plantations."[128] Although the appeal had only involved Virginia, Johnson drew a conclusion about the statute applicable to all the American colonies.

The appeal indicates the significant transformation in the substance to this constitutional law after the Constitution. During the colonial period, what we would think of as common-law and private law issues arose in this constitutional framework. In other appeals, the Privy Council ultimately decided whether colonial constitutional law required two witnesses or three to a will or whether colonies had to follow primogeniture. With the Constitution, these issues fell out of the national constitutional framework. What had been a colonial constitutional issue—whether a colony had to follow the Statute of Fraudulent Conveyances, the Statute of Frauds, other English statutes, and common law—became by default a matter of state common law. Neither the Constitution nor federal law attempted to occupy much of the substantive legal space previously occupied by the "laws of England." In property, contract, and commercial law and bankruptcy, "English" and "American" rules came into existence as states followed colonial decisions or reached new conclusions. The Constitution's inclusion of criminal jury trials, habeas corpus, and bills of attainder would transfer colonial constitutionalism in these areas, and national criminal common-law jurisdiction remained a subject of much contest.[129] Yet for most "private" law matters, nineteenth-century American law thus de-constitutionalized colonial constitutional law.[130]

The late eighteenth-century Supreme Court did not quickly replace these traditional constitutional cases with a new substantive constitutional jurisprudence. According to Julius Goebel, the small size of the Philadelphia bar and the absence of reports meant that the practice was conducted "in a manner approximating the club-like atmosphere that prevailed contemporaneously in the English High Court of Admiralty."[131] In short, the Court continued to operate in the early years in a manner not markedly different from the Privy Council. The absence of printed reports limited jurisprudential knowledge of the decisions largely to the Philadelphia bar.[132] Volume 2 of Dallas's *Reports* (1798) included cases to 1793; volume 3 (1799) included cases through 1799. Volume 4, including *Cooper v. Telfair* and other cases from 1799 to 1800, however, did not appear until 1807, while William Cranch's competing volume of Supreme Court reports from 1801 to 1803, including *Marbury v. Madison*, preceded it in 1804. The types of cases also left constitutional law somewhat underwhelming. The Court disposed of eighty-seven cases between 1789 and 1801. Thirty-five of these were admiralty cases; forty-two were various law cases (debt, assumpsit, ejectment, case, covenant, and dower), nine equity cases, and one probate case to affirm a will.[133] These cases raised issues arising under the Constitution: *Chisolm v. Georgia* was an assumpsit case; *Ware v. Hylton* was a debt case. Yet, repeatedly, the issues explored in these early cases remained jurisdictional rather than substantively constitutional. Constitutional law would become jurisprudential—but not for some years.

REVIEW OF LAW TO JUDICIAL REVIEW

American Constitutional law is the province of courts. Unlike the other two transformations, this aspect of constitutionalism was the product of 1787. In a book on control of colonial legislation, D. B. Swinfen defined review broadly as the process by which "colonial laws could either be ratified, amended, or rejected by the Crown or have their constitutional validity tested by the courts, colonial and imperial."[134] The functional loss of Privy Council review of legislation left control and constitutional validity of state legislation to courts alone. The rejection at the Philadelphia Convention of various models for negativing both state and congressional legislation left the Supreme Court the most plausible arbiter of constitutional issues.

In the British Empire, review of legislation was ubiquitous. The Board of Trade (under the Privy Council) oversaw review in the seventeenth and eighteenth centuries; the Colonial Office oversaw it in the nineteenth. Review was conducted usually pursuant to a requirement that colonial laws be not repugnant to the laws of England. During the nineteenth century, the Colonial Office reviewed thousands of colonial laws, disallowing significantly fewer than 5 percent a year. Swinfen argues that the process was helpful in "pruning colonial laws" of "provisions which might be, probably inadvertently, repugnant," encouraged in "individual cases" some desirable uniformity of law, and could be used as an instrument of political control.[135] For the sympathetic Swinfen, these fall into categories such as "imperial affairs," "humanitarianism" (under which Swinfen saw the Privy Council as a "champion" for "slaves, apprentices, immigrants, criminals, and ex-convicts"), or protecting "vested interests." In 1865, this review became substantively formalized under the Colonial Laws Validity Act, the "great legal landmark in colonial constitutional law."[136] The act "clarified and narrowed" the understanding of repugnancy and left to "the colonial legislatures the responsibility for managing their own affairs."[137]

In the colonies, review was *the* significant form of imperial legislative control and an omnipresent aspect of colonial government. Privy Council instructions, governors' correspondence, and legislative sneakiness (suspension acts, etc.) reveal this reality. During the American colonial period, 8,563 acts were reviewed. As a statistical piece, the number of disallowed laws was not large: 469, or 5.5 percent.[138] (This number is similar to the statistics during the later empire.) In comparison, the Supreme Court needs to review only a relatively small number of cases to have a significant influence. In the 2006 term, the Supreme Court heard oral arguments in 78 of the 8,857 cases filed and issued signed opinions in only 67.[139]

Review of legislation conjures up a list of specific acts being sent to England. As practiced, review was far more comprehensive—at least with respect to transmission of information. Between the late seventeenth century and the Revolution, the American colonies—with the noticeable exception of Rhode Island and Connecticut—sent the legislation and minutes of their legislative bodies. In 1909, Charles Andrews published a list "of the journals and acts of the councils and assemblies of the thirteen original colonies, and the Floridas, in America, preserved in the Public Record Office, London." The list was over one hundred pages long with twenty to forty collections of laws on each page. Massachusetts, for example, sent their printed collections of the charter, acts, and laws (often in duplicate); various manuscript acts; minutes of the council; and the journals of the assembly. Tens of thousands of pages of legislative records sailed to England.

Unfortunately, despite review's overwhelming importance in the colonial period, comparably little study has been given to the topic. Even to date, the only significant, admittedly outstanding, work remains Elmer Russell's *Review of American Colonial Legislation by the King in Council* of 1915. There is no comprehensive list of disallowed acts. Volumes 2 through 5 of *Acts of the Privy Council: Colonial Series* contain appendices with acts confirmed or disallowed between 1680 and the Revolution.[140] Only a few contain titles, leaving the substance of many to the imagination. Although Russell's discussion suggested categories of the types of acts disallowed or confirmed, a general colonial historian has little way of easily learning whether the act being referred to remained in force, and there has been no verification of Russell's conclusions. Similarly, outside of a few specific instances, no one has sought to combine the extant law officer opinions and comments of the counsel to the Board of Trade and Plantations with the acts.[141] Moreover, although Russell discussed general colonial evasion (for example, failure to transmit laws, temporary laws, reenactment), no one has investigated systematically the colonial response to disallowance of particular acts.

This neglect is due largely to review's abandonment with the Convention. As has been often remarked on, the 1787 Constitution did not replace this practice. James Madison, and others at the Convention, wanted it to continue. In one of his many comments about the negativing power, he wrote, "This was the practice in Royal Colonies before the Revolution and would not have been inconvenient; if the supreme power for negativing had been faithful to the American interest, and had possessed the necessary information."[142] After the Convention, Madison offered an additional rationale: "A constitutional negative on the laws of the States seems equally necessary to secure individuals agst. encroachments on their rights."[143] Yet for various and divergent reasons, the different negativing proposals eventually lost. The executive veto alone survived.

Near the end of the Convention, once the negative had been abandoned, two lawyers familiar with imperial practice added the "Constitution" to the grant of the Supreme Court's jurisdiction and the clause respecting state legislation. William Samuel Johnson, author of the comments on the appeals briefs, and John Rutledge, who had studied in London at the Middle Temple, ensured that the Supreme Court at least would inherit some aspect of the review of colonial legislation.[144] Connecticut's Oliver Ellsworth then ensured that the First Judiciary Act would explicitly give jurisdiction over state legislation respecting the Constitution explicitly to the Supreme Court.[145]

The transformation of colonial constitutionalism was largely the result of this loss of legislative review. Rhode Island and Connecticut alone had had charters that barred Privy Council review of legislation and permitted review only of judicial appeals. The loss of legislative review placed the new Supreme Court—a court comprised of judges, not judges and other members of the legislative and executive branches—with a jurisdiction peculiar to the colonial world. The Court—and the Court alone—became the arbiter of the Constitution. By the nineteenth century, printed reports of the Court's decisions began to create a constitutional jurisprudence that turned away from "private law." The Constitution as an interpretable public law document grew out of these other practices.

Horwitz correctly saw a transformation in American private law between 1780 and 1860. This transformation, however, did not occur against a stable or preconceived notion of Constitutional law that sprang into being with the 1787 written Constitution. The transformation in American private law was dependent on an intertwined transformation of colonial constitutionalism to American Constitutionalism. The transformation of American law between 1780 and 1860 was not only *in* private law but *of* the very notion of private and public law itself. Out of the great binary pairs of English law—*lex scripta* and *lex non scripta,* common law and statutory law—slowly grew another far more powerful legal construct, Constitutional law, with unconstitutional its sole opposing companion.

NOTES

1. Morton J. Horwitz, *The Transformation of American Law, 1780–1860* (Cambridge, Mass.: Harvard University Press, 1977), xii. Horwitz, with characteristic incisiveness, described colonial law as a "known and determinate body of legal doctrine" (4). In particular, he emphasized the colonists' success in "establishing the proposition that they carried the English common law with them" and the "authority of common law rules" (6). He concluded, "The overwhelming fact about American law through most of the eighteenth century is the extent to which lawyers believed that English authority settled virtually all questions for which there was no legislative rule" (8). In addition, Horwitz noted a distinction between "common law doctrines . . . derived from natural principles of justice" and statutes as "acts of will" and perceived a "strict conception of precedent" (7–8).

2. Stanley N. Katz, "The Problem of a Colonial Legal History," in *Colonial British America: Essays in the New History of the Early Modern Era,* ed. Jack P. Greene and J. R. Pole (Baltimore, Md.: Johns Hopkins University Press, 1984), 463.

3. See Lauren Benton, *Law and Colonial Cultures: Legal Regimes in World History, 1400–1900* (Cambridge: Cambridge University Press, 2002); Alexander Haskell, *Colonization as Commonwealth-Building: The Legal and Constitutional Implications of an Early-Seventeenth-Century Anglo-American Political Discourse* (paper presented at the American Society for Legal History, 2006); Daniel J. Hulsebosch, *Constituting Empire: New York and the Transformation of Constitutionalism in the Atlantic World, 1664–1830* (Chapel Hill: University of North Carolina Press, 2005), 254; Daniel J. Hulsebosch, "The Ancient Constitution and the Expanding Empire: Sir Edward Coke's British Jurisprudence," *Law and History Review* 21 (2003): 439–82; Alison LaCroix, "The Authority for Federalism: Madison's Negative and the Transition from Imperial to Federal Supremacy" (unpublished manuscript); David Thomas Konig, "Virginia and the Imperial State: Law, Entitlement, and the 'Crooked Cord of Discretion,'" in *The British and Their Laws in the Eighteenth Century,* ed. David Lemmings (Woodbridge, Suffolk, UK: Boydell

Press, 2005), 230, 249; David Thomas Konig, "Constitutional Contexts: The Theory of History and the Process of Constitutional Change in Revolutionary America," in *Constitutionalism and American Culture: Writing the New Constitutional History,* ed. Sandra F. VanBurkleo, Kermit L. Hall, and Robert J. Kaczorowski, 3–28 (Lawrence: University Press of Kansas, 2002); Bernadette A. Meyler, "Towards a Common Law Originalism." *Harvard Law Review* 59 (2006): 551–600; William M. Offutt, "The Atlantic Rules: The Legalistic Turn in Colonial British America," in *The Creation of the British Atlantic World,* ed. Elizabeth Mancke and Carole Shammas, 160–81 (Baltimore, Md.: Johns Hopkins University Press, 2005); Ellen Holmes Pearson, "Revising Custom, Embracing Choice: Early American Legal Scholars and the Republicanization of the Common Law," in *Empire and Nation: The American Revolution in the Atlantic World,* ed. Eliga H. Gould and Peter S. Onuf, 93–111 (Baltimore, Md.: Johns Hopkins University Press, 2005); Carla Pestana, *The English Atlantic in an Age of Revolution, 1640–1661* (Cambridge, Mass.: Harvard University Press, 2004); Claire Priest, "Creating an American Property Law: Alienability and Its Limits in American History," *Harvard Law Review* 120 (2006): 387–458; James S. Hart and Richard J. Ross, "The Ancient Constitution in the Old World and the New," in *The Worlds of John Winthrop: Essays on England and New England, 1588–1649,* ed. Francis J. Bremer and Lynn A. Botelho, 237–89 (Boston: Massachusetts Historical Society, 2005); George Van Cleve, "Somerset's Case and Its Antecedents in Imperial Perspective," *Law and History Review* 24 (2006): 601–46 (with comments by Hulsebosch and Ruth Paley); Craig Yirush, *Conquest Theory and the Metropolitan Assertion of Authority in the first British Empire* (paper presented at the American Society for Legal History, 2006); Mary Sarah Bilder, *The Transatlantic Constitution: Colonial Legal Culture and the Empire* (Cambridge, Mass.: Harvard University Press, 2004).

4. See, e.g., Bernard Bailyn, *The Ideological Origins of the American Revolution* (Birmingham, Ala.: Palladium Press, 2001); Gordon Wood, *The Creation of the American Republic* (Chapel Hill: Published for the Institute of Early American History and Culture at Williamsburg by the University of North Carolina Press, 1998); Gerald Stourzh, "Constitution: Changing Meanings of the Term from the Early Seventeenth Century to the Late Eighteenth Century," in *Conceptual Change and the Constitution,* ed. Terence Ball and J. G. A. Pocock, 34–54 (Lawrence: University Press of Kansas, 1988) (and Stourzh's other essays on this subject). This shift may account for the late eighteenth-century rise and fall of both the words "constitutionalist"—"one who studies or writes" on constitutions or was an "adherent" of constitutional principles—and "constitutionist"—a zealot for an established constitution. See *The Oxford English Dictionary,* 2d ed., s.v. "Constitution."

5. Hulsebosch, *Constituting Empire,* 254. Given the nature of the British constitution as dependent on history, "constitutional history" was often the phrase used to describe the change over time in the British constitution. See, e.g., *The parliamentary or constitutional history of England; being a faithful account of all the most remarkable transactions in Parliament, from the earliest times. Collected from the journals of both Houses, the records* (London: T. Osborne and W. Sandby, 1751–61); Gilbert Stuart, *Observations concerning the Public Law, and the Constitutional History of Scotland* (London: John Murray, 1779); Joseph Story, *Commentaries on the Constitution of the United States: With a preliminary review of the constitutional history of the colonies and states, before the adoption of the Constitution* (Boston: Hilliard, Gray, 1833).

6. On the historiography of the invention of judicial review, see Mary Sarah Bilder, "Idea or Practice: A Brief Historiography of Judicial Review," *Journal of Policy History* 20 (2008): 6–26.

7. Henry Sumner Maine, *Ancient Law: Its Connection with the Early History of Society, and Its Relation to Modern Ideas* (London: John Murray, 1861).

8. Hulsebosch, *Constituting Empire,* 9–10.

9. Henry St. John Viscount Bolingbroke, *A Dissertation upon Parties* (1735), 108; see Donald Lutz, ed., *Colonial Origins of the American Constitution: A Documentary History* (Indianapolis, Ind.: Liberty Fund, 1998), xxiii, xxxiv–xxxv.

10. *Essay on Political Society* (1800), 197 (contested attribution to Samuel W. Dana).

11. J. R. Pole's recent edition retains this original capitalization.

12. Clinton Rossiter modernized punctuation and capitalization in his version of *The Federalist Papers,* resulting in a consistently capitalized "Constitution."

13. Hulsebosch, *Constituting Empire,* 8–9.

14. 2 U.S. 419, 479 (1793); see Hulsebosch, *Constituting Empire,* 254. In 1800, the author of *Essay on Political Society* somewhat similarly writes, "Expounding and administering the constitutional law, the American tribunate is of various use in the order of society" (197).

15. For adjectival uses, see, e.g., *The Federalist Papers, No. 57* (James Madison, referring to "just and constitutional laws"); Edmund Burke, *Reflections on the Revolution in France* (Dublin: W. Porter, 1791), 135 ("They do not hold the authority they exercise under any constitutional law of the state"); *The Petition of the Freemen of the Town of Hartford in the State of Connecticut* (1796) ("our duty, as the faith of the nation is pledged in the Constitution, in a manner equally solemn, as in the case of any constitutional law whatever"). The *OED* does not include a reference for "constitutional law" but does include one for "constitutionality" in 1801. See *The Oxford English Dictionary,* 2d ed. (citing the Ann. Reg. 1800 at 60).

16. 25 U.S. 213 (1827) ("Cotemporaneous construction had always been considered as of great weight in matters of constitutional law; and in the question relating to the power of Congress to establish such corporations as the Bank of the United States, was considered as decisive"). The plural adjectival "constitutional laws" appeared more frequently.

17. Henry St. George Tucker, *Lectures on Constitutional Law: For the Use of the Law Class at the University of Virginia* (Richmond, Va.: Printed by Shepherd and Colin, 1843); see also William Goodell, *Views of American Constitutional Law: In Its Bearing upon American Slavery,* 2d ed. (Utica, N.Y.: Lawson & Chaplin, 1845); Daniel Raymond, *The Elements of Constitutional Law* (Baltimore, Md.: Cushing, 1845); E. Fitch Smith, *Commentaries on Statute and Constitutional Law and Statutory and Constitutional Construction* (Albany, N.Y.: Gould, Banks & Gould, 1848); Theodore Sedgwick, *A Treatise on the Rules which govern the Interpretation and Application of Statutory and Constitutional Law* (New York: J. S. Voorhies, 1857). The first treatise to use the term in the title appears to have been J. E. Hall's *Tracts on the Constitutional Law of the United States* (Philadelphia: J. Maxwell, 1817), in which the word never arises in the text; see also *Constitutional law: Comprising the Declaration of Independence, the Articles of Confederation, the Constitution of the United States, and the constitutions of the several states . . .* (Washington: Gales and Seaton, 1819); Thomas Sergeant, *Constitutional law: Being a View of the Practice and Jurisdiction of the Courts of the United States, and of Constitutional Points Decided,* (1822); George Tucker, *The Life of Thomas Jefferson, Third President of the United States: With . . . Notices of his Opinions on Questions of Civil Government, National Policy, and Constitutional Law* (Philadelphia: Carey, Lea & Blanchard, 1837).

18. Joel Parker, *Constitutional law: With reference to the present condition of the United States* (Cambridge: Welch, Bigelow, 1862).

19. See, e.g., H. von Holst, *The Constitutional Law of the United States,* trans. Alfred Bishop Mason (Chicago: Callaghan, 1887; J. I. Clark Hare, *American Constitutional Law* (Boston: Little, Brown, 1889).

20. For early uses, see works by Edwin Seligman and John W. Burgess. See, e.g., Edwin R. A. Seligman, "Changes in the Tenets of Political Economy with Time," *Science* 7 (1886): 377; John W. Burgess, *Recent Changes in American Constitutional Theory* (1923), 56.

21. Andrew C. McLaughlin, *The Foundations of American Constitutionalism* (1932; Union, N.J.: Lawbook Exchange, 2002), 135; see also Ray Forrest Harvey, *Jean Jacques Burlamaqui: A Liberal Tradition in American Constitutionalism* (Chapel Hill: University of North Carolina Press, 1937).

22. Charles Howard McIlwain, *Constitutionalism: Ancient and Modern* (Ithaca, N.Y.: Cornell University Press, 1947), 21; see also McIlwain, *Constitutionalism and the Changing World* (Cambridge: University Press, 1939).

23. McIlwain, *Constitutionalism: Ancient and Modern,* 15 (noting that "limitations on arbitrary rule have become so firmly fixed in the national tradition that no threats against them have seemed serious enough to warrant the adoption of a formal code"). McIlwain suggested that the early written constitutions "consist mainly of a codification of institutions and principles long in actual force," and that "our independence constituted a break in continuity here requiring a written code" (15).

24. Robert Livingston Schuyler, *Parliament and the British Empire: Some Constitutional Controversies concerning Imperial Legislative Jurisdiction* (Hamden, Conn.: Archon Books, 1929), 117–18. McIlwain's interest in constitutionalism had previously led to his argument over the "correctness" of the American Revolutionary claim that Parliament had no lawful authority over the colonies. Charles Howard McIlwain, *The American Revolution: A Constitutional Interpretation* (Clark, N.J.: Lawbook Exchange, 2005). For revision of this debate, see articles by Barbara Black and Liam Seamus O'Mellin.

25. Walton Hamilton, "Constitutionalism," in *Encyclopedia of the Social Sciences,* ed. Edwin R. A. Seligman and Alvin Johnson (New York: Macmillan, 1931), 4:255; see Richard S. Kay, "American Constitutionalism," in *Constitutionalism: Philosophical Foundations,* ed. Larry Alexander (Cambridge: Cambridge University Press, 2001), 16 (quoting Hamilton); Gerhard Casper, "Constitutionalism" in *Encyclopedia of the American Constitution,* 2d ed., ed. Leonard W. Levy and Kenneth L. Karst (New York: Macmillan Reference, 2000), 480 (quoting Hamilton). For other definitions, see, e.g., Francis D. Wormuth, *The Origins of Modern Constitutionalism* (New York: Harper, 1949), ix (discussing a series of "devices, the most familiar of which are the separation of powers, bicameralism, the written constitution, and judicial review"); David A. J. Richards, *Foundations of American Constitutionalism* (New York: Oxford University Press, 1989) (exploring foundations in political theory, particularly that of John Locke).

26. See James R. Stoner Jr., *Common-Law Liberty: Rethinking American Constitutionalism* (Lawrence: University Press of Kansas, 2003); Wormuth, *The Origins of Modern Constitutionalism,* 207–8 (suggesting the seventeenth-century common-law limits as the origins of judicial review); Lois G. Schwoerer, "British Lineages and American Choices," in *The Bill of Rights: Government Proscribed,* ed. Ronald Hoffman and Peter J. Albert, 1–41 (Charlottesville: Published for the United States Capitol Historical Society by the University Press of Virginia, 1997) (discussing multiple lineages of common law, Magna Carta, petition of right, the Bill of Rights,

commonwealth ideology, and natural law). On the ancient constitution, see, e.g., J. G. A. Pocock, *The Ancient Constitution and the Feudal Law: A Study of English Historical Thought in the Seventeenth Century* (Cambridge: University Press, 1957); Ellis Sandoz, ed., *The Roots of Liberty: Magna Carta, Ancient Constitution and the Anglo-American Tradition of Rule of Law* (Columbia: University of Missouri Press, 1993); Glenn Burgess, *The Politics of the Ancient Constitution* (University Park: Pennsylvania State University Press, 1992); Glenn Burgess, *Absolute Monarchy and the Stuart Constitution* (New Haven, Conn.: Yale University Press, 1996), chaps. 5 and 6; Corinne C. Weston, "England: Ancient Constitution and Common Law," in *The Cambridge History of Political Thought, 1450–1700,* ed. J. H. Burns, 374–411 (Cambridge: Cambridge University Press, 1991); J. W. Tubbs, *The Common Law Mind: Medieval and Early Modern Conceptions* (Baltimore, Md.: Johns Hopkins University Press, 2000); Colin Kidd, *British Identities before Nationalism: Ethnicity and Nationhood in the Atlantic World, 1600–1800* (Cambridge: Cambridge University Press, 1999), 75–98; Janelle Greenberg, *The Radical Face of the Ancient Constitution: St. Edward's "Laws" in Early Modern Political Thought* (Cambridge: Cambridge University Press, 2001).

27. Harold Hazeltine, "The Influence of Magna Carta on American Constitutional Development," *Columbia Law Review* 17 (1917): 1–33; John Phillip Reid, "Another Origin of Judicial Review: The Constitutional Crisis of 1776 and the Need for a Dernier Judge," *New York University Law Review* 64 (1989): 963 (discussing Pownall's book as "the leading treatise on colonial constitutional law"); Jonathan A. Bush, "Free to Enslave: The Foundations of Colonial American Slave Law," *Yale Journal of Law & the Humanities* 5 (1993): 417. See also "Comments," *Green Bag* 17 (1905): 373 (describing a colonial case as "colonial constitutional law").

28. See, e.g., Eliga H. Gould, *Lines of Plunder or Crucible of Modernity: Towards a Legal History of the English-Speaking Atlantic, 1660–1825* (paper presented at Seascapes, Littoral Cultures, and Trans-Oceanic Exchanges, Library of Congress, Washington, D.C., Feb. 12–15, 2003), http://www.historycooperative.org/proceedings/seascapes/gould.html.

29. For a variety of examples, see Patrick McAuslan's discussion in "In the Beginning," *Federal Law Review* 21 (1992–93): 272; Christopher Staker, "Australian Cases Involving Questions of Public International Law, 1992," *Australian Year Book of International Law* 14 (1992): 321 (*Mabo v. Queensland*); W. P. M. K., "Notes and Documents: Colonial Constitutional Law," *University of Toronto Law Journal* 6 (1945–46): 234 (complaining of the absence of a treatise on colonial constitutional law); Jocelyn Gagne, "The Content of Aboriginal Title at Common Law: A Look at the Nishga Claim," *Saskatchewan Law Review* 47 (1982–83): 310 (discussing aboriginal title and "theories of colonial constitutional law"); Bernard O'Brien, "The Law Applicable in Federal Jurisdiction," *University of New South Wales Law Journal* 2 (1977–78): 56 (describing colonial constitutional law as "divided into two major divisions" of conquered or settled colonies); W. S. Holdsworth, "The History of the Law as to the Status," *Tijdschrift voor Rechtsgeschiedenix* 3 (1922): 188 (describing principles of colonial constitutional law, including *Calvin's Case*); R. D. Lumb, "The Bicentenary of Australian Constitutionalism: The Evolution of Rules of Constitutional Change," *University of Queensland Law Journal* 15 (1988–89): 3 (discussing "colonial constitutional law" involving the doctrine of extra-territoriality and the doctrine of repugnancy); John Salmond, "The Limitations of Colonial Legislative Power," *Law Quarterly Review* 33 (1917): 117, 120. However, we should recall that in "its early years the British Empire wasn't an empire and it wasn't British." Jerry Dupont, *The Common Law Abroad: Constitutional and Legal Legacy of the British Empire* (Littleton, Colo.: F. B. Rothman, 2001), xiii.

30. William Forsyth, *Cases and Opinions on Constitutional Law, and Various Points of English Jurisprudence* (London: Stevens & Haynes, 1869); George Chalmers, *Opinions of Eminent Lawyers on Various Points of English Jurisprudence, chiefly concerning Colonies, Fisheries, and Commerce of Great Britain* (London: Reed and Hunter, 1814). A century later, decolonization led the update by D. P. O'Connell and Ann Riordan to describe itself as *Opinions on Imperial Constitutional Law* (Melbourne: Law Book, 1971).

31. Thomas Pownall, *The Administration of the British Colonies,* 3d ed. (London: Printed for J. Walter, 1766), table of contents, 53, 62.

32. Jack P. Greene, Charles F. Mullett, and Edward C. Papenfuse Jr., eds., *Magna Charta for America: James Abercromby's "An examination of the acts of parliament relative to the trade and the government of the American colonies" (1752),* (Philadelphia: American Philosophical Society, 1986), 306.

33. *To the Freeholders and Electors of the City and County of Philadelphia* (Oct. 1, 1764), quoted in David L. Jacobson, "John Dickinson's Fight against Royal Government, 1764," *William and Mary Quarterly* 19 (1962): 64, 81.

34. Letter of Stephen Hopkins et al. in *Freebody v. Brenton,* Dec. 1772, PC 1/60/10.

35. H. Jefferson Powell, *A Community Built on Words: The Constitution in History and Politics* (Chicago: Chicago University Press, 2002), 7.

36. See, e.g., McLaughlin, *The Foundations of American Constitutionalism,* 47 (accounting among other factors "the probable effect—psychological effect . . . of living for years under a government whose authority was confined, in theory, within written limitations"); Benjamin F. Wright Jr., "The Early History of Written Constitutions in America," in *Essays in History and Political Theory in Honor of Charles Howard McIlwain,* 344–71 (Cambridge, Mass.: Harvard University Press, 1936).

37. See the work of Catherine Patterson and Paul Halliday.

38. John George Bourinot, *Builders of Nova Scotia* (Toronto: Copp-Clark, 1902), 104–21; "Translation of the Charter of Nova Scotia, 1621," *Transactions of the Royal Canadian Institute* 14 (1922): 89–116 (reprinting document). The charter described itself as "hanc nostrum cartam" (112–13).

39. *An Incorporacion of Prince Rupert . . . into one body politique by the name of Governours and Adventurers trading to Hudsons baye* (1670) has been described as "nearly seven thousand words of tortured English legal phrases, lettered in eye-straining characters on five large sheets of parchment, and a gigantic seal." Douglas MacKay, *The Honorable Company: A History of the Hudson's Bay Company* (London: Cassell, 1936), 36, 37–38. On early efforts in Canada, including the Northwest Passage Company, the Bristol efforts for Newfoundland, the Nova Scotia Company (1622), and the Canada Company (1627), see E. E. Rich, *Hudson's Bay Company, 1670–1870* (New York: Macmillan, 1960), 1:1–8. Charters did not govern all English colonies, only those where no "Christian Prince or State" had an initial prior claim. Seventeenth-century settlements acquired from another European power were governed initially pursuant to treaties. Jamaica, for example, fell under the Treaty of Madrid (1670). Frances Gardiner Davenport, ed., *European Treaties Bearing on the History of the United States and Its Dependencies* (Washington, D.C.: Carnegie Institution of Washington, 1929), 2:187–97.

40. See also Tasmania's Charter of Justice.

41. See C. H. Philips, *The East India Company, 1784–1834* (Manchester, 1940); H. V. Bowen, *The Business of Empire: The East India Company and Imperial Britain, 1756–1833* (Cambridge: Cambridge University Press, 2006).

42. See E. C. S. Wade and G. Godfrey Phillips, *Constitutional Law,* 4th ed. (London: Longmans, Green, 1952), 400 (noting that constitutions could arise by formal instructions from the Crown to the governor).

43. For documents relating to the nineteenth-century constitutions of the "British imperial commonwealth," see James Brown Scott, *Autonomy and Federation within Empire: The British Self-Governing Dominions* (Washington, D.C.: The Endowment, 1921). For discussion of the imperial model and the U.S. Constitution, see the letter of A. Inglis Clark, Sept. 2, 1891, in David Eastman, *The Founding Documents of the Commonwealth of Australia* (Australia: D. Eastman, 1995), 1 (explaining influential draft for the Constitution). The Australian "constitution" also includes various letters patent.

44. 30–31 Vict., c. 3; see B. L. Strayer, *Judicial Review of Legislation in Canada* (Toronto: University of Toronto Press, 1968), 5.

45. A nice example of this shift appears on the title page of a document of the Australian attorney general and solicitor department. "Constitution" is in a larger font; "letter patent" and "acts" are in smaller font. See *The Constitution as in Force on 1 June 2003* . . . (Canberra, Australia: Office of Legislative Drafting, Attorney-General's Department, 2003).

46. Albert Carlos Bates, *The Charter of Connecticut* (Hartford: Connecticut Historical Society, 1932), 5.

47. Thanks to Catherine Patterson for assistance with this point.

48. *Worshipful Company of Shipwrights* (c. 1612) (including charter, acts and ordinances, and confirmation of them by Ellesmere, Fleming, and Coke).

49. Shelagh Bond and Norman Evans, "The Process of Granting Charters to English Boroughs, 1547–1649," *English Historical Review* 91 (1976): 102–20; *Royal Grants: Letters Patent and Charters, 1199–Present Day,* National Archives. For early charters, see *Calendar of Charter Rolls,* 2 vols. (1906).

50. See *An Act concerning Monopolies and Dispensations with Penal Laws, and the Forfeitures,* 21 Jac. 1, c. 3, sec. 6 (1622) (compare fourteen-year "patents" with excluded "charters, customs, corporations, companies, fellowships, and societies, and their liberties, privileges, powers, and immunities").

51. Bates, *The Charter of Connecticut*. On the Great Seal, see H. C. Maxwell-Lyte, *Historical Notes on the Use of the Great Seal of England* (London: H. M. Stationery Office, 1926).

52. For discussion of whether or not this occurred, see Reginald L. Poole, "The Publication of Great Charters by the English Kings," *English Historical Review* 28 (1913): 444, 449–53.

53. William Bradford referred to Virginia and Plymouth documents as patents. See William Bradford, *Of Plymouth Plantation, 1620–1647: The Complete Text* (New York: Knopf, 1952), 38; see also 215 (concerning "Mr. Allerton's proceeding about the enlarging and confirming of their Patent"); Sherley and Haterford to Bradford, Mar. 16, 1629/30 (describing "our main business, the patent, was granted" and adding that they had made them a corporation so "to enable you to make and execute laws in such large and ample manner as the Massachusetts Plantation hath it"). What we think of as the Peirce Patent, Thomas Weston called a "charter, the best we could, which is better than your former, and with less limitation." Thomas Weston to Bradford, July 6, 1621, *Of Plymouth Plantation,* 93. See also Copy of Order of the Privy Council (Jan. 19, 1632/33), 421–22 (discussing problems with the New England "Patents").

54. "Orders and Constitutions . . . 1619 and 1620," in *The Records of the Virginia Company of London,* ed. Susan Myra Kingsbury (Washington, D.C.: U.S. Government Printing Office,

1906), 3:352–53; see also 1:257 ("the Inhabitants hauing had great ioy by the Charters of Graunts and Liberties lately sent by Sr Geo: Yeardley," Quarter Court, Nov. 3, 1619).

55. John Pory, "A Reporte of the Manner of Proceeding in the General Assembly convented at James City 1619," in Kingsbury, *The Records of the Virginia Company,* 3:158; "Treasurer and Company, An Ordinance and Constitution for Council and Assembly in Virginia, July 24, 1621," in Kingsbury, *The Records of the Virginia Company,* 3:484.

56. See, e.g., Kingsbury, *The Records of the Virginia Company,* 2:469 (Court Record, Oct. 1623).

57. *For the colony in Virginea Britannia. Lavves diuine, morall and martiall, &c.* (London, 1612) contained no references to the charter or patent.

58. Form of Government, quoted from Young's "Chronicles of Massachusetts," in Charles Deane, "The Forms in Issuing Letters Patent by the Crown of England," *Proceedings of the Massachusetts Historical Society* 11 (1871): 166, 178. The 1628 grant by the Council of Plymouth to Rosewell was described as a "Charter" in the docket accompanying the 1629 charter. Docket (Feb. 1628/29), in Deane, "The Forms," 173.

59. "The Agreement at Cambridge (Aug. 1629)," in John Winthrop, *Winthrop Papers* (Boston: Massachusetts Historical Society, 1931), 2:151, 152.

60. John Winthrop, *Arbitrary Government Described* (1644). On the controversy, see Ronald Dale Karr, "The Missing Clause: Myth and the Massachusetts Bay Charter of 1629," *New England Quarterly* 77 (2004): 89–107.

61. William Wood, *New Englands Prospect* (1634), 44; see also Thomas Lechford, *Note-book kept by Thomas Lechford, Esq., lawyer in Boston . . . (1638–1641),* ed. Edward Everett Hale Jr. (Cambridge, Mass.: J. Wilson and Son, 1885), 278.

62. Emmanuel Downing to Hugh Peter, July 29, 1641, in *Winthrop Papers* (1944), 4:340, 341; see also [Unknown] to John Winthrop Jr., ca. May 1637, in *Winthrop Papers* (1931), 3:397, 403 (noting that "your Patent is called in and condemned, and the Patentees haue renounced").

63. See Michael P. Winship, "Godly Republicanism and the Origins of the Massachusetts Polity," *William and Mary Quarterly* 63 (2006): 427, 443–52.

64. *Proceedings of the Council of Maryland, 1636–1770* (Baltimore: Maryland Historical Society, 1885), 3:1–12.The language is very similar to that used in the early proprietary charters of Nova Scotia and Avalon.

65. Thomas Cecil, *A Relation of Maryland* (1635), title page. The twenty-five pages of the charter appear following page 56.

66. The Maryland Archives includes an early corrected copy of the 1632 charter in English. Constitutional Records, 1632–1851, http://aomol.net/megafile/msa/speccol/sc4800/sc4872/003145/html/m3145–0012.ht m l. The Archives implies the printing is London 1632; however, that date does not appear on the document.

67. *Proceedings of the Council of Maryland,* 3:43–44.

68. John Winthrop, "Discourse on Arbitrary Government" (1644), in *Winthrop Papers,* 4:468.

69. Ibid., 471. Winthrop notably remarked that he "might shewe a clear Rule out of the Patent it selfe" (472).

70. Ibid., 483.

71. Edward Winslow, *The danger of tolerating levellers in a civil state* (1649), 78 (a later publication of *Hypocrisy Unmasked*).

72. *[Acts and statutes] of the island of Barbados made and enacted since the reducement of the same, unto the authority of the Common-wealth of England and set forth the seventh day of September, in the year of our Lord God 1652, by the Honourable governour of the said island, the worshipfull the council, and gentlemen of the assembly; together with charter of the said island, or articles made on the surrender, and rendition of the same; published for the publick good* (1654). The East India Company Charter was published in 1661, and that of the Bahama Islands in 1670.

73. *Virginia and Maryland; or, The Lord Baltamore's printed case, uncased and answered shewing the illegality of his patent and usurpation of royal jurisdiction and dominion there* (1655). Baltimore's own pamphlet also used patent language. *The Lord Baltemores case concerning the province of Maryland, adjoyning to Virginia in America* (1653).

74. Bates, *The Charter of Connecticut,* 11–21.

75. Ibid., 21–24.

76. Bilder, *The Transatlantic Constitution.*

77. Session laws 1665, p. 2; 1661.

78. Linda A. Ries and Jane Smith Stewart, "The Charter to William Penn: This Venerable Document," *Pennsylvania Heritage* (Winter 2000): 18–25. Nonetheless, distinguishing charters from patents on the basis of seal color is a less-than-fruitful endeavor. The seal of the 1629 Massachusetts Bay charter, for example, looked "mustard-color" in the early twentieth century, and the current archivist reports that it is now best described as brown. Yet the Massachusetts Bay document stated repeatedly that the grant was "forever," and a company was obviously incorporated. "The Charter of Massachusetts Bay," *Proceedings of the Massachusetts Historical Society* 92 (1930): 228, 233.

79. The letters patent from the Crown to Virginia is unusual in this respect in declaring itself only a "letters patent." John Burk, *The History of Virginia* (Petersburg, Va.: Dickson & Pescud, 1805), 2:lxi–lxii.

80. Catherine F. Patterson, *Urban Patronage in Early Modern England: Corporate Boroughs, the Landed Elite, and the Crown, 1580–1640* (Stanford, Calif.: Stanford University Press, 1999), 165. On the ancient constitution in colonial Massachusetts, see Hart and Ross, "The Ancient Constitution."

81. On Magna Carta in the colonies, see A. E. Dick Howard, *The Road from Runnymede: Magna Carta and Constitutionalism in America* (Charlottesville: University of Virginia Press, 1968).

82. Lois G. Schwoerer, *The Ingenious Mr. Henry Care: Restoration Publicist* (Baltimore, Md.: Johns Hopkins University Press, 2001), 232 (describing American and English reception). As Schwoerer notes, the document provided "constitutional documents, English precedents, and compelling language on the rights and liberties of Englishman" and served as a "handbook that made Magna Charta and other documents readily available." She points out that Penn "silently lifted a sizeable portion" into *The Excellent Priviledge of Liberty & Property* (1687). (233). One of the early advocates of the *ch* spelling appears to have been, not surprisingly, Edward Coke.

83. Gershom Bulkeley, *The People's Right to Election; or, Alteration of Goverment [sic] in Connecticut* (1689), 2, 15.

84. Paul D. Halliday, *Dismembering the Body Politic: Partisan Politics in England's Towns, 1650–1730* (Cambridge: Cambridge University Press, 1998), 26. Halliday writes that those "spec-

ulating on the nature of corporations liked to say that the exact form of words in the charter was unimportant to establishing the corporation or to defining its privileges. But in the decades after 1660, charter terms were more thoroughly defined." As he quotes, Sir Robert Atkyns stated, "The charter gives the only rule" (40–41).

85. See, e.g., *The abridgement of the charter of the city of London being every free-man's privilege / exactly translated from the original record and rendered faithfully into English according to the said record itself from the time of William the Conquerour . . . to the time of our now Sovereign Lord King Charles the Second . . .* (London, 1680); *The royal charter of confirmation granted by King Charles II to the city of London. Wherein are recited verbatim, all the charters to the said city, granted by His Majesties royal predecessors, kings and queens of England. / Taken out of the records, and exactly translated into English by S.G. gent.; Together with an index or alphabetical table, and a table explaining all the obsolete and difficult words in the said charter* (London, 1680).

86. A copy of *The Kings Majesties charter, for incorporating the Company of the Massachusets Bay in New-England in America granted in the fourth year of His Highness reign of England, Scotland, France and Ireland, anno Dom. 1628* (1689); *The Answer of the subscribers to the declaration given in by the representatives, of the several towns of the colony of the Massachusets, which was publickly declared at the town-house. Boston, May 24. 1689. Upon the occasion of the revolution of the late government under Sir Edmond Andros. . . . We who are of the persons chosen and sworn governour, deputy governour, and assistants (according to charter) in the year 1686 . . . do consent to accept the care and government of the people of this colony . . .* (1689).

87. *The charter granted by Their Majesties King William and Queen Mary, to the inhabitants of the province of the Massachusetts-Bay, in New-England* (1692). The charter was reprinted in 1699. *The charter granted by Their Majesties King William and Queen Mary, to the inhabitants of the province of the Massachusetts-Bay in New-England* (1699). For other charters, see Hudson Bay (1690), the City of New York (1694), and Carolina (1698).

88. See, e.g., *The charter granted by Their Majesties King William and Queen Mary, to the inhabitants of the province of the Massachusetts-Bay in New-England* (1714) (preceding *The Acts and Laws).* For others, see *A Collection of charters and other publick acts relating to the province of Pennsylvania, viz. I. The royal charter to William Penn, Esq. II. The first frame of government, granted in England, in 1682. III. Laws agreed upon in England. IV. Certain conditions or concessions. V. The act of settlement, made at Chester, 1682. VI. The second frame of government, granted 1682. VII. The charter of the city of Philadelphia, granted October 25. 1701. VIII. The new charter of privileges to the province, granted October 28, 1701* (1740)*; A Defence of the legislative constitution of the province of Pennsylvania, as it now stands confirmed and established, by law and charter. With some observations on the proceedings published by sixteen members of Assembly, in a paper, entitled, The votes and proceedings of the House of Representatives: Recommended to the consideration of all the free-men of the province* (1728); *The charter granted by His Majesty King Charles the Second, to the colony of Rhode-Island, and Providence-Plantations in America* (Boston, 1719); *The charter granted by His Majesty King Charles II. to the governour & company of the English colony of Connecticut in New-England in America* (1718).

89. Jeremiah Dummer, *A defence of the New-England charters* (1721).

90. John Dickinson, "Speech on a Petition for a Change of Government of the Colony of

Pennsylvania, May 24, 1764," in *The Writings of John Dickinson,* ed., Paul Leicester Ford (Philadelphia: Historical Society of Pennsylvania, 1895), 1:44, quoted in Jacobson, "John Dickinson's Fight," 73–74.

91. *The Laws of Maryland* (1765).

92. *Journal of the Continental Congress,* Oct. 10, 1774; June 2, 1775; June 9, 1775.

93. Thomas Paine, *Common Sense* (1776), sec. 4.

94. Ibid., sec. 3.

95. Emphasis added.

96. On the evolving distinction between constitution and government, see Willi Paul Adams, *The First American Constitutions: Republican Ideology and the Making of the State Constitutions in the Revolutionary Era,* trans. Rita and Robert Kimber (1973; Lanham, Md.: Rowman & Littlefield, 2001), 19.

97. *Documentary History of the Constitution* (Washington, D.C.: Department of State, 1900), 3:7 (May 14, 1787). Madison subsequently revised this phrase to be "federal system of Government."

98. Other colonies wrote new documents that were little more than reworked versions of the charter. Those in New Jersey, for example, according to one commentator, "while freely admitting the absurdities and defects of their constitution were content to retain their archaic charter," which "did violence to the dogma of the Separation of Powers." Charles R. Erdman Jr., *The New Jersey Constitution of 1776* (Princeton, N.J.: Princeton University Press, 1929), vii. At the Convention, Ellsworth referred to the Articles of Confederation as a charter.

99. Madison to Judge Roane, Sept. 2, 1819, *The Records of the Federal Convention,* ed. Max Farrand (New Haven, Conn.: Yale University Press, 1966), vol. 3, doc. 131. He continued, "More especially those which divide legislation between the general and local governments; and that it might require a regular course of practice to liquidate and settle the meaning of some of them. But it was anticipated, I believe, by few, if any, of the friends of the Constitution, that a rule of construction would be introduced as broad and pliant as what has occurred."

100. See Patrick H. Hutton, "The Print Revolution of the Eighteenth Century and the Drafting of Written Constitutions," *Vermont History* 56 (1988): 154; Michael Warner, *Letters of the Republic: Publication and the Public Sphere in Eighteenth-Century America* (Cambridge, Mass.: Harvard University Press, 1990).

101. Morris L. Cohen and Sharon Hamby, "A Bibliography of the Early Reports of the Supreme Court of the United States," *Legal Reference Services Quarterly* 1 (1981): 43–144.

102. "Judicial Committee: Overview," http://www.privy-council.org.uk/output/page5.asp.

103. For recent discussion, see Paul von Nessen, "Is There Anything to Fear in Transnationalist Development of Law? The Australian Experience," *Pepperdine Law Review* 33 (2006): 883–92.

104. Privy Council Office, http://www.privy-council.org.uk/output/Page34.asp.

105. See, e.g., Dennis Morrison, "Caribbean Legal Affairs: The Judicial Committee of the Privy Council and the Death Penalty," *Nova Law Review* 30 (2006): 403–25; Mia Amor Mottley, "Caribbean Legal Affairs: Walking the Tightrope," *Nova Law Review* 30 (2006): 425–43; Brian D. Tittemore, "The Mandatory Death Penalty in the Commonwealth Carribbean and the Inter-American Human Rights System," *William and Mary Bill of Rights Journal* 13 (2004): 445–521; Joanna Harrington, "The Challenge to the Mandatory Death Penalty in the Commonwealth Caribbean," *American Journal of International Law* 98 (2004): 126–40.

106. *Watson v. The Queen,* 2004 WL 1372515 (Jamaica); Caroline Byrne, "UK Privy Council

Loses Appeal in Modern Commonwealth," Caribbean Net News (Aug. 17, 2006), http://www.caribbeannetnews.com/cgi-script/csArticles/articles/000028/002822.htm.

107. See New Zealand Business Roundtable, *Submission on Appeals to the Privy Council* (2001) (noting in particular the concern that "in a small country judges cannot always be relied on to uphold the rule of law, as opposed to being swayed by politically correct or even majority opinion").

108. Privy Council judgments begin to be reported around 1808 but even after 1833, Judicial Committee judgments were not officially reported. In 1865, the Privy Council appeals appear. Ellis Ames and Joseph Willard, "The Case of *Phillips v. Savage*," *Proceedings of the Massachusetts Historical Society* 5 (1860–62): 165, 170.

109. See "Unreported Judicial Decisions of the Privy Council, on Appeal from the Australian Colonies before 1850," Macquarie Law, http://www.law.mq.edu.au/pc/Introduction.htm (containing records of twenty cases); Bruce Kercher, "Unreported Privy Council Appeals from the Australian Colonies Before 1850," *Australian Law Journal* 77 (2003): 309.

110. E-mail to author (Oct. 17, 2006).

111. George Chalmers (1742–1825) probably assumed he would become an American colonial lawyer. After studying law in Edinburgh, Chalmers moved to Maryland in 1763 and began to practice law. Only in the fall of 1775 did Chalmers return to England. Chalmers, *Opinions of Eminent Lawyers*. Sharon O'Connor is currently compiling a finding guide to the American Privy Council appeals.

112. Paris to James Allen, July 26, 1738, in *Collections of the Connecticut Historical Society* (1892), 5:78–79; see Bilder, *The Transatlantic Constitution,* 122–36, 136–37 (discussing *Winthrop*).

113. See Ames and Willard, "The Case of *Phillips v. Savage*," 170 (suggesting distinction as reason for different result in *Winthrop* and *Phillips*).

114. Apart from scattered appeals briefs in various archives, collections remain in the British Library, the New York Public Library, the Library of Congress, and the Columbia Law School Library, each with handwritten notations. Unfortunately, some of the notes on the Columbia collection were shaved to fit the bound volume. See [Charles Yorke] briefs, Additional Mss. 15489, 36216–8220, British Library; [George Lee], Great Britain, Privy Council, Judicial Committee, Library of Congress, Law Division, Rare Books; [William Lee and George Lee], "Prize Appeals, 1736–1758," 2 vols., New York Public Library; William Samuel Johnson Collection, Diamond Law Library, Columbia University.

115. See Bilder, *The Transatlantic Constitution;* Mary Sarah Bilder, "The Corporate Origins of Judicial Review," *Yale Law Journal* 116 (2006): 502

116. Bilder, *The Transatlantic Constitution,* 137–38.

117. *Gillam Phillips v. Faith Savage (The Case of the Respondent Faith Savage)* (Jan. 1737), Henry Phillips Papers, 1728–38, Harvard Law School, handwritten notations (noting also that it created a new jurisdiction over real estates by allowing the probate judge to partition the property).

118. Appellant's case, *Gillam Phillips* v. Hannah Phillips (Jan. 1737), Phillips Papers. The brief correlated closely to the opinion that Ryder had previously given to Phillips's agent relating to the case in 1734. Jonathan Sharpe to Silas Hooper, Nov. 7, 1734 (Copy of Ryder Opinion), Folder 1–11, Phillips Papers.

119. Bilder, *The Transatlantic Constitution,* 139 (discussing *Clark v. Tousey*).

120. Lord Chancellor Hardwick had declared himself against the result in *Winthrop*. Allen to Gov. Talcott, Nov. 13, 1738, in Joseph Talcott, *Joseph Talcott Papers: Correspondence and Documents during Joseph Talcott's Governorship of the Colony of Connecticut, 1724–41*, Connecticut Historical Society Collections 4 (Hartford: Connecticut Historical Society, 1895), 5:71–72.

121. Johnson's notes on noncolonial appeals emphasized legal interpretations that affected colonial legal interpretations. See case of the appellant William Earl of Chatham (describing dispute among judges over whether the words "heirs male of the body" were words of limitation or of purchase and the consequence for perpetuities).

122. *Brenton v. Freebody* (1769), William Samuel Johnson Collection, Diamond Law Library, Columbia Law School; see Joseph Henry Smith, *Appeals to the Privy Council from the American Plantations* (New York: Octagon Books, 1965), 296 (mentioning note).

123. Smith, *Appeals to the Privy Council,* 495. Smith framed the legal question as whether "acts of Parliament disabling Roman Catholics extended" to Grenada (493). Smith discusses *Scott v. Brebner* at 493–95.

124. Al. Wedderburn and J. Dunning, brief in *Scott v. Brebner,* 5, Johnson Collection.

125. *Scott v. Brebner* (July 1771), Johnson Collection.

126. Bruce Kercher, "Judges and the Application of Imperial Law in Eastern Australia, 1788–1836," in *The British and Their Laws in the Eighteenth Century,* ed. David Lemmings (Woodbridge, Suffolk, UK: Boydell Press, 2005), 230, 249.

127. Charles Yorke represented the appellant, Corbin, who had lost in the Virginia courts. Johnson wrote: "Estate Tail Confirmed." Smith again thought the committee had failed to understand the technical distinctions involved. Smith, *Appeals to the Privy Council,* 493 (citing Add. Ms. 36,220/19). He noted, "Yorke appears to have questioned the soundness of this holding on the ground that Virginia was not colonized until more than twenty years after the passage of the statute, which was a useful regulation of property in an infant or an improved colony." Unclear is whether Smith is referring to Yorke's argument or his comment with respect to the holding going against him.

128. Smith discusses *Corbin* as part of a discussion (in which there seems to have been little pattern) over whether the pre-settlement statutes extended to the colonies. Smith, *Appeals to the Privy Council,* 487–95.

129. See Wilfred J. Ritz, *Rewriting the History of the Judiciary Act of 1789: Exposing Myths, Challenging Premises, and Using New Evidence* (Norman: University of Oklahoma Press, 1990).

130. For two interesting recent discussions of this common-law struggle, see Meyler, "Towards a Common Law Originalism"; Pearson, "Revising Custom, Embracing Choice." Another application would be in the fight over whether the Supreme Court had jurisdiction over common-law crimes.

131. Julius Goebel Jr., *History of the Supreme Court of the United States: Antecedents and Beginnings to 1801* (New York: Macmillan, 1971), 666.

132. Goebel notes that the newspaper account of *West v. Barnes* provided exceptionally unusual coverage. Ibid., 666 n. 7.

133. Ibid., 804.

134. D. B. Swinfen, *Imperial Control of Colonial Legislation, 1813–1865* (Oxford: Clarendon Press, 1970), 2.

135. Ibid., 6–7.

136. Wade and Phillips, *Constitutional Law,* 420; 28–29 Vict., c. 63 s. 2 (requiring colonial

laws to be void for repugnancy to "any Act of Parliament extending to the Colony to which such Law may relate, or . . . to any Order or Regulation made under Authority of such Act of Parliament, or having in the Colony the Force or Effect of such Act"). The act responded to actions of Justice Boothby of the Supreme Court of South Australia in striking down colonial laws under a wider definition of repugnancy. See Wade and Phillips, *Constitutional Law,* 6–8. Beginning in 1859, Justice Boothby declared a right to decide on the validity of colonial legislation. Boothby adopted a broad notion of repugnancy under which "English law should control that enacted by the local legislature" (171). Swinfen adds, "To him repugnancy meant more than conflict with imperial acts extending to the colony or with fundamental principles of English law" (171). Thus he concluded that the Australian legislatures could not "override the common law of England." *Liebelt v. Hunt,* SAPP 141 L.C. (1861).

137. Wade and Phillips, *Constitutional Law,* 183.

138. Elmer Russell, *Review of American Colonial Legislation by the King in Council* (New York: Columbia University, 1915), 221.

139. *2007 Year End Report on the Federal Judiciary* (Jan. 2007), 9.

140. *Acts of the Privy Council of England: Colonial Series* (Hereford, UK: Printed for H.M.S.O. by Anthony Brothers, 1908–12).

141. Opinions appear in Chalmers, *Opinions of Eminent Lawyers*. The comments of Francis Fane on the Connecticut laws appear in his *Reports on the Laws of Connecticut,* ed. Charles M. Andrews (New Haven, Conn.: Tuttle, Morehouse & Taylor Press, 1915).

142. *Records of the Federal Convention* (June 8, 1787), 1:168. Before the Revolution, Pownall had written that a colonial administration should have a court for "a constitutional conformity to the laws of the mother country; but would also maintain that dependency therein, which is the essence of colonial administration." Pownall, *The Administration of the British Colonies,* 85. Jack Rakove describes Madison's suggestion as "his most radical proposal of all: to give the national government an unlimited negative (or veto) over all state laws." Jack N. Rakove, *Declaring Rights: A Brief History with Documents* (Boston: Bedford Books, 1998), 105. For the classic article on the negativing power, see Charles Hobson, "The Negative on State Laws: James Madison, the Constitution and the Crisis of Republican Government," *William and Mary Quarterly* 36 (1979): 215–35.

143. Madison to Jefferson, Oct. 24, 1787, in *The Records of the Federal Convention,* 3:131, doc. 137. **yes**

144. For brief discussion, see Bilder, "The Corporate Origins of Judicial Review," text accompanying notes 249–252.

145. Sec. 25 of the *First Judiciary Act,* 1 Stat. 73, ch. 20 (1789).

3

Drawing and Redrawing the Line: The Pre-Revolutionary Origins of Federal Ideas of Sovereignty

ALISON LACROIX

THIS ESSAY EMERGED OUT OF CONVERSATIONS THAT BEGAN DURING preparation for my graduate school general examinations (supervised in part by Morton Horwitz) and that continued through the writing of my dissertation (under the same invaluable guidance). In its previous incarnation as a dissertation chapter, the essay served not only as the topic of discussion during multiple afternoon meetings in Griswold Hall, but also as the subject of a memorable and illuminating telephone call in September 2005, conducted while I was on a train north of Manhattan and Professor Horwitz was in Boston. He had sent me an e-mail message saying that he had thought of a new angle from which to approach Thomas Hutchinson's confrontation with the Massachusetts assembly and suggested that I call him to discuss it. I had been in the process of writing the chapter for several weeks and hoped that it would be central to the argument of the larger dissertation, so I was extremely grateful to have the benefit of Professor Horwitz's wise observations. I look back on that phone conversation not only as a critical moment in which Professor Horwitz helped me to understand the story I was trying to tell, but also as just one example of the type of devotion and attention that he has always shown to his students—even when they were far away and at the mercy of rail travel in the Northeast Corridor.

January 1773 might strike observers, then and now, as hardly the most propitious moment for a British imperial official to initiate a public debate regarding the constitutional basis of the empire. Yet that month, a desire for such a debate simmered near the surface of everyday life in the Massachusetts capital. Since at least the Stamp Act crisis of 1765, the question of the extent of Parliament's power to regulate the colonies—most notably, through taxation—had formed the subtext of political discussion in British North America. To be sure, Boston's newspapers that January featured the usual advertisements for imported wares such as chocolate, "choice West India RUM," Irish linens, "new Raisins & Currants," and "Teneriffe and Madeira WINES." By the end of the first week of the year, however, a new political debate had begun a slow burn in the upper chambers of the Province House. Soon reports of this great controversy began to fill the columns alongside the merchants' solicitations. The debate would help to end the career of Governor Thomas Hutchinson, finishing the work of destruction that the Stamp Act mobs had begun eight years earlier. And, significantly for the development of American federalism, the political conflict of early 1773 would highlight a growing divergence between the colonists' and their imperial cousins' conceptions of sovereignty.

The constitutional debate between Hutchinson and the Massachusetts colonial assembly, or General Court, unfolded between January 6 and March 6, 1773, in a series of widely publicized speeches and responses between Hutchinson and the General Court, the latter acting sometimes in its collective capacity and sometimes in its component parts of upper (Council) and lower (House of Representatives) houses. These three months provide a glimpse into a moment of significant crisis in prewar America. That crisis was both political, inasmuch as it concerned contemporary arrangements of power and regulation, and constitutional, inasmuch as it concerned the structure of imperial governance itself.

At the heart of the controversy lay the issue of sovereignty: that is, the question "What is the highest authority to which an individual owes duties and from which an individual can demand fulfillment of rights?" Both Hutchinson and the General Court sought to identify the "final and absolute political authority in the political community" such that "no final and absolute authority exists elsewhere."[1] As each side of the debate articulated its vision of the scope of parliamentary power, and the concomitant scope of the colonial assemblies' power, allegiances hardened, and visions of sovereignty began to diverge.[2] While Hutchinson hewed to a unitary view of sovereignty possessed exclusively by Parliament, the members of the General Court struggled to construct a workable scheme by which sovereignty could be apportioned between Westminster and the colonies. When, by 1774, this scheme proved elusive, the colonists applied their fledgling conception of divisible sovereignty to their efforts to promote union among the colonies.

The debate between Hutchinson and the General Court brought together some of the most theoretically sophisticated minds of the day in a public dispute over the nature of government power, a dispute that would expose a widening schism between the British imperial view of sovereignty and the colonial view. Spokesmen for the British Empire took their cues from developments in domestic political theory, which by the late eighteenth century increasingly insisted that sovereignty was both indivisible and possessed by Parliament alone. The great debate of 1773 thus illustrates an important break with the metropolitan conception of authority and an early instance in which colonists began to grope toward a conception of multilayered sovereignty in reaction to the theory of unitary sovereignty that they saw gaining ground among British officials.[3] This multilayered sovereignty, in turn, would provide a crucial theoretical underpinning for the development of American federalism.[4]

The Boston debates of 1773 should be understood as continuing this long history of confrontation while also signaling a new urgency in the tone of the debate—a shift from a state of relatively regular, if unsettling, dissent and discussion to a heightened atmosphere of strife in which first principles of government and constitution seemed to contemporaries to require redefinition and reexamination. John Phillip Reid, in an essay on the debate, refers to the addresses that each of the three sides delivered as "legal briefs" submitted on "the one occasion when the constitutional controversy was joined." For this reason, Reid notes, "these briefs may well be the most important legal documents of the prerevolutionary era."[5]

In their detail, their comprehensiveness, and—perhaps most important—their origin as speeches delivered in the context of an actual debate, the addresses offer valuable insight into the developing schism between imperial and colonial visions of the nature of British sovereignty. The debates served, on one side, as a rehearsal of post–Glorious Revolution British political theory and, on the other side, as a debut for creole constitutional notions that pointed toward a new understanding of the nature of authority within a composite political entity. In this way, the standoff between governor and assembly in Massachusetts helps to illuminate the path of colonial constitutional thought from the oppositional mode of the 1760s to the more daring and experimental assertions of the possibility of divided sovereignty that would characterize the period between 1774 and 1787.

Having served as lieutenant governor of Massachusetts Bay Colony since 1758, Thomas Hutchinson became acting governor in August 1769, and governor in March 1771. In keeping with the antagonistic relationship that he had developed with the people of Boston throughout his time as chief justice of the Massachusetts Superior Court of Judicature and then as lieutenant governor, Hutchinson immediately became a lightning rod for the increasingly voluble critics of the imperial administration. As Bernard Bailyn, Hutchinson's leading biographer, puts it, "He was embroiled in argument with the opposition from almost the first day of his acting governorship."[6]

By late December 1772, confrontation between the governor and the assembly appeared imminent. When the Boston town meeting, led by Samuel Adams, formed a committee of correspondence to caucus with other towns on the issue of the Crown's assumption of the salaries of royal officials, Hutchinson attempted to stanch radical sentiment by immediately exercising his prerogative to prorogue, or suspend, that session of the General Court. Despite the General Court's hiatus, dissent continued to brew. Faced with this continued intransigence,

Hutchinson shifted strategies from muting to engaging the assembly. In a December 22 letter to William Legge, second Earl of Dartmouth and secretary of state for the colonies, Hutchinson proposed a new approach. "I am brought to a necessity of requiring the Assembly to be more explicit in declaring how far they approve or disapprove of such proceedings and what sense they have of their dependence upon the Supreme Authority of the B[ritish] isles and Dominions than they have ever yet been," the governor wrote.[7] Explicit declarations such as these would require open public debate.

Two weeks later, on January 6, 1773, the General Court convened in a special emergency session called by the governor. Opening the session, Hutchinson wasted no time in reaching the gravamen of the matter, presenting a forceful case for the supremacy of metropolitan rule. Adhering to post–Glorious Revolution, Whig-influenced political theory, he took as his premise the notion that the paramount authority of the British government was vested in Parliament, by which he meant the unified political entity of king, Lords, and Commons—a political version of the Holy Trinity in which three seemingly distinct entities operated as one.[8]

Dismissing claims that the colonial assemblies possessed any powers apart from those granted to them by Parliament, Hutchinson embraced the view that was at that time becoming orthodoxy among many British political theorists: sovereignty must be undivided and indivisible within any given state.[9] Hutchinson based this argument on a twofold vision of the empire that saw the colonies as British satellites, and Parliament as the center of British imperial power. Power could be delegated from the central government to agents such as royal governors, but such delegations were only temporary; power could not truly be shared. "In sovereignty there are no gradations," Samuel Johnson would write in 1775, echoing Blackstone's *Commentaries*, published a decade earlier. Instead, Johnson insisted that every society must contain "some power or other, from which there is no appeal, which admits no restrictions, which pervades the whole mass of the community."[10] Hutchinson's January 6 speech to both houses of the General Court expressed the same conviction that civil society required a single, supreme, unlimited rule-making and -enforcing power.

Despite his lack of formal legal training, Hutchinson began with a narrow reading of the provision of the colonial charter that had established a provincial legislature.[11] "The General Court has, by Charter, *full* Power to make such Laws as are not repugnant to the Laws of England," Hutchinson stated. Finding no specific statement in the charter denominating the colonial legislature the "*sole* Power" governing the province, he argued that the General Court's lawmaking power was supplemental to, not exclusive of, the legislative authority of Parliament. "Surely then this is by Charter a Reserve of Power and Authority to Parliament . . . and, consequently, is a Limitation of the Power given to the General Court," he concluded.[12]

This line of argument illustrates the zero-sum nature of the debate for Hutchinson. He appears to have believed that in order to make his case for the complete supremacy of Parliament, he had to prove the total subordination of the General Court. Any limit on the power of the colonial assembly—especially if that limit stemmed from the province's founding charter—would, he hoped, dispose of all challenges to the broad sweep of metropolitan power. Absent an express grant of sole power, or sovereignty, to the colonial assembly, Hutchinson argued that any claim of independent legislative power by colonial legislators must fail.

At this point, the published accounts of the January 6 session convey the sense that Hutchinson had reached the climax of his polemic. The colonial assemblies existed at the pleasure of metropolitan authorities, he argued. Imperial officials, Hutchinson among them, had never envisioned the colonial governments as anything more than "subordinate Powers," corporations "formed within the Kingdom" with the limited brief of "mak[ing] and execut[ing] such Bylaws as are for their immediate Use and Benefit."[13] The governor then summed up his vision of sovereignty in a statement that would ring in his own ears and the ears of his fellow colonists for years to come. "I know of no Line that can be drawn between the supreme Authority of Parliament and the total Independence of the Colonies," Hutchinson declared. "It is impossible there should be two independent Legislatures in one and the same State, for although there may be but one Head, the King, yet the two Legislative Bodies will make two Governments as distinct as the Kingdoms of England and Scotland before the Union."[14]

The governor thus made his case clear: despite their recent pretensions to power, the colonial assemblies were nothing more than the creatures of the supreme assembly housed along the Thames. Hutchinson, like Dr. Johnson, viewed sovereignty as containing no gradations; the power pervading the whole mass of the British Atlantic community emanated from the center and tolerated no provincial competition. No line could be drawn between imperial and colonial power because, simply put, colonial power had no independent existence. No line could be drawn because, according to eighteenth-century British political theory, parliamentary power had to be absolute and plenary in order to fulfill its ancient constitutional mandate.[15] No line could be drawn, because to delineate sovereignty was to deny sovereignty.

With his pronouncement in the Council Chamber, Hutchinson declared his allegiance to a vision of sovereignty that had emerged over the course of two centuries of English political conflict. Sovereignty was, by the eighteenth century, a highly contested and fraught concept. The issue of sovereignty—its nature and its location—had lain at the heart of much of the constitutional struggle that had gripped England since the sixteenth century. Early modern definitions of English sovereignty typically invoked the Act in Restraint of Appeals of 1533, according to which England denominated itself an "empire," meaning—in the words of J. G. A. Pocock—a political entity "exercising a final and unappealable jurisdiction over itself in both church and state."[16] A state that possessed "sovereignty," then, was a state complete in itself, over which no other state (ecclesiastical or political) could claim authority.

With the establishment of a notion of sovereignty as a species of final dominion over the state that precluded interference from any putatively higher power, the next inquiry was where in the structure of government that dominion ought to be lodged. Conflict over this issue underlay the English Civil War and the Glorious Revolution, two watershed constitutional moments that continued to exert tremendous influence on the minds of eighteenth-century Britons both at home and in the colonies. In 1642, Parliament's declaration of a theory of its own sovereignty helped to spark war but nevertheless laid the foundation for the theory of parliamentary sovereignty that would gain currency while continuing to cause strife over the subsequent decades.[17] By the latter half of the eighteenth century, some commentators viewed parliamentary sovereignty as an accepted part of British constitutional theory. Citing Sir Edward Coke, Blackstone observed, "The power and jurisdiction of parliament . . . is so transcendent and absolute, that it cannot be confined, either for causes or persons, within any bounds."[18]

Blackstone's *Commentaries on the Laws of England*, published between 1765 and 1769, aimed to enshrine the unitary vision of sovereignty in late eighteenth-century British legal thought.[19] Blackstone inveighed against the concept of *imperium in imperio*, by which he meant multiple sources of authority sharing the same political space. At the time of the Hutchinson–General Court debate, political theorists routinely denounced the notion of *imperium in imperio*, variously translated as "an empire within an empire" or "dominion within dominion," as a "solecism."[20] The specter of the *imperium in imperio* principle appealed to the early modern desire for clear rules according to which governments ought to be constructed. It provided an analytical framework by which to assess the success (or, more often, the failure) of any given political arrangement.

Yet this orthodox principle of sovereignty had only recently become established, having begun as the centerpiece of anti-Stuart Parliamentarian ideology during the Civil War of the 1640s and cementing its place as the fundament of Whig—and therefore English—constitutionalism in the Glorious Revolution of 1688–89.[21] By the nineteenth century, British theorists of government viewed parliamentary sovereignty as integral to the nation's political and constitutional structure. In 1773, however, the unitary vision of sovereignty still required assertion and argument by such luminaries as Blackstone to establish its hegemony after the turmoil and uncertainty of the past century and a half.

But there was another way of looking at sovereignty—a Continental view that acknowledged certain systems of divided authority as legitimate, or at least plausible, governmental structures. Beginning with the work of Hugo Grotius in the early seventeenth century, and continuing with the writing of Samuel von Pufendorf in the later seventeenth century and Emer de Vattel in the mid-eighteenth century, European thinkers had offered an alternative to this all-or-nothing unitary vision of sovereignty.[22] Using the natural law concept of *fœdera*—that is, treaties or positive agreements among political entities—these theorists presented an alternative to the English (later British) belief that multiple sovereignties always spelled solecism and disaster.[23] Instead, they argued that leagues, compacts, and confederations could be viable modes of political cooperation among sovereign bodies.

Throughout both Europe and America, this Continental notion of divisible sovereignty had been bumping up against the common-law vision of unitary sovereignty throughout the middle decades of the eighteenth century. Despite the insistence of Blackstone, Johnson, and others that a single sovereign power must be acknowledged to "pervade the whole mass of the community," and—perhaps more important—their insistence that this was not an argumentative claim but a descriptive claim about the essence of the common law, the truth was that the nature of sovereignty was a contested, not a settled, issue in Anglo-American constitutional thought during this period.

Even before Hutchinson invited the General Court to parley, some colonists in Massachusetts and beyond had the tools to assess Parliament's claims of unlimited authority in light of these alternative theories of sovereignty. For example, Vattel's *Droit des gens* (*Law of Nations*) of 1758 was translated and published in an English edition in 1759. This version was followed in 1775 by an edition that was published in Amsterdam and distributed by Benjamin Franklin to the Library Company of Philadelphia, Harvard College, and the Library of Congress.[24] Richard Bland, writing in 1766, included a citation to Vattel in his *Inquiry into the Rights of the British Colonies*.[25] George Washington's library contained a copy of Grotius's *Rights of War and Peace* in its English translation of 1738.[26]

Indeed, the House of Representatives cited both Grotius and Pufendorf during the course of the debate with Hutchinson. The House answer of March 6 deployed both theorists against the governor's assertion that the colonies constituted part of the realm.[27] "We beg Leave, upon what your Excellency has observed of the Colony becoming Part of the State, to subjoin the Opinions of several learned Civilians," the House stated: "Colonies, says Puffendorf, are settled in different Methods. For either the Colony *continues a Part* of the Common Wealth it was [sent] out from; or else is obliged to pay a dutiful Regard to the Mother Common Wealth, and so to be in Readiness to defend and vindicate its Honor, and so is *united by a Sort of unequal Confederacy*; or lastly *is erected into a separate Common Wealth* and *assumes the same Rights*, with the State it descended from." Immediately following this passage (which the House noted came from "a very able Lawyer in this Country"), the answer cited Grotius for a similar proposition. "King Tullius, as quoted by the same learned Author from Grotius, says, 'We look upon it to be neither Truth nor Justice that Mother Cities ought of Necessity and *by the Law of Nature* to *rule over the Colonies*.'"[28] Hutchinson parried the reference with his own interpretation. "Your Attempt to shew that new discovered Countries do not become Part of the State, from the Authority of Puffendorff &c., will fail," he replied. "The Instance given by him of a Colony erected into a separate Common Wealth plainly appears by the Context to be by the Leave or Consent of the Parent State."[29]

As this exchange demonstrates, European theory formed an important conceptual background to the Boston debates.[30] The Grotian vision of the law of nations emphasized what Edward Keene terms an "extra-European order" of colonial and imperial systems based on "the principle that sovereignty should be divided across national and territorial boundaries."[31] Pufendorf's *De jure naturae et gentium* (*Law of Nature and Nations*) (1672) offered a similar vision of non-unitary authority based on study of the German Empire. For Pufendorf, German fragmentation was an invitation to revise the traditional Aristotelian categories of political bodies (monarch, aristocracy, democracy) to take into account the real—if unharmonious—structure of the empire.[32] Generalizing from the specifics of the empire and certain classical leagues of states, Pufendorf developed a new category: the "system of states" in which "several States are joined to each other, each by a perpetual League or Alliance" pursuant to which the states agree that "they shall not exercise some Part of that Sovereignty there specified, without the general Consent of each other." Sovereign powers that did not implicate the common interest, however, were left to each member state. "These Unions submit only some certain Parts of the Sovereignty to mutual Direction," Pufendorf noted, recommending that "the particular States reserve to themselves all those Branches of the supreme Authority, the Management of which can have little or no Influence (at least directly) on the Affairs of the rest."[33] In contrast to a unitary theory of sovereignty, therefore, Pufendorf's conception allowed for the possibility that political authority might cross jurisdictional boundaries and, on occasion, be shared among multiple states tied together in a single system.

Hutchinson's speech fanned controversy among Bostonians as they awaited the responses of the Council and the House of Representatives. While newspapers throughout the colonies debated the consequences of Hutchinson's remarks, the members of the Council and House of Representatives considered their responses. Each house designated a committee to craft written replies to be delivered to Hutchinson.[34] Slightly more than two weeks after Hutchinson's address to the General Court, the two houses delivered their answers, the Council on January 25, and the House on January 26. Each answer had received unanimous approval in its respective house, as the *Boston-Gazette* gleefully noted.[35]

The Council's answer took up Hutchinson's theme of lawmaking supremacy but resisted his conclusion by invoking traditional imperatives of limited governmental authority. Citing Magna Carta, the Council argued that Hutchinson's phrase "supreme authority" actually translated into "unlimited authority" and then charged that this was an untenable proposition according to the ancient fundamental law of England, which held that no authority could legitimately claim to be unlimited.[36] "If Supreme Authority includes unlimited Authority, the Subjects of it are emphatically Slaves," the Council argued. Moreover, the Council objected to Hutchinson's use of the term "supremacy," contending that the word was a term of art with specific nonterrestrial meaning. "Supreme or unlimited Authority can with Fitness belong only to the Sovereign of the Universe. . . . But with Truth this can be said of no other Authority whatever."[37] After thus chiding Hutchinson for confusing mere political power with divine dominion, the Council moved on to consider the limits that must necessarily attach to the former species of authority.

As these claims suggest, Anglo-Americans in the 1770s did not consider the terms "sovereignty" and "supremacy" to be necessarily synonymous.[38] In general, the idea of sovereignty in this period can be seen as an ill-defined concept relating to the legitimate source of "right," as opposed to mere "power," within a given polity.[39] "Supremacy," in contrast, was a more relative term that dealt with the question whether a particular lawmaking body was the final authority within its jurisdiction.[40]

Whatever difference existed between sovereignty and supremacy did not matter greatly, however, as long as the British nation and the British Empire were viewed as coterminous.[41] And this was precisely the view of British officials. From the standpoint of imperial administrators, because Parliament was domestically sovereign, it was imperially supreme.[42] Sovereignty and supremacy therefore *were* synonymous for imperial spokesmen, which allowed them to make the type of sweeping claims that Hutchinson's speech asserted. The colonial opposition, however, sought to break this equivalence between rule over nation and rule over empire, especially in the wake of the Stamp Act crisis of 1765. Still desirous of remaining British in the larger sense, they accepted Parliament's authority over them, but only to the extent that that authority did not trench on that of their local assemblies.

The willingness of these American theorists to contemplate a system in which the colonists lived under two layers of legislative authority suggests that they had begun to abandon the concept of supremacy, with its all-or-nothing emphasis on a single dominant power. They were also rejecting the emerging Blackstonian concept of indivisible sovereignty, insofar as they acknowledged only a limited authority of Parliament to regulate trade but reserved the other legislative powers for the colonial assemblies. Although the members of the colonial opposition might have agreed with Hutchinson that the colonies were part of Britain (whether empire, realm, or dominions was a separate issue), they disagreed with the governor's assertion that no line could be drawn between submission and independence. Parliament's authority over England, Scotland, and Wales could and must, they argued, be distinguished from its authority over America.

The House's answer to Hutchinson displayed this more aggressive tone. The answer, which numbered twenty-six pages when it was published in pamphlet form, met Hutchinson's brief for parliamentary authority with a point-by-point rebuttal of his theory of the empire. Their critique comprised several lines of argument, but two of their most significant targets were Hutchinson's interpretation of the original Massachusetts charter and his larger theory of sovereignty.

The House began its investigation into the colony's early history by disputing one of Hutchinson's key premises: his claim that because the charter had not contained an express grant of "sole power" to the colonial assembly, it had therefore reserved the bulk of the legislative power to Parliament, which in turn obligated the colonial assembly to pass only such acts as were not repugnant to the laws of England. In Hutchinson's view, therefore, the colonial assembly was entirely the creature of Parliament. House members challenged this hierarchy by offering their own construction of the charter based on seventeenth-century political understandings. At the time of the English arrival in America, the House reply contended, the prevailing theory held that the new colonial lands belonged to the king's dominions, not to the kingdom. They therefore possessed a special legal status that placed them under Crown authority alone. "The Right of disposing of the Lands was in the Opinion of those Times vested solely in the Crown," the House stated.[43]

The chain of argument proceeded thus: if the colonies were under the exclusive control of the Crown at the time of the charter, then they were at that time not part of the realm; if they were not then part of the realm, they could not now be part of the kingdom of Great Britain; if they were not now part of the kingdom of Great Britain, they were not now under the control of Parliament. "If then the Colonies were not annexed to the Realm, at the Time when their Charters were granted, they never could be afterwards, without their own special Consent, which has never since been had, or even asked," the House stated. "If they are not now annexed to the Realm, they are not a Part of the Kingdom, and consequently not subject to the Legislative Authority of the Kingdom."[44] The House thus refused to take a historicizing view of the original text, insisting instead that the constitution of 1629 and the constitution of 1773 were one and the same.

This argument made historical sense: the Massachusetts Bay Company had obtained its charter from Charles I in 1629, sixty years before the Glorious Revolution supplanted royal prerogative with parliamentary sovereignty as the basis of English government. At the time of the charter's drafting, therefore, English constitutional theory placed the king at the top of the ladder of sovereignty. Hutchinson's argument, in contrast, read the parliamentary sovereignty of his own post-

1688 period backward based on the assumption that the revolution settlement had applied retroactively and for all time.[45] Hutchinson's approach might have been good Whig orthodoxy, but the House's answer charged that it was not good history.

By challenging Hutchinson's interpretation of the charter, the House attacked imperial officials' assumption of equivalence between parliamentary sovereignty at home and supremacy over the colonial assemblies. Just as the Council had invoked Magna Carta as a talisman of the ancient constitution against overweening parliamentary power, the House sought refuge in the traditional pre-1688 vision of Crown prerogative. The Massachusetts colonial legislature therefore invoked what John Phillip Reid terms the "authority of custom" that openly challenged Parliament's authority both at home and in the far reaches of the empire.[46]

Was this argument in favor of Crown rule purely instrumental? Perhaps; after all, England had fought a savage civil war over the very issue of Crown prerogative versus parliamentary sovereignty. Yet members of the colonial opposition routinely pledged loyalty to the king during this debate, adhering to what scholars have variously termed the theory of dominion status or the "doctrine of allegiance" that emphasized membership in a loosely defined association with the monarch alone rather than membership in the British nation.[47] As the eminent Scots-American jurist James Wilson would put it in 1774, "All the different members of the British empire are distinct states, independent of each other, but connected together under the same sovereign in right of the same crown."[48] Adams made a similar distinction between the kingdom of Britain and the dominion of the king: "We are within the dominion, rule, or government of the King of Great Britain," he acknowledged; however, he added, "We are not . . . a part of the British kingdom, realm, or state."[49] Although they chose different terms, Wilson and Adams endorsed what Randolph Adams terms the "commonwealth of nations" view of empire, which held that the colonies were independent states, "that their sole connection with Great Britain lay in the crown; that the parliament at Westminster was but one of many co-equal legislatures, analogous, for example, to the General Court of Massachusetts Bay."[50] Rather than a choice *for* the Crown, such arguments should be seen as a choice *against* Parliament: the colonists sought to place their own legislatures directly under royal authority by cutting Parliament out of the hierarchy altogether.[51]

The central role played by James Wilson, who emigrated from Scotland to America in 1765 at the age of twenty-three, in developing the doctrine of allegiance was not a coincidence. For Wilson and other colonists who argued that the colonists owed loyalty to the king alone, the example of Scotland provided a rich trove of legal arguments. The union of crowns of 1603, in which James VI of Scotland also became James I of England, "united the kingdoms only to the extent that it gave them 'one Head or Sovereign'; it did not unite them in one body politic."[52] By 1707, when the Act of Union formally dissolved both the English and the Scottish parliaments and brought England and Scotland into a new entity called the British Parliament, English subjects—and, after 1607, American colonists—had lived through more than a century's worth of debates about the practical meaning of sovereignty, and the many varieties of Pufendorfian "systems of states" that could join two polities.[53]

The transformation from what David Armitage terms the "composite monarchy" of England to the "multiple kingdom" of Great Britain caused observers throughout Anglo-America to consider seriously the possibility of multilevel political and legal authorities besides the old feudal arrangements.[54] Moreover, because the era of the Anglo-Scottish unions coincided with the era of English colonization in North America, political thinkers on both sides of the ocean frequently drew analogies between the status of Scotland and that of the colonies. (Recall Hutchinson's January 6 statement that he "kn[ew] of no line" that could be drawn between parliamentary supremacy and colonial independence that would not create "two Governments as distinct as the Kingdoms of England and Scotland before the Union.") In this way, as Armitage notes, the same ideology that accompanied the melding of the multiple kingdom at home drove the expansion of the empire overseas. Thus, "British state-building and British empire-building" were "continuous with one another in their origins as in their outcomes."[55]

This ideological connection between state and empire building informed both sides of the debate between Hutchinson and the General Court. While Wilson's experience as a Scot informed his entire political outlook, Adams explicitly used the Scottish case to bolster his arguments against parliamentary authority.[56] In particular, Adams focused on the period following the union of crowns but before the Act of Union, which he believed provided useful precedents for the situation of the colonies in the 1760s and early 1770s. Just as Scotland had shared a king but not a legislature with England between 1603 and 1707, Adams contended, the American colonies should be seen as owing allegiance to George III, but not to Parliament. Just as Scotland had maintained its sovereignty until it formally merged with England in 1707, the colonies remained sovereign in 1774. In each case, one state had contracted its own arrangement with a sovereign who just happened to be the sovereign of another state—a fact that did not affect the relationship between the sovereign and the first state, which existed independent of the sovereign's relationship with any other state. "Distinct states may be united under one king. . . . Massachusetts is a realm, New York is a realm, Pennsylvania another realm, to all intents and purposes, as much as Ireland is, or England or Scotland ever were," Adams wrote in his "Novanglus" letters. "The King of Great Britain is the sovereign of all these realms."[57] Should Britain and the colonies mutually determine that a complete union was desirable, the full formalities of annexation—notably, consent in the form of legislative acts on each side—would be required.[58]

The House draftsmen went on to offer their own version of the line-drawing metaphor, confirming its role as a leitmotif of the debate. Obviously struck by Hutchinson's pronouncement, the House members adapted it for their own purposes: "Indeed it is difficult, if possible, to draw a Line of Distinction between the universal Authority of Parliament over the Colonies, and no Authority at all," the response observed.[59] The blandness of the statement belied its radical divergence from Hutchinson's imperial orthodoxy. Drawing lines remained difficult, but suddenly it was possible. Rather than pointing to the vast political boundary that encompassed Britain and its dependencies and then concluding that the lines of law and constitution must necessarily follow the lines of might and rule, the colonial opposition attempted to separate political lines from constitutional ones. Even John Adams agreed that the colonies were part of the British nation. But Adams, Wilson, and their contemporaries in the General Court did not view this political authority as necessarily decisive of final legal authority. Instead of accepting Hutchinson's all-or-nothing, totalizing vision of imperial structure, the colonists sought to adapt what originally had been an ad hoc structure of royal charter and local assembly into a newly conceived vision of Britishness. In so doing, they were—albeit unknowingly—laying the groundwork for a novel understanding of divisible sovereignty and, eventually, federalism.

The 1773 debates are significant because they marked the beginning of a transition, not because they witnessed the completion of that transition. Despite the slowly shifting meaning of the term "sovereignty," the members of the House feared—or at least pretended to fear—the unnatural creature of the *imperium in imperio* sufficiently to deploy it against Hutchinson in their reply of January 26. To bolster their claim that the original charters had placed the colonies under the exclusive control of the king, the members of the House committee reinterpreted the *imperium in imperio* principle as precluding Parliament from exerting its power over the colonies. "To suppose a Parliamentary Authority over the Colonies under such Charters, would necessarily induce that Solecism in Politics, *Imperium in Imperio*," the House answer contended. Premising their argument upon the existence and authority of the assemblies from the earliest moments of colonial settlement, the House members demurred to Hutchinson's claims, using his own argument to conclude "that the Colonies were by their Charters made distinct States from the Mother Country."[60]

Throughout the debate, then, both sides employed the *imperium in imperio* argument. Hutchinson relied on it to underpin his claim that the colonial assemblies did not possess legislative sovereignty; the members of the General Court, for their part, relied on it for their challenge to parliamentary authority. Both sides espoused the underlying principle that multiple sovereigns could not exist within the same political entity. Yet while Hutchinson took this principle to mean that the sovereignty of Parliament at home must translate into its supremacy abroad, the members of the General Court used it to build a novel argument for the sovereignty of the colonial assemblies based on a reconfiguration of the lines of authority between Britain and America. And, the House added, if such line drawing proved beyond the capacities of the royal governor, Massachusetts—in concert with the other colonies—was prepared to essay it.

Hutchinson addressed the General Court twice more before proroguing the legislative session on March 6; between his two speeches, each house issued a response. The issue of sovereignty dominated the remainder of the discussion. In his February 16 speech, Hutchinson first addressed the Council before directing the bulk of his comments to the House. As his comments to the Council suggest, his "drawing a line" phrasing had again returned to haunt him. The Council's "Attempts to draw a Line as the Limits of the Supreme Authority in Government, by distinguishing some natural Rights as more peculiarly exempt from such Authority than the rest, rather tend to evince the Impracticability of drawing such a Line," Hutchinson stated.[61] The governor thus stuck to his original observation that the sovereignty of Parliament was complete and indivisible. Addressing the House, Hutchinson noted that Massachusetts Bay Colony was "holden as feudatory of the Imperial Crown of England."[62] Thus, the colony was "subject to one supreme legislative power"—Parliament—along with the rest of the one entire dominion of the British Empire.[63]

Just over a week after Hutchinson's second speech, the Council issued what would be its final salvo; the House followed with its answer five days later. Previously, the House had produced the fierier response. Here, however, the Council struck directly at the heart of the issue: whether two coordinate authorities, in this case Parliament and the colonial assemblies, could ever exist within the same polity. The Council based its argument on Hutchinson's previous statement, uttered as part of his initial address on January 6, that "although from the Nature of Government there must be one Supreme Authority over the whole, yet this Constitution will admit of Subordinate Powers with Legislative and Executive Authority, greater or less, according to Local and other Circumstances." The Council heartily endorsed this assertion. "This is very true," the Council noted, adding that allowing for the existence of subordinate as well as supreme powers implied that "the Supreme Power has no rightful Authority to take away or diminish" the authority of the subordinate power. The supreme power lacked such authority to police the subordinate power because, the Council argued, the subordinate power was constituted independently of the supreme power. If the subordinate power were not independently constituted, then it would not need to be denominated a subordinate power; instead, it would be a subset of the supreme power. But this was not the case. Each power had its own grant of authority and its own zone of responsibility. Therefore, the Council observed, "The two Powers are not incompatible, and do subsist together, each restraining its Acts to their Constitutional Objects." The constitutional objects of each power were distinct, and they were defined by their subject matter.[64]

In other words, the colonists might consider consenting to Parliament's supremacy if that supremacy were accompanied by an independent acknowledgment of the colonial assemblies' subordinate authority. Such an arrangement would keep the two levels of legislative authority separate by assigning to each a specific array of responsibilities: Parliament would supervise, regulate, and legislate for the entire British Empire, including America; the colonial legislatures, meanwhile, would oversee all matters that did not relate to the empire as a whole.

This arrangement tracked the distinction between internal and external affairs that observers such as Richard Bland, Daniel Dulany, and Thomas Pownall had articulated since the Stamp Act debates had raised the issue of the scope of Parliament's authority over the colonies.[65] In the context of the 1773 debates, however, the Council's delineation between superior and subordinate powers moved beyond the specific issue of taxation and toward the theoretical problem of *imperium in imperio* as well as the practical difficulty of having two legislatures operating over the same territory. Without necessarily intending it, the members of the Council had taken a crucial step toward articulating a new vision of sovereignty. This reconception permitted sovereignty to be divided—not simply along the territorial lines that some early modern thinkers had posited, but along substantive subject-matter-defined lines. Parliament would regulate matters relating to the empire as a whole, while the colonial assemblies would have authority over all other matters. The Council's proposal, then, rebutted Hutchinson's claim that one could not draw a line between complete parliamentary sovereignty and complete colonial independence by arranging Parliament and the General Court along parallel rather than overlapping planes.

In a broader sense, the proposal laid the foundation for American federalism's parallel arrangement of national and state legislatures. Hutchinson's equivalence between political and legal boundaries based on territory would begin to give way to legal boundaries based on subject matter: in 1773, imperial versus colonial matters; sixteen years later, national versus state matters. Such an arrangement would satisfy Blackstone's maxim that "there is and must be in all [governments] a supreme, irresistible, absolute, uncontrolled authority, in which the *jura summi imperii*, or the rights of sovereignty, reside" through the granting of the aforementioned supreme authority to a specific arm of government, depending on the particular substantive issues at stake.[66] No *imperium in imperio* would result—and there would be no need for recourse to the type of unitary, monolithic sovereign enshrined in the British constitution.[67]

As these debates demonstrate, a transformation in the understanding of sovereignty itself preceded—or, at minimum, accompanied—American discussions of a revesting of sovereignty in the people. The essence of the General Court's break with imperial constitutional theory was its members' insistence that the ultimate source of political authority could be *divided*, rather than that it could be shifted wholesale to reside, still unitary, in a different location within the political community.

To his credit as a servant of the empire, Hutchinson resisted to the end the Council's reformulation of the concept of sovereignty. On March 6, he delivered the final installment in the exchange with the General Court. The Council's distinction between supreme and subordinate powers was specious, he insisted, citing the "Inconsistency" of "supposing a *subordinate* Power without a Power *superior* to it." Adhering to the Blackstonian idea of sovereignty, the governor refused even to consider the possibility that authority could be divided along subject-matter, as opposed to territorial, lines. "If you are still of Opinion that two Jurisdictions, each of them having a Share in the Supreme Power, are compatible in the same State, it can be to no Purpose to Reason or Argue upon the other Parts of your Message," Hutchinson asserted. "It is essential to the Being of Government that a Power should always exist which no other Power within such Government can have Right to withstand or controul."[68] And, as had been the case since 1688, when the English nation "*returned* to a just Sense of the Supremacy of Parliament," that uncontrollable, supreme power resided at Westminster.[69] Having made his last stand, the governor, in the words of one pamphlet, "was pleas'd to put an End to the Session."[70]

By the spring of 1773, Hutchinson seems to have realized that the debate with the General Court had strayed far beyond the bounds of whatever initial approval his plan had received from imperial administrators. Significantly, his correspondence with Lord Dartmouth became increasingly strained. Since taking office as secretary of state for the colonies in 1772, Dartmouth had followed a policy of conciliation in his dealings with the colonies.[71] Faced with a royal governor whose zealous advocacy of the official government position had clearly ignited the simmering colonial opposition, Dartmouth appears to have reconsidered the limited approval of Hutchinson's plan that his own March 3 letter had conveyed. News of Whitehall's increasing disapproval, as well as the firestorm of public commentary that the debate had sparked, seems to have begun to affect Hutchinson at around the time of his March 6 speech to the General Court. A marked decline in the quality of his handwriting, in addition to his self-exculpatory letters to correspondents such as Gage, suggests the governor's anxiety. Yet he continued to alternate between ringing affirmations and defensive justifications of his own conduct. On March 10, he wrote to an unknown correspondent that the "contagion" that had begun in the town meeting "seems to have been stopped by my speech to the Assembly and the consequent Proceedings there."[72] By April 25, however, a letter to Dartmouth contained the following apologia: "If I could, consistent with my duty to the King, have avoided any controversy with the Assembly upon Constitutional Points, it would have been most agreable to me. . . . It affords me relief that the propriety of the measure appears to His Majesty and that he is pleased to approve of it."[73]

Hutchinson's fears were well founded. By June of 1773, his imperial superiors had moved to sacrifice him in the hope of stanching the flow of unrest in Massachusetts. In letters dated April 10 and June 2, Dartmouth essentially ordered Hutchinson to halt the debate before he caused more damage to the delicate imperial arrangement. In late June, the subject of Hutchinson's resignation entered the official correspondence, when Hutchinson requested Dartmouth's permission to visit England in order to seek an alternative post.[74] Nearly a year later, on June 1, 1774, Hutchinson departed for England, leaving Massachusetts to the military governorship of General Gage. That day, Hutchinson's son-in-law Peter Oliver Jr., who remained in Boston, noted in his diary, "Nothing but mobs and riots all this summer."[75]

The competing ideologies articulated by the parties to the Hutchinson–General Court debate demonstrate the collision between the Blackstonian vision of sovereignty as indivisible and unitary and the colonists' increasingly federal vision in which divided authority was not a solecism but a foundational principle.[76] In order to escape the snares of the *imperium in imperio* principle, American colonists in the 1760s and 1770s reconceived that principle. "The key doctrine of federalism could survive criticism only to the extent that it could somehow be distinguished from the ancient belief that *imperium in imperio* was an illogical and unresolvable solecism," as Bernard Bailyn has observed. "So [Americans] reexamined that old formula, took it apart, and showed, not its falsity, but its irrelevance in the American situation."[77] They did this by breaking away from the early modern conception of sovereignty as lodged exclusively in a single supreme authority. If governmental authority could be divided among several parallel institutions, it could therefore be tied to subject-specific objects. In this way, as Bailyn puts it, "The two governments would intersect only where they exercised *concurrent* powers, and *concurrence* is not the *repugnance* that lay at the heart of the ancient precept."[78]

What scholars have not adequately recognized, however, is the significance of the debates between Hutchinson and the General Court in, first, establishing the respective sides of the sovereignty argument and, second, in providing a forum for colonial innovation. The post-1773 forays of a few individuals into this novel conception of sovereignty spoke in language strikingly similar to that used by the General Court. Writing in 1774, John Dickinson adopted the metaphor of line drawing that Hutchinson had first employed and that both houses of the General Court then adapted for their own use.

> The authority of parliament has within these few years been a question much agitated, and great difficulty, we understand, has occurred in tracing the line between the rights of the

> mother country and those of the colonies. . . . Whatever difficulty may occur in tracing the line, yet we contend that by the laws of God and by the laws of the constitution a line there must be beyond which her authority cannot extend. . . . We assert, a line there must be, and shall now proceed, with great deference to the judgment of others, to trace that line.[79]

As in his widely circulated *Letters of a Farmer in Pennsylvania* of 1768, Dickinson then proceeded to draw a line between regulating trade and legislating for the colonies' internal affairs. The former, he contended, was permissible; the latter was not. Dickinson thus emphasized a subject-matter distinction separating the areas that a legislature might permissibly oversee and those that it might not.

Hutchinson had refused to grant such a distinction, arguing that Parliament's sovereignty at home translated into full authority over the colonies because the colonies, like the British Isles, were part of the realm. In other words, Hutchinson understood legislative authority as coterminous with territorial boundaries, while Dickinson, Wilson, and the members of the General Court permitted legislative authority to be segmented according to the boundaries of subject matter.[80] Hutchinson might have scored a temporary victory for the empire in 1773 (albeit at the immense personal cost of his own career), but the substantive inquiry proposed by the General Court and embraced by Dickinson lived to fight—and win—another day. In 1787, Alexander Hamilton would describe the powers of the proposed federal government as similarly bounded by subject matter, not by political space: "The laws of the confederacy, as to the *enumerated* and *legitimate* objects of its jurisdiction, will become the SUPREME LAW of the land."[81] The enumerated, legitimate objects of an authority's jurisdiction, not the reach of its might over a given piece of territory, would determine whether its laws or those of a concurrent authority would apply.

The debates of early 1773 signified an important transition in Anglo-Americans' thinking about sovereignty, a moment of divergence between imperial and colonial theory, and an illustration of a key conceptual breakthrough that helped to bring about the development of federalism. Whether the General Court or Hutchinson—or neither—had the better constitutional arguments at the time is less relevant for the story of the intellectual history of federalism than the following two facts: first, each side was deeply committed to its particular constitutional vision; and second, one can clearly see here elements of the political-theoretical moves that would enable the General Court and their successors to develop a domestic version of Pufendorf's system of states.

Federalism required a belief that lines could be drawn between sources of authority. Imperial officials, citing the increasingly powerful theory of parliamentary supremacy, argued that such delineations were impossible. The General Court suggested, however, that not only could lines be drawn around sovereign authorities, but they could be drawn according to novel subject-matter-specific principles. Despite their tendentious origins, arguments such as these would in subsequent years provide the foundation for the American federal experiment. The Constitutional Convention delegates' enumeration of the powers of the national government, and their accompanying reservation of powers to the states, expanded on the Massachusetts General Court members' assertion, fourteen years earlier, that sovereignty could be apportioned among authorities—and preserved against competing claims—according to the substantive ends toward which that sovereignty was directed.

NOTES

1. The leading contemporary exponent of this view was, of course, William Blackstone, who argued, "There is and must be in all [governments] a supreme, irresistible, absolute, uncontrolled authority, in which the *jura summi imperii,* or the rights of sovereignty, reside." See William Blackstone, *Commentaries on the Laws of England* (1765–69; Chicago: University of Chicago Press, 1979), 1:49. For a modern view, see Stephen D. Krasner, *Sovereignty: Organized Hypocrisy* (Princeton, N.J.: Princeton University Press, 1999), 11, quoting F. H. Hinsley, *Sovereignty,* 2d ed. (Cambridge: Cambridge University Press, 1986). Krasner terms this "domestic sovereignty," in contrast to three other species of sovereignty (Westphalian, international legal, and interdependence).

2. On the provincial assemblies and the decades-long history of institutional conflict within the colonial governments, see Evarts B. Greene, *The Provincial Governor in the English Colonies of North America* (Cambridge, Mass.: Harvard University Press, 1898); Jack P. Greene, *The Quest for Power: The Lower Houses of Assembly in the Southern Royal Colonies, 1689–1776* (New York: W. W. Norton, 1963); Michael G. Kammen, *Deputyes and Libertyes* (New York: Knopf, 1968); Leonard Woods Labaree, *Royal Government in America: A Study of the British Colonial System before 1783* (New Haven, Conn.: Yale University Press, 1930); Herbert Osgood, *The American Colonies in the Eighteenth Century* (New York: Columbia University Press, 1924).

3. On the broader context of changing ideas of authority and state power in the eighteenth-century British Atlantic world, see Peter N. Miller, *Defining the Common Good: Empire, Religion and Philosophy in Eighteenth-Century Britain* (Cambridge: Cambridge University Press, 1994).

4. Antagonism between colonial assemblies and governors was common throughout the eighteenth century, arising out of institutional competition for power at a provincial level, as well as the friction between the governor's (and sometimes the Council's) role as an imperial agent and the assembly members' status as imperial subjects. See, e.g., Christine A. Desan, "The Constitutional Commitment to Legislative Adjudication in the Early American Tradition," *Harvard Law Review* 111 (1998): 1381–503.

5. John Phillip Reid, "The Ordeal by Law of Thomas Hutchinson," in *Law in the American Revolution and the Revolution in the Law,* ed. Hendrik Hartog (New York: New York University Press, 1981), 33–34. The debates are reprinted in their entirety in John Phillip Reid, ed., *The Briefs of the American Revolution: Constitutional Arguments between Thomas Hutchinson, Governor of Massachusetts Bay, and James Bowdoin for the Council and John Adams for the House of Representatives* (New York: New York University Press, 1981).

6. Bernard Bailyn, *The Ordeal of Thomas Hutchinson* (Cambridge, Mass.: Belknap Press of Harvard University Press, 1974), 196.

7. Hutchinson to Dartmouth, Dec. 22, 1772, *Hutchinson Correspondence* (Massachusetts State Archives, microform). An earlier letter of October 30, 1772, characterized the town meeting—or "the Inhabitants of the Town of Boston," as the ever-punctilious Hutchinson referred to it, possibly demonstrating his growing antipathy for that body—as addressing the governor in the language "of the News papers which have so much inflamed the minds of the people."

8. In a 1775 draft of what he termed a "Vindication" of his conduct, Hutchinson wrote, "Britain and its Colonies are alike dependent upon the supreme authority of the whole Empire." Using the third person to refer to himself, he continued, "The King, Lords, and Commons—this supreme authority appeared to him to be the sole bond which kept the several parts of the Empire together." Thomas Hutchinson, *The Diary and Letters of His Excellency Thomas Hutchinson, Esq.*, ed. Peter Orlando Hutchinson (1884–86; New York: Burt Franklin, 1971), 1:577. On the consequences of the Glorious Revolution for metropolitan and colonial political theory, see Jack P. Greene, "The Glorious Revolution and the British Empire, 1688–1783," in *The Revolution of 1688–1689: Changing Perspectives,* ed. Lois G. Schwoerer, 260–71 (Cambridge: Cambridge University Press, 1992); David S. Lovejoy, *The Glorious Revolution in America* (Middletown, Conn.: Wesleyan University Press, 1987); Jack M. Sosin, *English America and the Revolution of 1688: Royal Administration and the Structure of Provincial Government* (Lincoln: University of Nebraska Press, 1982).

9. In particular, "the British had developed since the Glorious Revolution the constitutional doctrine of the sovereign legislature of king-in-parliament as the ultimate, absolute and irresistible authority in the state." H. T. Dickinson, "Britain's Imperial Sovereignty," in *Britain and the American Revolution,* ed. H. T. Dickinson (London: Longman, 1998), 81.

10. Samuel Johnson, *Taxation No Tyranny: An Answer to the Resolutions and Address of the American Congress*, 4th ed. (London: T. Cadell, 1775), 24.

11. The fact that Hutchinson, scion of one of Boston's elite merchant families and a layman in the field of law, had been appointed chief justice of the superior court stoked the ire of many of his contemporaries at the Boston bar, especially John Adams. Adams rarely missed a chance to demonstrate his scorn for Hutchinson throughout the crisis of the early 1770s, even in passing. Indeed, Adams began the "Novanglus" series by referring to Hutchinson by name as a "destroying angel" whose "hypocrisy and perfidy" had long become apparent to the people of Massachusetts. John Adams, "Novanglus No. I" and "Novanglus No. V," in *The Works of John Adams, Second President of the United States,* ed. Charles Francis Adams (Boston: Little, Brown, 1851), 4:12, 72. In Bailyn's view, however, Adams's dislike of Hutchinson was "obsessive" and rooted more in Adams's own "excruciatingly sensitive self-esteem," especially his tendency to believe in "dangerous, secret forces" that would "block the aspirations of powerless but honest and able new men." Bailyn, *The Ordeal of Thomas Hutchinson*, 50–51. And so the debate, begun in the 1760s, continues.

12. *The Speeches of His Excellency Governor Hutchinson, to the General Assembly of the Massachusetts-Bay . . . with the Answers of His Majesty's Council and the House of Representatives . . .* (Boston: Edes and Gill, 1773), 8. On the concept of repugnancy in the British Empire, see Mary Sarah Bilder, *The Transatlantic Constitution: Colonial Legal Culture and the Empire* (Cambridge, Mass.: Harvard University Press, 2004).

13. Ibid., 5.

14. Ibid., 11.

15. On the rise of the theory of parliamentary sovereignty, see J. G. A. Pocock, *The Ancient Constitution and the Feudal Law: A Study of English Historical Thought in the Seventeenth Century: A Reissue with a Retrospect* (New York: W. W. Norton, 1987), especially the conclusion to part 1, titled "1688 in the History of Historiography."

16. 24 Hen. 8, c. 12 ; J. G. A. Pocock, "A Discourse of Sovereignty: Observations on the Work in Progress," in *Political Discourse in Early Modern Britain,* ed. Nicholas Phillipson and Quentin Skinner (Cambridge: Cambridge University Press, 1993), 381.

17. See Michael Mendle, "Parliamentary Sovereignty: A Very English Absolutism," in Phillipson and Skinner, *Political Discourse in Early Modern Britain,* 97.

18. Blackstone, *Commentaries on the Laws of England,* 1:156–57.

19. Cf. Morton J. Horwitz, "Why Is Anglo-American Jurisprudence Unhistorical?" *Oxford Journal of Legal Studies* 17 (1997): 555 ("Blackstone's *Commentaries* (1765), written two generations after the Glorious Revolution, expressed Blackstone's desire to mediate between several major tensions or contradictions. . . . Blackstone also needed to reconcile the waning seventeenth century Whig tradition of fundamental law with the gradually unfolding recognition during the second half of the eighteenth century of the reality of parliamentary supremacy"). On the relationship between Blackstone, the common law, and emerging ideas of popular sovereignty, see Horwitz, *The Transformation of American Law, 1780–1860* (Cambridge, Mass.: Harvard University Press, 1977), 19–20.

20. Bernard Bailyn refers to the "ancient belief that *imperium in imperio* was an illogical and unresolvable solecism." Bernard Bailyn, *The Ideological Origins of the American Revolution,* enl. ed. (Cambridge, Mass.: Belknap Press of Harvard University Press, 1992), 358. Why the term "solecism" should so often have been employed to dismiss the concept of *imperium in imperio* remains a question. As Daniel Hulsebosch has demonstrated, the pejorative dated back at least to 1720, when Henry St. John, Viscount Bolingbroke, referred to *imperium in imperio* as a "Solecism in Politicks." Daniel J. Hulsebosch, "*Imperia in Imperio*: The Multiple Constitutions of Empire in New York, 1750–1777," *Law and History Review* 16 (1998): 340 n. 58 (citing [Bolingbroke], *The Country Journal; or, The Craftsman,* Oct. 18, 1729).

21. See Bailyn, *Ideological Origins,* 198–202. The combination of parliamentary sovereignty with empire yielded a situation following the Seven Years' War that Bailyn describes as "anomalous": "extreme decentralization of authority within an empire presumably ruled by a single, absolute, undivided sovereign" (204).

22. See Patrick Thomas Riley, "Historical Development of the Theory of Federalism, 16th–19th Centuries" (PhD diss., Harvard University, 1968), 119–90; Peter S. Onuf and Nicholas Onuf, *Federal Union, Modern World: The Law of Nations in an Age of Revolutions, 1776–1814* (Madison, Wisc.: Madison House, 1993), 65–66.

23. See Richard Tuck, introduction to *The Rights of War and Peace,* by Hugo Grotius (Indianapolis, Ind.: Liberty Fund, 2005), 1:xxxiii; see also Edward Keene, *Beyond the Anarchical Society: Grotius, Colonialism, and Order in World Politics* (Cambridge: Cambridge University Press, 2002), 3 (discussing Grotius's views of "divisible sovereignty" and arguing these ideas both informed and grew out of European colonialism and imperialism).

24. David Armitage, *The Declaration of Independence: A Global History* (Cambridge, Mass.: Harvard University Press, 2007), 41. Armitage notes that Franklin informed the volume's editor in December 1775 that the book "has been continually in the hands of our congress, now sitting."

25. Richard Bland, *An Inquiry into the Rights of the British Colonies* (1766; Richmond, Va.: Appeals Press, 1922), 9 (misidentifying the title of Vattel's work as *Law of Nature*).

26. Tuck, introduction to *The Rights of War and Peace*, xi.

27. The question of the precise legal status of the colonies and the distinctions between membership in kingdom, realm, and dominion (the last distinguishable between the dominions of England and those of the king himself) is treated in Joseph Henry Smith, *Appeals to the Privy Council from the American Plantations* (New York: Octagon Books, 1965), especially chap. 8, "The Privy Council and the Extension of English Law." For a discussion of pre-Revolutionary Americans' own understandings of the status and origin of the colonies, see Michael Kammen, "The Meaning of Colonization in American Revolutionary Thought," *Journal of the History of Ideas* 31 (1970): 337–58. Kammen notes that by 1763, "it was manifest to imperial bureaucrats in London that colonization was somehow a subversive process viewed altogether differently by men living on opposite sides of the Atlantic" (351).

28. *The Speeches of His Excellency Governor Hutchinson*, 96–97 (emphasis to "united by a Sort of unequal Confederacy" added).

29. Ibid., 121–22.

30. Evidence that John Adams was the author of the House's statements comes from the obvious familiarity with the works of Grotius and Pufendorf that Adams displayed in his "Novanglus" letters. No. VI, for example, provided not just a passing reference but an actual footnote to *The Law of Nature and Nations* (vol. 1, book 7, chap. 8, secs. 5–6) on the question of the subject's power to resist a tyrannical prince. Adams, "Novanglus No. VI," in *The Works of John Adams*, 4:79. Adams's footnote also cited a note by Jean Barbeyrac, the French translator of Pufendorf, whose notes were included in the English translation by Basil Kennet that Adams and his peers read. On Barbeyrac and the complex history of his translations, see David Saunders, "The Natural Jurisprudence of Jean Barbeyrac: Translation as an Art of Political Adjustment," *Eighteenth-Century Studies* 36 (2003): 473–90.

31. Keene, *Beyond the Anarchical Society*, xi.

32. See Peter Schröder, "The Constitution of the Holy Roman Empire after 1648: Samuel Pufendorf's Assessment in His Monzambano," *Historical Journal* 42 (1999): 961–83. On fragmentation as "the abiding constitutional principle of the Holy Roman Empire," see Hagen Schulze, foreword to *German Federalism: Past, Present, Future*, ed. Maiken Umbach (Basingstoke, Hampshire, UK: Palgrave, 2002), viii.

33. Samuel von Pufendorf, *The Law of Nature and Nations; or, A General System of the Most Important Principles of Morality, Jurisprudence, and Politics*, trans. Basil Kennet, 5th ed. (1672; London, 1749), 2:681–83, secs. 16, 18.

34. The members of the House, in particular, went to great lengths to ensure that their response would meet the challenge that Hutchinson's dense polemical address posed. House leaders did not scruple to search beyond the chamber's membership to find the strongest advocate for their cause. After their overtures to Daniel Dulany and John Dickinson were rejected, House managers selected members Samuel Adams and Joseph Hawley to lead the opposition. Bailyn, *The Ordeal of Thomas Hutchinson*, 208. They also drafted rising Boston lawyer John Adams to aid in drafting arguments to rebut Hutchinson's vision of parliamentary sovereignty.

35. *Boston-Gazette and Country Journal*, Feb. 1, 1773.

36. *The Speeches of His Excellency Governor Hutchinson*, 18. By invoking the ancient constitution to rebut claims of parliamentary sovereignty, the council was both embarking on a

novel interpretation of traditional English constitutional arguments and returning to old understandings of those arguments. The trope of the ancient constitution had emerged in the early seventeenth century as a challenge to Stuart absolutism, a means of outflanking the claims of James I that his power and prerogative were based not on his will but on ancient custom. Promoted by Coke, the myth of the ancient constitution became ascendant after Parliament succeeded in forcing out James II and installing William and Mary as constitutional monarchs in 1689. The Council's use of the ancient constitution to oppose parliamentary sovereignty therefore turned the principle to the very opposite of its original objective. See Pocock, *The Ancient Constitution and the Feudal Law*, 233–36. John Phillip Reid terms this a "constitutional step backwards from the Glorious Revolution," but it is possible to see this revolution of the ancient constitution as an adaptation to changed circumstances rather than as a retreat along a linear spectrum of constitutional progress. John Phillip Reid, *Constitutional History of the American Revolution*, abridged ed. (Madison: University of Wisconsin Press, 1995), 98.

37. *The Speeches of His Excellency Governor Hutchinson*, 18–19.

38. John Phillip Reid, *The Authority to Legislate*, vol. 3 of *Constitutional History of the American Revolution* (Madison: University of Wisconsin Press, 1991), 8, 82 ("The concept of 'supremacy' was more a topic of dispute than an element of definition. It was used as much to argue about constitutionalism as to explain it").

39. Ibid., 85.

40. Ibid., 83 (discussing the relative nature of the term "supreme").

41. On the relationship between nation and empire in this period, see Eliga H. Gould, *The Persistence of Empire: British Political Culture in the Age of the American Revolution* (Chapel Hill: University of North Carolina Press, 2000).

42. Randolph G. Adams points out that John Adams's "Novanglus" letters made this distinction between the dual nature of Parliament as both an imperial and a national legislature. In John Adams's view, "Parliament had a double capacity, and when it acted as a Parliament of Great Britain, it had no relation to the colonies. When acting in its imperial capacity it had only such relation to the colonies as they by their consent accorded to it." Britain, meanwhile, "conceived the empire as a unicellular state wherein sovereignty was possessed, according to the Lockeian dogma, by the legislative, that is, by the High Court of Parliament at Westminster. Britons talked about 'our sovereignty' over the colonies." Randolph G. Adams, *Political Ideas of the American Revolution: Britannic-American Contributions to the Problem of Imperial Organization, 1765 to 1775*, 3d ed. (New York: Barnes & Noble, 1958), 120, 175.

43. Ibid., 38.

44. Ibid., 40. Parliament's own Navigation Act of 1660 endorsed the theory of the king's dominions, characterizing the colonies as "Lands, Islands Plantations or Territories to his Maiesty belonging or in his possession.'" Quoted in Smith, *Appeals to the Privy Council*, 470. As Smith's discussion makes clear, the House's use of this history was somewhat opportunistic, for the status of English law in the colonies was the subject of much confusion as late as 1700 (473–75). Yet again it is worth noting the imprecision of eighteenth-century syntax. The terms "realm" and "kingdom" were often used in perplexingly similar contexts during this period. Even such a clear thinker as John Adams seems to have been aware of this lack of precision. "Is America incorporated into the realm? Is it a part of the realm? Is it a part of the kingdom? Has it any share in the legislature of the realm?" he queried in "Novanglus No. VII," his use of both terms suggesting a subtle difference between them. In "Novanglus No. XII," however, an

exasperated-sounding Adams appeared to acknowledge the confusion. Of the Massachusetts Bay Company, he commented, "As soon as they arrived here, they got out of the English realm, dominions, state, empire, call it by what name you will, and out of the legal jurisdiction of parliament. The king might, by his writ or proclamation, have commanded them to return; but he did not." Adams, "Novanglus No. VII" and "Novanglus No. XII," in *The Works of John Adams*, 4:102, 177. *The Oxford English Dictionary* offers little help; the first definition listed under the heading "realm" is "kingdom," citing Blackstone for authority. The third definition listed under "kingdom" is "realm." *The Oxford English Dictionary*, 2d ed., s.v. "Realm" and "Kingdom."

45. Cf. Bailyn, *Ideological Origins*, 201. Daniel Hulsebosch notes that the colonists cited royal prerogative "just as such rhetoric was becoming anachronistic in England." Nevertheless, that principle, not the notion of parliamentary sovereignty, "was their mainstay throughout the colonial period." Hulsebosch, "*Imperia in Imperio*," 328–29.

46. Reid, *Constitutional History of the American Revolution*, abridged ed., 5.

47. The phrase "dominion status" comes from Charles Page Smith, who notes in his biography of James Wilson that Wilson may "be credited with formulating the idea of dominion status six years ahead of [John Adams] and some seventy years ahead of the British Foreign Office." Charles Page Smith, *James Wilson: Founding Father, 1742–1798* (Chapel Hill: University of North Carolina Press, 1956), 58. The phrase "doctrine of allegiance" is that of Adams, *Political Ideas of the American Revolution*, 116–17.

48. James Wilson, "Considerations on the Nature and Extent of the Legislative Authority of the British Parliament," in *The Works of James Wilson*, ed. Robert Green McCloskey (Cambridge, Mass.: Belknap Press of Harvard University Press, 1967), 2:745. The advertisement that announced the publication of this work noted that Wilson had originally written this pamphlet in 1768, during the nonimportation controversy that followed the passage of the Townshend Acts, but it was not published until 1774.

49. Adams, "Novanglus No. VII," in *The Works of John Adams*, 4:107. Adams took great care to distinguish between the British Empire, the existence of which he questioned, and the situation of the American colonies with respect to the king, which he termed sui generis. "I say we are not a part of the British empire; because the British government is not an empire. . . . It is a limited monarchy. . . . The British constitution is nothing more nor less than a republic, in which the king is first magistrate." Adams, "Novanglus No. VII," in *The Works of John Adams*, 4:106.

50. Adams, *Political Ideas of the American Revolution*, 44. Adams notes that at the time of his writing, in 1919, the commonwealth idea was widely discussed with respect to the dominions of the British Empire and the establishment of the League of Nations (36, 44 n. 6).

51. This move to establish something more like a commonwealth system, according to which the colonies would be subject to the Crown alone, gained momentum in 1774. See Thomas Jefferson, *A Summary View of the Rights of British America* (1774); see also John Cartwright, *American Independence the Glory and Interest of Great Britain* (1774); Joseph Galloway, *A Plan of a Proposed Union* (1774).

52. Brian P. Levack, *The Formation of the British State: England, Scotland, and the Union, 1603–1707* (Oxford: Clarendon Press, 1987), 1.

53. On the resonance of the Scottish union debates for the American struggle with Britain, see Ned Landsman, "The Provinces and the Empire: Scotland, the American Colonies and the Development of British Provincial Identity," in *An Imperial State at War*, ed. Lawrence Stone,

258–87 (London: Routledge, 1994); Ned Landsman, "The Legacy of British Union for the North American Colonies: Provincial Elites and the Problem of Imperial Union," in *A Union for Empire: Political Thought and the British Union of 1707,* ed. John Robertson, 297–317 (Cambridge: Cambridge University Press, 1995); and John Robertson, "Empire and Union: Two Concepts of the Early Modern European Political Order," in Robertson, *A Union for Empire*, 3–36.

54. David Armitage, *The Ideological Origins of the British Empire* (Cambridge: Cambridge University Press, 2000), 20.

55. Ibid., 60.

56. On the influence of Wilson's Scottish background on his political thought, see Mark David Hall, *The Political and Legal Philosophy of James Wilson, 1742–1798* (Columbia: University of Missouri Press, 1997), 68–72; McCloskey, introduction to Wilson, *The Works of James Wilson*, 1:14–16.

57. Adams, "Novanglus No. VII" and "Novanglus No. VIII," in *The Works of John Adams,* 4:113, 123. Levack explains how such an arrangement functioned during the reign of James VI and I: "The crown of England remained distinct from the crown of Scotland, even though James possessed and embodied both of them. James held the two crowns in the way that an ecclesiastical pluralist held two benefices. . . . The Union of the Crowns should, in fact, be considered primarily as a dynastic achievement." Levack, *The Formation of the British State*, 1–2, 3.

58. Adams, "Novanglus No. VIII," in *The Works of John Adams*, 4:124.

59. *The Speeches of His Excellency Governor Hutchinson*, 35.

60. Ibid., 39, 56.

61. Ibid., 61.

62. Ibid., 73.

63. Ibid.

64. Ibid., 86–87.

65. See, e.g., Richard Bland, *An Inquiry into the Rights of the British Colonies* (1766; Richmond, Va.: William Parks Club, 1922), 20 (describing the colonies' long-standing identity as "a distinct State, independent, as to their *internal* Government, of the original Kingdom, but united with her, as to their *external* Polity, in the closest and most intimate LEAGUE AND AMITY, under the same Allegiance, and enjoying the Benefits of a reciprocal Intercourse"). See also Adams's argument in "Novanglus No. VII": "We are a part of the British dominions, that is, of the King of Great Britain, and it is our interest and duty to continue so. It is equally our interest and duty to continue subject to the authority of parliament, in the regulation of trade, as long as she shall leave us to govern our internal policy . . . and no longer." Adams, "Novanglus No. VII," in *The Works of John Adams*, 4:120–21. See also Bailyn, *Ideological Origins*, 215.

66. Blackstone, *Commentaries on the Laws of England,* 1:49.

67. Several scholars have pointed to the theory of popular sovereignty as the key that allowed the colonists to circumvent the problem of *imperium in imperio*. Most notably, Edmund Morgan has argued that during the founding period, Madison and other advocates of the Constitution used popular sovereignty to justify the creation of a national, rather than a confederational, government. Edmund S. Morgan, *Inventing the People: The Rise of Popular Sovereignty in England and America* (New York: W. W. Norton, 1988), 267. Placing the rise of popular sovereignty somewhat earlier, Bernard Bailyn argues that by the 1770s, Americans' questioning of the idea of unitary, indivisible sovereignty had been followed by a new belief "that the ultimate sovereignty . . . rested with the people." Bailyn, *Ideological Origins*, 228. On a related note,

Larry D. Kramer has emphasized colonists' growing belief throughout the 1760s and 1770s that popular sovereignty was "the central principle of American constitutionalism." Larry D. Kramer, *The People Themselves: Popular Constitutionalism and Judicial Review* (New York: Oxford University Press, 2004), 35–36. Cf. Morton J. Horwitz, "A Historiography of *The People Themselves* and Popular Constitutionalism," *Chicago-Kent Law Review* 81 (2006): 817 ("If for Bailyn and Wood, the basic change in political theory brought about by the American Revolution was the shift from British parliamentary to American popular sovereignty, for Kramer popular sovereignty was already a powerful force even before the conflicts leading up to the Revolution").

68. *The Speeches of His Excellency Governor Hutchinson*, 115.

69. Ibid., 124 (emphasis added). Although he subscribed to the orthodox but ahistorical Whig view that the Glorious Revolution settlement had declared for all time the transcendent authority of Parliament, Hutchinson's interest in history here compelled him to distinguish between the feudal system as practiced on the Continent and the "corrected" feudalism that emerged after 1066, when—he argued—English custom tempered European feudalism to produce, among other things, mixed government and a distinct legislative power (118).

70. Ibid., 114.

71. Bailyn, *The Ordeal of Thomas Hutchinson*, 212.

72. Hutchinson to ——, *Hutchinson Correspondence*, Mar. 10, 1773.

73. Hutchinson to Dartmouth, *Hutchinson Correspondence*, Apr. 25, 1773.

74. Hutchinson to Dartmouth, *Hutchinson Correspondence,* June 12 and 26, 1773.

75. Hutchinson, *The Diary and Letters of His Excellency Thomas Hutchinson, Esq.*, 151. Hutchinson's departure was almost certainly a melancholy occasion for the governor, who was, after all, a creole by birth and a great-great-grandson of the religious dissident Anne Hutchinson.

76. Occasionally, a modern scholar has argued that divided sovereignty violates the *imperium in imperio* principle, and that therefore American federalism must be based on some other premise. See, e.g., Andrew C. McLaughlin, *The Foundations of American Constitutionalism* (New York: New York University Press, 1932), 135–36 ("Since the doctrine of divided sovereignty is now discredited as a principle of political science . . . it may seem best to speak of the federal state, not as one characterized by the distribution of sovereignty itself, but characterized by the distribution of sovereign powers").

77. Bailyn, *Ideological Origins*, 358.

78. Ibid.

79. John Dickinson, "An Essay on the Constitutional Power of Great Britain over the Colonies in America," in *Pennsylvania Archives*, 2d ser., ed. John B. Linn and William H. Egle (Harrisburg, Pa.: B. F. Meyers, 1875), 3:565, 569.

80. This distinction between subject-matter and territorial bases of sovereignty is conceptually similar to Daniel Hulsebosch's distinction between "jurisdictional" and "jurisprudential" visions of law. According to the former, as articulated by Sir Edward Coke, "the common law was inseparable from the institutions that applied, practiced, and taught the common law." A jurisprudential notion of law, in contrast, "refers to a rationally organized body of rules and principles defined primarily in reference to each other, not to the remedies and personnel enforcing them." Daniel J. Hulsebosch, "The Ancient Constitution and the Expanding Empire: Sir Edward Coke's British Jurisprudence," *Law and History Review* 21 (2003): 445–46.

81. [Alexander Hamilton], "The Federalist No. 27," in *The Federalist,* ed. Jacob E. Cooke (Middletown, Conn.: Wesleyan University Press, 1961), 174. This effort to divide lawmaking

authority along substantive lines subsequently influenced the drafting of the supremacy clause of the federal Constitution. The clause distinguishes between "this Constitution, and the Laws of the United States," which the clause denominates "the supreme law of the land," and all other laws (e.g., state laws), which are necessarily relegated to subordinate status insofar as they conflicted with the supreme law. U.S. Const. art. 6, cl. 2.

4

DeSaussure and Ford: A Charleston Law Firm of the 1790s

SALLY E. HADDEN

THOUGH THERE HAVE BEEN MANY STUDIES OF AMERICAN LAW FIRMS IN the nineteenth and twentieth centuries, none has been attempted for the eighteenth century. In part, any such effort is stymied by the lack of available sources to draw upon. Though legal partnerships existed during the eighteenth century, typically they left behind few if any records that are useful for research. In most instances, partnerships formed between family members (like the Cranches, father and son, in Boston) or between mentors and students were fleeting.[1] The volume of legal business would not always support the addition of younger attorneys to those who were already in practice; when families engaged in partnerships, it was typically for the generational transfer of assets and clients from older to younger men, lasting but a short time. Other reasons could draw men away from these early law firms as well: military service during wartime, all too common in the colonial era, and the lure of political office could bring an abrupt close to even a prosperous partnership. Only in the largest cities and towns, like Boston and Philadelphia, did these brief legal associations flourish—and even then, the archival material left behind for scrutiny by historians can be considered only minimal at best.

One exception to this poor evidentiary pattern can be found in Charleston, South Carolina, in the partnership formed between Henry William DeSaussure

My thanks to the organizers of the Seventeenth Biennial British Legal History Conference (upon the theme "Law and the City"), held at University College London in 2005; the Workshop in Early American History and Culture hosted by the University of Georgia; and Florida State University History Department's Works in Progress seminar, where I presented earlier versions of this work and received valuable comments from those present. I also acknowledge the assistance of Robert Berkhofer, Rachelle Friedman, and Charles Upchurch, who each offered suggestions that improved this essay.

and his brother-in-law Timothy Ford. The two men shared similarities with many others born in the 1760s: both were confirmed Revolutionary patriots with wartime service that resulted in wounds or imprisonment. In their respective home states of New Jersey and South Carolina, the Ford and DeSaussure clans were well connected to individuals in the middle and upper classes through family ties and education, giving both men a solid start in their adult earning capacities, though Timothy Ford chose to forgo his New Jersey advantages in order to forge new associations in his adopted Southern home. Both men rose to elective office at the city and state levels on multiple occasions and, by the time they left active legal practice in the 1820s, had gained the admiration of citizens living across South Carolina. But the details of their many years in politics are by no means as full and vibrant as the financial records and correspondence that the two created during their thirty-year partnership practicing law in Charleston.

This essay offers an initial exploration of the DeSaussure and Ford law firm's activities in the late 1780s and early 1790s, as well as a broader consideration of the sorts of legal expenses that would be incurred by two men in this transitional period for the legal profession. The partners adapted to a changing legal landscape by taking on numerous law students, expanding their practice, engaging in highly visible political activities, and establishing ties to Charleston's elite by joining various social and religious groups that would guarantee them a steady stream of clients. In a society that thrived upon tradition, DeSaussure and Ford advanced to the forefront of Charleston's legal practitioners by playing upon the strengths of partnership in an era when solo practice was still the rule of thumb. In addition, their intertwined family connections allowed the two men to pool financial resources and benefit from the labor of their wives and slaves, maximizing their earning power as lawyers.

BACKGROUND ON HENRY WILLIAM DESAUSSURE AND TIMOTHY FORD

Born August 16, 1763, Henry William DeSaussure was the descendant of émigré Swiss Protestants who came to South Carolina during the 1730s and settled in the Beaufort district.[2] Daniel DeSaussure, Henry William's father, was a hardy, flourishing merchant trader first in Beaufort and later in Charleston, prominent in local politics during the colonial period and outspoken in his opinions about the negative effects of British rule. His commitment to the American cause during the Revolution doubtless had some influence upon his son, who was only an adolescent when he followed his father into military service during the war against Britain. The war took a dreadful toll on the DeSaussure family: two of Henry's uncles died from either battlefield wounds or disease, while Daniel and his son Henry were both taken captive by the British after the fall of Charleston in 1780. Separated from his father, who was interned in St. Augustine, seventeen-year-old Henry was placed by the British in one of the prison hulks moored in Charleston

Harbor and later sent to Philadelphia for exchange in 1781. In Philadelphia, he was reunited with family members, including his mother and sister, who had been banished by the British from their home, and his father.

It was in Philadelphia that young DeSaussure decided upon a career in the law and at his father's urging entered the office of Jared Ingersoll, the Connecticut-born attorney who made his home in Pennsylvania.[3] After a three-year period of training in Ingersoll's office, DeSaussure was admitted to the Philadelphia bar (1784), and then he determined to return to South Carolina. Before doing so, he married a New Jersey woman, Elizabeth Ford, whom he met while he was studying law in Philadelphia; she, too, was in Philadelphia for her own education. The marriage was by all accounts a happy one, eventually producing twelve children who lived to adulthood.[4] Following DeSaussure's return to South Carolina, he was admitted to the South Carolina bar in 1786 and established his practice in the state's largest city.

Settled in Charleston, DeSaussure embarked on a career in politics that continued with few interruptions almost until his death in 1839. In 1789, when he was twenty-six, Charlestonians elected him to the state's constitutional convention. He served multiple terms in the House of Representatives of the South Carolina General Assembly and was later named intendant (mayor) of Charleston itself in 1797. Although he continued to practice law well into the 1820s, he was elected to the chancery bench, where he served for nearly thirty years (1808–37). To the student of early American law, DeSaussure is probably best known for publishing four volumes of South Carolina's chancery proceedings covering the years from the Revolution to 1817, which led one commentator to compare him with Chancellor Kent of New York for his central role in establishing many rules of equity for the new state.[5]

Information about Timothy Ford's background is more limited. Eight months older than DeSaussure, Ford was born in December 1762 to Jacob and Theodosia Ford of Morristown, New Jersey. He was educated at Princeton, in large part because his father had so directed in his 1776 will, ordaining that all three of his sons were to receive "liberal educations" and that his daughters likewise were to be given the "best English educations," though his wife might have them taught Latin in addition if she so desired.[6] As a result of this provision in Jacob Ford's will, Elizabeth Ford was in Philadelphia to be educated when she met her future husband, DeSaussure. After Princeton, Timothy Ford studied law in New York with Robert Morris. He fought in the Revolution, as DeSaussure did, being wounded in action at the battle of Springfield, New Jersey. It was through his sister, Elizabeth, that he first met Henry William DeSaussure (or "Billy," the name by which Ford called his brother-in-law), and after Elizabeth's marriage to DeSaussure, all three traveled to Charleston in October 1785. Whether Ford intended at the time for the journey to be a short vacation or a permanent relocation to the South cannot be stated with certainty, but his decision to settle in Charleston was doubtless heavily influenced by the ties that Elizabeth's marriage created for him with the DeSaussure extended family.[7]

Ford's first impressions of Charleston are well documented, for he kept a diary of his experiences during 1785 and 1786.[8] Upon arriving in Charleston, Ford found several Princeton graduates he knew, including Richard Hutson, Thomas Gibbes, John McCrady, and Patrick Noble—lawyers and men of standing within the community. Work and family connections eventually redoubled some eight years later, for just as his sister Elizabeth had married Henry William DeSaussure, Ford married DeSaussure's sister, Sarah Amelia (or "Miss Sally," as Ford called her), in January 1793. Sarah Amelia had been present in New Jersey at the time of her brother's wedding to Ford's sister and when the group set off for the South, so the acquaintance between Ford and his future wife was of long standing.[9]

Why Ford chose to leave New Jersey for South Carolina on a permanent basis is not obvious. His brother Gabriel wrote in January 1788 that problems continued to delay the settlement of their father's estate. However, enough money remained from their father's estate for their youngest brother, Jacob, to attend Princeton at this time; for Gabriel—and later Jacob—to study law and be admitted to the bar; and for their mother to visit Timothy in South Carolina in 1789. All three events indicate that money was readily available within the Ford family. Thus it is unclear why Timothy Ford decided to leave the place where he was trained and where he was (through his mentor Robert Morris, if not his own family) well connected. Perhaps Ford thought there were already too many lawyers practicing in New York and New Jersey for him to be hopeful about future prospects. That Gabriel and Jacob also intended to enter the legal profession may have encouraged him to seek his fortunes elsewhere, to avoid the possibility of conflict within the family about money and professional advancement. In any case, he chose to accompany his sister, her new husband, and his future wife to Charleston in 1785.

DESAUSSURE AND FORD IN PROFESSIONAL ENVIRONS

Following their arrival in Charleston in October 1785, the Fords and DeSaussures were feted by family and friends alike, but the young attorneys soon put their minds to business matters. Even before Ford was admitted to the South Carolina bar (which did not occur until the following year), he and his brother-in-law made good use of their legal skills on circuit. In April 1786, the two began the long trek from Charleston to Beaufort, a distance of about seventy miles, to attend the sitting of the circuit court. Along the way, the pair stayed with DeSaussure's relations each night, finally arriving at the court house a few days later. DeSaussure clearly intended to introduce Ford to all the right people, opening doors for him among the Huguenot network of families who would help Ford earn a living in the colony and make him a wealthy man. The two would have to scrap for their living, however, for other lawyers rode the circuit too and had been doing so for years when DeSaussure and Ford first appeared. Ford described meeting "Messrs. Holmes, Colhoon, Majr. Frazier and Majr Pinckney" upon arrival—the four men who were the "gentl. of the Bar that rode this circuit."[10] It would have been hard for him to avoid encountering the other legal practitioners as they arrived in Beaufort: a town of nearly thirty houses, Beaufort was not merely a small village but also a place where the residents were tightly bound by family ties. Ford discovered that "A stranger taken notice of by one gains an early access to all."[11]

Ford was singularly unimpressed by some of the men he met on circuit. In particular, when he was introduced at dinner to Aedanus Burke, the judge in eyre at Beaufort, Ford succumbed to making some sweeping condemnations of the man. Ford wrote, "I found him an arrant Irish man whose conversation though well enough aimed never contained a sentence of good English but on the contrary abounded with blunders vulgarisms & Hibernianisms." Ford's incredulity only increased once he saw Burke in action on the bench. "His ideas seem'd amazingly confused & he neither look'd spoke nor acted like a judge. In short he carries with him less dignity than I have seen for a man of his learning & station—I am told however that he is a Lawyer."[12] His disdain for the idleness and sloth of the youths he met, trained at law or not, was likewise severe. "Many send their sons to England for education from whence they generally return but little more improved & much more dissipated than they went—& after this much expense has been lavished upon them."[13] Ford did not reserve his views on diligence and hard work for Southern dandies: in a letter to his brother Gabriel, Ford censured their brother Jacob, whom Ford considered to be "wasting his time" and "dreaming away the term" at Princeton in 1792.[14]

Only newly arrived in the state, Ford was critical of the situation he found in South Carolina, not just on a personal level, but also concerning the proposed reorganization and codification of its laws. The legislature had recently appointed three men to digest all state laws into a more easily understandable form. Ford rejected this method of simplification, to be carried out by "Judges Pendleton Burk and Grimke."[15] Ford claimed that such a code "must be both deficient & faulty." In part he blamed the great variety of materials such a code must be built out of, but he also faulted (having now visited Beaufort court with his brother-in-law) "the looseness & irregularity of legal Practice: owing I believe partly to the method of administering justice in the several parts of the state and partly to the carelessness of practitioners." Ford thought that, in South Carolina generally, legal practices meant that no code could satisfy the needs of lawmakers and lawyers alike. In a comment deserving its own lengthy excerpt, Ford claimed that the incestuous nature of legal practice in Charleston made for sloppy legal proceedings.

> The state is divided into two districts the Northern & Southern, each of which is subdivided into circuits; where circuit courts are held twice a year including sessions common pleas goal delivery & presided over by one of the associate judges of whom there are four. For these Courts all the business is prepared & causes brought to issue in Charleston; & then the lawyers & judges set off together taking the requisite papers with them & are generally absent for 5 weeks. The consequence of this mode is that all the attorneys centre in Charleston, are acquainted with one another & practice upon so liberal a footing as only to adopt so much of the English practice as suits their case & convenience & compound for the rest—so that no errors or omissions of that kind are taken advantage of; & the judges do not make it their business to scrutinize into these niceties. The practice is of consequence as slovenly & unsettled as the laws themselves.[16]

Ford's condemnation of legal practice in South Carolina, so soon after his coming to the state, was only partially qualified. "The late introduction of county courts in two or three of the districts, by distributing the attorneys through the country will probably retrieve the practice in some measure from this state of confusion; at least as far as the deviations from the [E]nglish mode of administering justice will admit of. This deviation is however considerable."[17]

Ford's observations on legal practice extended not only to defects in laws, legal practice, and lawyers, but also to the—from his perspective—spendthrift practices giving rise to many lawsuits that individuals pursued through the courts. As was true in all parts of the new nation, the majority of all lawsuits filed during the 1780s and 1790s in civil courts were contests about debt and credit.[18] This continued a practice common throughout the eighteenth century in South Carolina, as research by Michael Woods has demonstrated.[19] Ford thought that debt and credit were ubiquitous in the state, intrinsically bound up in the culture of honor that he recognized when he arrived in the state that operated in equal part with the determination of most men of property never to pay their debts if possible. The close alignment of credit interests with legislative power seemed obvious to even as new a visitor as Ford: "The debtor interest is however prevalent, and operates in all the forms of injustice [to create] oppressions. . . . While men are madly accumulating enormous debts, their legislators are making provisions for their nonpayment."[20] It was the Revolution, Ford thought, that encouraged men to stop being honorable in the repayment of debts: "The planter who had been accustomed to live at his ease found himself much distressed at the conclusion of the war; involved in debt, his plantation torn to pieces . . . & his creditors pushing for repayment: the legislature immediately interfered & opened a new source of hope as well to the imprudent & fraudulent as to the unfortunate." From this beginning, Ford theorized, the cycle of indebtedness that a legislature might have prevented had spiraled out of control. "They learnt new lessons of fraud from legislative interference," the young man concluded, and "their apostacy is magnified thro the medium of their former integrity."[21]

Ford's concern about the willingness of men to put themselves in debt, relying upon the legislature to bail them out of impecunious circumstances, would actually work to his own benefit. The vast majority of legal work done by Ford and DeSaussure during their legal partnership consisted of cases for debt collection. The pair also carried on extensive legal business for family members, serving as executors for individuals like Henry William's half-brother Alexander Edwards and Edwards's wife, Mary McPherson DeSaussure, who was also his cousin.[22]

DeSaussure and Ford also entered into political disputes in the first decade of their legal partnership, possibly as a means to increase public awareness of their firm and improve their odds of gaining new clients. In the 1790s, when South Carolina's legislature began to reconsider apportionment, such that the backcountry might receive greater representation in the General Assembly, powerful interest groups opposed any redistricting that might diminish the power of low country planters. Though one-fifth of the free whites in South Carolina lived in the low country, they elected the majority of the state's legislators, a situation that upcountry residents found intolerable.[23] When residents of the backcountry launched a pamphlet war in 1793–94 with Robert Goodloe Harper arguing their case as "Appius," low country planters responded with their own volley of pamphlets, including one written by Ford, who signed himself "Americanus."[24] Arguing for the status quo, Ford tried to justify the continued unequal representation of the low country and the upcountry. He urged that in South Carolina, a state of nature had never existed prior to the formation of the Revolutionary government: individuals possessed rights and property before they formed any sort of government. Thus, if they had these possessions when they created a government, each interest group—mercantile, planting, farming, and manufacturing—present when the government formed could set the terms of the original compact. Therefore, planters who had been in the state long before backcountry residents had the right to determine the government structure and power arrangements. Latecomers, such as new immigrants settling the backcountry, must agree to existing arrangements, or they were free to go elsewhere.[25] DeSaussure echoed these sentiments in his own anonymous pamphlet, asserting that unequal representation was common in other states and had long been common practice in South Carolina. Any change from this was unnecessary.[26]

The efforts of DeSaussure and Ford in their pamphleteering paid off: the upcountry would remain underrepresented in the state assembly for several more decades. These political accomplishments did not stunt the partners' efforts to win business in the backcountry, however: they could rely upon circuit work to provide a steady stream of revenue, enough to justify having each man travel the northern or southern circuit in turn through successive years. Roughly one-third of all cases in South Carolina were now being heard on circuit, a fact not lost on the pair as they struggled to represent clients from diverse parts of the state. Indeed, the increasing numbers of cases being tried outside Charleston may have been what prompted DeSaussure to encourage Ford to join him in partnership, though Ford's ultimate inducement to move south will probably never be known. As lawyers and partners, however, the two men would see their family fortunes rise steadily through nearly thirty years of professional and personal association.[27]

PARTNERSHIP INCOME AND EXPENSES

A close investigation of the first two of a set of five cash and day books for the DeSaussure and Ford law firm, which cover the years from 1786 to 1821, reveals detailed information about expenses and income from all manner of clients, plus the names of the students who were taken into the law firm as apprentices.[28] Not all lawyers thrived economically in the new Republic: overcrowding at the bar and increased competition could drive down fees, though success as an orator and legal draftsman would attract clients in the long run.[29] Generally speaking, however, lawyers in the pre- and post-Revolutionary era had a greater opportunity to increase their wealth than did men in the other professions, and some individuals became quite affluent.[30]

In Charleston, DeSaussure and Ford managed to earn a handsome living in the first decade of their partnership, despite having an occupation theoretically regulated by the government. State law set the fees lawyers could charge at relatively low levels, which certainly may have caused less scrupulous practitioners to encourage appeals and multiple lawsuits. In the 1770s, attorneys attending district courts could charge only ten shillings for attending and arguing a suit, plus three shillings more for the paperwork required to initiate the suit.[31] After the Revolution, in county court causes, the state permitted lawyers to charge £1 1s. 9d. per suit. Stiff penalties applied to lawyers who presumed to charge more: loss of fee, plus a fine of £50 could be recovered by any informer who should turn in the overcharging attorney.[32] The regulation of fees did not stop lawyers in urban areas from earning sizeable incomes, as can be seen in Charleston and elsewhere: in the single year 1773, James Duane of New York City earned £1,860, and he too worked in a fee-regulated environment.[33]

Although it is unclear when the regulation of fees ceased to be enforced, by the mid-1780s, DeSaussure and Ford were obviously charging more than the law permitted.[34] The fees paid by clients appear to have varied mostly by the intricacy of the case, more than any other factor. Simple consultations started at £3, and that was also the standard retainer the two men charged virtually everyone who engaged them for legal work in the next decade. Rarely did any client receive a discount for legal work completed, though it may have been the case that clients were billed at "official" rates, and the partners then later wrote off the fees as uncollectible debts. Frequently, the partners collected retainers when they appeared and were able to argue a suit already begun by the plaintiff and defendant. This commonly occurred when they were riding circuit, where locals might commence a lawsuit only to discover they did not possess the legal knowledge with which to finish it. DeSaussure and Ford's income usually swelled in April and November, in months when the men attended the courts away from Charleston. The bulge in income roughly correlates to their being retained by individuals as soon as they arrived at a court town such as Beaufort. No suit appears to have been too large or too small for DeSaussure and Ford's attention, and their clients came from all social groups, male and female, though wealthy men predominated. The two partners appear to have taken on virtually every kind of legal work, from debt and property conveyancing to admiralty and criminal cases, so long as the client could afford to pay.

Henry William DeSaussure's penchant for careful bookkeeping is revealed in the minute details he recorded for over thirty years of the two men's working partnership. The five volumes he used to note daily expenditures and receipts are filled with his fine level handwriting, each line concealing the hours of toil he and Ford exerted to improve their fiscal situation. A lengthy portion of each DeSaussure and Ford cashbook is devoted to moneys paid to the partners on behalf of their clients.[35] These funds were usually received from the sheriff, who collected on their behalf, although sometimes money came into their hands straight from the losing parties themselves. This money was kept in a locked drawer, in the top of DeSaussure's desk, until it could be disbursed to clients or spent for their use. In addition to collecting legal fees owed by their clients, DeSaussure handled money destined for other purposes on a routine basis. Multiple entries in the firm's cashbooks suggest that he served as a financial middleman of sorts, paying off the bills of clients with Charleston grocers and factors, to whom they owed still more money. The careful collection and payment of clients' funds was a task he faithfully performed, year in and year out. As his biographer, Judge John Belton O'Neall, wrote, DeSaussure was "always careful to be fully informed of the exact state of his affairs, that he might not expose himself to embarrassment, and to avoid all risk of doing injustice to others."[36]

Given his attention to financial detail, it is hardly surprising that DeSaussure made the same meticulous arrangements with Ford when they commenced their partnership together. The articles establishing the law firm stipulated that during the years 1787 to 1792, profits would not be divided evenly between DeSaussure and Ford. In recognition of DeSaussure's South Carolina family connections, his existing legal practice (though he had been a solo practitioner for a single year), and the likelihood that Ford would only slowly acquire clients on his own merit, the men agreed that DeSaussure would receive two-thirds of the profits in the first eighteen months, and Ford one-third. This division of profits most likely acknowledged DeSaussure's advantageous Charleston background, as both men were newly minted from their legal studies in the North and neither could be considered experienced. In the next eighteen months Ford's share would increase to two-fifths of the firm's profits, and in 1791 and 1792, the men would begin sharing the firm's profits on an equal basis.[37] To calculate their shares of partnership income on so precise a basis, DeSaussure would have had to record every shilling received and spent with exacting detail, regardless of its source, and he did so.

Income was not exclusively derived from clients. In the first bound book, supplied by James Hawkins, stationer, of Queen Street, London, DeSaussure listed the names of all the young men who apprenticed themselves to the partners. Every few years, a new young man would join their office for a three-year training period. The first to arrive was William Tennant, son of the late Reverend William Tennant, in 1789. Two more young men, named Colcock and Ward, came in June and August of the same year. Each young man paid a fee of one hundred guineas, plus board if he lived with the DeSaussures, as Colcock did in his first year, and Dan Waring did in 1792. The fee might be negotiated to a lesser amount, if family circumstances did not permit payment all at once, or in full: the Colcocks could not afford the usual fee of one hundred guineas, and negotiations ensued between DeSaussure and Colcock's widowed mother, who managed to persuade DeSaussure to accept her son for a mere seventy guineas.

The arrangements to accept apprentices were not always immediately recorded, but DeSaussure usually remedied the defect with later detail. Mr. Darrell "came into the office late in 1789 or [b]eginning of 1790" undecided if law was his true calling. By June 1790 he notified DeSaussure that he intended to make the law his profession. Such notice was important, for the teaching attorney had to certify before Charleston's court of common pleas that the young man had served three years of serious apprenticeship in his office; thus, the month and year of his commencing legal studies were of critical importance. The large number of young men who were taken into the office gives a rough indication of the thriving nature of DeSaussure and Ford's practice, even in their first decade together. In total, the partners trained nine young men as apprentices during the first ten years they practiced, from 1786 to 1796.[38] Not all their trainees were cut out for legal practice, however: a Mr. Fripp who joined the men in 1792 "merely to be made acquainted with business" discovered that "his disposition soon compelled him to quit the study."[39]

The partners encouraged able men to join their firm as apprentices whenever they could. Vacationing with his family in Boston in 1804, Ford spent an afternoon with John Blake White, a young Charlestonian visiting Boston who was uncertain about his professional future. Despite White's misgivings about what future vocation he might undertake, "Mr. Ford recommended that I should again turn my mind to the study of the Law. He proposed that I should immediately return to Carolina & enter my name as a student; which he said, if I chose, I might immediately do in his office." When they discussed the proposal a second time, White noted that Ford heartily advocated entering the legal profession and "recommended it with the warmth of a friend." Such an endorsement was not completely selfless, however. New apprentices who had the means to travel—and could likely afford the fees of a three-year training period—were always prized.[40]

Several of the young men who served their clerkships with DeSaussure and Ford lived in the men's shared household with Elizabeth Ford DeSaussure.[41] The financial contributions of women who lived in middle-class households with men who were attorneys have been overlooked until recently.[42] However, without the daily assistance that Elizabeth offered the partners by washing, shopping, and tending to the needs of all members of the household, including apprentices who lived in the DeSaussure-Ford home, the fees earned from boarding apprentices would not have been acquired. Indeed, even before apprentices began arriving, DeSaussure and Ford could only devote their energies to reading, writing, and speech making because Elizabeth was engaged full-time in cooking, cleaning, and marketing. "The provision of meals and linens for such a household, at a time when there were no mechanical aids and not even piped water, must have been an enormously time-consuming activity."[43] It would be appropriate to consider the partnership they established a three-person business, a family enterprise in which the law of coverture and social norms relegated Elizabeth to the historical shadows.

Those shadows would have been familiar territory to the slaves who worked and lived in Charleston in the eighteenth century. Whether Elizabeth DeSaussure had the assistance of slave women to share the burdens of domestic chores in the first five years that she lived in Charleston is unknown; Henry William DeSaussure's records for the late 1780s do not reveal whether he required any of the slaves he owned who routinely worked on his father's indigo plantation outside Charleston to assist Elizabeth on a daily basis. However, the strong divide that existed between field and house servants, based upon notions of genteel behavior current in the eighteenth century, suggests that he probably would not have called upon a field slave to work in a city-based household. On the other hand, the labor of slaves could be easily rented, as every Charleston newspaper of the day attested.[44]

Physical labor was not the only sort of assistance female members of the household might render the typical middle-class enterprise. So long as the house and office shared the same physical environs—as the DeSaussure-Fords did through at least 1793—Elizabeth's presence as the eldest female of the household gave her responsibility for overseeing the apprentices' moral and emotional development, particularly if they boarded with the family. Beyond guiding young law students safely along the paths of correct behavior, Elizabeth DeSaussure's mere presence in the household as a partner's wife and sister quickly entangled her with clients. Elizabeth might be called upon to witness documents, take messages, or order supplies. Her advanced education in Philadelphia perhaps aided her in performing these tasks, allowing her to function as an unseen yet valuable de facto partner.[45] Elizabeth could also collect fees from clients or pay creditors who arrived at the partners' offices when one or both men were absent. Her management of money on a daily basis, noted through Henry William's repeated accounts of money allocated to Elizabeth for marketing, the purchase of clothing, and the payment of small bills at local shops, suggests her ready acquaintance with safely handling money and expenses. Regardless of how hard they worked, the partners depended upon Elizabeth's efforts to contain costs on as low a level as possible, so that they might see a profit at year's end.[46]

The business of making a living at the law was not exactly an easy one, as data drawn from the DeSaussure and Ford cashbook for 1786 and 1787 reveal. In 1786, following his return from the North, Henry William DeSaussure recorded the expenses and income listed in table 1 for the year.

A stray comment made in an entry for 1788 reveals that the partnership and sharing of moneys began in 1787, though the precise date that the partnership formed remains uncertain.[47] DeSaussure's decision to go into partnership with Ford began paying immediate dividends, however, with the firm earning £616 9d., nearly double his 1786 income. Unfortunately, expenses for the two men also rose, outpacing income by nearly £60.[48] An increase in business did not automatically lead to a profitable bottom line.

During the first few years of their association, the partners discovered that balancing income and expenses was difficult, with expenses frequently winning the battle. This may account for their willingness to accept apprentices so readily in the first decade of their partnership. In December 1788, DeSaussure toted up net income and expenses, and the inadequacy of legal practice to his current needs must have been blindingly apparent to him: income from legal work amounted to £368, while the expenses filling his ledger book came to nearly £629. How did he resolve the discrepancy? DeSaussure had a total personal income of nearly £300, which included other sources of revenue, like the sale of a slave and profits made on a crop of indigo harvested on land near his father's estate. In April 1788, DeSaussure sold a "wench Sarah" for £42 4s. 8d.

DeSaussure also continued to receive money from cases he had handled in

Table 1 DeSaussure and Ford Expenses and Income, 1786

Month	*Expenses (£. d. s.)*	*Receipts (£. d. s.)*
Carried forward from January–Augusts 1786 (cumulative)	135.2.9	146.2.1
September 1786	13.13.7	28.7.3
October 1786	18.10.10	7.10.0
November 1786	113.18.5	82.9.2
December 1786	33.14.11	43.18.5
Annual Totals	314.13.8[a]	308.6.11

[a] DeSaussure's addition is slightly off: the total should read £315 6d., a mistake of 6s. 10d.

1786, before commencing his partnership with Ford, but according to their agreement, the two men shared these profits nonetheless. In a singularly revealing moment, DeSaussure vented his resentment at pooling these earnings from his previous solo practice in the shared account he had established with Ford. Their articles of partnership must have stipulated this arrangement, yet it rankled DeSaussure to have the profits divided when he alone had been responsible for the original outlay in expenses. "The money then paid me must come into the general acct with Mr. Ford as I have debited myself in our joint books with every farthing I ever paid away, tho' paid out of these private funds of my own." The combined income from land, loans, the sale of the slave woman Sarah, and profits from their partnership pushed the revenues of DeSaussure and Ford to more than £666, barely enough to match their combined 1788 expenses.[49]

This pattern of expenses rarely equaling income continued through the next few years for the two men, despite the steady increase of legal business, which spiked sharply upward in the months when courts were in session. In 1791, Henry William DeSaussure recorded the expenses and income in table 2.

As one can readily see, the expenses for the firm in 1791 exceeded income by a healthy amount, nearly 10 percent, and the shortfall was made good only through money that DeSaussure received from other ventures. Indeed, DeSaussure indicated that he received money from land he rented and loans he made, by far the largest source of income he received aside from his legal work. The crops made by the few slaves he owned rarely yielded large profits, though they helped cover the shortcomings of DeSaussure and Ford's legal practice. In October 1791 he received £24 from his father for a portion of the crop worked with slaves DeSaussure owned.

Table 2 DeSaussure and Ford Expenses and Income, 1791

Month	*Expenses (£. d. s.)*	*Receipts (£. d. s.)*
January 1791	242.6.1	165.1.3
February 1791	144.8.4	102.3.5
March 1791	191.11.1	293.15.9
April–May 1791	833.10.2	676.9.0
June 1791	91.4.7	71.16.0
July 1791	102.0.11	105.15.8 ½
August 1791	119.19.1	198.12.7
September 1791	416.4.5	396.6.5
October 1791	202.0.9	129.10.4
November–December 1791	501.1.7	489.4.3
Yearly Totals	2844.7.0	2628.14.8
	"Plus cash receipts in my private account"	213.16.5
		2842.11.1

By comparing the receipts of 1788 and 1791, one can readily observe the overall rise in DeSaussure and Ford's income, from roughly £660 to nearly £2,600 in only a few short years. No major depreciation or governmental devaluation of local currency occurred during this time, so the figures can be interpreted as roughly comparable. Their hard work as attorneys seemed to be paying off: additional legal work and new clients kept the two men busy as they traveled on circuit and worked in the courts of Charleston. Yet their expenses continued to outrun their joint income by a steady amount. What were the expenses that increased so rapidly between 1788 and 1791?[50]

In part, personal expenses in the household continued to increase, boosting the firm's expenses. The costs included all the clothing, food, firewood, and sundries that individuals might need in an urban area like Charleston.[51] Prior to his own marriage in January 1793, Ford lived with DeSaussure and his wife Elizabeth, Ford's sister, in the same household. In March 1789, to take a single month as an example, the combined expenses of all three adults were £74 5s. 2d., which included the purchase of a second horse so that Ford could ride the northern circuit without having to hire a horse to do so. The horse cost £20, but only £10 was paid upon delivery—the other £10 of its purchase price was paid in kind as a retainer fee to DeSaussure and Ford by the horse's original owner. Aside from the purchase of the horse, only another five shillings was expended on paper for the office. The rest of the money went for household goods, nondurables like food and drink. In months like March, when the men did not ride circuit, personal expenses could easily outpace income. Again in January 1790, the same pattern holds true: the vast majority of outlays in that month were for food and clothing for persons in the household, plus a few other related items. Thus, the appearance that the law firm was not doing well financially actually masks great success: the income of the two lawyers continued to rise from year to year. It was their personal expenses that ate up much of the profit that the two men generated through their legal practice, even as it expanded.

Part of the household's rising expenses came from the extra mouths that had to be fed. One legal apprentice, Colcock, lived with the DeSaussure-Ford clan in 1789, though any costs associated with his board should have been offset by the additional fees paid to house and feed him. Two others, however, could not be charged for the expenses incurred on their behalf. By 1790, Henry William and Elizabeth DeSaussure had two small children, Anna and Henry Alexander, born in 1786 and 1788 respectively, who also needed to be fed, clothed, and cared for. They were the first two of twelve children that the couple had, practically guaranteeing that DeSaussure and Ford would need to work hard for there to be any money left at a year's conclusion.[52] Although precise figures are not available for the American South, estimates for early nineteenth-century Britain suggest that food and servants could take up to half of a typical middle-class family's income.[53] The family that expanded every few years with another child, or that purchased a slave to perform household work, could not continue to enjoy the same level of prosperity from earlier years unless its income increased on a commensurate basis. But even if domestic expenses could be contained through Elizabeth's skillful penny-pinching, professional expenses could not always be contained. Every new case might generate additional funds but came with associated costs.

What might be considered professional expenses? The typical range of expenses for the law firm can be divided into six categories: writing supplies, like paper, pens, ink, sealing wax, and wafers; the costs associated with circuit travel, including lodging and fodder, and payments incurred to others while on circuit, such as judge's or sheriff's fees for the service of warrants and witnesses' summons; books and durables, like bookcases, inkstands, chairs, and cloth to be made into pleaders' robes; professional memberships and fees, such as the firm's membership in the Charleston Library Society, which brought access to further volumes of law, and taxes paid upon their office (the Charleston city tax for a lawyer in business was £1 5s., so the firm collectively paid £2 10s.); printing and publication, like the formal legal notices that had to be inserted into the newspaper on a regular basis for clients; and finally, an unexpected cost: a scrivener. Even during years when the firm had one or two apprentices in the office, a scrivener was hired to do copyist work on behalf of DeSaussure and Ford. Though he did not handle many assignments, the scrivener reappeared from time to time during the period from 1789 to 1795, which suggests that he may have been used for specialty items, such as large engrossed charters or deeds of conveyance that had particular importance. Of the six categories, by far the largest of these expenses were court costs and sheriff's fees, consuming nearly 80 percent of all the moneys laid out for professional expenses. Printing bills, by contrast, were relatively small costs, as a bill from December 1790 demonstrates: the partners paid Mrs. Timothy, printer of the *Charleston Courier* after her husband's death, £3 for various advertisements and legal notices that were placed on behalf of their clients during the entire year.

One particularly interesting charge appears in June 1789, and then again in October 1790, when DeSaussure noted a contribution to John Drayton, another Charleston lawyer, for a subscription to a law library.[54] Although there is no evidence that such a law library ever came into existence, the possibility that Charleston lawyers might club together to purchase legal volumes suggests that city attorneys wanted to defray the costs of purchasing law books as well as create a social gathering spot.[55] Had it been established, a Charleston law library would have been older than the Social Law Library, formed in 1803 and the first such organization created by legal practitioners in Boston, or the Jenkins Law Library, founded by Philadelphia's city lawyers in 1802. Both of these legal libraries (which still exist) were set amidst larger populations that were home to many more practitioners than those in Charleston. However, given the existence of the Charleston Library Society, one has to wonder whether this new society would have been created primarily as a social venue, or to promote legal knowledge.[56] As it was, no such society appears to have ever come into existence, and older, more successful firms like DeSaussure and Ford continued to buy books for their own use as well as that of their law students.[57] In June 1789, DeSaussure recorded the expense of £1, spent for purchasing a volume of Blackstone's *Commentaries,* probably a duplicate copy given to a law clerk for study.

In March 1790, the firm made another purchase that might be considered personal and might be considered professional—it is a difficult expenditure to categorize. On March 15, Timothy Ford purchased a slave, as did Henry William DeSaussure. Ford purchased a man, Bob, while DeSaussure purchased a woman, Amelia. Both slaves passed through the hands of long-time clients of the two men, Thomas Cordes, and Colcock & Graham, though they were not transferred to settle any legal debts. The two slaves together cost over £130, and DeSaussure carefully recorded how much the partners paid for each slave, as well as for whom each had been purchased. That Bob and Amelia arrived together, as a pair, may indicate that they were husband and wife and were expected to function within the household as cook and butler. Indeed, by this time, Elizabeth DeSaussure was tending two small children and could probably no longer manage all the cooking or marketing necessary for the household without daily assistance. The arrival of Bob and Amelia no doubt shifted much of the household's labor from Elizabeth's shoulders to theirs, at the same time that it increased the expenses borne by the law partnership of DeSaussure and Ford.

Indeed, slave purchases consumed a considerable portion of DeSaussure and Ford's profits in the first five years of their partnership. A memorandum of agreement drawn up in May 1793, shortly after the marriage of Ford to DeSaussure's sister, describes how the partners bought slaves to be held "as our mutual property" from General Huger. As with Bob and Amelia, however, the two men also spent money separately to purchase slaves for their individual use. The document noted that Ford had previously bought five slaves from Job Colcock and Mr. Penman, and the agreement the partners made secured "Pat, Meram, Adam, Cyrus and Frank" as Ford's exclusive property. Pat's daughter, according to the document, became DeSaussure's separate property.[58] To what purpose Ford used the labor of two female and three male slaves prior to his marriage is uncertain; they may have been hired out to work in Charleston's thriving postwar economy to generate an additional stream of income. Possibly the purchase of slaves also permitted Ford to enter the ranks of the upper middle class more clearly, for it was the status of slave ownership that typically marked the closer alliance of the middle class with the planters who dominated South Carolina's political and social elite. Ford, the transplanted Northerner, experienced no difficulty in embracing his new role as slave owner.

Certainly, both men considered slavery to be part of the backbone of South Carolina society. In their pamphleteering efforts, both men defended the institution rigorously. Writing under the pseudonyms "Americanus" and "Phocion," they focused upon the reasons why preservation of property and the continued inequality of representation in the state legislature actually ensured a continuing spirit of liberty. In his pamphlet, Ford claimed that "where inequality of property prevails, the citizens are more jealous and watchful of their liberties from that very circumstance." DeSaussure repeated this sentiment the following year in his own publication, urging that in societies where domestic slavery was known, freemen were "more fiercely jealous of their liberties than any other people of the world."[59] Naturally, DeSaussure would urge that slavery was a benign institution, as he was born into a slave-holding family and continued to acquire slaves with Ford to labor for their mutual benefit. Only rarely did DeSaussure assist the enslaved to throw off their shackles: the law firm's cashbooks indicate that on a few occasions he handled the preparation of manumission and freedom papers for African Americans in Charleston at little or no cost.

CONCLUSIONS

There are a few preliminary conclusions that can be reached from this brief examination of the legal affairs of DeSaussure and Ford during their first decade together. The partners made a healthy living from their legal work, and their rising income level from 1786 through 1795 attests to this. In part, their increasing wealth resulted from their shared willingness to go out and ride both the northern and southern circuits, which were created shortly before the Revolutionary War, taking their expertise out of Charleston to build up a larger client base. Each man rode a different circuit after that first venture in 1786 when they traveled together: Ford routinely took the northern circuit, while DeSaussure rode the southern. If one partner was absent on circuit business, the other could keep the firm's office open for business in Charleston, providing legal services to those who might be in the city and need assistance. The thriving nature of their firm can also be seen in their ability to take nine apprentices into their offices during a ten-year period. Few students would be drawn to work for a firm where clients rarely came or the library they might learn from was out of date. The labor of Elizabeth DeSaussure and the slaves working in the household additionally increased the profitability of the firm.

However, the expenses DeSaussure and Ford incurred matched or exceeded their income on a regular basis, in part because of the addition of new family members and the steadily rising costs of professional practice. Not all their expenses were fixed, like these, however. The purchase of slaves ultimately was a discretionary matter. Similarly, some expenses incurred by the partners may have been linked to the need to appear as members of the upwardly mobile middle class. Their decision to purchase memberships in the Charleston Library Society, the St. Cecilia Society (a music and social group), and the Hibernian Society (another exclusive social group) and pews at St. Michael's Church was probably driven by the need to see and be seen by others who were members of Charleston's elite, and who would need their legal services in the future.[60]

Despite expenses that routinely outstripped income, both Ford and DeSaussure shared the opinion that their firm's prospects were steadily improving. The two men's outlook can be inferred from their decision in 1793 and 1803 to renew the partnership arrangements for additional five-year periods. After the initial articles of partnership in 1787 that divided their receipts in DeSaussure's favor, in later years, the pair agreed to divide the income evenly between their respective households. Each would have an equal share "in the profits & emoluments of all professional business to be done in town or country" regardless of who handled the specifics of a given case. Withdrawals from their shared income could be made by either the men or their families, as needed. At the close of every year, a settlement of accounts would reveal whether one or the other partner had drawn too heavily upon the firm's funds. The partners ensured that if either of them died, the widow and children left behind would continue to receive a portion of the partnership's profits.[61] These farsighted provisions ensured the financial security of family members, who would continue to benefit from the firm after the death of a partner, while tightening the bonds that drew DeSaussure and Ford together by emphasizing the communal nature of their enterprise. Doubtless Elizabeth DeSaussure and Sarah Amelia Ford approved of these measures, perhaps reflecting upon their own contributions to the family venture over the years and considering the arrangements their due reward.

The initial decision to create a partnership in legal practice put DeSaussure and Ford at the forefront of a new movement among businessmen of the early Republic. In the early nineteenth century, partnerships between two and three men grew rapidly in popularity, as individuals sought to establish themselves in commerce without taking on subservient roles that were socially disdained. In addition to the preference young men had to avoid positions of dependence in established firms, DeSaussure and Ford had other incentives to encourage the creation of a new two-man partnership. A family-based law firm could avoid problems associated with the moral hazards of an unscrupulous or lazy partner, while providing, as DeSaussure and Ford thoughtfully did, for the family relations of partners who might inconveniently die. Interestingly enough, though their incomes continued to rise through successive decades, the men never invited a third person into their partnership arrangements, suggesting that a family-run business contained the most trustworthy individuals of all. Small was risky, however, particularly when both partners lacked experience at the start of their venture, as DeSaussure and Ford did. Economist Naomi Lamoreaux has shown that small firms in which both partners were initially inexperienced had the highest failure rates in the early nineteenth century.[62] But for DeSaussure's slave-based profits, the firm might have foundered at the outset. Despite their somewhat rocky beginning, however, DeSaussure and Ford managed to beat the odds and became one of the earliest examples of a prosperous law partnership.

NOTES

1. Julius Goebel and Joseph Smith, eds., *The Law Practice of Alexander Hamilton: Documents and Commentary* (New York: Columbia University Press, 1964–81), 1:1, noting the short duration of legal partnerships in New York.

2. Arthur H. Hirsch, *The Huguenots of Colonial South Carolina* (1928; Columbia: University of South Carolina Press, 1999), 223. See also "Copy of the Memoir of the American Branch of the Family of DeSaussure, Drawn up by the Hon. Chancellor Henry Wm. DeSaussure," undated, DeSaussure Family Papers, South Carolina Historical Society, Charleston (hereafter SCHS). The DeSaussures were descended from French-speaking Calvinists who sought refuge near Lausanne, Switzerland, following the persecution of French Huguenots in the 1680s. Numerous pamphlets urging these nonconformists to emigrate to South Carolina circulated in Switzerland as well as southern France. Bertrand Van Ruymbeke, *From New Babylon to Eden: The Huguenots and Their Migration to Colonial South Carolina* (Columbia: University of South Carolina Press, 2006), 37–41.

3. William Harper, *Memoir of the Life, Character, and Public Services of the late Hon. Henry Wm. DeSaussure, prepared and read on the 15th February, 1841 at the Circular Church, Charleston, by appointment of the South Carolina Bar Association* (Charleston, S.C.: W. Riley, 1841), 11. Copy consulted in the DeSaussure Genealogy Files, SCHS.

4. Harper, *Memoir,* 11.

5. "Henry William DeSaussure," *Dictionary of American Biography* (New York: Charles Scribner's Sons, 1928–36), 5:253–54; "Henry William DeSaussure," *Biographical Directory of the South Carolina House of Representatives,* ed. N. Louise Bailey (Columbia: University of South Carolina Press, 1984), 4:154–56. See also *Appleton's Cyclopaedia of American Biography* (New York: D. Appleton, 1900), 2:150; *Who Was Who in America: Historical Volume 1607–1896,* rev. ed. (Chicago: Marquis, 1967), 215. The comparison between DeSaussure and Kent was drawn by John Belton O'Neall, celebrated South Carolina jurist of the nineteenth century and author of *Biographical Sketches of the Bench and Bar of South Carolina* (Charleston, S.C.: S. G. Courtenay, 1859), 1:245. On family movements during the Revolution, see Edward McCrady, *The History of South Carolina in the Revolution, 1780–1783* (New York: Macmillan, 1901), 378. Other information drawn from DeSaussure's obituary in the *Charleston Courier* (Apr. 1, 1839). Henry William DeSaussure, *Reports of the Court of Chancery and Court of Equity in South Carolina from the Revolution till 1813,* 4 vols. (Columbia, S.C.: Cline and Hines, 1817–19).

6. Jacob Ford will, July 10, 1776, Ravenel Family Papers, SCHS. The testator died in January 1777.

7. The decision of middle-class individuals to visit and eventually relocate to the South in this period has been well documented by Jonathan Wells, *The Origins of the Southern Middle Class, 1800–1861* (Chapel Hill: University of North Carolina Press, 2004), 19–40. The possibility of economic opportunity was widely acknowledged, and ties among the professional classes encouraged South-bound emigration (29–30).

8. Joseph W. Barnwell, ed., "Diary of Timothy Ford, 1785–1786," *South Carolina Historical*

and Genealogical Magazine 13 (1912): 132–47, 181–204. The existence of the diary for only a single year argues for the interpretation that Ford intended to make only a short visit to the South and subsequently decided to relocate permanently. Other Ford biographical data drawn from *Princetonians: A Biographical Dictionary* (Princeton, N.J.: Princeton University Press, 1976–91), vols. 3 and 4. "Miss Sally" reference from Barnwell, "Diary of Timothy Ford," Oct. 13, 1785: 139. See also Bailey, *Biographical Directory of the South Carolina House of Representatives*, 4:208–9.

9. The marriage of cousins and siblings associated with a business enterprise served to "counteract the centrifugal tendencies of partible inheritance. In a sense it was an alternative to elaborate marriage settlements," although in the case of DeSaussure and Ford, this was offset by the existence of elaborate partnership arrangements renewed at five-year intervals. Family ties ensured the continuity of business personnel, which was essential to a lasting commercial venture. Leonore Davidoff and Catherine Hall, *Family Fortunes: Men and Women of the English Middle-Class, 1780–1850* (London: Hutchinson, 1987), 218, 221.

10. Barnwell, "Diary of Timothy Ford," Apr. 4, 1786: 145. The men were John B. Holmes, John Ewing Calhoun (later senator from South Carolina), Alexander Fraser, and Thomas Pinckney. See 145 n. 7.

11. Ibid, 146. Ford's introduction to riding circuit stands as a sharp contrast to the more typical experience of Waightstill Avery, who in 1769 recorded that circuit travel entailed many a night in "nasty" log cabins or sharing a room with disgraceful drunks who frequented the same taverns as lawyers and judges. Clement Eaton, "A Mirror of the Southern Colonial Lawyer: The Fee Books of Patrick Henry, Thomas Jefferson and Waightstill Avery," *William and Mary Quarterly,* 3d ser., 8 (1951): 526.

12. Barnwell, "Diary of Timothy Ford," Apr. 4, 1785: 145. Burke's educational background is somewhat murky, according to his biographer John Meleney. He never formally studied law at the Four Courts in Dublin or the Inns of Court in London, but he reported in a letter to North Carolinian Thomas Burke (no relation) that he "Read with the greatest application, [and] the common law takes up the most of my time." A. Burke to T. Burke, Dec. 2, 1769, in *The State Records of North Carolina,* ed. Walter Clark, 16 vols. (Raleigh: State of North Carolina, 1895–1914), 15:676–80, as cited in John Meleney, *The Public Life of Aedanus Burke: Revolutionary Republican in Post-Revolutionary South Carolina* (Columbia: University of South Carolina Press, 1989), 20. Unlike Ford, Francisco de Miranda, a Spanish visitor to Charleston, considered Burke a man of sound abilities and intelligence. John Ezell, ed., *The New Democracy in America: Travels of Francisco de Miranda in the United States, 1783–1784* (Norman: University of Oklahoma Press, 1963), 29. However, Burke's penchant for jokes and ribald behavior that may not have comported with Ford's expectations are well documented. Meleney, *Public Life of Aedanus Burke*, 26–27, 33.

13. Barnwell, "Diary of Timothy Ford," Nov. 28, 1786: 192.

14. T. Ford to G. Ford, May 15, 1792, Ravenel Family Papers, SCHS.

15. Barnwell, "Diary of Timothy Ford," Nov. 28, 1786: 192.

16. Ibid., 199. The creation of circuit courts outside Charleston was the subject of numerous efforts in the 1760s, largely resulting from the Regulator movement. In 1769, the colony finally succeeded with the Circuit Court Act, designating seven districts that would have twice-yearly court sessions (April and November), while Charleston's courts would continue to meet on a quarterly basis. The 1769 act is reprinted in its entirety in Richard M. Brown, *South Carolina*

Regulators (Cambridge, Mass.: Harvard University Press, 1963), 148–58. Georgetown, Camden, and Cheraws were the northern circuit courts, while Beaufort, Ninety-Six, and Orangeburg were the southern circuit courts. Hoyt Canady, *Gentlemen of the Bar: Lawyers in Colonial South Carolina* (New York: Garland, 1987), 133.

17. Barnwell, "Diary of Timothy Ford," Nov. 28, 1786: 199.

18. This continued pre-Revolutionary trends in South Carolina of debt cases representing nearly 50 percent of all civil litigation in the colony. Canady, *Gentlemen of the Bar,* 96, table 2. On the overall increase in debtors' litigation in the early national period, see Bruce Mann, *Republic of Debtors: Bankruptcy in the Age of American Independence* (Cambridge, Mass.: Harvard University Press, 2002).

19. Michael Woods, "The Culture of Credit in Colonial Charleston," *South Carolina Historical Magazine* 99 (1998): 358–80. Woods showed that the average suit for indebted amounts rose from £55 before 1710 to more than £1,600 between 1764 and 1769 (359, table 1). Nearly 40 percent of all suits from 1700 to 1770 settled prior to final judgment. Merchants comprised 40 percent of all plaintiffs, and book accounts or written promises to pay were the preferred methods of indebtedness.

20. Barnwell, "Diary of Timothy Ford," Nov. 28, 1786: 200.

21. Ibid., 202–3.

22. Mary P. Fenhagen, "John Edwards and Some of His Descendants," *South Carolina Historical Magazine* 55 (1954): 22–23. Debt collection comprised the majority of work done by Southern colonial lawyers. Eaton, "A Mirror of the Southern Colonial Lawyer," 525.

23. James Haw, "Political Representation in South Carolina, 1699–1794: Evolution of a Lowcountry Tradition," *South Carolina Historical Magazine* 103 (2002): 125.

24. On Harper's side of the pamphlet war, see Eric Papenfuse, "The Evils of Necessity: Robert Goodloe Harper and the Moral Dilemma of Slavery," *Transactions of the American Philosophical Society* 87 (1997): 1–160.

25. Americanus [Ford], *The Constitutionalist; or, An Inquiry How Far It Is Expedient and Proper to Alter the Constitution of South Carolina* (Charleston, S.C.: Maryland, M'Iver, 1794), 3–10, 15–16, summarized in Haw, "Political Representation in South Carolina," 126–27.

26. Phocion [DeSaussure], *Letters on the Question of the Justice and Expediency of Going into Alterations of the Representation in the Legislature of South Carolina* (Charleston, S.C.: Maryland, M'Iver, 1795), 15–16, cited in Haw, "Political Representation in South Carolina," 127.

27. Canady, *Gentlemen of the Bar,* 131–132.

28. Ravenel Family Papers, SCHS. The five volumes of records in 11/131A/1 are all in the handwriting of Henry William DeSaussure and cover the following dates: cashbook 1786–95 (vol. 1); day book 1790–92 (vol. 2); cashbook 1797–1801 (vol. 3); cashbook 1804–20 (vol. 4); cashbook 1812–21 (vol. 5). Despite the slight variations in their names, the volumes all record the flow of money in and out of the partnership on a daily, monthly, and yearly basis. Lawyers' fee books have been recognized as a rich source of information on legal practice for over fifty years, though rarely have they been culled for what they might reveal. Eaton, "A Mirror of the Southern Colonial Lawyer," 520.

29. Anton-Hermann Chroust, *The Rise of the Legal Profession in America* (Norman: University of Oklahoma Press, 1965), 2:87–88.

30. Jackson T. Main, *The Social Structure of Revolutionary America* (Princeton, N.J.: Princeton University Press, 1965), 101–3.

31. *An Act for Establishing Courts, building Gaols, and Appointing Sheriffs and other officers for the more convenient administration of Justice in this province,* enacted April 1768, cl. 4, in *The Statutes at Large of South Carolina; Edited, under Authority of the Legislature,* ed. Thomas Cooper and David J. McCord (Columbia, S.C.: A. S. Johnston, 1840), 7:200.

32. *An Act for Establishing County Courts, and for regulating the proceedings therein,* enacted March 1785, cl. 61, in Cooper and McCord, *The Statutes at Large of South Carolina,* 7:242. By 1788, county court cases theoretically paid only £1 per case, and £2 upon appeal. *An Act to Alter and Amend the Several County Court Acts,* enacted January 1788, cl. 9 (248).

33. Milton M. Klein, "From Community to Status: The Development of the Legal Profession in Colonial New York," *New York History* 60 (1979): 149.

34. Even prior to the Revolution, fee regulation did not stop lawyers in North Carolina and Virginia from charging more than the law permitted. Eaton, "A Mirror of the Southern Colonial Lawyer," 528–31.

35. The second half of each cashbook covered disbursements, loans, and repayments of loans. The cashbooks strongly resemble those in volume 5 of Goebel and Smith, *The Law Practice of Alexander Hamilton,* although the minutiae of disbursements are much more thorough in the DeSaussure and Ford books, detailing precisely what Elizabeth Ford spent the household funds to purchase. At the same time, the type of work done for each client is provided in much less detail by Henry William DeSaussure than by Alexander Hamilton.

36. O'Neall, *Biographical Sketches of the Bench and Bar of South Carolina,* 1:250.

37. Untitled memorandum of agreement between Henry William DeSaussure and Timothy Ford, May 21, 1793, Ravenel Family Papers, SCHS. This document repeated the terms of the initial partnership agreement before spelling out further financial arrangements between the two men. Young men typically joined partnerships by moving into the household of the senior partner and living where they both worked. This may have delayed marriage for some men who were junior partners, as was the case of Timothy Ford during the first five years of the DeSaussure-Ford partnership. Davidoff and Hall, *Family Fortunes,* 222.

38. This number is comparable to the ten men trained by John Adams in his law practice from 1766 to 1775. As Adams recalled, he had "never been without three Clerks in my office." John Adams, *Legal Papers of John Adams,* ed. L. Kinvin Wroth and Hiller B. Zobel (Cambridge, Mass.: Harvard University Press, 1965), 1:lxxxi.

39. DeSaussure and Ford cashbook, 1786–95, Ravenel Family Papers, SCHS. All entries for the first five years were recorded in pounds, shillings, and pence. Thereafter, DeSaussure appears to have used a mixed method of English and American currencies to record moneys collected and disbursed.

40. Paul R. Weidner, ed., "The Journal of John Blake White," *South Carolina Historical and Genealogical Magazine* 42 (1941): 107.

41. Until Timothy Ford's marriage in January 1793 to DeSaussure's sister Sarah Amelia, he lived with Elizabeth and Henry William DeSaussure. The two men likewise shared joint ownership of a house purchased on Sullivan's Island, and a house built after 1800 on Meeting Street, until 1805, when they divided their physical assets. "Arrangement between T. Ford & H. W. DeSaussure," July 10, 1805, Ravenel Family Papers, SCHS. The entry of young men into the households of their legal tutors was common, even before the Revolution. See the experiences of John Thaxter, Nathan Rice, and Jonathan Mason with John and Abigail Adams, in Adams, *Legal Papers of John Adams,* 1:lxxxii.

42. See particularly the scholarship of Catherine Hall on the women of English middle-class families and the often unnoted economic, social, and cultural contributions they made to their households. Davidoff and Hall, *Family Fortunes*, and Catherine Hall, *White, Male, and Middle-Class: Explorations in Feminism and History* (New York: Routledge, 1992).

43. Hall, *White, Male, and Middle-Class*, 113.

44. The purchase of two slaves, one male and one female, by DeSaussure and Ford in 1790 suggests that Elizabeth did not continue to work alone in the household economy. See below.

45. Davidoff and Hall, *Family Fortunes*, 200.

46. Wells, *Origins of the Southern Middle Class,* 115. On the emotional, moral, and working contributions of women to the middle-class household, see Davidoff and Hall, *Family Fortunes*, 264, 282–83.

47. Nov. 11, 1788, DeSaussure and Ford cashbook, 1786–95, Ravenel Family Papers, SCHS.

48. Income for 1787 totaled only £616 9d., while expenses rose to £677 3d. DeSaussure and Ford cashbook, 1786–95, Ravenel Family Papers, SCHS.

49. Total expenses for the year 1788 came to £628 8s.3d. DeSaussure and Ford cashbook, 1786–95, Ravenel Family Papers, SCHS.

50. Indeed, if one looks forward to 1802, similar patterns prevail: the partners received £4,202 1s. 11d. and expended £4,931 9s. 3d. In this one year, DeSaussure broke down expenses based upon whether they were his, Ford's, or the partnership's together. Ford and his wife accounted for £1,023 of expenses, while DeSaussure and his family spent £1,293. The partners together incurred over £2,600 in expenses, suggesting that the costs associated with the business outstripped the money spent on family needs. "Account of DeSaussure and Ford for the Year 1802," Ravenel Family Papers, SCHS.

51. In partnership records, it was fairly common for middle-class households to mix personal and professional moneys together indiscriminately. So long as businesses operated in the same physical space as homes, the intermingling of financial records remained a commonplace. Davidoff and Hall, *Family Fortunes*, 202.

52. "Copy of the Memoir of the American Branch of the family of DeSaussure," DeSaussure Family Papers 1022.00.

53. Davidoff and Hall, *Family Fortunes*, 361.

54. The identity of the John Drayton to whom this refers cannot be determined with absolute certainty, as there were two men bearing this name in 1790 who were active in Charleston. However, this record most likely refers to the John Drayton (1766–1822) who eventually served as state governor in 1800. He studied law at the Inner Temple in London shortly after the American Revolution. John A. Garraty and Mark C. Carnes, eds., *American National Biography* (New York: Oxford University Press, 1998), 6:888–89.

55. Whether the law library might be associated with a city bar is similarly shrouded in mystery. On August 20, 1789, DeSaussure contributed nearly £2 for his share of a "bar dinner," but no records of an eighteenth-century Charleston bar have been located. DeSaussure and Ford cashbook, 1786–95, Ravenel Family Papers, SCHS.

56. DeSaussure and Ford were members of the Charleston Library Society, founded in 1748 and widely considered the "center of intellectual life" in the seaport. George C. Rogers, *Charleston in the Age of the Pinckneys* (Columbia: University of South Carolina Press, 1969), 99.

57. James Raven's analysis of the holdings of the Charleston Library Society shows that only 6 percent of the books owned by the association were devoted to law or politics. Most were

classic studies, like Blackstone, rather than the more narrowly technical treatises that became available in the late eighteenth century. James Raven, *London Booksellers and American Customers: Transatlantic Literary Community and the Charleston Library Society, 1748–1811* (Columbia: University of South Carolina Press, 2002), 185, figure 3.

58. Untitled memorandum of agreement between Henry William DeSaussure and Timothy Ford, May 12, 1793, Ravenel Family Papers, SCHS.

59. Quotations from Americanus, *The Constitutionalist,* 39–40, and Phocion, *Letters,* 9, 18, cited in Jack P. Greene, "'Slavery or Independence': Some Reflections on the Relationship among Liberty, Black Bondage, and Equality in Revolutionary South Carolina," *South Carolina Historical Magazine* 80 (1979): 204–5.

60. The St. Cecilia Society was an exclusive male-only social group that admitted only Charleston's elite to membership. The Hibernian Society was likewise a group with restricted membership that catered to upper-class men. Both societies still exist today. The interlocking nature of these social groups provided elite Charlestonian men with networks of information and financial support, as well as cultural stimulation. See Rogers, *Charleston in the Age of the Pinckneys,* 98–112; Nicholas Butler, "Votaries of Apollo: The St. Cecilia Society and the Patronage of Concert Music in Charleston, South Carolina 1769–1820" (PhD diss., University of Indiana, 2004).

61. Untitled partnership agreements dated May 21, 1793, and Dec. 31, 1803, Ravenel Family Papers, SCHS. Presumptively there was another partnership agreement in 1798 extending the partnership for the period 1798–1803, but it has not been located in either the Ford or DeSaussure family papers. Similarly, there were likely partnership agreements extending the arrangement until 1821 (not located), as the financial records indicate that both partners continued to draw money from the pooled income until that date. One peculiarity of the 1803 agreement was that Ford was no longer required to attend courts in person; "that part of the professional duty to be performed by Henry William DeSaussure except he be disabled by sickness or necessary absence." Why the two men decided that Ford was not to travel circuit or take part in oral arguments before the courts after that date is unclear from the remaining records.

62. Naomi R. Lamoreaux, "The Partnership Form of Organization: Its Popularity in Early-Nineteenth-Century Boston," in *Entrepreneurs: The Boston Business Community, 1700–1850,* ed. Conrad E. Wright and Katheryn P. Viens (Boston: Massachusetts Historical Society, 1997), 271, 279–80, 290, 293.

5

Utility, History, and the Rule of Law: The Fugitive Slave Act of 1850 in Antebellum Jurisprudence

ALFRED L. BROPHY

IN HARRIET BEECHER STOWE'S 1852 NOVEL *UNCLE TOM'S CABIN,* THE slave Eliza hears that her child, Harry, will be sold and sent away from her. She takes Harry and flees across the Ohio River, where she ends up seeking refuge at the home of Senator and Mrs. Byrd. The senator and his wife have been debating whether fugitive slaves should be returned to their owners. The senator has just voted for a bill in the Ohio legislature that would require them to be returned. In response to his pleas to listen to "reason," Mrs. Byrd says, "I hate reasoning," for reasoning is only "a way you political folks have of coming round and round a plain right thing; and you don't believe in it yourselves, when it comes to practice."[1] Indeed, Mrs. Byrd is correct, for the senator takes in Eliza and little Harry. The Byrds give Harry some clothes and toys that belonged to their own son, who has recently died. And then the senator himself drives a wagon carrying Eliza and Harry to a Quaker settlement—a stop on the Underground Railroad. Thus, when confronted by the inhumanity of the Fugitive Slave Act, the senator rebels against it. He realizes that he is breaking his own counsel. Yet, as Mrs. Byrd concludes, "Your heart is better than your head, in this case." And she asks, "Could I ever have loved you, had I not known you better than you know yourself?"[2] This vi-

---

I would like to thank Morton J. Horwitz, whose work has guided my thinking in law and legal history since I read *The Transformation of American Law, 1780–1860* in my first semester of law school. In more recent years, it has been my enormously good fortune to be his student in a more conventional sense. His humanity guides my work. I would also like to thank Mary Sarah Bilder, Adrienne Davis, David Holland, Daniel J. Hulsebosch, Daniel W. Hamilton, David Millon, and David Tanenhaus for reading this paper.

gnette at the center of *Uncle Tom's Cabin* shows Stowe's optimistic belief that if she could just make people *feel* the injustice of the Fugitive Slave Act—and of slavery more generally—they would oppose the act and the institution.

Much of *Uncle Tom's Cabin* is about the sentiment-based critique of slave law.[3] Stowe sought to overturn respect for slave law by pointing out how inconsistent it is with considerations of humanity. The Fugitive Slave Act of 1850, Stowe tells us, is what inspired her. For it was in the wake of the act that she heard "Christian and humane people" recommending that fugitives be returned to slavery. Stowe was surprised, and she thought they could not understand slavery; if they did, such a question could never be open for discussion. And from this arose a desire to exhibit it in a *"living dramatic reality."*[4]

The Fugitive Slave Act of 1850 inspired, then, one of the most important novels ever written by an American, for the act led to a conflict between sentiments of humanity toward the individual slaves and the cold logic of the rule of law and utilitarian considerations that underlay pro-slavery advocacy. Though Stowe touched the emotions of her readers, Northerners and Southerners, she was at the time on the losing end of the political and legal struggle over slavery. As Ralph Waldo Emerson told the citizens of Concord in 1851, many forces were aligned in favor of the act and in favor of slavery. "The learning of the Universities, the culture of the eloquent society, the acumen of lawyers, the majesty of the Bench, the eloquence of the Christian pulpit, the stoutness of Democracy, the respectability of the Whig party are all combined" in the pro-slavery mission of kidnapping a fugitive slave, Emerson said.[5]

The act had several key provisions. It established federal commissioners who had the authority to require private citizens to pursue fugitives. They also had jurisdiction to issue certificates of removal for fugitive slaves. The commissioners took testimony from the slave owner in person and from affidavits; the alleged slaves were not permitted to testify. The commissioners were to issue the certificates of removal once they established the identity of the slave as the person claimed to be a fugitive. There was no jury trial, and no defenses were permitted. Thus, the commissioners' function was limited to determining the identity of the person being returned, not whether the person actually *was* a fugitive. Commissioners received more compensation ($10) if they ordered the slave returned than if they found the alleged fugitive was not the person the slave owner claimed him or her to be ($5). The act preempted the personal liberty laws of several Northern states, which prohibited state officers from cooperating in the return of fugitive slaves. Those who interfered with the return of fugitives were subject to a $1,000 fine and six months' imprisonment.[6] Such provisions led Henry David Thoreau to say on July 4, 1854, that "there are perhaps a million slaves in Massachusetts."[7] It was thus a limitation of the rights of accused fugitives and the impressment of private citizens.

The Fugitive Slave Act of 1850 occupies an important place in our thinking about the coming of the Civil War and antebellum jurisprudence.[8] The majority of jurisprudential writing about the act has focused, however, on those opposed to it and why people comply with unjust laws. For example, Robert Cover focused on the variety of antislavery responses to the act in his 1975 book *Justice Accused.*[9] Cover sought to understand not the antislavery forces who were motivated by conscience to violate the law, like Stowe's fictional Senator Byrd, but the judges who followed the law, no matter the dictates of their internal moral compass. He emphasized the importance of studying those people, for they were among the leaders at the time. And while they may have been antislavery in private, many worked within the pro-slavery legal system. Henry David Thoreau recognized as much the year before the act was passed, as Americans debated the return of fugitive slaves. Thoreau criticized those who refused to take action against slavery: "There are thousands who are in opinion opposed to slavery and war, who yet in effect do nothing to put an end to them; who, esteeming themselves children of Washington and Franklin, sit down with their hands in their pockets, and say that they know not what to do, and do nothing; . . . What is the price-current of an honest man and patriot today? They hesitate, and they regret, and sometimes they petition; but they do nothing in earnest and with effect."[10]

Cover addressed the problem of individuals' complicity in evil, so prevalent in the era of slavery. There are important issues about how the law constrained and channeled those who were antislavery in private. Stowe addressed such issues in her second novel, *Dred: A Tale of the Great Dismal Swamp*, in which she set up a judge who was antislavery in private but issued a pro-slavery decision.[11] But largely left out of Cover's discussions are the ways that Americans discussed law outside the judiciary, as well as the ideas of those who supported slavery.

The debates over the act fit with the picture that Morton J. Horwitz's *Transformation of American Law, 1780–1860* created. Horwitz examined the ideas at the heart of American law. Before historians began to revisit the conservative and dominant ideas in the antebellum South,[12] *Transformation* depicted the architecture of a particular variety of conservative thought: legal thought. Across the common law, from torts and contracts to property, judges remade—or at least reaffirmed—the law to bring it in line with the dominant philosophy of the era, which sought to promote economic growth. Their opinions subordinated concerns for individuals to considerations of precedent and to an increasing respect for considerations of utility. Judges rarely employed the sentiment urged by Stowe and Thoreau, for law was a stable field of thought concerned with preservation of vested rights, with expansion of the economy, and with the "rule of law." The ideology of utility and cold legal reasoning that Stowe criticized in her antislavery trilogy—*Uncle Tom's Cabin, A Key to Uncle Tom's Cabin*, and *Dred*—was central to Horwitz's story as well.[13]

Even before the act, debate about the rendition of fugitive slaves centered around the admiration for utility that Horwitz identified among judges. Henry

David Thoreau's "Resistance to Civil Government" (popularly known, though not in Thoreau's time, as "Civil Disobedience"), delivered in 1849, illustrates the considerations of utility at the base of the rendition of fugitive slaves. Drawing upon a passage in William Paley's *Moral Philosophy*, which was a guiding text in moral philosophy for antebellum Americans, Thoreau spoke of Americans' respect for utility: "Paley resolves all civil obligation into expediency; and he proceeds to say that 'so long as the interest of the whole society requires it, that is, so long as the established government cannot be resisted or changed without public inconvenience, it is the will of God . . . that the established government be obeyed—and no longer.'"[14]

Thoreau, however, thought there were places where "the rule of expediency" is not the guide, places "in which a people, as well and an individual, must do justice, cost what it may." He concluded that "this people must cease to hold slaves, and to make war on Mexico, though it cost them their existence as a people." Thus Thoreau reached the central point of the debate: should we do justice to individual slaves or do what maximized the utility of the actor (in this case the nation). Many abolitionists, obviously, thought that justice to the individual also maximized the utility of the nation, but that was not what most Americans thought. Thoreau's Transcendental project was to replace the collective law with an individual conscience. He asks, "Is it not possible to take a step further towards recognizing and organizing the rights of man? There will never be a really free and enlightened State until the State comes to recognize the individual as a higher and independent power, from which all its own power and authority are derived, and treats him accordingly."[15] We see the centrality of utility from judicial opinions to legislative debates to literary addresses. Everywhere one looked in the antebellum period, one saw Americans in love with the idea of utility. As William Goddard told the Brown University Phi Beta Kappa Society in 1836, "we, as a people, . . . seem to make a regard to utility almost a part of our religion."[16]

This essay returns to the debates in Congress and the early responses in the public with the goal of reading them for insight into the nature of legal thought. Where Horwitz's and Cover's subjects were judges, this paper looks to legislators, lawyers, and ministers, with the goal of understanding the ideas supporting the act and the rule of law more generally. We see support for the rule of law not just because it supported slavery (though of course that is important), but because it supported the idea of a republic as a place where property rights are of primary importance. So even many who were not pro-slavery supported the act. Exploration of the reasons that people urged support of the act tells us about the power of the idea of law. Many legislators, moreover, employed considerations of utility to support slavery (because in their minds slaves were better off in slavery, and certainly everyone else was, too).

The debates illuminate the intersection of constitutionalism, law, and slavery in American thought.[17] Together, the debates and the response to the act illustrate key points of contention in antebellum thought: the roles of practical utilitarian considerations, based on a reading of history and a society's current mores, and the opposition: a religiously inspired search for moral perfection and individual humanity. Several key points of conflict emerge. First is a conflict between the considerations of utility to society and humanity to individuals. This is part of a calculation of the entire effects—a cost-benefit analysis. Second, and closely related to that, is the centrality of utilitarian calculations in legislation, particularly in legislation supporting slavery and considerations in the abstract of rights. Finally, in determining the values to plug into the utility calculus, historical evidence was central to the believed necessity of slavery in opposition to Bible- and morality-based critiques of slavery.

Let us begin with the most famous speech related to the Fugitive Slave Act, Daniel Webster's March 7, 1850, speech, which is concerned with supporting a moderate position, stepping back from the brink of disunion by recognizing that Southern states had a legitimate complaint about the loss of their slaves, and noting that well-intentioned abolitionists were, nevertheless, harming the slaves.[18] We might also recall that Thoreau referred to the act as "Webster's Fugitive-Slave Bill."[19]

So Webster first exculpates the pro-slavery ministers of the South: thousands believed slave-holding not sinful, and thousands more—maybe even more numerous—found "slavery to be an established relation of the society in which they live, can see no way in which, let their opinions on the abstract question be what they may, it is in the power of the present generation to relieve themselves from this relation."[20] Thus, a central element is the practical in politics and law: take the world as it is, rather than as it ought to be. That focus on the "practical reason" is, as Stowe pointed out, a central tenet of antebellum jurisprudence. And it is, as Ralph Waldo Emerson pointed out in his 1841 lecture, "The Conservative," the difference between conservatism and reform: "Reform is affirmative; conservatism is negative; conservatism goes for comfort, reform for truth. Conservatism is more candid to behold another's worth; reform more disposed to maintain and increase its own. Conservatism makes no poetry, breathes no prayer, has no invention; it is all memory. Reform has no gratitude, no prudence, no husbandry."[21]

Webster juxtaposed that practical reason with abolitionist extremism. Abolitionists "saw the right clearly; they think others ought so to see it also, and they are disposed to establish a broad line of distinction between what is right and what is wrong." Webster said starkly: "I think their operations for the last twenty years have produced nothing good or valuable. I cannot but see what mischiefs their interference with the South has produced." Webster surveyed Virginia legislature's 1832 debate in the wake of Nat Turner's rebellion as evidence that the South was moving toward the termination of slavery. He urged his audience

> to recur to the debates in the Virginia House of Delegates in 1832, and . . . see with what freedom a proposition made by Mr. [Thomas] Jefferson Randolph for the gradual abolition

> of slavery was discussed in that body. Every one spoke of slavery as he thought; very ignominious and disparaging names and epithets were applied to it. The debates in the House of Delegates on that occasion, I believe, were all published. They were read by every colored man who could read, and to those who could not read, those debates were read by others. At that time Virginia was not unwilling or unafraid to discuss this question, and to let that part of her population know as much of discussion as they could learn. That was in 1832.[22]

Then the abolition societies began in 1835 to send literature to Southern states. And the South retreated from discussion of termination in response to abolitionist societies.

> They attempted to arouse, and did arouse, a very strong feeling; in other words, they created great agitation in the North against Southern slavery. Well, what was the result? The bonds of the slave were bound more firmly than before, their rivets were more strongly fastened. Public opinion, which in Virginia had begun to be exhibited against slavery, and was opening out for the discussion of the question, drew back and shut itself up in its castle. . . . Every thing that these agitating people have done has been, not to enlarge, but to restrain, not to set free, but to bind faster the slave population of the South.[23]

Webster found that their fanaticism led them to see moral absolutes in stark and distinct terms: "They are not seldom willing to establish that line upon their own convictions of truth or justice; and are ready to mark and guard it by placing along it a series of dogmas, as lines of boundary on the earth's surface are marked by posts and stones." The reference to boundaries—to bright lines—and to monuments is itself a central part of antebellum thinking. There are intellectual monuments, like judicial decisions and even great orations (Webster's 1830 reply to Hayne became one), that coincide with physical monuments, like the Bunker Hill monument, the Washington Monument then under construction, and the city of Washington itself. And we hear of judges speaking of precedents as monuments that guide through a labyrinth.[24]

Yet those lines—boundaries—between right and wrong are central to abolitionist thinking and to the evangelical mind more generally. In fact, perfectionism was a central trope of the religious excitement of the 1840s and 1850s. We hear much mocking of that perfectionism in Webster, as well as others. Abolitionists were fanatics[25]—monomaniacs, to use the term that science developed at the time to label and stigmatize their behavior—and that single-minded pursuit of a goal led to larger harm.[26] For they "do not see how too eager a pursuit of one duty may involve them in the violation of others, or how too warm an embracement of one truth may lead to a disregard of other truths equally important." That is a crucial distinction between antebellum Americans: whether they do justice in individual cases or look at the picture as a whole. Many politicians spoke about this calculus: their vision of morals is such that they should do justice on the whole. That utilitarian calculus appeared in moral philosophy texts.[27] Thus, the debate related in what was perhaps its key part to the individual versus the collective. Abolitionists thought that such questions could be answered with a mathematical certainty:

"These persons are disposed to mount upon some particular duty, as upon a war-horse, and to drive furiously on and upon and over all other duties that may stand in the way. There are men who, in reference to disputes of that sort, are of the opinion that human duties may be ascertained with the exactness of mathematics. They deal with morals as with mathematics; and they think what is right may be distinguished from what is wrong with the precision of an algebraic equation."[28]

And that narrow mathematical reasoning admitted of few opportunities for compromise.

> They are apt, too, to think that nothing is good but what is perfect, and that there are no compromises or modifications to be made in consideration of difference of opinion or in deference to other men's judgment. If their perspicacious vision enables them to detect a spot on the face of the sun, they think that a good reason why the sun should be struck down from heaven. They prefer the chance of running into utter darkness to living in heavenly light, if that heavenly light be not absolutely without any imperfection. There are impatient men; too impatient always to give heed to the admonition of St. Paul, that we are not to "do evil that good may come"; too impatient to wait for the slow progress of moral causes in the improvement of mankind.[29]

So there is a practicality, a consideration of the complete picture rather than issues by themselves, and then there is one other key legal element in the speech: a sense of the duty that the Constitution imposes on Congress and on individual citizens.

That world of law involved an analysis of history in its consideration of the effects of legislation. Their practical world[30] took a bold look at the world as it is, for which history was an important teacher. The lessons were conservative—that slavery was ubiquitous and could not be ended. That practicality, looking to overall considerations of utility, is a piece of what Horwitz described for common-law judges. Where they altered the law to provide for economic progress, politicians took their institutions from considerations of utility. The Fugitive Slave Act debates appear, then, as part of a larger world of thought about law.[31] Part of that thought rested on the knowledge that the world was imperfect and it held that nothing could be done about such suffering. Or, as Senator R. M. T. Hunter said, "Some suffering . . . belongs to our condition; it is a part of the lot of humanity."[32] Senator John Bell of Tennessee reasoned from his understanding of history to argue that slavery was both morally just and practically necessary. Bell found that slavery had contributed "in a hundred various forms and modes, through a period of thousands of years, to the amelioration of the condition of mankind generally." Though Bell found that slavery was "sometimes abused and perverted, as all human institutions, even those of religion, are," it was "still contributing to advance the cause of civilization." Though Bell acknowledged that slavery had its origins in "individual cupidity," it was "still mysteriously working out a general good."[33] The conclusion that slavery was immoral, Bell thought, could not be proved, for the moral condemnation of slavery "is not arrived at in accordance with the Baconian method of reasoning, by which we are taught, that from a great many particular and well-established facts in the physical economy, we may safely deduce a general law of physical nature; and so of morality and government."[34]

Like Webster, Bell also focused on the fanaticism among the abolitionists: "There is a fanaticism of liberty as well as a fanaticism of religion and philanthropy—a fanaticism exhibiting itself in theories which admit no distinction of races and claims for all a perfect equality, social and political; theories which reject all practical or useful schemes of government which have ever existed, or can be devised."[35] In contrast with abolitionists' moral absolutes, supporters of the Fugitive Slave Act saw slavery as conferring more benefits than harms. Representative Miller of New Jersey emphasized the benefits of the rule of law's protection of property rights. His focus was on the rights of slaveholders. "Twenty millions of freemen are living under the best system of laws ever devised by man; their daily avocations un-oppressed by any tyrannical laws, undistributed by any high-handed aggression upon their rights, and sending up no complaints against arbitrary government. From the extreme North, where the Yankee whaler strikes the monster of the deep, to the South, where the slave labors contentedly in the cotton-fields for his master—everywhere throughout this mighty empire, the rights of property and the rights of the citizens are protected and defended by the Constitution and the laws of slavery."[36]

There might come a time when social and moral progress would allow the termination of slavery, but the time had not yet arrived. Or, as Senator Underwood argued, "Were I disposed to concede that to hold slaves was a sin on the part of the master, I am not sure that he would not aggravate his guilt, and deserve a hotter punishment by taking the prescription of *immediate abolition*."[37]

The attack on abolitionist fanatics was in part an attack on sentimental novelists. Even before Harriet Beecher Stowe wrote her sentimental novel, *Uncle Tom's Cabin*, Senator Bell linked sentimental writers, readers of sentimental literature, and abolitionists. He criticized sentimental literature for contributing to the agitation against slavery, indeed, against life as it was more generally: "But there is another class of enthusiasts which cannot be justly called fanatical, yet exercises a far more extensive and mischievous influences. Those are the subjects of a morbid sensibility, recluses—readers and authors of sentimental literature, who cannot bear the contemplation of the ordinary ills and hardships of real life, without a shock of their nervous system. They sigh for a state of society where wrong and injustice can never enter. Slavery at the south becomes the natural and favorite theme of the tongues and pens of these sentimentalists."[38]

While the pro-slavery sentimental novels were ineffective, there was also mocking literature, which in imitation of the sensationalist literature of the 1850s attacks the virtue of the reformers.[39] Indeed, abolitionists had developed a sophisticated and powerful critique of slavery—and of pro-slavery law in particular. One of Stowe's first published stories, entitled "Love versus Law," was a comparison of warm sentiments of the heart with the cold logic of property law. *One Thousand Lashes for Freedom* relied on cases to illustrate the brutality at the base of slavery. William Goodell's *American Slave Code in Theory and Practice* developed an important critique of the slave law. He focused on the "legal relation" of slavery based on an understanding of the statute law and how the statutes are applied.[40] He looked to statutes rather than the norms of behavior (so often characterized as benign by pro-slavery writers). Thus, it is law, not norms, that are critiqued. And then, after showing the harshness of the law, he argues that the legal relations structure the actual practice of master-slave relations. His vision of slave law was that it influenced treatment of slaves and that harsh treatment of slaves in turn influenced statutes. So harsh treatment went from norms to law. As Goodell said, the slave code "is a vigilant guardian of the legal relation of master and slave—even as the role of law ought to be to restrain power."[41] The role of law was to protect the weak, though it failed to do so.[42] *The American Slave Code in Theory and Practice*, like other important works on law in the antebellum era, discloses a sophisticated understanding of the relationship between law, history, and culture. One might construct a sophisticated picture of the relationship between history, precedent, and social norms by looking at Goodell and such pro-slavery works as Thomas Roderick Dew's *A Digest of the Laws, Customs, Manners, and Institutions of Ancient and Modern Nations*, Thomas R. R. Cobb's *An Inquiry into the Law of Negro Slavery in the United States of America*, George Sawyer's *Southern Institutes,* and John Fletcher's *Studies in Slavery.*[43] Together those works give us a picture of the rich understanding of jurisprudence that existed in the antebellum era.[44]

While Senator Bell phrased his speech as an attack on sentimentalism, its larger point was that concern for the suffering of individuals was not the appropriate consideration. Instead, we should have cold considerations of utility. Bell's reasoning was that everyone suffers and we cannot alleviate the suffering. These are the break-points, the places where the clashing view matters. While utilitarianism is the dominant value, there are other possible paths, which might have led to a "jurisprudence of sentiment." That jurisprudence based on sentiment, which was advanced by abolitionists black and white, received few adherents within the judiciary, however.

There also needed to be an understanding of what was possible, what was practical, and an understanding of the history of slavery and its current practice, which put it into a context for understanding how moral or immoral it was in reality. Senators looked to examples of history and what had happened and was happening. Senator John Bell of Kentucky read "the law of nature" by the "lights" and necessity of history. He analogized the dispossession of Natives from their land and found that acceptable with the law of nature.

> As to the lawfulness or sinfulness of the institution of slavery—whatever . . . the disciples of a transcendental creed of any kind may hold or teach . . . I must claim the privilege of interpreting the law of nature by what I see revealed in the history of mankind from the earlier period of recorded time, uncontradicted by Divine authority. But above all I have seen here, on this continent, and in these United States, the original lords of the soil subdued . . . and the remnant still held in subordination; and all this under an interpretation of the law of nature which holds good at this day among our northern brethren.

Senator Bell then looked to the institution of slavery and found it necessary. "There are three millions of the African race, whose labor is subject to the will of masters, under such circumstances that their condition cannot be changed, though their masters should will it, without destruction alike to the interests and welfare of both master and slave. These are the lights by which I read and understand the law of nature."[45]

This vision of utility was intertwined with a theological strand of belief in divine benevolence. Huntsville, Alabama, Presbyterian minister Frederick A. Ross's *Slavery Ordained of God* told of the good that slavery brought to masters and slaves, and he predicted it would continue until it passed away in the "fulness of Providence."[46] Senator Bell concluded with a plea for society to put slavery into context and understand the practicalities: "These examples show that there are certain abstract truths and principles which, however incontrovertible in themselves, like every other good thing, may be and often are misconceived and abused in their application. It is the business of statesmen to apply them with safety and to give them the utmost practical influence of effect consistent with the existing state of society."[47]

So the debates on the act contain much about the connections of morality and legislation. They also contain the grammar of constitutional interpretation. The Constitution enjoins a duty upon states and state legislators, also. Bell thought that Northerners did not have the right to interfere with Southern constitutional and property rights.

> I put it to all the sober and sound minds at the North as a question of morals and a question of conscience. What right have they, in their legislative capacity or any other capacity, to endeavor to get round this Constitution, or to embarrass the free exercise of the rights secured by the Constitution to the persons whose slaves escape from them? None at all; none at all. Neither in the forum of conscience, nor before the face of the Constitution, are they, in my opinion, justified in such an attempt. Of course it is a matter for their consideration. They probably, in the excitement of the times, have not stopped to consider of this. They have followed what seemed to be the current of thought and of motives, as

> the occasion arose, and they have neglected to investigate fully the real question, and to consider their constitutional obligations; which, I am sure, if they did consider, they would fulfill with alacrity.[48]

The proponents of that act thought that the Constitution enjoined on the legislature the duty of protecting slave property.

In the debates we also learn about the rule of law: why should people abide by a law if they disagree with it? Some of the reasons for abiding are religious: it is the duty, as many interpreted Paul's second letter to the Corinthians to say, to abide by the commands of human governments. For, as Senator Underwood of Kentucky said, "it is generally combined arrogance and folly for a minority to denounce the legislation of the majority, and to threaten resistance and defiance in consequence of an alleged conflict with the law of God."[49] He concluded that "government is ordained of God; . . . it is a duty to submit to the powers that be, and to render unto Caesar the things which are Caesar's."[50] There is a proper and constitutional mode by which bad laws "may be assailed and repealed; but until repealed, they must be obeyed, or it is the end of government."[51] Moreover, following the law is a duty that will hold the government together. Many recognized the close connection between morals and legislation and worried that because the act would not have the support of the community, it would be ineffective. As Senator Robert C. Winthrop of Massachusetts concluded, "It is the daily experience of this and of every other Government, that where laws are repugnant to the moral sense of the community, it is almost impossible to execute them."[52] Or, as Senator Rhett said, "A law to have its practical effect must move in harmony with the opinions and feelings of the community where it is to operate."[53]

After enactment, the Fugitive Slave Act of 1850 became a centerpiece of discussion about the rule of law. The debate focused on under what, if any, circumstances someone can violate the rule of law. A vibrant antislavery jurisprudence that emphasized the right to violate the law and demonstrated both the truth of legislators' predictions that the law would be a nullity and the limits of the power of law emerged around the act. Antislavery ministers discussed the ways that human-created laws were limited and subordinate to conscience.[54] Some, like Samuel Spear, saw a middle path between abiding all law and violating it: he suggested that judges who opposed the act should resign.[55]

Much of the debate appeared in pulpits. John Lord of Buffalo's First Presbyterian Church delivered a widely distributed sermon, "'The Higher Law,' in Its Application to the Fugitive Slave Bill," in 1851.[56] Lord's sermon proceeded from the fear that the decision to follow a "higher law" would result in an "open and forcible resistance by arms."[57] He believed, based on his reading of Matthew, that "obedience to governments, in the exercise of their legitimate powers, is a religious duty, positive enjoined by God himself."[58] Much of Lord's reasoning was based on his interpretation of the Bible, which held that government is divinely constituted, that government has jurisdiction over contemporary affairs, and that the decisions of governments within their jurisdictions are absolute. But Lord also reasoned that the higher law doctrine was unworkable, for it would abrogate all law. "Freedom of opinion by no means involves the right *to refuse obedience to law*; for, if this were so, the power to declare war and make peace; to regulate and levy taxes; in short, to perform the most essential acts of government, would be a mere nullity."[59] The state may enact laws for slavery, and one had to abide by those laws. Anything else would "contradict the decision of the Apostle—[and] subvert every established principle, whether human or divine, on which rests the authority of civil government." Lord looked to U.S. history, such as the ubiquity of slavery during the colonial period, to conclude that slavery did not violate any "higher law." He also looked to other countries, such as China, to conclude that slavery, at least in some circumstances, was permissible.[60]

Ichabod Spencer explained in even more detail the purposes and functions of law (and why it must be obeyed) in his November 1850 sermon at the Second Presbyterian Church in Brooklyn.[61] Laws are necessary to restrain those who do evil. Therefore, "Law is a friend of the human race. It is the protector of the good man; and it punishes the bad man, only for the purposes of securing rights,—property, liberty, life. And even the bad would be worse off thousand fold than they are, if there were no efficient Law to restrain them by its authority and sanctions."[62] Spencer embraced law as what facilitates and creates happiness and property. Though he acknowledged that in some instances one might violate an unjust law, those situations were few and far between. "Law is too important and delicate a thing to have its majesty trifled with by the wicked nonsense of a half-obedience."[63] He urged against rebellion, for that would lead to even greater harm. Revolutions "bring horrid evils along with them." Spencer engaged in the balance of harm and benefit at the center of utilitarian reasoning. "It would be better to bear the injury for a while, than to involve the nation in confusion and blood."[64] And when he looked around, he thought the law, on balance, brought substantially more benefit than harm. "Government with all its unavoidable imperfection and errors, on the whole is beneficial—indispensable—we could not do without it. And rarely, very rarely indeed, is there a single instance of an individual man . . . whom Law has injured *more* than it has benefitted."[65]

Nevertheless, law was losing some of its majesty.[66] The public's increasing condemnation of the Fugitive Slave Act was leading to further contempt of law. Emerson dismissed appeals to law books in his 1851 address at Concord. "A few months ago, in my dismay at hearing that the Higher Law was reckoned a good joke in the courts, I took pains to look into a few law books." Indeed, he reported that he looked for signs that "immoral laws are void" and found that "the great jurists, Cicero, Grotius, Coke, Blackstone, Burlamaqui, Montesquieu, Vattel, Burke, Mackintosh, Jefferson, do all affirm this." Yet Emerson did not cite those passages in defense of his argument, for "no reasonable person needs a quotation from Blackstone to convince him that white cannot be legislated to be black."[67]

As cases of fugitive slaves began to appear in courts, the debates increasingly took on the question of whether individuals should actively stop rendition of fugitive slaves. The most famous case arose in Boston in 1854 when Anthony Burns was arrested as a fugitive slave, and after Judge Edward Loring ordered him returned, abolitionists set about plans to free him.[68] President Pierce employed federal troops to make sure that Burns was put on a ship to return to Virginia.[69] Burns brought into relief the obligations that law imposed. While some courts found creative ways to avoid the law, most often they followed it.[70] Thoreau was led to ask in the wake of Anthony Burns's trial, "Does anyone think that justice or God wait on Mr. Loring's decision?"[71] As those courts upheld law, its credibility declined.

Yet while some like Thoreau and Emerson questioned the Fugitive Slave Act's pro-slavery jurisprudence, others supported it. Timothy Walker, founder of the Cincinnati Law School and author of the important *Introduction to American Law,* lectured on the need to abide by the law in the wake of the act in his 1851 Phi Beta Kappa lecture at Harvard. His lecture, "The Reform Spirit of the Age," mocked the reformers' ideas:

> We have been priest-ridden, and king-ridden, and judge-ridden, and school-ridden, and wealth-ridden, long enough. And now the time is come to declare our independence in all these respects. We cannot, indeed, change the past,—that is for ever immutably fixed; but we can repudiate it, and we do. We can shape our own future, and it shall be a glorious one. Now shall commence a new age,—not of gold, or of silver, or of iron, but an age of emancipation. We will upheave society from its deepest foundations, and have all but a new creation. In religion and politics, medicine and law, morals and manners, our mission is to revolutionize the world. And therefore we wage indiscriminate war against all establishments. Our ancestors shall no longer be our masters. We renounce all fealty to their antiquated notions. Henceforth to be old is to be questionable. We will hold nothing sacred which has long been worshiped, and nothing venerable which has long been venerated. These are the glad tidings which we the reformers of the age, are commissioned to announce.[72]

Walker wanted no such reform. The rest of his talk was about the need to return to a steady following of precedent and law. And without the rule of law, William Greene warned a Brown University literary society at the same time, the United States would descend from democracy into revolution.[73]

Subsequent events vindicated the moral perspective of abolitionists, but for people looking from the perspective of the early 1850s, the crisis over fugitive slaves touched central issues of moral philosophy. Abolitionists were pessimistic. The language of moral philosophy and those modes of thinking were employed from the university lecture hall to the pulpit to the halls of Congress and the courtrooms throughout the nation. For a time those pro-slavery ideas triumphed.

They emphasized a version of history that taught the ubiquity and, therefore, inevitability, indeed necessity, of slavery. They then tied that pro-slavery vision of history together with a moral philosophy that emphasized considerations of utility and rested on a belief in the need to abide by the rule of law. A sobering assessment was left by Louisa McCord, writing in the *Southern Quarterly Review* about the problems with abolitionists' attempts to end slave law: "a revolution that seeks to abolish law will end necessarily in despotism."[74]

Despite the efforts made to justify slavery and make it look acceptable, commonplace, and legal, others saw through this. Senator Charles Sumner of Massachusetts spoke about the violence inherent in the institution. "Slavery is an institution of force and not of right, as our law books teach—the private force of the master being made efficient and sufficient by the public force of the state."[75] One triumph of the antislavery position was that it made people see the considerations of force and brutality that pro-slavery politicians, judges, academics, and intellectuals tried to justify. And so abolitionists undid, through the process of the Civil War and constitutional amendment, a part of antebellum American law.

NOTES

1. Harriet Beecher Stowe, *Uncle Tom's Cabin,* in *Three Novels* (1852; New York: Library of America, 1982), 102.

2. Ibid., 108.

3. See Alfred L. Brophy, "'Over and Above There Broods a Portentous Shadow,—the Shadow of Law': The Critique of Law in *Uncle Tom's Cabin,*" *Journal of Law & Religion* 12 (1995–96): 457–506.

4. Stowe, *Uncle Tom's Cabin,* 513.

5. Ralph Waldo Emerson, "The Fugitive Slave Law: Address to the Citizens of Concord, 3 May, 1851," in *The Complete Works of Ralph Waldo Emerson* (Cambridge, Mass.: Riverside Press, 1904), 11:177.

6. *Fugitive Slave Act,* 9 Stat. 462 (Sept. 18, 1850).

7. Henry David Thoreau, "Slavery in Massachusetts," in *The Writings of Henry David Thoreau* (Boston: Houghton, Mifflin, 1906), 4:388.

8. On the act's place in history, see David Potter, *The Impending Crisis* (New York: Harper & Row, 1976), 112–14, 130–40; William Freehling, *The Road to Disunion: Secessionists at Bay* (New York: Oxford University Press, 1990), 1:497–505; Stanley L. Campbell, *The Slave Catchers* (Chapel Hill: University of North Carolina Press, 1973); Mark Graber, *Dred Scott and the Problem of Constitutional Evil* (Cambridge: Cambridge University Press, 2006); Merrill D. Peterson, *The Great Triumvirate: Webster, Clay, and Calhoun* (New York: Oxford University Press, 1987), 457–66; Thomas J. Brown, "The Fugitive Slave Act in Emerson's Boston," *Law & Social Inquiry* 25 (2000): 669–92; Laura R. Mitchell, "'Matters of Justice between Man and Man': Northern Divines, the Bible, and the Fugitive Slave Act of 1850," in *Religion and the Antebellum Debate over Slavery,* ed. John R. McGivigan and Mitchell Snay, 134–65 (Athens: University of Georgia Press, 1998). On the Southern reaction to the act, see John Hope Franklin, *The Militant South, 1800–1861* (Cambridge, Mass.: Belknap Press of Harvard University Press, 1961), 223–26;

William J. Cooper, *The South and the Politics of Slavery* (Baton Rouge: Louisiana State University Press, 1978), 301–21.

9. Robert Cover, *Justice Accused: Antislavery and the Judicial Process* (New Haven, Conn.: Yale University Press, 1975).

10. Thoreau, "[Resistance to Civil Government] Civil Disobedience," in *The Writings of Henry David Thoreau,* 4:306.

11. Harriet Beecher Stowe, *Dred: A Tale of the Great Dismal Swamp* (Boston: Phillips, Simpson, 1856); Alfred L. Brophy, "Humanity, Utility, and Logic: Harriet Beecher Stowe's Vision of Southern Legal Thought in *Dred: A Tale of the Great Dismal Swamp*," *Boston University Law Review* 78 (1998): 1113–61.

12. Among the many examples of this are Drew Gilpin Faust, *A Sacred Circle: The Dilemma of the Intellectual in the Old South* (Baltimore, Md.: Johns Hopkins University Press, 1977); Eugene Genovese and Elizabeth Fox-Genovese, *The Mind of the Master Class* (Cambridge: Cambridge University Press, 2005); Michael O'Brien, *Conjectures of Order: Intellectual Life and the Old South* (Chapel Hill: University of North Carolina Press, 2004); Timothy Huebner, *The Southern Judicial Tradition, 1790–1870* (Athens: University of Georgia Press, 1998).

13. Decades of subsequent research have revealed the basic validity of Horwitz's picture. See Gregory Alexander, *Commodity and Propriety: Competing Visions of Property in American Legal Thought, 1776–1970* (Chicago: University of Chicago Press, 1997); William W. Fisher, "Ideology, Religion, and the Constitutional Protection of Private Property, 1760–1860," *Emory Law Journal* 39 (1990): 65–132. Susanna Blumenthal has recently extended the story of moral philosophy into wills. See "The Deviance of the Will: Policing the Bounds of Testamentary Freedom in Nineteenth-Century America," *Harvard Law Review* 119 (2006): 959–1034. See also Lawrence Friedman, "Losing One's Head: Judges and the Law in Nineteenth-Century American Legal History," *Law & Social Inquiry* 24 (1999): 253–79; Alfred L. Brophy, "Reason and Sentiment: The Moral Worlds and Modes of Reasoning of Antebellum Jurists," *Boston University Law Review* 79 (1999): 1161–213.

14. Thoreau, "Civil Disobedience," 361. Thoreau credits Paley as "a common authority with many on moral questions." He went through a number of American editions. See Donald H. Meyer, *The Instructed Conscience* (Philadelphia: University of Pennsylvania Press, 1972), 8–9; Wilson Smith, *Professors and Public Ethics: Studies of Northern Moral Philosophers before the Civil War* (Ithaca, N.Y.: Published for the American Historical Association by Cornell University Press, 1956). On antebellum moral philosophy, see Rush Welter, *The Mind of America, 1820–1860* (New York: Columbia University Press, 1975); Louis Perry, *Boats against the Current: American Culture between Revolution and Modernity, 1820–1860* (New York: Oxford University Press, 2003); Theodore Dwight Bozeman, "Inductive and Deductive Politics: Science and Society in Antebellum Presbyterian Thought," *Journal of American History* 64 (1977): 704–22; John M. McFaul, "Expedience vs. Morality: Jacksonian Politics and Slavery," *Journal of American History* 65 (1975): 25–39.

15. Thoreau, "Civil Disobedience," 387. Emphasis on slaves' suffering was the center of abolitionists' thought. See Elizabeth Clark, "'The Sacred Rights of the Weak': Pain, Sympathy, and the Culture of Individual Rights in Antebellum America," *Journal of American History* 84 (1995): 463–93.

16. William G. Goddard, *An Address to the Phi Beta Kappa Society of Rhode Island, Delivered September 7, 1836* (Boston: John H. Eastburn, 1837), 22. We can learn much about antebel-

lum ideas from such lectures. See, e.g., James Perrin Warren, *Culture of Eloquence: Oratory and Reform in Antebellum America* (University Park: Pennsylvania State University Press, 1999); Donald M. Scott, "The Popular Lecture and the Creation of the Public in Mid-Nineteenth-Century America," *Journal of American History* 66 (1980): 791–809; Alfred L. Brophy, "The Intersection of Slavery and Property in Southern Legal Thought, from Missouri Compromise through Civil War" (PhD diss., Harvard University, 2001), chap. 1 (discussing conceptions of economic, moral, and legal progress in antebellum literary addresses).

17. The act appears as part of the rich public debate about the meaning of the Constitution, which was mediated by legislators and judges. See, e.g., Larry D. Kramer, *The People Themselves: Popular Constitutionalism and Judicial Review* (New York: Oxford University Press, 2004); Daniel W. Hamilton, "A Symposium on the People Themselves," *Chicago-Kent Law Review* 81 (2006): 809–1186.

18. "Speech of Mr. Webster," *Congressional Globe,* 31st Cong., 1st sess., 1850, 269.

19. Thoreau, "Walden," in *The Writings of Henry David Thoreau,* 2:257.

20. "Speech of Mr. Webster," 270.

21. Ralph Waldo Emerson, "The Conservative," in *Ralph Waldo Emerson: Essays and Lectures,* ed. Joel Porte (New York: Literary Classics of the U.S., 1983), 174–75. Emerson continued:

The conservative assumes sickness as a necessity, and his social frame is a hospital, his total legislation is for the present distress, a universe in slippers and flannels, with bib and pap spoon, swallowing pills and herb-tea. Sickness gets organized as well as health, the vice as well as the virtue. Now that a vicious system of trade has existed so long, it has stereotyped itself in the human generation, and misers are born. And now that sickness has got such a foot-hold, leprosy has grown cunning, has got into the ballot-box; the lepers outvote the clean; society has resolved itself into a Hospital Committee, and all its laws are quarantine. . . . Its social and political action has no better aim; to keep out wind and weather, to bring the day and year about, and make the world last our day; not to sit on the world and steer it; not to sink the memory of the past in the glory of a new and more excellent creation; a timid cobbler and patcher, it degrades whatever it touches.

22. "Speech of Webster," 270–71, 275.

23. Ibid. Senator Underwood responded to the illusion that abolitionists might create a "moral railroad" in the South. But he did "not see that the first speck of dirt has been moved to make the grade and foundation of the great moral railroad." "Speech of Mr. Underwood," *Congressional Globe,* 31st Cong., 1st sess., 1850, 531.

24. *Green v. Biddle,* 21 U.S. (8 Wheat.) 1, 101 (1823). Those who critiqued the common law thought it provided much less in the way of guides. William Sampson demystified the common law by insulting it. The common law, he wrote, was the one "pagan idol to which [the English] daily offered up much smokey incense. They called it by the mystical and cabalistic name of Common Law. A mysterious essences. Like the Dalai Lama, not to be seen or visited in open day: of most indefinite antiquity; sometimes in the decrepitude of age, and sometimes in the bloom of infancy, yet still the same that was, and was to be, and evermore to sit cross-legged and motionless upon its antique alter, for no use or purpose but to be praised and worshiped by ignorant and superstitious votaries." William Sampson, *Sampson's Discourse, and Correspondence with Various Learned Jurists, upon the History of the Law: With the Addition of Several Essays, Tracts . . .* (Washington, D.C.: Gales & Seaton, 1826), 11–12. Or, as Sampson speculated in argument in *People v. Martin,* Yates Sel. Cas. 112, 153 (N.Y. Sup. Ct. 1810), "Cicero wondered

how two soothsayers could look each other in the face. I wonder how the two learned expounders of the common law opposed to us can do so without laughing."

25. See, e.g., "Speech of James L. Orr," *Congressional Globe,* 31st Cong., 1st sess., 1850, 544: "Their course can have no other effect than to fan the flames of fanaticism until they shall burn out the vitals of the Constitution and Union." Indeed, "fanaticism" was a favorite word used to describe those who urged a restriction on private property. See, e.g., *In re New Orleans Draining Co.,* 11 La. Ann. 338 (1856): "So, too, fanaticism under the plea of philanthropy and the public good, is ready to purge and renovate society-revolutionize governments, and reconstruct the world according to its new ideas, provided that the cost and the consequent pain and sufferings, shall be borne by its beneficiaries"; *People v. Gallagher,* 4 Mich. 244 (1856) (lamenting inability of penal laws to take away property used to manufacture alcohol: "In 1831 there were over 4,000 organized temperance societies, and more than 600,000 members. In the mean time over 1,000 distilleries had been entirely stopped by their owners; about 5,000 drunkards had been entirely reclaimed, and over 1,000,000 of people in the United States were entirely abstaining from the use of all kinds of intoxicating drinks. . . . But the fate of these societies was sealed when they were induced by political demagogues, in conjunction with fanatical clergymen, to enter the political field, and take political action as a party."

26. In *Thompson v. Thompson,* 21 Barb. 107 (N.Y. Sup. Ct. 1855), one New York Supreme Court judge explained the presence of "monomanism":

Some maniacs . . . are rational on all subjects except one, and, until affected by that, exhibit the ordinary deportment and sagacity. These latter are monomaniacs. This partial insanity is prevalent to a very great extent; . . . I see no other way of accounting for the wide prevalence of whimsical and fantastical opinions, the transcendental speculations, the wild vagaries of faith, the intolerant fanaticism, the rash obtrusion upon regions of knowledge, palpably beyond the limits of the human faculties, the profane contempt manifested by some men, and, alas! by some women, for all that experience has rendered sure and steadfast, rushing with wild avidity into the espousal of any thing new, because it is new, and substituting the phantoms of a diseased imagination for all that the Christian and philosophic world has heretofore regarded as most dear and sacred.

The Georgia Supreme Court attributed the "growing policy of Northern states to free slaves who set foot in their state while passing through them, to fanaticism. . . . This fungus," the court said, "has been engrafted upon Northern States Codes by the foul and fell spirit of modern fanaticism." *Cleland v. Waters,* 19 Ga. 35 (1855).

27. See, e.g., Albert Taylor Bledsoe, *An Essay on Liberty and Slavery* (Philadelphia: J. B. Lippincott, 1856), 69–70; Jasper Adams, *Elements of Moral Philosophy* (Cambridge, Mass.: Folsom, Wells, and Thurston, 1837), 15 ("By this theory [of utility], the jurisdiction of conscience is abolished, her decisions are classed with those of the superannuated judge, and determination of moral causes is adjourned from the interior tribunal of the breast to the noisy forum of speculative debate. Nothing is yielded to the suggestions of conscience, nothing to the movements of the heart; every thing is dealt out with a sparing hand, under the stint and measure of calculation"); Joseph C. Stiles, *Modern Reform Examined; or, The Union of North and South on the Subject of Slavery* (Philadelphia: J. B. Lippincott, 1857) (pointing out ways that abolitionists want change). Compare Laurens P. Hickok, *A System of Moral Science,* 3d ed. (1853; New York: Ivison, Blakeman, Taylor, 1873), 410 (antislavery text that noted of the duties of slaves that "If running away is prospective of less evil than staying in slavery, it is right to run").

28. *Congressional Globe,* 31st Cong., 1st sess., 1850, 271. Stowe uses similar language to describe the antislavery lawyer Edward Clayton in *Dred: A Tale of the Great Dismal Swamp*: he is "mounted [on] his war-horse, and is coming upon us, now, like leviathan from the rushes. . . . He is a great seventy-four pounder, charged to the muzzle with goodness! But, if he should be once fired off, I'm afraid he'll carry everything out of the world with him. Because, you see, abstract goodness doesn't suit our present mortal condition. But it is a perfect godsend that he has such a case as this to manage for his maiden plea, because it just falls in with his heroic turn" (37).

29. *Congressional Globe,* 31st Cong., 1st sess., 1850, 271.

30. "Speech of Hon. T. G. Pratt," *Congressional Globe,* 31st Cong., 1st sess., 1850, app., 1238: "The American people are essentially a practical people, I never shall believe that they are willing to risk the destruction of this Government upon a mere abstraction."

31. Id. at 1616: "The legislator who shuts his eyes to all consequences, who does not look at all into the probabilities of *efficiency* or *inefficiency,* in connection with the measure to which he is about to impart his sanction, is unfit for the law-making functions."

32. "Speech of R. M. T. Hunter," *Congressional Globe,* 31st Cong., 1st sess., 1850, 1632. See also id. at 1633.

33. *Congressional Globe,* 31st Cong., 1st sess., 1850, app., 1105.

34. Id. at 1106.

35. Id. at 1102.

36. *Congressional Globe,* 31st Cong., 1st sess., 1850, app., 311. Representative Miller used language of landscape to speak of the fear of some of the "gathering clouds that darken these bright skies."

37. Id. at 531.

38. Id. at app., 1102.

39. See, e.g., D. W. Bartlett, *Modern Agitators; or, Pen Portraits of Living American Reformers* (New York: Miller, Orton & Mulligan, 1855).

40. William Goodell, *The American Slave Code in Theory and Practice* (New York: American and Foreign Anti-Slavery Society 1853).

41. Ibid., 400, 337. See also William Goodell, *History of Slavery and Antislavery: A History of the Struggle* . . . (New York: William Goodell, 1852). Goodell's *Views of American Constitutional Law: In Its Bearing upon American Slavery,* 2d ed. (Utica, N.Y.: Lawson & Chaplin, 1845), argued that the spirit of the Constitution did not support slavery. Moreover, it urged a more humane common law. See, e.g., 150–51.

42. Goodell, *American Slave Code,* 157. See also Richard Hildreth, *Atrocious Judges. Lives of Judges Infamous as Tools of Tyrants and Instruments of Oppression* . . . (New York: Miller, Orton & Mulligan, 1856).

43. Dew and Sawyer have received less attention than they deserve, given the sophisticated picture of legal development they exhibit. See, e.g., George Sawyer, *Southern Institutes; or, An Inquiry into the Original Early Prevalence of Slavery and the Slave-Trade* (Philadelphia: J. B. Lippincott, 1858), 16–29; Thomas R. Dew, *A Digest of the Laws, Customs, Manners, and Institutions of Ancient and Modern Nations* (New York: Appleton, 1853); Thomas R. R. Cobb, *An Inquiry into the Law of Negro Slavery in the United States* . . . (Philadelphia: T. & J. W. Johnson, 1858); Fox-Genovese and Genovese, *The Mind of the Master Class,* 201 (discussing Sawyer) and 201–3, 265–71 (discussing Dew).

44. Antebellum jurisprudence has not yet received all the attention it deserves. See, e.g., Michael Hoeflich, "Law & Geometry: Legal Science from Leibniz to Langedell," *American Journal of Legal History* 30 (1986): 95–121.

45. *Congressional Globe,* 31st Cong., 1st sess., 1850, app., 1105.

46. Fred A. Ross, *Slavery Ordained of God* (Philadelphia: J. B. Lippincott, 1857), 7. Ross wrote that "*slavery is of God,* and to continue for the good of the slave, the good of the master, the good of the whole American family, until another and better destiny be unfolded." I am indebted to David Holland for reminding me of the importance of Providence in this debate.

47. *Congressional Globe,* 31st Cong., 1st sess., 1850, app., 1106.

48. Id. at app., 1105.

49. Id. at 530.

50. Id. at 533.

51. Id.

52. Id. at app., 1593.

53. *Congressional Globe,* 31st Cong., 2d sess., 1851, 317.

54. See, e.g., Nathaniel Colver, *The Fugitive Slave Bill; or, God's Laws Paramount to the Laws of Men. A Sermon, Preached on Sunday, October 20, 1850* (Boston: J. M. Hewes, 1850); George Barrell Cheever, *God against Slavery: And the Freedom and Duty of the Pulpit to Rebuke it . . .* (Boston: Crosby & Nichols, 1850); Theodore Parker, *The Function and Place of Conscience in Relation to the Laws of Men: A Sermon for the Times; . . . Sunday, September 22, 1850* (Boston: Crosby & Nichols, 1850); John M. Krebs, *The American Citizen: A Discourse on the Nature and Extent of Our Religious Subjection to the Government under Which We Live . . . Delivered in the Rutgers Street Presbyterian Church . . . December 12, 1850 . . .* (New York: Charles Scribner, 1851), responding to John C. Lord, *"The Higher Law," in Its Application to the Fugitive Slave Bill . . .* (New York: Union Safety Committee, 1851); William Hosmer, *The Higher Law, in Its Relations to Civil Government . . .* (Auburn, N.Y.: Derby & Miller, 1852).

55. Samuel T. Spear, *The Law-Abiding Conscience, and the Higher Law Conscience: With Remarks on the Fugitive Slave Question. A Sermon, Preached in the South Presbyterian Church, Brooklyn, Dec. 12, 1850* 32 (New York: Lambert & Lane, 1850). See also Edward Pringle, *The Proceedings of the Union Meeting, Held at Brewster's Hall, December 24, 1850 . . .* (New Haven, Conn.: W. H. Stanley, 1851).

56. Lord, *"The Higher Law."* See also William Adams, *Christianity and Civil Government* (New York: Charles Scribner, 1851); Albert Barnes, *The Church and Slavery* (Philadelphia: Parry & McMillan, 1857); Moses Stuart, *Conscience and the Constitution: With Remarks on the Recent Speech of the Hon. Daniel Webster in the Senate of the United States on the Subject of Slavery* (Boston: Crocker & Brewster, 1851).

57. Lord, *"The Higher Law,"* 4.

58. Ibid., 6.

59. Ibid., 7.

60. Ibid., 10–11.

61. Ichabod S. Spencer, *The Religious Duty of Obedience to Law: A Sermon, Preached . . . Nov. 24, 1850* (New York: M. W. Dodd, 1850).

62. Ibid., 13.

63. Ibid., 15.

64. Ibid., 16.

65. Ibid., 20.

66. See, e.g., Calvin Colton, *A Voice from England to America by an American Gentleman* (London: Henry Colburn, 1839), 38–60 (discussing increasing public concern with statutory law); Timothy Walker, "Advice to Law Students," *Western Law Journal* 1 (1844): 481, 482.

67. Emerson, "The Conservative."

68. See, e.g., James Freeman Clarke, *The Rendition of Anthony Burns: . . . A Discourse on Christian Politics* (Boston: Crosby & Nichols, 1854).

69. See Albert J. Von Frank, *The Trials of Anthony Burns: Freedom and Slavery in Emerson's Boston* (Cambridge, Mass.: Harvard University Press, 1998), 203–19 (describing Burns's case from Loring's decision to Burns's departure from Boston).

70. Robert Cover and, more recently, Mark Tushnet detail such conflicts between law and sentiment. See Cover, *Justice Accused*; Mark Tushnet, *Slave Law in the American South:* State v. Mann *in History and Literature* (Lawrence: University Press of Kansas, 2004).

71. Henry David Thoreau, "Slavery in Massachusetts," 389.

72. Timothy Walker, *The Reform Spirit of the Age* (Cambridge, Mass.: J. Munroe, 1851).

73. William Greene, *Some of the Difficulties in the Administration of a Free Government: A Discourse, Pronounced before the Rhode Island Alpha of the Phi Beta Kappa Society, July 8, 1851* (Providence, R.I.: John F. Moore, 1851).

74. Louisa McCord, "British Philanthropy and American Slavery," *DeBow's Review* 14 (1853): 258–80.

75. *Congressional Globe,* 31st Cong., 1st sess., app., 1621.

6

Stability and Change in Antebellum Property Law: Stare Decisis in Judicial Rhetoric

POLLY J. PRICE

JUDGE-MADE PROPERTY AND CONTRACT LAW IN THE ANTEBELLUM PERIOD is a central focus of Morton Horwitz's *Transformation I,* and historical inquiry concerning antebellum law in the United States continues to engage the main themes of Horwitz's work. In this essay, I explore one aspect of judicial methodology inspired by the challenge of *Transformation I*—the extent to which judges viewed themselves to be primarily responsible for stability in the law. The context is the development of the rhetoric of stare decisis for property rights in the antebellum period. I suggest here that the rhetoric employed by judges in the United States diverges markedly from the development of stare decisis in English law. In this era, state courts tended to preserve property rules that they believed were necessary to avoid disrupting a large number of transactions. When this larger potential effect was missing, however, they were not necessarily concerned with the vested rights of the parties immediately before the court.

Stability has long been viewed as an essential quality of law. As William O. Douglas observed in 1949, "Uniformity and continuity in law are necessary to many activities. If they are not present, the integrity of contracts, wills, conveyances and securities is impaired." In the antebellum United States, judges, in their rhetoric at least, expressed a profound interest in maintaining stability in order to preserve property rights.

Beginning early in the nineteenth century, state court judges articulated what they termed a "rule of stare decisis" for common-law property rights. This view self-consciously recognized the undesirability of changing common-law rules that had created property reliance interests. State court judges gave the concept of stare decisis a distinct "vested rights" flavor and viewed the protection of settled expectations about property and contracts to be essential to the preservation of property rights. The founding period and later generations viewed stare decisis to be an important tool to protect reliance interests.

On the other hand, it is well documented that state courts prior to the Civil War modified existing common-law property rules with some frequency. Grant Gilmore portrayed a "Grand Style" of adjudication in which judges openly and "joyously" made law, in contrast to the formalism of the later nineteenth century. Change in the American common law of property created the possibility of a disjuncture with judicial rhetoric espousing settled rules of property. Although state courts, as well as the attorneys who argued before them, frequently articulated the view that stare decisis mandated adherence to rules that had generated settled property interests, such rhetoric seems inconsistent with other cases in which courts changed property rules, whether for utilitarian or instrumentalist reasons, to rationalize the common law, or in response to statutory changes.

The evidence here suggests that most state judges in the first half of the nineteenth century considered judicial abandonment of precedent to be a potentially retroactive impairment of property rights. Courts were willing to change property rules if they were first satisfied that the change would improve the law, usually in the sense that it would better reflect community practice, and if they were also satisfied that the change would not greatly disturb settled expectations. This preference for legislative change in property law indicates great awareness of the difference between the retroactive nature of judicial decision making and the prospective nature of legislation, a critical distinction for the reliance interests these courts identified.

Stare decisis was never absolute, even with respect to property interests. Nonetheless, the rhetoric of courts indicates that in this period stare decisis was viewed to be a property "meta-rule," or a rule about rules. This essay offers a tentative explanation for judicial action: the quest is to explain the types of cases in which judges seem constrained by stare decisis in the interest of protecting settled property expectations, while recognizing that in other cases they did not.

THE RHETORIC OF STARE DECISIS: EXAMPLES

Debates about adherence to precedent during the antebellum era reflect concern with stability of the common law. The codification debates in the first half of the nineteenth century provide ample illustrations. It was common, for example, for the radical codifiers (those who wanted to codify existing common law not only to make it more intelligible to non-lawyers, but also to reform it) in the 1820s and 1830s to argue that the very problem they sought to remedy was a moribund, slavish adherence to precedent that prevented needed reforms: "It would be unfair to press an objection of this description against an ancient system, if the rigid principle of adherence to precedent only manifested itself in a few rare and extravagant instances, of the nature of that which we have just cited. But the truth is not so. Large portions of the law receive their character from this principle, and it is to a great extent infused into the whole mass. . . . The question which now concerns us, is, whether an extreme deference to precedent and authority does not rather increase than diminish this uncertainty?"

Codification was a means to "reliev[e] judges from the obligation now imposed upon them of obeying precedents not consonant to the spirit of the age." The radical codifiers probably exaggerated the extent to which courts in fact followed stare decisis, but objections to the practice commonly focused upon particular areas of the law that state legislatures had not yet found the will to change. As early as 1805, at least one writer termed "surreptitious" any action by a court to "undertake without statute [to] alter the common law."

In an 1848 article in the *Western Law Journal,* Daniel Raymond noted the ability of judges to avoid or hide behind stare decisis by manipulation of prior precedent:

> [Stare decisis] is a very convenient and comfortable maxim for an ignorant or lazy Judge, as it saves him the trouble and labor of investigating a case and forming his own opinion. It is a wholesome maxim when judiciously followed and faithfully applied, but a most pernicious one when the letter and not the spirit is regarded. There is often an apparent resemblance or analogy between cases, when upon closer scrutiny they are found to be entirely diverse, and hence it is a matter of daily experience, that while Courts profess to follow the decisions, they merely follow their letter, and not their spirit and meaning; the consequence of which is, that they are perpetually running themselves into difficulties and absurdities, from which they cannot extricate themselves, without the aid of the Legislature.

Opponents of codification, on the other hand, stressed the changeability of the common law, probably equally overstating the extent to which judges reacted to changed social preferences in reforming the American common law, or at least purging it of its undesirable English elements. Few seemed fully persuaded by the argument that the "binding authority of precedent" was a safeguard to judicial integrity: "If judges may be supposed to be in fact corrupt, the slender web of authority and precedent is wholly insufficient to restrain them."

State courts enunciated the stare decisis property rule (less commonly referred to as a "maxim," "doctrine," or "policy") from an early period and throughout the antebellum era. Although there is some evidence of the existence of this concept in colonial decisions, in the post-founding period the rule appears in a Pennsylvania opinion in 1788, followed a few years later by an articulation of the rule by a North Carolina court. The Pennsylvania opinion articulated the common theme: "It is essential to private justice and to public peace and order, that the rules of property, as well as of the other objects of society, should be settled. . . . An attempt of that kind [to change the common-law rule] would shake the very foundations of property." From 1788 through 1860, courts in Pennsylvania, New York, South Carolina, and Virginia refer to the stare decisis property rule most frequently, but cases from Alabama, California, Connecticut, Illinois, Louisiana, Massachusetts, Mississippi, Missouri, New Hampshire, Tennessee, Texas, and Vermont also provide evidence of relatively widespread recognition of the rule, at least as a principle worthy of consideration.

A notable champion of stare decisis in rules of property and contract was James Kent. In the first volume of his *Commentaries on American Law,* published in 1826, Kent recognized the desirability of overruling "hasty and crude decisions," yet he emphasized that a light regard for prior judicial decisions "should disturb and unsettle the great landmarks of property":

> If a decision has been made upon solemn argument and mature deliberation, the presumption is in favor of its correctness; and the community have a right to regard it as a just declaration or exposition of the law, and to regulate their actions and contracts by it. It would therefore be extremely inconvenient to the public, if precedents were not duly regarded and implicitly followed. It is by the notoriety and stability of such rules that professional men can give safe advice to those who consult them; and people in general can venture with confidence to buy and trust, and to deal with each other. If judicial decisions were to be lightly disregarded, we should disturb and unsettle the great landmarks of property.

An author in the *North American Review,* writing contemporaneously with the publication of Kent's *Commentaries,* seemed to believe that American courts widely embraced this principle: "The rule of stare decisis, so strictly adhered to wherever title to property, and not the mere mode of procedure, is concerned, has given to that system its certainty and general equity, though at the expense of occasional individual hardship."

Judges in the United States diverge from their English counterparts quite markedly in their use of property "rights" rhetoric supporting stare decisis before the Civil War. William Blackstone's *Commentaries on the Laws of England* of 1765, an influential treatise on the English common law widely available in the United States, discusses stare decisis but does not suggest that it is important for stability of property rights, or that courts should consider the extent to which property transactions may have relied on previous court decisions. Instead, Blackstone's view was that a precedent need not be followed "where the former determination is most evidently contrary to reason. . . . For if it be found that the former decision is manifestly absurd or unjust, it is declared, not that such a sentence was bad law, but that it was not law."

The stare decisis property emphasis by American state court judges in the antebellum period, then, did not originate from their study of Blackstone's *Commentaries.* Moreover, a number of state courts articulated the stare decisis property rule well before the publication of Kent's *Commentaries* in 1826. Hugh

Henry Brackenridge discussed stare decisis at some length in his 1814 treatise on Pennsylvania law. If anything, the treatise admonishes American judges for too strict an adherence to stare decisis, especially to cases from English law not applicable to conditions and practices in the new United States. Brackenridge attributes the expediency of adhering to stare decisis in cases involving property reliance interests primarily to judicial opinions of Lord Ellenborough (1750–1818) and Lord Mansfield (1705–93).

The earliest statements of the stare decisis property rule by American courts usually do not attribute the principle to a particular source, although in 1808 a Pennsylvania court cites an English case. After the publication of the first volume of Kent's *Commentaries* in 1826, courts more commonly cite this source as authority for the rule. Another frequent reference is the 1823 New York case *Lion v. Burtiss*, quoted for the proposition that "Stare decisis is a maxim essential to the security of property." Other judicial opinions suggest that the rule spread primarily from the earlier decisions of other state courts. On rare occasion, courts later in this period locate the rule in English authority, but for the most part the concept seems to have taken on a life of its own in American courts.

Even if some of the earliest articulations of the stare decisis property rule by American courts rely upon English origins, the question of judicial motivation for adopting this stance remains. Further, if the primary motivation for invocations of stare decisis by judges was to legitimate common-law rule making in general, it is not necessarily obvious why courts would develop a distinction between property cases and other kinds of cases. I suggest that the predominant political discourse about vested rights of property is mirrored in judicial rhetoric by the concept that courts should not change rules that would unsettle property transactions. The particular rhetoric used by courts echoes larger themes about property rights in this period. This rhetoric indicates that state judges had internalized founding-era concern for the stability of property rights as a necessary element of economic prosperity.

A sampling of the rhetoric used by some courts supports these conclusions. Courts variously termed stare decisis "essential to the repose of property," the "great landmarks for the safety and regulation of real property," and a maxim "invaluable as applied to the great principles affecting the right of property." Changing property rules "would greatly interfere with the enjoyment of property," particularly those "on the faith of which an immense property has been advanced," or, as stated by a New Hampshire judge, "Upon the faith of an established rule, and the acquiescence of judges and of the whole nation in it, property to the amount of millions may depend." A Pennsylvania judge stated: "This doctrine has been so constantly repeated by our Courts, and so generally acted upon by the people, that it has become a rule of property which cannot be changed without a manifest disregard of the principle of stare decisis, producing in its result an alarming violation of the right of property, and a disastrous disturbance of the quiet of the community."

The rhetoric associated with invocation of stare decisis with respect to property rules is evident relatively early in this period. For example, in 1808 a Pennsylvania judge declared: "Unless the rule of stare decisis is adhered to in the administration of justice under a government of laws, all property must be rendered insecure." The following year, the same court declared that "it is better for the public that the intention of one individual should be defeated, than a series of decisions on which the property of this country depends should be shaken." A South Carolina court contended in 1810 that stare decisis was "of great importance to the security of property." A Tennessee court linked unsettled property rules to "despotism," noting it was "too late to change the course of thinking" with respect to rules of first entry on public lands, because "hundreds of titles have been acquired without any person suspecting that modern notions were to be applied to them." The alternative, Judge Overton maintained, would be to "prove that with extreme labor, after the lapse of thirty years, we have been enabled to construe our laws differently from all who practiced under them, and thereby defeat or unsettle most of our titles to land. This . . . will not promote the true interest of society." Instead, he continued, "we will . . . leave society to fight their way through scenes of litigation in the establishment of new principles which must eventuate in great loss to individuals."

Other rhetoric locates the work of courts within a larger commitment to protection of vested property rights. In *Lion v. Burtiss*, for example, Chief Justice Spencer declared: "Stare decisis is a maxim essential to the security of property," a phrase cited by later courts, including the California Supreme Court in 1860. A few years after *Lion*, an attorney arguing before the same court referred to the maxim stare decisis as "the ark of our safety." Senator Cramer, in response, wrote of the "particular evil" of departing from the maxim:

> We have not, in my view of the subject, the power (and by power I mean right) now to question or impeach that judgment rendered by this Court and founded on the uniform decisions of the Supreme Court during a period of more than seventeen years. Wills have been made, and estates settled, on the principles of those cases, which have been deemed and treated as the settled law of the land. They have been solemnly recognized by this Court, of the last resort, published to the world, held out to our citizens as the sure and established land-marks by which they might, with perfect safety, regulate their conduct in acquiring or perfecting titles, or dispose of estates upon their dying beds, in such a manner that their honest intentions could not be defeated. . . . Can any good citizen, for a moment contemplate the consequences of such a measure without alarm?

Similarly, in 1836 a New York court declared that "the maxim, stare decisis, ought to govern on the present occasion. Litigation can never be repressed, nor can the rights of property ever be secure, if this court of the last resort departs from its own solemn adjudications."

Although by far the majority of cases in which judges invoke stare decisis for stability of property rights involve real estate transactions and devises, judges also emphasized the importance of stare decisis for contracts and commercial cases. In his *Commentaries,* James Kent had specifically noted the "right" of the community to regulate their contracts based upon prior court pronouncements. This equation of contract reliance interests with certainty of land title further established a contract as a property right, underscoring the spread of contracts clause ideology to non-constitutional doctrines. It also suggests the tendency of the vested rights concept in this period to include almost anything as a right of property.

Judge Tucker of Virginia, in a dispute over assignment of a bond and the insolvency of one of the debtors, noted the "elevated ground" of property rules to argue that stare decisis imposed similar obligations with respect to contracts: "The decisions of the courts on such questions, if they do not stand upon the elevated ground of being rules of property, are at least the law of contracts. Those who buy and those who sell, look for the obligations which are assumed by the assignor, to those decisions. Hence the principle stare decisis, is peculiarly applicable to cases of this description." A few years later the Virginia court noted that lease terms must receive consistent interpretations by courts: "The principle stare decisis is in these matters not merely proper, but it is vital; since counsel advise, and conveyancers proceed, and parties contract, with reference to the declared construction of the language of an instrument."

In 1823, the Supreme Court of Errors for Connecticut considered a case in which the efficacy of an endorsement of a promissory note was at issue. A dissenting opinion by Chief Justice Hosmer believed that the majority had departed from prior law. He thought the majority's willingness to consider future cases in a similar light worthy of mention:

> If the maxim stare decisis is any thing more than a name; if the people of this state have the privilege of certain rules of action, and are not the sport of a perpetual vacillation and ruinous uncertainty; the law of Connecticut concerning endorsements of notes, as before expressed, is stable and unquestionable. There are many hundreds of such contracts, now, and at all times, existing among us,—the standing and almost universal mode of guaranty,—which will be evidence of obligations new and unthought of, if the present attempt at the bar to change the construction of such engagements, shall meet with success.

In *Garner v. Stubblefield,* a concurring judge wrote separately on the doctrine of stare decisis to distinguish between "erroneous" decisions of recent vintage and those of longer usage, specifically including "contracts":

> If by its long usage and its having entered into the contracts of mankind it has become the law of property, it ought not to be disturbed. The court in such cases could say with great propriety, stare decisis. But if the decision was but recently made, and was not from its nature calculated to enter into the contracts of the country or to have regulated the

> transmission of property, should the decision be thought to have been wrong, it would in such case be the duty of the court to overrule it. The policy of not disturbing the settled law of property, and more especially real property, is the only argument in favor of permitting a wrong decision to stand that common sense can approve.

An 1821 opinion from Maryland, *Hammond v. Ridgely's Lessee,* emphasized that contracting parties relied upon settled interpretations of law: "Sound policy does indeed require, that principles laid down, and acted upon by courts of last resort, should not be lightly shaken, as it is to established principles, and not to isolated opinions, that parties look in making their contracts."

In several cases in this period, the stare decisis property rule appears in dissenting opinions as an argument against the result reached by the majority. In some instances, the dissent suggests that the majority's decision was in fact a departure from settled law, rather than the legitimate distinction that the majority claimed. In a Virginia case, for example, Judge Tucker wrote:

> The efforts of the appellants' counsel, therefore, has rather been to keep the present case clear of the influence of those adjudications, than to attempt to call in question, what the interests of society so emphatically require to be regarded as no longer questionable. It must be admitted on all hands, that the principle stare decisis, is of peculiar importance in whatever relates to the title to property, and to real property in particular. Among other things, a continual fluctuation in the decisions of the courts on the construction of wills, is calculated to produce the most serious evils.

Other dissenting opinions take issue with conclusions that particular rule changes will not greatly affect settled expectations about property. In *Lemacks v. Glover,* for example, the dissenting opinion discussed the majority's overruling of a prior decision of that court: "That case settled a rule of property which it was dangerous to interfere with. Estates had been divided in conformity with it, and purchases made on its faith." The judge "urged the policy of adhering to the maxim stare decisis, especially where the decision laid down a rule of property."

A dissenting opinion in a case in South Carolina suggested that adherence to settled law in property cases was of constitutional obligation. The majority in that case had noted that stare decisis required adherence to rules under which property has been transacted, but it believed the prior case at issue "has not settled any great rule of property under which rights have been acquired, which the reversal would defeat." The dissenting judge believed otherwise: "The shield against the introduction of this great evil is placed, by the constitution, in the hands of the judiciary."

Attorneys appearing before courts also argued in favor of the stare decisis property rule with considerable frequency. An attorney is reported to have argued in 1800 to the Pennsylvania Supreme Court that stare decisis "is a maxim to be held forever sacred, on questions of property." Similarly, in Massachusetts in 1807, counsel argued, "The maxim stare decisis is of peculiar weight in commercial questions, in which, perhaps more than in any others, it is more important that the law be settled, than how it is settled." Authority for these arguments is not recorded in the reporters' notes of these and similar cases.

No court in this period appears to have challenged the basic proposition that stare decisis was an important principle for the stability of property rights, and courts are openly utilitarian about their purpose. Judge Tucker, for example, noted that fluctuation in law produces bad results for "what the interests of society so emphatically require to be regarded as no longer questionable." A Connecticut court was concerned that property rights were "the sport of a perpetual vacillation and ruinous uncertainty." Another judge suggested that abandoning "landmarks" of the law would "greatly interfere with the enjoyment of property" and "open the door to fraud and litigation." They meant, in their rhetoric at least, that instability of the common law potentially unsettled security of land title and frustrated the intentions of devisors.

We cannot be certain, of course, that judges actually accomplished what their rhetoric suggested—that they in fact promoted certainty in legal rules. The perception that stare decisis protected settled expectations about property may have been partly a legitimation covering other purposes. This may be true for the stare decisis property rule if the underlying doctrines at issue were not so widely known that people acted upon them, or if the judges misrepresented the prior precedent.

Nonetheless, the rhetoric accompanying invocation of the stare decisis property rule—that property rights were dependent upon stability of judicial rules—is surely significant, even if the effect cannot be precisely measured. Stare decisis in property cases was a powerful form of argument for attorneys, one that was difficult for courts to ignore, given the wider political emphasis on vested rights. The stare decisis property rule is symbolic of a larger reification of property associated with the vested rights doctrine.

ACCOUNTING FOR CHANGE IN THE COMMON LAW: THREE CATEGORIES FOR RELIANCE INTERESTS

In a number of instances, state courts cited the stare decisis property rule but explained why that proposition was not applicable to the case at hand. On the basis of these cases, one can generalize about the specific circumstances in which courts citing the stare decisis property rule would nonetheless entertain arguments that a precedent should be overruled. First, if the precedent in question was a recent case, judges noted that there would be less disruption to settled expectations if it were to be changed. Second, courts would also depart from stare decisis if the change in the law was needed to more closely reflect actual practices with respect to property transactions. Third, and most important, courts would overrule prior precedent only if they believed an insignificant number of persons would be affected by the change. Examples from each category below provide further elaboration of these concepts.

Isolating the Aberrant Recent Case

Judges expressed a greater willingness to overrule or decline to follow a particular property rule if it was relatively recent and conflicted with the weight of authority. For example, in Taylor's *Adm'r v. Spindle*, the Court was satisfied that a single recent decision had not been accepted in practice, and so the stare decisis property rule was not applicable. Counsel often proposed (and courts accepted) that a particular precedent was not subject to the stare decisis property rule because it was inconsistent with a line of cases, so that little reliance interest was likely to have occurred. The quest to determine "reliance" interest is a relatively uniform feature in judicial opinions. The more recent aberrational precedent could be excused by the "crowd of business which presses upon this court," but courts must correct "isolated blunders" because "they may invade the inviolability of contracts." But if "by long usage" a precedent had been accepted in legal practice, then it should be preserved.

Change in Law Needed to Reflect Community Practice

Often the more recent case was considered "erroneous" not as an abstract question of the "right answer" under some declaratory theory of law, but in the sense that it did not adequately reflect the law in practice. As expressed by the court in *Kottman v. Ayer*:

> The effect of this [decision] is a reversal of the case of Hillegas v. Hartley. I feel the full force of all that has been said on the rule of "*stare decisis*," but the case of Hillegas v. Hartley has not settled any great rule of property under which rights have been acquired, which the reversal would defeat. Its only effect will be in a few instances to restore rights honestly, in most cases, acquired, but which would have been defeated by accident or by ignorance that the law required such deeds to be recorded within six months. It defeats no right; it only avoids a forfeiture.

On occasion, judges also expressed more specific ideas about when precedent ought to be abandoned in favor of improved utility. The issue most frequently arose with respect to the expediency of following English precedent, when judges seemed to look to American customs to decline to follow an English rule. In other instances, courts employed the technique of distinguishing a case to avoid extending a principle that "if pressed to an extreme, would be introductory of very great mischiefs." But it is more common for judges to state that they must maintain "incorrect" rules or wrongly decided cases even when a change in the rule would be better. For example, a Connecticut court stated: "Stare decisis, is a sound judicial maxim, especially in settlement cases, where the stability of a rule is of more importance than its technical correctness." Even a bad rule must be maintained if changing the rule would result in greater disruption to property expectations.

Effect on a Small Number of Property Transactions

At least in cases in which stare decisis is explicitly discussed, judges consistently stated that property rules should not be changed if the effect would be to unsettle the expectations of a relatively large number of property owners. Courts tended to avoid departing from precedent that "must eventuate in great loss to individuals." Citing *McCulloch v. Maryland,* the Missouri Supreme Court was unwilling to revisit a prior judicial opinion "on the faith of which an immense property had been advanced." According to this court, "It is of little importance to the public whether a tract of land belongs to A. or B. In deciding their titles, strict rules of construction may be adhered to, though sometimes at the expense of justice, because certainty of title is thereby produced, and individual inconvenience is richly compensated by general good; but when multitudes are affected by the construction of an instrument, great regard should be paid to the spirit and intention."

Counsel pressed these arguments as well. In *Wilkes v. Lion,* an attorney for the defendant suggested: "Perhaps hundreds of wills may have been drawn in reference to that very decision." Allowing that decision to be questioned, he argued, would "impair that confidence in your stability which should be jealously maintained."

If, on the other hand, the change in rule was not perceived to have much effect in the larger community, courts were willing to change it. In *Kirk v. Dean,* Judge Brackenridge did not consider the court to be departing from the maxim stare decisis because "the consideration which is expressed by the court, the 'unsettling estates,' does not weigh so much in the case of dower, which is but a life estate." Courts also on occasion relaxed technical formalities in acquisition of property titles, particularly when the deficiency was the fault of a government agency, to avoid court rulings that would affect a large number of property transactions. In addition, courts were less concerned with the stare decisis property rule in questions of remedy and procedure.

To summarize, these courts were willing to change property rules if they were first satisfied that the change would improve the law, usually in the sense that it would better reflect community practice, and if they were also satisfied that the change would not greatly disturb settled property expectations. If a change in a common-law property rule would disrupt transactions and settled expectations, these courts stated a strong preference for the legislature to be the agent of change.

Typical is *Sparrow v. Kingman,* in which the court stated: "Questionable as I think this doctrine was at the first, it has prevailed too long in this State to be now overturned by a judicial decision. If there is any good reason for changing the rule, the change should be made by the Legislature, and not by the Courts." Another judicial opinion, *Bayard v. Malcolm,* merits a more extended quotation:

> Believing the law to be well settled by the numerous authorities introduced, and finding those authorities founded on principles calculated to afford a remedy, where one ought to exist; believing that certainty in the law is of more real importance, than the fancied improvements which ingenuity may suggest, and which, in their nature, must be fluctuating, I have neither the disposition, nor the boldness, to depart from the rule "stare decisis." This court, I would say, is emphatically called on to pronounce what the law is, not what it ought to be.

This preference for legislative change indicates great awareness of the difference between the retroactive nature of judicial decision making and the prospective nature of legislation, which was a critical distinction for the reliance interests these courts identified.

Several issues merit further exploration. Do these cases represent groups with conflicting economic interests? To what extent do these cases reflect the notion that there were limits on all government actors—judges as well as legislators—by the constraints of higher law? These questions are important because we know that courts changed property law in this period, and legislatures effected even greater changes. I do not suggest that on the basis of the cases examined here one could conclude that the property rules that were changed by courts always followed the general precepts that I have identified. However, if changes in common-law property rules usually occurred only in instances in which few settled expectations were disrupted, then the rhetoric of the stare decisis property rule probably did have both a standard meaning and a constraining effect in this period.

CONCLUSION

Stare decisis, developed in the immediate post-founding period of American law, was a useful guide to avoid making decisions that would have the effect of changing common-law rules in ways that property owners would find objectionable. As a rhetorical tool, at least, the stare decisis property rule reflects the dominant discourse concerning rights of property in other arenas. Political ideology played some role in shaping legal rules. This ideology mediated between existing precedent and judges' desires to create a uniquely American law.

To be sure, judicial statements about adherence to precedent occur primarily in cases potentially affecting title to property, not the use to which the property might be put. Changes in property use doctrines that did not affect one's physical possession of land or a contract right—for example, nuisance, water allocation, and ancient lights, all subjects of primary importance in *Transformation I*—did not seem to be of as much concern to judges. Such views are consistent with nineteenth-century takings clause jurisprudence with respect to legislative action. Laws that restricted the use of one's property but did not constitute a physical invasion or forced taking of title were not considered by judges to violate takings clauses contained in the federal or state constitutions and thus did not require compensation.

Although the rhetoric associated with the stare decisis property rule no doubt served a legitimating function, and it was probably ignored when for instrumental reasons courts wanted to change the rules, the concept is invoked frequently enough that one can draw more general conclusions about judicial attitudes toward the stability of property rights. Judges viewed abrupt changes in precedent to be undesirable when settled property expectations would be disturbed. This view was consistent with the legitimation of the existing distribution of property rights in American society. Stability of law no doubt mainly benefited men of property. These, after all, were the usual litigants.

At another level, the rhetoric of stare decisis employed by antebellum jurists in questions relating to property rules was not a concern that private property might be redistributed generally, or taken for public benefit without compensation, but instead expressed the absolute prohibition to the taking of property from A to give to B—a power courts expressly denied to the legislature in this period. Many judges, however, believed it was important to honor the "reasonable expectations" of property owners and those engaged in commercial transactions based upon their general understanding of common-law rules, or at least the settled understanding as those judges could discern it.

State court judges in the antebellum period claimed to abhor sudden changes in common-law rules that disrupted certain property reliance interests. The historical conclusion, however, is mixed. Judges clearly showed an appreciation of the potential effect of their decisions on property reliance interests, but they were also utilitarian in such a way that their focus was not necessarily upon the vested rights of parties before the court, but upon the potential for disrupting a larger number of transactions—a pragmatic concern for economic stability in addition to the reliance interest of a particular individual.

7

"The Benefits and Evils of Competition": James Coolidge Carter's Supreme Court Advocacy

LEWIS A. GROSSMAN

JAMES COOLIDGE CARTER (1828–1905) WAS PERHAPS THE MOST RESPECTed appellate advocate in the country at the end of the nineteenth century. He argued approximately three dozen matters before the Supreme Court, including some of the most important cases of the Gilded Age. He defended the federal income tax in the first phase of *Pollock v. Farmer's Loan & Trust Company*, the case in which the Supreme Court declared the tax unconstitutional.[1] He argued the *Chinese Exclusion Case*, in which he represented a Chinese immigrant who was denied reentry into the United States pursuant to a racist immigration restriction statute.[2] Carter also argued seminal cases concerning the Fifth Amendment privilege against self-incrimination and the recognition of foreign judgments in American courts.[3] This essay will focus on Carter's advocacy in three other important matters: his 1896 and 1898 briefs for the railroad defendants in *United States v. Trans-Missouri Freight Association* and *United States v. Joint Traffic Association*, two important early interpretations of the Sherman Antitrust Act, and the brief he filed in 1897 on behalf of the railroads in *Smyth v. Ames*, the case that established substantive due process limits on the legislative power to set railroad and utility rates.[4]

As I have explored in detail elsewhere, Carter, in addition to being a renowned practitioner, was also the preeminent American champion of historical jurisprudence, an important strain of Gilded Age legal thought. In his jurisprudential work, Carter equated the common law with the evolving customs of the people. He contended that statutory enactments, by contrast, often conflicted with custom and that legislation contrary to custom not only was futile but also promoted grave mischief as the people strove to evade its enforcement. Carter thus argued that the regulation of private affairs should remain primarily the province of unwritten law. These jurisprudential ideas grew out of Carter's celebrated leadership of the successful fight against the efforts of his nemesis, David Dudley Field, to replace New York State's decisional private law with a civil code. Finally, Carter was also one of the nation's most prominent municipal and legal reformers, an influential activist against party-based corruption in city government and the courts.[5]

In this essay, I will explore the ways in which Carter's jurisprudential and political views shaped his forensic arguments. In particular, I will examine how his briefs in *United States v. Trans-Missouri Freight Association, United States v. Joint Traffic Association,* and *Smyth v. Ames* reflected the mugwump political culture to which Carter, and many other late nineteenth-century urban lawyers, belonged.

The intellectual historian must, of course, be cautious when analyzing what an attorney said as an advocate. The positions taken by a lawyer arguing on behalf of a client are determined primarily by that client's needs, and the language the lawyer uses to advance these positions is shaped largely by tactical considerations. Nevertheless, the content and style of an attorney's forensic arguments can reveal a great deal about his personal ideology and that of his age. As Robert Gordon has argued, even late nineteenth-century classicist lawyers, who embraced the notion of neutral "legal science," both reflected and generated ideology in the documents they drafted.[6] Carter was not a classicist, and one need not be as sophisticated an analyst as Gordon to see the imprint of ideology on Carter's work product.[7]

Carter did not view legal argument as a logical discipline, but rather as an attempt to appeal to the emotions of the decision maker. Moreover, he insisted that an attorney who feigned sincerity could not be convincing. He told the graduating students of Columbian (now George Washington) Law School: "I think that the first requirement [of commanding the decision maker's attention] is that the man should really believe what he says."[8] Carter's longtime friend and colleague Joseph Choate observed: "Having once undertaken the conduct of a case [Carter] made a careful study of it to try to build upon the facts a theory consistent with his own sense of right and justice, which he might fairly and earnestly present to the favorable consideration of the court—and in this he generally succeeded—and having once convinced himself, he could apply all the clearness, force, and earnestness of which he was master to convince the tribunal, whether court or jury."[9]

Although Carter believed attorneys were less effective on behalf of clients with whom they disagreed, he also believed that this problem rarely arose. He explained to the graduating Columbian students:

> Some may ask how [earnest advocacy] is possible in those cases where the side which the lawyer is called upon to support happens to be, in his own belief, the wrong one. *There are not many such cases.* . . . Law suits are not conflicts in which all arguments upon the one side are right and upon the other wrong; they are conflicts between rival and competing rules and principles, all of which are true within certain limits, but some of which must

> give way to the superior force of others. The office of the contending advocates, as necessary to justice as it is useful to the litigants, is to discover and display the full force of the competing views. It is for the court to weigh and determine upon which side the balance falls.[10]

In other words, Carter viewed the resolution of legal disputes, even on moral grounds, as a process characterized by such nuance and complexity that a lawyer could find justice-based arguments for almost any position.

Because Carter demanded of himself that he genuinely embrace every assertion that he made to a judge, his written briefs offer a strikingly clear window into his personal views. There was undoubtedly a fair amount of self-delusion in Carter's conviction that his statements in court were invariably sincere. Nonetheless, because he strove to conform his forensic arguments to his beliefs, these arguments reveal a great deal about the beliefs themselves.

MUGWUMP IDEOLOGY

Defined narrowly, the mugwumps were northeastern urban gentleman reformers who, in the 1884 presidential election, bolted the Republican Party to vote for Democrat Grover Cleveland because they considered the Republican candidate, James Blaine, to be a corrupt spoilsman. More broadly, the mugwumps were late nineteenth-century gentlemen reformers who prided themselves on their independence and their noble adherence to principle rather than party.[11]

The mugwumps' reformist program was based largely on their moralistic opposition to the capture of the political process by unscrupulous party bosses and nouveau-riche corporate plutocrats. Carter's generation of genteel liberal reformers tended to embrace the following series of causes: first, abolition of slavery; then civil service reform, free trade, and sound currency; and, finally, anti-imperialism.[12] According to the standard view, the mugwumps' free trade and sound money positions reflected a broader embrace of laissez-faire. John Sproat, for example, asserts that the mugwumps "believed nature had created a perfectly balanced economic order, governed by immutable laws. Left alone, the order ideally served man's needs; any tampering with a single component would destroy the entire system or radically alter it. Free to function naturally, the system worked in perfect harmony to provide the greatest possible good to mankind."[13]

Undoubtedly, the mugwumps viewed the activist state with suspicion. They believed that government regulation often redounded to the benefit not of the public, but of the plutocratic and corrupt interests that controlled the political system. As other scholars have recognized, however, for many mugwumps, laissez-faire was not so much a scientific law as a "handy rule of practice," useful for deflating the power of the interests that inevitably captured the legislative process.[14] The Yankee gentry often supported positive government when they were confident it was being exercised for pure and unselfish reasons. Moreover, the number of mugwumps who favored active government grew as the problems of urban industrialism became more apparent after 1890. Many genteel reformers eventually decided that a limited night-watchman state did not satisfy the needs of modern civilization.[15]

The mugwumps had a deep commitment to private, as well as public, morality.[16] As in the public context, the keys to ethical behavior in the private realm were the avoidance of self-interest and the pursuit of the public good. The gentry reformers rejected the ethos of rapacious and selfish individualism that they thought characterized the new breed of industrialists and financiers. Instead, they advanced a competing vision of market behavior based on self-restraint, mutual dependence, and fair dealing. In the words of one scholar, the mugwumps "knew the normal marketplace not as a Hobbesian war of all against all, but, instead, as a moral endeavor governed by restraint and the golden rule."[17] They considered themselves to be the heirs to deep-rooted family traditions of gentlemanly business practices and high-minded community leadership.

James Coolidge Carter epitomized the mugwump worldview in almost every respect.[18] Matthias Reimann, along with most of the other scholars who have considered Carter, is thus mistaken in concluding that his "protest against legislation was protest against the infringement on the economic freedom of his wealthy clients."[19] Carter was not in fact motivated by a desire to advance the interests of big business. On the contrary, he, like his mugwump brethren, condemned the excessive wealth of the very rich and their corrupt control of the government.[20] He considered the upward redistribution of wealth to be more prevalent and more troublesome than the downward variety.

Moreover, if Carter was a laissez-faireist, he was certainly an ambivalent one. He set forth a variety of circumstances in which legislation was a desirable, or even necessary, supplement to the common law in the regulation of private affairs.[21] He argued that the development of custom "results in tracing out a sphere of conduct within which the individual can move and act with freedom and security, and beyond which he cannot pass without encroaching upon the like sphere of another and exciting resentment with its consequences."[22] Law, as a mere reflection of custom, had the same purpose. Therefore, for Carter, restrictions on individual autonomy were a corollary to the protection of individual rights. The role of "society's organised power" was to maintain customary restraints on private conduct objectionable to others.[23] In earlier times, social sanctions and occasional recourse to the courts had been sufficient to enforce these customary norms. As the country urbanized and industrialized, however, "men touch each other in a vastly greater number of ways and may consequently the more encroach upon and abridge the individual liberty of each other." Therefore, "additional and more complex legislation" was needed.[24]

Carter, like mugwumps generally, was impelled by a commitment to private as well as public morality. And his vision of the market as a cooperative and ethical realm made him quite receptive to certain types of regulation. Surprisingly, these attitudes emerge clearly even in the briefs Carter wrote for his railroad clients.

SMYTH V. AMES

In the words of William C. Wiecek, "The 1898 case of *Smyth v. Ames* completed the triumph of substantive due process."[25] For Progressive historians, the judiciary's use of substantive due process to strike down economic regulations exemplified the heartless, pro-corporate, antimajoritarian character of American law in the Gilded Age. Carter's role as the victorious lawyer in *Smyth v. Ames* has probably contributed to scholars' mistaken impression that he promoted an extreme form of laissez-faire.[26] In fact, however, Carter's argument for the railroad appellees in the case was hardly so ambitious; as in his nonforensic writings, he acknowledged a fairly broad province for legislative power. Nevertheless, Carter expressed a greater faith in the free market in his *Smyth* brief than in perhaps any other document.

Smyth v. Ames was commonly referred to as the Nebraska Rate Case, because it addressed an 1893 act of the Nebraska legislature "to regulate railroads, to classify freights, to fix reasonable maximum rates to be charged for the transportation of freights upon each of the railroads in the State of Nebraska, and to provide penalties for the violation of this Act."[27] The statute included detailed tables setting forth the state's "Schedule of Reasonable Maximum Rates."[28] Carter represented three groups of railroad stockholders who sued to enjoin enforcement of the rates on the ground that the statute violated the United States Constitution.

Smyth v. Ames was a politically charged matter. The Nebraska legislature had enacted the statute in the midst of the financial panic of 1893, which had wreaked havoc on the agricultural Midwest and had prompted farmers to demand legislative control of the rates they paid to ship their goods. The panic had triggered an economic depression that still afflicted the nation in April 1897, when the Supreme Court heard the case. One of the lawyers opposing Carter was the populist leader William Jennings Bryan. Just months before the argument, Bryan, running as the Democratic Party candidate, had lost the 1896 presidential election to William McKinley.

Despite the passion surrounding the issue of railroad rate regulation, Carter's argument was not particularly provocative, from a legal perspective. By the time the Court heard *Smyth*, it had already effectively abandoned its 1877 holding, in *Munn v. Illinois*, that state legislatures had unreviewable authority to set rates with regard to property "affected with the public interest."[29] In 1890, in *Chicago, Milwaukee and St. Paul Railway Co. v. Minnesota*, the Court had declared that the reasonableness of state-established rates "is eminently a question for judicial investigation, requiring due process of law for its determination."[30] Consequently, in *Smyth*, even Bryan, arguing in favor of rate regulation, did not contend that the Nebraska rate tables were simply immune from judicial review.[31] The only open questions for the Court were, first, the standard that courts should use to assess the reasonableness of rates and, second, the reasonableness of the Nebraska rates themselves.

Carter prevailed in *Smyth*; the Court invalidated the rate tables. The decision's main importance was its establishment of the principle, applicable to all regulated industries, that courts should determine whether the set rates represented a "fair return" on the "fair value" of the property in question.[32] In the words of one scholar, "This mired the Court in a half-century of resolving ever more esoteric issues of accounting."[33] Carter, however, did not advocate the "fair return on fair value" formula to the Court. Instead, as discussed below, he advanced a much less precise principle for courts to use in assessing the constitutionality of legislated rates.[34]

Before we consider Carter's analysis of the constitutional restrictions on rate setting, however, it is interesting to examine a portion of his *Smyth* brief in which he discussed the limits of state power more generally. Carter frequently could not resist offering judges a lengthy discourse on the area of law at issue, even if the digression was irrelevant, or perhaps even harmful, to his client's cause. In *Smyth*, Carter's excursus concerned the police power of the state. He articulated a broad vision of the state's regulatory authority over health, safety, and morals.

> [The police power] represses evil practices and ill-doing generally. It aims to do, as its name imports, about what a wise policeman would do if he were charged with the duty of walking about among men as they are engaged in the ordinary and useful callings of life, and repressing mischievous and unfair practices which every one, except the guilty parties, would agree should not be permitted.
>
> But it also acts on a larger scale. It regulates the construction of buildings, the hours of labor, compels manufacturers and producers to submit their wares to inspection to stamp them, &c., requires carriers to provide safe vehicles and keep them in repair, employers of labor to make the buildings in which their operations are carried on safe and comfortable for workingmen, &c., &c.[35]

Readers of the brief may have expected Carter next to draw a distinction between the permissible types of regulation he discussed in this passage, on one hand, and the unconstitutional regulation of prices and wages, on the other. Instead, he proceeded to affirm the state's broad power to issue the latter sorts of controls, as well. Indeed, he asserted that the Court had unduly *restricted* the police power in *Munn v. Illinois*!

> Language has sometimes been used, for instance in the case of Munn *vs.* Illinois . . . which seems to *suggest*, although it by no means so declares, that the exercise of [the police]

> power, so far as it seeks to touch *prices*, is limited to certain pursuits obscurely defined as "*affected with a public interest*." This is a misleading phrase. . . .
>
> . . . From the very nature of the power it has no other limitation than the *necessities* of society. . . . Instead of saying that whatever things are affected with the public interest may be subjected to the regulation of [the police] power, we might better say that whatever *requires* the regulation of that power is *affected* with a public interest. The primary inquiry always must be whether the *regulation is necessary*.
>
> The purchase and sale of wheat, or other provisions, are not ["affected with the public interest"]; but were there peril of a famine, and great proprietors had accumulated the whole supply, and were holding it at a price which the people could not afford to pay . . . none could doubt the right of the State to take it compulsorily for a fair price and with it to accommodate the public necessities.[36]

This was a striking concession. After all, Nebraska might cogently have contended that the panic of 1893 represented just the sort of crisis posited by Carter that would justify price controls. Carter's discussion was even more curious in light of the fact that it was extraneous to the core of his argument—as he himself acknowledged. "It may be asked what the use is of talking about *police powers* . . . if, after all, the real inquiry is . . . whether the legislation invades some right which it was the design of the constitution to protect *against legislative* action. . . . This is a fair question."[37] The very superfluousness of Carter's police power analysis suggests that it simply reflected his personal views.

This is not to say that Carter's *Smyth* brief was a progressive one. He based his argument that the Court should strike down the Nebraska rates on an idealized vision of the free market. As James May has shown, many late nineteenth-century jurists embraced the principles of classical economics, according to which truly free competition inevitably produced results that were both efficient and fair.

> Within [the] natural economic world of unimpeded production and exchange, the disparate interests of consumers, capital, and labor were coordinated and ultimately harmonized through the operation of the powerful and pervasive natural law of competition. . . . Both academic and popular texts repeatedly asserted that freely competitive production and exchange powerfully tended to produce just results consonant with God's will and the dictates of morality. As long as individuals were not impeded in their free pursuit of economic opportunity, abnormally high prices and returns temporarily prevailing in any particular market would attract new entrants. Such new entry would expand available supply, intensify horizontal competition, and force prices downward until supply and demand once again achieved an equilibrium generating fair, normal prices and returns.[38]

In *Smyth,* Carter embraced the classical economic model with respect to railroad rates. He asserted: "The prices of carriage are everywhere fixed, not by the railroads nor by shippers, but by the same imperious power which fixes the price of all other articles or services, namely, the pressure of competition. Against this determination it is irrelevant to argue justice or injustice; or, to speak more correctly, the decision of this power is always just."[39] Carter repeatedly contended that because railroads operated in a free market, the state should treat railroad rates no differently from the price of boots or shoes. "It is said that the rates in Nebraska are too high. But how can this be? It is not pretended that free competition is not in full operation in that State; on the contrary, it is known that between the main lines an energetic competition exists. Of course, in the sparsely settled regions there is less of it; but if rates were so high that the carriers were making great profits, there would be."[40]

Carter did not contend that the state had no authority at all to regulate railroad rates. He readily acknowledged the government's power to repress "extortion," a term that encompassed a seller's "undue, unreasonable and oppressive" exaction of money from customers.[41] Such conduct violated Carter's mugwump vision of the market as a moral sphere characterized by self-restraint and fair dealing. He analogized the charging of extortionate prices to a grocer's use of false weights, contending that the state could properly repress either one as an "immoral" and "petty" practice to which "fair men will not stoop."[42]

Carter maintained, however, that only "palpably and grossly excessive" charges qualified as extortionate.[43] "Extortion, as applied to *prices* of things or services, *means* the *wrongful exaction*, under *color of right*, of excessive compensation. And as it necessarily implies *guilt*, it must and does mean that the sum exacted is, in some way, so *manifestly* disproportionate to the value received that any man having the ordinary use of reason who exacts it must be *conscious* that he is doing wrong."[44] Carter thus argued that a state legislature had the power to set maximum rates only if it set them at an extremely high level. It did not have the authority to cap rates, as the Nebraska legislature had, within the wide range that the market might naturally establish. "The necessary limitation of the power to establish rates for a carrier . . . is that the [set] rates must be so high as to plainly permit him to charge a *reasonable* price, as that would be determined in a suit between him and the shipper; for that is his indubitable *right*. And inasmuch as that price is, in nearly every case—we might justly say in every case—fixed by the stress of competition, the maximum rates fixed by the law must leave *clear and manifest room for the play of the competitive forces beneath them*."[45]

Carter maintained that extortion was, in reality, extremely uncommon. One disincentive to extortion, he argued, was that unethical commercial actors "suffer in their reputation and are avoided. Other people decline to have relations with them."[46] Carter thus incorporated into his *Smyth* argument his jurisprudential theory that societal customs tended to reflect ideal norms.[47] Carter also used classical economic principles to explain why extortion was rare. He contended that so long as there was free competition, a seller could not impose extortionate prices on a buyer, because the buyer could instead purchase the good or service from a rival seller. Consequently, in a free market, extortion "becomes impossible and even *unthinkable*."[48] The opportunity for extortion arose only if the seller had a monopolistic position or if the buyer's desperate need for the good or service in question rendered him powerless to negotiate.[49]

Carter acknowledged to the Court that rate setting would usually be superfluous if the legislated maximum rates were high enough to pass constitutional muster under his approach. The pointlessness of such laws did not trouble him, however. "It proves only that where the price of transportation is as subject to the laws of free competition as those in any other occupation or employment, there is no more need of statutes against extortion than in such other occupations."[50]

Gilded Age economists and jurists struggled with the question of whether classical economic theory, and the legal principles intertwined with it, continued to be relevant in the face of the dramatic economic and social changes that characterized the era. They asked whether, in an increasingly urbanized, industrialized, and centralized nation, it was still reasonable to assume that unregulated economic activity would produce harmonious and just results.[51] Carter himself acknowledged that modern conditions were expanding the zone of justifiable government regulation far beyond its traditional bounds.[52] Nevertheless, Carter continued to adhere to the core principles of classical economic theory even as he tentatively acknowledged its limitations.

By the 1890s, there was thus an intrinsic tension in Carter's economic worldview—a tension he could exploit in the forensic setting. The fluid and conflicted nature of his economic vision allowed him to deploy it, with blinkered earnestness, on behalf of either side in almost any case about business regulation. Classical economic notions were more clearly applicable to an economy of small producers, basic goods, and arm's-length exchanges. Consequently, when arguing on behalf of a client who was resisting government rate regulation, Carter would stress the traditional aspects of that client's business. This was his strategy in *Smyth*, in which he contended that the "railroad business is . . . one of the common and free pursuits of life, just as much as the manufacture of boots and shoes."[53] To advance his argument in other sorts of cases, however, Carter would point, with equal sincerity, to the special problems that the railroad industry confronted, and he would challenge the classical view that unfettered competition inevitably produced just and harmonious results. The most striking example of the latter approach was Carter's performance in two major antitrust cases, discussed in the following section.

UNITED STATES V. TRANS-MISSOURI FREIGHT ASSOCIATION AND *UNITED STATES V. JOINT TRAFFIC ASSOCIATION*

In 1890, Congress enacted the Sherman Antitrust Act, the first section of which banned "every contract, combination in the form of trust or otherwise, or conspiracy, in restraint of trade or commerce among the several States, or with foreign nations."[54] This critically important statute was the federal government's first attempt to address the growing problem of collusive, exclusionary, and monopolistic business practices that undermined free-market competition. Before the passage of the Sherman Act, only the states imposed restrictions on trusts, primarily through common-law prohibitions against agreements in restraint of trade.

United States v. Trans-Missouri Freight Association and *United States v. Joint Traffic Association* were the second and third cases in which the United States Supreme Court considered the scope and meaning of the Sherman Act.[55] In each case, Carter represented railroad defendants who had been prosecuted under the act for engaging in price-fixing activities. He argued, unsuccessfully, for a restrictive interpretation of the law that would have absolved his clients of wrongdoing.

The cooperative conduct of Carter's railroad clients that the United States challenged under the Sherman Act grew out of Congress's enactment of the Interstate Commerce Act (ICA) in 1887.[56] The ICA was designed primarily to address the rampant phenomenon of discriminatory pricing in the railroad industry. Railroads charged higher rates for short haul traffic than for long haul traffic. Moreover, they offered preferred rates to major shippers in order to secure their business, often under great pressure from the shippers themselves. The ICA attacked these problems by requiring each railroad to publish uniform rates and file them with the newly formed Interstate Commerce Commission. Railroads were forbidden to depart from these rates without publishing and filing new rate sheets. The ICA did not mandate that different railroads charge identical rates, however, and on competitive routes, there continued to be an extreme, and in some instances unsustainable, downward pressure on prices. Railroads, to gain as much market share as possible, frequently underbid their rivals secretly, in direct violation of the ICA's requirement that they follow their published rate schedules.[57]

Trans-Missouri and *Joint Traffic* concerned similar efforts by groups of railroads to address this situation by imposing obligations on themselves to supplement those mandated by the ICA. In each instance, the railroad companies of a particular region formed an association that agreed on rates for competitive routes. The member railroads were permitted to deviate from these rates only after notifying the association of the intended change and then waiting a designated period of time. The associations levied monetary penalties on members who violated these requirements.[58] The United States sued both associations under the Sherman Act, seeking to enjoin further implementation of their agreements.

In December 1896, Carter argued in defense of the Trans-Missouri Association in the Supreme Court.[59] He asserted that the Sherman Act should be interpreted simply as incorporating preexisting common law.[60] The question for the Court, Carter contended, was whether the Trans-Missouri agreement was "under the class of contracts void at common law as against public policy."[61] This strategy reflected Carter's general preference for the common law over statutes and his support for the interpretive canon that statutes in derogation of the common law should be construed narrowly.[62]

Based on his contention that the Sherman Act incorporated the common law, Carter urged the Court to apply a "rule of reason" to the statute's prohibition on "contracts in restraint of trade." He observed: "There is not at the present time, nor has there ever been, any doctrine or principle [at common law] declaring all contracts which might restrain trade to any extent . . . illegal. . . . The settled law of the present day is, and indeed always has been, that whenever a contract confessedly creating *some* restraint is asserted before a legal tribunal to be unlawful, and is defended on the alleged ground that the restraint is a *reasonable* one, the Court has always considered that question, and upheld or condemned the contract according to its views touching the reasonableness of the restraint."[63]

Carter then explained why the Trans-Missouri agreement was a reasonable restraint on trade. His 125-page brief focused on the economics of the railroad business and explained why the formation of the association was a perfectly sensible response to the industry's particular problems. His efforts were to no avail; the Supreme Court voted 5–4 in favor of the United States. Justice Rufus Peckham, writing for the majority, refused to confine the Sherman Act's prohibitions to "unreasonable" restraints of trade or commerce.[64] The Court thus did not address the question of whether the association's activities were, in fact, reasonable ones.

Two years later, in *Joint Traffic*, Carter got a second chance. He subtly reframed the statutory interpretation question in a manner that, somewhat surprisingly, persuaded the Court to revisit it.[65] Carter asserted that in the previous case, the Trans-Missouri Association, while arguing that the Sherman Act banned only "unreasonable" restraints, had implicitly conceded that its agreement was, in fact, a "restraint of trade or commerce." Now, on behalf of the essentially identical Joint Traffic Association, Carter contended that the Sherman Act did not apply because the agreement actually *promoted* commerce rather than "restraining" it. He explained: "[The Joint Traffic Association] does, indeed, purport to restrain *competition*, . . . and if competition and commerce were *identical*, in assuming to restrain competition . . . it would be assuming . . . to restrain commerce, but surely no such identity will be pretended."[66] Carter defined commerce as the "interchange of commodities," and he maintained that competition was only an "incident" of commerce. Commerce, he observed, "can and does take place on a large scale in numerous forms without competition." Indeed, a well-designed restraint on competition frequently "enlarges, increases, and benefits" commerce.[67]

In the guise of explaining why the Joint Traffic Association's activities promoted commerce rather than restraining it, Carter essentially restated and expanded his arguments from *Trans-Missouri*. His *Joint Traffic* brief was a massive 205-page treatise that dwarfed even his *Trans-Missouri* filing. It consisted almost entirely of economic policy analysis and was nearly devoid of legal citations. Justice Peckham, in his majority decision, was moved to describe Carter's work as "masterly."[68] Nonetheless, the Court once again ruled, 5–4, in favor of the United States, refusing to abandon the strict literalist approach to the Sherman Act it had embraced in *Trans-Missouri*. Carter's approach would not prevail until six years after his death, when the Court embraced the "rule of reason" in *Standard Oil v. United States*.[69]

One might assume that Carter's work for antitrust defendants, which was not limited to the railroad association cases, conflicted directly with his mugwump agenda. After all, Carter, like other gentry reformers, harbored a deep suspicion about the motives, morals, and machinations of the new class of plutocrats. It is important to note, however, that the mugwumps generally did not enthusiastically embrace strong antitrust regulation, at least initially. Despite their misgivings about huge accumulations of wealth and the disproportionate political influence of business magnates, the mugwumps were largely silent on the wisdom of antitrust laws, even after the "trust problem" became a central issue of public policy in the middle of the 1880s.[70] As John Sproat has observed, most liberal reformers "simply ignored the Sherman Anti-Trust Act when it passed Congress. . . . Not one word on the measure appeared in the pages of *The Nation*."[71]

When mugwumps had anything at all to say about antitrust regulation, they were ambivalent or, in some cases, fervently opposed. They tended to believe that the primary cause of monopolies was illegitimate government assistance to big business and that excessive corporate consolidation would not occur in a truly free market.[72] Around the turn of the century, however, with the problem of consolidation growing ever more evident, mugwumps increasingly began to embrace antitrust enforcement, along with other sorts of regulation of industrial capitalism.[73] Nevertheless, when Carter fought to limit the force of the Sherman Act in the late 1890s, few if any denizens of the gentlemen's clubs he frequented would have downright condemned his efforts.

Some of Carter's friends may have been uncertain about the wisdom of his course, however. After all, since the Erie Railroad wars of the late 1860s, liberal reformers had viewed the railroads with more suspicion and hostility than any other industry. Many mugwumps considered the railroad industry to be a special case, a "natural monopoly" exempt from the effects of free competition and thus more properly subject to government regulation than other businesses.[74] Nonetheless, even with regard to railroads, the mugwumps remained genuinely torn about the appropriate degree of state intervention. They almost unanimously favored safety regulation, but few sanctioned rate setting, and fewer still advocated a direct attack on railroad consolidation itself.[75]

The reformers' ambivalence was understandable, for antitrust laws, more than other types of economic regulation, challenged traditional political and philosophical boundaries. The Sherman Act, as one of the first major instances of federal intervention into the economy, was a strikingly modern measure.[76] Nonetheless, many who supported the law had a traditionalist motive for doing so; they desired to preserve a competitive economy of small producers.[77] As Morton Horwitz has explained, the critical dividing line in the area of antitrust was not between conservative opponents of government regulation and Progressive proponents of an activist state. Rather, it was between those who wanted to preserve America's decentralized economic and political institutions and those who embraced the inevitability of large-scale concentrations of capital.[78] On one hand, there were both "old conservatives" and "old Progressives" who favored vigorous antitrust enforcement because of their hostility to big business.[79] On the other hand, there were both "new conservatives" and "new Progressives" who opposed a literalist interpretation of the Sherman Act because they thought that economic concentration was a natural and, in many cases, beneficial development.[80]

Regardless of where Carter fell on the spectrum between conservative and Progressive, he was clearly, if reluctantly, "new" with regard to corporate consolidation. Although he sometimes seemed to lament the rise of centralized industrial capitalism, he invariably recognized its inevitability and occasionally acknowledged its advantages. In *Law: Its Origin, Growth, and Function*, for example, Carter identified the "division of employments" and the "increase of co-operation, and crowded populations" as unavoidable incidents of an "advancing civilisation."[81]

Carter's *Joint Traffic* brief reflected his personal acceptance of modern economic developments. In the document, he explicitly set forth his feelings about urbanization, industrialization, and business concentration. He remarked: "Those who, like the writer of this brief, prefer a society of which the characteristic feature is a large number of small, but independent, proprietors, look with regret upon the substitution in place of it of organized masses of human beings, who seem to be mere parts of a great industrial machine; but this means they don't like a densely peopled world, and do not stop to think that we actually have one, and must adapt ourselves to its requirements."[82] In another passage, Carter observed:

> There is no doubt that prior to and at the time of the passage of the [Sherman Act] there were, as there still are, certain tendencies in the industrial world which drew widespread attention and excited, in some minds, much alarm. Many industries were seen, or supposed, to be under the control of great aggregations of capital. . . .
>
> Undoubtedly it may be possible for a large aggregated capital to wield a greater power in many ways than would be possible for the same amount distributed among many separate owners or managers, and the suspicion was entertained that such power was employed in controlling markets, and perhaps in controlling legislation, and it was also thought to be an instrumentality by which the unequal distribution of wealth was fostered and increased. The disfavor thus excited was, as was natural, turned to political account. . . .

> While, therefore, all, or nearly all, professed themselves in favor of repressive legislation, the question what legislation could be contrived was a difficult one and suggested some difficult questions. . . . Was it certain that these so called *trusts* were, in every instance, necessarily mischievous? Indeed, sensible legislators for the most part understood very clearly that the things complained of were but the necessary incidents and consequences of the progress of industry and civilization and could not be arrested without checking the advance of the nation and crippling it in the fierce competitions with other nations, and that any useful effort to remedy the supposed evils must be directed against the abuses of the power of aggregated capital and not at the aggregations themselves.[83]

In other words, Carter maintained that business concentration was not only ineluctable, but in some ways beneficial. He extended this reasoning to all industries, not just railroads. In *Joint Traffic*, he remarked, "An enormous aggregation of capital may indeed control, to a certain extent, and for a limited time, the production of a great staple, such for instance as sugar; but this . . . may be only the fair reward of the superior advantages which belong to a large capital and the successful practice of economies in production."[84]

Interestingly, Carter's embrace of economic "bigness" was not restricted to the sphere of business; it also extended to labor organization. He appeared to adopt a theory of countervailing powers similar to that articulated by Oliver Wendell Holmes. In 1896, Holmes, then a justice on the Supreme Judicial Court of Massachusetts, dissented with the following words from the decision in *Vegelahn v. Gunther* upholding a labor injunction: "One of the eternal conflicts out of which life is made up is that between the effort of every man to get the most he can for his services, and that of society, disguised under the name of capital, to get his services for the least possible return. Combination on the one side is patent and powerful. Combination on the other is the necessary and desirable counterpart, if the battle is to be carried on in a fair and equal way."[85] Two years later, Carter made a strikingly similar point in his *Joint Traffic* brief.

> [Labor unions] go infinitely further in restraint of competition than the agreement under attack. . . . But would any one say that if there were a State statute condemning contract and combinations in restraint of trade generally in the same terms as those employed in the Anti-Trust Act in relation to inter-State trade, the labor union agreements would be held illegal under it? And yet the main object of these unions is to do away with competition. The ground upon which they are best defended is that by combination they enable laborers to command higher wages, and thus a larger share of the comforts of life. Formerly this was thought to be against public policy, as being injurious to trade; but more reasonable views have succeeded, and the universal belief at present is that they greatly increase the efficiency of labor [and] lead to a more just distribution of the products of industry.
>
> Associations of employers are rendered necessary as a counter-pose to those of laborers.[86]

In short, the social and economic changes Carter witnessed in his later years led him to endorse increased private cooperation, as well as more state regulation.[87] In *Trans-Missouri* and *Joint Traffic,* Carter discussed at great length why uncontrolled competition did not necessarily produce just and harmonious results under modern conditions. Although some of his arguments focused on the particular characteristics of the railroad business, he also voiced doubt about the beneficence of competition in general. Carter's growing ambivalence about classical economic principles was embodied by the title he gave one of the major sections of his *Joint Traffic* brief: "Competition: Its Benefits and Evils."[88]

In *Trans-Missouri,* Carter contended, "Nothing is more fully recognized at the present day than that there is a species of competition to which railroads are specially subject, which is ruinous, not only to private, but to public interests, and that agreements designed to check it and prevent the resulting mischiefs are entitled to judicial favor and support."[89] He asserted that railroads were especially vulnerable to destructive competition because the industry was one in which the bulk of capital was invested in permanent physical structures.[90] In his *Joint Traffic* brief, Carter explained:

> The reason why railroads are greater sufferers than other industries from the destructive effects of free competition is that the latter have several defences and protections against it while the former have but one. Manufacturers, for instance, of certain descriptions of goods, when there is a low price in consequence of an over supply, may hold their goods for another time and a better market, or, if the competition is so fierce that they feel unable to continue it, they may, at a sacrifice indeed, sell out and transfer their capital to some other quarter. This they can generally do, for their buildings and water or steam power have a value for many other purposes. . . .
>
> Of these defences, the first is not open to a railroad. It cannot hold its goods for a better market. The provision for a certain amount of transportation has already been made and the expense fully incurred. All that is received is clear gain; that is to say, it will make the loss so much less, even if it fails to make a profit. Nor is the second any more open. The railroad owner cannot find any purchaser for his plant who may profitably employ it for some other purpose. It can only be used as a railroad.[91]

According to Carter, these characteristics of the railroad industry resulted in oversupply, plunging prices, catastrophic business failures, and devastation of communities.[92] In sum, "Railroad competition . . . always tends to, and, unless resisted by tacit or express agreement, will certainly degenerate into, deadly strife."[93]

The economic phenomenon to which Carter referred was an authentic one, and it was not limited to the railroad industry. As James May explains with regard to the final decades of the nineteenth century, "New production technologies and expanded operations often demanded heavy fixed investments and created a situation of periodic, severe 'overcapacity' or 'overproduction' in many lines of commerce. As a result, competitive rivalry in various forms intensified and threatened the viability of many firms, as businesses with fixed investments not easily transferred to other uses struggled to maintain market share and recover at least something beyond their variable expenses."[94] Modern scholars agree that one of primary reasons why American firms increased their mutual cooperation in the Gilded Age was to avoid the very real perils of cutthroat competition.[95]

Carter's exploration of the "evils of competition" in his *Trans-Missouri* and *Joint Traffic* briefs was not limited to railroads. Instead, he issued a broad-based challenge to the classical faith in competition, at least under modern conditions. He observed, "A common notion is that competition tends to secure *lower* prices to the consumers of commodities, and thus to benefit them; but this proceeds upon the assumption that it is more desirable to benefit consumers than producers."[96] Carter declared that "there is a point beyond which competition may not only cease to be beneficial, but become exceedingly injurious, not only to private individuals, but to the public also."[97] Instead of portraying the market as a harmonious Eden, he depicted it as a Darwinian jungle.

> Mischiefs and miseries [flow] from the eager prosecution of competition which sometimes seem, for the moment at least, to equal, or outweigh, the benefits. The predominating motive in the rivalry being private and individual gain, no tenderness, or even thought, for the welfare of others is encouraged. Many are striving for the same thing, and every available weapon will be employed. Scruples are apt to be silenced, and "to get there" is a vulgar phrase which well describes the character of the struggle. In such a struggle the weakest goes first to the wall, but if the struggle is protracted all will go in their order until the field shows a single combatant only with no rival. The defeated, where they have any strength left, go into an inferior class to renew the same contest with less powerful antagonists, and the champion soon receives a challenge from other quarters which will put his powers to a severer test. This operation is constantly going on in the industrial world, and the law of the survival of the fittest seems to exercise everywhere its pitiless sway.[98]

Carter urged the Court to countenance economic cooperation that was designed not to inflate prices artificially, but "to *maintain reasonable prices*, and thus to prevent *the unnecessary and mischievous destruction of invested capital* by securing a living chance to the weaker parties to a deadly competition (and there must always be weaker parties in every competition)."[99]

As discussed earlier, Carter and other mugwumps viewed the market as a cooperative and moral realm, an attitude they inherited from antebellum moral philosophers such as Francis Wayland.[100] The Gilded Age liberal reformers' belief that unimpeded economic activity tended to produce just and harmonious results—a belief they clung to as long as possible—was premised on the assumption that market actors embraced an ethic of self-restraint and fair dealing, rather than one of rapacious competitive individualism. The mugwumps' political economy grew out of an idealized image of the America of their youth—a nation in which small producers and gentleman merchants made face-to-face exchanges in accordance with community moral standards. In this nostalgic vision, customary morality and the natural laws of economics worked together to create a stable, prosperous, and fair society, and there was little need for coordinated regulation, either public or private.

As Carter's antitrust briefs demonstrate, however, by the end of the nineteenth century, the gentry elite were increasingly dubious that an unimpeded market would promote justice and harmony in an industrial economy characterized by voracious plutocrats and swarming urban masses. In these briefs, Carter stressed man's inherent selfishness, which he described as worse than that of animals. "The brute cares only for the wants of his body, and when these are satisfied he lies down contended. . . . But the desires of man have no such limitations. However much he may acquire, he is still greedy for more, and is never absolutely satisfied."[101] Carter chose a telling example to illustrate the decline of market ethics and the consequent need for regulation.

> Take the case of the hack service at the railway stations in an ill-conditioned city. It happens, in the absence of regulation, that great opportunities are offered for exacting excessive charges from passengers wishing that service, especially strangers. A crowd of rough and disreputable fellows with wretched conveyances, avail themselves of it, and the respectable drivers, who would prefer greatly to conduct their business with decency, are compelled to enter into competition with them, or abandon their business. Passengers, upon their arrival, are set upon by an ill-mannered crowd, outbidding each other in their pretences as to charges and conveniences, and such as take a conveyance find themselves, when set down, in dispute with half-ruffians as to the charge agreed upon. The consequence is that although many really wish the facility, few make use of it, except in case of sheer necessity, and the thought of every passenger is how he, or she, may best escape the rude annoyance sure to be met with on reaching the station. The business is effectually ruined. Where a dozen decent men might be employed usefully to themselves and others, a half dozen ruffians are engaged in plunder.
>
> A proper municipal ordinance is passed and enforced under which the charges are fixed at a reasonable rate, and a passenger wishing the service is quietly shown to a decent vehicle. This of course is a *restraint*, and a restraint upon competition, but no one would think of it as a restraint upon *trade*. On the contrary it *creates* trade, and is indeed the necessary condition under which anything properly called trade in that branch of industry can exist.[102]

In *Trans-Missouri* and *Joint Traffic*, Carter thus emphasized the need for "restraints" (a word he used repeatedly) that would "set bounds upon this pursuit of material power and wealth and check its destructive tendencies while still preserving its beneficial effects."[103] He remarked that such restraints were most essential "in the industrial pursuits of life . . . [where] the mercenary and individual desires and ambitions are most earnest and active, and where ungoverned action is likely to prove most injurious."[104] Self-restraint deriving from "tacitly recognized customs" was no longer sufficient under modern conditions.[105] In late nineteenth-century America, custom had to be supplemented by either government mandates or "voluntary organizations . . . which frame rules for the conduct of their members."[106] Carter contended that these two forms of restraint, public and private regulation, "are essentially of the same character, and have the same objects in view; in other words, they are *modes of government*."[107]

In short, although Carter's antitrust briefs were directed against aggressive federal antitrust regulation, they were not antiregulatory in spirit. On the contrary, Carter maintained that "most of the industries and interests of life when they assume great magnitude need *regulation*, which must be provided either by law or private effort, or by both."[108] He portrayed the development of cooperative restraints as an entirely natural societal response to "pitiless and destructive competition."[109]

> Those who look with disfavor upon such checks upon competition, generally base their views upon the notion that they are restraints upon the *natural* course of trade, and that it is necessary, or, at least, highly desirable, that what is called the *order of nature* should not be interfered with. What they understand by the *order of nature* is not very clear, but a just definition certainly would be that order which would follow, if men were left free to act as they chose, subject of course to the rules of morality, without interference by positive law. But the making of agreements for the conduct of business is as much in the order of nature as anything else. Wherever men encounter a difficulty or mischief which can be done away with only by mutual agreement, can anything be more natural than that they should make agreements for such purposes?[110]

Although Carter did not here use the term "custom," he was, in essence, asserting that the very act of cooperating to restrain cutthroat competition was itself a societal custom that the law must reflect. For obvious reasons, he did not suggest to the Supreme Court in *Trans-Missouri* or *Joint Traffic* that his clients would continue their associative activities regardless of how the Court interpreted the Sherman Act. Several years later, however, in *Law: Its Origin, Growth, and Function*, he discussed the aftermath of his defeat in these railroad antitrust cases to demonstrate the futility of law inconsistent with custom.

> What effect has the decision had upon the conduct of the presidents, directors, and managers of the railroad companies? None whatever. They have indeed abrogated their formal written agreements, but they still confer and fix uniform rates by concert—that is, they are in the daily practice of forming the combinations and conspiracies which the [Sherman Act] condemns! And no attempt is made to bring any one of the criminals to justice! The artillery of the Attorney-General's office is as silent as if every gun were spiked. It was easy for the Government to pretend to execute the law, but when it found out what executing the law really involved it recoiled. And both the railroad officers who made, and make, themselves criminal, and the Government that fails to punish them, are right. Both yield to a necessity which is absolutely imperious. What creates the wrong is the statute; that is, with the interpretation the Supreme Court has placed upon it.
>
> This illustration gives a clear notion of the anomalous conditions thrust upon society when the written law commands one thing and the universal custom another.[111]

Throughout his antitrust briefs, Carter remained true to his jurisprudence by insisting that voluntary regulation was generally preferable to government regulation, or at least was a necessary supplement to it. He maintained that "complete regulation by law is neither possible nor desirable; . . . the necessary regulation of great industries conducted by private individuals is in most respects better worked out by private agencies."[112] Nevertheless, by presenting public and private regulation as alternative modes of legitimate restraint on excessive competition, Carter acknowledged a wide scope for the former as well as the latter. He thought that municipal regulations restricting hack services were valid and wise,[113] and by the same token, he believed that the federal Interstate Commerce Act was "admirable in its main purposes, and excellent in many of its provisions."[114] While consistently rejecting populist approaches such as government ownership of the railroads, Carter insisted that even socialism was preferable to a system in which individuals had no choice but to engage in a vicious struggle with each other until there was only one survivor.[115]

CONCLUSION

Carter's arguments in *Trans-Missouri* and *Joint Traffic*, premised on the assertion that rate wars destructive to railroads inevitably arose in the absence of regulation, occurred shortly before and shortly after his appearance in *Smyth*, in which he proclaimed that railroad rates were always fair to shippers in a freely competitive system. He thus risked appearing inconsistent with regard to the beneficence of the free market. The overall thesis of his arguments in these three cases was that railroads needed protection from market failures, but shippers did not. In other words, in a free market, railroad rates could never be too high, but they could be too low.

In the antitrust briefs, Carter did not, despite his lengthy discussions of ruinous competition, altogether deny that the free market tended to produce fair and harmonious results. Instead, he selectively espoused precisely this thesis. He used classical economic reasoning to assure the Court that the railroads' cooperative activities would not result in rates that were unfairly high for shippers. In *Trans-Missouri*, for example, he asserted, in language similar to his argument in *Smyth*:

> We find that the operation of [competition] in all other cases has the effect of reducing prices to the point of equilibrium. Why should it not have the same effect here? There are scarcely any of the great industries of the country which are not, to a greater or less degree, united together by agreements to maintain prices; but we do not find that thereby prices of commodities are increased to an unreasonable point. They cannot be; for if they were, new capital would flow into them from other pursuits and increase the supply of the commodities and necessarily reduce the price. This law is absolutely inexorable and it is not within the power of man to control it.[116]

Carter's embrace of the classical law of supply and demand was conveniently partial, however. He contended that a railroad combination would not charge excessive rates because such a tactic would dry up the demand for shipping services, but he dismissed the possibility that abnormally low rates would increase the demand for shipping services and that prices would consequently rise toward a sustainable equilibrium. In other words, Carter treated the demand for shipping services as extremely elastic in response to high prices, but as almost entirely inelastic in response to low prices.[117] On the supply side of the equation, Carter emphasized that certain peculiarities of the railroad business artificially inflated the supply of shipping services and forced rates down, but he was silent about other characteristics of the industry that created barriers to entry for competitors, thus creating upward pressure on rates.[118]

The distinctions drawn by Carter were not necessarily unfounded; there might have been a legitimate basis for distinguishing between the effect of market forces on railroads and shippers. But, in any event, the point of this essay has not been to condemn Carter for being inconsistent; he was, after all, a lawyer with a duty to his clients. Rather, I have sought to examine how Carter, in court, earnestly voiced his personal (and typically mugwump) philosophy regardless of the identity of his client and the nature of that client's cause. He was able to do so because his belief system comprised opposing, but sincerely held, tendencies. His political economy emphasized both classical free-market concepts and limits on those concepts necessitated by late nineteenth-century changes in American society. As a scholar, Carter struggled to reconcile these conflicting tendencies.[119] As a lawyer, by contrast, his goal was not to make his philosophy coherent, but rather to achieve victory in court. He thus accentuated those aspects of his conflicted worldview that happened to advance the interests of the client at hand. Each of his briefs represented an accurate, though partial and simplified, picture of the workings of his mind.

NOTES

1. 157 U.S. 429 (1895). Carter actually argued on behalf of the Continental Trust Company, the appellee in the closely connected case of *Hyde v. Continental Trust Co.*, 157 U.S. 654 (1895). The Supreme Court heard *Hyde* simultaneously with *Pollock* and decided them on identical grounds, but it reported the two cases separately. The cases were formally consolidated on rehearing. *Pollock v. Farmer's Loan and Trust Co.* (rehearing); *Hyde v. Continental Trust Co.* (rehearing), 158 U.S. 601 (1895). The matter as a whole is familiarly known as *Pollock*, and for the sake of simplicity, I refer to the entire matter under that name. Carter did not participate in the rehearing phase, for reasons discussed in Lewis A. Grossman, "The Ideal and the Actual of James Coolidge Carter: Morality and Law in the Gilded Age" (PhD diss., Yale University, 2005), 211–17. For an analysis of Carter's argument in this case, see 251–61.

2. *Chae Chan Ping v. United States*, 130 U.S. 581 (1889).

3. The self-incrimination cases were *Counselman v. Hitchcock,* 142 U.S. 547 (1892), and *Brown v. Walker,* 161 U.S. 591 (1896). The case concerning foreign judgments was *Hilton v. Guyot,* 159 U.S. 113 (1895). For a discussion of Carter's argument in *Hilton,* see Grossman, "The Ideal and the Actual," 224–30.

4. *United States v. Trans-Missouri Freight Association,* 166 U.S. 290 (1897); *United States v. Joint Traffic Association,* 171 U.S. 505 (1898); *Smyth v. Ames,* 169 U.S. 466 (1898). For a description of Carter's entire career as a trial and appellate lawyer, see Grossman, "The Ideal and the Actual," 184–223.

5. See Lewis A. Grossman, "James Coolidge Carter and Mugwump Jurisprudence," *Law and History Review* 20 (2002): 577–629.

6. Robert W. Gordon, "Legal Thought and Legal Practice in the Age of American Enterprise, 1870–1920," in *Professions and Professional Ideologies in America,* ed. Gerald L. Gerson (Chapel Hill: University of North Carolina Press, 1983), 110.

7. For an extended analysis of the contrast between Carter's jurisprudence and classical legal thought, see Lewis A. Grossman, "Langdell Upside-Down: The Anticlassical Jurisprudence of Anticodification," *Yale Journal of Law & the Humanities* 19 (2007): 149–219.

8. James Coolidge Carter, *Hints to Young Lawyers: Address to the Graduating Class of the Law School of the Columbian University at Commencement* (Washington, D.C.: Columbian University Press, 1894): 12.

9. Joseph H. Choate, "Memorial of James Coolidge Carter," in *Association of the Bar of the City of New York: Annual Reports* (1906), 126.

10. Carter, *Hints to Young Lawyers,* 12–13 (emphasis added).

11. Gerald W. McFarland, *Mugwumps, Morals, and Politics, 1824–1920* (Amherst: University of Massachusetts Press, 1975), 11; John G. Sproat, *"The Best Men": Liberal Reformers in the Gilded Age* (New York: Oxford University Press, 1968), 126; John M. Dobson, *Politics in the Gilded Age: A New Perspective on Reform* (New York: Praeger, 1972), 111; Grossman "Mugwump Jurisprudence," 581–84.

12. Tucker identifies these five issues as the core issues of genteel liberal reform. David W. Tucker, *Mugwumps: Public Moralists of the Gilded Age* (Columbia: University of Missouri Press, 1998), viii. Hoogenboom remarks, "These reformers . . . started their careers as free soilers and finished them as anti-imperialists." Ari Hoogenboom, *Outlawing the Spoils: A History of the Civil Service Reform Movement, 1865–1883* (Urbana: University of Illinois Press, 1961), x. Carter embraced all five causes. Grossman, "Mugwump Jurisprudence," 584.

13. Sproat, *"The Best Men,"* 146. On mugwumps and laissez-faire, see also 142–68, 206–8; Richard Hofstadter, *Age of Reform: From Bryan to F.D.R.* (New York: Knopf, 1955), 142; Tucker, *Mugwumps,* 59, 62, 83–84; Grossman, "Mugwump Jurisprudence," 619–24.

14. Tucker, *Mugwumps,* 84.

15. On increasing mugwump support for active government after 1890, see McFarland, *Mugwumps, Morals, and Politics,* 107–23.

16. Grossman, "Mugwump Jurisprudence," 602–4.

17. Tucker, *Mugwumps,* 24. On mugwump market ethics, see Tucker, *Mugwumps,* 4; Richard J. Ellis, *American Political Cultures* (New York: Oxford University Press, 1993), 111; Hoogenboom, *Outlawing the Spoils,* 99.

18. See Grossman, "Mugwump Jurisprudence."

19. Matthias Reimann, "The Historical School against Codification: Savigny, Carter, and the

Defeat of the New York Civil Code," *American Journal of Comparative Law* 37 (1989): 116. For similar comments on Carter, see Roscoe Pound, "The Scope and Purpose of Sociological Jurisprudence," *Harvard Law Review* 24 (1911): 601; Roscoe Pound, "Common Law and Legislation," *Harvard Law Review* 23 (1908): 382 n. 3, 388 n. 1, 396 n. 2, 404 n. 6; Roscoe Pound, review of *Law: Its Origin Growth and Function,* by James C. Carter, *Political Science Quarterly* 24 (1909): 318–19; Benjamin R. Twiss, *Lawyers and the Constitution: How Laissez Faire Came to the Supreme Court* (New York: Russell & Russell, 1962), 179; Sidney Fine, *Laissez Faire and the General-Welfare State* (Ann Arbor: University of Michigan Press, 1969), 164; Martin J. Horwitz, *The Transformation of American Law, 1870–1960: The Crisis of Legal Orthodoxy* (New York: Oxford University Press, 1992), 119. Perhaps the only scholar to recognize that Carter should not be neatly pigeonholed as a pro-business conservative is Robert Gordon, who has written, "A leading Mugwump in the '80s, Carter turned into a leading, though relatively conservative, Progressive in the '90s." Robert W. Gordon, "The Ideal and the Actual in the Law: Fantasies and Practices of New York City Lawyers, 1870–1910," in *The New High Priests: Lawyers in Post–Civil War America,* ed. Gerard W. Gawalt (Westport, Conn.: Greenwood Press, 1984), 51–52.

20. Grossman, "Mugwump Jurisprudence," 586–87.

21. Ibid., 619–26.

22. James C. Carter, *Law: Its Origin, Growth, and Function* (New York: G. P. Putnam's Sons, 1907), 126–27.

23. Ibid., 135.

24. Ibid., 336.

25. William M. Wiecek, *Liberty under Law: The Supreme Court in American Life* (Baltimore, Md.: Johns Hopkins University Press, 1988), 119.

26. Benjamin R. Twiss, for one, specifically mentions Carter's participation in the case. Twiss, *Lawyers and the Constitution,* 166.

27. *Smyth v. Ames,* 169 U.S. 466, 470 (1898). The Nebraska Constitution declared railways to be "public highways . . . free to all persons for the transportation of their persons and property thereon." It also provided that "the legislature may from time to time pass laws establishing reasonable maximum rates of charges for the transportation of passengers and freight on the different railroads in this state." Id., at 471–42.

28. Id. at 473.

29. *Munn v. Illinois* upheld the state regulation of grain elevator rates. Chief Justice Waite explicitly rejected the argument that the reasonableness of the rates was a judicial question, stating, "For protection against abuses by legislatures the people must resort to the polls, not to the courts." *Munn v. Illinois,* 94 U.S. 113, 126, 134 (1877).

30. 134 U.S. 418, 458 (1890). The Court ruled similarly in *Reagan v. Farmer's Loan & Trust Co.,* 154 U.S. 362 (1894). Justice Bradley, along with two other justices, dissented from the decision in *Chicago, Milwaukee and St. Paul Railway Co.,* because the majority "practically overrules *Munn.*" 134 U.S. at 461 (Bradley, J., dissenting).

31. *Smyth,* 169 U.S. at 486–94 (Bryan argument).

32. Ibid., 546–47.

33. Wiecek, *Liberty under Law,* 135. The Supreme Court effectively overruled *Smyth* in 1942, when it asserted, "We think this is an appropriate occasion to lay the ghost of [*Smyth*], which has haunted utility regulation since 1898." *Federal Power Commission v. Natural Gas Pipeline Co.,* 315 U.S. 575, 602 (1942).

34. Carter's co-counsel, J. M. Woolworth, hinted at the formula. He did not dwell on it, however, because he asserted that Nebraska's statutory rates would not permit the railroad appellees to recover even their costs of doing business, let alone provide them a fair return on their investment. See *Smyth*, 169 U.S. at 498–99.

35. James Coolidge Carter, brief for appellees, *Hastings v. Ames* (Supreme Court of the United States, 1895), 39. After Carter wrote the brief, Nebraska attorney general Hastings was succeeded in his office by Constantine Smyth, who became the defendant and appellant. The name of the case thus became *Smyth v. Ames*.

36. Ibid., 40–41.

37. Ibid., 42–43.

38. James May, "Antitrust in the Formative Era: Political and Economic Theory in Constitutional and Antitrust Analysis, 1880–1918," *Ohio State Law Journal* 50 (1989): 271–72.

39. Carter, brief for appellees, *Hastings*, 16–17.

40. Ibid., 23. Carter also referred to the competition posed by other forms of carriage (48). Interestingly, Carter went further than many classical economists by arguing that railroad prices were bound to be reasonable even in the absence of competition. "A plain regard for self interest will and does prevent [excessive charges before competitors enter the field]. Moderate charges yield more profit by the greatly increased business they draw. . . . A sound policy, perfectly well known to railroad managers, advises them that it is best to tempt and draw out a large traffic by low prices than to try to make a large profit on a small business" (17).

41. Ibid., 44.

42. Ibid., 45.

43. Ibid., 88.

44. Ibid., 46.

45. Ibid., 71.

46. Ibid., 45.

47. See Grossman, "Mugwump Jurisprudence," 606–9.

48. Carter, brief for appellees, *Hastings*, 48.

49. Ibid., 44.

50. Ibid., 88–89.

51. For a discussion of the challenges that late nineteenth-century economic developments presented for classical economic theorists, see May, "Antitrust in the Formative Era," 281–83.

52. Grossman, "Mugwump Jurisprudence," 620–24.

53. Carter, brief for appellees, *Hastings*, 69. For other references to boot and shoe manufacturers, see ibid., 67, 70. Carter's opponent in *Smyth*, William Jennings Bryan, took on the task of highlighting the unique features of the railroad industry that arguably made classical economic theory inapplicable to it. As paraphrased in the report of *Smyth v. Ames*, 169 U.S. 466, 493–94 (1898), Bryan contended:

A railroad is to a certain extent a monopoly; it is only because it is a monopoly that it can collect unreasonable rates. Competition can only act within certain limits. If a railroad is built between two points, no other road can be built between those points . . . unless the first road is realizing an income practically double a reasonable return upon the value of the road, because a new road would require an investment equal to the value of the first road, and until transportation rates on business done would pay running expenses and a reasonable profit on both investments competition would be prohibited. When two roads are built they must necessarily collect more in tolls than one road would be justified in collecting. . . . The very existence of the road prevents the building of a new road capitalized at present cost, and, even if a new road should be built, commerce would be compelled to bear a higher burden than it would if this road were limited to a scale of charges which produce a reasonable return on its actual value.

54. *Sherman Antitrust Act*, ch. 647, 26 Stat. 209 (1890).

55. *Trans-Missouri Freight Association*, 166 U.S. 290 (1897); *Joint Traffic Association*, 171 U.S. 505 (1898). Before the Supreme Court heard these cases, it addressed the Sherman Antitrust Act in *United States v. E. C. Knight Co.*, 156 U.S. 1 (1895), in which it declared that the act did not reach manufacturing monopolies (in this instance, the Sugar Trust), because manufacturing was a local activity that fell outside Congress's constitutional power to regulate interstate commerce. By contrast, the regulated activities of the railroads at issue in *Trans-Missouri* and *Joint Traffic* clearly fell within Congress's interstate commerce power.

56. *Interstate Commerce Act of 1887*, ch. 104, 24 Stat. 379 (1887).

57. The literature on late nineteenth-century railroad economics and regulation is voluminous. Prominent examples include Gabriel Kolko, *Railroads and Regulation* (New York: W. W. Norton, 1970); Herbert Hovenkamp, *Enterprise and American Law, 1836–1937* (Cambridge, Mass.: Harvard University Press, 1991); and James W. Ely Jr., *Railroads and American Law* (Lawrence: University Press of Kansas, 2001).

58. The Trans-Missouri Freight Association agreement capped fines at one hundred dollars, a level so absurdly low that the association cannot have intended to use the fines as a deterrent. See *Trans-Missouri*, 166 U.S. at 296. The Joint Traffic Association, by contrast, provided that a member could be required to forfeit the receipts from any transaction that violated the agreement. See *Joint Traffic*, 171 U.S. at 508.

59. Carter's co-counsel were John F. Dillon and Edward J. Phelps.

60. James Coolidge Carter, brief for appellees, *United States v. Trans-Missouri Freight Association* (Supreme Court of the United States, 1897), 62.

61. Ibid., 64.

62. Carter, *Origin, Growth, and Function*, 308.

63. Ibid., 65.

64. *Trans-Missouri*, 166 U.S. at 327–42

65. Although the Trans-Missouri and Joint Traffic cooperative agreements were substantially identical, Joint Traffic also persuaded the Court to consider the significance of some of the differences in the details of the agreements *Joint Traffic*, 171 U.S. at 562–65. Finally, the *Joint Traffic* Court also considered constitutional arguments that Trans-Missouri had not advanced. Id. at 565–73.

66. James Coolidge Carter and Lewis Cass Ledyard, brief for appellee, *United States v. Joint Traffic Association* (Supreme Court of the United States, 1898), 41. Although Carter's much younger partner, Lewis Cass Ledyard (1852–1932), co-signed the brief, Carter was clearly the principal author of it. Indeed, at least once, the brief referred, in the singular, to the personal views of "the writer of this brief" (48).

67. Ibid., 41–42.

68. *Joint Traffic*, 171 U.S. at 575.

69. 221 U.S. 1 (1911).

70. For a general discussion of the rise of public concern about industrial concentration, see Horwitz, *Transformation II*, 80–85.

71. Sproat, *"The Best Men,"* 165.
72. Ibid., 158–59.
73. McFarland, *Mugwumps, Morals and Politics,* 154.
74. Sproat, *"The Best Men,"* 159, 162.
75. Ibid., 162–64. Even socialist-leaning thinkers to the left of the mugwumps acknowledged the inevitability of railroad concentration. Henry Carter Adams, for example, viewed railroads as unavoidably monopolistic because of their increasing returns to scale. He favored government regulation of the industry, however. Indeed, he thought the ineluctable concentration of the railroads, which immunized them from the effects of competition, was in and of itself the primary reason why the government should regulate them. See Horwitz, *Transformation II,* 81–82.
76. Congress's only previous large-scale effort at economic regulation was its enactment of the Interstate Commerce Act in 1887.
77. Morton J. Horwitz, "Progressive Legal Historiography," *Oregon Law Review* 63 (1984): 682–83.
78. Ibid.; Horwitz, *Transformation II,* 80–85.
79. Supreme Court justice Rufus Peckham, who ruled against Carter's clients in both *Trans-Missouri* and *Joint Traffic,* was an example of an "old conservative." Louis Brandeis, particularly in his guise as informal advisor to President Wilson, epitomized the "new Progressives."
80. Many of the titans of industry were, of course, "new conservatives" who resisted almost all government regulation of business and were particularly opposed to "trust busting." See Horwitz, *Transformation II,* 83. Another apparent "new conservative" was Justice Edward G. White, who dissented in favor of Carter's clients in *Trans-Missouri* and *Joint Traffic* and who later, as chief justice, wrote the majority opinion in *Standard Oil v. United States,* applying the "rule of reason" standard to the Sherman Act. The prototypical "new Progressive" was President Theodore Roosevelt. His distinction between "good trusts" and "bad trusts" almost exactly paralleled the Court's "rule of reason." On this basis, in a 1984 article, Horwitz termed Roosevelt a "new conservative." Horwitz, "Progressive Legal Historiography," 682–83. In later lectures at Harvard Law School, however, Horwitz properly distinguished "new Progressives" like Roosevelt from the "new conservatives," based on the former group's much greater enthusiasm for government regulation in general, if not for antitrust regulation in particular. Lewis A. Grossman, personal notes from Professor Horwitz's American Legal History course at Harvard Law School, winter term, 1990.
81. Carter, *Origin, Growth, and Function,* 336.
82. Carter and Ledyard, brief for appellee, *Joint Traffic,* 48.
83. Ibid., 19–20.
84. Carter and Ledyard, brief for appellee, *Joint Traffic,* 146–47. Carter defended, through a trial and two appeals, the North Sugar Refining Company against New York's effort to revoke its charter because of its participation in the notorious price-fixing Sugar Trust. *People v. North River Sugar Refining Co.,* 3 N.Y.S. 401 (N.Y. Cir. Ct. 1889); *People v. North River Sugar Refining Co.,* 7 N.Y.S. 406 (N.Y. Gen. Term 1889); *People v. North River Sugar Refining Co.,* 24 N.E. 834 (N.Y. 1890). I was unable to find any of Carter's briefs or transcripts of any of his oral arguments in this matter. For a discussion of New York State's legal efforts against the Sugar Trust, see May, "Antitrust in the Formative Era," 325–27.
85. 44 N.E. 1077, 1081 (Mass. 1896) (Holmes, J., dissenting).

86. Carter and Ledyard, brief for appellee, *Joint Traffic*, 131–32. Despite Carter's confident assumption that antitrust laws did not restrict labor unions, the Supreme Court would subsequently uphold the use of the Sherman Act for precisely this purpose. See *Loewe v. Lawlor*, 208 U.S. 274 (1908).

87. Carter's recognition of the country's unstoppable evolution toward "a highly developed industrial life" led him to "doubt the soundness of the maxim that the best government is that which governs least." Carter, *Origin, Growth, and Function*, 335.

88. Carter and Ledyard, brief for appellee, *Joint Traffic*, 43.

89. Carter, brief for appellees, *Trans-Missouri*, 79.

90. Ibid., 75.

91. Carter and Ledyard, brief for appellee, *Joint Traffic*, 60–61.

92. Carter, brief for appellees, *Trans-Missouri*, 74–75; Carter and Ledyard, brief for appellee, *Joint Traffic*, 60.

93. Carter, brief for appellees, *Trans-Missouri*, 101.

94. See May, "Antitrust in the Formative Era," 283–84.

95. See ibid. and sources cited therein.

96. Carter, brief for appellees, *Trans-Missouri*, 72.

97. Ibid., 75–76.

98. Carter and Ledyard, brief for appellee, *Joint Traffic*, 47.

99. Carter, brief for appellees, *Trans-Missouri*, 76–77.

100. Grossman, "Mugwump Jurisprudence," 594–95.

101. Carter and Ledyard, brief for appellee, *Joint Traffic*, 50.

102. Ibid., 51–52.

103. Ibid., 50.

104. Ibid., 51.

105. Ibid., 51.

106. Ibid., 51.

107. Ibid., 51.

108. Ibid., 105.

109. Carter, brief for appellees, *Trans-Missouri*, 102.

110. Carter and Ledyard, brief for appellee, *Joint Traffic*, 70. For a discussion of how late nineteenth-century opponents of a strict interpretation of the Sherman Act based their arguments on traditional notions of freedom of contract and private economic ordering, see May, "Antitrust in the Formative Era," 285, 304–5.

111. Carter, *Origin, Growth, and Function*, 212.

112. Carter and Ledyard, brief for appellee, *Joint Traffic*, 131.

113. Ibid., 52. He also remarked, however, that "a voluntary union of the honest and respectable drivers . . . might be quite as effective as the ordinance, and even more so" (52–53).

114. Ibid., 86.

115. Ibid., 69. With regard to the notion of government ownership, Carter remarked, "This . . . was not to be thought of. Besides other insuperable obstacles, no ownership, except that of *all* railways by the United States, would be effective; and the United States had no power to acquire the ownership" (98). In *Smyth v. Ames*, Carter contended that if the state owned the railroads and established the rates, "the result would be universal corruption, high rates, and an enormous deficit to be paid by taxation." Carter, brief for appellees, *Hastings*, 31.

116. Carter, brief for appellees, *Trans-Missouri,* 115–16.

117. In explaining why the laws of supply and demand would not correct abnormally low rates, Carter contended that the railroads could not "by a small diminution of price, enlarge the demand, at least, immediately. The world is not open to them. . . . There is a certain amount of business to be done by all, and the struggle of each is to get as much of that as possible." Carter and Ledyard, brief for appellee, *Joint Traffic,* 62. But in the same brief, in explaining why railroad rates could not go too high, he stated, "The very existence of a large part, perhaps the largest part, of railroad traffic depends upon the price expected for it. It would immediately disappear if the price were raised" (123).

118. Throughout his *Smyth* and *Trans-Missouri* briefs, Carter intimated that establishing a competing railroad was akin to establishing a competing candy store. But the very same necessity of enormous initial capital investment that, Carter argued, compelled railroads to accept freight at perilously low rates could also discourage new railroads from entering the field in the first place. William Jennings Bryan referred to the latter phenomenon in his argument in favor of rate regulation in *Smyth v. Ames*. See note 53 above.

119. Grossman, "Mugwump Jurisprudence," 580–81, 619–26.

8

On Limited Liability: A Speculative Essay on Evolution and Justification

GREGORY MARK

LIMITED LIABILITY IS THE LEGAL DOCTRINE THAT THE OWNERS OF A BUSIness corporation's equity are not liable for the debts of the corporation beyond what they have paid for their shares. This doctrine is now so taken for granted that a separate, special, and extraordinary doctrine, called piercing the corporate veil, has developed to create an exception to limited liability and to render shareholders liable for corporate debts. The exception requires that those who own the corporation ignore its independent legal existence and, usually, do something nefarious on top of that. Successful invocation of the piercing doctrine is rare. Indeed, so episodic is its use by courts that conservative commentators have termed it "freakish."[1] Both as a matter of economic culture and law, it is little questioned, save on occasion by a legal academic. Why it is so accepted and how that acceptance arose is a matter of some curiosity. Limited liability is far from the norm for owners in other circumstances, even for owners of other business entities. At common law, partners are liable for one another's debts accumulated during the activities of the partnership. Only statutory action generally changes the nature of partnership liability. The advent of limited partnerships, the limited liability company, and other such intermediary business entities where limited liability is a statutory matter ought to alert us to the continuing unusual status of limited liability.

That limited liability is an unusual matter should be apparent to any lawyer, at least any lawyer who can reach into the recesses of her mind and remember her basic corporation law class. The theoretical problems posed by limited liability become evident as soon as the student ponders the simple question posed by contrasting the liability of owners for differing types of business entities. How is it that a partnership's partner-owner is fully liable for the judgments against his partnership while a corporation's share owner is liable only for the value she paid for her shares? Why provide a protection against liability that shifts costs from owner to victim? Why is there no difference for debts arising from tort as opposed to contract, where at least one might make the plausible claim that the counterparty has, or at least has access to, knowledge that would allow it to contract around limited liability?

In everyday life, of course, the theoretical conundrums may matter very little. The theory that matters most to a wronged party is the theory of the deep pocket. As an ordinary matter if, for example, one is to be a victim of a tortfeasor, better that the one harming be the agent of a wealthy entity than a marginal sole proprietor. Not only, of course, is the entity likely to have more money, or at least a bigger insurance policy, but it is impersonal and therefore less likely to arouse jury sympathy. Thus, who, if the choice actually arose, would not, sitting behind the veil of ignorance, prefer to be the victim of a corporate entity than not? The other practical theory, the theory of the scattered and impersonal owner, has a similar practical impact. Suppose, for example, that a relatively large public corporation were held liable for a judgment greater than its capacity to satisfy. How would one proceed against its owners as a practical matter? Would the owners at the time of the violation be those liable? At the time of judgment? Would liability be joint and several or pro rata? Would one simply pursue under joint and several liability only a subset of all owners, say the impersonal owners of a plurality of the equity—for example, mutual funds and pension funds—rather than pursue the hard (and inefficient) to-track-down individual owners? Better a doctrine that moots such questions.

Neither of these practical theories, however, tells us much about why limited liability exists in the first place. They may, however, suggest why, in an era of expanding constructs of liability more generally, corporate limited liability is not much of a practical issue to contracting counterparties or litigants. Simply put, the possibility of pursuing the ultimate owner for a corporate liability simply may hold little appeal when contrasted with other forms of protection.

Nonetheless, limited liability is foundational to corporate law. Why does it exist? More to the point, why does it continue to exist? Does it fulfill some psychological need to conceive of the entity as responsible for itself? Is it merely vestigial?

The "why" question, however, yields two classes of answers. The first class is one that observers might be tempted to label theoretical. That label would be analytically unsound, because it suggests that questions of theory play no role in the other class of answers. Better to call the first class ahistorical, since the first class of answers has a universal sound to them. Since the answers tend to be framed in terms that would appear to apply across temporal and cultural circumstance, they also carry an implicit normative claim. To wit, if a phenomenon exists independent of time and culture, it must be axiomatic, and deviation from the axiom will lead to difficulties. Thus, explanations of this type have a justificatory quality to them. The second class of answers might be helpfully termed evolutionary and historical. "Evolution," while a word with its own terminological difficulties, has the advantage of suggesting adaptation to circumstance, as well as change over time. In this sense, the term evokes a scientistic understanding of change, calling to mind the "laws of history" so fashionable to those who sought to divine the rules of societal transformation. By contrast, while the term "historical" preserves an aspect of contingency and choice, it also connotes to many ears the narrative randomness in which history is just "one damned thing after another." An answer that invokes the meaning of both terms preserves the analytic utility of theory while preserving the narrative richness of a story in which many variables, leading among them the variables of human choice that partake of a humanistic understanding, play a role. In short, an explanation of how we got to our current state of affairs may be quite different from an explanation of the current state of affairs. What's more, the evolutionary exploration should explicate the full potential range of owner liability, from unlimited liability, through intermediate forms of liability beyond the purchase price of the shares, through liability limited to share value.

Explanations for the existence of limited liability in the United States have generally tended to sound in the former rather than the latter category, even if given the gloss of a discussion of law ranging into the nineteenth century. Roughly speaking, three explanations have been put forth. First, the explanation from necessity: Those who hold (or held, if one is speaking of the past) capital are reluctant to hand it over to another to engage in risky, albeit potentially profitable, enterprises without some limit on risk. That is, capital is risk averse. This explanation, the most traditional, holds that limited liability acts to attract reluctant capital that would not otherwise be forthcoming to risky enterprises by holding out the prospect of unlimited gain while setting a floor on losses. Since not every shareholder can or does play a managerial role, that function being delegated to directors (and ultimately hired managers), limited liability, along with the fiduciary responsibility of directors, works to ensure that those in whom capital is entrusted will act to maximize profit while leaving the investor immune beyond initial investment for managerial defalcation. (One interesting twist on whether limited liability actually acts to insulate the original shareholders from liability arises when one considers the possibility, mentioned in some of the prominent cases considered by every law student studying the matter, that the creditors of the forming corporation, notwithstanding limited liability, could demand a personal guarantee of one or more of the original shareholders. So far as I am aware, however, no one has ever sought out the evidence that this type of guarantee was typical of early business corporations.) Second, the argument from efficiency: Those who hold capital are dispersed and hold their capital in insufficiently large quantities to make monitoring of those who are entrusted with the capital either possible or efficient. That is, limited liability is efficient. This explanation, of more recent vintage, holds that limited liability reduces the transaction costs of monitoring by reducing the risk associated with failure to monitor and by facilitating the holding of a diversified portfolio. Monitoring will be performed by intermediary institutions with the right incentives, for example the financial press, or investors with stakes large enough to warrant the cost. In the end, it matters only that monitoring is done and that the market for a firm's equity is sufficiently liquid that the price of the equity accurately reflects the relative risks and rewards of the individual corporation and its management. Third, the argument from democracy: Those who hold capital seek wealth as a vehicle for fostering their own growth. That is, limited liability creates opportunity. This explanation, the least known of the three, brings together strands of evidence that go beyond the immediate wealth-creating questions of the other two theories and posits a public attitude linking wealth creation to other ends. Limited liability facilitates the aggregation of the capital of many individuals of modest means, creating the preconditions for opportunity and prosperity, thus independence and cooperative interdependence rather than hierarchical dependence.

An evolutionary understanding would employ explanatory tools, including the tools of the social sciences, economics among them, but would situate that understanding in the evolving context of the legal doctrine. Instead of just once asking, "What are the aims of limited liability?" anyone seeking an evolutionary understanding would ask that question over and over in time, seeking to explain change rather than stasis. So let me suggest that, as a speculative matter, we should reconsider the explanation for limited liability. We should ask what the aims of the doctrine might have been, whom it was designed to protect, and whom it in fact protected. We should ask what attributes of the corporation helped create the landscape in which legislatures and the courts came around to granting full limited liability. We should ask why limited liability aroused as little opposition as it did in the markets and among commentators, both legal and political. We can then discern whether its intended consequences actually occurred and, as important, what the doctrine's unintended consequences might have been. In so doing, we might learn of the reactions to those consequences, intended or not, entailed by the doctrine, and how they in turn acted to change the doctrine itself. That understanding is possible only by placing the doctrine inside the history of the corporation itself and alongside other doctrinal histories, especially those of tort and contract. This essay does not do those things. It merely suggests how. In so doing, however, I hope to demonstrate how impoverished our current view of limited liability is.

Roughly speaking, the legal history of the business corporation has three periods. The first of these, from roughly the founding of the country through the fourth decade of the nineteenth century, is the era of the legislatively chartered corporation. In this era the predominant mode for bringing a corporate body into existence was to obtain a charter from the state legislature. These charters tended to be limited grants, limiting both corporate activities and the capacity of the shareholders to alter the corporate body. From that period through, again very roughly, the beginning of the 1890s, the mode shifted to one of administrative incorporation, in which a department of (usually) the state's executive branch was empowered, sometimes exclusively, to grant corporate charters. In this period the charters became both more expansive, in the sense that the corporation was permitted a broader range of activities, and more permissive, in the sense that greater discretion was granted to the incorporating shareholders, their managers, and each of those group's successors, to shape the corporation. And, since roughly that period, the administrative charter has come to be virtually exclusive and enabling, in the sense that the charter facilitates, not regulates, the aims of the incorporating parties.

THE EARLY CORPORATION

For the first half century of the country's existence, corporations received their charters from state legislatures, and those charters specified the activities in which the corporation might engage and greatly restricted the corporation in other ways. Typically, for example, charters limited the capitalization of the entity and its life span and regulated the voting power of its owners, among other things. Charters were strictly construed by the courts. Very few powers or rights passed by implication, and notwithstanding the incremental and accretive nature of the common law, the courts were generally quite slow to expand the powers and rights of corporations by implication from those stated in the charter. The rights of share owners vis-à-vis the corporate entity and against those who dealt with the entity were among the rights contained in the corporate charter. Limited liability was not inherent in a charter nor in the rights of a share owner. Thus, the question for historians is not simply what the charters that spoke to the question of limited liability actually said, but what the rule was if the charter did not speak clearly to the question of shareholder liability.

The modern explanations of limited liability do little to explain either why the legislatures might grant limited liability or what understanding would inform the courts absent a clear legislative statement. While the early corporation and its attributes have been described on many occasions, few explanations of the status of limited liability have been proffered. Rather than seeking to apply modern explanations, however, any historical examination should hypothesize based on conditions at the time. One possibility is to draw inferences from attributes of contemporary corporate jurisprudence. First among those would be corporate personality. It would seem to follow that if a corporation existed as a person at law, then a legitimate inference would be a certain independence, indeed autonomy. An independent or autonomous person would be responsible for its own acts, or at least responsible for the acts its agents committed on its behalf. Under this approach, it would be within the authority of courts, faced with a corporation that could not satisfy a judgment against it, to refuse to look to the owners. Even a strictly construed charter would, under this approach, carry with it an implication of limited liability. Thus, courts might, even in a regime of strict construction, infer limited liability. Unfortunately, that inference depends on an anachronistic understanding of corporate personality, for corporate personality was itself an attribute said to be bestowed by the charter. The bounds of corporate personality were, as the courts said, a product of the powers and rights granted through the charter. This "artificial entity" understanding would long outlast even the strict construction of charters by the courts.

A personality conception as the basis for limited liability is not simply a straw man, but rather a speculative construct that compels historians to look at the very attributes that form the corporate personality in order to find the basis for the construction of limited liability. Chief among those attributes, one might well imagine, would have been the right to sue and be sued. Itself an aspect of corporate personality, the right seems to imply what artificial corporate personality more generally failed to imply—that if a corporation can be sued for wrongs it committed or that were committed in its name, then no other person could be so sued. This bit of speculation has an explanatory advantage over simply deriving limited liability from the personified entity itself. The inference is a tighter one, drawn not from a construct itself derived from the positive attributes granted the entity, but from one of the attributes itself. It would be a first-level derivation rather than a second, hence a more legitimate product of strict construction. The difficulty with the hypothesis is, however, a paucity of evidence. Limited liability was often a legislative act, and we lack the records that tell us much about what legislators were thinking as shareholder liability arose as an issue. What the courts did absent legislative authorization is an even more difficult question.

What is striking about the judicial record is how few suits even address the question of limited liability. Perhaps corporate personality in general or the specific inference from the right to be sued led lawyers and the public to assume a regime of corporate autonomy and limited shareholder liability. While possible, of course, such an explanation discounts both lawyerly imagination and the depth of public anti-corporate suspicion. Similarly, one could posit an even more unusual theory. Suppose that the proper analogy for collective economic endeavor was not an individual person, but a government. That is not such a far-fetched notion when one considers both the mercantilist history of the corporation—after all, the jurisprudential legitimation of the Bank of the United States was that it was an entity created to carry out the aims of the United States, and the conceit of state chartering was that the legislature granted charters to individuals to facilitate state aims. Furthermore, of course, state enterprise was itself common in this era. Under this understanding, the grant of the right to sue *and to be sued* carried a very important implication not usually associated with such a pedestrian right, the waiver of sovereign immunity. It is precisely that right that makes the entity private and not public.

If one remembers that the state itself was often a shareholder of the corporations it created, and that ownership of the corporation would revert to the state upon expiration of the charter, then the inference gains some plausibility, since the state would not be extending the waiver to the shareholders, of which it was one. The state would privatize the entity, but not itself as a shareholder; the private shareholders shared in the inference that liability would not extend beyond the corporate body unless the legislature expressly extended it. Of course, the waiver of sovereign immunity implicit in the corporate right to be sued need not have applied to the state as shareholder or residual owner. If it did not, then the state would have retained immunity while private shareholders would have become liable. Remember, however, that the traditional explanation of limited liability, indeed in some ways all current explanations, posits that the corporation was a vehicle to reassure private investors by limiting their potential losses and maximizing potential gains. Any explanation that left all shareholders winners but only private shareholders losers beyond investment contradicts those theses. If only the private shareholders were left liable for losses, but those shareholders had to share gains with the governmental shareholders, then their liability would be magnified, not reduced, and the incentives posited by every current explanation of limited liability turned on their heads.

These tortured games of legal logic, however, do little to explain what it might have been that those who committed their capital, the state included, would have feared from a regime of owner liability. Put aside for a moment the question of liability for the uncontrolled action of others. In a partnership the premise is that of owner control, hence liability. All owners can participate in control; therefore all are on notice that they have an owning and controlling party's liability for the acts of the entity. Shareholders, by definition, delegate authority. Of course, some partners were more powerful than others, and some shareholders, especially in the early years, participated in entity governance. The formal distinctions, however, as with the distinction between creditor and passive owner, mattered. What liability was there to fear?

No answer to that question would be complete without an antecedent understanding of what activities and markets corporations participated in and what legal regimes governed those activities and markets. Then, as now, corporations could be liable for their agreements and the harms they caused.

Agreements—contracts—are usually considered an undifferentiated mass for purposes of limited liability. Nonetheless, for purposes of considering which liabilities mattered the most, one distinction is important: that of the financial creditor and the trade creditor, including employees. As a matter of common law, the distinction means and meant next to nothing. As a matter of the politics of limited liability, the distinction could well matter a great deal, since the grant of limited liability was legislative in character. At various times and in various jurisdictions, the tension between passive capitalist and entrepreneurial capitalist defined political relations, even more so than the capital-labor division. Indeed, in some cases a political alliance existed between labor and entrepreneurs. In a world in which capital was scarce and distant, the desire to protect local entrepreneurs from distant capital might well lead to a regime of limited liability, even if it limited the desire of capital to invest as creditor. In a world in which most businesses, and thus most corporations, were creatures of their locality, local owners would prefer a regime that protected them from distant creditors, and their employees and customers might share in the desire to protect local businesses. In a jurisdiction, such as Pennsylvania, that contained geographically dispersed concentrations of both entrepreneurs and capital, the tension might also lead to both legislative and doctrinal swings as one group gained and then lost ascendance in the legislature and the judiciary. Trade creditors, on the other hand, especially employees, were more likely to be local, and their contractual claims more limited, thus less of a financial danger to owners, even if unsatisfied by the entity. Trade creditors and employees, of course, also had much more to gain from the continued existence of the entity than from attempting to recover an unpaid debt from a shareholder.

The businesses in existence for the first fifty years of the country's existence were also much less capable of inflicting harms that would cause liability sufficient to endanger the enterprise. Modern consumer liabilities, such as products liability, were unknown. Other than infrastructural and mining entities, the activities of business were also unlikely to cause extensive harms. Mines might collapse, canals overflow their banks, dams burst, and the like, but even those catastrophes had relatively limited capacity to damage in largely rural America. Limits on consequential damages went further in limiting potential entrepreneurial liability. Under such circumstances, the need for limited liability in tort was small.

Thus, demand for a regime of unlimited liability in America's early years was likely small. Large-scale judgments for the deliberate or inadvertent infliction of harm would have been exceedingly rare. Judgments on behalf of trade creditors would generally have been small and unlikely to require attempts to get at owners. Ownership was, in any case, generally a local matter in which those seeking corporate charters often were politically allied with those whose principal antagonists were passive capital. The juridical conception of the corporation was one that, if it did not mandate, at least hinted at a limit on shareholder liability. And the public aims of, and public participation in some, complicate any understanding of limited liability. Under such circumstances what is interesting is that much protection was afforded finance creditors at all, as charters often limited liability to a multiple of the value of the shares purchased. But, of course, the expectation of a limited liability—as opposed to unlimited liability—was created even where liability was limited to a multiple of the value of shares purchased. It was that understanding that became the norm.

THE COMING OF GENERAL INCORPORATION

The period in which incorporation became less an activity of state legislatures and more generally an administrative matter dates from the 1840s through the 1890s. While many states retained the legislative capacity to issue charters well beyond the last decade of the nineteenth century, in some jurisdictions state legislatures were barred from issuing charters by their state constitutions, and in many others the legislatures vested the capacity in a state administrative agency, even while maintaining the right to issue a charter. Certainly in the largest commercial and industrial jurisdictions the process became one of administrative routine by the end of the century. Again, the outlines of this story have been often told. For purposes of thinking about the evolution of limited liability, however, the transformation of chartering has been little explored.

What virtually every commentator agrees on, however, is that this period marks the complete privatization of the understanding of the business corporation. The sheer number of incorporations; the retreat of the state from enterprise, given the Jacksonian opposition to the national bank and the bankruptcy of many canal projects; the increasingly administrative and pro forma consideration of charters, meaning, among other things, that the state's consideration of what the grant meant declined precipitously; and the increasing breadth of corporate objects in the face of the first industrial revolution all contributed to a declining view that corporations existed for public rationales. Nor were many of the country's largest enterprises widely held. Apart from railroads, few of the largest businesses in the country were owned by a dispersed set of shareholders. Whatever vestigial remnants of the public conception of the corporation had existed in the formative years had largely disappeared, save one—the belief that corporations were a tool to facilitate enterprise and that enterprise was an important public good.

In this half century, no one really doubted that corporations were responsible for their own debts. In both politics and law the question became what protections were appropriate for those who were on the receiving end of corporate malfeasance should the corporation be unable to satisfy a judgment. In both the political and market spheres the owners of corporations sought protection. In politics, of course, implicit and explicit subsidies limited the ultimate liability of owners to creditors. An ideology of growth inhibited restraints on the behavior of the owners and managers of enterprises. Increasingly, especially where railroads and other forms of interstate enterprises were concerned, the alliance between entrepreneurs and local communities evaporated. As industrialism's promise revealed its concomitant dangers, new forms of potential liability also revealed themselves. In this era then, the question became what forms of protection for creditors could surmount the political and legal hurdles that a pro-entrepreneurial bias had embedded in American law, and whether limited liability would be among them.

Corporations could be held to damages in two spheres, contract and tort. Creditor protection became an important issue during the period leading to general incorporation. Rather than attacking limited liability, however, states resorted to a host of other protections to protect creditors. To the contrary, during this period limited liability in the modern sense became the norm. The expedient of leaving shareholders liable for a multiple of their contribution essentially disappeared. On the other hand, the problem of "watered stock," closely related to the question of limited liability, began to receive a great deal of attention. In the nineteenth century shares of stock had what was termed a par value. When each share's par value was multiplied by the number of shares issued and outstanding, the total became a kind of reserve held by the company for the benefit of creditors, should the company find itself in distress. The sum could not be invaded for purposes of paying dividends to common shares, for example. Alongside the law governing par value came a host of laws governing the circumstances under which dividends might be paid, usually requiring that dividends be paid only from current or cumulated profits, and often only after profits reached a certain level. The aim of all these regulations was to prevent equity—really equity's managerial agents, the directors—from declaring dividends so large that the company's capacity to pay its debts was compromised. These protective devices were statutory and have been termed the "trust fund doctrine." The courts, however, created a more capacious doctrine to cover managerial acts that acted as a fraud upon creditors: the doctrine of fraudulent conveyance. Briefly put, the doctrine made certain transfers revocable if they are made in detriment to creditors within a certain period before insolvency, for example, if a company borrowed a large sum of money and then immediately paid it out as a dividend and on the heels of the dividend became insolvent.

What is most interesting about the various acts creating these creditor protections is what we do not know about them. No systematic study of the statutory enactments has been done such that scholars could correlate the enactments with larger changes in the economic and political environment. The fifty years represented by the move to general incorporation are among the most economically dynamic in human history and the periodization is far too large to allow anything substantial to be said about triggering events or the back-and-forth that might have accompanied the preference for creditor over equity. What is clear, however, is that finance creditors, at least, did not rely on law alone. Moreover, finance creditors, in tandem with shareholders themselves, began to recognize a common threat to their interests: the defalcations of management. When businesses were local affairs and shareholders members of if not the family then the community, keeping track of one's investment was relatively easy. As markets for shares became national, shareholders faced the same issue as creditors, only with greater intensity—how to protect one's investment from managerial malfeasance, except that the protection for equity had more facets. Rather than ensuring simply the income stream from interest payments and the ultimate repayment of debt, shareholders also had to police against self-interested managerial acts that could diminish the value of their investment without necessarily driving the company to insolvency.

Paradoxically, the extralegal innovations that grew up to help protect dispersed shareholders served as much to protect creditors, especially finance creditors, as shareholders, by providing a continuous stream of information concerning the companies, the markets they operated in, and the nature of their management. Very briefly, journals covering commerce, common enough even in colonial times, greatly expanded. The first credit reporting agency, Dun and Bradstreet, reported on the state of companies and their management to those who purchased their reports. While the reports are far from a modern financial analysis, they did contain a great deal of information about the personal habits and reputations of business owners and managers. In an era when lending involved an assessment of the character of the debtor, this was not an insubstantial contribution to faith in the markets. The capacity to rapidly transmit information, first through a sophisticated mail system, quickly augmented by the telegraph, meant that markets could react relatively quickly to news created at even a great distance. Finally, of course, as enterprises became larger, the large enterprises set standards for accounting and internal transparency that were necessary in order for the firms to conduct business at all. These practices filtered down throughout the industrial and commercial arenas. As information became more available, exact, and relevant, the capacity of markets to price risk became greater and the need for legal protections declined somewhat.

The "somewhat" is an important caveat, for not all creditors were created equal. What emerged over the course of the nineteenth century was an increasingly glaring gap in creditor capacity to take advantage of the protections of information and market efficiency. Not every finance creditor, of course, took advantage of the information available. Nonetheless, even an only mildly effective market would roughly price in available information. But not every market every creditor operated in was effective in that sense. Many trade creditors could not take advantage of the information available in the capital markets because they had a much more limited capacity to change their counterparty. For example, while suppliers of fungible commodities could sell their goods on open markets, more specialized suppliers of goods to an enterprise often had few alternative markets. Once committed to supplying something designed for limited use by the customer, a supplier had few alternative markets save the salvage and scrap markets. Even more obvious, however, was the plight of labor. In the face of managerial failure to pay their salaries, labor was, like a supplier, a creditor and an unsecured creditor, low on the totem pole at that. When corporate resources were exhausted, unsecured creditors got little or nothing in insolvency.

In a marked reversal of the alliance between entrepreneurs and labor that marked the end of the charter and the beginning of the free incorporation eras, labor now found itself on the side of passive capital, seeking easier access to shareholder wealth. Unlike passive capital, which had many extralegal protections where labor had few, labor successfully, in at least a few instances, appealed to the political system. Some of the same state legislatures that created the grants of limited liability created a notable exception. Those jurisdictions responded to the plight of labor by making owners, or at least some owners, liable for unpaid employee wages, skipping entirely the necessity for an action piercing the corporate veil. These little-known statutes appeared in important jurisdictions, New York most notably, and, while rarely invoked, nonetheless remind us of the contingent nature of the basic doctrine itself.

The other remarkable transformation in these fifty years was in the nature of liability itself. Whereas the corporations of the early twentieth century were local and commercial affairs, save for the larger infrastructural and financial entities, by century's end industrial concerns were among the leading entities. Even where the country's infrastructure was concerned, plank roads and canals had been supplanted by railroads and streetcars. These new systems of transportation posed far greater threats to life and property that did roads and canals. Not only did the cars move at greater speeds, threatening those in their path, but their sources of power posed threats even when operating as expected, spewing ash and fire and threatening electrocution. When they crashed, passengers died and were maimed in unprecedented numbers and freight was destroyed. Similarly, large industrial concerns concentrated danger from pollutants in enterprises operating as expected to fires, explosions, and spectacular outflows of toxins when they did not. Tort liability became an enormous question confronting businesses, and corporate actors sought to minimize responsibility. While a railroad accident usually did not threaten insolvency, industrial calamity could well render a corporation insolvent, simultaneously destroying the source of wealth and creating liability. Why, then, did these accidents not threaten limited liability? After all, tort victims could not choose the variety of entity that harmed them. While one might reconcile oneself to a regime in which risk of loss shifts from entrepreneur to contractual counterparty because everyone, more or less, knows what they are getting into, the same cannot be said of accident victims. Since piercing the veil usually requires an "injustice" on top of failure to observe formalities, why was the lack of notice not injustice enough?

One answer, which may be unsatisfying, is that judgment creditors all look alike in the eyes of the law. No court has ever held that mere incapacity to satisfy a judgment is sufficient injustice to warrant veil piercing. As limited liability was often a legislative creation, such a distinction would have to be made legislatively, as some jurisdictions did with unpaid wages. Lying in the background, too, may have been the judicial incapacity to formulate a good remedy. For example, in the case of the New York statute providing for liability for unpaid wages, only the largest stockholders may be pursued. Courts might well have been reluctant to impose a liability scheme that was so obviously radically redistributive. In any case, evidence has not yet been uncovered that would allow scholars to make judgments, much less definitive judgments, about the answers to such questions.

Shareholders, and their agents who managed businesses, nonetheless sought protections from liability in tort. This is not the place to rehash the many legal and market protections, but they ranged from judicially constructed limits on causation of harm to extensive programs of insurance. These protections, of course, in the first instance benefited the business and only in some cases provided a benefit to the victims of industrial accidents. Nonetheless, legal buffers to liability reduced the pressure on the doctrine of limited liability by reducing the number of cases in which a judgment would go unsatisfied while not placing primary pressure for reform on the doctrine itself. Rather, of course, the pressure was on the underlying scheme of liability in the first place. Moreover, market forms of security also took pressure off the doctrine. Life, property, and casualty insurance provided some relief to victims, decreasing the political pressure to undermine the statutory scheme of limited liability. The insurance companies quickly calculated that they would be better off adjusting the price of insurance rather than seeking either to litigate to pierce the veil or to use their political clout to alter the scheme. In any case, their political position was unclear and hardly uniform throughout the industry. A property and casualty insurer was as likely to sell policies to a company whose property (say, freight) was damaged in a railroad accident as it was to sell a policy to a railroad whose property (say, locomotives) might be damaged in the same accident. Accident victims, dispersed and unorganized, suffered episodically, whereas corporation shareholders were, by definition, organized into entities that sought to further shareholder interests. It is therefore not surprising that limited liability survived, even if it provided minimal protection to shareholders.

MODERN INCORPORATION

The modern public corporation was born in the statutes of New Jersey in the last decade of the nineteenth century. In the modern public corporation shareholders are passive, playing only episodic managerial roles. They are dispersed. Ownership of the corporation is also widely dispersed, with few corporations having dominant shareholders. Corporate charters, especially in the most important chartering jurisdictions, are almost uniformly a matter of administrative action. The laws that govern the internal relations of the corporate organization are uniformly facilitative in nearly all the important chartering jurisdictions. They do not so much regulate the internal balance of power as allow the shareholders and managers to create a balance. The existence of a market for charters—corporations can reincorporate at will, moving their legal home from one jurisdiction to another—is said to police the capacity of jurisdictions to tilt corporate law too much in favor of certain corporate actors over others. They are completely private in nature, and their nature is the single-minded quest for profit.

Limited liability is largely irrelevant to the modern public corporation, save in one instance. That instance is itself a product of the New Jersey legal template of the 1890s. That instance is parent-subsidiary liability, when one corporation owns the majority of the shares of another company. Otherwise, for a variety of reasons, public corporations seem to be immune to veil piercing. According to those who have conducted systematic searches of the records, in no instance has the veil of a public corporation with widely held shares been pierced. Limited liability, it would seem, is a fact in search of a theory.

Veil piercing by financial creditors has become exceedingly rare. Modern financial theory and legal practice have rendered the question of watered stock essentially irrelevant by rendering the concept of par value irrelevant. Prior to the New Jersey acts of the 1890s, a corporation had to get something objectively valuable in return for the shares it issued. The New Jersey statutes, by contrast, left the judgment about the value of the consideration paid for shares in the hands of the directors. Moreover, their word was the last word. Thenceforth, watering stock became hard to do, and the easy avenue to recovery from shareholders disappeared, leaving only a piercing action.

The "trust fund" thought necessary to protect creditors itself became largely irrelevant. Finance creditors could much more easily understand who was borrowing their money, for what purpose, and how the money would be managed. Dun and Bradstreet reports were supplemented by credit evaluation agencies, today Standard and Poor's, Moody's, and Fitch. These companies graded public debt for creditworthiness, giving systematic reassurance to market pricing of debt. Financial markets became ever more transparent, with the rise of the ticker tape giving nearly instant securities prices. The financial press became both more sophisticated and national in scope, with the rise of the *Wall Street Journal* and later glossy magazines such as *Business Week, Forbes,* and *Fortune.* The securities exchanges, most notably the New York Stock Exchange, created listing requirements for the corporations the securities of which traded on their floors. The listing requirements included mandates for regularized financial reports. In short, creditors could more easily know the risks they were entertaining, and the markets could better price those risks.

As corporate activity became more transparent and markets more fluid, finance creditors sought safety not in so-called trust funds but in allocating their investments according to their appetites for risk. Corporations responded at first by regularly decreasing the par value for which shares were issued, minimizing the trust fund itself. The states responded, albeit more slowly than the corporations, by allowing corporations to issue shares for nominal par value or none whatsoever. That avenue for creditors to recover from shareholders became ever more evanescent. The disappearance of the trust fund also profoundly underlined the practical difficulty of recovery from shareholders. At least the par value fund was centralized and policed by laws governing dividend payouts and the like. To levy on the fund was easy. To pierce the veil and go after dispersed shareholders was difficult—so difficult, evidently, that it has never been done. Yet one searches in vain for strong protests in the finance community for this loss of protection.

Trade creditors, by contrast, benefited to a much smaller degree from the availability of market information. Perhaps they have been unable to price in risk—and they certainly lacked the capacity to do it with the precision and certainty of finance creditors—or perhaps the same factors that limited their capacity to limit risk still applied. In any case, when one reviews the piercing-the-veil cases, trade creditors predominate as plaintiffs.

The transformation of tort liability and the rise of the class action have combined to create veil piercing questions that never before existed. Modern products liability has given potential liability in tort a new dimension, emphasizing again the distinction between the contract counterparty, at least some of whom might be able to investigate the solvency of the corporation, and the tort victim, who cannot, unless the victim is aware of the corporate identity of the producer in the first place, and who, even then, presumably does not anticipate being the victim of a corporate tortfeasor. The fruits of the second industrial revolution have also spawned liability unheard of in the industrial era. For example, chemicals with unknown or long-term effects make liability assessment difficult and complicate enormously questions of notice not present even for trade creditors. Moreover, latent damage triggered decades after contact with a product further complicates questions of liability and notice.

The most salient issue for the modern corporation where limited liability is concerned, however, is not whether tort victims should more easily pierce the veil. Nor is it that veil piercing should be even more stringently limited for contractual counterparties because of their capacity to investigate the corporations they deal with. It is instead a product of an innovative feature of modern corporate law introduced by New Jersey in the 1890s. New Jersey made it possible for one corporation to buy and sell the shares of another. While antitrust issues were the primary concern triggered by this newfound corporate flexibility, limited liability was another. It was one thing for a state to make the decision that limited liability would act as a catalyst for growth, even widespread growth, by providing protection for individual investors. It was quite another for a parent corporation to be shielded from liability for the acts of a subsidiary, acts the parent caused to happen, no matter the risks to the external parties. In the first instance, risk aversion would be the product of fear of loss of all assets, reducing the individual and all dependent on the individual to penury. In the second, risk aversion would mean only that a parent corporation would be shielded from the losses beyond investment generated by the activities of the subsidiary but would entail no special gain, for the corporations would have no fears akin to that of individuals. Beyond that consideration, of course, are the possibilities for taking outsized risks in subsidiaries and substantially externalizing losses while internalizing gains.

EVOLUTION, JUSTIFICATION, AND MODERN LAW

Limited liability is best understood as the product of a wide variety of legal and market forces. It remains in place even if the rationales for its creation have long since been superseded by other legal and market protections. Rationales for its continued existence can be, and are, therefore markedly different from explanations for the existence of the doctrine. To read back current rationales is just an intellectual mistake, an example of anachronism. It distorts our understanding of the past, limits our imagination by suggesting a certain timelessness to contemporary ideas that may be misplaced, and adds to contemporary hubris about our capacity to understand the unintended consequences of our acts by suggesting an exaggerated superiority of knowledge over our predecessors. To continue to accept rationales from the time of a doctrine's creation may, however, entail other dangers.

Limited liability is a contingent facet of corporate existence. When first enacted, it had a tentative quality. It was neither sweeping in scope nor absolute in its protection. It its various manifestations it was designed to strike a balance between the desire to embolden entrepreneurs by limiting the risks associated with their endeavors and the desire to protect fearful capital from the predations of business owners. It was part of a world of vastly different capital markets, a wildly different industrial and commercial structure, nascent corporate law, and a system of recompense for accidents that could not begin to contemplate the vicissitudes of modern life. Limited liability changed as each of the factors that bore on corporate existence changed. Limited liability has probably been an exaggerated benefit to entrepreneurs. That claim notwithstanding, the contemporary and later accounts all attributed great importance to it, so that we may fairly surmise that contemporaries thought it important. If so, then it probably was part of the compendia of phenomena that "released energy" in the nineteenth century. It also probably acted to redistribute rewards, though, again, probably not in fact to the degree supposed. In the end, scholars should break down the cases not by doctrinal category, but in other ways, to find out who benefited and who did not.

NOTE

1. Frank H. Easterbrook and Daniel R. Fischel, "Limited Liability and the Corporation," *University of Chicago Law Review* 52 (1985): 89.

9

Transformations: Pluralism, Individualism, and Democracy

DALIA TSUK MITCHELL

IN 1952, A MERE TWO YEARS BEFORE CHIEF JUSTICE EARL WARREN DELIVered a per curiam decision in *Brown v. Board of Education*,[1] Adolf A. Berle Jr. pointedly noted that "protection of life, liberty and property contained in the Fifth and Fourteenth Amendments, though speaking the old language of possessory property and of individuals defending themselves against arbitrary feudal government, does at least set up the implication that corresponding protection exists when the individual derives his economic life not from possessory property but from position in the modern industrial world."[2] Berle went on to argue that just as corporations could not adopt rules that interfered with Congress's regulation of interstate commerce, such as preferential railroad rates, they also could not adopt rules burdening or denying "civil rights whose preservation is constitutionally guaranteed."[3] According to Berle, an individual's constitutional rights trumped not merely the exercise of state power but also the exercise of private power. As he put it, "a corporation, having achieved economic power making discrimination possible," should be "subject[ed] to constitutional tests as to its practices and regulations" if the latter "really invade[d] personality contrary to some constitutional privilege."[4]

According to Berle, the U.S. Supreme Court endorsed this principle in two cases decided in the late 1940s: *Marsh v. Alabama*, which declared that a company-owned town could not deprive individuals of freedom of speech and religion, and *Shelley v. Kraemer*, in which the Court refused to enforce a restrictive covenant.[5] Yet while today we typically associate the decisions in these cases with the doctrine of state action, it is important to recognize that Berle's argument was

I wish to thank Morty for sparking my interest in American legal history, for many conversations about the subject, and for his ongoing enthusiasm about my work. I am also grateful to Al and Dan for organizing this collection and to Larry for comments on drafts and for listening to my endless musings about pluralism. All errors are mine.

not grounded in this doctrine. Rather, Berle's argument was based on a legal pluralist understanding of public and private power. Its insight was that groups and other associations were powerful, perhaps even sovereign, entities. The success of American democracy thus demanded recognition of group autonomy as well as limitations on group power.

As I have argued elsewhere and will shortly summarize in the first part of this essay, the vision of legal pluralism was informed by early twentieth-century theories of political pluralism as well as the legal realist critique of classical legal thought. In fact, legal pluralism was an important strand of legal realism that immensely influenced the policies of the early New Deal.[6] The second part of this essay explores the influence of legal pluralism, indirect as it might have been, on the development of the modern discourse of civil rights and liberties in the post–World War II era. As I will demonstrate, in the 1940s and 1950s, focusing on the discriminatory practices of private organizations allowed scholars and the Court to advance the protection of individual rights under the First and Fourteenth Amendments without disturbing the tacit balance between state rights and federal power or the legitimacy of the Court itself. Ironically, the Warren Court's revolution, which legitimized the Court's role in protecting individual rights and liberties from state infringement, helped eclipse, albeit inadvertently, the vision of legal pluralism. The third part of this essay explores how by the 1960s, as the individual became the focus of legal and political analysis, the protection of property rights, now seen as entitlements, returned to the forefront of American legal thought. Rapidly growing unease about limiting individuals' as well as groups' and associations' interests in their property overshadowed the legal community's earlier concerns about private power. The fourth part concludes by examining how by the 1970s, the reconceptualization of groups as associations of individuals helped secure the guarantees of the First and Fourteenth Amendments to all associations, irrespective of their power. More than three decades later, in *Boy Scouts of America and Monmouth Council v. Dale*, such an understanding allowed the Court to hold that applying New Jersey's public accommodations law to prohibit the Boy Scouts from discriminating against individuals based on their sexual orientation would violate that association's First Amendment rights.[7]

1920s–1930s: LEGAL PLURALISM

The law's treatment of diverse interests received renewed and changed attention at the turn of the twentieth century. In the nineteenth century, the recognition of diversity in society was tied to a belief in progress and the assignment of subordinated positions to certain social and cultural groups.[8] At the turn of the twentieth century, the critique of absolutism led to growing skepticism toward existing social norms and values (what historians have described as cultural and ethical relativism, respectively) and toward "traditional foundations of thought and structures of understanding" (what Peter Novick labeled cognitive relativism).[9] This was the core of the legal realists' critique of classical legal thought. But when realists tried to describe ways to improve the legal system, they were confronted with the normative implications of their skepticism: does skepticism toward one's own legal system and ideals imply a nonjudgmental attitude toward all customs and values?

Legal realists argued that the law should aim to accommodate the different visions, interests, and experiences of modern American society. Yet no legal realist embraced a nonjudgmental attitude toward all cultures, values, and structures of understanding. Without dwelling on it, they simply refused to accept that skepticism necessarily implied a relativist stance toward all aspects of life. That which was intellectually possible, and maybe inevitable, was not only practically impossible but also personally destabilizing. A nonjudgmental view of all customs, values, and forms of knowledge involved a level of uncertainty about law and the world that very few could endure. It produced an existential crisis. Still, to recognize a degree of absolutism in the cultural, ethical, or cognitive realms undermined the critique of classical legal thought. Recognizing the tension, legal scholars struggled to find a middle ground—to avoid an emotional and intellectual crisis (maybe even nihilism) on one hand, and absolutism on the other.

The social scientists among the realists, including Herman Oliphant, Hessel Yntema, and Underhill Moore, set out to collect data about the diverse interests, customs, and viewpoints that characterized society. They overcame the uncertainties produced by relativism in part by postponing the normative and in part by departing from cognitive relativism. They put their trust in science as the ultimate form of knowledge and in empiricism as an objective way to verify facts and learn about the world.

Major critics of legal realism throughout the twentieth century focused on this group of social scientists, noting that in a heterogeneous and changing society, the social sciences offered little guidance as to which customs or principles to adopt. When forced to engage normative questions, these legal realists indeed evaded the difficult task of choosing between competing interests and values by portraying society as homogenous, and law as a mirror of congruent social interests. Their legal realism, grounded as it was in objective empiricism and nonjudgmental attitudes toward customs and values, helped obscure the critical stance of the legal realists (their cognitive relativism) and the realists' reformist zeal. In the hands of these social scientists, realism became increasingly apologetic.[10]

Other legal realists, like Robert Hale, Adolf Berle, and Morris Cohen, held on to a stronger cognitive relativist approach but continued to believe in the power of certain norms and customs and the disadvantages of others. They sought "to combine a pre-modern, prophetic and essentialist moralistic passion for social justice with a critical modernist sense of the socially constructed character of social categories and institutions."[11] To reconcile their skepticism toward traditional structures of knowledge (or cognitive relativism) with their acceptance of certain ethical norms, many of these realists, whom I label legal pluralists, made the group rather than the individual the basis for political and legal analysis. As I will elaborate below, by focusing on the diversity of groups in society, legal pluralists endorsed a certain amount of skepticism toward the prevailing legal system and ideals. Yet they also believed that by allowing individuals to unite to promote their interests, subject to certain universal requirements, disparities of power, particularly economic power, could be minimized, if not eliminated. By viewing group autonomy as a means to political and economic equality, legal pluralists were able to embrace skepticism without also sanctioning a nonjudgmental attitude toward all customs and values. Rather than choosing between relativism and absolutism, they saw their task as defining the appropriate balance between group autonomy and the limits of group power—the normative limits of their celebration of diversity.

Legal pluralists were informed by theories of political pluralism that developed in the early decades of the twentieth century. Resisting both the radical collectivist vision of Marxists and socialists and the individualism of traditional liberal thought, political pluralists described groups, specifically functional groups such as labor unions, as the fora where individuals found meaning for their ideas and actions. As farmers, workers, professionals, consumers, women, and ethnocultural groups formed a variety of associations to protect and advance their interests, political scientists argued in favor of adding groups, organizations, and associations to the existing array of local and state governments as the bases of the modern American state.[12]

Some political theorists, such as Arthur Bentley, argued that because individuals organized themselves into groups to pursue their interests, groups and organizations were loci of participation and representation. They believed that by exploring the role of groups in society they could offer a more realistic description of liberal democratic politics and the limited role of the liberal state.[13] Other political theorists, among them John Dewey, Mary Parker Follett, and Harold Laski, not only recognized the existence of a multiplicity of centers of self-government in society but also embraced it as a constitutive element of democracy. These theorists argued that the state was too broad and abstract a body to command loyalty and allegiance from individuals, who associated more easily with diverse groups and organizations than with a unified state entity. By conceiving of sovereignty as distributive or multiple and by encouraging the growth of organizations such as labor unions, these political theorists sought to guarantee the flourishing of diverse and valuable forms of identities, ways of life, experiences, and viewpoints.[14]

Drawing on political pluralism, legal pluralists recognized the significant role of associations such as churches, political parties, neighborhood groups, corporations, and trade unions in an industrialized society either as promoters of individual autonomy and protectors of individuals against an otherwise omnipotent state or as economic bases for democracy. In this vein, advocates of the workers' right to organize and corporate law scholars portrayed labor unions and corporations, respectively, as real entities whose existence was both real and distinct from their individual members.[15] But while for the most part political pluralists were not concerned about the power that collective entities might exercise (trusting labor unions and corporations to self-regulate their activities), legal pluralists exposed organizations, associations, and corporations as loci not only of individual self-government but also of coercive power over their members, nonmembers, and other associations, power that liberal legal thinkers cloaked as free contractual arrangements between individuals.[16]

The legal pluralists' concerns about potential abuses and excesses of group power produced a variation on the dilemma engendered by relativism. On one hand, the role of groups in promoting individual autonomy supported deference to group authorities. To allow the state to exercise power over diverse groups risked imposing one set of concededly partial interests and beliefs in the name of a general public good. On the other hand, the ability of large organizations, especially corporations, to amass great economic, political, and social power made them, like the sovereign state, threatening to the rights of other groups and their members. Such assumptions seemed to justify normative intervention in the internal governance structure of groups and organizations, government intervention being seen as enhancing individual freedom.[17]

Legal pluralists mediated these tensions by arguing that the role of the state and the legal system was to guarantee that individuals could associate with others to pursue their needs and that no one association or collective entity could use its power to oppress individuals who belonged to other groups (oppression being defined, at least initially, as economic oppression). Moreover, legal pluralists argued that, in principle, collective entities should be allowed to exercise their powers freely but that courts should tame potential abuses of power by imposing on organizations limitations resembling the constraints on sovereign power. They wanted collective entities to exercise their power to benefit the community at large.[18]

The Depression and the New Deal gave legal pluralists a chance to try out their ideas in practice. Recast as New Dealers in Franklin Roosevelt's administration, they sought to combine decentralized economic and political power with national planning. By legitimating the activities of collective entities, New Dealers hoped both to endorse the multiplicity of interests and viewpoints that characterized modern society and to promote economic progress while entrusting national planning to limit the destructive potential of capitalism. The securities acts of 1933 and 1934 were based on cooperation between government and big business, the Tennessee Valley Authority combined centralized government planning with regional bureaucracy, and the National Industrial Recovery Act of 1933 created the National Recovery Administration to oversee cooperative programs among business, labor, and government (this scheme was declared unconstitutional in 1935).[19]

Legal pluralists never fully resolved the tension between their commitment to group autonomy or self-government and their concerns about inequities of group power. As New Dealers, they struggled to mediate this tension by requiring organizations such as labor unions and corporations to act to benefit society. By the late 1930s, they also began to explore the relationship between groups and individuals. As the next part elaborates, in these endeavors they drew on their legal pluralist understanding of private power to promote the protection of individual rights and liberties.

1940s–1950s: LEGAL PLURALISM AND INDIVIDUALISM

The 1940s were a crucial decade in the development of the modern discourse of civil rights. In the early half of the twentieth century, legal scholars associated rights with economic and social needs, specifically the rights of individuals to work, to livelihood, to social insurance, and to economic independence. The so-called cultural politics of the 1920s, including the rebirth of the Ku Klux Klan and the passage of restrictive immigration laws, turned American intellectuals away from direct engagement with racial problems. Race and culture were seen as divisive issues, especially after racial and cultural battles almost destroyed the Democratic Party in 1924. But in the second half of the twentieth century, the concept of civil rights became associated with the rights of ethnic and religious minorities, specifically the right to be different.[20] As I elaborate below, the shift from class to ethnicity took place, for the most part, in the 1940s.

Several factors helped turn the attention of lawyers, legal scholars, and government officials from economic and social rights to the rights of ethnic and racial minorities. Most dominant among them were apprehension about the potential spread of European totalitarianism, fears of Japanese propaganda directed at African Americans, and increased African American organization and protest. Despite the strong correlation between racial discrimination and economic inequality and the combined ascendance of both racial- and labor-related rights during the 1940s, the concept of liberty in the postwar years became associated with the right not to suffer racial and ethnic discrimination. The concept of social and economic citizenship gradually lost its primacy.[21]

The shift from social and economic rights to racial and ethnic equality was paralleled by a change in the perception of the roles of the three branches of government. In the early twentieth century and during the New Deal, legal scholars emphasized the roles of the executive and legislative branches in promoting social and economic rights. With totalitarianism in Europe, legal scholars grew concerned about the relationship between statism and tyranny.[22] Limiting the power of the legislative and executive branches became the underlying theme of scholarly writings about rights.

By the 1960s, the transformation was complete. The concept of civil rights was no longer associated with an affirmative obligation of the government to protect social and economic rights; rather, it was associated with the (liberal) judicial role of imposing constitutional constraints on the government to prevent it from discriminating against members of ethnic, racial, and religious minorities. This latter concept became pronounced in the decisions of the Warren Court as it championed a vision of democracy that focused on individual rights and liberties.[23] As this part explores, the vision of legal pluralism helped legitimate these transformations.

Strong ties connected the vision of legal pluralism and the decisions of the Warren Court. Both rested on the assumption that the role of law was not only to enforce majoritarian rule, but also, and perhaps more essentially, to protect the rights of historically marginalized or underprivileged groups. Legal pluralists and the Warren Court shared what Morton Horwitz labeled "a substantive conception of democracy," that is, the understanding that "greater social inclusiveness and empowerment of minorities" was not in tension with democracy but rather "an extension of democratic values."[24] As to the shift from class to ethnicity, it is important to remember that political pluralism, which informed legal pluralism, was the mirror image of theories of cultural pluralism, which conceived of ethnic and cultural groups as constitutive elements of American democracy. If political pluralism was important to the early twentieth-century debates about workers' rights, the cultural pluralist ideal, articulated by Horace Kallen as early as 1915, became more pronounced in the postwar conversations about ethnic and racial equality.[25] In short, viewed through pluralist lenses, the shift from class to ethnicity was only a shift in emphasis.

Legal pluralists continued to embrace groups and organizations as constitutive elements of American democracy while remaining concerned about private collective power. Influenced by the ongoing distress about individual rights, their solutions changed. In addition to requiring organizations to exercise their power to benefit the community and encouraging collaboration of groups such as labor unions and corporations with the federal government as a means of taming group power, legal pluralists began to emphasize the need to protect the individual from group power. Throughout the 1940s and 1950s, the Court, informed by similar concerns, subjected private organizations and associations to constitutional constraints, specifically to the requirements of the First and Fourteenth Amendments. As we will see, these decisions, which legal pluralists such as Adolf Berle, Robert Hale, and William Douglas wholeheartedly endorsed, also helped substantiate decisions protecting the constitutional rights of individuals against state encroachment.

Take, for example, *Steele v. L.&N.R. Co.* In this 1944 decision, the Court intimated that unions authorized under a federal statute to be bargaining representatives could not discriminate against African American employees without violating the equal protection clause.[26] Two years later, in *Marsh v. Alabama*, the Court held unconstitutional restrictions on freedom of speech imposed by a company-owned town. According to Justice Black, who delivered the Court's opinion, "the corporation's right to control the inhabitants" of the company-owned town was not "coextensive with the right of a homeowner to regulate the conduct of his guests."[27] Reviewing the two cases, Robert Hale suggested that due to the ability of unions and corporations to exert pressure on employers to refuse to hire African American workers, they should be subjected to constitutional limitations imposed on the states, whether or not they could be viewed as state actors.[28]

As Hale saw it, imposing constitutional constraints on private organizations was the obvious implication of his (and the realists') earlier rejection of the distinction between a supposedly non-coercive private sphere of individual rights and a coercive public sphere of state regulation as fundamentally misguided. According to Hale, all relations among private parties were premised on the existence and enforcement of the law of contracts and property by the state. Private law was thus a form of regulatory public law. Property rights were a means by which the government indirectly coerced some individuals to produce income to the property owners.[29] This was especially true in the case of corporations and other organizations that could amass property and power over individuals, other groups, and even the state. While Hale's early twentieth-century critique focused, for the most part, on the rights of workers and, more specifically, labor unions against corporations, in the 1940s, he turned to racial discrimination. As he pointedly put it, "racial discrimination practiced by private groups, though it does not even nominally violate state law, may be just as effective as if it were practiced by the state itself." Among Hale's examples were the discriminatory practices of labor unions that prevented African Americans from taking up certain occupations, as well as those of political parties that denied African Americans the right to vote in their primaries.[30]

Hale went so far as to argue that protecting African Americans from discrimination required prohibiting hostile acts by private individuals.[31] At a minimum, he and Berle agreed that even if a private wrong, as distinguished from state action, could not offend the Constitution, certain organizations, especially corporations, because their economic power gave them discriminatory power, should be subjected to constitutional limitations. As Berle put it, "if there is power, accompanied by invasion of an individual right guaranteed by the Constitution, then it would seem that the mere enjoyment of a state corporate charter is a sufficient justification for invoking operation of the Fourteenth and Fifteenth Amendments."[32]

The Court did not go so far as to impose constitutional constraints on organizations merely because of their power, but throughout the 1950s and 1960s the liberal wing of the Court came rather close, extending the analysis of *Steele v. L.& N.R. Co.* and *Marsh v. Alabama* beyond the realm of corporations and labor unions. For one thing, in *Terry v. Adams*, a 1953 case addressing the exclusion of African Americans from voting in the primaries of the Jaybird Democratic Association (the Jaybird party), a Texas county political organization, the Court refused to view the Jaybird party as a private organization to which constitutional constraints did not apply. Writing for the Court, Justice Black noted that "the only election that has counted in this Texas county for more than fifty years has been that held by the Jaybirds from which Negroes were excluded. . . . The effect of the whole procedure, Jaybird primary plus Democratic primary plus general election, is to do precisely that which the Fifteenth Amendment forbids."[33] Fifteen years later, in *Amalgamated Food Employees Union Local 590 v. Logan Valley Plaza, Inc.*, the Court declared unconstitutional the exclusion of picketers from a privately owned shopping mall.[34]

Decisions rendering the discriminatory practices of private entities unconstitutional had a significant effect on the developing role of the Court as protector of individual rights from state infringement. For a Court that was repeatedly accused of judicial activism and concerned about its ability to strike down laws effecting discrimination without damaging the delicate balance between Northern and Southern Democrats, cases limiting the power of organizations and groups were at the forefront of the fight for equal rights. Take, for example, *Tucker v. Texas*. This 1946 case involved a criminal conviction of a Jehovah's Witnesses minister for "refusing to leave the premises" of a federal government–owned town after being "notified to do so" by a representative of the government. Noting the similarities of the case to *Marsh v. Alabama*, which was decided the same day and involved a company-owned town, the Court reversed the conviction.[35] Two years later, in *Saia v. New York*, in which the Court held unconstitutional a city ordinance forbidding the use of sound amplification devices without the police chief's permission, Justice Douglas relied on *Marsh v. Alabama* to proclaim that "courts must balance the various community interests in passing on the constitutionality of local regulations," "but in that process they should be mindful to keep the freedoms of the First Amendment in a preferred position."[36]

Reaching even further, the legal pluralist vision informed the Court's developing state action doctrine. The amicus brief that the American Civil Liberties Union submitted to the Court in support of the petitioners' claim in *Shelley v. Kraemer* drew on Hale's argument about the sovereign power of property owners, especially owners who joined efforts, to argue that restrictive covenants were unconstitutional.[37] While the Court held that "restrictive agreements standing alone cannot be regarded as violative of any rights guaranteed to petitioners by the Fourteenth Amendment," it viewed the required enforcement by the courts as constituting state action subject to the constraints enumerated in the Constitution.[38]

Moreover, the legal pluralists' analysis of inequities of group power helped pave the road to the Warren Court's rejection of formal equality. Take, again, the American Civil Liberties Union brief in *Shelley v. Kraemer.* Informed by Hale's analysis of group power, it also challenged the long-standing argument that society could achieve equality by providing different ethnic groups with similar opportunities. "Restrictive covenants may not be granted enforcement on the principle of reciprocity expressed to the effect that Negroes have an equal right to establish and enforce restrictive covenants barring White people from their areas," the brief noted. "The allowance of such a theoretical right to exclude is no answer to a Negro family which cannot find a place to live."[39] The Court agreed. Rejecting on the facts the respondents' argument that the state's enforcement mechanism was equally available to restrictive covenants excluding white persons, the Court also noted "more fundamental considerations": "The rights created by the first section of the Fourteenth Amendment are, by its terms, guaranteed to the individual. The rights established are personal rights. It is, therefore, no answer to these petitioners to say that the courts may also be induced to deny white persons rights of ownership and occupancy on grounds of race or color. Equal protection of the laws is not achieved through indiscriminate imposition of inequalities."[40]

In short, the Court recognized the role of law in correcting the imbalances of group power that permeated social, cultural, and legal relationships. In the early 1950s, several cases challenging the practice of establishing separate educational facilities for African Americans drew upon similar "fundamental considerations."[41] These were the foundations upon which Chief Justice Warren could announce that "separate educational facilities are inherently unequal."[42]

Ironically, however, by turning its reasoning away from group power to the argument that the rights enumerated in the amendments to the Constitution were granted to individuals, the Court also helped lay the foundation for the destruction of the state action doctrine and the legal pluralist vision, more broadly. As late as 1968, Charles Black noted that "'separate but equal' and 'no state action'—these fraternal twins have been the Medusan caryatids upholding racial injustice."[43] Like Hale and Berle, Black believed that the fight for equal protection required an extension of the state action doctrine to actions of powerful organizations, if not also to actions of powerful individuals. But, as I explore in the following parts, the legal community's distress about ethnic discrimination, seen by legal pluralists as a mere shift in emphasis, ultimately helped eclipse concerns about private power. In the intellectual atmosphere of the 1960s and 1970s, the focus on individual rights also brought about a renewed interest in the rights of groups and associations. Gradually, the Court moved from balancing group autonomy with group power to protecting the rights of groups (and their members), specifically their rights in their property and their rights of expressive association. By the 1970s, groups and organizations were no longer subject to constitutional constraints but were rather the object of constitutional rights.

1960s: INDIVIDUALISM

In a 1959 article entitled "Race Relations and Group Interest in the Law," Jack Greenberg, a lifelong crusader for civil rights, noted that "a discussion of the jurisprudence of race relations appears in [a] symposium on group interests largely as a paradox." According to Greenberg, the struggle for ethnic and racial equality demanded the elimination of "socially enforced group identity."[44] As he more pointedly put it, "The state may not, because of race, treat a Negro individual differently from a white individual, no matter what the treatment of Negroes as a group. . . . The constitutional discrepancy of the personal right of freedom from racial discrimination being nullified by a group right philosophy cannot endure."[45]

Greenberg's argument was meant to attack the Court's acquiescence in the states' attempts to stagger desegregation of schools. Like the legal pluralists, he believed that "the jurisprudence of group rights unquestionably serves to advance individual rights" in cases involving members of minority groups invoking "claims to intragroup equality." Using as examples *Steele v. L.& N.R. Co.* and *Terry v. Adams*, Greenberg explained that "members of the minority group" belonging to labor unions, or political parties, "may draw upon sanctions to shed their minority group status."[46]

The legal community could have embraced two different jurisprudences—one seeking to limit the power of groups such as labor unions and corporations, the other seeking to empower ethnic, racial, and religious minorities. But particular intellectual transformations during the postwar years created an atmosphere in which such bifurcated analysis was impossible.[47] As this part explores, beginning in the late 1930s, different developments helped shift the attention of American scholars away from groups and associations and toward the individual as the basis for legal and political analysis. In this intellectual environment, distress about property rights—of individuals as well as organizations—gradually overshadowed concerns about group power (including corporate and union power). As the following part will explore, similar developments also substantiated the portrayal of groups as associations of individuals whose freedom of intimate and expressive association could trump the rights of those excluded from participating.

First among these developments was the widespread acceptance of Keynesian economics beginning in the late 1930s and continuing until the mid-1970s. It provided economic justification for the later New Deal fiscal policies, which attempted to regulate the economy not through planning but by "accepting existing consumer preferences" and "manipulating aggregate demand."[48] As Michael Sandel recently explained, Keynesian economics was predicated upon the belief that governments should not choose among competing individual visions of the public good. Its celebration both reflected this image—the image of the night-watchman state—and helped deepen its hold on American public life. The individual consumer became the foundation of economic thought.[49]

The individual was also the focus of a new pluralist image of the modern state, which political theorists such as Robert Dahl developed in the postwar years. While informed by the early pluralists, Dahl and his colleagues reduced collective entities into individual arrangements (viewing organizations and groups as allowing individuals more effectively to socialize and to pursue their ends). Drawing upon models of equilibria derived from economics, their pluralist image of the state rested on the assumption that individuals formed multiple interest groups that interacted, competed, and traded ends in neutral political markets. The American state was, accordingly, a political compromise between various pressure groups. Presumably free political markets were trusted to produce shared public goods.[50]

The neo-pluralist image of the state was traceable to "a loss of faith in the ideals of *laissez-faire* capitalism," specifically the idea that "self-interest pursued in economic transactions would inure to the common good." Yet ironically, neo-pluralists embraced a similar faith in the structure of political markets and political bargains. Accordingly, the public interest would result from "the unregulated pursuit of private interests in the legislatures."[51]

Indeed, proponents of both Keynesian economics and interest group pluralism hoped to create "a social order that was neither intrusive nor anarchistic, that provided opportunities for cooperative action and crevices for personal freedom."[52] John Kenneth Galbraith described the countervailing demands of different economic interests (producers, labor unions, consumers) as the fuel that made American capitalism work.[53] And Daniel Bell noted that "the growing complexity of society necessarily multiplied . . . interests, regional or functional, and in an open society the political arena . . . [was] a place where different interests [fought] it out for advantage."[54] In short, postwar intellectuals viewed interest groups, organized along economic or political axes, as ensuring social, political, and economic stability.[55]

While Keynesian economics and the neo-pluralist vision of the state emphasized the role of the individual (consumer or group member), they also retained a role for the group in economic and political analysis. Yet their faith in the power of economic and political markets to produce the common good, coupled with the growing emphasis on individual rights and liberties, made individual preferences the focus of their analysis. As legal scholars' concerns shifted from wealth and class toward a wide range of indicia of lack of privilege, including "race, extremist political or social views, indigent criminal defendants, alienage, and eventually gender, affectional preferences, and disabilities," they, too, found individual preferences to be the only common thread uniting their thought.[56]

With individual preferences as a common thread, the protection of property rights rapidly returned to the forefront of American legal discourse. Take, for example, Charles Reich's "The New Property," the most important article on the subject of property since the legal realists challenged the classical conception of property as a natural right that deserved utmost protection from state infringement. "In the final analysis," Reich wrote, "the Bill of Rights depends upon the existence of private property. Political rights presuppose that individuals and private groups have the will and the means to act independently. But so long as individuals are motivated largely by self-interest, their well-being must first be independent. Civil liberties must have a basis in property, or bills of rights will not preserve them."[57]

Reich's goal was to protect individuals against abuses of government power, especially in the allocation of government benefits. He wanted his readers to recognize that traditional forms of wealth were being replaced by government largesse—"money, benefits, services, contracts, franchises and licenses."[58] Drawing on the legal realists' critique of the distinction between a public sphere of coercive power and a private sphere of free individual interactions, Reich attacked the traditional distinction between private, pre-political property rights and public, governmentally created privileges. If, as the realists demonstrated, all property was governmentally created, then, Reich proclaimed, the constraints on the allocation of private property should be applied to government largesse. Accordingly, the fact that government benefits were public property could not mean that such benefits could be withheld completely.

By characterizing government largesse as property, Reich hoped to establish procedural constraints that would bolster the welfare state while strengthening its rule-of-law character. He was reacting to the abuse of governmental power during the McCarthy era, specifically to denials of benefits to people accused of communist associations. Viewing "the role of the new property, as well as the old," as satisfying "individuals' needs—not necessarily their wants—so that they can contribute to the commonwealth as independent citizens,"[59] Reich sought to use procedural constraints to support the welfare state.

Reich's "The New Property" was compatible with the legal pluralist vision. Indeed, Reich recognized the significant role organizations played in the modern state. "Today," he commented, "it is the combined power of government and the corporation that presses against the individual."[60] Yet unlike the pluralists who encouraged collective ownership while seeking to limit the power of collective entities, Reich's postwar critique of the public-private distinction used the liberal protection of private property to advocate the creation of individual entitlements in public (or collective) property. In this vein, Reich pointed out the need to allocate the benefits created by collective entities (and the government) to individuals. It is thus perhaps not surprising that, despite Reich's goals, his theory was quickly interpreted as advocating the idea that "property is a negative claim that the owner has against others, including the state, not to interfere with her use, possession, and enjoyment of her property."[61]

A concept of property associated neither with collective ownership nor with individual ownership but with individual entitlements sat well with a description of liberty as the freedom to pursue individual interests away from government regulation. According to the libertarians' vision of the new property, the state's role was thus not to seek to provide individuals with a set of particular goods, but rather to protect individuals' entitlements and expectations. As the conservative wing of the Court saw it, groups and organizations were equally entitled to the protection of their rights, especially their property rights.

Take, for example, Justice Minton's dissent in *Terry v. Adams,* the case addressing the exclusion of African Americans from the primaries of the Jaybird party. Relying on *Shelley v. Kraemer*'s analysis of the state action found in the courts' enforcement of restrictive covenants, Minton accused Justice Black of reaching beyond *Shelley* to redress wrongs involving only individual action. As he pointedly put it, "the majority has found that this pressure group's work does constitute state action. The basis of this conclusion is rather difficult to ascertain. Apparently it derives from a dislike of the goals of the Jaybird Association. I share that dislike. I fail to see how it makes state action."[62]

Ironically, by the 1960s, Justice Black, who wrote the Court's opinions in *Marsh v. Alabama* and *Terry v. Adams,* became progressively worried that allowing civil rights to trump property rights, even collective property rights, might lead to anarchy. After the passage of the Civil Rights Act of 1964 and the Voting Rights Act of 1965, Black viewed the civil rights movement's continuing acts of civil disobedience with growing suspicion. Fears about anarchy, lawlessness, and mob rule led Black to recant his earlier position. In a series of decisions in the mid-1960s about the constitutionality of private segregation in restaurants, lunch counters, and motels, Black separated from the liberal wing of the Court.[63]

One of the most important of these opinions was delivered in the 1964 case *Bell v. Maryland,* in which the Court held unconstitutional the conviction for trespass of African Americans who were asked to leave a Baltimore restaurant because of their race and refused to do so. Writing in dissent, Black distinguished cases such as *Shelley v. Kraemer,* where the exercise of state power would prohibit a willing property owner from selling his or her property on the grounds of the race of the buyer, from situations where "the property owner chooses *not* to sell to a particular person or *not* to admit that person." In the latter cases, according to Black, the property owner, even a corporation, "is entitled to rely on the guarantee of due process of law, that is, 'law of the land,' to protect his free use and enjoyment of property and to know that only by valid legislation, passed pursuant to some constitutional grant of power, can anyone disturb this free use." Without such legislation, Black did not see how the Court could compel a property owner "to allow people to force their way into his restaurant and remain there over his protest." "We must never forget," he stressed, "that the Fourteenth Amendment protects 'life, liberty, or property' of all people generally, not just some people's 'life,' some people's 'liberty,' and some kinds of 'property.' "[64] Four years later, in *Amalgamated Food Employees Union Local 590 v. Logan Valley Plaza, Inc.*, again in dissent, Black distinguished the company-owned town (in *Marsh v. Alabama*), where the "property has taken on *all* the attributes of a town," from a privately owned shopping center. "To hold that store owners are compelled by law to supply picketing areas for pickets to drive store customers away is to create a court-made law wholly disregarding the constitutional basis on which private ownership of property rests in this country," Black proclaimed.[65] The power that certain property owners, backed by the state, could exercise over individuals was no longer Black's concern.

The liberal wing of the Warren Court continued to limit the power of property owners to effect racial discrimination. In his concurring opinion in *Bell v. Maryland,* Justice Douglas came close to embracing Hale's and Berle's argument that corporations should be subjected to constitutional tests simply because they were corporations. "The facts of these sit-in cases have little resemblance to any institution of property which we customarily associate with privacy," Douglas stressed. In fact, as he saw it, *Shelley v. Kraemer* and its progenies involved "preferences . . . far more personal than the motivations of the corporate managers in the present case when they declined service to Negroes." Calling attention to the separation of ownership from control in large public corporations (as Berle in collaboration with Gardiner C. Means did more than three decades earlier[66]), and to the fact that the corporation itself had no personal preferences, Douglas insisted that upholding the convictions "*would make corporate management the arbiter of one of the deepest conflicts in our society*: corporate management could then enlist the aid of state police, state prosecutors, and state courts to force *apartheid* on the community they served, if *apartheid* best suited the corporate need; or, if its profits would be better served by lowering the barriers of segregation, it could do so."[67]

Douglas's argument was grounded in the early twentieth-century legal pluralists' concerns about inequities of economic power. While he celebrated groups and associations as centers of participation and representation, he also recognized the power that organizations could exercise over their members and other individuals. For Douglas, as it was for Hale and Berle, racial discrimination was another example of the power that certain groups in society, typically through the aggregation of property, could exercise over others.

But by the late 1960s, the legal pluralists' argument was losing ground. First, perhaps because it recognized the growing opposition to its imposition of constitutional constraints on private organizations, the Court changed its rhetoric. While in *Tucker v. Texas*, the case involving a federally owned town, and similar 1940s decisions, the Court drew an analogy from the constitutional limitations to which it subjected private power to restrict the power of public entities, by the late 1960s the Court reversed its comparison. In 1968, relying on *Marsh v. Ala-*

bama, the Court declared that "under certain circumstances property that is privately owned may, at least for First Amendment purposes, be treated as though it were publicly held."[68] Growingly confident about its power to strike down discriminatory state laws, the Court made constitutional limitations on publicly held property the norm; similar constraints on privately held property were derived, if at all, only by analogy.

Moreover, by the mid-1970s, the conservative wing of the Court was able to overcome the legal pluralists' influence. In *Hudgens v. National Labor Relations Board,* the Court held that union members did not have a First Amendment right to enter a private shopping mall to picket one of the stores. Writing for the Court, Justice Stewart announced: "It is, of course, a commonplace that the constitutional guarantee of free speech is a guarantee only against abridgment by government, federal or state. Thus, while statutory or common law may in some situations extend protection to provide redress against a private corporation or person who seeks to abridge the free expression of others, no such protection or redress is provided by the Constitution itself."[69]

For all practical purposes, Stewart's decision, which relied on Black's dissent in *Amalgamated Food Employees Union Local 590 v. Logan Valley Plaza, Inc.,* overruled the majority opinion in that case. As to *Marsh v. Alabama,* Stewart announced it to be a unique case where "a private enterprise" assumed "all of the attributes of a state-created municipality," and "the owner of the company-owned town was performing the full spectrum of municipal powers and stood in the shoes of the State." In all other cases involving privately owned property, the public, even when invited as customers, did not have First Amendment rights as it would have "on the similar public facilities in the streets of a city or town."[70] No longer concerned about the power that groups and associations, including corporations and labor unions, could exercise over individuals, the Court chose to protect the property rights of collective entities as if they were individuals.

In 1924, Horace Kallen argued that the protection of private property in twentieth-century America was not about wealth but about "people, qualities of race, heritage and attitude."[71] For Kallen, the equation of property and identity was meant to convey the power that certain ethnic and cultural groups shared. A similar understanding underlay the postwar decisions imposing constitutional constraints on private organizations. But, as the following part explores, in the 1970s, identity, like property, became an entitlement, devoid of social or cultural power. Powerful distinctions among ethnic and racial groups disappeared, and in their turn, all that was left were groups. Rapidly, protecting freedom of association became the focus of the Court's analysis of constitutional challenges to groups' discriminatory practices; for the most part, associations, irrespective of their power or privileged status, were to be immune from government regulation.

1970s: FREEDOM OF ASSOCIATION

The reconceptualization of property rights as entitlements was one obstacle to the legal pluralists' agenda. Perhaps more devastating was the Court's growing anxiety about attempts to limit the freedom of civil rights associations. Cases involving Southern officials seeking to break down the NAACP by demanding to see its membership lists raised the need to protect, perhaps make sacred, the freedom of association.

In 1958, in *NAACP v. Alabama,* the Court announced that "freedom to engage in association for the advancement of beliefs and ideas is an inseparable aspect of the 'liberty' assured by the Due Process Clause of the Fourteenth Amendment, which embraces freedom of speech." In this case, freedom of association required granting immunity to the NAACP from state scrutiny of its membership lists.[72] Five years later, Douglas expressed similar sentiments when he wrote: "A Free Society is made up of almost innumerable institutions through which views and opinions are expressed, opinion is mobilized, and social, economic, religious, educational, and political programs are formulated."[73] Accordingly, Douglas also proclaimed that "government can neither legislate with respect to nor probe the intimacies of political, spiritual, or intellectual relationships in the myriad of lawful societies and groups, whether popular or unpopular, that exist in this country."[74]

As Douglas emphasized in his concurring opinion in *Bell v. Maryland, NAACP v. Alabama,* which involved a corporation asserting "the constitutional rights of its members," was easily distinguished from the sit-in cases, which involved "the corporate owners of a restaurant, like the corporate owners of streetcars, buses, telephones, and electric light and gas facilities," who were "interested in balance sheets and in profit and loss statements." Moreover, unlike *NAACP v. Alabama,* cases like *Bell v. Maryland* involved a powerful organization imposing its power on individuals.[75] But, as I explore below, the legal community's ongoing obsession with individual entitlements, coupled with contemporaneous developments in political and legal theory, helped obliterate Douglas's value-based distinctions among groups and associations.

First among these developments was the legal process school. Its members, including Alexander Bickel, Herbert Wechsler, Harry Wellington, Albert Sacks, and Henry Hart, sought to move legal analysis away from values and toward process as a means of ensuring the continuing success of American democracy. Drawing on the neo-pluralist vision of the state as composed of multiple interest groups, they concluded that the legislature was the governmental body best situated to make policy choices that would accommodate the needs of diverse interest groups. The role of the judiciary was thus limited to offering guidance to the legislature, specifically about appropriate processes, and to guaranteeing that legislative processes would not unfairly exclude certain groups, specifically African Americans.[76] If legal pluralists wanted the Court to ensure that the rights of minority groups were protected from infringement by the states or by powerful organizations, legal process scholars insisted that only where universal suffrage was wanting should the Court intervene to protect the rights of those excluded from the political process. In this vein, as Wellington put it, the Court should not impose constitutional constraints "whenever any organization or group performs a function of a sufficiently important public nature."[77] Only as "a last resort" could the Court strike down legislation to promote values that "most people in society desired in the long run."[78]

Members of the legal process school endorsed the Court's protection of African Americans from discrimination because the latter were not adequately represented in the political sphere. Still their analysis of the Court's limited role helped shift the attention of the legal community from concerns about the rights of minority groups and about private power to apprehension about the Court's power of judicial review—from substantive evaluations of power and vulnerability to obsession with process and procedure.

At the same time, a different group of scholars, also influenced by the neo-pluralist vision of the state, argued that the Court should protect group autonomy and refrain from interfering with group affairs. In 1953 Mark DeWolfe Howe described "private groups" as "sovereign" and called on the Court to respect their autonomy. Moreover, reflecting on the decision in *Terry v. Adams*, Howe noted that the decision properly concluded that when a group "so exercises its powers as to infect the blood-stream of official sovereignty its exercise of power may be treated as the assertion of state authority." But Howe was rather tentative about limiting group power. Concerned about the rights of groups, he was more inclined to embrace the political pluralists' celebration of group autonomy than the legal pluralists' imposition of constraints on group power.[79] Robert Horn of Stanford followed suit, urging the Court to protect groups from government regulation as well as from individuals who claimed rights against them.[80] And Thomas Cowan announced that "modern life is lived associatively. The new democracy is an aggregation of sub-groups, not primarily of individuals."[81]

These group theorists remained very interested in protecting the rights of African Americans as a group. They also recognized that some groups were more powerful than others. But they assumed that power inequalities could be overcome if all individuals were allowed to associate to promote their collective interests. In their opinion, as long as all groups were treated equally, American democracy would thrive.

By the late 1960s, the different schools informed by the neo-pluralist vision of the state came under direct attack as social scientists argued that public policy was not determined through struggles among interest groups but rather through "the manipulation of the power of the state by certain entrenched elites." As these scholars saw it, a political order premised upon interest group pluralism failed to represent the vast majority of Americans, who "sat on the sidelines, dispirited, bored, and apathetic." To reempower individuals, they called on the government to respond to the people—not to groups, but to individuals. While urging a more participatory political process, they also called on the judiciary to protect individual rights and liberties.[82]

At the same time, the growing faith in economic markets to produce the common good helped transform the nature of the corporation, the archetype of legal pluralism. Drawing on microeconomics, neoclassical economists found a way around the need to tame corporate power and instead described corporate entities as nexuses of private contractual relationships.[83]

In this context, it is perhaps not surprising that the Court, as we have already seen, displayed unease when asked to impose constitutional constraints on organizations. Informed by the legal process school, it was concerned that subjecting private entities to constitutional limitations would risk its legitimacy. Influenced by market theories, it could escape earlier generations' concerns about private power, especially collective property power. As if reconciling the differences between group theorists and their critics, the Court reenvisioned organizations as associations of individuals rather than collective entities. Accordingly, the Court viewed organizations' constitutional rights as derived from the rights of their individual members and thus on a par with the rights of the individuals whose lives they affected. Drawing on *NAACP v. Alabama*, the Court used the individual's freedom of intimate and expressive association to sanctify the rights of all associations.

Associational rights were not absolute. In 1984, in *Roberts v. United States Jaycees*, the Court held that the application of the Minnesota Human Rights Act to compel the United States Jaycees to admit women as regular members did not violate the group members' freedom of association.[84] Similarly, in *Board of Directors of Rotary Int'l v. Rotary Club of Duarte*, decided three years later, the Court held that the California civil rights statute did not violate the First Amendment rights of Rotary International by requiring California Rotary clubs to admit women.[85]

But both cases were unique. Both involved a conflict between a local branch seeking to admit women and the national organization's attempt to restrict their ability to do so.[86] In this respect, both cases required the Court to resolve an intragroup disagreement. More important to my argument here is the Court's analysis of Jaycees' and Rotary's associational rights. The holding in each case was not justified by reference to the public role of the association or to its ability to exert power over individuals. Rather, the Court attempted to balance the interests of each of these two organizations with the interests of the individuals or groups they excluded (more specifically, the compelling state interest in protecting these individuals or groups).[87]

Balancing tests were commonly used by the legal realists earlier in the twentieth century. But their 1980s application was different. Realists, and legal pluralists, used such tests to correct imbalances of power between different groups, specifically corporations and labor unions. Similarly, the Warren Court's state action doctrine focused on the power that organizations could exert over members of minority groups. It was meant to protect individual rights from group power, not to balance the rights of individuals and groups. But in the 1980s the Court saw it appropriate to balance the interests of different groups without necessarily taking into account the power that certain groups and associations might wield.

This transformation in the Court's approach to evaluating group interests might seem rhetorical, especially given the outcome in cases such as *Roberts v. United States Jaycees* or *Board of Directors of Rotary Int'l v. Rotary Club of Duarte*. To explain the significance of the development, let me turn to Herbert Wechsler's 1959 article, "Toward Neutral Principles of Constitutional Law." The article was Wechsler's attempt to justify the Court's controversial and seemingly ends-driven ruling in *Brown v. Board of Education* by reference to "neutral principles." Finding it difficult to accept that "racial segregation is, in principle, a denial of equality to the minority against whom it is directed," Wechsler wrote: "For me, assuming equal facilities, the question posed by state-enforced segregation is not one of discrimination at all. Its human and its constitutional dimensions lie entirely elsewhere, in the denial by the state of the freedom to associate, a denial that impinges in the same way on any groups or races that may be involved."[88]

As Wechsler recognized, "if the freedom of association is denied by segregation, integration forces an association upon those for whom it is unpleasant or repugnant." Indeed, he was at a loss to provide a neutral principle for holding that "where the state must practically choose between denying the association to those individuals who wish it or imposing it on those who would avoid it . . . the Constitution demands that the claims for association should prevail."[89] Still, his insistence that the freedom of association was a neutral principle while antidiscrimination could not serve this function was the best articulation of what had become, by the 1970s, a dominant view. As Morton Horwitz aptly put it, "Discrimination analysis entailed choosing between victims and victimizers—in other words, being forced to choose between conflicting moral positions." While Wechsler recognized that there was "no basis for choosing on neutral grounds between denying or imposing freedom of association,"[90] by focusing on freedom of association, he was able to evade the moral question that had troubled legal pluralists since the turn of the twentieth century—in a diverse world, are some cultural and moral practices more valid than others?[91]

Indeed, by turning its back on concerns about group power and status and, instead, assuming that different groups' claims to freedom of association were equally legitimate, the Court, too, was able to evade this moral question. In so doing, it brought an end to the legacy of twentieth-century legal pluralism.

EPILOGUE

In 1998, in a review of Morton Horwitz's *The Warren Court and the Pursuit of Justice*, Linda Greenhouse labeled Horwitz "an unapologetic liberal for whom the Warren Court era remains 'a time when American idealism showed its most generous and hopeful face.'"[92] For readers of Horwitz's *The Transformation of American Law, 1870–1960: The Crisis of Legal Orthodoxy*, Greenhouse's characterization must have seemed awkward. *Transformation II*, as we have all come to label it, was the work of a critical legal historian,[93] not of "an unapologetic liberal." While a complete intellectual biography of Morton Horwitz awaits its author, I would like to suggest that the differences between Horwitz's approaches in the two books might be settled once we recognize that Horwitz is, at heart, a legal pluralist.

Take, for example, Horwitz's heroes in *Transformation II*: Adolf Berle, Robert Hale, William Douglas, and Morris and Felix Cohen—all, as I have argued here and elsewhere, were legal pluralists. Recognition of their legal pluralism substantiates Horwitz's argument that legal realism was not merely a methodology but also an ideology. In a similar manner, Horwitz's respect for the Warren Court is grounded in Horwitz's own embrace of the postwar cultural variation of legal pluralism. Most important, however, is Horwitz's lifelong rejection of procedural understandings of democracy and his celebration of a substantive democratic ideal, that is, the idea that tolerance of political, cultural, ethnic, and religious minorities does not "derive from non-democratic sources, but rather [is] part of the task of creating a pluralistic version of democratic culture."[94] For Horwitz, the American ideal of democracy is grounded in the celebration of diversity. Perhaps lyricist Abel Meeropol (Lewis Allan) and composer Earl Robinson best captured this ideal in their 1943 song, "The House I Live In," popularized by Frank Sinatra:

> What is America to me?
> The house I live in,
>
> . . . . .
>
> The faces that I see,
> All races and religions,
> That's America to me.
>
> . . . . . .
>
> The house I live in,
> My neighbors white and black,
> The people who just came here,
> Or from generations back;
>
> . . . .
>
> That's America to me.[95]

NOTES

1. 347 U.S. 483 (1954).

2. Adolf A. Berle Jr., "Constitutional Limitations on Corporate Activity: Protection of Personal Rights from Invasion through Economic Power," *University of Pennsylvania Law Review* 100 (1952): 942.

3. Ibid., 948.

4. Ibid., 951.

5. *Marsh v. Alabama,* 326 U.S. 501 (1946); *Shelley v. Kraemer,* 334 U.S. 1 (1948).

6. Dalia Tsuk Mitchell, *Architect of Justice: Felix S. Cohen and the Founding of American Legal Pluralism* (Ithaca, N.Y.: Cornell University Press, 2007). Felix Cohen, a brilliant legal realist and the guru of federal Indian law, was the voice of legal pluralism. While I refrain from making additional references to Cohen's work and scholarship in this essay, my argument here draws on my analysis in *Architect of Justice* to examine, albeit from a different angle, the significance of legal pluralism.

7. 530 U.S. 640 (2000).

8. Lynn Dumenil, *The Modern Temper: American Culture and Society in the 1920s* (New York: Hill and Wang, 1995), 145.

9. Peter Novick, *That Noble Dream: The "Objectivity Question" and the American Historical Profession* (New York: Cambridge University Press, 1988). See also Morton J. Horwitz, *The Transformation of American Law, 1870–1960: The Crisis of Legal Orthodoxy* (New York: Oxford University Press, 1992), 180–82; Richard H. Pells, *Radical Visions and American Dreams: Culture and Social Thought in the Depression Years* (Urbana: University of Illinois Press, 1998), 4.

10. Horwitz, *Transformation II,* 210–12.

11. Morton J. Horwitz, "Jews and Legal Realists" (unpublished manuscript), 9–10. Cf. Morton J. Horwitz, "Why Is Anglo-American Jurisprudence Unhistorical?" *Oxford Journal of Legal Studies* 17 (1997): 581.

12. See, for example, W. Y. Elliott, *The Pragmatic Revolt in Politics: Syndicalism, Fascism, and the Constitutional State* (New York: Macmillan, 1928); Paul Q. Hirst, ed., *The Pluralist Theory of the State: Selected Writings of G. D. H. Cole, J. N. Figgis, and H. J. Laski* (New York: Routledge, 1989).

13. Arthur Bentley, *The Process of Government* (Bloomington, Ind.: Principia Press, 1908), 465–80. See also Earl Latham, *The Group Basis of Politics* (Ithaca, N.Y.: Cornell University Press, 1952), 12–13.

14. See John Dewey, *The Public and Its Problems* (New York: H. Holt, 1927); Mary P. Follett, *The New State: Group Organization the Solution of Popular Government* (New York: Longmans, Green 1918); Harold J. Laski, *Studies in the Problem of Sovereignty* (New Haven, Conn.: Yale University Press, 1917). For a recent analysis of theories of political pluralism, see Avigail I. Eisenberg, *Reconstructing Political Pluralism* (Albany: State University of New York Press, 1995).

15. Mark M. Hager, "Bodies Politic: The Progressive History of Organizational 'Real Entity' Theory," *University of Pittsburgh Law Review* 50 (1989): 579–80.

16. The classic critique of the distinction between public and private power remains Robert L. Hale, "Coercion and Distribution in a Supposedly Non-coercive State," *Political Science Quarterly* 38 (1923): 470–94.

17. Cf. Daniel R. Ernst, "Common Laborers? Industrial Pluralists, Legal Realists, and the Law of Industrial Disputes, 1915–1943," *Law and History Review* 11 (1993): 59–100.

18. See Dalia Tsuk, "Corporations without Labor: The Politics of Progressive Corporate Law," *University of Pennsylvania Law Review* 151 (2003): 1861–912; Dalia Tsuk, "From Pluralism to Individualism: Berle and Means and 20th Century American Legal Thought," *Law & Social Inquiry* 30 (2005): 179–225. For a detailed analysis of the relationship between legal realism and pluralism, see Tsuk Mitchell, *Architect of Justice*, chap. 2.

19. Michael J. Sandel, *Democracy's Discontent: America in Search of a Public Philosophy* (Cambridge, Mass.: Belknap Press of Harvard University Press, 1996), 252–55. On collectivism in the New Deal, see Gary Dean Best, *The Retreat from Liberalism: Collectivists versus Progressives in the New Deal Years* (Westport, Conn.: Praeger, 2002).

20. Alan Brinkley, *The End of Reform: New Deal Liberalism in Recession and War* (New York: Knopf, 1995), 165; Risa L. Goluboff, "The Work of Civil Rights in the 1940s: The Department of Justice, the NAACP, and African Americans Agricultural Workers" (PhD diss., Princeton University, 2003); Risa L. Goluboff, *The Lost Promise of Civil Rights* (Cambridge, MA: Harvard University Press, 2007).

21. John T. Elliff, *The United States Department of Justice and Individual Rights, 1937–1962* (New York: Garland, 1987); William E. Forbath, "Civil Rights and Economic Citizenship: Notes on the Past and Future of the Civil Rights and Labor Movements," *University of Pennsylvania Journal of Labor and Employment Law* 2 (2000): 697–718; Risa L. Goluboff, "The Thirteenth Amendment and the Lost Origins of Civil Rights," *Duke Law Journal* 50 (2001): 1609–85; Herbert Hovenkamp, "The Political Economy of Substantive Due Process," *Stanford Law Review* 40 (1988): 379–447.

22. See, for example, Brinkley, *End of Reform*, 154–65.

23. Morton J. Horwitz, *The Warren Court and the Pursuit of Justice* (New York: Hill and Wang, 1998).

24. Morton J. Horwitz, "Foreword: The Constitution of Change: Legal Fundamentality without Fundamentalism," *Harvard Law Review* 107 (1993): 62–63.

25. Horace M. Kallen, "Democracy versus the Melting-Pot," in *Culture and Democracy in the United States* (New York: Boni and Liveright, 1924), 67, 125, originally published in the *Nation* (Feb. 18 and 25, 1915). See also Louis Menand, *The Metaphysical Club: The Story of Ideas in America* (New York: Farrar, Straus and Giroux, 2001), 388–93; Werner Sollors, *Beyond Ethnicity: Consent and Descent in American Culture* (New York: Oxford University Press, 1986), 66, 97; David A. Hollinger, "Ethnic Diversity, Cosmopolitanism and the Emergence of the American Liberal Intelligentsia," *American Quarterly* 27 (1975): 142; Elmer N. Lear, "On the Unity of the Kallen Perspective," in *The Legacy of Horace M. Kallen*, ed. Milton R. Konvitz (London: Associated University Presses, 1987), 116; Sidney Ratner, "Horace M. Kallen and Cultural Pluralism," in Konvitz, *The Legacy of Horace M. Kallen*, 50.

26. 323 U.S. 192, 198–99 (1944).

27. 326 U.S. at 505–6.

28. Robert L. Hale, *Freedom through Law: Public Control of Private Governing Power* (New York: Columbia University Press, 1952), 379.

29. Hale, "Coercion and Distribution."

30. Robert L. Hale, "Rights under the Fourteenth and Fifteenth Amendments against Injuries Inflicted by Private Individuals," *Lawyers Guild Review* 6 (1946): 627–28. Cf. W. E. B. DuBois, "Civil Rights Legislation before and after the Passage of the 14th Amendment," *Lawyers Guild Review* 6 (1946): 642 (noting that "the most discouraging situation that faces us are the cove-

nants based on the organized action of real estate interests to curtail the housing rights of Negroes and to insure the perpetuation of slums").

31. Hale, "Rights under the Fourteenth and Fifteenth Amendments"; Robert L. Hale, "Our Equivocal Constitutional Guarantees," *Columbia Law Review* 39 (1939): 563–94.

32. Berle, "Constitutional Limitations," 951–52. See also A. A. Berle Jr., "The Developing Law of Corporate Concentration," *University of Chicago Law Review* 19 (1951–52): 661 (noting the need to protect "the basic rights of individuals" against corporations "as they were against the erstwhile political state").

33. 345 U.S. 461, 469–70 (1953).

34. 391 U.S. 308 (1968).

35. 326 U.S. 517, 518–20 (1946).

36. 334 U.S. 558, 562 (1948).

37. Philip B. Kurland and Gerhard Casper, eds., *Landmark Briefs and Arguments of the Supreme Court of the United States: Constitutional Law,* vol. 46 (Arlington, Va.: University Publications of America, 1975).

38. *Shelley,* 334 U.S. at 13–21.

39. Kurland and Casper, *Landmark Briefs and Arguments*, 46:424.

40. *Shelley,* 334 U.S. at 21–22.

41. See, for example, *Sweatt v. Painter,* 339 U.S. 629, 634–35 (1950) (holding that a newly established state law school for African American students did not provide them with educational opportunities equivalent to those offered to white students at the University of Texas. Drawing on *Shelley v. Kraemer,* the Court declared that "It may be argued that excluding petitioner from that school is no different from excluding white students from the new law school. This contention overlooks realities. It is unlikely that a member of a group so decisively in the majority, attending a school with rich traditions and prestige which only a history of consistently maintained excellence could command, would claim that the opportunities afforded him for legal education were unequal to those held open to petitioner. That such a claim, if made, would be dishonored by the State, is no answer"); *McLaurin v. Oklahoma State Regents for Higher Education*, 339 U.S. 637, 641–42 (1950) (holding that the University of Oklahoma deprived an African American student of the equal protection of the laws by requiring him to eat apart from other students. Citing *Shelley v. Kraemer,* the Court noted that while "the removal of the state restrictions will not necessarily abate individual and group predilections, prejudices and choices[,] . . . at the very least, the state will not be depriving appellant of the opportunity to secure acceptance by his fellow student on his own merits").

42. *Brown*, 347 U.S. at 495.

43. Charles L. Black Jr., "Foreword: 'State Action,' Equal Protection, and California Proposition 14," *Harvard Law Review* 81 (1967–68): 70.

44. Jack Greenberg, "Race Relations and Group Interest in the Law," *Rutgers Law Review* 13 (1959): 503.

45. Ibid., 505–7.

46. Ibid., 509–10.

47. My argument in this part is developed in Tsuk, "From Pluralism to Individualism."

48. Alan Brinkley, "The New Deal and the Idea of the State," in *The Rise and Fall of the New Deal Order, 1930–1980,* ed. Steve Fraser and Gary Gerstle (Princeton, N.J.: Princeton University Press, 1989), 85–98.

49. Sandel, *Democracy's Discontent*, 251–62.

50. See Robert A. Dahl, *A Preface to Democratic Theory* (Chicago: Chicago University Press, 1956); Robert A. Dahl, *Pluralist Democracy in the United States: Conflict and Consent* (Chicago: Chicago University Press, 1967). See also Edward A. Purcell Jr., *The Crisis of Democratic Theory: Scientific Naturalism and the Problem of Value* (Lexington: University of Kentucky, 1973), 253–66.

51. J. M. Balkin, "Some Realism about Pluralism: Legal Realist Approaches to the First Amendment," *Duke Law Journal* (1990): 388–91.

52. Pells, *Radical Visions*, 143–44.

53. John Kenneth Galbraith, *American Capitalism: The Concept of Countervailing Power* (Boston: Houghton Mifflin, 1952), 115–39.

54. Daniel Bell, *The End of Ideology: On the Exhaustion of Political Ideas in the Fifties* (Glencoe, Ill.: Free Press, 1960), 60.

55. Davita Silfen Glasberg and Michael Schwartz, "Ownership and Control of Corporations," *Annual Review of Sociology* 9 (1983): 325.

56. Herbert Hovenkamp, "The Mind and Heart of Progressive Legal Thought," *Iowa Law Review* 81 (1995): 159.

57. Charles A. Reich, "The New Property," *Yale Law Journal* 73 (1964): 771.

58. Ibid., 733

59. Gregory S. Alexander, *Commodity and Propriety: Competing Visions of Property in American Legal Thought, 1776–1970* (Chicago: University of Chicago Press, 1997), 375.

60. Reich, "The New Property," 773.

61. Alexander, *Commodity and Propriety*, 373–75.

62. 345 U.S. at 484–85, 494.

63. Horwitz, *The Warren Court*, 37–51.

64. 378 U.S. 226, 330–32 (1964).

65. 391 U.S. at 332–33.

66. See Adolf A. Berle Jr. and Gardiner C. Means, *The Modern Corporation and Private Property* (New York: Macmillan, 1932)

67. 378 U.S. at 242–66.

68. *Amalgamated Food Employees Union Local 590*, 391 U.S. at 316.

69. 424 U.S. 507, 513 (1976).

70. Id., at 519.

71. See Kallen, "Postscript—Culture and the Ku Klux Klan," in *Culture and Democracy in the United States*, 23.

72. 357 U.S. 449, 460–66 (1958).

73. William O. Douglas, "The Right of Association," *Columbia Law Review* 63 (1963): 1373.

74. Ibid., 1375.

75. 378 U.S. at 267–71.

76. Reuel E. Schiller, "From Group Rights to Individual Liberties: Post-war Labor Law, Liberalism, and the Waning of Union Strength," *Berkeley Journal of Employment and Labor Law* 20 (1999): 13–16. See also Alexander M. Bickel, "Foreword: The Passive Virtues," *Harvard Law Review* 75 (1961): 40–79; Herbert Wechsler, "Toward Neutral Principles of Constitutional Law," *Harvard Law Review* 73 (1959): 1–35.

77. Harry H. Wellington, "The Constitution, the Labor Union, and 'Governmental Action,'" *Yale Law Journal* 70 (1961): 374.

78. Schiller, "From Group Rights to Individual Liberties," 15–16.

79. Mark DeWolfe Howe, "Foreword: Political Theory and the Nature of Liberty," *Harvard Law Review* 67 (1953): 91–95.

80. Schiller, "From Group Rights to Individual Liberties," 16–17.

81. Thomas A. Cowan, "Group Interests," *Virginia Law Review* 44 (1958): 331.

82. Schiller, "From Group Rights to Individual Liberties," 48–57; Tsuk, "Corporations without Labor," 1908 n. 217.

83. Tsuk, "From Pluralism to Individualism," 210; Tsuk, "Corporations without Labor," 1898.

84. 468 U.S. 609 (1984).

85. 481 U.S. 537 (1987).

86. Cf. Lois M. McKenna, "Freedom of Association or Gender Discrimination: *New York State Club Association v. City of New York*," *American University Law Review* 38 (1989): 1073–79.

87. See, e.g., *Roberts*, 468 U.S. at 475 ("We are persuaded that Minnesota's compelling interest in eradicating discrimination against its female citizens justifies the impact that application of the statute to the Jaycees may have on the male members' associational freedoms"); *Board of Directors of Rotary Int'l*, 481 U.S. at 549 ("Even if the Unruh Act does work some slight infringement on Rotary members' right of expressive association, that infringement is justified because it serves the State's compelling interest in eliminating discrimination against women").

88. Wechsler, "Toward Neutral Principles of Constitutional Law," 33–34.

89. Ibid., 34.

90. Horwitz, *Transformation II*, 265–68.

91. Cf. ibid.

92. Linda Greenhouse, "A Miracle Very Much of Its Time" (Books of Our Times), *New York Times*, Aug. 5, 1998, p. E8.

93. Cf. Robert W. Gordon, "Critical Legal Histories," *Stanford Law Review* 36 (1984): 57–125.

94. Horwitz, "Foreword: The Constitution of Change," 63–64.

95. *The House I Live In,* By Earl Robinson and Lewis Allan Copyright © 1942 (Renewed) by Music Sales Corporation (ASCAP) International Copyright Secured. All Rights Reserved. Used By Permission. Sinatra's version of "The House I Live In" was used in a short 1945 film, with the same title, in which he starred. The stanza including the words "my neighbors white and black" was omitted from the film version, apparently because its sentiment (equality for African Americans as well as recent immigrants) seemed too radical at the time. See Owen McNally, "Our 'House': Populist World War II Anthem Resonates Anew, Capturing Essence of American Unity," *Hartford Courant,* Sept. 8, 2002; Ivy Meeropol, "The (Unexpurgated) House I Live In," letter to the editor, *The Nation*, Sept. 11, 2002, http://www.thenation.com/doc/20020805/letter (accessed Aug. 18, 2008). I thank Morty for telling me about this song. See also "Popular Harvard University Course Looks at the Supreme Court during the Warren Years," *All Things Considered,* National Public Radio, Jan. 3, 2005.

10

The Death and Rebirth of the Clear and Present Danger Test

STEPHEN A. SIEGEL

I WOULD LIKE TO TAKE THE OCCASION OF OUR HONORING MORT HORWITZ to celebrate some of the people and legal doctrines he celebrates and to disdain some of the people and legal doctrines he disdains.

Justice William Brennan certainly is among the people Mort admires. Mort places Brennan alongside John Marshall, Oliver Wendell Holmes Jr., and Louis Brandeis at the pinnacle of American judicial greatness.[1] Among the doctrines Mort appreciates is the "clear and present danger" test, at least the version that emerged from Justice Brennan's rewrite of Justice Fortas's opinion in *Brandenburg v. Ohio*.[2] Mort has described Brennan's statement of the danger rule as "the most speech-friendly test yet devised,"[3] and I interpret that as a compliment.

Justice Brennan and the clear and present danger test are the heroes of my piece.

Concomitantly, among the people Mort disdains are the justices who responded to cold war security concerns and McCarthyism with a First Amendment jurisprudence that was deferential to repressive legislative enactments and government action.[4] In that vein, *Dennis v. United States*[5] and that case's version of the danger rule[6] certainly are among the cases and doctrines that Mort dislikes the most.[7]

Deference in First Amendment jurisprudence during the cold war and the *Dennis* case are the villains of my piece.

In this paper, what ties these heroes and villains together is the doctrine of strict scrutiny. In a recent paper, I argued that strict scrutiny did not originate in the equal protection clause. Rather, it originated in the First Amendment in the late 1950s and early 1960s and migrated from there to equal protection litigation in the late 1960s.[8] That paper credits Justice Brennan with being the key figure in establishing strict scrutiny in the First Amendment in two 1963 cases, *NAACP v. Button*[9] and *Sherbert v. Verner*.[10] He also was the key figure in moving strict scrutiny to the equal protection clause, in 1969, in *Shapiro v. Thompson*.[11]

My thesis in this paper is that once it is appreciated that strict scrutiny originated as a First Amendment doctrine, we can—by taking a close look at First Amendment history—come to appreciate strict scrutiny, rather than the rule in the *Brandenburg* case, as the clear and danger test reborn. It was in the cases establishing strict scrutiny in the First Amendment that Justice Brennan "shook off McCarthyism,"[12] revived the danger test in a new and expanded guise, and ended the reign of *Dennis* and deferential civil liberties jurisprudence. The "real" Warren Court dates from these opinions.[13]

That Justice Brennan was a fan of strict scrutiny and used it widely,[14] but not indiscriminately,[15] is well known. But I do not think his leadership in establishing it as a facet of constitutional law is sufficiently appreciated.[16] In attributing strict scrutiny to Justice Brennan, and claiming a connection to the pre-*Dennis* clear and present danger rule, I am arguing uphill in several regards. One certainly is that in 1965, as the Meiklejohn lecturer at Brown University, Justice Brennan reviewed the Warren Court's development of First Amendment doctrine and discussed the danger rule without suggesting that it had any relation to strict scrutiny.[17] Indeed, in that lecture, Brennan never mentioned strict scrutiny as a First Amendment doctrine. Nevertheless, contemporary commentators noted the connection between the pre-*Dennis* clear and present danger precedents and the Warren Court's new direction in First Amendment jurisprudence.[18]

The first part of this paper reviews First Amendment history, emphasizing the central role of the clear and present danger test in the 1940s and the shift to a jurisprudence of judicial deference in the 1950s. The second part reviews the origin of strict scrutiny in First Amendment litigation in the late 1950s and early 1960s. The third part argues that strict scrutiny should be understood as the rebirth of the 1940s' danger test. The fourth part assesses the history of the danger rule for the light it sheds on current developments in the law of strict scrutiny. Finally, I conclude with remarks on the relation of this paper to a few themes in Mort Horwitz's scholarship.

THE CLEAR AND PRESENT DANGER TEST AND THE RISE, DECLINE, AND REVIVAL OF THE FIRST AMENDMENT

To understand the death of the clear and present danger test and its rebirth as strict scrutiny, it is best to divide First Amendment history into three periods: 1919–39, 1939–49, and 1949–63.

1919–39: The First Movement toward Heightened Protection of First Amendment Liberties

Before the 1930s, First Amendment liberties received scant protection under the United States Constitution.[19] One reason was that until 1925, freedom of speech was not considered sufficiently fundamental to receive protection against state infringement under the Fourteenth Amendment's due process clause.[20] Another was the Supreme Court's disposition to interpret the First Amendment as a restriction only on "prior," not "subsequent," restraints on speech.[221] A final reason was that the Court generally applied the "bad tendency" test, which was very permissive of governmental power to regulate speech.[22]

It is true that between 1919 and 1927, Holmes and Brandeis formulated the clear and present danger test, which offered more substantial protection for speakers voicing unpopular and even illegal sentiments.[23] Yet while Holmes and Brandeis were on the Court, the danger test was embraced neither by the Court nor even by a substantial minority of its justices.[24] The clear and present danger test's importance lay in the future, not in the decade of its formulation.

Nonetheless, for reasons that are just beginning to be canvassed,[25] the Court became somewhat more protective of First Amendment values in the 1930s.[26] Although the Court was more speech protective than ever before, the modest protections it implemented were "largely *ad hoc* with no discernible thread of doctrinal continuity."[27] Holmes and Brandeis's danger rule played almost no role. The most prominent doctrinal development was the Court's expanded use of "Blackstone's old doctrine of 'prior restraint' as the essence of forbidden censorship"[28] to bar injunctions prohibiting defamatory speech,[29] to strike down taxes specifically levied on newspapers and magazines,[30] and to void municipal ordinances creating standardless parade permit systems.[31]

Because the protections afforded speech, press, and assembly during the 1930s were still quite modest, the most important development was at the level of principle rather than practice. Toward the end of the decade, the Court began articulating a theoretical foundation for increased judicial protection for First Amendment liberties. In 1937, in *Palko v. Connecticut*, Justice Cardozo noted that "freedom of thought and speech" occupies an exalted position in the Constitution's framework of values as "the matrix, the indispensable condition, of nearly every other form of freedom."[32] The following year, in *United States v. Carolene Products Co.*,[33] when then Justice Stone first suggested dividing judicial review into domains of deferential and nondeferential scrutiny, he indicated that First Amendment liberties were among the few areas in which there might be active judicial review.[34] First Amendment liberties were involved in every one of the rationales Justice Stone put forth as justifying heightened judicial protection. First Amendment liberties were part "of the first ten Amendments"; were important to "those political processes which can ordinarily be expected to bring about repeal of undesirable legislation"; and frequently protected "particular religious . . . or national, . . . or racial minorities" from hostile legislation.[35]

In the 1930s, the Court was groping toward a new direction in constitutional review. On one hand, the Court was contracting economic liberties;[36] on the other, it was modestly expanding speech and other civil liberties.[37] By the end of the

1930s, the groundwork had been laid for the major expansion of First Amendment liberties that occurred in the next decade.

1939–49: The First Amendment Comes of Age

It was in the 1940s that the First Amendment came to occupy a "preferred position" in the pantheon of American constitutional values.[38] Speech received protection through a number of doctrines. The Court continued to void handbill, parade, and sound truck licensing schemes as impermissible prior restraints if they lacked sufficiently clear standards to control official decision making.[39] In addition, the Court protected speech by straining its construction of statutes to avoid possible conflicts with the First Amendment,[40] loosening its requirements for facial challenges and standing to sue,[41] and invalidating statutes for vagueness[42] and overbreadth.[43] Most importantly, the Court protected speech by adopting "balancing of interests" as its general approach to First Amendment issues.[44]

Balancing of interests is an approach to judicial decision making that begins by identifying the societal and personal interests implicated by a legal conflict and assigning differing weights to those interests based on their varying importance to social and individual flourishing.[45] Then, balancing-of-interests jurisprudence resolves legal conflict by allowing the more important interests to prevail over the less important, or by allowing each interest to prevail to an appropriate extent.

Balancing-of-interests jurisprudence comes in two styles: ad hoc and categorical.[46] Ad hoc balancing determines controversies by weighing the interests at stake in each particular case.[47] Categorical balancing weighs conflicting interests as a step toward formulating a standard or rule that is applied in subsequent controversies without further balancing.[48]

In the late 1930s and the 1940s, balancing of interests (both ad hoc and categorical) was the dominant form of constitutional jurisprudence in First Amendment controversies.[49] Before that time, most judges approached constitutional adjudication as involving the analytical elaboration of legal definitions, categories, principles, and rules.[50] This formalistic jurisprudence was founded on the belief that even when they were instrumental tools fashioned to effectuate constitutional policy, legal rules ultimately rested on differences in natural kind, not debatable differences of degree.

Rooted in developments in social philosophy, private law jurisprudence, and national politics,[51] balancing of interests entered constitutional law through the dissents of Holmes, Brandeis, and Stone in the 1920s.[52] With the New Deal revolution and the departure of the "Four Horsemen of Reaction"[53] from the Court, balancing of interests became the dominant approach to several areas of constitutional law.[54] The First Amendment was preeminent among them. What Professor Aleinikoff calls "the Age of Balancing" fully arrived in First Amendment controversies by the early 1940s.[55]

Similarity in overall technique, however, masked important jurisprudential, political, and substantive differences among the justices who embraced balancing-of-interests jurisprudence. Although all justices in the 1940s adjudicated First Amendment controversies through a balancing approach, they were divided into three distinct camps based on the extent to which their balancing deferred to the government's determination that the defendant's exercise of a First Amendment freedom could be regulated or proscribed. One group, lead by Justice Felix Frankfurter, employed an ad hoc balancing technique that was extraordinarily deferential to the government's decision to enforce rules that directly or indirectly limited First Amendment liberties.[56] At times, Frankfurter wrote as if he meant to adjudicate First Amendment claims through the same rational basis test that the Court used to review legislation regulating economic interests.[57] In practice, Frankfurter and his allies, which included Justices Burton, Reed, and Jackson, never went that far.[58] On occasion, the Frankfurter bloc found government regulations of First Amendment freedoms had gone too far.[59] But generally, they were unlikely to find that legislatures had struck the wrong balance. Acutely aware that in constitutional cases the Court played the secondary role of reviewing the balance struck by the more democratically accountable branches of government, the deferential balancers were willing to intervene only to keep "the democratic process . . . open and unobstructed."[60]

Underlying the deferential-balancing position was the belief that "judicial review [was] itself a limitation on popular government," that "to the legislature no less than to courts is committed the guardianship of deeply-cherished liberties," and that "education in the abandonment of foolish legislation is itself a training in liberty . . . [that] serves to vindicate the self-confidence of a free people."[61] For these reasons, the justices led by Frankfurter concluded that deferential balancing, something nearly equivalent to rational basis review, was the proper judicial stance in all but a few cases implicating First Amendment freedoms. As a result, they gave First Amendment liberties only modestly more protection than economic interests.[62] Inevitably, the justices who advocated deferential ad hoc balancing were low protectionists when it came to reviewing First Amendment cases.

Frankfurter's low-protectionist group was opposed by a group of high-protectionist justices who subjected legislation to searching scrutiny and, in balancing the conflicting interests, freely substituted their own constitutional judgment for that of the legislature. This group of activist balancers, composed of Justices Black, Douglas, Murphy, and Rutledge, provided a solid bloc of four votes in favor of robust First Amendment values during most of the 1940s.

The four high-protectionist justices employed a categorical balancing technique.[63] These justices believed "that, when balancing interests, speech was to be given an especially heavy weight because of its central function in the preservation of the democratic process."[64] In balancing to create a doctrine for application in subsequent controversies, the high-protectionist justices determined that speech could not be regulated unless it created a "clear and present danger" of harm to an interest the state was entitled to protect.[65] They developed a rigorous form of the danger test, which allowed only an imminent threat of substantial harm to outweigh the individual and public interest in the exercise of First Amendment liberties.[66] As Justice Rutledge wrote in *Thomas v. Collins*:

> Any attempt to restrict [First Amendment freedoms] must be justified by clear public interest, threatened not doubtfully or remotely, but by clear and present danger. . . . Only the gravest abuses, endangering paramount interests, give occasion for permissible limitation. . . .
>
> . . . [Our] tradition . . . support[s] an intrusion upon this domain, only if grave and impending public danger requires [it].[67]

Between these two blocs was a small group of justices who thought the Court's judgment in First Amendment cases should be independent of the legislature's, but not stringently protective of First Amendment values. This group, consisting of such jurists as Chief Justice Stone and Justice Roberts, treated speech differently from economic regulation. When First Amendment values were involved, their review was more searching than that of Frankfurter and his allies. At the same time, they required something far less than a clear and present danger to tip the balance in the state's favor. They occupied an intermediate position between the low protectionists' deferential stance and the high protectionists' stringent stance. They imposed a reasonableness standard, or what might be called "a rationality standard with some teeth,"[68] on legislation that trenched on First Amendment rights.[69]

This moderate-protectionist group held the balance of power. By necessity, the low and high protectionists competed for their votes.[70] To attract and hold the moderate center, low and high protectionists had to restrain their words when they wrote for the Court.[71] Sometimes opinions for the Court written by high-protectionist justices employed the rhetoric of moderate balancing without any suggestion that a clear and present danger was necessary for the state to limit First Amendment freedoms.[72] Conversely, when Court opinions by low-protectionist justices found the balance of interests came out in favor of the government, they sometimes did so without any hint of a deferential stance.[73]

Throughout most of the 1940s, the high protectionists attracted and held the moderate center more frequently than the low protectionists did. This was especially true after the spring of 1943, when the low-protectionist Justice Byrnes resigned and the high-protectionist Justice Rutledge joined the Court.[74] With Justice Rutledge, there was a critical mass of four high-protectionist justices on the Court, enough to grant writs of certiorari and only one vote short of the majority for disposition of the cases.[75]

Over the next six years, the Court handed down more First Amendment decisions than during its entire previous history.[76] Of the approximately twenty-nine cases involving serious First Amendment claims that were decided on constitutional rather than statutory grounds,[77] the First Amendment claim prevailed in twenty of them.[78]

At least until the formation of the "real" Warren Court in 1962,[79] the appointment of Justice Rutledge to the Court "mark[ed] the era *par excellence* of civil liberties . . . in American jurisprudence."[80] As Wallace Mendelson has observed, if the high-protectionist "clear and present danger [test] was ever the law, it was while the four libertarians—Justices Black, Douglas, Murphy, and Rutledge, were together on the bench."[81]

1949–63: The First Amendment Recedes and Is Reborn

The 1940s' high-protection era ended in the summer of 1949 when Justices Murphy and Rutledge died and were replaced by the low-protectionist Justices Clark and Minton.[82] Murphy's and Rutledge's deaths coincided with a shift in First Amendment litigation from cases involving the speech of labor organizers and religious minorities to cases focused on communist speech and organizing.[83] The new appointments and shift in issues led to a threefold revolution in the First Amendment analysis, all within the confines of the balancing test.

First, the new low-protectionist majority subverted the clear and present danger test into a formula for low-protectionist balancing.[84] Presaged in a number of cases in 1950 and early 1951,[85] the locus classicus of the Court's "reinterpretation" of the danger test was *Dennis v. United States*.[86] In *Dennis*, the Court upheld the Smith Act convictions of the Communist Party leadership for conspiring to form an organization to teach and advocate the violent overthrow of the United States government.[87] Chief Justice Vinson, writing for the Court's plurality, adopted the reformulation of the danger test that Judge Learned Hand had suggested when the case was before the Second Circuit: "In each case [courts] must ask whether the gravity of the 'evil,' discounted by its improbability, justifies such invasion of free speech as is necessary to avoid the danger."[88] This reinterpretation of the danger test removed the crucial requirement of immediacy, which was the very heart of the danger test, the element that made the danger formula a stringent standard.[89] In lessening the stringency of the test, the Court turned what had been a speech-protective test into a formula for ad hoc balancing ripe for deferential application.

Second, having subverted the danger rule, the new low-protectionist majority entirely jettisoned it as an influential approach to First Amendment controversies. In its place, the new majority formally ensconced ad hoc deferential balancing as the universal metric for First Amendment controversies.[90]

Justice Frankfurter advocated jettisoning the danger rule in *Dennis* in a concurrence attacking the constitutional bona fides of the clear and present danger standard. "The demands of free speech in a democratic society," he wrote, "are better served by candid and informed weighing of the competing interests, within the confines of the judicial process, than by announcing dogmas too inflexible for the non-Euclidian problems to be solved."[91] In Frankfurter's view, the judicial "weighing" was not to be a process of bringing independent judgment to the issue at bar. Rather, in "assessing" and balancing "the competing interests . . . full responsibility for the choice cannot be given to the courts. Courts are not representative bodies. They are not designed to be a good reflex of a democratic society."[92] Therefore, "Primary responsibility for adjusting the interests which compete in the situation before us of necessity belongs to the Congress. . . . We are to set aside the judgment of those whose duty it is to legislate only if there is no reasonable basis for it."[93]

From Frankfurter's *Dennis* concurrence, deferential balancing flowered into the general mode of analysis for First Amendment issues. It governed cases involving not only communists, but also other unpopular speakers and groups. In these years, for example, the Court allowed states to arrest speakers for addressing hostile audiences,[94] proscribe group libel,[95] investigate camps that invited leftists to speak at their campfires,[96] and compel observant Jews not to work on the Christian day of rest.[97] Throughout the 1950s, and into the early 1960s, deferential balancing dominated the Court's response to most First Amendment controversies.[98]

Barenblatt v. United States[99] illustrates the Court's ad hoc and deferential-balancing approach to the First Amendment during this illiberal part of the Warren era.[100] Lloyd Barenblatt, a Vassar College professor, was called before the House Un-American Activities Committee as part of its investigation into communist infiltration into education. On First Amendment grounds, Barenblatt refused to answer questions about his present or past membership in the Communist Party, membership in particular clubs when he was a student at the University of Michigan, and knowledge of "Francis Crowley as a member of the Communist Party."[101] The Supreme Court upheld his conviction for contempt of Congress in an opinion written by Justice Harlan for the low-protectionist majority composed of himself and Justices Clark, Frankfurter, Stewart, and Whittaker.

As articulated by Harlan, the Court's approach was that "where First Amendment rights are asserted . . . resolution of the issue always involves a balancing by the courts of the competing private and public interests at stake in the particular circumstances of the case."[102] In making that balance, "the critical element" in each case "is the existence of, and the weight to be ascribed to, the interest of the" government, as compared to "the individual interests at stake."[103] In Barenblatt's case, because HUAC was investigating "Communist activity in this Country,"[104] the government interest was nothing less than "the right of self-preservation,"[105] a right that easily "subordinate[d]"[106] Barenblatt's privacy interest[107] or even the social interest in academic freedom.[108] Because the trial record contained no evidence that HUAC had abused its power "to conduct appropriate investigations in aid"[109] of Congress's "wide power to legislate in the field of Communist activity,"[110] the validity of Barenblatt's contempt conviction was "beyond question."[111]

As many contemporaries noted, Harlan's balancing analysis in *Barenblatt* weighed the whole society's interest against Barenblatt's individual concerns.[112] This weighing process violated the norms of balancing as described by the jurists who first advocated that approach in preference to legal formalism. According to them, balancing is a valid technique only when the interests involved are defined at the same level of generality so that, for example, social interests are weighed against social interests and individual interests are balanced against competing individual interests. Weighing the state's social interests against individual concerns almost always makes the state's interests seem paramount. It was this violation of the norms of balancing that made the Court's approach to balancing so deferential that it bordered on rational basis review in many First Amendment cases of the 1950s and early 1960s.

The third aspect of the revolution in First Amendment jurisprudence brought about by the Court's change in personnel was that the new majority's imposition of a deferential-balancing approach drove Justices Black and Douglas to abandon balancing entirely in favor of an "absolutist" approach to the First Amendment.[113] The deferential majority's First Amendment decisions in the 1950s convinced Black and Douglas that the Court's balancing formula "was so constructed as to bend in times of crisis, when constitutional protection was needed most."[114] Speaking of Justice Black, Charles Reich observed that his eventual "reluctance to allow judges to evaluate competing social interests was intensified by his observation that judges could not be counted on to give a fair evaluation to these interests; frequently the interest representing liberty was inadequately assessed."[115] Black said this was especially so "in times of emergency and stress."[116]

For Black, the inherent flaw with balancing was that "if the need is great, the right of the Government can always be said to outweigh the rights of the individual."[117] History taught that balancing "has been the excuse for practically every repressive measure that Government has ever seen fit to adopt."[118] And so, although Black agreed with his deferential colleagues that "the decision to provide a constitutional safeguard for a particular right, such as . . . the right of free speech, involves a balancing of conflicting interests,"[119] he came to insist that "the Framers themselves did this balancing when they wrote the Constitution and the Bill of Rights. They appreciated the risks involved and they decided that certain rights should be guaranteed regardless of these risks. Courts have neither the right nor the power to review this original decision of the Framers and to attempt to make a different evaluation of the importance of the rights granted in the Constitution."[120]

Thus, throughout the 1950s and into the early 1960s, the Court was split on First Amendment issues between a low-protectionist majority and a high-protectionist minority. In the early years, the low protectionists held a 7–2 advantage. With the replacement of Chief Justice Vinson and Justice Minton by Earl Warren and William Brennan, respectively, the low protectionists' voting advantage was reduced to 5–4.[121] Then in 1962, Justices Whittaker and Frankfurter resigned for health reasons.[122] Whittaker was replaced with Byron White, who did not vote consistently with the liberal bloc.[123] Frankfurter, however, was replaced with Arthur Goldberg, who unwaveringly favored individuals in First Amendment cases. With Goldberg's appointment, high protectionism achieved a dominant voice for the first time since Murphy and Rutledge left the Court in 1949.

The return to high protection, however, did not mean a turn to First Amendment absolutism. Absolutism was the approach of Justices Black and Douglas, who certainly were an important part of the new majority. Nonetheless, absolutism had no appeal to Chief Justice Warren and Justices Brennan and Goldberg. They preferred a categorical balancing approach to First Amendment issues.[124] Employing a categorical balancing approach, the new high-protectionist majority vastly increased the Constitution's protection of First Amendment values by, among other things, reviving the clear and present danger rule;[125] adopting the actual malice rule to limit public official and public figure defamation actions;[126] vigorously enforcing the void for vagueness, overbreadth, chilling effects, facial challenge, and symbolic speech doctrines;[127] and, on occasion, imposing the requirements of strict scrutiny on government activity that burdened First Amendment rights.[128]

It was in 1963 that the reconstituted Warren Court, with a civil liberties–friendly majority for the first time in Supreme Court history, started the First Amendment on its course of sustained growth that has continued exponentially to the present day.

THE RISE OF STRICT SCRUTINY AS PART OF THE REVIVAL OF THE FIRST AMENDMENT

When, in 1963, "history's Warren Court"[129] began to give substantial protection to First Amendment values, it did so through a panoply of doctrines. Although it was not particularly prominent, strict scrutiny was among them.[130] Indeed, that strict scrutiny played any role tends to be overlooked in scholarly commentary.[131]

Still, it is important that strict scrutiny was a part of the Warren Court's First Amendment doctrinal resources, and the three cases in 1963 that employed strict scrutiny were especially significant.[132] They were the cases in which the Warren Court's new civil rights–protective majority first manifested its formation,[133] and they were the cases that established strict scrutiny as part of constitutional law.[134]

It is conventionally believed that strict scrutiny originated in equal protection cases dealing with racial discrimination.[135] But if strict scrutiny is the doctrine that requires government action to promote a compelling state interest through means that are narrowly tailored to that end, then the first equal protection case to employ strict scrutiny was *Shapiro v. Thompson*, decided in 1969.[136] *Shapiro*, in which Justice Brennan spoke for the Court,[13137]7 was a fundamental rights case involving the right of interstate travel. No racial discrimination case used strict scrutiny until *Palmore v. Sidoti* in 1984.[138]

It is true that the term "strict scrutiny" traces back to *Skinner v. Oklahoma*[139] and *Korematsu v. United States*,[140] in 1942 and 1944, respectively. But in those cases the Court did not actually employ the test or flesh out any element of it.[141] *Skinner* and *Korematsu* originated the name but not the actual doctrine or practice of modern strict scrutiny.

It is also true that in the 1950s the Warren Court began dismantling the system of Jim Crow with its landmark opinions in *Brown v. Board of Education*[142] and *Bolling v. Sharpe*.[143] Those cases, however, involved a shift in the Court's application of its traditional equal protection doctrine that classifications needed to be "reasonably related to [a] proper governmental objective."[144]

Finally, it is true that the Warren Court imported the narrow tailoring branch of strict scrutiny into equal protection clause jurisprudence in the 1964 racial discrimination case *McLaughlin v. Florida*.[145] But because *McLaughlin* did not require the state to have a compelling interest,[146] it was only a step toward making the modern doctrine of strict scrutiny a part of equal protection analysis. Moreover, even if *McLaughlin* were considered a strict scrutiny case, strict scrutiny's appearance in equal protection analysis would still postdate its instantiation in the First Amendment in 1963 in opinions written for the Court by Justices Brennan and Goldberg.[147]

Brennan's and Goldberg's 1963 opinions established strict scrutiny as part of First Amendment jurisprudence, but they did not originate it. This is readily apparent if we consider separately the development of strict scrutiny's two component branches.

As a constitutional standard, narrow tailoring is not unique to modern strict scrutiny.[148] The demand for narrow tailoring first appeared in the Gilded Age commerce clause and *Lochner*-era due process cases.[149] By 1940, the New Deal Court had made narrow tailoring analysis a prominent part of First Amendment jurisprudence.[150] The Warren Court's narrow tailoring precedents, in First Amendment cases, trace to *Talley v. California*[151] and *Shelton v. Tucker*.[152] Narrow tailoring was a venerable part of First Amendment analysis well before Justices Brennan and Goldberg combined it with the robust compelling interest standard to establish strict scrutiny.

As for the compelling state interest branch of strict scrutiny, its first appearance in civil liberties litigation was in 1957, in a concurrence by Justice Felix Frankfurter to *Sweezy v. New Hampshire*.[153] In *Sweezy*, Justice Frankfurter was moved by the importance he placed on academic freedom to temporarily desert his low-protectionist stance and vote to protect the right of a college professor to refuse to answer questions posed by the state attorney general about his classroom lectures.[154] "Political power," he wrote, "must abstain from intrusion into this activity of freedom . . . except for reasons that are exigent and obviously compelling."[155] This is the seminal statement of the compelling interest standard in the *United States Reports.*

After 1957, Frankfurter never again voiced the compelling interest standard. Nevertheless, between 1958 and 1962, it was picked up by other justices and, shorn of its connection with the term "exigent,"[156] was used six times in opinions for the Court, always in First Amendment cases.[157]

These uses, however, did not establish the compelling interest standard as part of First Amendment law. Four of them were by Frankfurter's low-protectionist colleagues,[158] and in two of the cases the First Amendment claimant lost.[159] In the hands of the Court's low-protectionist majority, the compelling interest standard was not meant to be a stringent test. It was used, for example, by Justice Harlan in that most classic of 1950s deferential-balancing opinions, *Barenblatt v. United States.*[160] As stated in *Barenblatt*'s companion case, *Uphaus v. Wyman*, what the low-protectionist majority meant by the compelling interest requirement was that the state's justification needed to be "sufficiently compelling"[161] to justify the government's free speech restriction. For the deferential justices, a free speech restriction was "sufficiently compelling" if it had a "reasonable relationship to a proper governmental objective."[162]

Moreover, by 1962, the low-protectionist majority was in the process of abandoning any notion that in First Amendment cases the government's burden of justification needed to be "compelling."[163] Only the fortuity of Frankfurter's and Whittaker's resignations, and Goldberg's appointment, with its attendant shift in power to high-protectionist justices, saved the compelling interest test as a constitutional standard.

Thus what Brennan and Goldberg did in their 1963 opinions was not originate the "compelling interest" formula but breathe real life into it.[164] Brennan, for his part, was immediately attracted to the compelling standard after it was articulated by Justice Frankfurter in *Sweezy v. New Hampshire.*[165] In 1958, Brennan mentioned the standard in passing in *Speiser v. Randall.*[166] In 1961, arguing in dissent in *Braunfeld v. Brown*[167] that Sunday closing laws violated the free exercise rights of Orthodox Jews, Brennan used the compelling interest standard in a way that anticipated its future stringency.[168]

Thus two years later, in 1963, when Brennan and Goldberg wrote for the reconstituted Warren Court majority in *NAACP v. Button,*[169] *Gibson v. Florida Legislative Investigation Committee,*[170] and *Sherbert v. Verner*[171] they drew from, but essentially altered, existing precedent by interpolating a robust compelling interest standard into First Amendment analysis. Their transformation of the compelling interest standard established strict scrutiny as an undoubted part of First Amendment jurisprudence and set the stage for its migration into the equal protection clause and general legal consciousness.

STRICT SCRUTINY AS THE CLEAR AND PRESENT DANGER TEST REBORN

The 1940s' clear and present danger test and strict scrutiny have more in common than their First Amendment origins and the fact that each is its era's hallmark doctrine of civil liberties law. The links and affinities between the two doctrines are such that it is appropriate to consider strict scrutiny as the danger rule's successor doctrine, as the clear and present danger test reborn.

First, Justice Brennan specifically relied on the 1940s' danger rule[172] in his seminal opinions that established strict scrutiny as part of First Amendment analysis. It is telling that Justice Brennan, in his dissent in *Braunfeld v. Brown*, laid the foundation for his pathbreaking question, "What, then, is the compelling state interest which impels the [state] to impede appellants' freedom of worship?"[173] by quoting Justice Jackson's classic statement of the danger rule in *West Virginia State Board of Education v. Barnette*: "The right of the state to regulate, for example, a public utility may well include . . . power to impose all the restrictions which a legislature may have a 'rational basis' for adopting. But freedoms of speech and of press, of assembly, and of worship may not be infringed on such slender grounds. They are susceptible of restrictions only to prevent grave and immediate danger to interests which the state may lawfully protect."[174]

Similarly, in *Sherbert v. Verner*,[175] the case that settled strict scrutiny as a part of First Amendment analysis, Justice Brennan relied on *Thomas v. Collins,* another danger rule precedent from the 1940s. In *Sherbert*, after determining that Sherbert's free exercise rights were significantly burdened,[176] Justice Brennan asserted: "We must next consider whether some compelling state interest . . . justified the substantial infringement of appellant's First Amendment right. It is basic that no showing of a rational relationship to some colorable state interest would suffice; in this highly sensitive constitutional area, '[o]nly the gravest abuses, endangering paramount interest, give occasion for permissible limitation.' "[177] In sum, it was when Justice Brennan, in *Sherbert*, quoted Justice Rutledge's statement of the danger rule in *Thomas v. Collins* that he announced the birth of modern strict scrutiny.

Scholars who witnessed the birth of what we now call strict scrutiny recognized the analytic kinship between the two tests and spoke of strict scrutiny in terms of the danger rule. Writing just after modern strict scrutiny's emergence in 1963, Martin Shapiro spoke of its demand for "an 'overriding and compelling . . . immediate, substantial and subordinating state interest' "[178] as "a return to preferred position balancing,"[179] which is how he understood the clear and present danger rule.[180] Writing in 1969, Frank Strong saw the narrow tailoring doctrine, which was then the most developed branch of strict scrutiny, as "another facet in the life of 'clear and present danger,'"[181] and as "a role that 'clear and present danger' could play in the future."[182]

Of course, one difference between strict scrutiny and the danger rule is that strict scrutiny came to play a central role in equal protection analysis. There is evidence, however, that the civil libertarian justices on the Stone and Vinson Courts contemplated such an expanded role for the danger rule. Justice Murphy, dissenting in *Korematsu*, expressly applied the danger rule as the test for the military's explicit racial classification.[183] According to Murphy, "depriv[ing] an individual of any of his constitutional rights" requires "a public danger that is so 'immediate, imminent, and impending' as not to admit of delay and not to permit the intervention of ordinary constitutional processes to alleviate the danger."[184] In all likelihood, the danger rule is what Justice Black had in mind when, in applying the "most rigid scrutiny" in *Korematsu*, he said, "Nothing short of apprehension by the proper military authorities of the gravest imminent danger to the public safety can constitutionally justify" the racial restriction at bar.[185]

Strict scrutiny's kinship with the danger test is not just historical; it is also analytical. Strict scrutiny may be conceived as a generalization of the danger test. Under the danger rule, speech may be restricted only when it is necessary to prevent the imminent occurrence of a grave evil.[186] This is the equivalent of saying that a restriction on speech must be narrowly tailored to promote a compelling state interest. Under the danger rule, the Court has predetermined that the only interest sufficiently compelling to justify restricting speech is "a clear and present danger that [speech] will bring about the substantive evils that [the state] has a right to prevent."[187]

Finally, the danger rule and the strict scrutiny test are both standards that implement constitutional norms through what scholars call categorical balancing.[188] As categorical balancing, the danger rule was constantly challenged, on one hand by jurists who adhered to a jurisprudence of ad hoc balancing,[189] and on the other hand by jurists who advocated an absolutist approach.[190]

The same is true for strict scrutiny. It too has been constantly criticized, on one side, by jurists who would prefer to implement the equal protection clause by a "sliding-scale" approach,[191] which is a form of ad hoc balancing, and on the other side, by jurists who prefer that the Constitution be entirely colorblind, which is a form of absolutism.[192]

In the 1940s, the danger rule was the leading exemplar of the "more exacting judicial scrutiny" called for by Justice Stone in *United States v. Carolene Products*' Footnote 4.[193] When the foes of bifurcated review came to power, the danger rule had to be, and was, destroyed in *Dennis v. United States*.[194] A decade later, it rose from the ashes, transformed by a new generation of civil libertarian justices into strict scrutiny.

LEARNING ACROSS THE GENERATIONS: WHAT THE CLEAR AND PRESENT DANGER TEST TEACHES US ABOUT STRICT SCRUTINY

Like the civil libertarian justices who fashioned the 1940s' danger rule, the justices who established strict scrutiny in the 1960s meant it to be highly protective of constitutional values and easily applicable. The gap between the precise tailoring and exigent interest it required and the means and ends usually associated with governmental action normally was so vast that application of the test was straightforward. For decades, constitutional scholars recognized that selection of strict scrutiny as the appropriate level of review was outcome determinative. Shortly after strict scrutiny's appearance in equal protection litigation, Gerald Gunther famously described it as "'strict' in theory and fatal in fact."[195]

More recently, however, in both First Amendment and Equal Protection cases, Justice O'Connor has taken to saying that Gunther's comment is not true.[196] And after observing the recent course of affirmative action decisions,[197] commentators have begun to describe strict scrutiny as plastic,[198] as "functional" rather than "wooden,"[199] and as tending toward either "intermediate scrutiny"[200] or a "sliding scale" test.[201] In the words of one commentator, in affirmative action "the Supreme Court has been unwilling to apply strict scrutiny strictly."[202] A similar development is occurring in the First Amendment where a leading scholar has criticized strict scrutiny as "pernicious" because "it risks leading courts and legislators to the wrong conclusions, it causes courts to apply the test disingenuously, and it distracts us from looking for a better approach."[203]

Moreover, given the emergence of meaningful minimal scrutiny review in *Romer v. Evans*[204] and *Lawrence v. Texas*,[205] there are renewed calls for, or predictions of, the overall transformation or demise of tiered scrutiny.[206] Understanding what is happening to strict scrutiny and fashioning the appropriate response are very much on the scholarly agenda.

As part of that inquiry, this paper suggests that this is the second time in post–New Deal constitutional law that a stringent doctrine of heightened scrutiny has decayed into a less stringent balancing test. The first occurrence was *Dennis v. United States*,[207] which in the eyes of contemporary commentators reduced the clear and present danger test to the "probable danger" test[208] and then to a form of deferential ad hoc balancing.[209] Given the close relationship between the danger rule and strict scrutiny,[210] there is good reason to expect that the danger rule's life cycle holds lessons for the strict scrutiny standard. Much can be learned about the current debate surrounding strict scrutiny from the writings of scholars who observed the danger rule's travails.

The first lesson derives from scholars in the 1950s and 1960s who extensively analyzed Justices Black's and Douglas's eventual opposition to both the danger rule and ad hoc balancing in the name of constitutional absolutism.[211] Some of these scholars preferred to approach First Amendment problems through the jurisprudence of ad hoc balancing, and they criticized Black and Douglas accordingly.[212] Other scholars decried ad hoc balancing as a jurisprudence of judicial abnegation and generally supported what Black and Douglas were doing.[213] But whatever their jurisprudential and substantive positions, most of these scholars agreed that absolutism was impossible and that Black and Douglas really addressed the First Amendment through the jurisprudence of categorical balancing.[214] As Thomas Emerson said, First Amendment absolutists really meant to insist

> on focusing the inquiry upon the definition of "Abridge," "the freedom," and if necessary "law," rather than on a general de novo balancing of interest in each case. And the text gives weight to the constitutional decision made in adopting the First Amendment by emphasizing that the entire question of reconciling social values and objectives is not reopened. This approach of "defining" rather than "balancing" narrows and structures the issue for the courts, bringing it more readily within the bounds of judicial procedures. It is true that the process of "defining" requires a weighing of various considerations, but this is not the same as open-ended "balancing." On this aspect of the absolute test all proponents of the doctrine appear to be in agreement.[215]

The same is true of the many justices who have leaned toward finding in the equal protection clause a per se rule against racial classification. In the 1960s, it was Stewart and Douglas.[216] More recently it has been Scalia and Thomas.[217] But Stewart limited his principle to statutes defining crime and upheld, for example, racial segregation in municipal "drunk tanks,"[218] and laws "requiring the keeping of racially segregated public records for statistical or other valid public purposes."[219] Douglas, in turn, in opposing affirmative action and arguing that the compelling state interest standard was too discretionary a doctrine to cabin racial classifications,[220] had to acknowledge that "racial susceptibility to certain diseases . . . [and] sensitiveness to environmental conditions . . . may in an extreme situation justify differences in racial treatment that no fairminded person would call 'invidious' discrimination."[221] Similarly, Justices Scalia and Thomas recently categorically exempted racial classifications imposed by prison officials from strict scrutiny.[222]

The rich literature of the 1950s and 1960s critiquing the strengths and weaknesses of First Amendment absolutism provides valuable insight into constitutional absolutism for any constitutional value in any age. With the advance of originalist,[223] textualist,[224] and "new formalist"[225] approaches to constitutional interpretation, we would profit from the skepticism expressed about the possibility of absolutism in that extensive literature.[226]

The second lesson derives from the scholars in the 1950s and 1960s who extensively analyzed the danger rule as a form of categorical balancing to show that because categorical balancing is a form of balancing, any rule derived from categorical balancing can easily change into an ad hoc balancing test. That, they said, is what happened to the danger rule in the confrontation between national security and communist speech in the 1950s.[227] Apparently, that is what is happening today with strict scrutiny in the confrontation between the proponents of affirmative action and the proponents of a colorblind constitution.[228]

With regard to the danger rule, some scholars saw it as essentially a balancing test years before it was officially reconfigured as such in *Dennis v. United States*.[229] As early as 1941, Herbert Weschler described the Court's approach to protecting speech as a balancing test and observed: "If this is the clear and present danger test for which liberals have fought and bled, it needs no argument to show that the formula which it provides does little more than to state the general principle of justice which would be accepted in evaluating any legislation which interferes with individual freedom. . . . What the clear and present danger test can do, and all that it can do, is to require an extended judicial review in the fullest legislative sense of the competing values which the particular situation presents."[230]

After the disaster of *Dennis*, more scholars came to see that "the clear and present danger test, even with its original emphasis on the immediacy of the threatened harm, was always a 'balancing' test," and that "the Justices who used the language of clear-and-present-danger did not shrink from making the legislative judgments which are inescapable in our system of judicial review."[231] Years later, T. Alexander Aleinikoff generalized their insight as a failing of all categorical balancing tests. "New situations," he observed, "present new interests and different weights for old interests. If these are allowed to re-open the balancing process, then every case becomes one of an 'ad hoc' balance, establishing a rule for that case only. Balances are 'definitional' only if the Court wants to stop thinking about the question."[232]

These scholarly critics were challenged by an array of commentators who advocated categorical balancing as a far better mechanism for defending civil liberties than the alternative of ad hoc balancing, which they saw as inevitably resulting in a supine response to legislative infringements of the First Amendment.[233] In their view, categorical balancing did not guarantee that a court would not buckle "under sufficient internal or external pressure in some 'hard' case."[234] Their point was that, as compared to balancing ad hoc in every case, balancing categorically was more likely to focus judges on the societal rather than the individual interests burdened by the government's restriction of First Amendment activity.[235] In addition, the existence of a rule previously established by categorical balancing could "insulate a judge from legally irrelevant pressures to a considerable degree."[236]

The interplay between these two camps filled the law reviews and bookshelves of the 1950s and 1960s with sustained and insightful analyses of the comparative strengths and weaknesses of ad hoc and categorical balancing as approaches to constitutional decision making. Their debate foreshadowed, and could well inform, the developing controversy between the proponents and opponents of sliding-scale and tiered scrutiny.

The final lesson for strict scrutiny's present travails derives from the denouement of the contest among the 1950s and 1960s absolutists, categorical balancers, and ad hoc balancers.[237] Their extended debate faded away as commentators came to realize that the jurisprudential struggle masked a controversy over substantive differences. As Martin Shapiro noted, the First Amendment controversy was not over balancing as a judicial technique. It was "an oversimplification to view the clear-and-present-danger and balancing formulas purely as rivals."[238] They were, in fact, rather "compatible."[239] Indeed, "the balancing technique frequently appears in the cases in which the Roosevelt Court reintroduced the clear-and-present-danger test and subscribed to the preferred position doctrine."[240] In short: "The proponents of clear-and-present-danger and preferred position were perfectly willing to balance interests as long as it was understood in advance that freedom of speech was an especially important interest, and that the state's interest in suppression only became weighty enough to justify suppression when the speech clearly and immediately threatened actual damage to other fundamental interests of society. This might be called balancing *within* the clear-and-present-danger and preferred position approaches."

At bottom, the controversy between the ad hoc and categorical balancers was an argument over "the place of the Supreme Court in American politics."[241] Truly, it was a "conflict between the judicially modest and the judicial activitsts."[242] In Shapiro's view the "judicially modest . . . feel that [judicial] review is undemocratic"[243] and the jurisprudential debate was "little more than a facade behind which role of the Court problems lurk."[244] Or, as Elliott Richardson said in the immediate aftermath of *Dennis,* "the foregoing discussion has shown a number of points at which the degree of deference paid to the legislative judgment may make a critical difference."[245]

Deference, of course, is the key not only to why the danger test collapsed into the "probable" danger test in *Dennis v. United States*.[246] It is also the given explanation as to why strict scrutiny morphed into intermediate scrutiny in *Grutter v. Bollinger*[247] and was cast aside in favor of rational basis scrutiny in Justice Thomas and Justice Scalia's dissent in *Johnson v. California*.[248] To a student of the history of the danger rule, the present moment in the evolution of strict scrutiny "is like deja vu all over again."[249]

CONCLUSION

As the life cycle of the danger test shows, and as the rise and present state of strict scrutiny reenact, constitutional doctrine and approaches to judicial decision making are important for giving direction to resolving disputes at any given moment. But they, and the direction they give, are impermanent. Inevitably, the justices' changing substantive vision of American society and the Court's place in it shape the Court's jurisprudence and doctrines. As Mort Horwitz has taught throughout his career, law cannot be separated from politics.[250]

Also as Mort has taught, the history of the danger test and strict scrutiny shows that "the central problem of modern constitutionalism is how to reconcile the idea of fundamental law with the modernist insight that meanings are fluid and historically changing."[251] In the interwar years, when the First Amendment rule was the "bad tendency" test, balancing-of-interests jurisprudence was more civil liberties protective. In the years after World War II, when the dominant rule was the danger test applied by civil libertarians like Justices Black, Douglas, Murphy, and Rutledge, balancing was less protective. Judicial deference was a progressive doctrine when applied to disputes involving economic legislation before the New Deal, a conservative doctrine when applied to First Amendment disputes during the McCarthy era, and a progressive doctrine, once again, when applied to the late twentieth-century affirmative action cases.[252] Strict scrutiny, obviously a progressive doctrine at its inception, has increasingly been devoted to promoting conservative policies in the Rehnquist Court.[253] Because social and historical contexts change, legal concepts and doctrines are constantly subject to what Jack Balkin has called "ideological drift."[254] Constant attention to how established doctrines and concepts function in an ever-changing social reality is necessary to prevent law from "los[ing] touch with life,"[255] turning into a "desert of increasingly abstract conceptualism,"[256] and "sliding from legal fundamentality into legal fundamentalism."[257]

Finally, the judicial and scholarly controversy in the 1950s and 1960s concerning the danger rule and deferential balancing confirms the wisdom of Mort Horwitz's advice that, when confronting an extended debate about some aspect of the law, we should stop "to ask what [is] at stake in proving or disproving" that person's thesis.[258] Arguments among lawyers, law professors, and judges, Mort says, "often serve as 'stand ins' for more general controversies" in the political and social culture.[259] I have tried to ask the "what was at stake" question with regard to the voluminous literature generated in the late 1950s and early 1960s on the merits and demerits of the danger rule, First Amendment absolutism, ad hoc and categorical balancing, and judicial deference. We would do well to do the same with the contemporary literature regarding strict scrutiny and all our pressing legal questions.

These are but a few of the many lessons that I thank Mort for teaching me.[260]

NOTES

1. Morton J. Horwitz, "In Memoriam: William J. Brennan, Jr.," *Harvard Law Review* 111 (1997): 28 n. 42; E. Joshua Rosenkranz et al., "Remembering a Constitutional Hero," *New York Law School Law Review* 43 (1999): 18 (comments of Morton J. Horwitz).

2. 395 U.S. 444 (1969).

3. Horwitz, "In Memoriam," 28.

4. Morton J. Horwitz, *The Transformation of American Law, 1870–1960: The Crisis of Legal Orthodoxy* (New York: Oxford University Press, 1992), 252, 260–65; Morton J. Horwitz, *The Warren Court and the Pursuit of Justice* (New York: Hill and Wang, 1998), 56–65.

5. 341 U.S. 494 (1951).

6. See text accompanying notes 86–90 below (discussing how *Dennis* reduced the danger rule to a deferential-balancing test).

7. Horwitz, *Transformation II,* 260 (*Dennis* was the "post-war nadir of Supreme Court protection of free speech"); Horwitz, *The Warren Court,* 57–59; Morton J. Horwitz, "Commentary: 'Contracted' Biographies and Other Obstacles to 'Truth,'" *New York University Law Review* 70 (1995): 715–17 (saying *Dennis* was "the nadir of civil liberties in the 1950s; that it represented the triumph of Cold War hysteria; that it was a capitulation by the Supreme Court to Cold War paranoia").

8. See Stephen A. Siegel, "The Origin of the Compelling State Interest Test and Strict Scrutiny," *American Journal of Legal History* 48 (2006): 355; text accompanying notes 135–68 below (discussing the origin of strict scrutiny).

9. 371 U.S. 415 (1963), discussed in text accompanying notes 132 and 169.

10. 374 U.S. 398 (1963), discussed in text accompanying notes 132 and 171 below. Justice Goldberg provided an assist with a third opinion, *Gibson v. Florida Legislative Investigation Committee*, 372 U.S. 539 (1963), but he acknowledges Brennan's leadership. See Arthur Goldberg, "Mr. Justice Brennan and the First Amendment," *Rutgers-Camden Law Journal* 4 (1972): 8 (saying Brennan was the "principal architect" of the Court's First Amendment jurisprudence).

11. 394 U.S. 618 (1969).

12. Horwitz, "In Memoriam," 28 (speaking of *Brandenburg*).

13. David Currie, *The Constitution in the Supreme Court: The Second Hundred Years, 1888–1986* (Chicago: University of Chicago Press, 1990), 415. See also Horwitz, *The Warren Court,* 65–67 (discussing the phases of the Warren Court); text accompanying notes 122–23 below (discussing formation of the Warren Court's civil libertarian majority).

14. See, e.g., Edward Heck, "Justice Brennan and Freedom of Expression Doctrine in the Burger Court," *San Diego Law Review* 24 (1987): 1175–78 (describing Brennan's extensive use of strict scrutiny in the Burger Court's First Amendment decisions).

15. Brennan opposed using strict scrutiny in affirmative action cases—see *Metro Broadcasting, Inc., v. FCC*, 497 U.S. 547 (1990); *City of Richmond v. Croson*, 488 U.S. 469, 528, 561 (1989) (Brennan, J., joining Marshall, J.'s and Blackmun, J.'s dissents)—and eventually agreed not to use it in gender discrimination decisions. Compare *Craig v. Boren*, 429 U.S. 190, 197–98 (1976) (intermediate scrutiny), with *Frontiero v. Richardson*, 411 U.S. 677, 688–90 (1973) (strict scrutiny). On campaign finance, see Richard Hasen, "The Untold Drafting History of *Buckley v. Valeo*," *Election Law Journal* 2 (2003): 241–45, 250 (rebutting the view that Brennan was the opinion's "primary author" and placing him among the minority of justices who were sympathetic to both contribution and expenditure limits because "FECA[,] by limiting the role of money in politics, furthered First Amendment values").

16. See, e.g., Horwitz, *The Warren Court,* 65–73 (reviewing Brennan's contribution to First Amendment doctrine and mentioning strict scrutiny only in regard to *Speiser v. Randall,* 357 U.S. 513, 524–26 (1958)); Lucas A. Powe Jr., *The Warren Court and American Politics* (Cambridge, Mass.: Belknap Press of Harvard University Press, 2000), 221, 303–78 (reviewing Warren Court First Amendment doctrine and mentioning strict scrutiny only in regard to *NAACP v. Button,* 371 U.S. 415 (1963)); Harry Kalven Jr., *A Worthy Tradition: Freedom of Speech in America* (New York: Harper & Row, 1988) (focusing on First Amendment doctrine in the 1950s and 1960s and not mentioning strict scrutiny at all). But see Goldberg, "Mr. Justice Brennan," 13 (describing Brennan's early First Amendment jurisprudence using the terms, but not the label, of strict scrutiny).

17. William Brennan, "The Supreme Court and the Meikeljohn Interpretation of the First Amendment," *Harvard Law Review* 79 (1965): 8–11.

18. See text accompanying notes 178–82 below (discussing the literature).

19. See, e.g., David Rabban, *Free Speech in Its Forgotten Years* (New York: Cambridge University Press, 1997), 129–76; Geoffrey Stone, *Perilous Times: Free Speech in Wartime from the Sedition Act of 1798 to the War on Terrorism* (New York: W. W. Norton, 2004), 136–233.

20. See *Gitlow v. New York,* 268 U.S. 652, 665 (1925) (assuming that freedom of speech is protected by the due process clause); *Gilbert v. Minnesota,* 254 U.S. 325, 331 (1920) (discussing a freedom of speech claim against state legislation "without . . . deciding" whether speech was protected against state action).

21. See, e.g., *Patterson v. Colorado,* 205 U.S. 454, 462 (1907). The Court also gave very limited protections under the First Amendment's free exercise clause as a restraint only on governmental regulation of religious belief, not religiously motivated practices. See, e.g., *Hamilton v. Regents of the University of California,* 293 U.S. 245, 262 (1934) (upholding state's refusal to grant an exemption for a religiously motivated refusal to engage in required military training at a state university); *Reynolds v. United States,* 98 U.S. 145, 165 (1878).

22. The "bad tendency" test allowed the state to criminalize any statement that had a "natural tendency and probable effect . . . to bring about the substantive evil which the legislative body might prevent." *Gitlow,* 268 U.S. at 671. See also Stone, *Perilous Times,* 170–73 (discussing the "triumph of 'bad tendency'").

23. See, e.g., *Whitney v. California,* 274 U.S. 357, 372–80 (1927) (Brandeis, J., concurring); *Gitlow,* 268 U.S. at 672–73 (Holmes, J., dissenting); *Abrams v. United States,* 250 U.S. 616, 626–29 (1919) (Holmes, J., dissenting).

24. Robert McKay, "The Preference for Freedom," *New York University Law Review* 34 (1959): 1205–7; Wallace Mendelson, "Clear and Present Danger—from *Schenck* to *Dennis,*" *Columbia Law Review* 52 (1952): 315.

25. See Michael Klarman, *From Jim Crow to Civil Rights: The Supreme Court and the Struggle for Racial Equality* (New York: Oxford University Press, 2004), 110–12; G. Edward White, *The Constitution and the New Deal* (Cambridge, Mass.: Harvard University Press, 2000), 128–63 (discussing heightened protection for speech during the 1930s); Howard Gillman, "Preferred Freedoms: The Progressive Expansion of State Power and the Rise of Modern Civil Liberties Jurisprudence," *Political Research Quarterly* 47 (1994): 623, 625, 640–50 (discussing the rise of modern civil liberties); G. Edward White, "The First Amendment Comes of Age: The Emergence of Free Speech in Twentieth-Century America," *Michigan Law Review* 95 (1996): 303–30 (discussing First Amendment freedoms in the 1930s and 1940s); Geoffrey Berman,

"Note: A New Deal for Free Speech: Free Speech and the Labor Movement in the 1930s," *Virginia Law Review* 80 (1994): 299–303, 312–22.

26. The rise of labor unions is generally associated with this development, though the inclusion of racial and religious minorities in the governing Democratic coalition were factors. See Klarman, *From Jim Crow,* 110–12; Berman, "A New Deal for Free Speech," 299–303, 312–22; Gillman, "Preferred Freedoms," 625 (discussing impact of industrialization); Ken Kersch, *Constructing Civil Liberties* (New York: Cambridge University Press, 2004), 211–17, 227 (discussing labor picketing as speech).

27. Mendelson, "Clear and Present Danger," 317. See also 319.

28. Ibid., 317.

29. *Near v. Minnesota,* 283 U.S. 697 (1931).

30. *Grosjean v. American Press Co.,* 297 U.S. 233, 249–51 (1936).

31. *Lovell v. City of Griffin,* 303 U.S. 444 (1938). For a comprehensive discussion, see Thomas Emerson, "The Doctrine of Prior Restraint," *Law and Contemporary Problems* 20 (1955): 652–55, 660–63.

32. 309 U.S. 319, 327 (1937).

33. 304 U.S. 144 (1938).

34. Id. at 152 n. 4.

35. Id.

36. See, e.g., *West Coast Hotel Co. v. Parish,* 300 U.S. 379 (1937) (women's minimum wage legislation is constitutional), rev'g *Adkins v. Children's Hospital,* 261 U.S. 525 (1923) (women's minimum wage legislation is unconstitutional).

37. See notes 26–31 above (discussing expanding speech protections); Klarman, *From Jim Crow,* 117–70 (on racial equality, voting rights, and criminal procedure).

38. See White, *The Constitution,* 143–54 (discussing the "preferred position" debate); Gillman, "Preferred Freedoms," 640–50 (same); White, "The First Amendment," 332–42 (same); Alpheus Mason, "The Core of Free Government, 1938–1940: Mr. Justice Stone and 'Preferred Freedoms,'" *Yale Law Journal* 65 (1956): 597–628. The phrase "preferred position" was first used in *Jones v. City of Opelika,* 316 U.S. 584, 608 (1942) (Stone, C. J., dissenting), but reflects a transition that was noticeable a bit earlier.

39. Mendelson, "Clear and Present Danger," 324–25; McKay, "The Preference for Freedom," 1215–17; Thomas Emerson, *Toward a General Theory of the First Amendment* (New York: Random House, 1966), 63–65, 66–67. The Court also used several procedural devices, such as loosening standards on standing to sue and procedural due process (including proscriptions on vagueness). See McKay, "The Preference for Freedom," 1217–22.

40. Mendelson, "Clear and Present Danger," 321 (citing *United States v. CIO,* 335 U.S. 106 (1948)). See also Samuel Krislov, *The Supreme Court in the Political Process* (New York: Macmillan, 1965), 120 (discussing the 1930s through the 1950s); McKay, "The Preference for Freedom," 1214–15 (citing cases in the 1950s).

41. See, e.g., *Saia v. New York,* 334 U.S. 558 (1948) (facial invalidation of ordinance prohibiting amplified sound devices); *Thornhill v. Alabama,* 310 U.S. 88, 96–98, 101–4 (1940) (permitting facial challenge of statute regulating picketing); *Lovell v. Griffin,* 303 U.S. 444, 447 (1938) (allowing facial challenge to standardless handbill distribution licensing ordinance).

42. See, e.g., *Winters v. New York,* 333 U.S. 507, 509–20 (1948); *Herndon v. Lowry,* 301 U.S. 242, 259 (1937).

43. See, e.g., *Martin v. City of Struthers,* 319 U.S. 141, 147–48 (1943); *Schneider v. Town of Irvington*, 308 U.S. 147, 162 (1939). Overbreadth encompasses the related requirements of "narrow tailoring" and the use of the "least restrictive means." See Francis Wormuth and Harris Mirkin, "The Doctrine of the Reasonable Alternative," *Utah Law Review* 9 (1964): 271–79 (showing that overbreadth encompasses a number of now separate doctrines and discussing its importance in First Amendment litigation in the 1940s).

44. For a survey of the various techniques by which the Court established speech as a preferred freedom and their relationship to balancing of interests, see McKay, "The Preference for Freedom," 24.

45. For the remarks in this paragraph, see Martin Shapiro, *Freedom of Speech: The Supreme Court and Judicial Review* (Englewood Cliffs, N.J.: Prentice-Hall, 1966), 83–87; T. Alexander Aleinikoff, "Constitutional Law in the Age of Balancing," *Yale Law Journal* 96 (1987): 945–48.

46. For the remarks in this paragraph, see Shapiro, *Freedom of Speech,* 76–77, 83–87, 90–92 (discussing balancing "at the 'defining' stage" and balancing "of particular factors in each case"); Aleinikoff, "Constitutional Law," 948 (discussing "definitional" and "ad hoc" balancing); Goldberg, "Mr. Justice Brennan," 9–11, 25 (same); Melville Nimmer, "The Right to Speak from *Times* to *Time*: First Amendment Theory Applied to Libel and Misapplied to Privacy," *California Law Review* 56 (1968): 938–48 (same).

47. Aleinikoff, "Constitutional Law," 948, 962–63.

48. See ibid., 948 (citing *New York v. Ferber,* 458 U.S. 747 (1982) as illustrating an approach in which balancing leads to a rule that can be applied in subsequent cases without additional balancing); Nimmer, "The Right to Speak," 942–44 (discussing *New York Times v. Sullivan,* 376 U.S. 255 (1964) as illustrating the "definitional" approach).

49. For the remarks in this paragraph, see Shapiro, *Freedom of Speech,* 76–78; Aleinikoff, "Constitutional Law," 948–52, 953–54, 959–60, 963–64.

50. Aleinikoff, "Constitutional Law," 949–52; Stephen Siegel, "Lochner Era Jurisprudence and the American Constitutional Tradition," *North Carolina Law Review* 70 (1991): 23–52. This paralleled private law jurisprudence. See Stephen Siegel, "Comment: The Revision Thickens," *Law and History Review* 20 (2002): 631–37.

51. Aleinikoff, "Constitutional Law," 952, 955–63; Gillman, "Preferred Freedoms," 633–50; White, "The First Amendment," 302–10.

52. Aleinikoff, "Constitutional Law," 953–54.

53. Fred Rodell, *Nine Men: A Political History of the Supreme Court from 1790 to 1955* (Littleton, Colo.: F. B. Rothman, 1955), 217. See also Peter H. Irons, *New Deal Lawyers* (Princeton, N.J.: Princeton University Press, 1982) 13.

54. Aleinikoff, "Constitutional Law," 963–64.

55. Ibid., 948. See also 966–67 (discussing the First Amendment).

56. On Frankfurter's position, see Melvin Urofsky, *Division and Discord: The Supreme Court under Stone and Vinson, 1941–1953* (Columbia: University of South Carolina Press, 1997), 37, 165–66; Mason, "The Core of Free Government," 614–66; Mendelson, "Clear and Present Danger," 320; White, "The First Amendment," 333–34, 337–40. White aptly describes Frankfurter's position as "tortured and ambivalent" (340).

57. See, e.g., *West Virginia State Board of Education v. Barnette,* 319 U.S. 624, 648 (1943) (Frankfurter, J., dissenting), where Justice Frankfurter wrote: "The Constitution does not give

us greater veto power when dealing with one phase of 'liberty' than with another. . . . Judicial self-restraint is equally necessary whenever an exercise of political or legislative power is challenged. . . . Our power does not vary according to the particular provision of the Bill of Rights which is invoked." See also *Kovacs v. Cooper,* 336 U.S. 77, 89–96 (1949) (disputing the First Amendment's "preferred position"); McKay, "The Preference for Freedom," 1199–200 (quoting and analyzing Frankfurter's concurrence in *Dennis v. United States,* 341 U.S. 494, 524–25 (1951)).

58. See, e.g., *Saia v. New York,* 334 U.S. 558, 562 (1948) (Frankfurter, J., dissenting, joined by Reed, J., and Burton, J.); id. at 566 (Jackson, J., dissenting); *Craig v. Harney,* 331 U.S. 367, 384 (1947) (Frankfurter, J., dissenting, joined by Vinson, C. J.); id. at 394 (Jackson, J., dissenting); *Murdock v. Pennsylvania,* 319 U.S. 105, 117 (1943) (Reed, J., dissenting joined by Frankfurter, J.); id. at 134 (Frankfurter, J., dissenting, joined by Jackson, J.). Justice Jackson's well-noted differences with Justice Frankfurter in *Barnette,* 319 U.S. at 624, should not mask the fact that generally they were allied in First Amendment cases. Professor Urofsky describes Reed as a moderate, but the cases cited above show he frequently voted to restrict First Amendment freedoms.

59. *Thornhill v. Alabama,* 310 U.S. 88 (1940); *Schneider v. Town of Irvington,* 308 U.S. 147 (1939).

60. White, "The First Amendment," 333 (quoting Justice Frankfurter's opinion in *Minersville School District v. Gobitis,* 310 U.S. 586, 599 (1940)). See also Mason, "The Core of Free Government," 615–16 (same).

61. *Gobitis,* 310 U.S. at 600.

62. For other examples of deferential-balancing opinions or dissents that impose a standard close to rational basis review, see *Saia,* 334 U.S. at 564 (Frankfurter, J., dissenting); *United Public Workers of America v. Mitchell,* 330 U.S. 75, 100, 102 (1947) (per Justice Reed); *In re Summers,* 325 U.S. 561, 573 (1945) (per Justice Reed); *Barnette,* 319 U.S. at 624, 661–62 (Frankfurter, J., dissenting).

63. See Shapiro, *Freedom of Speech,* 77–78 (describing technique as "balancing *within* the clear-and-present-danger and preferred position approaches"). Illustrative cases include *Craig v. Harney,* 331 U.S. 376, 373 (1947); id. at 383 (Murphy, J., concurring); *Thomas v. Collins,* 323 U.S. 516, 531–32, 536 (1945); *Bridges v. California,* 314 U.S. 252, 361–62 (1941); *Thornhill,* 310 U.S. at 104–5. See also *Barnette,* 319 U.S. at 633–34 (per Jackson, J., for the majority, which included the four high-protectionist justices).

64. Shapiro, *Freedom of Speech,* 77.

65. Mendelson, "Clear and Present Danger," 320, 322–24; Shapiro, *Freedom of Speech,* 58–59.

66. See, e.g., *United Public Workers of America v. Mitchell,* 330 U.S. at 75, 124, 126 (Douglas, J., dissenting); *Thomas,* 323 U.S. at 530 (per Justice Rutledge); *Bridges v. California,* 314 U.S. at 352, 262 (per Justice Black); *Thornhill,* 310 U.S. at 105 (per Justice Murphy).

The libertarian justices also used a more rigorous application of the least restrictive means test than low-protectionist justices. *United Public Workers of America v. Mitchell,* 330 U.S. at 110 (Black, J., dissenting); Shapiro, *Freedom of Speech,* 59–60; Wormuth and Mirkin, "The Doctrine," 274–78 (discussing various cases and Justices Black and Douglas); "Note: Less Drastic Means and the First Amendment," *Yale Law Journal* 78 (1969): 469–70 (same).

67. *Thomas,* 323 U.S. at 530–32. For other examples of high-protectionist opinions or dis-

sents that employ the clear and present danger test, see *Craig v. Harney,* 331 U.S. 367, 371–72 (1947) (per Douglas, J.); *Prince v. Massachusetts,* 321 U.S. 158, 174–75 (1944) (Murphy, J., dissenting). The danger test even crept into opinions written by more moderate justices for majorities mainly composed of the high protectionists. See *Barnette,* 319 U.S. at 624, 633–34 (per Jackson, J.) (compulsory flag salute in grade school); *Cantwell v. Connecticut,* 310 U.S. 296, 308–11 (1940) (per Roberts, J.) (speech and free exercise of religion).

68. Barry Cushman, "Lost Fidelities," *William and Mary Law Review* 41 (1999): 142 (speaking of Justice Roberts's approach to constitutional review).

69. See, e.g., *Schneider v. Town of Irvington,* 308 U.S. 147, 161 (1939) (per Roberts., J.).

70. Mendelson, "Clear and Present Danger," 325–26, 332.

71. Conversely, when the high protectionists wrote in dissent, they tended not to moderate their language and more freely claimed imminent danger as what First Amendment balancing required for the government to prevail. Mendelson, "Clear and Present Danger," 326. Likewise, low protectionists more fully expressed their deferential jurisprudence when they wrote for themselves, either in a concurrence or a dissent. See, e.g., *Kovacs v. Cooper,* 336 U.S. 77, 89 (1949) (Frankfurter, J., concurring); *Murdock v. Pennsylvania,* 319 U.S. 105, 117 (1943) (Reed, J., dissenting); *Bridges,* 314 U.S. at 279 (Frankfurter, J., dissenting).

72. See, e.g., *Marsh v. Alabama,* 326 U.S. 501, 509 (1946) (per Black, J.); *Martin v. City of Struthers,* 319 U.S. 141, 143–49 (1943) (per Black, J.); Shapiro, *Freedom of Speech,* 77.

73. See, e.g., *Jones v. City of Opelika,* 316 U.S. 584, 593–98 (1942) (per Reed, J.); *Bridges,* 314 U.S. at 281–82, 293 (Frankfurter, J., dissenting).

74. See Mendelson, "Clear and Present Danger," 320.

75. Ibid.

76. Ibid.

77. See ibid., 320–21 (saying there were forty-one First Amendment cases but discounting seven "as involving only specious claims" and mentioning five more as settled "without reaching a First Amendment question"). I treat Mendelson's numbers as approximate because I note some unexplained double-counting of cases. See, e.g., Mendelson, "Clear and Present Danger," 321 n. 48, 324 n. 69, 326 n. 88 (setting aside *Musser v. Utah,* 333 U.S. 95 (1948) and *United Public Workers v. Mitchell,* 330 U.S. 75 (1947), as reaching only statutory issues, yet including them in later discussion).

78. If we include the five cases Mendelson treats as disposed of on statutory grounds, the statistics are twenty-five cases upholding First Amendment values and nine cases ruling against them. Including the "statutory" cases seems appropriate, as most of them involve determinations that the statutes were unconstitutionally vague or that the evidence did not support conviction. These determinations were decidedly influenced by First Amendment concerns. See, e.g., *Winters v. New York,* 333 U.S. 507 (1948); *Musser,* 333 U.S. at 95; *Keegan v. United States,* 325 U.S. 478 (1945).

79. Currie, *The Constitution,* 415. See also Powe, *The Warren Court,* 209–16, 497–501 (dating "history's Warren Court" to the 1962 term); Horwitz, *The Warren Court,* 65–67. (discussing the phases of the Warren Court).

80. Mendelson, "Clear and Present Danger," 320.

81. Ibid. (internal quotation marks omitted).

82. Horwitz, *The Warren Court,* 56; Krislov, *The Supreme Court,* 116; Urofsky, *Division and Discord,* 154–58; Mendelson, "Clear and Present Danger," 328, 332–33.

83. Urofsky, *Division and Discord,* 159–69; Mendelson, "Clear and Present Danger," 328–29.

84. See, e.g., Frank Strong, "Fifty Years of 'Clear and Present Danger': From *Schenck* to *Brandenburg*—and Beyond," *Supreme Court Review,* 1969, 54 (quoting *Konigsberg v. State Bar of California,* 366 U.S. 36, 64 (1961) (Black, J., dissenting); Mendelson, "Clear and Present Danger," 331.

85. See, e.g., *Feiner v. New York,* 340 U.S. 315 (1951); *American Communications Association v. Douds,* 339 U.S. 452 (1950); Mendelson, "Clear and Present Danger," 328–30 (discussing the cases); Urofsky, *Division and Discord,* 159–69 (same).

86. Shapiro, *Freedom of Speech,* 62–66, 80–81; Strong, "Fifty Years," 54–56; Laurent Frantz, "The First Amendment in the Balance," *Yale Law Journal* 71 (1962): 1428 ("This 'reinterpretation' of the 'clear and present danger test' appears to have killed it").

87. See Shapiro, *Freedom of Speech,* 63–64; Stone, *Perilous Times,* 396; Mendelson, "Clear and Present Danger," 330.

88. *Dennis v. United States,* 183 F.2d 201, 212 (2d Cir. 1950).

89. Mendelson, "Clear and Present Danger," 330.

90. Shapiro, *Freedom of Speech,* 79–83; Strong, "Fifty Years," 54–59; Frantz, "The First Amendment," 1432–33.

91. *Dennis v. United States,* 341 U.S. 494, 524–25 (1951).

92. Id. at 525.

93. Id.

94. *Feiner v. New York,* 340 U.S. 315 (1951). *Feiner* effectively reversed *Terminiello v. Chicago,* 337 U.S. 1 (1949), a hostile audience case decided in favor of the speaker just two years earlier.

95. *Beauharnais v. Illinois,* 343 U.S. 250 (1952).

96. *Uphaus v. Wyman,* 360 U.S. 72 (1959).

97. *Braunfeld v. Brown,* 366 U.S. 599, 610 (1961).

98. The general dominance of deferential balancing is masked by the Court's anomalous "Red Monday" decisions in 1957 and its occasional protection of the NAACP from hostile Southern legislation. See Powe, *The Warren Court,* 93–99, 135, 141–42, 154–56, 165–71.

99. 360 U.S. 109 (1959).

100. 99 100 Contemporaries treated *Barenblatt* as a paradigmatic case in part because of Justice Black's classic dissent. See *Barenblatt,* 360 U.S. at 134 (Black, J., dissenting); Powe, *The Warren Court,* 144–45; Shapiro, *Freedom of Speech,* 81, 97, 119. But see Daniel Farber and John Nowak, "Justice Harlan and the First Amendment," *Constitutional Commentary* 20 (1985): 425 (arguing that Harlan, who wrote for the Court in *Barenblatt,* did not "favor" case-by-case balancing).

101. *Barenblatt,* 360 U.S. at 114.

102. Id. at 126.

103. Id. at 126–27 (quoting *Watkins v. United States,* 354 U.S. 178, 198 (1957)).

104. Id. at 127.

105. Id. at 128.

106. Id. at 134.

107. Id. at 114, 126 (discussing "associational relationships").

108. Id. at 129–31.

109. Id. at 127.

110. Id. For the Court's short discussion of the record, see id. at 134.

111. Id. at 133. See also *Konigsberg v. State Bar of California*, 366 U.S. 36, 52–53 (1961) (balancing analysis upholds denial of bar membership for refusal to answer questions about Communist Party membership). At times the Court's ruling against First Amendment claims read more as if it was imposing only a rational basis standard. See *Lerner v. Casey*, 357 U.S. 468, 477–79 (1958) (upholding firing a subway conductor for failure to answer question about Communist Party membership); *Bauharnais*, 343 U.S. at 250 (per Frankfurter, J.) (upholding group libel laws through a balancing analysis).

112. For the comments in this paragraph, see, e.g., *Barenblatt v. United States*, 360 U.S. 109, 144–45 (1959) (Black, J., dissenting); Horwitz, *The Warren Court*, 68; Powe, *The Warren Court*, 144–45; Shapiro, *Freedom of Speech*, 83–87; Krislov, *The Supreme Court*, 115–16; Frantz, "The First Amendment," 1438–40, 143–44; Nimmer, "The Right to Speak," 939–41; Charles Reich, "Mr. Justice Black and the Living Constitution," *Harvard Law Journal* 76 (1963): 718–20; Edmund Cahn, "The Firstness of the First Amendment," *Yale Law Journal* 65 (1956): 479–80 (describing deferential justices as "laissez-faire jurists"); Strong, "Fifty Years," 57–59 (discussing the contemporary criticism). As Laurent Frantz expressed the point, "Irrespective of the ultimate merits of balancing, it will not do to treat freedom of speech as though it were a mere private interest of the individual before the court, as the majority did in *Barenblatt*. It is that, but it is also much more. And it is equally unsound to equate repression with national 'self-preservation' merely because government happens to be the adverse litigant. This lends to the government's interest such immediacy and magnitude that any other public interest would automatically have to give way, let alone one treated as though it were merely private." Frantz, "The First Amendment," 1438.

113. See Krislov, *The Supreme Court*, 116–17 (tracing Justice Black's adoption of an "absolute position on Free Speech"); L. A. Powe Jr., "Evolution to Absolutism: Justice Douglas and the First Amendment," *Columbia Law Review* 74 (1974): 384–401 (tracing the evolution of Justice Douglas's First Amendment jurisprudence); Reich, "Mr. Justice Black," 694–97, 720–22, 726–27 (tracing the evolution of Justice Black's First Amendment jurisprudence); Strong, "Fifty Years," 53–54 (dating Justice Douglas's embrace of First Amendment absolutism to 1961).

114. Reich, "Mr. Justice Black," 720.

115. Ibid., 719.

116. Hugo Black, "The Bill of Rights,' *New York University Law Review* 35 (1960): 878, quoted in Reich, "Mr. Justice Black," 720.

117. Ibid.

118. *Communist Party v. Subversive Activities Control Board*, 376 U.S. 1, 164 (1964) (Black, J., dissenting), quoted in Reich, "Mr. Justice Black," 720.

119. Black, "The Bill of Rights," 879, quoted in Reich, "Mr. Justice Black," 717.

120. Ibid. The split in the Court between deferential balancers and absolutists was analyzed in the late 1950s and early 1960s in a host of scholarly commentary defending and attacking both approaches. See, e.g., Shapiro, *Freedom of Speech*, 87–152; Charles Fried, "Two Concepts of Interests: Some Reflections on the Supreme Court's Balancing Test," *Harvard Law Review* 76 (1963): 755–78; Frantz, "The First Amendment"; Alexander Meiklejohn, "The First Amendment Is an Absolute," *Supreme Court Review*, 1961, 245–66; Wallace Mendelson, "On the Meaning of the First Amendment: Absolutes in the Balance," *California Law Review* 50 (1962): 821–28; Nimmer, "The Right to Speak," 935–48; Reich, "Mr. Justice Black," 733–54.

121. Horwitz, *The Warren Court,* 117 (chart of the changing political composition of the Warren Court); Powe, *The Warren Court,* 88–90.

122. Powe, *The Warren Court,* 205, 209–10.

123. See Horwitz, *The Warren Court,* 71, 117 (saying Justice White did not generally protect civil liberties and listing him among the Warren Court's conservatives); Powe, *The Warren Court,* 210–11, 304.

124. See Goldberg, "Mr. Justice Brennan," 9–11, 25 (discussing "definitional" and "generic" balancing); Nimmer, "The Right to Speak," 938–48 (discussing "definitional" balancing).

125. *Brandenburg v. Ohio,* 395 U.S. 444, 447–48 (1969); *Edwards v. South Carolina,* 372 U.S. 229, 237–38 (1963).

126. *Curtis Publishing Co. v. Butts,* 388 U.S. 130 (1967); *New York Times v. Sullivan,* 376 U.S. 254 (1964).

127. Horwitz, *The Warren Court,* 68–73, 104–6. See also Powe, *The Warren Court,* 303–79 (recounting free expression developments).

128. *William v. Rhodes,* 393 U.S. 23, 31 (1968) (political association); *DeGregory v. Attorney General,* 383 U.S. 825, 829 (1966) (legislative investigation); *Lamont v. Postmaster General,* 381 U.S. 301, 308–09 (1965) (Brennan, J., concurring) (right of addressees to receive communist propaganda); *Sherbert v. Verner,* 374 U.S. 398, 403, 406 (1963); *Gibson v. Florida Legislative Investigation Committee,* 372 U.S. 539, 546–47, 555, 557; *NAACP v. Button,* 371 U.S. 415, 438 (1963). See also *NAACP v. Overstreet,* 384 U.S. 118, 122 (1966) (Douglas, J., joined by Warren, C. J., Brennan, J., and Fortas, J., dissenting from cert. denial); *United States v. O'Brien,* 391 U.S. 367, 376 (1968) (discussing but rejecting using the compelling standard to decide symbolic speech cases).

129. See Powe, *The Warren Court,* 209–16, 497–501 (dating "history's Warren Court" to the 1962 term). See also Currie, *The Constitution,* 415 (discussing the "real" Warren Court); Horwitz, *The Warren Court,* 65–67 (discussing the phases of the Warren Court).

130. See note 128 above (citing all the First Amendment cases between 1963 and 1969 that used the compelling state interest standard). In other words, beginning in 1963, strict scrutiny was a part of the Court's First Amendment toolkit but rarely was the tool of choice. The prominent use of strict scrutiny in First Amendment analysis dates from the mid-1970s. See *First National Bank of Boston v. Bellotti,* 435 U.S. 765, 786, 795 (1978); *Buckley v. Veleo,* 424 U.S. 1, 66, 74–75 (1976); *Brazenburg v. Hayes,* 408 U.S. 665 (1972); *Wisconsin v. Yoder,* 406 U.S. 205 (1972).

131. See, e.g., Horwitz, *The Warren Court,* 65–73 (reviewing First Amendment doctrine and mentioning strict scrutiny only in regard to *Speiser v. Randall,* 357 U.S. 513 524–26 (1958)); Powe, *The Warren Court,* 221, 303–78 (same, but mentioning strict scrutiny only in regard to *NAACP v. Button,* 371 U.S. 415 (1963)); Harry Kalven, *A Worthy Tradition: Freedom of Speech in America* (New York: Harper & Row, 1988) (same, but not mentioning strict scrutiny at all). But see Goldberg, "Mr. Justice Brennan," 13 (describing the 1960s cases in terms readily identifiable as strict scrutiny but without using the label).

132. The three cases are *Sherbert v. Verner,* 374 U.S. 398 (1963); *Gibson v. Florida Legislative Investigation Committee,* 372 U.S. 539 (1963); and *NAACP v. Button,* 371 U.S. 415, 438 (1963).

133. Horwitz, *The Warren Court,* 65–66; Powe, *The Warren Court,* 209, 218–21.

134. This assertion, and the material in this part, is discussed at greater length in Siegel, "The Origin," 377–80.

135. See, e.g., Urofsky, *Division and Discord,* 89–90; Suzanne Goldberg, "Equality without Tiers," *Southern California Law Review* 77 (2004): 496–503; Greg Robinson and Toni Robinson, "*Korematsu* and Beyond: Japanese Americans and the Origins of Strict Scrutiny," *Law and Contemporary Problems* 68 (2005): 30–39; Larry Simon, "Racially Prejudiced Governmental Actions: A Motivation Theory of the Constitutional Ban against Racial Discrimination," *San Diego Law Review* 15 (1978): 1068 (saying strict scrutiny developed in cases challenging segregation).

136. 394 U.S. 618, 627, 634, 637 (1969).

137. Id. at 621.

138. 466 U.S. 429 (1984).

139. 316 U.S. 535, 541 (1942) ("strict scrutiny").

140. 323 U.S. 214, 216 (1944) ("most rigid scrutiny").

141. See, e.g., John Ely, *Democracy and Distrust: A Theory of Judicial Review* (Cambridge, Mass.: Harvard University Press, 1980), 145 n. 38 (saying *Skinner* failed rationality review); Michael Klarman, "An Interpretive History of Modern Equal Protection," *Michigan Law Review* 90 (1991): 232 (saying *Korematsu* used "rationality review"). In *Korematsu*, 323 U.S. at 216, Justice Black did say that "pressing public necessity may sometimes justify" racial classification without further defining or applying what it meant. See Siegel, "The Origin," 381–83 (discussing Justice Black's comment).

142. 347 U.S. 483 (1954).

143. 347 U.S. 497 (1954).

144. Id. at 499. See also Klarman, "An Interpretive History," 226–27, 229–30, 238–43, 227, 232–40 (discussing the traditional doctrine and its application to racial segregation).

145. 379 U.S. 184 (1964). *McLaughlin* also may have been the first equal protection case to shift the burden of proof to the government. See Siegel, "The Origin," 360. In this regard, it was anticipated by First Amendment burden shifting. See *Speiser v. Randall,* 357 U.S. 513 524–26 (1958) (seminal case shifting burden of proof in First Amendment cases); Siegel, "The Origin."

146. See *McLaughlin,* 379 U.S. at 196 (saying racial discrimination "will be upheld only if it is necessary, and not merely rationally related, *to the accomplishment of a permissible state policy*" [emphasis added]). See also *Loving v. Virginia*, 388 U.S. 1, 11 (1967) (saying if "racial classifications in criminal statutes . . . are ever to be upheld, they must be shown to be necessary to the accomplishment of *some permissible state objective*" [emphasis added]).

147. See text accompanying notes 169–71 below.

148. On the history of narrow tailoring, see Guy Struve, "The Less-Restrictive-Alternative Principle and Economic Due Process," *Harvard Law Journal* 80 (1967): 1463–88; Wormuth and Mirkin, "The Doctrine"; "Note: Less Drastic Means."

149. See Wormuth and Mirkin, "The Doctrine," 257–70 (discussing the development of the doctrine).

150. Ibid., 271–77. For Wormuth and Mirkin's complete discussion of narrow tailoring in First Amendment cases, see 270–93.

151. 362 U.S. 60, 63–65 (1960).

152. 364 U.S. 479, 485–90 (1960). Narrow tailoring, as a First Amendment doctrine, clearly predates its first use in equal protection cases in *McLaughlin v. Florida,* in 1964. See, e.g., *Schneider v. Town of Irvington,* 308 U.S. 147, 162 (1939); material cited above in note 150.

153. 354 U.S. 234 (1957).

154. Siegel, "The Origin," 364–68.

155. *Sweezy,* 354 U.S. at 262 (Frankfurter, J., concurring). See also id. at 265 (Frankfurter, J., concurring), quoted in note 156.

156. Frankfurter's *Sweezy* opinion invited the shearing. In addition to questions concerning his college lectures, Sweezy refused to answer questions regarding his involvement with the Progressive Party. In the part of Frankfurter's concurrence dealing with those questions, and not Sweezy's college lectures, Frankfurter stated the standard as: "For a citizen to be made to forego even a part of so basic a liberty as his political autonomy, the subordinating interest of the State must be compelling." *Sweezy,* 354 U.S. at 265.

157. *Bates v. City of Little Rock,* 361 U.S. 516, 524 (1960); *Scull v. Commonwealth of Virginia ex rel. Comm. on Law Reform and Racial Activities,* 359 U.S. 344, 352 (1959); *Barenblatt v. United States,* 360 U.S. 109, 127 (1959); *Uphaus v. Wyman,* 360 U.S. 72, 79–81 (1959); *Speiser v. Randall,* 357 U.S. 513, 529 (1958); *NAACP v. Alabama ex rel. Patterson,* 357 U.S. 449, 463 (1958). It was also used in an additional concurrence, *Talley v. California,* 362 U.S. 60, 66 (1960) (Harlan, J., concurring), and a dissent, *Braunfeld v. Brown,* 366 U.S. 599, 610 (1961) (Brennan, J., concurring and dissenting).

158. *Bates v. City of Little Rock,* 361 U.S. 516, 524 (1960) (opinion by Stewart, J.); *Barenblatt,* 360 U.S. at 127 (opinion by Harlan, J.); *Uphaus,* 360 U.S. at 79–81 (opinion by Clark, J.); *NAACP v. Alabama ex rel. Patterson,* 357 U.S. 449, 463 (1958) (opinion by Harlan, J.).

159. *Barenblatt v. United States,* 360 U.S. 109 (1959); *Uphaus,* 360 U.S. at 72.

160. 360 U.S. at 127. See text accompanying notes 99–112 (discussing *Barenblatt* as a deferential decision).

161. 360 U.S. 72, 81 (1959).

162. *NAACP v. Button,* 371 U.S. 415, 454 (1963) (Harlan, J., dissenting). See also *Talley v. California,* 362 U.S. 60, 69 n. 1 (1960) (Clark, J., joined by Frankfurter, J., and Whittaker, J., dissenting) (requiring a "reasonable relationship to the achievement of the government purpose asserted as its justification"). See also Siegel, "The Origin," 368–75 (discussing the low protectionists' view).

163. See Siegel, "The Origin," 373–75.

164. In this endeavor, Brennan, who provided the leadership, played the same role that Zechariah Chafee Jr. played in regards to Justice Holmes's clear and present danger test: he read a protective meaning into a phrase that in the precedents did not bear it. See Rabban, *Free Speech,* 7–8, 324–26 (discussing Chafee's transformation of Holmes's danger test).

165. 354 U.S. 234 (1957).

166. 357 U.S. 513, 529 (1958).

167. 366 U.S. 599, 610 (1961) (Brennan, J., concurring and dissenting).

168. Id. at 613–16 (Brennan J., concurring and dissenting). Professor Powe describes *Braunfeld* as reflecting Brennan's "emerging" jurisprudence. Powe, *The Warren Court,* 185.

169. 371 U.S. 415 (1963).

170. 372 U.S. 539 (1963).

171. 374 U.S. 398 (1963).

172. In the remainder of this paper I will use the term "danger rule" to mean "the 1940s' danger rule." I make no claim about the danger rule in other times. See, e.g., Strong, "Fifty Years," 44–53 (discussing the danger rule's changing meaning); Bernard Schwartz, "Justice

Brennan and the *Brandenburg* decision—a Lawgiver in Action," *Judicature* 79 (1995): 24–29 (same).

173. *Braunfeld v. Brown,* 366 U.S. 599, 613–14 (1961) (Brennan, J., concurring and dissenting).

174. 319 U.S. 624, 639 (1943), quoted in *Braunfeld,* 366 U.S. at 599, 612 (Brennan, J., concurring and dissenting).

175. 374 U.S. 398 (1963).

176. Id. at 403–6.

177. Id. at 406, quoting *Thomas v. Collins,* 323 U.S. 516, 530 (1945). For Justice Rutledge's full statement in *Thomas,* see text accompanying note 67 above.

178. Shapiro, *Freedom of Speech,* 151.

179. Ibid., 169. See also 151.

180. Ibid., 77, 173–74.

181. Strong, "Fifty Years," 63–64.

182. Ibid., 64. See also 80 (describing narrow tailoring as the fruit of the danger "test's trial and tribulations of a half-century").

183. 323 U.S. 214, 234–35 (1944) (Murphy, J., dissenting).

184. Id. at 234 (Murphy, J., dissenting).

185. Id. at 218. See also id. at 216 (saying "pressing public necessity may sometimes justify the existence of [racial] restrictions"); id. at 223 (speaking of "real military dangers," fear "of invasion," and "military urgency").

186. The requirements of "gravity" and "necessity" are discussed in Elliot Richardson, "Freedom of Expression and the Function of Courts," *Harvard Law Review* 65 (1951): 16–24.

187. *Schenck v. United States,* 249 U.S. 47, 52 (1919).

188. See text accompanying note 48 (discussing categorical balancing).

189. E.g., *Dennis v. United States,* 341 U.S. 494, 527–29 (1951) (Frankfurter, J., concurring); Paul Freund, *On Understanding the Supreme Court* (Boston: Little, Brown, 1951): 27; Learned Hand, *The Bill of Rights* (Cambridge, Mass.: Harvard University Press, 1958), 58–61; McKay, "The Preference for Freedom," 1203, 1205–12.

190. E.g., *Brandenburg v. Ohio,* 395 U.S 444, 449–50 (1969) (Black, J., concurring); id. at 450–55 (Douglas, J., concurring); Paul Kauper, review of *Political Freedom: The Constitutional Powers of the People,* by Alexander Meiklejohn, *Michigan Law Review* 58 (1960): 621.

191. E.g., *City of Cleburne v. Cleburne Living Center,* 473 U.S. 432, 451–52 (1985) (Stevens, J., concurring); id. at 455, 460, 472, 478 (Marshall, J., concurring and dissenting); *Massachusetts Board of Retirement v. Murgia,* 427 U.S. 307, 318–21 (1976) (Marshall, J., dissenting); Goldberg, "Equality without Tiers," 484–89; "Note: Justice Stevens' Equal Protection Jurisprudence," *Harvard Law Review* 100 (1987): 1146–65.

192. E.g., *Defunis v. Odegaard,* 416 U.S. 312, 333–34, 341, 343–44 (1974) (Douglas, J., dissenting); *Loving v. Florida,* 388 U.S. 1, 13 (1967) (Stewart, J., concurring); *McLaughlin v. Florida,* 379 U.S. 184, 198 (1964) (Stewart, J., concurring).

193. 304 U.S. 144, 152–53 n. 4 (1938).

194. 341 U.S. 494 (1951) (discussed in text accompanying notes 86–90).

195. Gerald Gunther, "Foreword: In Search of Evolving Doctrine on a Changing Court: A Model for a Newer Equal Protection," *Harvard Law Review* 86 (1972): 8. But see Adam Winkler, "Fatal in Theory and Strict in Fact: An Empirical Analysis of Strict Scrutiny in the Federal

Courts," *Vanderbilt Law Review* 59 (2006): 796, 813, 815 (saying that between 1990 and 2003 government action survived strict scrutiny 30 percent of the time, though survival rates vary depending on the area).

196. E.g., *Johnson v. California,* 125 S. Ct. 1141, 1151 (2005) (equal protection); *Grutter v. Bollinger,* 539 U.S. 306, 326–27 (2003) (same); *Adarand Constructors v. Pena,* 515 U.S. 200, 237 (1995) (same); *Employment Division v. Smith,* 494 U.S. 872, 904–5 (1990) (O'Connor, J., concurring) (showing strict scrutiny has not been fatal in First Amendment cases).

197. E.g., *Concrete Works of Colorado, Inc., v. City and County of Denver, Colorado.,* 540 U.S. 1027 (2003) (Scalia, J., joined by Rehnquist, C. J., dissenting from denial of certiorari); *Grutter,* 539 U.S. at 306 (diversity in law school admissions); *Shaw v. Reno,* 509 U.S. 630 (1993) (racial gerrymandering); *Parents Involved in Community Schools v. Seattle School District No. 1,* 377 F.3d 949 (9th Cir. 2004) (upholding race as a tiebreaker in high school placement).

198. Calvin Massey, "The New Formalism: Requiem for Tiered Scrutiny?" *University of Pennsylvania Journal of Constitutional Law* 6 (2004): 977.

199. Luis Fuentes-Rohwer and Guy-Uriel E. Charles, "From *Brown* to *Bakke* to *Grutter*: Constitutionalizing and Defining Racial Equality," *Constitutional Commentary* 21 (2004): 166. See also Michelle Adams, "Searching for Strict Scrutiny in *Grutter v. Bollinger*," *Tulane Law Review* 78 (2004): 1944 (saying the Court in *Grutter* applied strict scrutiny "in an undeniably relaxed manner," not "the mechanical, outcome-determinative approach [it had previously] signaled").

200. Libby Huskey, "Note," *Wyoming Law Review* 4 (2004): 474–75.

201. Fuentes-Rohwer and Charles, "From *Brown* to *Bakke*," 163–64. See also Adams, "Searching for Strict Scrutiny," 1943 (exploring the ramifications of the Court's application of strict scrutiny "in an undeniably relaxed manner," not as before as "mechanical" and "outcome-determinative"); Wilson Huhn, "The Jurisprudential Revolution: Unlocking Human Potential in Grutter and Lawrence," *William and Mary Bill of Rights Journal* 12 (2003):, 96–97 ("sliding scale" approach).

202. Pamela Karlan, "Easing the Spring: Strict Scrutiny and Affirmative Action After the Redistricting Cases," *William and Mary Law Review* 43 (2002): 1602–3.

203. Eugene Volokh, "Freedom of Speech, Permissible Tailoring and Transcending Strict Scrutiny," *University of Pennsylvania Law Review* 144 (1996): 2417.

204. 517 U.S. 620 (1996).

205. 539 U.S. 538 (2003) (overturning laws that criminalize homosexual sodomy).

206. See, e.g., Goldberg, "Equality without Tiers," 481; Huhn, "The Jurisprudential Revolution," 96–97; Massey, "The New Formalism," 970–80. The predictions trace back at least to Jeffrey Shaman, "Cracks in the Structure: The Coming Breakdown of the Levels of Scrutiny," *Ohio State Law Journal* 45 (1984): 161–84. The calls for a sliding scale trace back to the 1970s. *Craig v. Boren,* 429 U.S. 190, 211–12 (1976) (Stevens, J., concurring); *San Antonio Independent School District v. Rodriguez,* 411 U.S. 1, 70, 98–99, 109–10 (1973) (Marshall, J., dissenting); *Dandridge v. Williams*, 397 U.S. 471, 508–30 (1970) (Marshall, J., dissenting); "Note: Justice Stevens' Equal Protection Jurisprudence."

207. *Dennis v. United States,* 341 U.S. 494 (1951).

208. Krislov, *The Supreme Court,* 119; McKay, "The Preference for Freedom," 1212, 1222. See also *Dennis v. United States*, 183 F.2d 201, 213 (2d Cir. 1950) ("We do not understand how one could ask for a more probable danger, unless we must wait till the actual eve of hostilities").

209. Strong, "Fifty Years," 53, 54, 57.

210. See text accompanying notes 172–94 (discussing the doctrines' historical roots and analytical similarities).

211. See text accompanying notes 113–20 (discussing Black's and Douglas's shift to absolutism).

212. Kenneth Karst, "Legislative Facts in Constitutional Litigation," *Supreme Court Review,* 1960, 77–86; Kauper, review of Meiklejohn, 624–26; Mendelson, "On the Meaning," 120, 826.

213. Shapiro, *Freedom of Speech,* 108–11; Frantz, "The First Amendment," 1429–36; Reich, "Mr. Justice Black," 742–50; Hans Linde, "'Clear and Present Danger' Reexamined: Dissonance in the *Brandenburg* Concerto," *Stanford Law Review* 22 (1970): 1167–68, 1174, 1179, 1183.

214. Emerson, *Toward a General Theory,* 56–58; Shapiro, *Freedom of Speech,* 90–91, 101–02; Frantz, "The First Amendment," 1434–38; Karst, "Legislative Facts," 79–80; Reich, "Mr. Justice Black," 742–44.

215. Emerson, *Toward a General Theory,* 57. See also Shapiro, *Freedom of Speech,* 90 ("It is in this process of defining or delimiting the scope of the First Amendment that balancing—that is, harmonizing the freedom of speech with other individual and social interests—should take place"); Reich, "Mr. Justice Black," 743–44 (saying absolutism involves a search for the balance created by the Constitution and grounds decisions in a less malleable frame of reference that is external to the judge).

216. *Loving,* 388 U.S. at 1, 13 (Stewart, J., concurring); *McLaughlin v. Florida,* 379 U.S. 184, 198 (1964) (Stewart, J., dissenting, joined by Douglas, J.)

217. *Grutter v. Bollinger,* 539 U.S. 306, 370 (2003) (Thomas, J., dissenting, joined by Scalia, J.)

218. *Washington v. Lee,* 263 F. Supp. 327, 331 n. 6 (D.C.M.D. Ala. 1966), upheld in *Lee v. Washington,* 390 U.S. 333 (1968). See also id. at 334 (Black, J., Harlan, J., and Stewart, J., concurring) (admitting that prison officials may employ racial segregation "in particularized circumstances . . . in maintaining security, discipline, and good order in prisons and jails").

219. *McLaughlin,* 379 U.S. at 198 (Stewart, J., dissenting).

220. *DeFunis v. Odegaard,* 416 U.S. 312, 343 (1974) (Douglas, J., dissenting).

221. Id. at 343.

222. *Johnson v. California,* 543 U.S. 499, 524 (2005) (Thomas, J., dissenting, joined by Scalia, J.).

223. See, e.g., Randy Barnett, "The Original Meaning of the Commerce Clause," *University of Chicago Law Review* 68 (2001): 105–8 (propounding "original meaning" as opposed to "original intent" originalism); Randy Barnett, "An Originalism for Nonoriginalists," *Loyola Law Review* 45 (1999): 620–53 (same); Antonin Scalia, "Originalism: The Lesser Evil," *University of Cincinnati Law Review* 57 (1989): 849–65 (defending originalism as opposed to non-originalist constitutionalism).

224. See Nancie G. Marzulla, "The Textualism of Clarence Thomas: Anchoring the Supreme Court's Property Rights Jurisprudence to the Constitution," *American University Journal of Gender, Social Policy, and the Law* 10 (2002): 353–62 (discussing Justices Black's and Thomas's textualism).

225. Thomas Grey, "The New Formalism" (Sept. 6, 1999), Social Science Research Network, http://ssrn.com/abstract=200732 (discussing originalism as a branch of the "new formalism").

226. I particularly suggest Emerson, *Toward a General Theory,* 56–58; Shapiro, *Freedom of Speech,* 81, 87–95, 101–4; Frantz, "The First Amendment," 1434–38; Karst, "Legislative Facts,"

77–86; Mendelson, "On the Meaning," 120; Powe, "Evolution to Absolutism," 371; Reich, "Mr. Justice Black," 727–54.

227. See, e.g., Shapiro, *Freedom of Speech,* 62–66, 80–81; Strong, "Fifty Years," 52–56.

228. See text above accompanying notes 197–203 (discussing affirmative action precedents).

229. 341 U.S. 494 (1951). On *Dennis*'s reconstitution of the danger test, see *Konigsberg v. State Bar of California,* 366 U.S. 36, 64 (1961) (Black, J., dissenting); text accompanying notes 86–90 (discussing *Dennis*).

230. Herbert Weschler, "Symposium on Civil Liberties," *American University Law School Review* 9 (1941):, 887, quoted in Strong, "Fifty Years," 86. See also Freund, *On Understanding,* 27–28:

The truth is that the clear-and-present-danger test is an oversimplified judgment unless it takes account also of a number of other factors: the relative seriousness of the danger in comparison with the value of the occasion for speech or political activity; the availability of more moderate controls than those which the state has imposed; and perhaps the specific intent with which the speech or activity is launched. No matter how rapidly we utter the phrase 'clear and present danger,' or how closely we hyphenate the words, they are not a substitute for the weighing of values. They tend to convey a delusion of certitude when what is most certain is the complexity of the strands in the web of freedoms which the judge must disentangle.

231. Kenneth Karst, "The First Amendment and Harry Kalven: An Appreciative Comment on the Advantages of Thinking Small," *UCLA Law Review* 13 (1960): 10. See also Shapiro, *Freedom of Speech,* 77; Richardson, "Freedom of Expression," passim (extended analysis of the danger test as requiring judicial balancing); Strong, "Fifty Years," 55–58 (reviewing the literature, but slightly misquoting Karst). Among the works cited by Strong are Samuel Krislov, *The Supreme Court and Political Freedom* (New York: Free Press, 1968), 121; McKay, "The Preference for Freedom," 1212, 1222.

232. Aleinikoff, "Constitutional Law," 980–81. Aleinikoff wrote in opposition to all forms of balancing. See 1002–5.

233. See Shapiro, *Freedom of Speech,* 2–3, 90–92; Frantz, "The First Amendment," 1434–35; Goldberg, "Mr. Justice Brennan," 9–11, 19, 25; Nimmer, "The Right to Speak," 942–45; Reich, "Mr. Justice Black," 740–44 (defending Justice Black as a categorical balancer).

234. Nimmer, "The Right to Speak," 945.

235. Emerson, *Toward a General Theory,* 55–60; Shapiro, *Freedom of Speech,* 83–87, 90–92, 97; Frantz, "The First Amendment," 1430–35; Goldberg, "Mr. Justice Brennan," 9–11, 25; Nimmer, "The Right to Speak," 945, 946–47; Reich, "Mr. Justice Black," 743; In other words, categorical balancing promised to counter ad hoc balancing's historic tendency to underweigh the cost to civil liberties when confronted with the immediate impact of the government's security concern. See text accompanying note 112 (critiquing ad hoc balancing in *Barenblatt*).

236. Nimmer, "The Right to Speak," 945. See also Emerson, *Toward a General Theory,* 54–56; Frantz, "The First Amendment," 1435; Reich, "Mr. Justice Black," 743.

237. For the comments in this paragraph, see, e.g., Emerson, *Toward a General Theory,* 51–58 (describing the competing theories as "clear and present danger test," "ad hoc balancing," and "absolute test"); Shapiro, *Freedom of Speech,* 46, 76, 87 (same); Brennan, "The Supreme Court," 4–9 (same).

238. Shapiro, *Freedom of Speech,* 77.

239. Ibid.

240. Ibid., 77.

241. Ibid., 2. See also Richardson, "Freedom of Expression," 43, 47–48 (discussing judicial deference to legislative judgments).

242. Shapiro, *Freedom of Speech,* 2

243. Ibid., 2

244. Ibid., 87.

245. Richardson, "Freedom of Expression," 43. See 44–54 (discussing the role of deference in First Amendment adjudication).

246. 341 U.S. 494 (1951).

247. 539 U.S. 306 (2003).

248. 543 U.S. 499, 524 (2005) (Thomas, J., dissenting, joined by Scalia, J.).

249. Yogi Berra, *The Yogi Book* (New York: Workman, 1998), 30.

250. See, e.g., Horwitz, *Transformation II* 3–7, 269–72; Morton J. Horwitz, "Transformation I: After 25 Years," *Law & Social Inquiry* 28 (2003): 1158.

251. Morton J. Horwitz, "Foreword: The Constitution of Change: Legal Fundamentality without Fundamentalism," *Harvard Law Review* 107 (1993): 116. See also 110 (quoting John Dewey that "ideas that at one time are means of producing social change have not the same meaning when they are used as a means of preventing social change") Indeed, Mort has urged us to "face the historicist critique that even truth changes over time" (33).

252. Horwitz, *Transformation II,* 252, 260–65 (discussing the *Lochner* and cold war eras); Morton J. Horwitz, "Commentary: 'Contracted' Biographies and Other Obstacles to 'Truth,'" *New York University Law Review* 70 (1995): 714–16 (same).

253. See, e.g., Horwitz, "Foreword: The Constitution of Change," 98–116 (discussing color blindness and hate speech).

254. Jack Balkin, "Some Realism about Pluralism: Legal Realist Approaches to the First Amendment," *Duke Law Journal,* 1990, no. 3, 375–86 (discussing "ideological drift").

255. Horwitz, "Foreword: The Constitution of Change," 40.

256. Ibid., 113.

257. Ibid., 116.

258. Morton J. Horwitz, "History and Theory," *Yale Law Journal* 96 (1987): 1826.

259. Morton J. Horwitz, "Republicanism and Liberalism in American Constitutional Thought," *William and Mary Law Review* 29 (1987): 57–74 (discussing controversies among legal historians).

260. A reminiscence relevant to this paper's treatment of the origin of the compelling state interest test: When I was a law student, it was Mort Horwitz's dazzling discussion of the doctrine of reasonable use in nineteenth-century water law that sensitized me to the phenomenon of a legal concept meaning one thing to the person who originates it and another thing to the people who develop it. See Morton J. Horwitz, *The Transformation of American Law, 1780–1860* (Cambridge, Mass.: Harvard University Press, 1977), 38–40 (discussing *Tyler v. Wilkinson*); text accompanying notes 153–64 (discussing strict scrutiny).

11

Hugo Black's Civil Rights Movement

CHRISTOPHER SCHMIDT

WHEN THE CIVIL RIGHTS MOVEMENT SWEPT ACROSS THE NATION IN THE early 1960s, Justice Hugo Black did not like what he saw. In reaction to African American students sitting down at "whites only" lunch counters, he worried about the threat to the property rights of the white proprietors. A demonstration outside a jail led Black to defend the right of government to protect its property. A peaceful protest in a segregated library raised concerns for him that library patrons would be disturbed. When he saw mass protest marches in cities across the nation, he warned that the streets were no place to pursue social reform. He opposed the Montgomery Bus Boycott, predicted the March on Washington would turn violent, and felt that Martin Luther King Jr. should abandon his campaign of public demonstrations.

In light of Black's early career on the Court, his uncompromisingly critical attitude toward the protests of the civil rights movement took by surprise many of his friends and supporters. Following his appointment to the Court in 1937, Black, in heroic fashion, rose above the bigotry of his upbringing and early career as a lawyer and politician in Alabama—a period during which he was a member of the local Ku Klux Klan—to become an unshakeable supporter of *Brown v. Board of Education* and its progeny. The justice stood as a monument to the principle of free speech during the hysterics of the McCarthy era, and he aggressively advocated extending the protections of the Bill of Rights to the states. Yet by the time of his retirement, his liberal credentials were under fire. In a series of defections from some of the most important of the Warren Court's decisions, Black expounded an increasingly strict commitment to textualism and originalism.[1] Particularly striking defections came when the Court evaluated the extent of constitutional protections for public protest. In these cases, Black announced, with characteristic passion and eloquence, his disapproval of the tactics of the civil rights protesters. By the middle of the decade, his disapproval had turned to outright condemnation of the civil rights movement.

In this essay I attempt to explain Black's reaction to the civil rights movement. The origins of his deep fear of social unrest and the pursuit of reform outside established institutional channels, I argue, can be traced to the same basic principles that drove his legendary commitment to civil liberties. His inability to understand the significance of the civil rights protests was as much the product of a stubborn consistency in his lifelong antagonism toward concentrated power and his commitment to the rule of law as it was the product of his growing conservative tendencies. An analysis of Justice Black's protest decisions offers important insights into not only the life and thought of a great, contradictory, and flawed figure of American history, but also the fundamental challenge the civil rights movement posed for the American legal system.

JUSTICE BLACK'S PROTEST DECISIONS

Reading Black's civil rights protest decisions is a bracing experience. The turn to direct-action protest by the leaders of the civil rights movement deeply disappointed the justice who, from his early years on the Court, demonstrated a growing commitment to judicial leadership in the struggle for racial equality. The protest decisions reveal a rawness of feeling that is rare for the *U.S. Reports.* They are eloquent, powerful, and disturbing. As Black described a nation that was spinning out of control, his words suggested that he himself was losing a sense of control. These were his jeremiads, his lay sermons from the pulpit of the Supreme Court. Black even treated the reading of his opinions from the bench as a kind of sermon to the nation. "Trembling with rage and shaking his finger at the courtroom audience," a reporter described the justice as he read his dissent in one of the protest cases, "Black blistered the majority with a 30-minute assault that made his strongly phrased written dissent pale by comparison."[2]

Between 1964 and 1966, Black wrote opinions in four major protest decisions. Each built upon its predecessors, repeating and expanding several basic themes. Each iteration was more uncompromising in his denunciation of the actions of civil rights protesters. Black's first public attack on the tactics of civil rights protesters came in *Bell v. Maryland* in 1964.[3] The Court was faced with the fundamental constitutional question raised by the student sit-ins that exploded across the South in early 1960: whether, under the Fourteenth Amendment, a state could prosecute African Americans for trespass for refusing to leave a privately owned public accommodation, such as a lunch counter, in which the owner refused to serve blacks. In earlier cases, the Court had been able to dodge the difficult "state action" question, finding a lack of evidence to support the conviction or locating enough official involvement in the nominally private exclusionary policy to attribute the discrimination to the state.[4] In *Bell,* however, Black insisted on squarely confronting the boundary between individual property rights and the equal protection clause, and his dissent gave him a platform for condemning the students for challenging the property rights of the business owners. The next major protest decision in which Black wrote was *Cox. v. Louisiana* in 1965.[5] Over another angry Black dissent the Court overturned the conviction, under an anti-picketing statute, of the leader of a civil rights protest that took place outside a courthouse. In 1966, in *Brown v. Louisiana* a bare majority of the Court overturned the conviction of five African Americans who took part in a peaceful sit-in protest in a public library, with Black again writing in dissent.[6] In the same year came *Adderley v. Florida*, a case in which protesters were arrested for trespassing for a demonstration outside a county jail.[7] Black secured his majority, and the Court, for the first time during the civil rights movement, upheld a state conviction of civil rights demonstrators.

Although the precise form of the protest and the legal issues changed from case to case, Black's opinions returned to several basic ideas. His dominant theme was clear: a fine line separated social order from chaos, and the only protection from anarchy was a strict, consistent application of the rule of law. "Experience demonstrates that it is not a far step from what to many seems the earnest, honest, patriotic, kind-spirited multitude of today, to the fanatical, threatening, lawless mob of tomorrow," he wrote in his *Cox* dissent.[8] "It would betray our whole plan for a tranquil and orderly society," he asserted in *Bell*, "to say that a citizen, because of his personal prejudices, habits, attitudes, or beliefs, is cast outside the law's protection and cannot call for the aid of officers sworn to uphold the law and preserve the peace."[9] Reading the Fourteenth Amendment to require business owners to serve blacks would "severely handicap a State's efforts to maintain a peaceful and orderly society."[10] The protection of public order, he explained in concluding his *Bell* dissent, was the primary goal of government.

> The Constitution does not confer upon any group the right to substitute rule by force for rule by law. Force leads to violence, violence to mob conflicts, and these to rule by the strongest groups with control of the most deadly weapons. Our Constitution, noble work of wise men, was designed—all of it—to chart a quite different course: to "establish Justice, insure domestic Tranquility . . . and secure the Blessings of Liberty to ourselves and our Posterity." At times the rule of law seems too slow to some for the settlement of their grievances. But it is the plan our Nation has chosen to preserve both "Liberty" and equality for all. On that plan we have put our trust and staked our future. This constitutional rule of law has served us well. Maryland's trespass law does not depart from it. Nor shall we.[11]

He made clear that when a protest resulted in disorder—or even just the threat of disorder—the government's first responsibility was to preserve the rule of law. In *Brown v. Louisiana* he wrote: "It is high time to challenge the assumption in which too many people have too long acquiesced, that groups that think they have been mistreated or that have actually been mistreated have a constitutional right to use the public's streets, buildings, and property to protest whatever, wherever, whenever they want, without regard to whom such conduct may disturb."[12] He feared that "powerful private groups" would interpret the majority opinion overturning the library sit-in conviction "as granting them a license to invade the tranquility and beauty of our libraries whenever they have quarrel with some state policy which may or may not exist."[13] "Governments like ours," he concluded, "were formed to substitute the rule of law for the rule of force."[14] Although one can always locate examples of peaceful protest demonstrations, "I say once more that the crowd moved by noble ideals today can become the mob ruled by hate and passion and greed and violence tomorrow. If we ever doubted that, we know it now. The peaceful songs of love can become as stirring and provocative as the Marseillaise did in the days when a noble revolution gave way to rule by successive mobs until chaos set in. The holding in this case today makes it more necessary than ever that we stop and look more closely at where we are going."[15]

For Black, the rule of law above all else had to be consistent in application. He insisted in each of his protest decisions that the Court evaluate the actions of the civil rights protesters without regard to the admirable goals of their protests. "The worst citizen no less than the best is entitled to equal protection of the laws of his State and of his Nation," Black explained in *Bell*.[16] The last thing the Court should be doing was to be creating some sort of legal double standard based on the Court's approval of the protesters' underlying message. "None of our past cases justifies reading the Fourteenth Amendment in a way that might well penalize citizens who are law-abiding enough to call upon the law and its officers for protection instead of using their own physical strength or dangerous weapons to preserve their rights."[17] In *Cox* he further elaborated on this theme: "The crowds that press in the streets for noble goals today can be supplanted tomorrow by street mobs pressuring the courts for precisely opposite ends. . . . Those who encourage minority groups to believe that the United States Constitution and federal laws give them a right to patrol and picket in the streets whenever they choose, in order to advance what they think to be a just and noble end, do no service to those minority groups, their cause, or their country."[18] "It has become automatic," he lamented, "for people to be turned loose as long as whatever they do has something to do with race. That is not the way I read the Constitution."[19]

An overriding commitment to law and order in fact protected the interests of civil rights protesters, Black explained. As he wrote in *Cox*: "The streets are not now and never have been the proper place to administer justice. Use of the streets for such purposes has always proved disastrous to individual liberty in the long run, whatever fleeting benefits may have appeared to have been achieved. And minority groups, I venture to suggest, are the ones who always have suffered and always will suffer most when street multitudes are allowed to substitute their pressures for the less glamorous but more dependable and temperate processes of the law."[20] He returned to this theme in *Brown v. Louisiana*: "It is an unhappy circumstance . . . that the group, which more than any other has needed a government of equal laws and equal justice, is now encouraged to believe that the best way for it to advance its cause, which is a worthy one, is by taking the law into its own hands from place to place and from time to time."[21]

The civil rights protest cases also allowed Black to develop his argument that the protection of property rights was the cornerstone of a stable, orderly society. A government that was serving its proper role in ensuring peace and tranquility for society had to be particularly vigilant toward encroachments on this fundamental but vulnerable right. "The experience of ages," he wrote in *Bell*, "points to the inexorable fact that people are frequently stirred to violence when property which the law recognizes as theirs is forcibly invaded or occupied by others. Trespass laws are born of this experience."[22] Challenges to the inviolability of physical property that was open to the public were central to the civil rights movement—and this was one of the elements of the movement that most disturbed the justice from Alabama. Black even extended his deference to property rights to publicly owned property. "The State, no less than a private owner of property, has power to preserve the property under its control for the use to which it is lawfully dedicated," he argued with regard to the protest outside the jail in *Adderley*. "The United States Constitution does not forbid a State to control the use of its own property for its own lawful nondiscriminatory purpose."[23]

Black also offered his views on the appropriate tactics for social reformers. The best way for government to serve its essential function of protecting social order was to channel all protest into the political and legal process. "Our society has put its trust in a system of criminal laws to punish lawless conduct. To avert personal feuds and violent brawls it has led its people to believe and expect that wrongs against them will be vindicated in the courts."[24] He was passionately committed to the idea that the foundation of a stable society was faith in the judiciary. "The very purpose of a court system," he explained in *Cox*, "is to adjudicate controversies . . . in the calmness and solemnity of the courtroom according to legal procedures. Justice cannot be rightly administered, nor are the lives and safety of prisoners secure, where throngs of people clamor against the processes of justice right outside the courthouse or jailhouse doors."[25]

MAKING SENSE OF BLACK'S PROTEST DECISION

What happened to Justice Black? Scholars who have looked at Black's protest decisions have generally divided into two camps: those who emphasize their continuities with his earlier civil rights and civil liberties decisions, and those who argue that Black's views took a sharp turn in the 1960s. The continuity interpretation is generally the territory of the justice's defenders,[26] although this was not always the case. Alexander Bickel, for example, a sharp critic of Black's jurisprudence, argued that his "rather aggrieved lecture to the demonstrators" in the demonstration cases is "a consistent and integral part of his conception of the legal order, and indeed serve[s] to complete and explain it."[27]

In contrast, proponents of the "new Black" thesis (or it might be described as the "old Black" thesis, since some see his later decisions as a revival of an earlier, more conservative "Alabama Black") argue that the justice changed in the last decade of his service on the Court. His previous commitment to protecting dissent and supporting the cause of African Americans was largely lost, as he was unable, or unwilling, to distinguish the peaceful protest actions of the civil rights movement from the extralegal violence of the white supremacists or the urban rioting that swept across the nation in the second half of the 1960s. Many of the justice's admirers concede that by the end of his life the great protector of individual liberty had retreated to the conservative terrain of defending law and order. His disappointed liberal colleagues certainly thought something had changed in him. "Black has hardened and gotten old," Chief Justice Earl Warren said in 1966. "It's a different Black now."[28] William Brennan concurred with the chief justice: "Hugo changed, the man changed, right in front of us."[29] And most scholars have emphasized Black's growing conservatism throughout the 1960s. Black's generally sympathetic biographer summarized the justice's new outlook: "No longer was he giving freedom to address public matters priority over appeals for public convenience and civic order. . . . Formerly he had treated dissenters as heroes indispensable to progress, who helped the country live up to its highest aspirations. Now he disparaged protest groups and their leaders: he considered them ambitious, misinformed, dangerous agitators. A very different Black was focusing on constitutional limitations of a very different sort."[30]

Yet the focus of this "new Black" versus "same Black" debate too often fails to recognize the various, often contradictory strands of thought contained within Black's jurisprudence throughout his career. Whether or not one concludes that Black's protest decisions were consistent with his earlier rulings largely depends on which of these strands one identifies as representative. Undoubtedly Black changed in some respects: most notably, he lost a measure of creativity in applying his unique mixture of textual commitment, history, principle, and common sense, which had made possible those legal opinions from the 1940s and 1950s that stood as monuments to civil liberty. Yet the continuities in his basic commitments must also be reckoned with.

The growing radicalism and violence of the 1960s pushed Black toward a visceral animosity toward the protest tactics, but his underlying distrust of street demonstrations was there from the beginning. His criticism of direct-action protest was not just a reaction to rioting and rising crime rates. For instance, the strict division between speech and conduct that he relied upon in rejecting the free speech claims of civil rights protesters was nothing new for Black. When critics challenged his unwillingness to find civil rights protests protected under the First Amendment, he would cite an opinion from 1949 in which he rejected the free speech claim of labor picketers as involving unprotected conduct.[31] Furthermore, his antagonism toward public protests predated the 1960s. When Black came under criticism for what some saw as his growing conservatism in the late 1960s, Virginia Durr, his sister-in-law from his first marriage, sought to set the record straight: "Hugo has been that way since the Montgomery Bus Boycott, he has admonished us each time we saw him to 'tell our friends to get off the streets and into the Courts' or it would be like Germany and 'our friends' would get it in the neck—so really he has not changed his mind."[32] It was therefore in character for him to disapprove of the sit-ins from the start, and to oppose the March on Washington.[33] "You better tell your friend Martin Luther King to stop marching," he told Virginia Durr.[34] After viewing television coverage of a civil rights demonstration in 1964, Black commented on the "looks of hatred and fanaticism" on the faces of the protesters.[35] He saw the urban rioting that swept across the nation in the following years as the logical, predictable extension of the protest tactics pioneered by the students and civil rights leaders.

To explain the emergence of Black's skepticism toward the civil rights movement even in the movement's earliest stages, when it was driven largely by a commitment to nonviolence and integration and when the dignity of the protests captured the sympathies of many liberal whites, it is necessary to look to the ideas that guided the justice through his first two decades on the Court. The origins of Black's critique of civil rights protest can be found in the same set of basic principles on which he based his great civil libertarian opinions of the 1940s and 1950s. Throughout his years on the Court, the dominant theme of Black's jurisprudence was a fear of concentrated power and the threat it posed for personal liberty. He nurtured this belief in his days as a populist politician railing against the greed of big business; once on the Court, he transformed it into a civil libertarian platform for his First Amendment and criminal procedure decisions; and during the civil rights movement he used it as the basis for his critique of public demonstrations, which, he concluded, created a dangerous source of extragovernmental power.

Black was guided by his study of history. He had always been largely self-taught, and upon his appointment to the Court he rededicated himself to his ever-increasing collection of books, immersing himself in the classics and in American history, particularly the history of the Revolution and founding era. Through his studies, Black constructed a general philosophy on human liberty that would guide him for the rest of his life. "The Americans who supported the Revolution and the adoption of our Constitution knew firsthand the dangers of tyrannical governments," Black explained in a 1960 lecture.[36] The Revolutionary experience created a generation of Americans with a particular fear of concentrated power; often this fear took on characteristics of a near-paranoid obsession.[37] Not surprisingly, when looking back to the Founders, it was the Anti-Federalists, the group whose "loud and irresistible clamor"[38] about excessive national power resulted in the Bill of Rights, with whom Black most identified. And no figure of history did Black revere more than Thomas Jefferson,[39] who dedicated his life to defending limited government as the best protection for individual freedom.[40]

Inspired by his study of the past, Black viewed the expansion of government power at the expense of liberty as a sign of impending tyranny. "Experience" and "history"—words that always signaled the analytical crux of a Black opinion—showed that those who gain some power will look for ways to secure more. It was this idea, containing a generous dose of both insight and paranoia, that gave such force and depth to his efforts to place the First Amendment as a roadblock in the face of the McCarthyite juggernaut. In a 1950 dissent, he wrote:

> Centuries of experience testify that laws aimed at one political or religious group, however rational these laws may be in their beginnings, generate hatreds and prejudices which rapidly spread beyond control. Too often it is fear which inspires such passions, and nothing is more reckless or contagious. In the resulting hysteria, popular indignation tars with the same brush all those who have ever been associated with any member of the group under attack or who hold a view which, though supported by revered Americans as essential to democracy, has been adopted by that group for its own purposes. . . . Under such circumstances, restrictions imposed on proscribed groups are seldom static, even though the rate of expansion may not move in geometric progression from discrimination to arm-band to ghetto and worse.[41]

Black saw fascism looming at every turn. "Experience all over the world has demonstrated that the distance between stable, orderly government and one that has been taken over by force is not so great as we have assumed," he noted in 1960.[42] With the specter of European fascism in the background, Black wrote in 1940 of the "tragic proof that the exalted power of some governments to punish manufactured crime dictatorially is the handmaid of tyranny."[43] In the mid-1940s he began to describe Jim Crow as a fascist regime;[44] he told the justices in discussing the segregation cases that separate but equal was "Hitler's Creed."[45] Black, like many others, saw ominous signs of American fascism in the anticommunist fervor of the McCarthy period. A decision upholding the breach of peace conviction of a speaker for making an inflammatory speech led him to warn in dissent that the Court was taking "a long step toward totalitarian authority."[46] He even feared that election of Eisenhower in 1952 would "bring on fascism and war."[47] "There are grim reminders all around this world," he wrote in a 1961 opinion, "that the distance between individual liberty and firing squads is not always as far as it seems."[48] The real and immediate threat of tyranny was nothing less than the dominant motif of his legal writings.

It was a tyranny of sorts that Black saw in the social movements of the 1960s. The dangers uncontrolled power posed to personal liberty were not limited to government power. Private actors could also exercise power that could be just as destructive to liberty. As Edmund Burke warned in *Reflections on the Revolution in France*, individual liberty, when exercised through concerted action, could become a new form of concentrated power.[49] When the rule of law broke down, liberty was threatened not only by government power, but also by disorder.[50] Anarchy—excessive liberty—bred new opportunities for oppression, for tyranny. Liberty itself may threaten liberty. "The regulation of picketing and marching," Black argued, "is essential since this conduct by its very nature tends to infringe the rights to others."[51]

The crucial difference between Black the civil libertarian and Black the critic of the civil rights movement was that the threat to the rule of law he now identified derived from private actors rather than the state. Too much liberty risked creating an environment in which that very liberty would be lost. Weakening the constraints of the rule of law created space in which new tyrannous relations could emerge. This was the "uncontrolled and uncontrollable liberty" that Black warned of in *Tinker v. Des Moines*.[52] Black echoed Burke's fears in *Brown v. Louisiana* when he warned that the "power of private nongovernmental groups"[53] would lead to a loss of liberty for others—in this case, protesters who occupied the public library took away the right of other patrons to use the facilities undisturbed. When Black concluded his dissent with the observation that "governments like ours were formed to substitute the rule of law for the rule of force,"[54] he referred not to the force of a tyrannical government, but the force of a free people, acting in concert toward a shared goal—albeit one that ran afoul of local laws designed to preserve order. The rule of law faced threats from all directions—from overbearing government, from a disorganized populace that was susceptible to dictators, and from an organized populace that sought to exercise power outside the formal institutions of governance.

If the threat to liberty could come from disorder just as it could come from oppressive government, then the solution, Black concluded, was to steer protest into traditional political and judicial channels. In the spring of 1965, he confided to his wife that he felt "people in this country subconsciously want a change in government, since all seem to want a 'government by demonstrations and marching.' . . . Hitler took to the streets before he took over."[55] For Black, pressing social change through the politics of mobilization was not complementary or even supplementary to institutionalized politics and litigation; it was an *alternative* form of government. And this renegade "government" threatened the very foundations of liberal democracy. "What we have in this country is a government of laws," he explained in a 1968 lecture, "designed to achieve justice to all, in the most orderly fashion possible, and without leaving behind a deluge of hate-breeding divisions and dangerous riots."[56]

There is a symmetry to the idealized vision of the courtroom in his early decisions arguing for more expansive protections for the rights of criminals and his later decisions denouncing the tactics of civil rights protesters. In 1940, in his first major civil liberties decision, Black wrote for the Court a ruling that overturned the convictions of African American defendants whose confessions had obviously been coerced. He concluded his opinion in *Chambers v. Florida* with perhaps the most quoted line he ever wrote, in which he described the courts as "havens of refuge for those who might otherwise suffer because they are helpless, weak, outnumbered, or because they are nonconforming victims of prejudice and public excitement."[57] Fifteen years later, in discussing *Cox* with the other justices, Black continued to emphasize the essential liberty-protecting role of the judiciary: "We are settling by law what used to be settled by combat. Congregating outside a courthouse can generate fear, and destroy a court. If this Louisiana mob can scare that court, a John Birch crowd can surround this courthouse. There is a limit to where they can go."[58] Although the courts are "not as glamorous as the streets," Black told his wife, they were the "route by which the only lasting civil rights will come."[59]

In applying this liberty-versus-power framework, Black, throughout his judicial career prior to the 1960s, found reasons to make modifications and exceptions. It was here that the evolution, discontinuity, and contradictions in Black's approach to the law emerge. Most notably, early in his time on the Court, he differentiated between the exercise of government power in the area of economic regulation and government action that infringed on personal liberties. This was his theory of "preferred freedoms," in which basic human rights were elevated above property rights or abstract due process rights.[60] In the balance of liberty and power, it was those without power who must be protected. Those whose property rights might be threatened by economic regulation were certainly not powerless in American society. As Black the populist, New Dealer, and avid reader of the books of Progressive historians Charles Beard and Vernon Parrington recognized, business interests were often a major obstacle to the realization of democratic liberty. The freedoms that the courts had to carefully protect were those related to free expression and criminal justice, for it was here that liberty of the most vulnerable was most threatened. In *Chambers,* he wrote: "Tyrannical governments had immemorially utilized dictatorial criminal procedure and punishment to make scape goats of the weak, or of helpless political, religious, or racial minorities and those who differed, who would not conform and who resisted tyranny."[61] On this theory Black built his justification for aggressive judicial action in the name of protecting civil liberties, while avoiding the *Lochner*-era pitfalls of judicial oversight of economic policy.

Another essential modification to his general theory came in the school desegregation cases, where Black recognized that the Fourteenth Amendment's equal protection clause could not be understood under the standard civil libertarian model of rights as a limit on government power. The framers of the amendment, Black concluded, intended to abolish officially sanctioned racial hierarchies, and it was obvious to Black that segregated education violated this principle.[62] "The Civil War Amendments have as their basic purpose the abolition of such castes, and to protect the Negro against discrimination on account of color," he told the justices in their conference following the first round of oral arguments in *Brown*.[63] This anti-caste reading of the Fourteenth Amendment had the potential to be an incredibly powerful constitutional tool for uprooting entrenched inequality.[64] In *Griffin v. Illinois*, Black had the opportunity to bring together his strong reading of the equal protection clause with his commitment to protecting the rights of criminal defendants. The result was one of the most sweeping proclamations of the equality principle ever made by a Court opinion: "There can be no equal justice where the kind of trial a man gets depends on the amount of money he has."[65] The strength of Black's jurisprudence in these decisions from the first two decades of his judicial tenure was the balance he achieved between a deep commitment to certain basic principles and a refusal to allow these principles to obscure the important role of the courts and the rule of law in a modern evolving democracy.

If there was a certain element of continuity in Black's defense of the rule of law as a limit on both government and private power, his newfound emphasis on property rights in the 1960s marked a shift in Black's thought. In the 1940s, Black approached property rights from the perspective of the fervent New Dealer that he had been while in the Senate. Senator Black had responded to critics of the New Deal who attacked economic regulation as a violation of property rights by arguing that basic human rights should be placed above property rights.[66] He extended this rationale while on the Court. In a draft of a 1940 opinion, he stated bluntly: "The power of the states to regulate property must be distinguished from constitutional procedural rights protecting human life and liberty."[67] In *Marsh v. Alabama*, a 1946 decision in which the Court struck down a ban on solicitation in a privately owned "company town," Black explained, "Ownership [of property] does not always mean absolute dominion. The more an owner, for his advantage, opens up his property for use by the public in general, the more do his rights become circumscribed by the statutory and constitutional rights of those who use it."[68]

The language of his *Marsh* opinion would seem to fit perfectly the situation of the lunch counter sit-ins, but by the early 1960s Black had moved from his New Deal roots, and he found new values in protecting property rights. When the sit-in cases arrived at the Supreme Court, Black began to talk more and more about the value of exclusion as a right of property owners. "I remember nigras had to come in the back door of my Pappy's store," he told his clerks. "They had no constitutional right to come in any place they wanted."[69] He returned to this theme repeatedly in considering the protest cases. "We have a system of private ownership of property—we should not turn down these rights by constitutional construction," he told the justices in a 1962 conference in which they discussed the latest batch of sit-in cases.

> I believe that a store owner, the same as a home owner, has a right to say who can come on his premises and how long they can stay. A store owner, like a house owner, can tell a customer to leave. If he has that right, he cannot be helpless to call the police and get help to throw the customer out. One man on another man's property can be thrown off with force, if necessary. That rule is necessary if private property is to be protected. I would rank stores along with homes, although there is, of course, a difference in history and sentiment.[70]

This deeply personal concern with the protection of property rights was new to Black's thought.

A striking aspect of Black's defense of private property in the sit-in cases was the sweeping terms with which he declared a restaurant owner's "right" to exclude patrons, even when that exclusion was based on racial animus. "When a man owns property, he owns it," Black told the justices in a 1963 conference in which they discussed the latest sit-in cases. Justice Joseph P. Bradley "was right in the *Civil Rights Cases*, when he said once the barrier of privacy is broken down then there is no stopping. If these businesses can be regulated by the Court in this way, so can private homes."[71] This emphatic language, and the constant refrain that the owner had a "right" to exclude,[72] hinted at a deeper fear that limiting an individual's ability to exclude others from private property might in and of itself trench upon some liberty interest. Yet such a conclusion was obviously untenable, as no one apart from the most fervent segregationists would question a state's right to require desegregation of stores or restaurants (indeed, there existed a long common-law tradition prohibiting racial exclusion at inns and on common carriers). Further, Black explicitly recognized the power of Congress, under both the commerce clause and the enforcement clause of the Fourteenth Amendment, to ban segregation in privately owned public accommodations and businesses.

In this effort to balance his New Dealer's commitment to ambitious legislative regulation of the economic sphere with his growing concern with the rights of private property, Black's jurisprudence revealed a discordance. If indeed the property owner had some kind of right to exclude, and if "the Constitution does not distinguish between a home and a store," then why does the restaurant owner's right to exclude survive against a constitutional claim but not against statutory intrusion? It is hard to imagine that Black's pappy would be any less aggrieved if he were required to open the doors of his store to blacks because of a court order based on the Constitution or federal legislation. Yet Black did not see it this way, at least not in 1964, when he argued that the property rights of restaurant owners could be constrained, as long as the constraints were the product of legislative, not judicial, initiative.[73]

By the end of the decade, he had moved toward reconciling this tension over the nature of the "right" to exclude from privately owned enterprises. In 1969 in *Daniel v. Paul*, Black, who during the height of the New Deal had been labeled "the most radical man in the Senate,"[74] argued for limiting the reach of the commerce power. In a lone dissent, he drew upon a nostalgic commitment to localism in arguing that the public accommodations provision of the Civil Rights Act of 1964 did not extend to a relatively isolated private recreation area. To apply the law to "this country people's recreation center, lying in what may be, so far as we know, a little 'sleepy hollow' between Arkansas hills miles away from any interstate highway, would be stretching the Commerce Clause so as to give the Federal Government complete control over every little remote country place of recreation in every nook and cranny of every precinct and county in every one of the 50 States. This goes too far for me."[75] Although this decision spoke more of local autonomy than property rights, by the late 1960s Black was repeatedly defending the right to exclude, even when such a right came into conflict with Black's beloved First Amendment. "No matter how urgently a person may wish to exercise his First Amendment guarantees to speak freely, he has no constitutional right to appropriate someone else's property to do so," Black explained in a lecture in 1968.[76] In the same year, he wrote a strongly worded dissent when the Supreme Court struck down a state court injunction of a peaceful demonstration in the parking lot of a shopping center, which the state court had justified as necessary to protect the property rights of the business owner.[77] Black rejected the Court's extension of his *Marsh* opinion to cover such a protest[78] and even went so far as to compare the majority's protection of the protesters to a taking of private property that required compensation under the Fifth Amendment.[79] "To hold that store owners are compelled by law to supply picketing areas for pickets to drive store customers away is to create a court-made law wholly disregarding the constitutional basis on which private ownership of property rests in this country."[80] By the end of the decade, Black had fully embraced his newfound commitment to protecting the rights of property owners.

Black's monumental achievements as a justice in the 1940s and 1950s derived from the creative tensions that emerged from his effort to identify timeless truths about the relationship of government and liberty while also recognizing the realities of economic and racial inequality in modern society. By the 1960s, this creativity was lost, as Black increasingly sought to resolve the underlying tensions in his jurisprudence. His growing fears that the unbridled power of the judiciary threatened society led him to embrace a sterile textualism. He revised and limited his rationale for school desegregation, now claiming that he had supported *Brown* solely on the basis that the framers of the Civil War Amendments intended to outlaw segregated schools.[81] He became concerned with the need for courts to protect property rights, and by the end of the decade he was arguing for limits to the scope of Congress's commerce power. While his liberal colleagues adapted the law to support the cause of civil rights activists, Black turned insistently formalistic in his quest for a universally applicable balance between power and liberty. As civil rights activists found new methods to demand recognition of the rights of

African Americans to equal treatment in society, in effect exercising a form of power from outside the institutions of government, Black turned his attention to the liberties of those whose rights he feared were diminishing in the face of the protests. Thus we see the remarkable development of Black passionately arguing on behalf of judicial protection for embattled groups of a very different kind from those he favored in his early years on the Court. He now spoke out on behalf of people who valued orderly streets, library patrons who wanted a quiet place to read, and business owners who did not want blacks sitting at their lunch counters.

JUSTICE BLACK AND PROFESSOR HORWITZ

Not only the occasion for this essay but its topic and methodology are indebted to Professor Morton Horwitz.

One of the most intellectually exhilarating experiences of my life was when, as a graduate student in the History of American Civilization Program at Harvard preparing for my general examinations, I read a field in United States legal and constitutional history with Professor Horwitz. Once every week or two, I would walk across Harvard Yard to the law school. We would sit down in his office in Griswold Hall and talk about the readings he had assigned for our meeting. Our discussions were always free flowing, with Professor Horwitz drawing together seemingly disparate events and concepts, and describing the singular importance of certain individuals in history, even as he emphasized the inevitable constraints of one's historical epoch. It was history, law, and ideas on a grand scale. Every now and then we would come across some technical aspect of law, which he would carefully explain as I scribbled on my notepad. He would then gently suggest that if I was really so interested in legal history, I really ought to consider law school (advice I would eventually follow).

Recently, an observation Professor Horwitz made while talking about his work on the Warren Court volume of the Holmes Devise brought me back to these wonderful discussions. When I asked him if he had found anything particularly unexpected in his research, he mentioned his deepening appreciation for the contributions of Hugo Black. This intrigued me, as I recalled Professor Horwitz's rather scathing treatment of Black in *The Warren Court and the Pursuit of Justice*. The book's most memorable descriptions of Black are not of his contributions to the Warren Court's achievements, but of those critical moments when he abandoned his liberal allies. Black's turn clearly vexed Professor Horwitz. In a book that is a model of concision, totaling not much over one hundred pages of text, he dedicated over fifteen pages to the Court's treatment of civil rights demonstrations in a section titled "Justice Black Breaks with the New Liberal Majority."[82]

When I mentioned to Professor Horwitz my surprise about his revised opinion of Black, he spoke of a newfound respect for Black's commitment to civil rights and civil liberties in the 1940s and 1950s. As I imagined the great and contradictory portrait of Justice Black that seemed to be taking shape in Professor Horwitz's new book, my mind returned to the personal crash course in American constitutional history I had with Professor Horwitz in Griswold 310. Of the many illuminating discussions we had, I remember particularly well his contagious fascination with the lives of two major figures from early American history: James Otis, as portrayed in Bernard Bailyn's *Ideological Origins of the American Revolution,* and John Adams, as portrayed in Gordon Wood's *Creation of the American Republic*. Each of these men is generally remembered for his contributions to the struggle for independence and to the construction of the new nation, yet in the hands of Bailyn and Wood they become tragic heroes, significant for their failures as much as their accomplishments. Otis literally drove himself mad trying to come to terms with his prophetic insights about constitutional principles as constraints on, rather than reflections of, political institutions.[83] Adams never relinquished his belief in a "mixed" government that would reflect permanent divisions in society between the elites and the masses; his enthusiasm for the new Constitution, in one of the great ironies of the founding period, was largely a product of his misunderstanding of it. As a result, Adams found his ideas increasingly irrelevant to the new nation.[84] Otis and Adams read as widely and thought as deeply as any of their contemporaries, but in their commitment to the ideas they discovered in their books, they failed to fully understand the revolutions happening around them.

In much the same way, Hugo Black was a heroic and tragic figure who was eventually left behind by social, cultural, and intellectual changes—changes he played a major role in making possible in the first place. Like Otis and Adams, his flaws were the product of dedicated study and an unwavering commitment to certain basic principles, which they all felt transcended any particular historical moment. Black's faith in the Bill of Rights, particularly the First Amendment, as the cornerstone of American liberty made him into one of the great justices in the history of the Supreme Court. When he was faced with a dramatically new approach to social reform in the protests of the civil rights movement, he turned to the tools that had served him so well earlier in his judicial career—a deep wariness of power and a commitment to judicial protection of individual liberty—only now he found in these resources answers that struck many of his liberal supporters as deeply misguided.

Furthermore, as portrayed by Bailyn and Wood, Otis and Adams become touchstones by which to measure the overwhelming nature of the change happening around them. By highlighting these figures, Bailyn and Wood allow the reader to appreciate the intellectual upheaval of the Revolution and founding. They shared a common characteristic: they were serious, thoughtful students of philosophy and history who felt an unwavering commitment to the truths they discovered in these readings. Hugo Black, much like Adams and Otis, was a person whose flaws derived from a passionate commitment to a particular conception of liberty. In his reaction to the civil rights movement, we can better understand the changes this social and intellectual upheaval wrought upon the nation.

Black's frustration with the civil rights movement emphasizes a point that should be obvious but risks being lost beneath the veneer of nostalgia that too often obscures the events of that time: the protest tactics not only challenged a corrupt system of white supremacy but also challenged the premises of the system of legal reform. Black was certainly not the only person who distinguished the goals of the movement, which he generally supported, from the tactics of the protests, which he could not support. A particular commitment to public order is certainly not unusual among those who practice law. If lawyers "prize freedom much," Alexis de Tocqueville observed, "they generally value legality still more."[85] "The logical and inescapable end of civil disobedience is the destruction of the public order," explained president of the American Bar Association and future Supreme Court justice Lewis F. Powell Jr.[86] Thurgood Marshall expressed considerable skepticism toward direct-action tactics and civil disobedience—it took convincing, for example, for him to understand the value of the lunch counter sit-ins.[87] While Black stood out from his colleagues for the uncompromising fervor with which be attacked the protesters, he was far from alone among the justices in his commitment to preserving law and order in the name of individual liberty.[88] Justice Frankfurter, recently retired from the Court, wrote to Black to praise his stance on the sit-in cases.[89] Justices White and Clark wrote powerful opinions on the importance of the rule of law in the face of protests, "whether they be integrationists or white supremacists."[90] Even a committed supporter of the protesters such as Arthur Goldberg seemed to go out of his way to assert the need to limit excessive protest.[91] The culminating point of the Warren Court's efforts to steer protest into institutional pathways came in 1967 in *Walker v. City of Birmingham*, where Justice Stewart lectured movement activists that "respect for the judicial process is a small price to pay for the civilizing hand of the law, which alone can give abiding meaning to constitutional freedom."[92] As the urban rioting worsened, as the civil rights protesters' demands sharpened and their tactics became more aggressive, the majority of the Court came around to Black's position. And, as made clear by the presidential election of 1968, won by Richard Nixon campaigning on a law-and-order platform, the majority of the nation appeared to as well.[93]

The tendency in Black's thought to place contemporary situations into a timeless battle between liberty and power served him well when faced with matters of free speech and criminal procedure, where government action conflicted with protections identified in the Bill of Rights. A commitment to ahistorical theories of governance and human behavior can be severely limiting, however. Categories become more rigid over time. They take on a life of their own, detached from the basic ideas of justice that gave them life in the first place. This is what Professor Horwitz's writings demonstrate so powerfully: that those who embrace categories of thought that are disconnected from a vision of right and wrong end up with "snares and delusions,"[94] and that constitutional law has been particularly susceptible to the lure of "legal fundamentalism" based on "a pre-modern vision of timeless and unchanging truths."[95] In concluding the second volume of *The Transformation of American Law,* Professor Horwitz warned of the pattern in American legal theory in which "each generation continues frantically to hide behind unhistorical and abstract universalisms in order to deny, even to itself, its own political and moral choices."[96]

Black's great contribution to American constitutional law came when he negotiated the pitfalls of legal abstractions and acknowledged the need for "a dynamic understanding of the unfolding of principle over time."[97] This, in essence, was what he achieved in articulating his preference for personal rights over property rights and his reading of the Fourteenth Amendment as embodying an anticaste principle. Black gradually abandoned these insights, however, in his effort to remain consistent with his belief in the timeless truths about power and liberty. In the process, he lost his ability to understand the contribution of the civil rights movement to the cause of American freedom.

NOTES

1. See, e.g., *Griswold v. Connecticut,* 381 U.S. 479, 507–27 (1965) (Black, J., dissenting); *Harper v. Virginia State Board of Elections,* 383 U.S. 663, 670–80 (1966) (Black, J., dissenting); *Katz v. United States,* 389 U.S. 347, 364–74 (1967) (Black, J., dissenting).

2. John P. MacKenzie, "Louisiana Sit-In Conviction Reversed," *Washington Post,* Feb. 24, 1966, A1. In defense of Black, his ex-clerk A. E. Dick Howard explained that this was the way Black always read his opinions. A. E. Dick Howard, "Mr. Justice Black: The Negro Protest Movement and the Rule of Law," *Virginia Law Review* 53 (1966): 1045.

3. 378 U.S. 226 (1964).

4. See, e.g., *Bouie v. City of Columbia,* 378 U.S. 347 (1964); *Barr v. City of Columbia,* 378 U.S. 146 (1964); *Robinson v. Florida,* 378 U.S. 153 (1964); *Gober v. City of Birmingham,* 373 U.S. 374 (1963); *Avent v. North Carolina,* 373 U.S. 375 (1963); *Shuttlesworth v. Birmingham,* 373 U.S. 262 (1963); *Lombard v. Louisiana,* 373 U.S. 267 (1963); *Peterson v. Greenville,* 373 U.S. 244 (1963); *Taylor v. Louisiana,* 370 U.S. 154 (1962); *Garner v. Louisiana,* 368 U.S. 157 (1961).

5. 379 U.S. 559 (1965).

6. 383 U.S. 131 (1966).

7. 385 U.S. 39 (1966).

8. 379 U.S. at 559, 584.

9. 378 U.S. at 226, 327–28.

10. Id. at 327.

11. Id. at 346

12. 383 U.S. at 131, 162.

13. Id. at 167.

14. Id. at 168.

15. Id. When announcing this dissent from the bench, Black, who had largely abandoned his text, spoke even more directly about his fears when he warned, "The psalm-singing crowds that gather to express their views can be transformed into a loud, boisterous, arrant, dangerous mob." "Negro Protest Upheld by Court," *New York Times*, Feb. 24, 1966, p. 23.

16. *Bell*, 378 U.S. at 328.

17. Id. See also id. at 334 (warning of creating "one Fourteenth Amendment for the South and quite a different and more lenient one for the other parts of the country").

18. 379 U.S. at 584

19. "Negro Protest Upheld by Court" (quoting from the largely extemporaneous spoken version of Black's dissent in *Brown v. Louisiana*).

20. 379 U.S. at 583–84.

21. 383 U.S. at 167–68.

22. 378 U.S. at 346.

23. 385 U.S. at 39, 47–48.

24. *Bell*, 378 U.S. at 327; see also *Hamm v. City of Little Rock*, 379 U.S. 306, 318–19 (1964) (Black, J., dissenting) ("one of the chief purposes of the 1964 Civil Rights Act was to take such disputes [over access to public accommodations] out of the streets and restaurants and into the courts").

25. 379 U.S. at 583.

26. See, e.g., Howard, "Mr. Justice Black."

27. Alexander M. Bickel, *The Morality of Consent* (New Haven, Conn.: Yale University Press, 1975), 9.

28. Roger K. Newman, *Hugo Black: A Biography,* rev. ed. (New York: Fordham University Press, 1997), 570.

29. Ibid.

30. Ibid., 551.

31. *Giboney v. Empire Storage & Ice Co.,* 336 U.S. 490 (1949); Hugo Black, *A Constitutional Faith* (New York: Knopf, 1969), 55.

32. Patricia Sullivan, ed., *Freedom Writer: Virginia Foster Durr, Letters from the Civil Rights Years* (New York: Routledge, 2003), 399.

33. Newman, *Hugo Black,* 542.

34. Ibid.

35. Sheldon Hackney, "The Clay County Origins of Mr. Justice Black: The Populist as Insider," in *Justice Hugo Black and Modern America,* ed. Tony Freyer (Tuscaloosa: University of Alabama Press, 1990), 78.

36. Hugo L. Black, "The Bill of Rights," *New York University Law Review* 35 (1960): 867.

37. Edmund Burke observed that the American revolutionaries "augur misgovernment at a distance and snuff the approach of tyranny in every tainted breeze." Quoted in Gordon Wood, *The Creation of the American Republic, 1776–1787* (Chapel Hill: Published for the Institute of Early American History and Culture at Williamsburg by the University of North Carolina Press, 1969), 5.

38. Black, "The Bill of Rights," 869.

39. Daniel J. Meador, *Mr. Justice Black and His Books* (Charlottesville: University Press of Virginia, 1974), 17–19.

40. See, e.g., Bernard Bailyn, *To Begin the World Anew: The Genius and Ambiguities of the American Founders* (New York: Knopf, 2003), 55 ("For the fear of power—the very heart of the original Revolutionary ideology—was an animating spirit behind all of [Jefferson's] thinking, and ultimately the source of the deepest ambiguities"); see also Jack N. Rakove, *Original Meanings: Politics and Ideas in the Making of the Constitution* (New York: Knopf, 1996), 151 ("The genius of [the Anti-Federalists'] political ideology lay in its ability to locate danger lurking anywhere").

41. *American Communications Association v. Douds,* 339 U.S. 382, 448–49 (1950) (Black, J., dissenting).

42. Black, "The Bill of Rights," 880.

43. *Chambers v. Florida,* 309 U.S. 227, 241 (1940).

44. Gerald T. Dunne, *Hugo Black and the Judicial Revolution* (New York: Simon & Schuster, 1977), 325 (quoting Black in a 1945 speech before a meeting of the Southern Conference for Human Welfare: "The conditions which created fascism abroad must not be allowed to exist here—the placing of some groups in a preferred class of citizenship at the expense of other groups").

45. Del Dickson, ed., *The Supreme Court in Conference, 1940–1985* (Oxford: Oxford University Press, 2001), 639.

46. *Feiner v. New York,* 340 U.S. 315, 323 (1951).

47. Newman, *Hugo Black,* 416.

48. *Braden v. United States,* 365 U.S. 431, 445–46 (1961) (Black, J., dissenting).

49. Edmund Burke, *Reflections on the Revolution in France,* ed. J. G. A. Pocock (1790; Indianapolis, Ind.: Hackett, 1987), 8.

50. Tony Freyer has described "Black's conviction that individual rights depended on stable social relations and responsible behavior." Tony Freyer, *Hugo L. Black and the Dilemmas of American Liberalism* (Glenview, Ill.: Scott, Foresman/Little, Brown Higher Education, 1990), 140.

51. Black, *A Constitutional Faith,* 57.

52. 393 U.S. 503, 524 (1969). On his copy of Black's dissent, next to the passage on "uncontrollable liberty," an astonished Abe Fortas wrote, "Hugo Black!!" Laura Kalman, *Abe Fortas: A Biography* (New Haven, Conn.: Yale University Press, 1990), 290.

53. 383 U.S. at 131, 166.

54. Id. at 168.

55. Hugo L. Black and Elizabeth Black, *Mr. Justice and Mrs. Black* (New York: Random House, 1986), 112.

56. Black, *A Constitutional Faith,* 63.

57. 309 U.S. at 227, 241.

58. Dickson, *The Supreme Court in Conference,* 325.

59. Black and Black, *Mr. Justice and Mrs. Black,* 105.

60. See, e.g., *Marsh v. Alabama,* 326 U.S. 501, 509 (1946).

61. 309 U.S. at 227, 236.

62. Dickson, *The Supreme Court in Conference,* 639.

63. Ibid., 648.

64. See, e.g., Owen M. Fiss, "Groups and the Equal Protection Clause," *Philosophy and Public Affairs* 5 (1976): 107–77; Cass R. Sunstein, "The Anticaste Principle," *Michigan Law Review* 92 (1994): 241–55.

65. 351 U.S. 12, 19 (1956).

66. Newman, *Hugo Black,* 210–11.

67. Ibid., 295.

68. 326 U.S. at 501, 502.

69. Newman, *Hugo Black,* 541.

70. Dickson, *The Supreme Court in Conference,* 712.

71. Ibid., 720.

72. See ibid., 706 (Black, in conference discussion on *Burton v. Wilmington Parking Authority,* 365 U.S. 715 (1961), referring to "the common law right of a private owner [of a restaurant] to pick his own customers").

73. Ibid., 709 (Black, in conference discussion on 1961 round of sit-in cases, arguing, "The owner of a store has the right (*absent an act of Congress or state statute*) to say who can and cannot come into his store or stay there" [emphasis added]); 712 (Black, in conference discussion on the sit-in cases of the 1962 term, noting, "I would have no difficulty in sustaining a state law or a federal law under the Fourteenth Amendment [despite the *Civil Rights Cases*] that would prevent racial discrimination and require a retailer to serve all people. But it cannot make a constitutional difference"); and 720 (Black, in conference discussion on the sit-in cases of the 1963 term, stating, "If these businesses can be regulated by the Court in this way, so can private homes. I have no objection to regulation by a proper body of rights of policy, but we are not the proper agency to do it").

74. Newman, *Hugo Black,* 226 (quoting Joseph Alsop and Turner Catledge).

75. 395 U.S. 298, 315 (1969) (Black, J., dissenting) (footnote omitted).

76. Black, *A Constitutional Faith,* 57.

77. *Amalgamated Food Employees Union Local 590 v. Logan Valley Plaza, Inc.,* 391 U.S. 308 (1968).

78. Id. at 330–32 (Black, J., dissenting).

79. Id. at 330.

80. Id. at 332–33.

81. *Harper v. Virginia Board of Elections,* 383 U.S. 663, 677 n. 7 (1966).

82. Morton J. Horwitz, *The Warren Court and the Pursuit of Justice* (New York: Hill and Wang, 1998), 37–51.

83. Bernard Bailyn, *The Ideological Origins of the American Revolution,* 2d ed. (Cambridge, Mass.: Belknap Press of Harvard University Press, 1992), 176–81.

84. Wood, *The Creation of the American Republic,* 567–92.

85. Alexis de Tocqueville, *Democracy in America,* ed. Phillips Bradley (1835; New York: Knopf, 1945), 1:275.

86. Lewis F. Powell Jr., "A Lawyer Looks at Civil Disobedience," *Washington & Lee Law Review* 23 (1966): 230. Powell concluded his attack on the "doctrine" of civil disobedience with a description of Justice Black as "a great liberal judge, whose concern for civil rights and freedom of dissent is exceeded only by his concern for our country" and an excerpt from Black's dissent in *Brown v. Louisiana* (231).

87. Juan Williams, *Thurgood Marshall: American Revolutionary* (New York: Times Books, 1998), 241, 245–52; Mark V. Tushnet, *Making Civil Rights Law: Thurgood Marshall and the Supreme Court, 1936–1961* (New York: Oxford University Press, 1994), 301–13; Derrick Bell, "An Epistolary Exploration for a Thurgood Marshall Biography," *Harvard Blackletter Journal* 6 (1989): 55–56.

88. See Michal R. Belknap, "The Warren Court and Equality," in *Constitutionalism and American Culture: Writing the New Constitutional History,* ed. Sandra F. VanBurkleo, Kermit L. Hall, and Robert J. Kaczorowski (Lawrence: University Press of Kansas, 2002), 227–35.

89. Dunne, *Hugo Black,* 394–95.

90. *Cox,* 379 U.S. at 589 (Clark, J., concurring and dissenting).

91. Id. at 554 ("The constitutional guarantee of liberty implies the existence of an organized society maintaining public order, without which liberty itself would be lost in the excesses of anarchy").

92. 388 U.S. 307, 321 (1967).

93. See generally Rick Perlstein, *Nixonland: The Rise of a President and the Fracturing of America* (New York: Scribner, 2008).

94. Morton J. Horwitz, *The Transformation of American Law, 1870–1960: The Crisis of Legal Orthodoxy* (New York: Oxford University Press, 1992), 271.

95. Morton J. Horwitz, "Foreword: The Constitution of Change: Legal Fundamentality without Fundamentalism," *Harvard Law Review* 107 (1993): 34.

96. Horwitz, *Transformation II,* 272.

97. Ibid., 271.

12

Peregrinations of the Free Rider: The Changing Logics of Collective Obligation

ELIZABETH BLACKMAR

THE "FREE RIDER" IS A COMMON FIGURE OF SPEECH IN POLITICAL ECONomy, and if keyword searches of recent articles are any indicator, the term continues to gain currency in fields that range from community organizing to international affairs. In its contemporary usage, the "free rider" refers to a person who chooses not to contribute to a common good, because he or she will receive the benefits of that good regardless of any individual payment or effort—in other words, the person who says, "Why pay when you can ride free?" Where rational individuals are said to aspire to maximize their own self-interest, the free rider is simply one more version of Economic Man. Such an individual cannot be expected either to contribute or to sacrifice to a wider social good unless there is a direct return, a quid pro quo.

The rational behavior attributed to the free rider poses problems for theories of capitalism and democracy. In the classical tradition, free riding disrupts the reciprocity of rights and duties, since the public realm has no special claim on individual citizens. Within a bourgeois culture, the free rider implies a dangerous indifference to the disciplined calculus of costs and benefits on which social order rests. From the perspective of neoclassical economics, without individuals revealing what something is worth to them, it is not possible to establish the efficient price of public goods. Neoliberal theorists hold that free riders test the legitimacy of compulsion to sustain an organization, including government itself. At the same time, the presence of free riders can obstruct the private bargaining through which society achieves an optimal allocation of resources.

I thank Christine Desan, Louis Hyman, Jeffrey Sklansky, Kimberly Phillips-Fein, and William Leach for helpful comments on an earlier draft. Morton Horwitz taught his students, even the most entrenched historical materialists among them, that language, too, has a history.

Neoliberal logic asserts that the free rider is a problem best solved by the establishment of a regime in which everyone pays for what he or she wants, preferably through market exchanges, though occasionally through user fees paid to government suppliers. Only those public goods—for example, national defense—that cannot be individually allocated and from which no member of the public, broadly conceived, can be excluded should be paid for out of a system of general taxation. Thus, the free rider has figured in important ways in campaigns for privatization, which is to say in arguments against the use of state power to redistribute wealth more equitably by socializing public benefits. And advocates of deregulation also use the metaphor to set the terms for privately bargained solutions to the "social costs" of free enterprise.

As a figure of speech, the free rider has a much longer history in American popular speech than its contemporary use would suggest. The figure's value as a slogan, however, first became evident in debates over the status of organized labor in the United States and especially over the closed shop, a workplace in which only union members could get a job. Labor leaders insisted that no union member could be compelled to work alongside a non-union worker, who threatened collective well-being. In the course of debating labor policy during World War II and then specifically the Taft-Hartley Act, politicians and labor reformers used the metaphor of the free rider to translate this principle of solidarity into a liberal premise of fairness, the idea that everyone should pay a fair share in exchange for benefits received. Neoliberal intellectuals, in turn, dropped both collectivity and fairness and made the bargain everything.

This essay looks at how a single metaphor, one among many, has reduced the analysis of obligation in political, economic, and legal reasoning. It explores the logic of collective action in the labor movement as it was historically articulated, negotiated, and understood, and it looks at the multiple ethical valences of the figure of the free rider before it became a single term of art, associated with rational choice. Through its use of such figures of speech, neoliberal discourse has pried itself loose not only from the contingencies of history but particularly from questions of social power—in other words, from social reality. This essay is not about the history of the labor movement as such, nor about conditions that allow people to work together for a common good. Rather, this essay is about the ideological construction of common sense, how a particular use of commonplace language has erased mutual obligation from contemporary deliberations over democracy and the social relations of capitalism.

MEMBERSHIP AND OBLIGATION: HISTORICAL CONDITIONS OF COLLECTIVE ACTION

In the late nineteenth century, political theorists and social scientists, observing the turmoil of economic depressions, strikes, lockouts, unemployment, and workplace accidents, also contemplated the primacy of associations in modern industrial society. In seeking to make sense of the conflicts, Progressive reformers and legal commentators regularly compared corporations and labor unions, treating both as new kinds of "combinations" that were changing the relations of everyday life. On the face of things, such comparisons, implying as they did equal status if not power, were absurd. U.S. Steel, capitalized at one billion dollars in 1900, easily overmatched the assets of such unions as the United Mine Workers, one of the nation's strongest in 1902, when it raised some two million dollars to sustain a five-and-a-half-month strike in the anthracite fields.[1] Yet the popular comparison between corporations and unions did not just draw a parallel in organizational form or financial resources.

Both institutions represented the organized capacity to act and through action to shape labor markets or control productive resources. With the number of strikes increasing from 471 in 1881 to more than 3,000 strikes involving a half-million workers in 1902 and 1903 (including 175,000 coal miners), labor militancy defined social relations at the turn of the twentieth century.[2] (In the same twenty-five-year span a century later, with the workforce six times the size it had been, the number of strikes ranged from a high of 145 involving 729,000 workers in 1981 to lows of 17 in 1999 and 2004, affecting 73,000 and 171,000 workers respectively.[3]) The effective power of organized labor, though always vulnerable to police repression and court injunctions, could be measured both through the aggregate gains of real wages and shorter hours for millions of workers and by business reaction, especially the launching of the open-shop movement.[4]

American jurisprudence has consistently valued and protected the property rights of employers over and above any countervailing claims of workers to set the price or control the conditions of their own labor.[5] Because scholars today are so conscious of the defeat of the American labor movement, many have ceased to ask questions about how historically that movement gained (as well as lost) its capacity to act collectively and to change the balance of power at critical junctures. One reason to reconsider, however briefly, the organizational struggles of trade unions is to remind ourselves that voluntarism—or political mobilization—historically rested on concepts of effective affiliation or membership.

Unions had to learn how to bind workers to the obligations of membership. At the most basic level, shared work brought people into unions with a sense of the importance of sticking together when dealing with bosses. And membership surged during strikes. Whether in response to picket lines or out of hope of securing gains, once the battle was engaged, more workers joined, despite the direct sacrifice of paychecks and physical security. When there was less to lose, however, after battles had been won or lost, membership dropped. Facing this underlying rhythm, virtually every labor union in the country wrestled with ways to secure the long-term commitment of members. The sentiment, calculation, or even consciousness that sustained collective action also required organizing, which meant building collective financial resources and finding means of enforcing collective decisions.[6]

American unions came out of the world of nineteenth-century voluntary associations, from religious congregations to fraternal lodges, that rested on twin practices of self-taxing and discipline.[7] Self-taxing took the form of regular weekly or monthly contributions of collectively established dues; a secretary-treasurer kept careful track of each member's accounts, and those who fell in arrears lost the rights of membership. Initially formed as local mutual aid societies, trade unions, too, enforced obligations of membership by simply expelling anyone who failed to pay dues or assessments (which generally went toward death benefits or sick relief) or who failed to abide by the work rules or to join in collective actions, especially strikes. Before the mid-1880s, striking workers also depended on the extended reciprocity of their communities, with neighbors and other voluntary associations extending support in the form of credit; contributions of food and cash; and, in exceptional cases, sympathy strikes.

Building the social capacity of trade unions required coming to terms with the problem of financial capacity, what workers could be asked to contribute, and what they would agree to contribute in monthly dues to sustain a collective purpose. The leaders of national and international organizations for craft unions in the late 1880s and 1890s argued that only by building national treasuries of reserve funds could the labor movement counter the power of employers, whether local businesses or national corporations.[8] Delegates to union conventions spent hours and days writing and amending constitutions and bylaws that spelled out the rules for levying initiation fees, dues, special assessments, and especially the funds, known as the per capita tax, that locals collected and transferred to their national organizations.

Strategies for organizing varied widely according to the conditions and composition of different trades before World War I. Railroad brotherhoods, particularly the "Big Four" of engineers, conductors, brakemen, and firemen, borrowed rituals from fraternal associations, and like those lodges, trainmen linked membership to benefits, especially valuable in a dangerous trade in which numerous workers were maimed or killed.[9] The Big Four unions prided themselves on their voluntarism and famously did not establish closed shops, although they did draw the color line to maintain closed unions.[10] Both the work culture of railroading and the attraction of benefits sufficed to maintain remarkably high rates of affiliation among white workers in skilled railroad jobs, with 75 to 90 percent of eligible workers joining the brotherhoods through the 1920s.[11] At the same time, through their control of a dominant and strategic national industry, the railroad unions placed themselves in the most direct relation to the state. Twenty years of congressional deliberations culminated in the Railway Labor Act of 1926, which forbade discrimination against unionized workers; required employers to bargain in good faith with elected union representatives; established boards for arbitration; and, not incidentally, banned the closed shop. A decade later Congress extended its provisions to airlines.[12]

If the railroad brotherhoods were exceptional in their high rates of membership and relation to the federal government, they also built a distinctive organizational culture. Few unions so valued the trappings of membership, whether abundantly illustrated monthly journals or the morocco leather cases provided for membership cards.[13] Then again, in few unions did a membership card carry as much daily value: brakemen and conductors accepted membership cards in lieu of fare for trainmen traveling around the country. The brotherhoods were also among the first American unions to establish pensions as well as death and accident funds. Scholars who have concluded that insurance benefits seamlessly glued members to the railroad unions, however, overlook the almost draconian rules that governed the brotherhoods. Conductors and engineers could lose all they had contributed to a pension simply by being late in paying their dues.[14] Indeed, local chapters created special pools to help cover the dues of members who fell behind due to sickness or other adversity.[15]

The railroad brotherhoods did little to support the less skilled trades in railroading, which were organized into as many as seventeen separate unions. The insularity of the Big Four contributed to the devastating defeat of the railroad craft shops in 1922. Repeated technological innovations and the aging of members further undermined the railroad brotherhoods and placed pensions funds and other benefits in jeopardy. Still, however self-regarding, however restricted by race and skill, and however vulnerable to technological obsolescence they might have been, the railroad unions did introduce a precedent and a practice of solidarity in the national transportation industries that was not decisively countered until the president of the United States broke the PATCO strike in 1981.

Trade unions affiliated with the American Federation of Labor also developed the principles of self-taxing and discipline for their national organizations. As late as 1904, fewer than half of American unions collected sufficient dues to maintain a strike fund or other benefits.[16] Hundreds of local and even national unions, moreover, followed the nineteenth-century tradition of passing the hat during conflicts with employers. But the sheer number, length, and incidence of strikes at the turn of the century strained extended reciprocity as far as it could go.

In the 1890s, unions in the construction trades and some light industries—boot and shoe makers, typographers, cigar makers—began adopting tactics developed in Great Britain, where national unions collected high dues from locals and provided members with strike funds and benefits.[17] In the aftermath of the anthracite strike, Samuel Gompers, president of the American Federation of Labor, urged trade unionists to pay attention to the "necessity of a good treasury," warning that "there is no greater source of weakness than to be compelled to make an appeal to others for financial assistance."[18] A decade later, leaders of craft unions spoke contemptuously of the "begging letter system" and declared that the failure to build a strike fund "amounts to a lack of conviction, cowardice, or indifference" on the part of unionized workers.[19]

As Gompers campaigned for higher dues in the name of *collective* self-interest, leaders of strong unions—cigar makers, iron mongers, boot and shoe workers, brewers, and granite cutters—explained in the *American Federationist* how their members had built defense funds through dues that ranged from $13 to $20 a year—3 to 4 percent of annual incomes—and additional assessments whenever necessary.[20] High dues supported burial, accident, and life insurance as well as strike benefits. But all agreed that the most substantial "return" to union members came in the form of what Gompers called "reserve power." "Power is necessary to influence. Power depends on resources," he wrote. "What wages are to the individual, dues are to the organization. The very existence of a sound financial organization constitutes a defense of its members. . . . Consciousness that they possess power puts moral courage and confidence into the workers, and it puts fear into the hearts of those who would wrong them."[21] This was the collective faith of "bread and butter," or business unionism.

Trade unionists in the mines even more ardently believed that collective organizing was a life-and-death matter, for whether facing the hazards of the trade or the extremity of poverty, mining communities subsisted on the industrial precipice.[22] With militant locals prepared to risk their lives confronting mine owners, no craft in the United States expressed a stronger ethos of sacrifice. The national United Mine Workers of America built strong regional organizations from locals in the bituminous coal fields, which stretched from western Pennsylvania to Kansas, and won industry-wide settlements with mine companies in the late 1890s. The miners also established informal closed shops through their method of collecting the dues that were essential to threshold fights for better wages, hours, and safety.

Union locals appointed an officer to stand at the gates of a coal field or at the head of a mine shaft once a month to make sure that every miner's membership card (and later the color of his union button) showed that he had paid his dues. With mine owners bemoaning the delays and even brawls that accompanied this direct personal enforcement of membership, the union proposed an alternative: employers could withdraw dues from each miner's pay and turn the funds over to union officers. The mine operators' own practice of deducting the debt workers owed the company store or rent for company housing offered a ready precedent for the dues checkoff. Winning the checkoff signaled union strength, but even without it, miners regarded enforcing membership as a foundation of collective action.[23]

"The non-unionist has no moral right to seek his own temporary advantage at the expense of the permanent interest of all workingmen," wrote John Mitchell, president of the United Mine Workers of America, in 1903. "It may pay an anti-unionist to defeat the hopes and aspirations of his fellowman, just as it may pay a man to be a traitor to his country, but neither is morally justified."[24] Finding that a number of anthracite workers had not continued their membership after the 1902 strike, Mitchell delivered a scathing indictment. "Let me say, and I wish that what I say could be heard throughout the length and breadth of the anthracite field, that I have more respect for the man who worked during the anthracite strike than I have for the man who refused to belong to the union now."[25] Mitchell's judgment prompted bitter protests from hard-pressed rank and filers: "It is not right for an organizer to say that he would prefer to shake the hand of a 'scab' or of a 'strikebreaker' than that of a man who fails to pay his dues in the union. It is not right for him to say that the man who receives the sliding scale and [is] not a member of the organization is a thief."[26]

Whatever the craft or industry, the single most effective means of organizing, disciplining, and maintaining union membership was the closed shop, whether formally recognized in a contract, informally established by direct enforcement, or solidified culturally through ritual and shaming. And it was this expression of union power that most disturbed employers. Industrialists who launched the open-shop drive in 1902 produced an avalanche of pamphlets, articles, and books denouncing "compulsory unionism" as an infringement on individual freedom and an unfair monopoly within the free labor market.[27] From the union perspective, however, the closed shop collectively protected individual activists and members from employers' reprisal—the very essence of solidarity *and* freedom. Trades that were most successful in establishing closed shops also were among the most robust when it came to strikes—or effective threats of a strike. The discipline of paying dues not only provided a "war chest"; it supported the discipline of maintaining a picket line.

The passion of union leaders who viewed paying union dues as a moral duty cannot obscure just how hard it was for these organizations to hold on to their rank and file, especially after World War I, when failed strikes and economic depression—as well as the "American plan" of corporate paternalism and company unions—combined to empty union treasuries and deplete membership rolls. Some organizers and labor editors tried to make the case for membership by turning to the language of salesmanship and business enterprise.[28] Thus, cigar makers who paid annual dues of $15.60 and saw a $78 wage increase due to union efforts were said to have earned a "dividend" of 500 percent.[29] Yet older members worried that the emphasis on insurance or individual returns subverted the principles of trade unionism. "We think too much of benefits in the organization," one machinists argued. "If I had my way I would abolish all benefits except the strike benefit."[30]

Even as they struggled to preserve their organizations in the 1920s, trade unionists continued a fifty-year political battle to stop the courts from issuing injunctions that barred collective actions. Success came at a point of labor's greatest vulnerability, when Congress passed the Norris–LaGuardia Act in 1932.[31] This recognition of the legitimacy of labor's collective action also marked a new strategic alliance of union leaders and middle-class labor reformers, who ultimately set the terms for what kinds of concerted actions counted. As Christopher Tomlins has shown, to the extent that large numbers of these labor reformers were also lawyers, the labor movement's new course was framed by a preoccupation with establishing legal and administrative procedures. Their efforts climaxed with the Wagner Act's creation of the National Labor Relations Board (NLRB), which in turn threw its support behind the Congress of Industrial Organizations (CIO), led by former miners.[32]

Still, the shift to a new labor regime, which from the perspective of the CIO provided essential state backing for organizing the mass production industries in the late 1930s, also happened at the moment of a larger break with the culture of voluntary association in the United States, a process already evident not only in unions but in congregations, lodges, clubs, and trade associations as well. "Instead of the mutuality of the fraternal order, in which brothers were obligated to protect and defend one another," sociologist Mary Ann Clawson writes, new kinds of service clubs and mass membership organizations "sought to reconcile individual self-interest with a more abstract notion of concern for the community."[33] Labor journals in the 1920s and early 1930s recorded the strains of this shift as both generational and cultural; younger union members did not share the commitment, bred of individual risk and sacrifice, of the generation that had built the American labor movement between 1890 and 1919, and the associational life of locals offered few attractions compared to automobiles or commercial amusements. In such a context, obligation itself could become an abstraction.

World War II marked the demise of a dominant associational culture based on participatory membership, self-taxing, and discipline. All the more curious, then, that voluntary associations, and most specifically unions, provided the key metaphor for a new discourse on the relation of citizens to the state and particularly for a theory of "collective action" that aimed to demonstrate that pursuit of collective goals could never be rational to the individual actor. Where did this metaphor—the free rider—come from, and why did it take hold?

THE TRAVELS OF A TROPE

The metaphor of the free rider popped up in a variety of contexts in the first third of the twentieth century, though not in the labor press.[34] Sportswriters used it regularly to refer to batters who got a walk to first base; in the late 1920s, it covered investors who speculated in bonds, and poker players who passed on a bet. Then too, the term "free rider" applied to a range of freeloading behaviors, including automobile hitchhiking and, according to H. L. Mencken, people who helped themselves to a free lunch on movie production sites.[35] But however much the term traveled, most usages pointed back to the railroads.

In the nineteenth century, the free rider had referred to individuals at two poles of the social scale. Wealthy or well-placed citizens—including stockholders, politicians, clergy, and journalists—received free passes from railroad executives to win goodwill from the "public." Poor citizens—"tramps"—hitched rides on the freight cars. Newspapers denounced both groups, the former for the abuse of privilege, and the latter as a menace to public safety.

Granger and Populist attacks on the railroad monopolies foregrounded the association of free riding with corporate corruption and the abuse of privilege.[36] In 1889, the Interstate Commerce Commission added its weight to the campaign to end free rides in exchange for favors or influence.[37] Over the decades, poor free riders, most visible during economic depressions, seldom encountered the same degree of opprobrium. Many of the workingmen who rode the rails for free did so at the sufferance of train workers, who were known for recognizing a union card as the equivalent of a ticket.[38] And in the late spring of 1932, when hundreds of veterans headed to Washington, D.C., to demand their bonus, they literally commandeered boxcars to demand a "free ride." While railroad officials threatened to call in the national guard, local townspeople provided food and encouragement to the demonstrators, who ultimately made it to Washington without paying fares.[39]

Meanwhile, free riding had taken on another connotation, once again associated with wealthy citizens' abuses of privilege. As part of the argot of Wall Street in the 1920s, "free riders" (virtually always in quotes) initially referred to investors who bought stock and sold it at a profit before having to pay the full price to the original seller. Far from worrying about ethical transgressions, brokers appear to have regarded windfalls from trading on the margins as a prerogative. The practice found an equivalent on the federal bond market in the 1930s: when the U.S. Treasury announced a new issue, investors put down a 10 percent payment and then flipped the bonds to new purchasers before the full payment was due. In the climate of the Depression, free riding lost its earlier panache for elites and signaled instead unsavory fast dealing, even fraud. Secretary of treasury Robert Morgenthau tried to stamp out the practice, which he thought distorted the bond market. Officers of the New York Stock Exchange persuaded the Security Exchange Commission and the Federal Reserve to let them regulate brokers themselves, rather than to have the SEC restrict stock purchases on the margins.[40]

Among wealthy Americans, who feared that the progressive income tax would leave them paying the tab for new federal programs, the dominant connotations of free riding also moved closer to the idea that everyone should pay his or her fair share. The political pundit Frank R. Kent, whose syndicated column "The Great Game of Politics" appeared in one hundred newspapers nationwide, called for a return to the balanced budget and repeatedly warned that New Dealers thought the "rich can be made to pay the bill incurred by governmental extravagance while the poor get a free ride."[41] The columnist, most famous for coining the term "fat cats," firmly tied the figure of the free rider to a critique of redistribution, a concern that resurfaced after World War II.[42]

Over two generations, free riding had a remarkable number of valences in public discourse, and sometimes it was even regarded as a legitimate windfall or reward for class solidarity—as for the "tramp" with a union card—or for public service. In many cities, policemen, firemen, and other uniformed public workers took streetcars and subways without paying.[43] Free rides could also express the bounty of public goods, as when transit systems provided children with free rides to museums and parks during the summer.[44] If, for the most part, free riding stood for chiseling, opportunism, or self-promotion at the expense of collective well-being, in the popular vernacular, the moral status of the free rider depended on who was offering the rides and on the wider context of reciprocity, including a pragmatic understanding of ability to pay. Still, on the eve of World War II, the notion that the free rider violated community standards of fairness had enough salience for labor reformers to seize the term to explain the principles of industrial democracy.

THE APPEARANCE OF THE FREE RIDER IN LABOR POLICY

In 1942, the free rider made one of its first full-fledged appearances as a synecdoche in *The Dynamics of Industrial Democracy* by Clinton Golden and Harold Ruttenberg, CIO organizers for the Steel Workers Organizing Committee. Describing a 1941 contract negotiation "with the management of a large steel corporation," Golden and Ruttenberg quote the fractured grammar of Tommy Morgan, a pipe fitter and the president of his local. "I had twenty-two years bargaining for myself, and I don't want no more of it." The steel company president reminded Morgan "that some of the employees did not belong to his union, and they had the right to bargain with management for themselves," the authors report. "Don't dignify them free-riders by sayin' it's a right for them to bargain as individuals. It's no right. It's a union-bustin' scheme; that's what it is," Morgan replied. "Sure, you deal with them free-riders as individuals; and you give in to them, sure. But why? 'Cause they've got any bargaining power? No. 'Cause most of the men are in the union. Take the union away, and see how much bargaining any of them individual employees of yours do."[45]

The authors then introduce Phil Murray, president of the CIO, who explicates "Tommy's remarks" for the steel president. "The terms of this contract, when they are finally agreed upon, will apply equally to nonmembers and members. Individual workers, not members of the union, can bargain with management for themselves because of the strength they derive from the union's organized power.

Take that out of the picture and they would be as helpless as they were before the union. That is why Tommy calls them 'free-riders,' individuals who enjoy the benefits of the union but refuse to join and assume their share of its hazards and costs."[46]

Historian Thomas Brooks describes *The Dynamics of Industrial Democracy* as "one long brief for the union shop as a vehicle of industrial peace."[47] Ruttenberg had used the same device of a worker's dialogue three years earlier in an article on industrial peace in the *Harvard Business Review*.[48] In that article, however, union members refer to non-union workers not as free riders but as scabs.[49] Two things had changed the labor lexicon by 1942: Ruttenberg and Golden, social democrats who believed achieving industrial democracy required forging alliances with liberal employers, may have aimed to clean up the language of their stories, since "scab" remained an inflammatory term to workers and employers alike. And the conditions of "union security," that is, both the right and the power of unions to demand the closed shop, had come under the jurisdiction of lay arbitrators charged with working out the terms of industrial peace in wartime.

Labor leaders found themselves fighting a new strategic battle, as disputes in war industries were referred to the National Defense Mediation Board and, after Pearl Harbor, to the National War Labor Board, composed of representatives of labor, business, and the public.[50] Labor leaders had pledged their cooperation and conceded their right to strike in exchange for the board's mediation of conflicts. Yet having given up the strike during a national emergency, what could organized workers do to secure the authority and power of their unions in negotiations with employers in the future? Without the strike, unions lost a galvanizing force in recruiting new members. There would be little sense of urgency, and even less of shame, in defying the collective will of the majority of fellow workers, when that will lost its most powerful expression in the capacity to strike.

The War Labor Board recognized this cost to labor and in the "Little Steel" case devised a new system for the "maintenance of membership." As a corollary to stabilizing union membership for the duration of contracts, and in an effort to end the dues picket lines thrown up by the Steel Workers Organizing Committee, the War Labor Board also endorsed the dues checkoff.[51] This compromise was far from acceptable to business leaders.[52] Sounding the keynote for what would be four years of employer dissent on board decisions, John Chamberlain attacked compulsory membership as inimical to democracy in an article in *Fortune* that made its way into the record of the Little Steel case. Once again impersonating labor's common sense through dialect, Chamberlain conceded the legitimacy of union members' complaint against "those who aren't 'sharing the load' or are 'snaking a free ride'" before comparing the closed shop to the one-party state.[53]

It is noteworthy that despite Chamberlain's characterization of labor's position on behalf of union security, Lee Pressman, the CIO's chief lawyer, did not argue for the fairness of bearing burdens in exchange for benefits. Pressman was a communist sympathizer who learned his union politics directly from John L. Lewis before the miners' leader resigned from the CIO in 1940. Pressman reminded the War Labor Board of the overarching context of employer hostility toward unions, a hostility that had led capital to destroy the labor movement after World War I. Preserving union security in exchange for the no-strike pledge meant protecting the very right to organize.[54]

CLOSING DOWN THE CLOSED SHOP

The doubling of membership in CIO unions during World War II and the upsurge of strikes following the war's end reinforced the determination of business leaders, congressional Republicans, and Southern Democrats, who had been fighting the Wagner Act for more than a decade, to rein in the labor movement. During the Senate hearings for the bills that became the Taft-Hartley Act in 1947, William Green, the former miner and president of the American Federation of Labor, was far from a compelling witness; his sometimes bumbling answers underscored the class difference and tensions in the hearing room.[55] Labor leaders repeatedly spoke of collective responsibility, mutual protection, and sacrifice to explain why unions had a claim on all the workers in a shop in which the majority of workers had achieved a contract. Even where Green noted that dues were needed to pay for experts who advised unions, his larger argument was far more direct: "You cannot make a man, a union man, work with a nonunion man against his will," he told the senators. Too many dead bodies lay between them. "You know, it is a religion for them—a lot of them. There have been almost as many martyrs to the cause of unionism as there have been to the church itself. It has not been long since 40 union workers at Latimer, Pa., were shot down because they stood up for their union. And at Pana, Ill., in the miners' situation, hundreds of them gave up their lives in defense of the union."[56]

John L. Lewis, who had led the 1946 coal miners' strike that many believed precipitated the barrage of anti-labor bills in 1947, insisted on the right of unions to protect themselves from employers who aimed "to destroy the union."[57] Lewis was not above using a veiled threat as he took senators back to basics: "A workman has a right to give or to withhold his labor. Unions have always had the legal right to ask for a closed or union shop or check off. On the basis of simple social justice they have a right to seek such provisions in collective bargaining contracts. Those who insist upon using the power of the State to compel union members to work with nonunion members against their will are inviting economic chaos in labor relations in America."[58]

The witnesses testifying against the ban on the closed shop spoke not only in terms of solidarity, sacrifice, or the faceoff of power, but in terms of fairness as well. After all, John L. Lewis himself (who admired Herbert Hoover and endorsed

Wendell Willkie) had argued in 1925 that the dues checkoff showed workers "in the most forceful way that something is never obtained for nothing and that the individual must pay for all collective benefits."[59] At the Senate hearings, Lewis's successor as president of the CIO, Phillip Murray, reiterated "the principle that those who share in the benefits should also share in the responsibilities."[60] When Green tried to explain what unions did for their members, Senator Joseph Ball indignantly asked whether he thought that "a substantial percentage of American workers . . . are such chiselers that they would object to paying the dollar or two a month dues to the union in return for those benefits?" "Well a nonunion worker will not pay any dues," Green answered. "Experience has shown that."[61]

Business leaders, who had spent decades honing arguments against union security, the dues checkoff, and especially the closed shop, felt most compelled to answer what they themselves designated "the free rider argument," sometimes putting the phrase into the mouths of labor witnesses. "Why should nonunion workers enjoy rights won by unions?" editors of *Modern Industry* asked. "There are 'free riders' among employers, too, who refuse to join trade associations." "Freedom is Cheap," the editors concluded in boldface. "Permitting no joiners to share the benefits won by a union is a cheap price to pay for a free society in which both employees and employers have the freedom to choose their own work."[62] In a forum in the same magazine, Senator Ball restated his own case:

> Another argument is the "free rider" one: that nonunion members get the benefits of union agreements without paying for them. In the first place, that assumes the premise that all unions are good for the workers, a premise which cannot be sustained. In the second place, if a union is really doing a job for its members, with the tremendous advantage it has in exclusive bargaining rights, it will have no trouble enrolling all workers covered except a few nonconformists. If the union cannot sell its own services then it isn't doing a job that merits support. The idea that a union, like Government, should have the power to tax all workers, is again totalitarian thinking.[63]

Leaving ideological purity to Senator Ball, Senator Robert Taft in the majority report on the Senate bill that became the Taft-Hartley Act emphasized that banning the closed shop remedied "the most serious abuses of compulsory union membership." He presented the bill's provision that unions could bargain for a contract clause that would require workers to join the union within thirty days of being hired, as a practical recognition that a large number of companies had already made their separate peace with some form of union security (covering some 77 percent of unionized workers in 1946[64]). The act gave "employers and unions who feel that such agreements promoted stability by eliminating 'free riders' the right to continue such arrangements."[65] During the floor debate Taft explained that he had chosen the "open union" over the "open shop," so that "the bill further provides if a man is admitted to the union and subsequently fired from the union for any reason other than nonpayment of dues, the employer shall not be required to fire the man."[66] As the minority report on Taft's bill observed, such a provision meant that a member could "act as a spy or stoolpigeon or strike-breaker, be a racketeer or a grafter, and yet the union would have no effective sanction against him."[67]

With evident relief, Senator Taft invoked another authority for permitting the union shop while outlawing the closed shop. In January of 1946, the Supreme Court of Canada had ruled in an arbitration between Ford Motor Company and the United Auto Workers that employees in a union shop had to pay dues whether or not they joined the union, because the union had an obligation to represent all the workers under the contract. (Justice Ivan Rand's ruling came to be known as the "Rand Formula.") If the worker "pays dues without joining the union, he has the right to be employed. That, in effect, is a kind of tax, if you please, for union support," Taft reported to his colleagues. "I must say that the argument made for the union shop, and against abolishing the closed shop, is that if there is not a closed shop those not in the union will get a free ride, that the union does the work, gets the wages raised, then the man who does not pay dues rides along freely without any expense to himself. Under the Canadian rule, and under the rule of the committee, we pretty much take care of that argument. There is not much argument left."[68]

METAPHOR AS LEGAL SLOGAN

The debates over the Taft-Hartley Act specialized the metaphor of the free rider in legal circles as well as in the textbooks of industrial relations.[69] As one who violated basic fairness by getting something for nothing, the free rider could be made to pay up, but very reliance on the metaphor bleached what it meant to belong to a union fighting for labor's collective interest in an industrial society. If fairness to the majority of coworkers required an employee to pay for the services of a union, what exactly were those services? What kind of obligations did they impose? And what kind of power could the union exert on members' behalf in the wider political arena? In the aftermath of the Taft-Hartley defeat, labor leaders understood a strategic opening when they saw one and built their own arguments on the principle of fairness embedded in the slogan of the free rider.[70] Yet as members of the National Labor Relations Board, union lawyers, and judges quoted Senator Taft to establish congressional intent, the solution to the "free rider problem" redefined union membership. By the 1980s, the labor movement found that far from being a scab or a chiseler, the free rider had acquired new status by becoming in the eyes of some observers a dissenter—a "non-conformist," even an exemplar of individual freedom.

Throughout the 1950s, employers and business associations, including the U.S. Chamber of Commerce, the National Manufacturers Association, the American Farm Bureau, the National Right to Work Committee, and the Southern Industrial Council, mobilized to consolidate their gains politically and legally.[71] As early as 1953, the Supreme Court found itself addressing the "scope of the phrase 'membership in any labor organization'" when construing Taft-Hartley.[72] "Congress recognized the validity of unions' concern about 'free riders,' i.e. employees who receive the benefit of union representation but are unwilling to contribute their share of financial support to such unions," Justice Stanley Reed wrote in what became the standard narrative of the legislative history, but the record also "clearly indicates that Congress intended to prevent utilization of union security agreements for any purpose other than to compel payment of union dues and fees."[73] The 1953 *Radio Officers' Union* ruling combined three lower court cases involving NLRB decisions. In one case Teamsters had tried to enforce prompt payment of dues by demoting the seniority of a member in arrears; in another, the radio officers had suspended a member for violating its rules by bumping another member at the hiring hall. The Court found that employers could not enforce these union actions, even though (or even because) they might be "an effective method of coercing compliance with union obligations or practices." Many unions turned to fines.

The pressures of the right-to-work movement pushed AFL and CIO unions to accept multiple and ever flatter concepts of membership. By 1947, a dozen states had adopted laws that forbade closed and union shops, a ban that the Taft-Hartley Act recognized and the Supreme Court upheld in 1949.[74] The Rand Formula, however, had suggested an end run around such restrictions by holding that all workers should contribute financially for the services of a union elected by the majority. The union was in effect acting as employees' agent in contract matters. In 1963, a unanimous Supreme Court ruled that even in states with right-to-work laws, unions could bargain for an "agency shop" in their contract so long as state legislators had not explicitly forbidden it.[75] Justice Byron White followed the lead of the union's brief in reviewing Taft-Hartley's "significant alterations in the meaning of 'membership' for the purposes of union-security contracts."[76] With "the burdens of membership" in an agency shop "expressly limited to the payment of initiation fees and monthly dues," he wrote, "'membership' as a condition of employment is whittled down to its financial core."[77]

The American labor movement may have made a devil's bargain when it settled for the agency shop, for the very idea that membership could be reduced to a "financial core" to cover specific services—collective bargaining or handling grievances—threw over a century's worth of organizing. In its amicus brief in the 1963 case, however, the AFL-CIO conceded that labor organizing could only be about the art of the possible. Stretching the legislative history of Taft-Hartley to create a proactive congressional concern with protecting unions from free riders, the brief stressed that this "sensible solution to the union security issue" had been upheld by the NLRB since 1950, had been adopted in as many as 60 percent of existing contracts, and provided a pragmatic "compromise," especially for businesses that opposed the union shop on principle.[78] Still, having accepted the labor movement's own strategic concession that membership could be a divisible as well as limited concept, state and federal courts, as well as the NLRB itself, steadily whittled away the legal scope of collective action, including unions' powers to defend the labor movement politically and to enforce the obligations of membership.

Since 1956, employers had argued (and Justice Hugo Black agreed) that laws permitting unions to spend members' dues on politics violated the First Amendment. The majority of the Court rejected the constitutional argument and instead held (in 1961 for railroad unions and in 1988 for all other unions under Taft-Hartley) that members could demand reimbursement for the portion of dues that went for political uses.[79] Justice William Brennan, who wrote the majority opinion in both cases, found that Congress, when permitting union shops, had "authorized the exaction of only those fees and dues that are necessary to performing the duties" of collective bargaining as such.[80] In his 1988 dissent, Justice Harry Blackmun's strenuously objected to the "narrow prism" of Brennan's interpretation of "a single-minded legislative purpose," which in turn defined the purpose of trade unionism. "Congress was not guided solely by a desire to eliminate 'free riders,'" Blackmun insisted. The "plain language" of Taft-Hartley permitted "union-security agreements that require the tender of full union dues and standard union initiation fees from nonmember employees, without regard to how the union expends the funds so collected."[81]

In 1961, Felix Frankfurter, joined by John Marshall Harlan, had also scoffed at Brennan's tortured reading of legislative history to bar "purposes that have uniformly and extensively been so long pursued as to have become commonplace, settled, conventional trade-union practices." The railway labor law had been written "against the background and presupposition of what is loosely called political activity of American trade unions in general and railroad unions in particular," Frankfurter observed. "To write the history of the Brotherhoods, the United Mine Workers, the Steel Workers, the Amalgamated Clothing Workers, the International Ladies Garment Workers, the United Auto Workers, and leave out their so-called political activities and expenditures for them would be sheer mutilation."[82]

Far from a labor champion despite his contribution to writing the Norris–LaGuardia Act, Frankfurter noted that unions arrived at their political decisions by majority rule, another "commonplace" of democratic organizations and governments. "No one's desire or power to speak his mind is checked or curbed," he wrote. "The individual member may express his views in any public or private forum as freely as he could before the union collected his dues." Moreover, it was "pre-Victorian" to think that economic and political concerns could be separated. "It is not true in life that political protection is irrelevant to, and insulated from, economic interests. It is not true for industry or finance. Neither is it true for labor."[83]

Congress itself certainly drew little distinction between political and economic matters when it came to the labor movement. In 1959, the AFL-CIO lost the political battle over the Landrum-Griffin Act, which required unions to "open the books" to the public by filing annual financial reports with the Department of Labor, a requirement that one self-confessed union buster described as an unalloyed boon to hostile employers.[84] Still, in the 1960s, the majority of the NLRB, appointed by Democratic presidents, supported union prerogatives. And by and large, the Supreme Court deferred to the NLRB, recognizing the unions' right to discipline members, so long as it did not cost anyone a job. Thus, in 1967 and 1969, the Supreme Court upheld union fines on members who crossed a picket line or who violated work rules that set a ceiling on piecework.[85] But in the 1970s, under Republican administrations, the politics of both the NLRB and the Supreme Court changed.[86]

In 1972, in an 8–1 decision, the Court barred the Textile Workers Union of America from fining thirty-one members who had resigned and crossed a picket line during a strike, finding that "when a member lawfully resigns from the union, its power over him ends."[87] Only Justice Blackmun dissented, noting that that all the resignees had participated in the strike vote, ratified the strikebreaking penalties, and participated in the strike. "Union activity, by its very nature, is group activity and is grounded on the notion that strength can be garnered from unity, solidarity, and mutual commitment." Key to the success of a strike, Blackmun wrote, is "the mutual reliance that adheres in the 'pact.'"[88]

By the mid-1980s, with industrial unions fighting an uphill battle made harder by a hostile president and an unsympathetic NLRB, even the most basic principle of workers' mutual obligation failed to move the majority of jurists intent on opposing individual freedom to collective action, historically understood. In 1976, the Pattern Makers' League of North America, in part responding to the Court's 1972 decision, had amended its constitution to bar members from resigning during a strike or lockout. A year later, when two locals in Wisconsin and Illinois fined members who had resigned and crossed the picket lines, the NLRB upheld employers' charge of an unfair labor practice. In 1985, the Supreme Court agreed, in a 5–4 decision written by Justice Lewis Powell Jr., that union rules, however democratically decided, could not restrict the right of individual members to resign under any circumstances.[89]

Once again Blackmun in dissent returned to the fundamentals of collective action and the obligations that unions imposed on members. "To be effective, the decision to strike, like the decision to bargain collectively, must be respected by the minority until democratically revoked." Before undertaking a strike, union members had to have some sense that they could rely on one another. "Once an employee freely has made the decision to become a member of the union, has agreed not to resign during a strike, and has had the opportunity to participate in the decision to strike, his faithfulness to his promise is simply the quid pro quo for the benefits he has received as a result of his decision to band together with his fellow workers and to join in collective bargaining. For the dissatisfied member to return to work in violation of his promise, while his fellows remain on strike—forgoing their wages and risking their jobs in a now-weakened effort to pressure the employer into making concessions—is to allow the breaching individual to become a free rider, enjoying the benefits of his bargain without having to live with the risks that all who sought those benefits agreed to share." In other words, the free-riding strikebreaker had turned back into a scab.[90]

Blackmun denounced the majority's willingness to set aside the "promise of solidarity" and "the right of all workers to take effective collection action."[91] But having, in effect, whittled all union membership down to the agency shop—individual payment of fees for explicit services—the majority of the Court concluded that workers could take or leave the union as they chose.

The fate of union membership in the United States was never a matter of law, of course. Unions collapsed for many reasons, foremost among them the sustained, organized, and professionalized half-century campaign of business to bust the labor movement.[92] This is what Lee Pressman told the War Labor Board in 1942, and in the end it had little to do with free riders. Closed shops might have preserved something of the discipline that maintained union strength, but within the wider political culture, conceptions of organized obligation had eroded. So, too, had the industrial economy. Solidarity may have built the labor movement in the United States, but in the postwar era, social scientists as well as jurists increasingly judged such a concept metaphysical or sentimental. By contrast, the "free rider argument" implied that union membership represented the quid pro quo of any market exchange, a direct return for individual contribution, the product of free choice.

PUBLIC FINANCE, PUBLIC CHOICE, AND THE NEOLIBERAL LOGIC OF COLLECTIVE ACTION

Debates over the closed shop had narrowed the stakes of the labor movement to a particular problem and then given that single problem a name: the free rider. Within twenty-five years, the trope left behind its association with contests over workers' rights in the United States and came to stand for a new problem, that of valuing and allocating goods and services produced outside the market, most often by the state. The free rider started its new journey in the literature of public finance and then moved more widely into the social science discourse of rational choice in the 1970s and 1980s. By the end of the twentieth century, it served as an intellectual shorthand that reduced all social and political relations to the terms of the market and then worried when rationally calculating individuals failed to bargain or cooperate.

In the 1950s, in the face of the vastly expanded capacity and responsibilities of the New Deal and cold war state, American economists took up the intellectual challenge of applying marginalist microeconomic price theory to macroeconomic fiscal policies. Microeconomic theory had proved its worth in managing wartime production and distribution, and economists continued to deploy their models, including the new techniques of game theory, to support strategic military planning.[93] Within the private sector, economists also analyzed the conditions of equilibrium that minimized waste, weighed risks and opportunity costs, and maximized individual satisfaction. Yet how could neoclassical models of market transactions account for the wealth produced, collected, or transferred through public agencies? Explaining how the value of public goods—and hence their price and distribution—could be established in the absence of market signals had important implications for the efficient operation of the public sector within the larger capitalist political economy.

The framing of these issues rested, as S. M. Amadae has shown, on the self-conscious repudiation of social democratic as well as communist alternatives.[94] Economists, who proudly claimed to purge moral judgments from their discipline, cemented "freedom" to individual choice, converting the free rider from a self-serving opportunist into a normative human being. In the process, even Robert Taft's concession to a notion of transactional fairness—the right, for example, of union shops to collect dues in exchange for collective representation—lost its purchase among those social scientists wwwwho regarded bargaining and obligation as antonyms. In the world of price theory, moreover, economists had few tools (and even less inclination) to grapple with concentrated corporate power as a social problem, let alone the idea of labor solidarity as an institutional counterpoint.

Two analogies gave the free rider its new platform and identity. Dismantling classical political economy's separation of public and private domains, as well as what they called "organic" (or metaphysical) theories of the state, public finance theorists proposed that markets and governments could be thought of as alternative—and implicitly interchangeable—mechanisms for the delivery of benefits to individual consumers. Citizens who achieved sovereignty as consumers had no obligations beyond the transactions that made their desires known. Indeed, connecting sovereign consumers to a traditional identity as constituents gave rise to a second analogy, which also carried a corollary. Social scientists suggested that governments and their publics could best be thought of as large social organizations, the diffuse end of a continuum of groups ranked by size. Given the limited impact of any one member's influence on the large group as a whole, in most instances, individuals could best realize their self-interest on their own, that is, through market bargaining rather than through a collective or political process.

The application of microeconomics, a theory of individual pursuit of satisfaction, to macroeconomics, a theory of politically mediated aggregate economic action, begged a new question. "Why is political or governmental organization required at all," economist James Buchanan asked, when it comes to the production of goods and services?[95] Classical theory replied that in addition to managing the rules and maintaining the playing field, government had to step in when markets failed to meet the demand for such things as defense, transportation, education, public health, or public parks. But because public goods could not be exclusively appropriated or diminished by individual consumption, because their supply was not determined by profitability, individual marginal utility had no bearing on their price and hence their efficient provision. Through the power of taxation, of course, the state could compel everyone to pay, regardless of how benefits were allocated. This practical reality, however, did not deter economists from pursuing the challenge of placing what Paul Samuelson called "collective consumption goods" into a neoclassical framework.

Yet in 1954, when Samuelson published "The Pure Theory of Public Expenditure," he demonstrated that "no decentralized pricing system can serve to determine optimally . . . levels of collective consumption."[96] In his authoritative 1959 text on public finance, Richard Musgrave amplified Samuelson's conclusion with a full lineage of German, Austrian, Italian, and Swedish economists who had grappled with how to apply marginal utility theory to government expenditures in the late nineteenth and early twentieth centuries.[97] The Europeans, most especially Swedish economist Knut Wicksell, had recognized that since citizens had no incentive to reveal what government goods and services were worth to them, both the distribution and the allocation of public benefits had to be addressed politically. Wicksell thought of himself as a social democrat; it took an American libertarian—his first English-language translator and greatest champion, James Buchanan—to reduce his multilayered deliberations on political economy to something called the free rider problem.

By the early1960s, what began as a theoretical conundrum had become part of the agenda of economists intent on challenging theories of "welfare economics," and most especially the growth of the state as an economic actor. Buchanan, who in his autobiography recalled as a boy reading his grandfather's Populist tracts in his Tennessee home, also described having a "conversion experience" under the ministrations of Frank Knight at the University of Chicago, who inspired a new faith in the market and an intense mistrust of government.[98] In his own writings and in collaboration with political scientist Gordon Tulloch, Buchanan drew a very different conclusion than Samuelson about the limits of neoclassical models for devising a theory of public expenditures. If it was not possible to establish individual preferences—and hence an efficient allocation—for public goods, one simple solution was to minimize the public goods.[99]

Although Buchanan suggested in a 1964 article that "this specter of the 'free rider'" was "found in many shapes and forms in the literature of modern public finance theory," he himself seems to have been the first economist not only to turn the specter into a term of art but to try to rehabilitate that figure as well.[100] Debates over right to-work laws in the late 1950s, if not the popular vernacular, surely familiarized Buchanan with the figure of the free rider in industrial relations. Yet he went out of his way to establish that far from being thieves or scabs, individuals who refused to pay for collective goods made a rational and ethically neutral choice. Couching his argument in terms of a dilemma in "large groups" that corresponded to an inclusive public, Buchanan noted that "the very usage of the term 'free rider' . . . suggests some deliberate effort on the part of the choosing individual to secure benefits at the expense of his fellows. In the only situation where the problem really emerges, however, the choosing individual enjoys no sensation of 'riding free,' or 'letting George do it.' There is no personal interaction present at all. The individual is simply reacting to an environment in which he finds himself, to 'nature,' so to speak, not in any way against his fellow citizens."[101] Thus, the free rider was cut loose altogether from a landscape of reciprocal social obligation and moved into the desert of market freedom.

Buchanan's theory entailed some other noteworthy inversions. Whereas conventional economic wisdom had held that government stepped in when markets failed—that is, government provided goods and services that could not be efficiently delivered through the market—he suggested that markets failed *because* government stepped in. Indeed, it was the rational choice of citizens to act as free riders that explained "the failure of the market process to produce optimal results when public goods are present." This failure in turn explained why individuals turned to "political government processes as substitute for market processes."[102] That being the circular case, Buchanan focused his attention on "political government processes," drawing on Wicksell's theories to call for new voting procedures that would protect individual citizens from having to pay taxes for public goods regardless of who enjoyed the benefit.[103]

As Buchanan and Tulloch established the "public choice" movement through their journal (given that name in 1968), other social scientists took up the challenge of reconciling the decision-making mechanisms of markets and states in the name of maximizing both individual freedom and social wealth.[104] No text was more important in the libertarian revival than Mancur Olson's *Logic of Collective Action*, published in 1965.[105] From the very selection of its title, the book offered itself as a provocation. Collective action historically referred to the solidarity of the labor movement. In Olson's hands, however, the *logic* of collective action established the impossibility of solidarity as either a condition or a goal of collective organizing. It was contrary to human rationality and antithetical to human freedom.

No logic of voluntary collective action for large groups could produce collective benefits, because no rational individual would choose to contribute to a collective good that, by definition, he or she could enjoy without making any contribution. Individual utility or self-interest could not be aggregated, generalized, or trumped outside markets any more than within them. Given this harsh reality, Olson argued, the provision of collective goods always rested on incentives—supplying exclusive individual benefits—or on coercion, whether that of government taxation or, in the case of unions, compulsory membership. Although he only used the term "free rider" in his discussion of the labor movement, for readers persuaded by Olson's larger account of a universal logic that applied to all forms of large association, the value of the trope was its very portability and plasticity.[106]

The tremendous influence of Olson's *Logic of Collective Action* marked one last inversion of the labor movement's inadvertent contribution to neoliberal political ideology. Theories of industrial democracy had stressed the correspondence between republican government and trade unions governed by constitutions and bylaws; Olson embraced the comparison of union discipline and the power of government in order to prove the impossibility of either institution democratically providing for collective well-being.[107] Olson believed in "freedom from any coercive control of an individual's economic life, no matter what the political implications or political arrangements of such control might be."[108] Thus, the economist analyzes how the free rider can be eliminated not because a scab weakens collective power, but because the free rider undermines the calculation of costs by which individuals freely bargain.

Since the 1960s, rational choice theorists have rung the changes on Buchanan's and Olson's briefs for methodological individualism and its implicit and explicit link to dismantling the conceptual apparatus of the regulatory welfare state. First within the pages of *Public Choice*, and by the early 1970s, in mainstream economic journals, as well as in the pages of such periodicals as *Public Interest* and *Commentary*, the free rider regularly appeared in discussions of vouchers, user fees, and the relative merits of direct government spending versus private contracts or subsidies to private parties.[109] Calls to eliminate free riders through privatization became the mainstay of opposition to the use of state power to redistribute wealth by socializing public benefits.

As rational choice swept through the social science disciplines in the late 1960s, the free rider was also quickly absorbed into game theory and merged with the "prisoner's dilemma" to explore how people made strategic decisions in relation to others. Game theorists embraced Buchanan's and Olson's ideas about the difference between small groups and large groups and put the free rider to work in ever more elaborate scenarios.[110] Unlike Buchanan in 1964, however, they saw that the decision not to contribute to collective effort also came at the expense of other players. If people were to cooperate or negotiate their way to a win-win outcome that maximized the benefits all around, the free rider, intent on getting something for nothing, had to be repressed, "incentivized," "bribed," co-opted, or punished. In different words, a trade unionist in 1920 might have said the same thing. But in game theory, the players are individual and equal, an illusion that no trade unionist ever had about negotiations between workers and employers.

In a 1972 article in the *Journal of Law and Economics,* Buchanan added the free rider problem to Ronald Coase's ideas about how the social costs of such things as pollution could be more efficiently allocated through the bargaining of private parties rather than by state regulations. A recent Virginia lawsuit had centered on the danger that a cedar tree rust posed to apple trees on adjacent properties.[111] Arguing against a state policy that decided whether cedar owners or apple growers deserved protection, Buchanan proposed that the parties might reach "mutually satisfactory agreements" based on compensation so long as everyone acknowledged and valued their individual stakes in a resolution. But if there were too many apple growers, "the familiar free rider obstructions to voluntarily negotiated solutions" arose, increasing transaction costs. If bargaining could not lead to optimal outcomes, the failure of a market solution would push the matter into the legislature or the courts. But the apple growers could themselves eliminate the free riders, Buchanan concluded, by getting rid of small proprietors and consolidating their land, thereby reducing the number of parties to the deal with the cedar owners. The concentration of wealth was part of the solution.[112]

As the metaphors of rational choice moved into the field of law and economics, Richard Posner and others used the free rider to consider how vested interests captured regulatory agencies, the problems of cartels, and the logic of a revised antitrust doctrine, which allowed, for example, manufacturers to control distributors who would otherwise undermine a corporate marketing strategy.[113] When legal theorists began to look to "social norms" as yet another private alternative to the historical function of the state—making and enforcing laws—they turned their backs on historical examples that exposed the difficulties of building and preserving collective norms in the face of more powerful opponents and opted for pastoral stories of farmers and cattlemen trying to get along.[114]

By 1997, when Richard Posner weighed in with his own "economic approach" to norms, the free rider problem verged on incoherence. Posner tried to theorize the "incentives of ostracizers" and worried that "unpaid norm-enforcers" might find that others benefited from their exertions. "The free rider problem that results from the fact that there is . . . no centralized authority to create or change norms," moreover, also meant an "innovator cannot capture most of the benefits" of "lumpy" cultural changes. Concluding that "law both complements and substitutes for norms," Posner arrived at a revelation: "many contracts are adhered to, even when there is no feasible means of legal enforcement, by considerations of reciprocity."[115]

"Solutions" to the free rider problem ranged from determining what sticks and carrots could bring free riders into the bargaining fold to working out the political procedures that ensured that everyone was satisfied that no one contributed more than a neighbor and each got from the public trough exactly what had been paid for. Still, by the 1990s, some social scientists, aspiring to make sense of the patent reality of social cooperation, began to tire of sterile metaphors and developed a robust critique of the rational choice paradigm.[116] European and Australian theorists, perhaps less constrained by the ideological agenda of American libertarians, also more readily turned the free rider problem back into questions about the historically situated and fluid nature of cooperation, the diffuse benefits of collective action, and even the practical possibilities of solidarity. Yet as they free themselves from the desiccated caricatures of rational choice, social scientists working in the shadows of the neoliberal revolution have been left with little space to imagine collective responses to the concentration of power.

"FREEDOM OF ASSOCIATION"

Over the last century, the free rider has traveled an uneven ethical path from an abuser of privilege to a thief, chiseler, or scab to the normative universal individual, in whose name public policy is being rewritten throughout the post-industrial world. The work of universalizing the free rider's characteristics into a dominant social logic required the suppression of older judgments about the obligations of members of defined communities that operated on principles of discipline, sacrifice, and majority rule—on concepts of solidarity that encompass rather than oppose self-interest. Such values run counter to the psychology of the calculating individual associated with a free-market regime. With the evisceration of older conceptions of membership and obligation, civil society as it was reconceived in the late twentieth century has few institutions that can claim and *enforce* the loyalty of members to achieve a collective purpose. Out of this impoverishment of civil society has come a parallel impoverishment of the state, which retains police powers but possesses less and less capacity to provide for the general welfare or, indeed, to call on its citizens to temper self-interest in order to produce a common good.

Since the 1980s, political theorists, jurists, and neoliberal politicians around the world have reexamined the meanings of membership and collective action in trade unions in light of universal principles of human rights, which include the "freedom of association."[117] Yet while the right to organize remains a starting point for discussions of the powers of unions to bind their members, it has been matched by arguments on behalf of the right of individuals to disassociate. Indeed, even the agency shop has come under attack as an infringement of individual freedom rather than a means of ensuring fairness. In such a climate it becomes harder and harder for unionists to argue that neither government nor employers can force a union member to work alongside a scab.

In the United States, the so-called rights revolution, disappointment at the ineffectiveness of trade unions, and recognition of the limitations of the Wagner Act's model for collective bargaining have prompted legal scholars to look for alternative strategies to address growing inequalities of income and wealth as well as the ongoing vulnerability of individual workers to exploitation.[118] None, however, has succeeded in working out a new route from individual rights to the collective strength necessary to counter the associated power of international capital.

In the meantime, despite recent critiques of neoliberal social science, the free rider continues to circulate as a flat, tired, yet ubiquitous explanation for the impossibility of collective action, the irrationality of socializing basic goods through a strong public sector, and the obstacles that government regulation poses to the maximization of social wealth. There have been opportunity costs to the heuristic thinking that allowed lawmakers, jurists, and social scientists to screen out history in favor of stick figures. Scholars have lost track of the ways people in the past thought about and acted on a sense of collective obligation, and they have lost sight of alternative ways of conceptualizing how people might pursue collective benefits today. In the face of growing concentrations of economic power and growing inequities in the distribution of wealth, it is hard not to conclude that there have been social costs to the neoliberal ascendency in law and society that cannot be bargained away.

NOTES

1. A. M. Sakoloski, *Finances of American Trade Unions* (Baltimore, Md.: Johns Hopkins Press, 1906), 43. The miners raised four-fifths of the total themselves, the rest coming from other unions and public sympathizers.

2. David Montgomery, *Workers' Control in America* (New York: Cambridge University Press, 1979), 18, 20, table 1.

3. U.S. Department of Labor, Bureau of Labor Statistics, "Work Stoppages Involving 1,000 or More Workers 1947–2005," http://www.bls.gov/news.release/wkstp.t01.htm (accessed July 26, 2006). For the size of the labor force, see U.S. Department of Labor, Bureau of Labor Statistics, introduction, "Report on the American Workforce," http://www.bls.gov/opub/rtaw/rtawhome.htm#introduction (accessed Dec. 18, 2006).

4. James Livingston, "The Social Analysis of Economic History and Theory: Conjectures on Late Nineteenth-Century American Development," *American Historical Review* 92, no. 1 (1987): 78–85. On the legal status of labor in the nineteenth century, see Christopher Tomlins, *Law, Labor, and Ideology in the Early American Republic* (New York: Cambridge University Press, 1991); William Forbath, *Law and the Shaping of the American Labor Movement* (Cambridge, Mass.: Harvard University Press, 1991).

5. James B. Atleson, *Values and Assumptions in American Labor Law* (Amherst: University of Massachusetts Press, 1983).

6. These generalizations, and most of the discussion that follows, stem from my reading of trade union journals and convention minutes, invaluably indexed by Lloyd Reynolds and Charles

C. Killingsworth, *Trade Union Publications: The Official Journals, Convention Proceedings, and Constitutions of International Unions and Federations, 1850–1941* (Baltimore, Md.: Johns Hopkins Press, 1945).

7. For a summary of the arguments as to contractual, property, and "relational" theories of voluntary associations, including unions, see Zechariah Chafee Jr., "The Internal Affairs of Associations Not for Profit," *Harvard Law Review* 43 (1930): 993–1029.

8. Sakolski, *Finances of American Trade Unions*, 9–12, 18, 35–37 (strike funds); Lloyd Ulman, *The Rise of the National Trade Union: The Development and Significance of Its Structure, Governing Institutions, and Economic Policies* (Cambridge, Mass.: Harvard University Press, 1955), 68–79.

9. Shelton Stromquist, *A Generation of Boomers: The Pattern of Railroad Labor Conflict in Nineteenth-Century America* (Urbana: University of Illinois Press, 1987). On the culture of railroading, see W. Fred Cottrell, *The Railroader* (Stanford, Calif.: Stanford University Press, 1940), and on risks and insurance, Reed C. Richardson, *The Locomotive Engineer 1863–1963: A Century of Railway Labor Relations and Work Rules* (Ann Arbor: University of Michigan, 1963), 272–78.

10. Black railroaders, including Pullman porters, organized their own unions. Eric Arnesen, *Brotherhoods of Color: Black Railroad Workers and the Struggle for Equality* (Cambridge, Mass.: Harvard University Press, 2001). In 1944, the Supreme Court ruled that under the Railway Labor Act the duty of fair representation meant that the brotherhoods could not restrict membership on the basis of race. See *Steele v. Louisville & Nashville R.R.*, 323 U.S. 192 (1944).

11. Jerome L. Toner, *The Closed Shop in the American Labor Movement* (Washington, D.C.: Catholic University of America Press, 1941), 108.

12. Richardson, *The Locomotive Engineer*, 281–85; David Montgomery, *The Fall of the House of Labor: The Workplace, the State, and American Labor Activism, 1865–1925* (New York: Cambridge University Press, 1987), 367–68.

13. E. W. Davis, "Fixed Amount of Dues Each Month," *Brotherhood of Locomotive Engineers Monthly Journal* 42 (1908): 302.

14. The brotherhoods' obsessive proceduralism mirrored the disciplinary regimes of their employers. See James H. Drucker, *Men of the Steel Rails: Workers on the Atchison, Topeka and Santa Fe Railroad, 1869–1900* (Lincoln: University of Nebraska Press, 1983), 30–41. Every January, the Brotherhood of Locomotive Engineers published the names of "backsliders" to shame them. See "House Cleaning Session," *Brotherhood of Locomotive Engineers Monthly Journal* 44, no. 1 (1910): 85–86, 94.

15. See, for example, F. M. Ryan, "Fund to Prevent Expulsion or Suspension," *Brotherhood of Locomotive Engineers Monthly Journal* 44, no. 3 (1910): 201–2; Thomas H. Hiner, "Duty and Dues," *Brotherhood of Locomotive Engineers Monthly Journal* 45, no. 6 (1911): 475–76. A member of the Order of Railway Conductors for twenty-three years warned this practice encouraged lax habits in a letter to the editor of the *Railway Conductor* 43, no. 1 (1926): 80.

16. Sakolski, *Finances of American Trade Unions*, 87.

17. Ibid., 45–67.

18. Samuel Gompers, "Necessity of a Good Treasury," *American Federationist* 10, no. 9 (1903): 836–38.

19. Frank Duffy, "The Carpenters and High Dues," *American Federationist* 22, no. 8, pt. 2 (1915): 595 (begging letters); G. W. Perkins (president of the Cigarmakers International Union), "A Well-Filled Union Treasury, *American Federationist* 22, no. 6 (1915): 428–29 (cowardice).

20. John F. Tobin, "Boot and Shoe Workers' Union," *American Federationist* 22, no 2 (1915): 101–2; Joseph F. Valentine, "Make Unionism Effective," *American Federationist*, 22, no. 4 (1915): 268–69; James Duncan, "Self-Sustaining Dues, *American Federationist* 22, no. 10 (1915), 846–48; Joseph Proebstle, "Labor's Best Investment," *American Federationist* 22, no. 12 (1915): 1048. See also the American Federation of Labor, *Encyclopedia Reference Book* (Washington, D.C.: A. F. of L. Building, 1919), s.v. "Dues, High Union."

21. Samuel Gompers, "The Advantages of High Dues," *American Federationist* 22, no. 2 (1915): 112–13.

22. Montgomery, *Fall of the House of Labor*, 338–39.

23. Button strikes were especially common in the anthracite fields in 1913 and 1916, when some 79,481 miners refused to work with non-union workers, costing the companies almost a million days' labor. Perry K. Blatz, *Democratic Miners: Work and Labor Relations in the Anthracite Coal Industry, 1875–1925* (Albany: State University of New York, 1994), 217.

24. Towner, *The Closed Shop*, quoting Mitchell, *Organized Labor* (Philadelphia: American Book and Bible House, 1903), 174.

25. Ibid., 180.

26. Blatz, *Democratic Miners*, 211, quoting Peter Kelly in a 1909 speech.

27. Montgomery, *Fall of the House of Labor*, 269–75; Sidney Fine, *"Without Blare of Trumpets": Walter Drew, the National Erectors' Association, and the Open Shop Movement, 1903–57* (Ann Arbor: University of Michigan Press, 1995). Beatrice and Sidney Webb used the term "compulsory unionism" in their highly influential 1897 book, *Industrial Democracy* (London: Longmans, Green, 1897).

28. The shift in the *American Federationist* was especially pronounced after William Green succeeded Samuel Gompers; see, for example, Green's editorial, "Problems of Modern Trade Unionism," *American Federationist* 33, no. 6 (1926): 659.

29. James Simpson, "Does It Pay to Belong to the Organized Labor Movement?" *American Federationist* 19, no. 9 (1912): 699–700. For other examples of the dividend analogy, see Charles Blaine, "Importance of Local Union Work," *Shoe Worker's Journal* 12, no. 11 (1911): 12–13; Charles L. Blaine, "Ten Wasted Years," *Shoe Worker's Journal* 24, no. 3 (1923): 9–10; James Wilson, "Report of the General President," *Pattern Makers' Journal* 41, no. 7 (1930): 13.

30. "Proceedings of the Fifteenth Convention of the Pattern Makers League of North American," *Pattern Makers' Journal* 37, no. 7 (1926): 78.

31. Staugton Lynd, review of *Values and Assumptions in American Labor Law*, by James Atleson, *Stanford Law Review* 36 (1984): 1292–93.

32. Christopher L. Tomlins, *The State and the Unions: Labor Relations, Law and the Organized Labor Movement in America, 1880–1960* (New York: Cambridge University Press, 1985). See also Harry A. Millis and Emily Clark Brown, *From the Wagner Act to Taft-Hartley: A Study of National Labor Policy and Labor Relations* (Chicago: University of Chicago Press, 1950); James A. Gross, *The Making of the National Labor Relations Board: A Study in Economics, Politics and the Law* (Albany: State University of New York Press, 1974); James A. Gross, *The Reshaping of the National Labor Relations Board: National Labor Policy in Transition* (Albany: State University of New York Press, 1981). On the miners' contribution to CIO organizing, see Len De Caux, *Labor Radical: From the Wobblies to CIO: A Personal History* (Boston: Beacon, 1970), 139.

33. Mary Ann Clawson, *Constructing Brotherhood: Class, Gender, and Fraternalism* (Princeton, N.J.: Princeton University Press 1989), 259–62.

34. In reading the journals of fifteen unions from 1895 to 1940, I found only one use of the analogy (but not the term) in Charles Blaine, "Ten Wasted Years," *Shoe Worker's Journal* 24, no. 3 (1923): 10. "The unorganized are in a sense passengers evading their fares but not enjoying full privileges."

35. H. L. Mencken, *The American Language: An Inquiry into the Development of English in the United States* (New York: Knopf, 1948), 699.

36. See, for example, "The Railroad Question," *Chicago Daily Tribune*, Mar. 18, 1873, p. 2; and "Albany," *New York Times*, Apr. 16, 1873, p. 7. The pass system was also known as "deadheadism," with reference to wilted flowers that needed to be lopped off their plants.

37. "Free Passes: The Interstate Commission Desires to Know Something," *Atlanta Constitution*, Apr. 18, 1889, p. 2. See also "Free Passes Shut Off," *Washington Post*, Jan. 1, 1992, p. 1; "Free Passes," *Los Angeles Times*, Jan. 1, 1892, p. 9.

38. De Caux, *Labor Radical*, 68–69, offers a vivid description of railroaders and union cards; for perceptions of free riders as nuisance, see *Los Angeles Times*, Sept. 24, 1893, p. 5; Nov. 5, 1893, p. 6; Nov. 29, 1893, p. 5; Dec. 21, 1893, p. 5.

39. See, for example, articles in the *Washington Post*, May 21, 1932, p. 2; *New York Times*, May 24, 1932, p. 1; *Chicago Daily Tribune*, May 25, 1932, p. 3.

40. For the general term in finance, see "Everyday Economics: 'Free Riding,'" *Chicago Daily Tribune*, Dec. 14, 1938, p. 31; "Free Riding-2," Dec. 15, 1938, p. 37. For bond speculation and regulation, see, for example, "New Treasury Loan Tops $1,500,000," *New York Times*, May 27, 1936, p. 35; "Treasury Moves to End 'Free Rides'," Dec. 11, 1938, p. 75. For the New York Stock Exchange, see "'Free-Ride' Usage May Be Retained," *New York Times* Jan. 15, 1937, p. 29; "Exchanges Adopt Rules to Prevent 'Free Riding,'" *New York Times*, Feb. 17, 1937, p. 1.

41. Kent appeared on the cover of *Time* on August 27, 1928, as a representative of politically influential journalists. Examples of his deployment of the formula appear in his column in the *Los Angeles Times*, July 29, 1935, p. 5, and *Wall Street Journal*, Sept. 11, 1935, p. 2; Sept. 2, 1936, p. 4.

42. "Who Pays Taxes?" *New York Times*, May 27, 1939, p. 8.

43. For discussions of free rides in exchange for public service, see, for example, Mrs. J. H. McPherson, "Free Riders," *Chicago Daily Tribune*, July 25, 1920, p. 8; "Taxing the Straphanger," *Chicago Daily Tribune*, Oct. 4, 1921, p. 8; "Free Rides Are Favored for Police and Firemen," *Atlanta Constitution*, July 3, 1908, p. 7; and for military service, "Free Rides for Old Soldiers," *Atlanta Constitution*, March 10, 1911, p. 7; "Free Rides for Soldiers," *New York Times*, Apr. 29, 1941, p. 10; "Soldiers' Free Ride Opposed by Mayor," *New York Times*, Apr. 24, 1942, p. 1. The carriers generally resisted giving free rides to ordinary public workers or service men.

44. For examples of such policies that began in the 1910s, see "IRT Free Service Breaks All Records," *New York Times*, Oct. 1, 1934, p. 19; "148,300 Free Rides Given by IRT," *New York Times*, Sept. 21, 1936, p. 25.

45. Clinton S. Golden and Harold J. Ruttenberg, *The Dynamics of Industrial Democracy* (New York: Harper and Brothers, 1942), 24–25.

46. Ibid., 25.

47. Thomas R. Brooks, *Clint: A Biography of a Labor Intellectual, Clinton S. Golden* (New York: Atheneum, 1978), 197.

48. Harold J. Ruttenberg, "The Strategy of Industrial Peace," *Harvard Business Review* 17 (1939): 159–76.

49. Ruttenberg, "Strategy of Industrial Peace," 172.

50. Nelson Lichtenstein, *Labor's War at Home: The CIO in World War II* (New York: Cambridge University Press, 1982).

51. Ibid., 78–81. A union maintenance plan gave employees fifteen days after taking a job or the signing of a contract to decide whether to join or remain in the union, and no members could resign during the duration of the contract. For a summary of the War Labor Board's union security policy, see *Humble Oil and Refining Co.*, 15 War Lab. Rep. 380 (1944), reprinted in Frank P. Graham, "The Union Maintenance Policy of the War Labor Board," in *Yearbook of American Labor; War Labor Policies*, ed. Colston E. Warne et al., 1:145–61 (New York: Philosophical Society, 1945). Graham also wrote the decision on union security in the Little Steel case.

52. 15 War Lab. Rep. at 391.

53. John Chamberlain, "Democracy and the Closed Shop," *Fortune* 25, no. 1 (1942): 64–65, quote on 131. Employers' counsel cited Chamberlain's article during the hearing; see 1 War Lab. Rep., 393–94. In 1950, Chamberlain helped establish the *Freeman*, a libertarian journal.

54. Gilbert J. Gall, *Pursuing Justice: Lee Pressman, the New Deal, and the CIO* (Albany: State University of New York, 1999), 134, 138–39. *Bethlehem Steel et al.*, July 16, 1942, 1 War Lab. Rep., 387–89, give the union's fourteen arguments on behalf of union security. Pressman also argued that efficient war production depended on the ability of unions to discipline their members, a formulation that was to have a long life in what some historians have described as the postwar labor-management accord in mass production industries. Lichtenstein, *Labor's War at Home*, 79, 241–45.

55. Hearings before the Senate Committee on Labor and Public Welfare, on S. 55 and S.J. Res. 22 "and all other bills and resolutions referred to the committee having the object of reducing industrial strife in the United States," 80th Cong., 1st sess. pt. 2, 979–80, 986.

56. Id. at pt. 2, 999.

57. Id. at pt. 3, 2016.

58. Id. at pt. 3, 2017.

59. John L. Lewis, *Miners Fight for the American Standards* (Indianapolis, Ind.: Bell, 1925), 139, 162.

60. Hearings before the Committee on Labor and Public Welfare, pt. 2, 1137.

61. Id. at pt. 2, 1006.

62. "Why the Closed Shop?" *Modern Industry* 13, no. 3 (1947): 206.

63. "Should the Closed Shop Be Outlawed?" *Modern Industry* 13, no. 3 (1947): 109.

64. Minority report, in *Legislative History of the Labor Management Relations Act, 1947* (Washington, D.C.: U.S. Government Printing Office, 1974), 470. According to the Bureau of Labor Statistics, six million workers were covered by some form of checkoff provision in 1947 (486).

65. Senate report no. 105 on S. 1126 in *Legislative History*, 412–13.

66. Ibid., floor debates, 1420, 1010.

67. Ibid., minority report, 471.

68. Ibid., floor debates, 1422. The Canadian case was *Re Ford Motor Co. of Canada and the International Union UAA & AIW of America (UAW-CIO)* (1946) 1 CCH Lab. Law Rep. P 2150.

69. A 1950 review noted new "terms largely developed in connection with recent federal and state labor laws," including the "free rider." Julius B. Bearnson, review of *Labor Dictionary*, by Paul Casselman, *Western Political Quarterly* 3, no. 3 (1950): 485.

70. Thus, in 1951, when the railroad unions secured an amendment to the 1926 Railway Act that permitted bargaining for a union shop, they repeatedly invoked the free rider problem as defined by the Taft-Hartley debates. The Supreme Court upheld the federal law over a right-to-work clause in Nebraska's constitution in *Railway Employees' Department, American Federation of Labor. v. Hanson,* 351 U.S. 225 (1956), but left the door open on whether the railroad unions could spend their dues for political purposes.

71. These groups submitted amicus briefs in *Hanson.*

72. *Radio Officers' Union of the Commercial Telegrapher Union, AFL v. National Labor Relations Board no 5,* 347 U.S. 17, 39 (1953).

73. Id. at 41.

74. Gilbert J. Gall, *The Politics of Right to Work: The Labor Federations as Special Interests, 1943–1979* (Westport, Conn.: Greenwood Press, 1988), 19–27, 34, 46–47. The Supreme Court upheld right-to-work laws in *Lincoln Federal Labor Union v. Northwestern Iron and Metal Company,* 335 U.S. 522 (1949).

75. *National Labor Relations Board v. General Motors Corp.,* 373 U.S. 734 (1963). In a companion case, the Court upheld the right of Florida's state courts to enforce an explicit ban on the agency shop along with other forms of union security mentioned in a right-to-work law; see *Retail Clerks International Association, Local 1625, AFL-CIO, et al., v. Schermerhorn et al.,* 375 U.S. 96 (1963).

76. *National Labor Relations Board v. General Motors Corp.,* 373 U.S. at 741–742; cf. "Brief for the American Federation of Labor and Congress of Industrial Organizations as Amicus Curiae," in *National Labor Relations Board v. General Motors Corp.* (United States Supreme Court, October term, 1962), at 15.

77. *National Labor Relations Board,* 373 U.S. at 742.

78. AFL-CIO brief v, 4–9, 12. The AFL-CIO lawyers argued that the Taft-Hartley Act tacitly recognized a "whittled down" definition of membership, since "it only permits discharge of those who do not pay dues and initiation fees, which amounts to the same thing as an agency shop" (16).

79. *International Association of Machinists et al. v. Street et al.,* 367 U.S 740 (1961); *Communications Workers of America et al. v. Beck et al.,* 487 U.S. 735 (1988).

80. *Communications Workers of America et al.,* 487 U.S. at 735.

81. Id. at 775, 779. Justices Scalia and O'Connor joined Blackmun's dissent. The court's dispute over how dues or "user fees" could be spent by unions in the public as well as private sector continued. In *Ellis v. Railway Clerks,* 466 U.S. 435, 448 (1984), the court examined whether the railroad union's political activities were "germain" to collective bargaining; with *Abood v. Detroit Board of Education,* 431 U.S. 209 (1977), and *Lehnert v. Ferris Faculty Association,* 500 U.S. 507 (1991), it turned to how public teachers' unions spent their funds.

82. *International Association of Machinists et al.,* 367 U.S. at 800.

83. Id. at 806, 808, 814–15. Citing the British laws that prevented trade unions from using dues for political purposes, Frankfurter also noted that Congress could pass a similar law providing that "dissenting members may contract out of any levies used for political purposes"; id. at 817.

84. Martin Jay Levitt, *Confessions of a Union Buster* (New York: Crown, 1993), 40–43; on Landrum-Griffin, see R. Alton Lee, *Eisenhower and Landrum-Griffin: A Study in Labor-Management Politics* (Lexington: University Press of Kentucky, 1990).

85. In *National Labor Relations Board v. Allis-Chalmers Manufacturing Co. et al.,* 388 U.S. 185 (1967), Justice Brennan found that imposing fines for crossing a picket line fit within the "contractual conception of the relation between a member and his union." *Scofield et al. v. National Labor Relations Board,* 394 U.S. 423 (1969), upheld fines to enforce a production ceiling.

86. For the politics of labor policy, see James A. Gross, *Broken Promise: The Subversion of U.S. Labor Relations Policy, 1947–1994* (Philadelphia: Temple University Press, 1995).

87. *National Labor Relations Board v. Granite State Joint Board, Textile Workers Union of America, Local 1029, AFL-CIO,* 409 U.S. 215 (1972).

88. Id. at 220, 221. Blackmun joined the majority of the Court in the companion case of *Booster Lodge No. 405, International Association of Machinists and Aerospace Workers, AFL-CIO v. National Labor Relations Board et al.,* 412 U.S. 84 (1973), because the union had not provided a notice of strikebreaking penalties and the fined workers had not participated in a strike vote or the strike itself. See also David Abraham, "Individual Autonomy and Collective Empowerment in Labor Law: Union Membership Resignations and Strikebreaking in the New Economy," *New York University Law Review* 63 (1988): 1268.

89. *Pattern Makers' League of North America, AFL-CIO v. National Labor Relations Board et al.,* 473 U.S. 95 (1985).

90. Id. at 129.

91. Id. at 130, 133.

92. Kimberly Phillips-Fein, "Top-Down Revolution: Businessmen, Intellectuals and Politicians against the New Deal, 1945–1964" (PhD diss., Columbia University, 2005); Michael Goldfield, *The Decline of Organized Labor in the United States* (Chicago: University of Chicago Press, 1987).

93. Michael A. Bernstein, *A Perilous Progress: Economists and Public Purpose in Twentieth-Century America* (Princeton, N.J.: Princeton University Press, 2001).

94. S. M. Amadae, *Rationalizing Capitalist Democracy: The Cold War Origins of Rational Choice Liberalism* (Chicago: University of Chicago Press, 2003).

95. James M. Buchanan, "Ethical Rules, Expected Values, and Large Numbers," *Ethics* 76, no. 1 (1965): 9.

96. Paul A. Samuelson, "The Pure Theory of Public Expenditure," *Review of Economics and Statistics* 36, no. 4 (1954): 387–89; Paul A. Samuelson, "Diagrammatic Exposition of a Theory of Public Expenditure," *Review of Economics and Statistics* 37, no. 4 (1955): 350–56.

97. Richard Musgrave, *Theory of Public Finance: At Study in Public Economy* (New York: McGraw Hill, 1959). The year before, Musgrave coedited with Alan Peacock an invaluable collection of primary texts, *Classics in the Theory of Public Finance* (New York: Macmillan, 1958).

98. James M. Buchanan, *Better than Plowing* (Chicago: University of Chicago Press, 1992), chap. 2.

99. James M. Buchanan, *The Demand and Supply of Public Goods* (Chicago: Rand McNally, 1968), especially chap. 5. In a fascinating exchange with Musgrave, Buchanan concedes that "empirically," people did not always seem to conduct themselves as the theory of the free rider predicted: see James M. Buchanan and Richard A. Musgrave, *Public Finance and Public Choice: Two Contrasting Visions of the State* (Cambridge, Mass.: MIT Press, 1999).

100. James Buchanan, "What Should Economists Do?" *Southern Economic Journal* 30, no. 3 (1964): 220.

101. Buchanan, "Ethical Rules, Expected Values, and Large Numbers," 9.

102. Ibid.

103. James Buchanan and Gordon Tulloch, *Calculus of Consent: Logical Foundations of Constitutional Democracy* (Ann Arbor: University of Michigan Press, 1962). Not the least irony of Buchanan's use of Wicksell was that the latter argued in 1896 that the democratic political reform of public finance would "transform into public activities proper many activities which today are left to private initiative" in "A New Principle of Just Taxation," in Musgrave and Peacock, *Classics in the Theory of Public Finance*, 73.

104. The journal began in 1966 as *Papers on Non-market Decision Making*

105. Mancur Olson, *The Logic of Collective Action: Public Goods and the Theory of Groups* (Cambridge, Mass.: Harvard University Press, 1965). Olson first distributed a draft through the U.S. Air Force Academy in 1963 as "The General Theory of Public Goods." For the influence of economists on political science, see also James A. Caporaso and David P. Levine, *Theories of Political Economy* (New York: Cambridge University Press, 1992), and Amadae, *Rationalizing Capitalist Democracy.*

106. Olson relished puncturing the arguments of the right-to-work movement by showing the logical necessity of the closed shop. He also went after liberal political theories of pluralistic interest or pressure groups and the broker state.

107. Olson, *Logic of Collective Action*, chap. 3.

108. Ibid., 93.

109. See articles in *Public Choice*, 1969–2004, passim; Jeffrey Henig, "Privatization in the United States: Theory and Practice," *Political Science Quarterly* 104, no. 4 (1989): 649–70.

110. See, for example, Geoffrey E. Nunn and Thayer H. Watkins, "Public Good Games," *Southern Economic Journal* 45, no. 2 (1978): 598–606; and Roy C. Evans and Frederick H. DeB. Harris, "A Bayesian Analysis of Free Rider Metagames," *Southern Economic Journal* 49, no. 1 (1982): 137–49.

111. James M. Buchanan, "Politics, Property, and the Law: An Alternative Interpretation of *Miller et al. v. Schoene*," *Journal of Law and Economics* 15, no. 2 (1972): 439–52, quotes on 443.

112. Although they rejected the very possibility of a collective subject, libertarians seldom troubled over the status of individual freedom within a corporate subject.

113. Richard A. Posner, "The Rule of Reason and the Economic Approach: Reflections on the Sylvania Decision," *University of Chicago Law Review* 45 (1977): 1–20; Richard A. Posner, "The Next Step in the Antitrust Treatment of Restricted Distribution: Per Se Legality," *University of Chicago Law Review* 48 (1981): 6–26. See also Posner, "Theories of Economic Regulation," *Bell Journal of Economics and Management Science* 5, no. 2 (1974): 344, 346–49; George J. Stigler, "Free Riders and Collective Action: An Appendix to Theories of Economic Regulation," *Bell Journal of Economics and Management Science* 5, no. 2 (1974): 359–65. For overviews, see Nicholas Mercuro and Steven G. Medema, *Economics and the Law*, 2d ed. (Princeton, N.J.: Princeton University Press, 2006); A. Allan Schmid, *Property, Power, and Public Choice: An Inquiry into Law and Economics* (New York: Praeger, 1987).

114. Robert C. Ellickson, *Order without Law: How Neighbors Settle Disputes* (Cambridge, Mass.: Harvard University Press, 1991); cf. an earlier pastoral tale by Terry Anderson and P. J. Hill, "The Evolution of Property Rights: A Study of the American West," *Journal of Law and Economics* 18, no. 1 (1975): 163.

115. Richard A. Posner, "Social Norms and the Law: An Economic Approach," *American Economic Review* 87, no. 2 (1997): 366, 368.

116. Hugh Stretton and Lionel Orchard, *Public Goods, Public Enterprise, Public Choice: Theoretical Foundations of the Contemporary Attack on Government* (New York: St. Martin's, 1994); Donald P. Green and Ian Shapiro, *Pathologies of Rational Choice Theory* (New Haven, Conn.: Yale University Press, 1994). For a response to Green and Shapiro, see Dennis C. Mueller, *Public Choice III* (Cambridge: Cambridge University Press, 2003), chap. 28.

117. Ferdinand von Prondyzynski, *Freedom of Association and Industrial Relations: A Comparative Study* (London: Mansell, 1987), and Lewis I. Leader, *Freedom of Association: A Study in Labor Law and Political Theory* (New Haven, Conn.: Yale University Press, 1992), provide valuable discussions of these debates and the practices of union security in different countries. See also M. G. Mitchnick, *Union Security and the Charter* (Toronto: Butterworths, 1987).

118. Among the salient law review articles, in addition to Abraham's "Individual Autonomy and Collective Empowerment in Labor Law," are Cynthia L. Estlund, "The Ossification of American Labor Law," *Columbia Law Review* 102 (2002): 1527–612; Karl E. Klare, "Judicial Deradicalizaiton of the Wagner Act and the Origins of Modern Legal Consciousness," *Minnesota Law Review* 62 (1978): 265–39; Karl E. Klare, "Labor Law as Ideology: Toward a New Historiography of Collective Bargaining Law," *Industrial Relations Law Journal* 4 (1981): 450–82; Katherine Van Wezel Stone, "The Post-war Paradigm in American Labor Law," *Yale Law Journal* 90 (1981): 1509.

13

Two Horwitzian Journeys

ASSAF LIKHOVSKI

FESTSCHRIFTS PROVIDE AN OPPORTUNITY TO ACKNOWLEDGE INTELLECTUAL debts, and my debt to Morty has been huge. Much of my academic career has been influenced by the Horwitzian depiction of antebellum American legal doctrines in *Transformation I.* The Horwitzian interest in judge-made law and the arguments made in that book about the ways in which common-law rules favored the powerful in society have been a source of inspiration for me ever since I first read his work as a law student in Israel in the early 1990s.

In this article, I would like to describe in some detail one of my first projects as a legal historian, written in the middle of the 1990s, as well as to briefly discuss one of my latest projects, which I have been working on in the last couple of years but have not yet completed. Both projects were inspired in some ways by *Transformation I.* Both are also about the transformation of *Transformation I,* as it migrated to non-American legal contexts and as its historiographical questions and interpretations were transformed as a result of their encounter with the specific legal texts and historical contexts that I was interested in.

Both of the projects that will be discussed in this article attempt to answer the question "What factors influence judicial decisions?" Both seek to show that class and economic interests, at least in some contexts, are not the major factors

---

I would like to thank Roy Kreitner, Pnina Lahav, and the participants of the law and politics workshop at Tel Aviv University for their comments, and Hephzibah Levine, Itamar Mann, and Adar Ortal for their assistance. Support for the research for this article was provided by the Israel Science Foundation (grant number 510/04). "An Arab, a Jew, and a Little English Girl" is based on chapter 3 of my book *Law and Identity in Mandate Palestine* (Chapel Hill: University of North Carolina Press, 2006). Segments of the project described in "A Duke, a Lady, and a Sofa" have been published in "Formalism and Israeli Anti-avoidance Doctrines in the 1950s and 1960s," in *Studies in the History of Tax Law,* vol. 1, ed. John Tiley (Oxford: Hart, 2004), 339; "The Story of Gregory," in *Business Tax Stories,* ed. Steven A. Bank and Kirk Stark (New York: Foundation Press, 2005), 89; and "Tax Law and Public Opinion: Explaining *IRC v. Duke of Westminster,*" in *Studies in the History of Tax Law,* vol. 2, ed. John Tiley (Oxford: Hart, 2007), 2:183.

that shape case law. This article is thus an opportunity for me to look back on more than a decade of work and reflect on how my work has been, to a large extent, an attempt to revisit the "Horwitz thesis" outlined in *Transformation I*, taking some explicit and implicit questions that Horwitz posed in that book, shifting their focus from legal doctrines and their economic effects to judicial minds and their relationship to culture and public opinion, and examining them in a number of non-American contexts. The ultimate lesson of this experience, I will conclude, is that the Horwitzian journey, a journey that seeks to study the links between politics and judge-made doctrines, is at once an inconclusive yet also a rewarding pursuit.[1]

AN ARAB, A JEW, AND A LITTLE ENGLISH GIRL

It was not easy being a student in Israeli law schools in the late 1980s and early 1990s. Back then there were very few Israeli scholars interested in legal history, and most of the courses offered by the Tel Aviv University Law School, where I was a student, were dry, black-letter, formalist courses. There were few exceptions to the generally stifling atmosphere that I encountered at the law school. One exception was a course on "legal systems"—a combination of comparative law, legal history, and sociology of law taught by Pnina Lahav and the late Leon Sheleff. Another exception was a course on American legal history taught by a visiting professor, Eben Moglen of Columbia Law School. Eben was the person who introduced me to Horwitz's work. At that time, I was studying for a joint history-law degree (a rare phenomenon in those days), and Eben's course convinced me that law was not as dry as I thought it was and that I could combine my interest in history and law and become a legal historian.

After graduating from the Tel Aviv University Law School, I went to Harvard in the fall of 1994. At first I thought that I would continue the work I had done as a history student in Israel. As a graduate student in the history department of Tel Aviv University, I wrote an MA thesis on Protestantism and radical reform of English law in the seventeenth century.[2] I was interested in examining the affinities between radical religious and legal thought, but I ultimately decided to abandon this topic and focus on colonial legal history instead. The decision to forsake law and religion and move to the study of law and colonialism was the result of my encounter with two books, one very famous and the other quite obscure.

When I came to Harvard, one of the first books I bought in one of the Harvard Square bookstores was Edward Said's *Orientalism*. I had been aware of the book for a long time, but in Israel I never read it. While Said's brand of cultural history is clearly flawed and problematic (as dozens of works have shown since *Orientalism* was first published thirty years ago), the book is also extremely interesting and challenging. The second book, the one that sealed my decision to focus on the legal history of colonialism rather than on law and religion, provided the perfect example of the power as well as the problems of the Saidian thesis. I still remember the day that I first encountered it in the library. It was autumn. The weather, which was fine when I arrived in Cambridge in the summer, had turned bitterly cold. Snow was falling, and I was sitting in the Widener library, searching the catalog for books on the subject "Palestine—Law." One of the entries that came up read *Palestine Parodies.*[3] The catalog said that the book was "printed for private circulation" in British-ruled Palestine in 1938. Its authors were identified as "Mustard and Cress." Who the hell were Mustard and Cress, and why was such a book cataloged under "law"?

When I found the book amid the dusty stacks, I discovered that it was written by a British judge in Palestine of the 1930s, and that the reason it was cataloged under "Palestine—Law" was that it was written in that particular English genre—the legal parody—well known from books like *Forensic Fables.*[4] The book contained numerous parodies of famous literary works transported to Palestine. For example, the first chapter of the book was entitled "Alice in Blunderland." It was modeled after Lewis Carroll's *Alice's Adventures in Wonderland*. One of the sections, called "Down the Souk," described Alice's visit to the Old City of Jerusalem, where she met with a group of scheming Arab politicians bent on establishing "the A.S.S." (Arab Supreme State). Another section of this chapter, called "The Pool of Tears," was about lazy British government officials frightened by the discovery of a lost government file. A third section, "The Municipal Tea Party," told the story of Alice's visit to the council room of the Jewish municipality of Tel Aviv, where the Mayor, the Engineer, and the Town Clerk (modeled after Lewis Carroll's Dormouse, Mad Hatter, and March Hare) conducted a demented council meeting. In one of the sections, entitled "A Visit to the Courts," Alice was taken to a government court in Tel Aviv, whose sleepy denizens acted as strangely as those who populated the court of the King and Queen of Hearts. This was exactly the kind of material I was looking for: a text that would allow me to gain access to the mentality of the British colonial rulers and would enliven the dry cases that later came to serve as the main sources of my history of law and colonialism in British-ruled Palestine.

Inspired by *Orientalism* and *Palestine Parodies*, Edward Said as well as Mustard and Cress, I embarked on a Horwitzian journey through the decisions of the Supreme Court of Mandatory Palestine, reading the reports of the court cover to cover, seeking to find in the hundreds of cases that were entombed in the dusty and crumbling pages of the law reports clues to the questions that intrigued me: Who were the strange and unfamiliar people who determined the fates of Arabs and Jews in Palestine in the early twentieth century? Was the colonial setting in which they functioned relevant to the legal doctrines they produced? Were the British judges animated by an Orientalist mentality of the type that Said was describing in his book? What other factors influenced the shape of judge-made doctrines in Palestine? Were their decisions connected to economic or political interests, or were they manifestations of cultural biases? And was it possible to write a history of judge-made law that ignored the personal and social background of specific judges and focused merely on the doctrines they produced?

Approaching the cases with these questions in mind, I soon discovered that among the hordes of cases of now long-forgotten litigants, one could indeed find real gems that were equal in many senses to the stories told in *Palestine Parodies*. Such gems were especially evident in tort cases that dealt with the application of Article XLVI of the Palestine Order in Council, 1922, which was the foundational constitutional document of British rule in Palestine. Three specific cases, one dealing with an Arab, another with a Jew, and a third with a little English girl, came to serve as the starting point of my story. This story would trace the transformation of a private law doctrine, but it would do so focusing on non-economic, cultural, and personal factors.

The Cases

In 1930, an Arab resident of Haifa, Dr. Caesar Khoury, fell into a hole dug by the municipality and fractured his shoulder blade. Would Dr. Khoury be compensated? The law of torts of Palestine was found in the Ottoman civil code, the *Mejelle*, which the British retained when they conquered the country at the end of the First World War. Did the *Mejelle* provide a remedy for cases of personal injury? No, said Judge Francis Baker, who wrote the opinion of the Supreme Court of Palestine. The *Mejelle* dealt with liability for damages caused by animals to property, but it was "silent" with regard to injuries caused to persons. Therefore, Dr. Khoury could not be compensated.[5]

In 1939, a Jewish resident of Tel Aviv, Feivel Danovitz, was run down by a truck. He sued the driver and the owner of the truck. The lower courts of Tel Aviv decided that because the *Mejelle* did not deal with liability for personal injury, there was a lacuna in the tort law of Palestine that could be filled by recourse to English common law in accordance with the provisions of Article XLVI of the Palestine Order in Council, 1922. According to Article XLVI, in the absence of Ottoman laws or local Palestinian legislation, the civil courts of Palestine were to exercise their jurisdiction "in conformity with . . . the substance of the common law, and the doctrines of equity in force in England . . . provided always that the said common law and doctrines of equity shall be in force in Palestine so far only as the circumstances of Palestine and its inhabitants . . . permit and subject to such qualifications as local circumstances render necessary." Because English common law recognized liability for personal injury, Danovitz could be compensated.

On appeal, however, the Supreme Court of Palestine rejected this argument. Judge Randolph Copland, who wrote the majority opinion, acknowledged that there was indeed a gap in the tort law of Palestine. But, said Copland, the proviso of Article XLVI prevented the importation of the English law of torts. The proviso stated that English law could be used by the courts only so far as "the circumstances of Palestine and its inhabitants . . . permit." The common law, said Copland, is a law based on the customs and habits of the English people, and "the customs and habits, mode of life, mode of thought and character of the English people are very different from those of the inhabitants of Palestine. . . . It would be a grave injustice to force on another country a customary law which is founded on the totally different customs and habits of a totally different race."[6]

Dissatisfaction with the *Sherman* decision led to the promulgation of the Civil Wrongs Ordinance of 1944.[7] The ordinance, however, came into effect only in July 1947. By then, the Supreme Court of Palestine had reversed the *Sherman* decision and declared that English tort law was indeed applicable to Palestine. This reversal was caused by a little English girl.

Stephanie Constance Orr, the daughter of the chief registrar of the Supreme Court of Palestine, was born in 1943 in a Jerusalem hospital belonging to the London Society for Promoting Christianity among the Jews. While she was still in the hospital, a hot water bottle was placed in Stephanie's cot. The bottle had a hole. It leaked and Stephanie Orr was permanently crippled. Her parents sued the London Society. At first glance, it appeared that in view of the *Sherman* decision, the Orrs were bound to lose.[8] The Supreme Court, however, decided otherwise. In May 1947, exactly a year before the end of British rule in Palestine, *Sherman* was overruled. In his decision, Chief Justice William FitzGerald explained that *Sherman* was no longer applicable. If in 1940 there were circumstances that prevented the application of the English law of torts, said FitzGerald, they did not exist anymore. "There is now in Palestine," he said "a population of 600,000 Jews with western ideas of culture and western ideas of commerce. There is a progressive Arab population of one and a half million, also with strong cultural and commercial ties with Europe." The circumstances of Palestine and its inhabitants did not bar the importation of the English law of torts.[9]

Law and Identity

How can the positions of different British judges on the applicability of English law to Palestine be explained? Would a Horwitzian instrumental explanation assist us? Obviously, it would be difficult to rely on a direct analogy to the American cases. British judges had little incentive to reshape the law of Palestine in order to promote economic growth or in order to serve the interests of local capitalists, be they Jewish or Arab. The economic and social setting of Palestine in the early twentieth century was simply not equivalent to that of the United States in the early nineteenth century. But what about the personal interests of judges? One possible way to explain the transformation of the law of torts of

Palestine between *Sherman* and *Orr* would be to view the decision in *Orr* as an example of the important role of empathy in judicial decisions. Judge Orr was the registrar of the Supreme Court, and British judges were obviously more inclined to rule in favor of the young daughter of a close British colleague than to assist an unfamiliar Arab or a Jew. There were also practical considerations that might have led to the different decisions in *Sherman* and *Orr*: the desire to let the public insure itself before imposing tort liability, or the fear of overloading the courts with tort claims.[10]

However, an explanation based simply on the role of judicial empathy is not sufficient. As I immersed myself in the cases and in the biographical and historical context of the decisions of the Supreme Court of Palestine, I came to realize that one could also read them as expressions of conflicting cultural images of British rulers and Jewish and Arab subjects. *Sherman* and *Orr* could not be read simply as manifestations of the direct interests of the judges who decided them. Instead, they reflected two conflicting notions about identity within the British judiciary in Palestine. After all, before looking for hidden motives, one needs to consider the explicit justifications used by the judges, and the contradictory justifications used in *Sherman* and *Orr* in order to reject and then to justify the importation of English tort doctrines into the law of Palestine manifested conflicting notions of identity based on different answers to the question whether "the character of the English people" was or was not "very different from [that] of the inhabitants of Palestine."

Notions of "Englishness," as well as notions of Arab and Jewish identity, I discovered, often influenced decisions concerning the importation of English law into Palestine. Because Article XLVI required the courts to determine whether the specific circumstances of Palestine and its inhabitants allowed the importation of specific English norms, it forced the judges of Palestine to reveal their opinions about the country and its inhabitants, to compare the English to Arabs and Jews, and to discuss similarities and differences between them. The cases that interpreted Article XLVI were, therefore, an important locus where law and identity interacted in the decisions of the courts of Palestine. One could thus trace a slow and gradual evolution in the willingness to import English law, a development that paralleled changes in the composition of the British judiciary in Palestine and in British notions of the identity of self and other. In this respect, a comparison between the Supreme Court of Palestine of the 1920s and early 1930s and the Supreme Court of the 1940s would be instructive.

During the 1920s and early 1930s, the Supreme Court of Palestine was usually quick to state that differences between the law of Palestine and the law of England prevented the application of English norms, and quantitatively, there was little importation of English law. Why did the Supreme Court of Palestine ignore Article XLVI during the first fifteen years of the mandate? There were some objective barriers to the introduction of English law. English legal literature was not readily available in Palestine at the time. Many local lawyers, as well as some British judges, were unfamiliar with English law.[11] Perhaps there was also less pressure to import English norms because the massive development of the economy occurred mainly in the 1930s (due to the influx of German Jewish immigrants and capital) and the 1940s (when Palestine became a major supply center of the British army in the Middle East). Finally, the reason may rest on the style of the early decisions of the courts of Palestine, which, in the 1920s, tended to be very brief. It is therefore often difficult to discern the specific reasons that led the judges to decide a case one way or the other. However, it is also possible to attribute the reluctance to use English law to British notions of self and other.

One can imagine a spectrum of British attitudes on the appropriate balance between local and English law in the colonies. On one end of this spectrum was a "traditional" approach that viewed English law as superior and local law as inferior. According to this approach, English law could not be introduced into the colonies because the natives were inferior and therefore had to be governed by their own local laws, which were appropriate to their level of civilization. A middle position on this spectrum would be that English law was superior to local law and therefore could be introduced into the legal system as part of the "civilizing mission" of the British. Finally, at the opposite end of the spectrum, one would find a position according to which the natives and the English were equal and English law and local law were comparable. Therefore, those parts of English law that were better than the comparable parts of local law should be introduced, and those parts that were inferior should not.

Many of the judges of the Supreme Court of Palestine in the 1920s and early 1930s came from a cultural and professional background that would have made them more amenable to the "traditional" approach. The first chief justice, Sir Thomas Haycraft, was a barrister and a veteran of the colonial service. Before coming to Palestine, Haycraft served as a judge in Cyprus, Gibraltar, Mauritius, and Grenada.[12] He was considered a conservative judge.[13] Age may have played an important role in his conservatism. Palestine was the last station in Haycraft's long colonial career. He came to Palestine in 1921, at the age of sixty-two.[14]

Another Supreme Court judge in the 1920s was Owen Corrie. Corrie was described by Judge Gad Frumkin, the only Jewish Supreme Court judge, as "a graduate of Eton and Cambridge and a member of the English bar" who "saw himself as superior to his British colleagues . . . and it goes without saying that he snubbed his non-British ones, and attempted to erect a barrier between himself and them." In 1936, Corrie became the chief justice of the Fiji Islands. "He liked ceremonies," said Frumkin, "and when he was transferred to Fiji as chief justice, he enjoyed the rites which accompany such an office in a far-away colony. He told his friends about the number of boats and servants he had and sent them a photo of himself in his official dress with a black boy holding the fringes of his gown."[15]

Similar comments were made about Michael McDonnell, the second chief justice. McDonnell was Irish. He was educated in a public school—St. Paul—and then at the University of Cambridge.[16] In 1909, when McDonnell was only twenty-seven years old, he wrote the official history of St. Paul.[17] The 500-page book was based on meticulous historical research, but in essence, it is merely a list of the achievements of St. Paul's graduates throughout the ages: the academic and athletic prizes they won, the books they wrote, the various positions they held in the British government. It is the work of a conservative young man convinced of the superiority of his education and the tradition he represents. It is no wonder that some contemporaries described him as a "hard-bound, die-hard conservative . . . full of tradition and precedents."[18] McDonnell's conservatism may have been augmented by a dislike for the "cosmopolitan" and "proletarian" Jews of Palestine and by a general pro-Arab inclination, which eventually led to his forced resignation during the Arab rebellion of 1936.[19]

Randolph Copland, who wrote the *Sherman* decision in 1940, was made in the same mold. Copland was a graduate of the University of Cambridge who had served for a long time as a judge in the district courts of Palestine, finally being appointed to the Supreme Court of Palestine in 1936. Frumkin described him as "cynical" and mainly interested in deciding cases in the fastest possible way (his nickname was "the Broom").[20]

Haycraft, Corrie, McDonnell, and Copland were all reluctant to use English law. They seem to have viewed Article XLVI as giving the judges discretion to turn to English law if they thought it appropriate. They rejected the idea that in certain cases the locals could claim English rights or remedies by virtue of the article. Their attitude, it seems, stemmed in part from their notions of identity, from a strong self-other view of the population of Palestine that prevented them from thinking that English law was applicable to the local population.

The Supreme Court of the late 1940s and especially its chief justice, William FitzGerald, were very different. FitzGerald was the former attorney general of Palestine. He was portrayed by contemporary observers as "a warm hearted eloquent Irishman," less committed to the preservation of British imperial traditions than the earlier generation of judges (his relatives were involved in the struggle for Irish home rule). Unlike the first generation of British judges, who tended to erect formal barriers between themselves and the local litigants and judges, FitzGerald viewed local judges as his equals and strove to abolish discrimination between native and British judges.[21] FitzGerald's decision in *Orr*, as well as many other decisions of his, reflected this background.

One can see the link between identity and attitudes toward the importation of English law even more clearly when one contrasts the *Orr* decision with its immediate predecessor, the Sherman decision of 1940. Judge Copland, who wrote the decision in *Sherman,* viewed Palestinian and English societies as static. He was unwilling to recognize changes in the composition of society, and he emphasized the more stable aspects of life ("customs and habits, mode of life, mode of thought and character").[22] FitzGerald's decision in *Orr* described Palestinian society as dynamic, both in recognizing changes in it and in focusing on those aspects of personality that could be changed easily, such as "ideas of culture and commerce" or "cultural and commercial ties."[23]

Copland based his decision on the traditional colonial dichotomy. His world was divided into two entities, each with its own distinct identity—the English on one hand, and the people of Palestine on the other. In his world, the barrier between colonial ruler and local subjects was impassable, because the subjects were required to change the most immutable aspects of their identity, their "race" or "character." FitzGerald lived in a different world. The English now belonged to a broader category—the West (or Europe). The inhabitants of Palestine were no longer an undifferentiated mass. Instead, they were divided into two categories—Jews and Arabs. The barriers between categories were not rigid. What was required of the Jews and Arabs now was not the impossible feat of changing their "character" or "race." All they had to do was adopt Western ways of commerce and culture. *Sherman* and *Orr* thus represented two different conceptions of Palestinian and English identity, both of which had supporters among the British judiciary in Palestine.

The decisions of the Supreme Court of Palestine on Article XLVI were thus not a product of rational doctrinal evolution, nor were they simply a reflection of nonlegal economic or political interests of the sort that Horwitz discussed in his description of antebellum American law. Instead, they were determined by the identities of various British judges, and their views of the local "others." The more conservative judges—those who refused to import English law and at the same time saw English law as superior to local law—were those judges who viewed the locals, both Arabs and Jews, in the familiar Orientalist fashion as different (and inferior). The less conservative judges, those who were both more willing to use English law and willing to recognize its defects, were those judges whose notion of identity was less rigid. Judicial interpretations of Article XLVI were thus mirrors of identity, in the sense that they reflected the self-definitions of British judges in Palestine, as well as their understandings of the identity of their others—the Jews and Arabs.

Colonial identities were obviously merely one factor among many. Institutional considerations (different perceptions of the role of judges and legislature or different perceptions of the independence of the law of Palestine), differences in knowledge of local law, and the narrow self-interests of judges (preventing as much litigation as possible or the desire to assist the daughter of a close colleague) all played a part in determining the specific path that the judicial interpretations of Article XLVI took. Ultimately, I came to realize, it would be impossible to estimate the specific weight of each factor, including identity, in influencing judicial outcomes.

A DUKE, A LADY, AND A SOFA

My early Horwitzian journey into the case law of Palestine provided me with an example of the difficulty of translating the class-based instrumental argument used in *Transformation I* to non-American settings, in which national identities rather than class may have played a major role in shaping the case law. But in some sense, the story I told was merely a variation of the Horwitzian thesis, since in the British Empire, race (or ethnic origin) replaced class as the major category used to create social hierarchy.[24]

However, whether it was race that played a major role in shaping the decisions or whether it was class, one thing that bothered me was the fact that I could not determine the relative weight of these and other factors in shaping the case law. Perhaps, I reasoned, the problem was found in my historiographical brush. A macro-history, albeit that of a single court (the Supreme Court of Palestine) during a relatively brief period of time (thirty years), is simply not accurate enough. It assumes a coherence in a set of decisions by a single court, or even a single judge, which simply cannot exist, given the fact that institutions and even personal views are dynamic rather than static.

My next Horwitzian journey would therefore focus on a small set of specific landmark cases, trying to provide as thick a description as possible of these cases, replacing historiographical breadth with depth. Such a description would, of course, be sensitive to the doctrinal context in which the cases were decided, but it would be more focused on the multiple layers of nonlegal contexts that influenced the judicial outcome. I would seek to uncover the economic, political, social, cultural, and institutional background of the cases, creating (so I believed at the time) a more precise description of judicial motivations. The project would also be comparative, enabling me to look at the way the same legal question was dealt with by different courts in different countries. What legal doctrines would I use?

When I came back to Israel, I began teaching comparative law and legal history, but I also had to teach a "real" legal subject. My dean at the time said that I could choose one of three subjects: civil procedure, conflict of laws, or taxation. Civil procedure and conflict of laws are taught in Israel in the fourth and final year of law school, when most law students have already long lost their interest in law. I was therefore not very happy with the first two choices. Fortunately, there was a third choice: I could teach taxation. This choice seemed to me more appealing. Taxation was a third- rather than a fourth-year course, and it seemed more interdisciplinary than the procedural courses. I therefore gladly embraced the offer to become a tax professor. Most of my colleagues, when they heard this, thought that I was either very brave or very foolish. At first I too was a bit apprehensive, but soon I discovered that unlike other areas of law, the legal history of taxation is an almost totally unexplored field, and I knew that I made the right choice.

One of my first projects as a tax historian was to reconstruct the history of tax avoidance doctrines in the Anglo-American world. Avoidance—the reduction of one's taxes through the abuse of gaps or loopholes in the law—is always a hot topic for tax scholars, but the history of the creation and transformation of judicial anti-avoidance doctrines, in the United States and elsewhere, has received very little attention.

One rare exception is a study of the judicial decisions of the House of Lords in the twentieth century. This study was written in 1978 by legal historian Robert B. Stevens.[25] Since a large portion of the cases heard by the House of Lords have been tax cases, Stevens had to pay close attention to the development of tax doctrines. Like Horwitz in *Transformation I,* Stevens's interpretation of the cases was a class-based one showing how judicial doctrines were tilted in favor of the wealthy. According to Stevens, the decisions of the House of Lords on tax avoidance could be read as a reflection of the political ideology of the law lords. In the late nineteenth century, Stevens argued, the courts did not treat tax statutes differently from other statutes, and their overall approach did not seem to favor the taxpayers. But then matters changed in the early twentieth century. With the introduction of a progressive income tax in Britain in 1909, a formalist, pro-taxpayer stance on tax interpretation and tax avoidance came to dominate the decisions of the House of Lords. This stance, which enabled the wealthy to avoid taxation, can be partly attributed to the fact that many of the law lords sought to serve the interests and protect the wealth of "the established sections of society."[26]

One of the major examples used by Stevens to illustrate this argument was the infamous *Duke of Westminster* case, decided by the House of Lords in 1935. In this case, the law lords used a formalist approach to avoidance in order to allow the wealthiest man in Britain to artificially reduce his tax burden. *Duke of Westminster,* argued Stevens, was the logical outcome of a long line of cases in which the law lords sought to prevent the use of taxation for the redistribution of wealth in Britain.[27]

After reading Stevens's book, I thought that it would be interesting to examine whether his argument was also relevant to the Israeli and American contexts. Ultimately, I also decided to revisit the English case and describe in more detail the legal and nonlegal contexts in which it was decided. My project thus became a comparative micro-history of landmark tax avoidance cases in three jurisdictions: the United Kingdom, the United States, and Israel. What I discovered was that while class interests certainly played a role in the outcome of these and many other tax avoidance cases, other factors, most notably the dynamics of public opinion at the time that a particular tax avoidance case was decided, as well as non-political tax administration concerns, were as important as politics and class in determining the shape of judicial anti-avoidance doctrines.

The Cases

Hugh Richard Arthur, the second Duke of Westminster, was a spoiled playboy and a Nazi sympathizer to boot. He was also the wealthiest man in Britain in the 1930s, and naturally, his legal advisers invested a great deal of effort in devising ways to protect his wealth from taxation.[28] One of the schemes he used was paying his servants deductable annuities instead of non-deductable salaries. This scheme became the subject of *IRC v. Duke of Westminster*, decided by the House of Lords in May 1935. The duke won. "Every man," said Lord Tomlin, "is entitled if he can, to order his affairs so as that the tax attaching under the appropriate Acts is less than it otherwise would be. If he succeeds in ordering them so as to secure this result, then, however unappreciative the Commissioners of Inland Revenue or his fellow taxpayers may be of his ingenuity, he cannot be compelled to pay an increased tax."[29]

At the very time at which the House of Lords was deciding the *Duke of Westminster* case, a similar tax avoidance case, that of a Brooklyn woman, was moving through the American legal system, with very different results. This was the case of Evelyn Gregory, the widow of the private secretary of the multimillionaire banker and philanthropist V. Everit Macy. *Gregory* involved a spinoff transaction pursued by Gregory merely to reduce her tax burden. However, in the American case, the judges decided in favor of the state rather than the taxpayer. In *Gregory v. Helvering,* decided by Judge Learned Hand of the Second Circuit in March 1934 and affirmed by the U.S. Supreme Court in January 1935, the court ruled that while the spinoff transaction in question was literally covered by the words of the Revenue Act of 1928, which exempted "corporate reorganizations" from taxation, it was not, in substance, one of the transactions that the Revenue Act intended to exempt.

Just "as a melody is more than the notes," said Judge Hand in his decision, so the "meaning of a sentence may be more than that of the separate words." The purpose of the section exempting reorganizations from taxation "is plain enough; men engaged in enterprises . . . might wish to consolidate, or divide, to add to, or subtract from, their holdings. Such transactions were not to be considered as 'realizing' any profit, because the collective interests still remained in solution. But the underlying presupposition is plain that the readjustment shall be undertaken for reasons germane to the conduct of the venture in hand, not as an ephemeral incident, egregious to its prosecution. To dodge the shareholders' taxes is not one of the transactions contemplated as corporate reorganizations."[30] *Gregory* was thus the exact opposite of the *Duke of Westminster* case. While the *Duke of Westminster* enshrined a formalist approach to tax avoidance in England and Commonwealth countries for most of the twentieth century, Learned Hand's substantive approach to avoidance came to dominate American cases ever since the 1930s.

The third and last case whose history I chose to examine was a case of *Mefi Ltd. v. Assessing Officer,* decided by Israel's Supreme Court in 1967.[31] This case marked the transition of Israeli tax avoidance doctrines from the formalist, pro-taxpayer, English-inspired *Duke of Westminster* approach to a more substantive, anti-taxpayer *Gregory*-like approach.

Mefi was a case involving the purchase of a loss-making corporation that manufactured furniture in order to offset its losses against income made by the purchasers. Israel has a legislative general anti-avoidance provision that allows the Revenue to disregard "artificial transactions."[32] The main question before the Israeli Supreme Court was, therefore, whether the transaction was indeed "artificial." Before the decision in *Mefi,* the term "artificial" was interpreted by the courts as referring to any transaction that was "uncommon." Such an approach, which examined the form of the transaction rather than the motivation of taxpayers, tended to favor taxpayers.

Justice Moshe Silberg, who wrote the leading opinion in *Mefi,* rejected this interpretation of the term "artificiality." Silberg noted that such an interpretation would protect tax avoidance transactions because once a transaction reduces one's taxes, it would become common. Silberg therefore suggested a new, substantive, purpose-oriented notion of artificiality. The question that should be asked, he said, was whether the transaction in question had any substance apart from its tax consequences.

Public Opinion and Tax Administration

How can one explain the decisions in the three cases? Robert Stevens read the English cases (and would probably read the American and Israeli ones) as reflecting the political ideology of the judges. While I did find a few indications that political ideology and class interests influenced the attitude of some English, American, and Israeli judges toward tax avoidance, I believe that the political ideologies of the judges were not the major explanatory factor. Instead, judicial responses to short-term fluctuations in public opinion in the English and American cases, and judicial concerns with the efficiency of the tax administration machinery in the Israeli case, played an important role in shaping the outcomes of the specific cases I studied.

Tax avoidance decisions are influenced by the complex pull of various factors. Avoidance undermines trust in government.[33] However, a substantive interventionist approach to avoidance by the courts blurs the boundary between the legislature and the other branches of government and undermines the notion of the rule of law.[34] The courts are thus constantly pulled in two opposite directions: on one hand, the desire to intervene in tax avoidance cases in order to contribute their share to the battle against tax avoidance and, on the other, a desire to preserve the notion of the rule of law by leaving this task to the legislature. These opposing forces mean that the specific result in tax avoidance cases is never predetermined but is instead the outcome of particular conditions existing at the time of the decision: when economic conditions worsen, tax avoidance often becomes a source of public concern and even public scandal. The courts are then forced to treat avoidance harshly. Conversely, when economic conditions improve, tax avoidance is no longer viewed as a matter of general public concern. Public opinion is not enraged by the use of tax avoidance schemes to undermine the fairness of the tax system. In such circumstances, courts tend to adopt a more formalist, pro-taxpayer, and passive attitude to avoidance, leaving the matter to the legislature.

This model of judicial behavior in tax avoidance cases is the one that I think can best explain the outcome of such cases as *Duke of Westminster.* In order to explain the decision, one has to trace the ebb and flow of public concern with tax avoidance and its companion phenomenon, tax evasion (that is, the reduction of the tax burden by criminal means) in Britain in the early twentieth century. Such a history of public opinion and tax avoidance, based on both quantitative and qualitative methods, reveals that British public opinion was not concerned with tax avoidance and evasion in the period leading up to the decision in *Duke of Westminster* in May 1935. While tax avoidance increasingly captured the attention of accountants and lawyers in the early 1930s, it was not until 1936 that the issue came to the attention of the general public. As long as there was no public pressure to deal effectively with avoidance, the law lords did not feel compelled to intervene.

In addition to the lack of pressure from public opinion, judicial passivity in the *Duke of Westminster* case was also the result of the specific institutional culture of English courts. In England, courts were not viewed as the proper institution to deal with the problem of avoidance. Instead, as some of the judges who decided such cases expressly said, the problem was seen as one that should be resolved by the executive and legislative branches of government. This was not merely a rhetorical ploy to justify judicial passivity. Revenue and treasury officials too did not consider the judiciary an appropriate forum for tackling tax avoidance. Indeed, following the rise to power of Nazism in 1933, judicial intervention became even more problematic, because at least some observers came to identify a substantive approach by the courts to tax avoidance with the legal practices of Nazi courts, especially after a German Supreme Fiscal Court case in 1935 declared that all tax laws should be interpreted according to the National Socialist weltanschauung and that tax avoidance was an offence against "the loyalty the citizens owe to one another and to the country."[35]

The same impact of short-term changes in public opinion can be seen in *Gregory,* the American case. *Gregory*'s substantive anti-taxpayer approach was the result of the immediate political context in which the case was decided, rather than any long-term ideological convictions of the judges in that case. Specifically, the decision was mainly the result of the influence of tax avoidance and tax evasion scandals that captured newspaper headlines in the United States in the period immediately preceding the decision, especially the attempt by the FDR administration to indict Andrew Mellon, the former secretary of the treasury, for tax evasion.[36] Thus, in the months and weeks before Judge Hand decided *Gregory*, leading American newspapers such as the *New York Times* contained many reports accusing the former secretary of treasury of tax evasion and tax avoidance. It seems therefore reasonable to speculate that these reports had some influence on Judge Hand's decision in *Gregory*.

The argument that there is indeed a direct link between short-term concerns of public opinion with avoidance and a substantive approach is enhanced by the fact that Learned Hand had no clear and consistent view on these matters. Thus, soon after *Gregory* was decided, Hand reverted to a more conservative approach to tax avoidance in *Chisholm v. Commissioner*, decided in July 1935, six months after the Supreme Court's decision in *Gregory*.[37] *Chisholm*'s facts—appreciated shares were sold indirectly through a partnership in order to minimize the taxes—were quite similar to the facts in *Gregory*. The Board of Tax Appeals found for the commissioner, based on the argument that the transaction was not "bona fide." This decision, however, was reversed by Judge Hand. Hand distinguished this case from *Gregory* by noting that the partnership in this case had continued existence, unlike the transitory nature of the spinoff corporation discussed in *Gregory*.[38] But the real reason that Hand distinguished *Chisholm* from *Gregory* may be found in the internal memos of the three judges who decided the case. These memos reveal that the judges apparently felt that they had released the substantive genie from its bottle and that they regretted having done so.[39]

Finally, in the Israeli study, which examined the transition from a formalist to a substantive approach to tax avoidance in Israel of the 1950s and 1960s, I show that while a liberal ideology and pro-taxpayer sentiments may have played a certain role in the propagation of a formalist approach to tax avoidance, the main cause of judicial formalism was administrative inefficiency—the inability of the Israeli Revenue to deal effectively with tax evasion, let alone tax avoidance.[40]

The social history of tax compliance in Israel in the first decade after Israeli independence in 1948 is one of widespread evasion and a massive breakdown in tax compliance. During the last decade of the British Mandate in Palestine, the Jews established a large-scale voluntary tax system that financed illegal Jewish immigration and an autonomous Jewish military apparatus. However, after independence, levels of compliance dropped dramatically. This drop can be attributed to the heavy burden of taxation, to economic hardship, and to the fact that the relative cohesiveness of pre-independence Israeli society disappeared as post-1948 Israel absorbed huge waves of non-ideological Jewish refugees fleeing post-Holocaust Europe and the Middle East.

When the government cannot collect taxes, judges are also reluctant to collect them or they view certain forms of noncompliance, such as tax avoidance (which seemingly is based on obedience to the law), as more benign. The inefficiency of the tax collection machinery and the fact that many Israelis were simply evading their taxes contributed to the adoption of a passive, formalist, pro-taxpayer approach to tax avoidance. Judges were not willing to aggressively intervene in tax avoidance transactions as long as the state was unable to crack down on the cruder, more deplorable, and far more widespread phenomenon of tax evasion. Once the Israeli tax collection machinery became more efficient in the early 1960s and tax compliance rose, judges renounced their previous formalist and passive approach to avoidance and adopted a substantive approach in cases such as *Mefi*.

CONCLUSION

Morty was one of my intellectual fathers. Like many sons, I tried to rebel, but as a historian I know that you cannot really escape your past. My research agenda was, and still is, influenced in various ways by his work.[41] Many of my research projects are based on questions that I first asked myself while reading *Transformations I* as a young law student in Israel of the early 1990s. These projects seek to understand judge-made law, its sources, and its impact and aim to show that at least in some (American and non-American) contexts, the political and redistributive functions of law are not the only or indeed the major ways to explain the development of judicial doctrines.

Looking back on more than a decade spent in Horwitzian journeys, I now understand that the journeys were more important than the destination. Having read countless decisions of courts around the globe, I realize that my research projects have, in certain ways, been misconceived. The attempt to uncover judicial motivations, which has been the major goal of my research in both of the projects described in this article, is futile.

There is no way to discover why judges decide the way they do. Autonomous legal considerations; policy preferences; political ideology; jurisprudential notions; institutional constraints; strategic behavior; cultural biases; the influence of public opinion; the personality of judges, litigants, and lawyers; and countless other factors are all involved. Sorting them out and determining which of these factors influenced a specific decision or indeed a series of decisions is often an impossible task. Whether we use the broad-brush Horwitzian approach to the history of judicial doctrines, such as the one applied in *Transformation I*; the more nuanced, complex, thicker, and culturally sensitive methodology used by Horwitz in his later work; a biographical approach focusing on specific judges rather than on the development of specific doctrines; a micro-history of specific landmark cases; or even the "hard" quantitative methodology so favored by political scientists engaged in the study of judicial behavior, we will never really solve the mystery and reach the promised land of certain answers to what is, ultimately, a literary, interpretative pursuit.[42] But as one of Morty's favorite lawyers, Oliver Wendell Holmes, said long ago in another context, "certainty generally is illusion, and repose is not the destiny of man."[43] I, at least, am certain that I will keep following the road that Morty first inspired me to explore.

NOTES

1. The Horwitzian project, of course, has itself changed in the three decades since *Transformation I* was published in 1977. Some of my other projects, such as my attempt to argue in favor of a comparative transnational history of modern legal thought, have also been written against the backdrop of Horwitz's work, especially the type of American-centered intellectual history of legal thought that characterizes *Transformation II.* See Assaf Likhovski, "Czernowitz, Lincoln and Jerusalem and the Comparative History of American Legal Thought," *Theoretical Inquiries in Law* 4 (2003): 621.

2. See Assaf Likhovski, "Protestantism and Radical Reform of English Law: A Variation on a Theme by Weber," *Law and Society Review* 33 (1999): 365.

3. Mustard and Cress, *Palestine Parodies* (Tel Aviv: Printed for private circulation by Azriel Press, 1938).

4. O, *Forensic Fables* (London: Butterworth, 1926).

5. CA 88/30 *Municipality of Haifa v. Khoury, Collection of Judgments of the Courts of Palestine,* ed. Max D. Friedman, comp. Leon Rotenberg (1932), 4:1343.

6. CA 113/40 *Sherman v. Danovitz,* 7 Palestine Law Reports 363, 367–68 (1940).

7. Gad Tedeschi and Abraham Rosenthal, *Pkudat ha-Nezikin le'or Toldot Hit'havuta ve-Tikuneha* [The Civil Wrongs Ordinance in Light of the History of Its Preparation and Amendments] (Tel Aviv: Masada, 1962/3), iii–vii.

8. The defendants moved to dismiss the case on the grounds that no cause of action had been shown. Judge Curry of the District Court of Jerusalem rejected their motion but nevertheless said that "it appears to me at present that the respondent [Orr] is unlikely to succeed." Motion 6/46 *Rendle v. Orr,* 1946 S.C.D.C. 94, 95 (1946) (Jerusalem District Court).

9. CA 29/47 *London Society for Promoting Christianity among the Jews v. Orr,* 14 Palestine Law Reports 218, 223 (1947).

10. Tedeschi and Rosenthal, *Pkudat ha-Nezikin,* vii.

11. Malchi, *Toldot,* 14, 144; Edward Keith-Roach, *Pasha of Jerusalem: Memoirs of a District Commissioner under the British Mandate,* ed. Paul Eedle (London: Radcliffe Press, 1994), 75; S. G. Kermack, "Memoirs of Time in Judicial Service, Palestine, 1920–30" (unpublished typewritten manuscript, Middle East Centre, St. Antony's College, Oxford), 2.

12. See A. H. M. Kirk-Greene, *A Biographical Dictionary of the British Colonial Service, 1939–1966* (London: H. Zell, 1991), 163; Gad Frumkin, *Derekh Shofet bi-Yerushalayim* [The Life of a Jerusalem Judge] (Tel Aviv: Dvir, 1954), 243–44; Eliakim Rubinstein, *Shofte Arets: Le-Reshito uli-Dmuto shel bet ha-Mishpat ha-'Elyon be-Yisra'el* [Judges of the Land: The Early Years of the Supreme Court of Israel] (Tel Aviv: Schocken, 1980), 20.

13. Horace B. Samuel, *Unholy Memories of the Holy Land* (London: L. and V. Woolf and Hogarth Press, 1930), 185; Eliezer Malchi, "Hitpathutam shel Bate ha-Mishpat be-Tel Aviv" [The Development of Courts in Tel Aviv], *Ha-Rashut ha-Shofetet* 28 (1998): 60, 63.

14. Frumkin, *Derekh Shofet*, 243–44.

15. Ibid., 238–39. See also Kirk-Greene, *Biographical Dictionary*, 78.

16. Norman Bentwich, *A Wanderer between Two Worlds* (London: Kegan Paul, 1941), 5–6; Helen Bentwich, *Tidings from Zion: Helen Bentwich's Letters from Jerusalem, 1919–1931,* ed. Jennifer Glynn (London: I. B. Tauris, 2000), 153; Kirk-Greene, *Biographical Dictionary*, 231.

17. Michael F. J. McDonnell, *A History of St. Paul's School* (London: Chapman and Hall, 1909).

18. Helen Bentwich, *Tidings from Zion*, 153.

19. Bernard Wasserstein, *The British in Palestine: The Mandatory Government and the Arab-Jewish Conflict, 1917–1929,* 2d ed. (Oxford: B. Blackwell, 1991), 214–15; Frumkin, *Derekh Shofet*, 343; Rubinstein, *Shofte Arets*, 20–21; Naomi Shepherd, *Ploughing Sand: British Rule in Palestine, 1917–1948* (London: John Murray, 1999), 187–89; Central Zionist Archives, Jerusalem, J 108/12, *Histadrut 'Orkhe ha-Din ha-Yehudim be-Erets Yisra'el: Protocol ha-Mo'etsa ha-Shishit* [Jewish Bar Association: Protocol of the Sixth Council, 1937], 1; HC 11/30 *Attorney General v. Rubashoff,* 1 Palestine Law Reports 876, 880, 882 (1930); HC 44/36 *El Qasir v. Attorney General,* 3 Palestine Law Reports 121 (1936); "Chief Justice to Retire," *Palestine Post*, Sept. 19, 1936.

20. Frumkin, *Derekh Shofet*, 348–49.

21. Norman Bentwich, *My 77 Years: An Account of My Life and Times, 1883–1960* (Philadelphia: Jewish Publication Society, 1961), 210; Frumkin, *Derekh Shofet*, 466; Haim Steinberg, "Zikhronot mi-Yom Petihat beyt ha-Mishpat ha-'Elyon bi-Yerushalayim u-Mishnotav ha-rishonot" [Memories from the Opening of the Supreme Court in Jerusalem and Its First Years], *Ha-Rashut ha-Shofetet* 28 (1998): 26, 30–31. An interesting summary of his views can be found in William FitzGerald, "The Law in the Era of Reconstruction," *Ha-Praklit* 1 (June 1944): 5–11.

22. CA 113/40 *Sherman v. Danovitz*, 7 Palestine Law Reports 363, 367–68 (1940).

23. CA 29/47 *London Society for Promoting Christianity among the Jews v. Orr*, 14 Palestine Law Reports 218, 223 (1947).

24. For a different argument, one that suggests that class was as important as race in the British Empire, see David Canadine, *Ornamentalism: How the British Saw Their Empire* (London: Allen Lane, 2001).

25. Robert Bocking Stevens, *Law and Politics: The House of Lords as a Judicial Body, 1800–1976* (Chapel Hill: University of North Carolina Press, 1978).

26. Ibid., 170–76, 264.

27. Ibid., 206–8. Stevens also mentions other factors that influenced judicial opinion such as the rise of a formalist, "scientific," "professional" approach to judicial lawmaking (183–84, 191–97).

28. See Leslie Field, *Bendor: The Golden Duke of Westminster* (London: Weidenfeld & Nicolson, 1983), 1–2, 100, 106–7, 146, 260, 263. See also G.E.C., *The Complete Peerage,* vol. 12, pt. 2 (London: St. Catherine Press, 1959), 541–44.

29. *IRC v. Duke of Westminster* (1936) AC 1. at 19–20.

30. *Helvering v. Gregory*, 69 F.2d 809, 811 (2d Cir. 1934), aff'd, 293 U.S. 465 (1935).

31. C.A. 265/67 *Mefi Ltd. v. Assessing Officer*, 21(2) P.D. 593.

32. *Income Tax Act*, art. 86.

33. On trust, see Joel Slemrod, "On Voluntary Compliance, Voluntary Taxes and Social Capital," *National Tax Journal* 51 (1998): 485. For historical discussions of the role of trust in the

development of the British tax system and especially the need of politicians to shape the tax system in ways that fostered the people's trust in the state and in fellow taxpayers, see Martin Daunton, *Just Taxes* (Cambridge: Cambridge University Press, 2002), xiii–xiv.

34. See generally R. Cocks, "Victorian Barristers, Judges and Taxation: A Study in the Expansion of Legal Work," in *Law, Economy and Society, 1750–1914: Essays in the History of English Law,* ed. G. R. Rubin and David Sugarman (Abingdon: Professional Books, 1984), 445, 464 (on revenue cases and the rule of law).

35. See H. Blumenthal, "A Tax-Evasion Frustrated," *Accountant Tax Supplement* 93 (Aug. 10, 1935): 335–36. See also H. Voit, "A Tax Avoidance Frustrated" (letter), *Accountant Tax Supplement* 93 (Sept. 28, 1935): 395. On the Nazi legislation of 1934, which declared that "the tax laws should be interpreted according to the conceptions of National-Socialism," see Paul Haensel, "The German Tax Reform of 1934–35," *Tax Magazine* 13 (1935): 705.

36. Assaf Likhovski, "The Duke and the Lady: *Helvering v. Gregory* and the History of Tax Avoidance Adjudication," *Cardozo Law Review* 25 (2004): 953.

37. *Chisholm* v. *Commissioner,* 79 F.2d 14 (2d Cir. 1935). See also Marvin A. Chirelstein, "Learned Hand's Contribution to the Law of Tax Avoidance," *Yale Law Journal* 77 (1968): 440, 445–47, 452.

38. *Chisholm*, 79 F.2d at 15.

39. Hand memo, May 27, 1935, File No. 194–10, Hand Papers, Harvard Law School Library.

40. Likhovski, "Formalism and Israeli Anti-avoidance Doctrines in the 1950s and 1960s," 339.

41. I use the term "influence" here in a variety of ways, some of which reflect the notion of influence expounded in Harold Bloom's famous discussion of modern poetic influence, *The Anxiety of Influence: A Theory of Poetry,* 2d ed. (New York: Oxford University Press, 1997).

42. On multifactored, thick description, see, e.g., Morton J. Horwitz, The *Transformation of American Law, 1870–1960: The Crisis of Legal Orthodoxy* (New York: Oxford University Press, 1922), vii–viii. On judicial biographies, see, e.g., Laura Kalman, "The Power of Biography," *Law & Social Inquiry* 23 (1998): 479–530. On the micro-history of specific cases, see, e.g., A. W. Brian Simpson, *Leading Cases in the Common Law* (Oxford: Oxford University Press, 1995). On judicial behavior, see, e.g., Nancy Maveety, ed., *The Pioneers of Judicial Behavior* (Ann Arbor: University of Michigan Press, 2003); Jeffrey A. Segal and Harold J. Spaeth, *The Supreme Court and the Attitudinal Model Revisited* (Cambridge: Cambridge University Press, 2002); Lee Epstein and Jack Knight, *The Choices Judges Make* (Washington, D.C.: Congressional Quarterly Press, 1998).

43. O. W. Holmes, "The Path of the Law," *Harvard Law Review* 10 (1897): 466.

14

Morton Horwitz: Legal Historian as Lawyer and Historian

WILLIAM MICHAEL TREANOR

THE GIFTS OF THE HISTORIAN AND THE GIFTS OF THE LAWYER ARE rarely found in the same person. The term "legal historian" is almost an oxymoron. The great historian has the ability to enter into the mind-set of those who lived before, to recover and analyze the details of the past, to synthesize what he or she finds and describe broad trends, to see cause and effect. The work of the great historian is marked both by a firm grasp of small things and by profound scope and ambition. But a legal historian, to be great, must possess not just the gifts of the historian, but the gifts of a lawyer. He or she must be able to understand and manipulate legal doctrine, to see connections between legal principles, to see where ambiguity lies and where the law is determinate, to be able to make the standard moves of legal argument, and to understand the limitations of those moves. Few people have the capacity to do both history and law well. Virtually none have the ability to perform at the highest level as both legal analyst and historian. In a generation of great legal historians, Morton Horwitz has the foremost place, and in assessing why, I think a primary reason is that he has the most extraordinary strength as both legal analyst and historian.

The standard analyses of Horwitz's work typically focus on its scope and ambition. In writing this essay, I looked at the reviews of *Transformation I* and *Transformation II,* and they generally stress the books' broad themes and judge the books in light of those themes.[1] Thus, the reviews center on the link in *Transformation I* between economic change and legal change; they probe the more complicated relationship among politics, culture, and legal change described in *Transformation II*. Obviously, these great themes are basic to the contribution of these books. Indeed, we have been debating the theses of Horwitz's work for forty years.

The success of these books is not, however, simply a product of their scope and ambition, of Horwitz's ability to think broadly in terms of changing worldviews and the factors that produce the changes. Their success reflects, as well, Horwitz's mastery of the law. His understanding of the complicated legal doctrine of the eras he has studied is dazzling—to read the footnotes in *Transformation I* and *Transformation II* is a humbling experience for any scholar. As impressive as his ability to recapture the doctrine of the past is his ability to recapture and apply the methods of legal analysis practiced in the past. Perhaps in part because he was trained at Harvard Law School at the height of the period during which its pedagogy was strongly process oriented, Horwitz has an insider's deep understanding of the legal craft.

Horwitz's great range is the key to his analytic approach, and it has enabled him to make contributions of the most fundamental importance. In this essay, I would like to illustrate that point by talking about his treatment of takings law. Takings law, the subject of much of my academic work, is a topic I became interested in when I read *Transformation I* and encountered Horwitz's claim, then novel but now generally accepted, that "the principle that the state should compensate individuals for property taken for public use was not widely established in America at the time of the Revolution."[2] I focus on takings doctrine here in part because it is the area of Mort Horwitz's work I am most familiar with, but I think it is an appropriate example of his approach and its strength.

Let me begin with a minor example drawn from my memory of Mort Horwitz as teacher, rather than author. Intrigued by *Transformation I*'s analysis of the rise of the just compensation principle, I decided to write my student note on the original understanding of the takings clause. When he read an early draft, Mort had countless insights that were of extraordinary value, but one comment stands out most clearly in my memory. At one point, as he was discussing various aspects of what I had written, he said to me, "Do you know Moore's *History of the Foreshore*?" It was a classic moment, of a type every one of his graduate students is certainly familiar with. The slight leaning forward, the low voice, the pause after the word "know," the slight twist of the head, and then the name of a book (or, in other cases, an article) that, although the question generously implied I might have encountered, was completely unknown to me. This happened to me countless times during my work with him. I don't think I had ever heard of any work mentioned in a sentence that began "Do you know." In this instance, not only did I not know the work; I did not know what a foreshore was.

Moore's *History of the Foreshore* is a book from 1888 that was a history of the law governing the area between the high- and low-water tide (i.e., the foreshore). The fact that Horwitz had heard of this book and read it exemplifies his mastery of a truly arcane part of the law. But what in the hands of another scholar would be simply legal trivia was in Horwitz's hands much more. He discussed with me how state ownership of the foreshore grew out of an older notion of property in which all property was the property of the king. He then discussed how this older version had evolved into a republican conception of property, under which property is held subject to the interests of the community. He explained that the law of the foreshore, once consistent with a dominant approach to property, was now an exception to the dominant rule—private ownership of property—and he linked the literal marginalization of the law of the foreshore with the emergence of liberalism.

Horwitz's discussion of the law of the foreshore was, of course, a tour de force. But, more significantly, it reflected an approach characteristic of much of Horwitz's work: a legal rule of apparently limited consequence is used to illuminate larger worldviews, showing both how the worldviews had practical consequence and how they were in tension, and the worldviews, in turn, illuminated the legal rule, placing it in a larger context of meaning.

This approach underlies Horwitz's treatment of the takings law in *Transformation I* and *Transformation II*, this linkage of small points of law with broad themes in a way that enriches the analysis of both. Moreover, in these books, his treatment is deepened further because not only does he understand broad questions of ideology and fine points of the law—the two extremes of legal history—but he also is a master of the middle ground of the law: he is both a gifted legal analyst and a profound student of the limits of legal analysis. No legal historian I know of is his rival in terms of understanding the basic legal moves lawyers make. At the same time, he also has a gift for deconstruction, for the close reading that reveals tensions and underlying ideology. This combination of close analysis and deconstruction leads to an acceptance of ambiguity, but not complete indeterminacy, to a recognition that there is a range of potential meanings of terms and a range of potential paths of legal evolution, but no more than a range. Horwitz's approach at the same time avoids both formalism and the indeterminacy that characterized the critical legal studies movement, neither of which accurately captures the realities of legal reasoning. This combination of classic analysis and deconstruction allows Horwitz to recapture how previous generations thought about the law and to reveal the underlying preconceptions of which they were not always aware.

Horwitz's treatment of the evolution of takings law in *Transformation I* and *Transformation II* tracks the interplay of two competing conceptions of property. As in his discussion with me of the law of the foreshore, Horwitz begins his historical analysis in *Transformation I* with this notion of what is at its origin a feudal conception of property. Under that theory, property is the creature of the state, and it can be taken back by the state in response to greater needs.[3] Horwitz contends that the acceptance of this conception of property underlies the surprising fact previously alluded to—one of his many discoveries in his book—that there was no just compensation principle established at the time of the American Revolution.[4]

Horwitz also finds, however, in the late eighteenth century the growing influence of a competing conception of property, reflective of both Blackstonian influence and the acceptance of natural law thinking, which conceived of property as an individual right.[5]

The competition between these two very different conceptions shaped legal evolution in the late eighteenth century and first half of the nineteenth century. Growing acceptance of the natural law–Blackstonian view led to the emergence of the just compensation principle and its general adoption, even in states in which it was not enshrined in constitutional text.[6] The continuing power of the older statist notion, however, led courts to limit the compensation principle even as that principle came to be firmly established.

For example, Horwitz finds in the second decade the emergence of the doctrine of consequential damages, under which government acts that did not involve direct trespass to land or physical appropriation did not give rise to a requirement of compensation, even when those acts harmed private property.[7] Thus, no compensation was owed if the government built a road and, in so doing, damaged the foundations of a property owner's house. Despite the obvious tension between this rule and the general compensation principle (and the opposition from such leading judges as Kent and Story to the rule that consequential damages did not necessitate compensation), the rule won broad acceptance in the years after 1825 and the rule was justified "as a vindication of the common good."[8]

Similarly, Horwitz finds the compensation principle strongly limited—at first—by the public use doctrine. The Fifth Amendment's takings clause provides: "Nor shall private property be taken for *public use* without just compensation"[9] and state constitutions have analogous public use requirements. Horwitz finds that in the years before 1840 the dominant approach was for courts to read the "public use" requirement in a way that permitted aggressive use of the eminent domain power. Thus, they routinely uphold government assertions of the power of eminent domain to aid privately owned turnpikes and canals over private property owners' claims that the government acts did not advance the public interest.[10] This interpretive approach accords with the view that "compensation clauses were gratuitous limitations on an otherwise inherent and unlimited sovereign power."[11] The traditional notion that property is held subject to the public good undergirds an analysis in which a utilitarian calculus is used to answer the question of whether a taking is a public use.[12]

Horwitz's treatment of the takings principle is not limited to an analysis of the case law and competing conceptions of the relationship between property and the state. He links the different views of the takings principle and its scope to larger political and economic movements. Thus, he sees the limitations on takings law as reflecting the drive for economic growth. He writes, "The basic source of early nineteenth century resistance to the compensation principle were those entrepreneurial groups who regarded it as a threat to low cost economic growth."[13] At the same time, the countervailing arguments *for* strengthening the takings principle came from those who feared the use of the eminent domain power for redistributive purposes.[14]

Having explicated the early takings case law, Horwitz then traces a doctrinal shift that begins to occur in the wake of the Panic of 1837. The Panic led to the end of the generous financing that had allowed the canal and turnpike companies and others to undertake new projects while at the same time producing a populist politics that engendered an increased fear among elites that governments would use the eminent domain power for redistributive purposes.[15] This rethinking led to an analytic shift in which courts moved from a deferential stance to one in which they more closely scrutinized whether exercises of the eminent domain power were public uses.[16] Horwitz also strikingly argues that in reviewing eminent domain cases, courts in a number of critical areas moved from an instrumentalism (in which acts that advanced overall economic well-being were seen as satisfying the public use requirement) to a formalist and facially apolitical approach in which only specific exercises of the eminent domain power were found to constitute public uses.[17]

In countless ways, Horwitz's treatment in *Transformation I* of the takings principle was pathbreaking. As I have pointed out, he made a major contribution with his recognition that the takings principle was not clearly established at the time of the adoption of the Fifth Amendment's takings clause. Similarly, his analysis of the "public use" requirement, written at a time at which neither lawyers nor historians were focusing on the issue, continues to be one of the best treatments of the topic, despite the passage of time and the fact that the issue has become one of great moment.[18] The larger point to recognize is that his analysis as a whole was pathbreaking. Before Horwitz, there had been relatively little historical analysis of the early history of takings case law, and nothing that matched its close treatment of doctrinal evolution.[19] Horwitz was plowing new ground here. The fact that takings case law is the subject of only a handful of cases in *Transformation I* and is but one of countless doctrinal areas he explores suggests how much new ground the book as a whole plowed.

Horwitz's treatment of takings merits accolades, however, not simply because of the depth of his research into the case law, but because of the sophistication of his analysis of that case law. On one hand, he recognizes that law evolves in a way that causes certain issues to come off the table. Thus, as the takings principle wins general acceptance and constitutional recognition, the legal claim that the government can take property without providing compensation loses all its force. At the same time, he recognizes areas of ambiguity. To be precise, he finds two competing conceptions of property, each tied to a broadly accepted ideology, each of which shapes the case law in areas where the application of the takings principle is unclear (consequential damages and public use doctrine). Horwitz's approach is a form of deconstruction as he sees the tensions present in the law. But he does not embrace indeterminacy. Instead, he sees a very defined series of moves that legal actors make. His analysis embodies what are recognizably the standard types of arguments that lawyers and judges employ.

As *Transformation II* brings the story of the takings principle forward in time, it employs a similarly subtle approach to legal analysis. At the start of *Transformation II*, the dominant physicalist conception of property—a conception that emerged in an agrarian society in which land was the most significant form of property—shapes takings law and means that compensation is owed only in cases of physical appropriation. Thus, neither consequential injuries (discussed in *Transformation I*) nor government regulations were seen as takings.[20] But an ideological shift (the rise of individualism in the 1870s) and an economic shift (the increasing significance of intangible and commercial forms of wealth in a "dynamic industrial society"[21]) led to a reconceptualization of property so that property was increasingly equated with value.[22] This dephysicalized conception of property caused the Supreme Court in *Pumpelly v. Green Bay Co.*,[23] a case involving the flooding of land, to reject the traditional rule that consequential damages were not compensable takings.[24] But once the notion of property as value had won acceptance, consequential damages, which involved physical interference with physical property, did not long serve as the boundary line between permissible and impermissible governmental actions. While one wing of the Court sought to limit *Pumpelly* to government acts with physical consequences,[25] ultimately, the logic of *Pumpelly* led the Court to use takings principles to analyze government actions that affected value, such as government regulation of utility and railroad rates.[26]

Transformation II thus mirrors *Transformation I*. Again, Horwitz recognizes the tension in the doctrine, a tension that must be understood in historical context and that emerges from that context. There is a precise area of ambiguity, and legal actors respond to that ambiguity in a discrete number of ways, ways that reflect standard legal moves.

I regard this combination of awareness of ambiguity, combined with a recognition of the constraining force of legal reasoning, as both a powerful model for thinking about legal history and an approach that is classically Horwitz's, rather than anyone else's. Much of Horwitz's approach in *Transformation I*, as Grant Gilmore points out in an influential *Yale Law Journal* review of the book,[27] resonates with what legal realists had done. But Horwitz adds legal teeth to the analysis, bringing in a recognition of legal determinacy that had not been present before.

At the same time, he also brings to his work a recognition of the legitimacy of divergent legal views as reflecting plausible moves within a structure of thought. Much of legal history is told as a story of declension. I think that, to some extent, *Transformation I* can be understood as a response to this, with its target being the consensus school and its view that this was a pro-people government intervention period (a kind of golden age) and then a falling away from it. Though they disagree on when declension sets in, the class treatments of the Handlins and Levy are declension stories.[28] This approach is a deeply flawed way to recover the past. It does not allow one to understand the full range of legal actors. If legal change is all about declension, what are the legal arguments of the people who are arguing for the falling away?

Horwitz takes seriously the competing arguments of legal actors who lived in the past in a way that never fails to amaze me. It is a credit to his skill as an historian, but it is also a credit to his skill as a lawyer. Both a lawyer and an historian of consummate gifts, he is able to recover lost legal worlds in a way that is a model for us all. Among his great contributions as a scholar, this is surely one of the greatest.

NOTES

1. Morton J. Horwitz, *The Transformation of American Law, 1780–1860* (Cambridge, Mass.: Harvard University Press, 1977); Morton J. Horwitz, *The Transformation of American Law, 1870–1960* (New York: Oxford University Press, 1992).

2. Horwitz, *Transformation I,* 63. On the acceptance of Horwitz's view, see, e.g., *Lucas v. S.C. Coastal Council,* 505 U.S. 1003, 1056–59 (1992) (Blackmun, J., dissenting) (citing Horwitz); id. at 1028 n. 15 (Scalia, J.) (accepting dissent's historical analysis).

3. Horwitz, *Transformation I,* 64–65.

4. Ibid., 63.

5. Ibid., 64.

6. Ibid., 64, 66.

7. Ibid., 71–74.

8. Ibid., 73.

9. U.S. Const. amend. V (emphasis added).

10. *Transformation I,* 65–66, 259–60.

11. Ibid., 65.

12. Ibid., 260.

13. Ibid., 66.

14. Ibid.

15. Ibid., 260.

16. Ibid.

17. Ibid., 261. The two lines of cases that Horwitz highlights here involve railroad exercise of the eminent domain power (which came to be justified as public uses because of public access to trains) and mill acts (which came to be justified on the grounds that they comported with riparian law).

18. For the decision that has been the source of much recent controversy, see *Kelo v. City of New London,* 545 U.S. 469 (2005).

19. The most important studies prior to Horwitz's were Joseph Sax, "Takings and the Police Power," *Yale Law Journal* 74 (1964): 36–76, and Fred Bosselman, David Callies, and John Banta, *The Takings Issue* (Washington, D.C.: U.S. Government Printing Office, 1973). Both are fine studies, but neither closely traces doctrinal evolution in the way that Horwitz does.

20. *Transformation II,* 145–46.

21. Ibid., 145.

22. Ibid., 148–51.

23. 80 U.S. (13) Wall. 166 (1871).

24. See *Transformation II,* 148.

25. Ibid., 304, n. 27.

26. Ibid., 160–64.

27. Grant Gilmore, "From Tort to Contract: Industrialization and the Law," *Yale Law Journal* 86 (1977): 788–97.

28. Oscar Handlin and Mary Flug Handlin, *Commonwealth: A Study of the Role of Government in the American Economy, Massachusetts, 1774–1861* (New York: New York University Press, 1947); Leonard Levy, *The Law of the Commonwealth and Chief Justice Shaw* (Cambridge, Mass.: Harvard University Press, 1957).

15

Whither Legal History?

CHARLES DONAHUE JR.

I LAST WROTE ON THIS TOPIC IN 1967, AND I DID SO WITH SOME SENSE OF desperation.[1] A number of law faculties—Harvard, Columbia, Pennsylvania, and Michigan come immediately to mind—had long had, or had recently introduced, first-year courses in legal history, and they were not going well. In some cases the problem was the teacher. The late Julius Goebel was a very good legal historian, perhaps even a great one, but his teaching style in large classes was pure Kingsfield, and he alienated a whole generation of Columbia law students from legal history. But the problem was not only the teacher. Jack Dawson, Spence Kimball, and John Honnold were all successful teachers of traditional law courses—Dawson was one of the great first-year teachers of his day—but none of them was able to pull off this course. When the students ceremonially burned Kimball's book in the courtyard of the school's Gothic quadrangle, the Michigan faculty voted to eliminate the requirement.

Part of the problem was the times. Some of my readers will remember the late 1960s, but for those who do not, it was the beginning of the era of the flower children. For a generation that was determined to make all things new—and not in the sense meant in the book of Revelation (21:5)—anything that smacked of history was abhorrent. History was what was wrong. History was hierarchy. History was oppression. History was what had produced the Vietnam War. In law schools, Holmes's aphorism that "It is revolting to have no better reason for a rule of law than thus it was so in the time of Henry IV" had become "It is revolting to have a rule of law that was so in the time of Henry IV."[2]

This paper was originally given as a lecture at the Center for Law and Legal History in the Washington and Lee School of Law in October of 2004. I have added some references but have tried to preserve the more informal and tentative style of the original lecture. The introduction to S. F. C. Milsom's *A Natural History of the Common Law* (New York: Columbia University Press, 2003), xiii–xxviii, is obviously important for what is said here, and it would be pointless to decorate the pages with specific references to it. Tom Green generously shared his reactions to the paper with me and saved me from a number of foolish statements. That he did not save me from more of them is the result of my stubbornness.

But the problem went deeper than that. Dawson and Goebel certainly, Kimball and Honnold probably, knew that the society that had produced the assize of novel disseisin was a very different society from the one that produced the action of ejectment, and that in turn was a very different society from the one that produced code pleading in ejectment, and from the society that produced the modern action to recover the possession of land, but they did not teach it that way, or if they did, they did not get it across. The lesson that first-year students learned from the basic legal history course was that there was a direct line from the assizes of Henry II to the action to recover possession of land today, and they quite rightly asked why they were being asked to learn that it was called the assize of novel disseisin in the reign of some medieval English king. If it was the same thing, why bother to learn its ancient name? If there is something about the way the action works today that can only be explained by the way it was in the time of Henry II, then we ought to get rid of it.

Although legal history was in rather bad shape in the law schools in this period, constitutional history was still taught to undergraduates in many colleges and universities. Although the English version of this course tended to have a Whiggish and diachronic bias, and the American an equally diachronic and somewhat New Deal bias, the course, when it was well taught, left little doubt that constitutional law and politics, broadly defined, had an intimate though subtle relationship. Since the course was highly recommended to those undergraduates who regarded themselves as pre-law, there were many law students who had had some exposure to legal history before they came to law school. What they got under the name of legal history when they got to law school was very different from what they expected, and this was, I think, a further reason that so many students were disappointed with the standard fare.[3]

In 1967, I was looking for a job, and I wanted to teach legal history in a law school. My desperation, then, was the desperation of a job seeker who wondered if his chosen career was going to exist. But there was more. Academic disciplines that are not taught tend to die. A marked decline in a major type of teaching of legal history was bound to have ramifications for the writing and practice of legal history in general.

Unbeknownst to me, a number of my contemporaries, including Morty Horwitz, were also looking for a position teaching legal history in a law school. Quite remarkably, because there was little communication among us, we all told our potential employers the same thing. We would teach any course they wanted us to teach, including any of the substantive first-year courses, but we did not want to teach a required first-year legal history course. The reason for this was partly the spirit of the times. If the students were rebelling, any required course needed to be justified, and rightly or wrongly, the students did not see the justification for this one. There was also another reason, more related to the contents of the required first-year course. The diachronic emphasis of these courses ended up force-feeding students the origins of doctrines and institutions, the modern versions of which they did not know or barely knew. Dawson, S. E. Thorne, and Mark Howe at Harvard, Stephan Kuttner and W. H. Dunham at Yale,[4] Goebel at Columbia, and Willard Hurst at Wisconsin, to name but a few, were all successfully teaching legal history to law students, but they were teaching it in relatively small advanced courses and seminars. There were law students who wanted to study legal history—principally, though not exclusively, those who had had some exposure to it in college—and they were quite willing to do it in their second or third years when they were looking, as it were, for a way to put the two halves of their lives together. Indeed, many of us who were looking for positions in legal history had taken such advanced courses and seminars.

Behind our reluctance to teach a first-year required course was also a considerable discomfort, if not outright hostility, to the type of history that those courses, perhaps necessarily, reflected. We were all convinced that law is intimately connected with the economy of ideas, the politics, and the social structure of the society that produces it. There was no way that that connection could be shown in a course that went from Aethelbert to Earl Warren, particularly if few, if any, of the students could be assumed to have any idea of the intellectual, political, and social histories of the periods before the American Revolution and might have quite spotty ideas about the intellectual, political, and social history of America since the Revolution.

Looking back on this moment from the perspective of forty years, our ploy seems to have worked. Most of us got jobs; at least enough of us got jobs that most of the larger law schools, and then some of the smaller ones, acquired a legal historian for their faculties. While the legal history that we taught varied, and still varies, greatly among us, it was almost always in second- and third-year courses and seminars that did not attempt to cover everything but that focused more narrowly in time and emphasized the connections between legal history and intellectual, political, or social history.[5] A quite large body of literature has developed, at least on the American side, that does the same thing. At gigantine Harvard, we now have seven faculty members who identify themselves as legal historians, and eight more who write or teach legal history more than occasionally. We have a wide range of curricular offerings in the field. No one takes all of them, but more than half of the students take at least one legal history course or seminar at some time during their careers at the law school. It would be overly optimistic to say we are witnessing a move to history among our students, but in marked contrast to the late 1960s and early 1970s, most students seem to tolerate a bit of it, and some are really drawn to it. The collapse of legal history in law schools that some of us feared in the late 1960s and early 1970s clearly has not happened, and considering the number of relatively young scholars in the field, such a collapse does not seem to be imminent.[6]

There have, however, been some changes that in my view are more problematical, and that I would like to use to set up the principal theme of this paper. Before we do so, it is well to sound a word of caution. It is relatively easy to survey the legal history courses being taught in law schools, and there is no doubt that they have increased in the past couple of decades. It is much more difficult to survey what is being taught in these courses, and I have not done so.[7] In the case of faculties of arts and sciences, a survey of the courses being taught is much more difficult, to say nothing of what is being taught. Such surveys, in my view, should be undertaken, but in their absence I am relying on impressions derived from discussions with other legal historians, and from what is being written in the field. What is taught and what is written do not always correspond, though they usually are related. Much, however, is being written, particularly in American legal history, and the variety of subjects and methods is great. My examples, particularly on the American side, are derived from my own quite limited reading, and I may have the general trends wrong. If I do, I apologize. To the extent, however, that I have them right, I hope to encourage others, both in teaching and in writing, to bridge a gap that may be emerging between legal history as practiced in history departments and legal history as practiced in law schools. In short, the story of legal and constitutional history courses will turn out to be a story about the discipline of legal history generally.

To return to the more problematical developments: In 1967, many, perhaps most, respectable colleges had a course in English constitutional history. Very few do now. The situation is more complicated with regard to American constitutional history, but I have the impression that there has been a decline in such courses as well.[8] There are a large number of young Americanists who teach in faculties of arts and sciences and who attend the annual meeting of the American Society for Legal History. Most of them are bringing legal or constitutional history into their courses in one way or another. There are fewer young non-Americanists who attend the meeting, but those who do also bring legal, less often constitutional, history into their courses. The undergraduate courses involving law that both groups are teaching tend, however, to be quite specialized. I have the impression that one is less likely to learn in college today about the history of United States Supreme Court from John Jay to William Rehnquist than one is about the legal reforms sought by the women's movement of the late nineteenth and early twentieth centuries, less likely to learn about the development of French institutions from Hugh Capet (987–996) to the French Revolution (1789) than one is to learn about the resolution of disputes in France in the eleventh and twelfth centuries or mercantile courts in the ancien régime. When this fact is coupled with the fact that fewer students, even pre-law students, are concentrating in history in college, this means that the level of preparation of law students who come into legal history courses in the law school has, on average, gone down.[9]

The virtual disappearance of courses in English constitutional history means that in law schools we can no longer count on having at least a couple of students in a large class who have some idea of the process that produced Magna Carta. Indeed, I have encountered rather large classes where no one in the room was willing to admit that he or she knew what Magna Carta was. This means, of course, that those of us who teach English legal history must begin at the very beginning and cannot get as far. It also means that in the veritable explosion of teachers of legal history in the last twenty years there are few who are willing to teach or write in the area of English legal history, much less continental European legal history.[10] The decline in preparation in history in general that characterizes many of our law students may also be contributing, at least in part, to the fact that many of those who wish to continue in legal history find it necessary, or advantageous, to get an advanced degree in history (a phenomenon with which we shall deal at the end of this paper).

Now what happened in history faculties is, in many ways, similar to what happened in law faculties, only it happened a bit later and with somewhat different results. When I arrived at the University of Michigan in 1968, a member of the history department was teaching both English and American constitutional history going, in two different courses, from Aethelberht to the New Deal. No respectable historian today would regard him- or herself as competent to teach over such a wide chronological range. Michigan still has undergraduate offerings in legal and constitutional history, but no one tries to cover the range that was being covered by one man in the late sixties.

The causes of the phenomenon of the decline of traditional constitutional history courses all seem to be related to how history is being written today. The first cause is specialization. As knowledge expands, the area that we can competently cover narrows. There are very few historians, even in law schools, who teach, much less write, about both England and America, and those few who do tend to be those who focus on the seventeenth and eighteenth centuries.

The second cause of the phenomenon is related to the first, but it is a bit different. The pioneers of English constitutional history, to take the example with which I am more familiar, tended to be Whiggish in their history, and Whig history has been out of fashion for at least fifty years. If the constitutional history of England from the witenagemot of the Anglo-Saxons to Queen Victoria could not be seen as a steady progression, despite occasional setbacks, in the direction of parliamentary democracy, the blessings of ordered liberty, and the rights of Englishmen, there was less reason put it all together in one package. Let us, rather, study the constitutional struggles—if you want to call them that—of the Middle Ages in the context of what was going on the Middle Ages, those of the seventeenth century in the context of seventeenth-century history, and so on. Over the past generation English historians, in particular, have become increasingly narrow in their chronological focus in order to broaden out synchronically. English records are extraordinarily rich. Even if we focus on the political and the constitutional, a great deal more can be learned about who was involved, what their relations were with each other, and how the events unfolded. The result of such studies has been to show how serendipitous some of the great constitutional moments were and how anachronistic was the interpretation of the Whig historians.

The third reason for the phenomenon, and this applies more to European history than it does to American, is an increasing discomfort with national history. The European nations of the nineteenth and early twentieth centuries wrote the history of their nations. Each tended to regard itself as unique, no one more so than the English. History departments in America have pioneered the movement away from this type of writing of history. In my field, for example, we all tend to regard ourselves as medievalists and try to keep abreast of developments all over at least Western Europe. Since there are just so many hours in the day, this broadening has had, once more, a tendency to narrow our focus chronologically while it broadens it geographically. The move away from national history has also produced a marked change in the hiring practices of history departments. Relatively few, particularly among the smaller ones, think that they must cover in depth every period of English history from the Anglo-Saxons to Elizabeth II. The early modernist is expected to be able to say something in survey courses about England but need not be a Tudor-Stuart specialist, particularly if the department lacks coverage in, say, the Iberian Peninsula or Eastern Europe, to say nothing of the non-Western world.

Now I have said that the present generation of legal historians in law schools began by moving in the same general direction. We wanted to relate developments in law to intellectual, political, and social developments synchronically. Indeed, most of us thought that that was the point of legal history: to show how law, nonlegal ideas, politics, and society interact. We differed among ourselves (and continue to differ) about the level of generality to which we wanted to take our studies or thought they could be taken, but what we wanted to study was that interaction. The reason why we wanted to teach in law schools was that we thought that puzzling over that interaction was a necessary part of a lawyer's equipment. Not every student would want to study that interaction historically, but the advantage of historical study is that it gives one some distance. It shows how at different times and in different places differences in all four elements—law, general ideas, politics, and society—have produced quite different mixes. Indeed, it may even show why we get such different mixes.

If this is the purpose of the enterprise, then there is no particular reason why we should focus on legal phenomena that are recognizably the ancestors of our own. There are, of course, limits as to how far one wants to range, but those limits are more the products of one's own knowledge. Some of us, including myself, will not write about, and are reluctant to teach, the legal history of any system where the primary materials are in a language of which we do not have at least some reading knowledge. Others of us may be willing to work with translated materials but realize that the history of, say, China, would require more time than we have to work it up. Similar limitations apply to our students. While we may be willing to let them work with translated materials, the further we get from what is vaguely familiar to them, the more difficult it is for them to get up to speed on the intellectual, political, and social background necessary for the exercise.

It must be admitted, moreover, that one of the fascinations of history is studying what is, at least in some sense, one's own. One can be firmly committed to the study of legal developments within their own periods and still include within that study a broader diachronic element. It is, however, tricky business. For example, most of the language of a seventeenth-century English case, even the technical language, is recognizably modern English. It takes considerable imagination to see how it may be that it was not being used in the same way that we use it today. It takes, perhaps, even more imagination to see how the legal institutions described in that language interacted with each other in the seventeenth century in ways that produced quite different results from what we get today, even if the language is describing institutions that are clearly the ancestors of our own, and, of course, to see how intellectual, political, and social differences made the meaning of that case quite different from what it would have been had it been decided the same way in the twenty-first century. But if one can identify carefully where the changes at all these levels took place, one can write or teach respectable diachronic history.

Let me illustrate that last point more specifically. Suppose that a colleague asks me when the holder in due course doctrine began. That is a question to which I think I have at least a partial answer. We first see the holder in due course doctrine in a form that is recognizably the ancestor of the modern doctrine in cases in the English central royal courts in the late seventeenth century. But I will try not to answer the question that way. I will try to persuade my colleague to sit with me for about ten minutes while I try to tell him or her about an historical context. There was competition for business among the various English courts, a competition that came to a head in the sixteenth and seventeenth centuries. In the later seventeenth century the central royal courts of common law were trying to oust the High Court of Admiralty of a substantial part of its lucrative mercantile business. The relationship between the common-law courts and the merchants had been problematical in the thirteenth century and for quite mysterious reasons became problematical again in the early seventeenth century. At least some of the merchants thought that they operated according to something that they called *lex mercatoria*, but that may be chimera, a phrase used more for polemical purposes than for identifying a genuine source of law. Over the course of the seventeenth century, a practice arose of using inland bills of exchange as a substitute for hard currency. This practice, coupled with the assurance from London merchants and bankers that the custom of merchants was that the holder of such paper took free of any defenses that the original obligor had against the original obligee, eventually led the central royal courts in the late seventeenth century to hold that this custom could be pleaded as part of the customary law of England and need not be proved as such, as it would have to have been if it had been pleaded as a custom among the merchants of London.[11] If the end result of this exercise is a realization by my colleague that the word "doctrine," as in "holder in due course doctrine," requires considerable translation when applied to the world of the late seventeenth century, that the combination of factors that can be legitimately argued to have played a role in the emergence of that doctrine was unique to the late seventeenth century, and that the function of that doctrine in the late seventeenth century was greatly different from what it probably is today—if I can persuade my colleague of this, I will have done my job.

What is the effect of the change in what is being written about and taught in history departments on this enterprise as I have just conceived of it? The problem, for the most part, is not that we are asking different questions. Both the historians who teach in faculties of arts and sciences and the historians who teach in law schools are, again for the most part, asking how law, general ideas, politics, and society interact. We would come closer to the mark if we said that the former group is methodologically committed to the proposition that legal phenomena can always be understood in relation to what is going on in the intellectual, political, or social realm. The history of law is a piece of general history. Either it fits into that general history (some would argue that it always does) or, if it does not, it is uninteresting.[12] The history that they write and teach is sometimes called "external history."

Historians who teach in law schools differ in that, for the most part, they regard the relationship between law, on one hand, and general ideas, politics, and society, on the other, as something that must be demonstrated rather than something that may be presumed. The vast majority of them have long given up the notion that law is autonomous, but they recognize that legal specialization in most periods of Western legal history has made the law semi-autonomous. With respect to some topics for some periods of time, the law proceeds without much direct reference to or much influence from what is going on in the world outside the legal system, and for those areas, to the extent that we focus on the intellectual, the political, and the social at all, it is to ask what effect on general ideas, politics, and society this semi-autonomous realm might have had. Even in those areas where ideological, political, or social influence is apparent or probable, there remain the questions how the legal system translated those influences into law, which of the arguments that were advanced were accepted, and how the acceptance of those arguments affected the overall system. The history that many of us write and teach is sometimes called "internal history."

The terms "external" and "internal" applied to legal history are in origin French, and as used by the French, they distinguish two types of study. External legal history is the history of institutions, at least those recognized as such by the law; the history of sources of law, both formal and informal; what is sometimes called the history of legal science (writing about law); and, perhaps, the history of procedure, at least as broadly conceived. Internal legal history is the history of doctrine or rules of law and their development. As used more recently in English, the two terms seem to distinguish the legal history that is written from the perspective of the relationship of law to the outside world as opposed to the legal history that is written from the perspective of the participants in the legal system without regard, or with little regard, to the world outside the legal system.[13] It has even been recently suggested that historians without formal legal training are best suited to the former, particularly to the history of constitutional and criminal law, whereas historians with formal legal training are best suited to the latter, particularly, private law.[14] The same author also seems to wonder why the history of institutions is part of legal history at all.[15]

I find both of these suggestions odd (and I might add that they seem to be belied by the general thrust of the articles in which they appear). Both constitutional and criminal law have a rich internal development (though in some periods in English legal history the development of formal doctrines of criminal law was stifled by institutional factors). Anyone who thinks that S. F. C. Milsom's masterly study of the development of the real actions in the early common law is not a book that makes an argument about the transformation of a society is not reading the same book that I am reading.[16] One of the principal points of Milsom's earlier work about the development of the action of trespass in the fourteenth century is that we are not looking at the transformation of a society; rather we are looking at a change in institutions—a point about external legal history, at least as defined by the French.[17]

The legal historian studying doctrinal developments must have a firm grasp of at least that kind of external history. Otherwise, he or she is likely to make huge mistakes. What looks like a major conceptual breakthrough in the mid-fourteenth century may be nothing more than a shift of jurisdiction from local courts to the central royal courts. The reason why what seem to us to be obvious questions were not asked by legal systems of the past, much less answered, is that these were questions of a type left to an inscrutable decision maker, like the jury of the English common law or the *iudex* of the Roman law.

But if the so-called internal legal historian cannot afford to ignore the external, at least as defined by the French, and, slightly more controversially, should commit him- or herself to what that internal history meant in the context of the general ideas, politics, and society in which it took place, the so-called external legal historian can hardly afford to ignore the internal. Let me illustrate with my hypothetical college course on the history of the women's movement of the late nineteenth and early twentieth centuries. One of the legal reforms that that movement sought was the strengthening of the married women's property acts. Now married women's property acts were not new in the late nineteenth century. There is some controversy about which was the earliest, but let us take one of the candidates for the first such act in the Anglo-American world, the Mississippi Women's Law of 1839.[18] The antebellum South is not the place where we would expect to find the first married women's property act, but there it is, and the purpose of the act does not seem to have been to announce a new vision of women's role in society but rather to protect married women in a debtor frontier state from their husband's creditors after the panic of 1837.

The acts themselves in their classic form declare that a married woman may deal with her property as if she were single, a solution perhaps more clever than wise, because, of course, a married woman is not single. The consequences of pretending that she is can be seen, among other places, in the tangled and conflicting answers that the courts gave to the question of what the adoption of the act did to the tenancy by the entirety. In fact, the story of the married women's property acts is a nice example of how statutory reform of a preexisting legal structure can lead to unintended and contradictory results, some of which, in this case, may be regarded as beneficial to women, and some not. I do not know whether any college course that deals with the legal reforms sought, and in many instances achieved, by the women's movement deals with this question. I know that relatively few of them do.

Why not? I am not sure that I have a satisfactory answer to that question. I do not think that one has to be trained as a lawyer in order to understand the doctrinal moves that were going on as appellate courts came to grips with a statute that raised all kinds of questions for which the legislature did not provide an answer, although we will see shortly that it takes some work. I would suggest that there are two initial barriers that prevent more legal historians who are trained only in history from doing it today. The first is the tendency—and it is only a tendency—that those who do not have legal training have to assume that law is a scheme of rather rigid rules that do not require much interpretation. The statute was passed, wasn't it? That's the end of the story, isn't it (unless, of course, the statute just wasn't enforced)? Now it is quite easy to disabuse oneself of this view. We knock it out of our students in the first month of law school. One need not go to law school to understand that interpretation is something about which one can have endless arguments. The problem, to the extent that there is a problem, is knowing that one has an attitude that needs correcting.

A second thing that is preventing more legal historians who are trained only in history from getting a grip on the full story is the modern tendency to focus on a rather narrow time frame. It may be possible to understand a legal system without having a sense of the broad changes that occur across rather long periods of time, but it is very hard to understand the *history* of a legal system without that sense. The specialist in the women's movement of the late nineteenth and early twentieth centuries may not realize that he or she has to go back at least to 1839 and forward well into the twentieth century to understand the long and complicated process by which the married women's property acts were incorporated into the American common law, a process that has never, so far as I am aware, been fully explored.[19]

My argument so far has been that pure external and pure internal legal history as recently defined are likely to be bad history, or, at least, incomplete history. Those who start with a political or social movement and discover that it had legal ramifications need to immerse themselves in legal sources that show how those ramifications were worked out. Those who start with a particular piece of legal discourse or change in legal discourse need to look outside the confines of the legal system to see both whether it is being pushed by developments within the realm of general ideas, politics, or the broader society, and what effect it may have had on general ideas, politics, or the broader society.

Doing that, however, turns out to be a rather tall order. Let me look at it from both sides. Let us imagine, first, our putative historian of the women's movement in America whom I have persuaded to look at the effect of the married women's property acts on the tenancy by the entirety. There are secondary sources that tell the story in a way that is probably comprehensible to a non-lawyer who is willing to make extensive use of a legal dictionary and to read very slowly,[20] but our historian knows that a secondary source is no substitute for a primary source. If the object is to understand the discourse that led to the dramatically different results that the states reached on the question, one must read the discourse, not someone else's summary of it. There are a rather large number of cases, none of them written with our historian in mind. Let us take the first paragraph of *King v. Greene*, a New Jersey case decided in 1959, relatively recent and hence more comprehensible than most, which comes toward the end of a long line of development in that state.[21]

> This is an action seeking possession of lands, damages for *mesne* profits and a declaration that a mortgage incumbrance held by defendant Margaretta P. W. Harrison is a nullity and directing its discharge of record. The Superior Court, Law Division, hearing the matter on stipulated facts, granted plaintiff's motion for summary judgment. Defendants appealed, and while pending and prior to argument in the Appellate Division, we certified the cause on our motion. After argument in this court, we directed that the cause be reargued and requested that the New Jersey Title Insurance Association appear as *amicus curiae*.

Each of these sentences is crucial to our historian's understanding of the case. The first two tell us what the court was called upon to decide and the standard of review. The second two indicate that the case was important and why it was important. But for someone for whom legal language and institutions are unfamiliar, the whole paragraph is gobbledygook, and explaining it to the undergraduates is going to be even harder. Our historian is likely to go back to something more familiar, like the difference between the feminism of Elizabeth Cady Stanton and Susan B. Anthony.

Now let me put the shoe on the other foot, illustrating with a case that I sometimes use in teaching about the medieval law of marriage. There is a marriage case dated to 1430 in the archives of the archbishop of York in England in which a woman succeeds in obtaining a divorce from her husband and a declaration that she is, in fact, married to a man who was married to someone else.[22] That other marriage, of course, also has to be dissolved. A marriage of sixteen years duration and another of twenty were dissolved on the basis of an informal marriage, which was nonetheless a marriage under the rules of the time, and which had taken place twenty-two years previously. The evidence for the first marriage in time is not particularly strong, but none of the parties contested it, and the record shows that the crucial male defendant, whom we might call the "swing man," confessed the plaintiff's action as soon as she brought it. It certainly looks as if this was a consent judgment.

But one is not supposed to be able to get consent judgments in medieval marriage cases. The court was supposed to see to it that the indissolubility of marriage was upheld, even if the parties did not want it to be upheld. Why did the court allow these parties to go through what is virtually a charade? One possible explanation is that the crucial male defendant's name was Robert Easingwold; his lawyer's name was also Robert Easingwold, and the judge's name was Roger Easingwold. When we couple these facts with the fact that the archbishop of York, the judge's superior, was relatively new on the job and chancellor of England at the time, we get a fairly plausible explanation of how such jiggery-pokery might have happened.

But did it? That question requires some investigation into who these Easingwolds were. Roger the judge and Robert the lawyer may have been related, although that is not certain. There is no evidence that either of them was related to Robert the defendant. The surname Easingwold is derived from a small town about twelve miles northwest of York. No fewer than thirteen men named Easingwold appear in the records of the city of York during this period. Blood relationship is possible in some cases, highly unlikely in others. What the surname suggests, and what the historical record in some cases confirms, is that they all had relatively recent origins in the town of Easingwold. What the records seem to be showing us is that men named Easingwold patronized other men named Easingwold, not necessarily because they were related by blood but because of their common origins in the town of Easingwold. It is even possible that this case and the scandal that it may have caused affected the fortunes of what we might call the "Easingwold gang," because shortly after this case men named Easingwold disappear from the York records.[23]

Now I am not telling you this story to convince you that any legally trained historian can do good social history. I am telling you this story because I am not sure that this is good social history. Assuming that one can read the case record and that one knows what the law was and what the requirements of proof were, anyone with legal training can figure out that this case is problematical. Three defendants, represented by the best lawyers that the court had, put in no defense to a weak case. The names of the chief defendant, the lawyer, and the judge are in the record. Tracing them into nonlegal sources takes some time and knowledge that such sources exist, but granted those two things, it is a relatively mechanical exercise. But my speculations involved more than that. They involved an assumption about an institution, patronage, and that it worked, at least in part, on the basis of a common origin rather than, or in addition to, kinship. That may or may not be right. One would certainly like to know what those who have studied patronage in the urban societies of late medieval England have said about the phenomenon. Ideally, one would like to find a study by someone competent who has worked on how social networks operated at York. I think I got this one right, but I am given pause by the fact that a very good social historian has also looked at this case and has connected it to a quite different set of social patterns.[24]

The argument has proceeded on the premise that the dichotomy that has recently been posited between external and internal legal history is a false dichotomy. I will accept the proposition that they frequently represent different starting points. Historically trained legal historians frequently start from outside and work in. That is fine, but they should not stop at the door of the courtroom or the law library if they want to see the whole picture, and the picture that they paint may frequently be misleading or even flat-out wrong if they do not penetrate what they sometimes regard as a black box. Those who start within the box tend to be legally trained legal historians. But they must look at what is outside the box if they want to see the whole picture; the story that they tell may be equally misleading or even flat-out wrong if they do not do so. Also, if you accept the premise with which we began, the most important thing that we can tell lawyers and law students today is how what is outside the box affects, and is affected by, what goes on inside the box.

I hope that I have convinced my readers that this is the only way that legal history can properly be done, because the last part is hard. The legal historian, I have said, has to be both an historian and a lawyer. To the extent that he or she tries to be one and dabble in the other, the result is likely to be at best incomplete and at worst a disaster. The question is how are we to get people properly trained to do the job? The great legal historians of the past were professionally trained in one field and autodidacts in the other. F. W. Maitland had no professional training as an historian; neither did Willard Hurst. T. F. T. Plucknett had no professional training as a lawyer; neither did Richard Brandon Morris. Such people are rare today.[25] I can boast no advanced degree in history, but I spent most of my third year in law school studying with two great legal historians who taught in Yale's arts and sciences faculty. The problem is that full professional qualification in both disciplines takes a large amount of time and can be fearsomely expensive. Unlike law and economics, in which students who wish to pursue the joint JD/

PhD are generously funded by a private foundation, legal history has no angel in the private sector. (We're working on it.) Despite these difficulties, a remarkable number of young people are pursuing and obtaining both degrees. The question is whether we can make it any easier for them.

A few law schools have been working on making the pursuit of joint or concurrent degrees a bit easier administratively, a bit less expensive, and a bit less time consuming. Yale is one of them; Harvard is another. Columbia has a JD/PhD program explicitly in legal history. There are probably others.

I have three reactions to these developments. The first is that I welcome them wholeheartedly. One of the reasons why I welcome them is not that I think that one cannot learn a discipline on one's own, or largely on one's own. If I thought that, I would not call myself an historian. But having done it, I can say that it's not very efficient. There is a reason why we have teachers in addition to bibliographies and books.

My second reaction is to wonder whether all of it is really necessary. Prescinding for a moment from the question whether any lawyer will believe you if you do not have a law degree, or any historian if you do not have a history degree, is it really necessary for what we have been talking about to go through the whole program? It is sometimes said that we teach everything that we have to teach in the first year and half of law school and that we spend the other year and half convincing the students of that fact. Similarly, the person with legal training who does a history PhD program through the general exams may not need to do the dissertation if he or she already knows how to do original historical research and write up a major piece of research.

My third reaction is more complicated. A degree in law does not a lawyer make, and I'm not sure that a degree in history makes one an historian. It takes some imagination to transfer the experience of appearing before the United States Court of Appeals for the Sixth Circuit to that of a serjeant-at-law appearing before Chief Justice Robert Belknap and his companions in the late fourteenth century, but if one has had the first experience, one is probably better able to imagine the second. On the other side, the social historian at York whose work with the York cases I find troublesome has examined a wide range of sources and has written widely about the experiences of women in later medieval England. I know his sources, but I cannot begin to put them together in the way that he has if I am also expected to teach first-year property and wills and trusts.

My fourth reaction is more complicated still. There is a certain kind of analytic smarts that is characteristic of good lawyers, which enables them to penetrate through a thicket of contradictory rules and see what is likely to be a winning argument within the institutional constraints that are imposed by whatever legal setting the lawyer happens to be in. The technique can be taught, but some lawyers are better at it than others. There is a certain kind of historical smarts that is characteristic of good historians, which enables them to see connections between people, between events, between ideas, between social groups and forces. Once more, the technique can be taught, but some historians are better at it than others. Excellence in one or the other technique may not be essential for being a good lawyer or historian, but the first characteristic may be essential for the best teaching and writing of what we have defined as internal legal history and the second for what we have defined as external legal history. Very few people are equally good at both; hence, even if one is trained in both disciplines but is moderately self-aware, one is likely to lean on the technique at which one is better. If that is right, joint degrees may help, but they will not solve the problem.

When I left Harvard with a bachelor's degree in 1962, there was a busy street that separated the area of the campus that contained the law school from that which contained the faculty of arts and sciences. One took one's life in one's hands crossing that street, in both a literal and a figurative sense. When I returned to Harvard in 1978, the street had been sent underground and there was a grassy pedestrian mall on top. I still, however, have to tell some third-year law students where Widener Library is located. Perhaps what is needed is more people crossing that mall, in both directions, and working with the people on the other side.[26] That is not going to be easy. Collaborative work is not the tradition in either law or history, but perhaps the next important step will be to get it to happen.

NOTES

1. Charles Donahue Jr., review of *The Life of the Law,* by John Honnold, *Columbia Law Review* 67 (1967): 1353–60.

2. Oliver Wendell Holmes Jr., "The Path of the Law," *Harvard Law Review* 10 (1897): 469. David Seipp (personal communication) reminds me that there may not be that much distance between Holmes and the skeptics of the 1960s: "History must be a part of the study [of law], because without it we cannot know the precise scope of rules which it is our business to know. It is a part of the rational study because it is the first step toward an enlightened scepticism, that is, toward a deliberate reconsideration of the worth of those rules. When you get the dragon out of his cave on to the plain and in the daylight, you can count his teeth and claws, and see just what is his strength. But to get him out is only the first step. The next is either to kill him, or to tame him and make him a useful animal. For the rational study of the law the black-letter man may be the man of the present, but the man of the future is the man of statistics and the master of economics. It is revolting to have no better reason for a rule of law than thus it was so in the time of Henry IV."

3. The version of Development of Legal Institutions that Mark Howe taught at Harvard was considerably more popular than the version taught by Dawson, perhaps because Howe confined himself pretty much to American developments.

4. These two from positions in the faculty of arts and sciences rather than from positions in the law school.

5. There are exceptions, or seeming exceptions, to every generalization. John Langbein has for many years taught a highly successful second- and third-year law school course in Anglo-

American legal history with a strong institutional emphasis. His class materials, currently entitled "History of the Common Law: The Development of Anglo-American Legal Institutions," are to be published in 2009 by Aspen (with Bruce Smith and Renée Lerner as coauthors) and may begin a return to Development of Legal Institutions as a course.

6. Philip Girard kindly shared with me an advance copy his article "Who's Afraid of Canadian Legal History?" now published in the *University of Toronto Law Journal* 57 (2007): 727–53. Despite differences that we can confidently attribute to the different colonial histories of the two countries, there seem to be remarkable similarities in what happened to legal history in law schools.

7. One can get an impression from the leading textbooks, e.g., Stephen B. Presser and Jamail Zainaldin, *Law and Jurisprudence in American History,* 6th ed. (St. Paul, Minn.: West, 2006); Kermit L. Hall, Paul Finkelman, and James W. Ely Jr., *American Legal History: Cases and Materials*, 3d ed. (New York: Oxford University Press, 2005); and J. H. Baker, *An Introduction to English Legal History,* 4th ed. (London: Butterworths LexisNexis, 2002). The first two emphasize the connections between legal history and broader history; the last does not. Most teachers I know of, however, pick and choose materials in these books, supplement extensively, and present quite different visions from those suggested in the books.

8. The Institute for Constitutional Studies at the George Washington University School of Law is premised on the proposition that there has been a marked decline in such courses. See Institute for Constitutional Studies, http://docs.law.gwu.edu/ics/index.htm (accessed Dec. 17, 2006).

9. I have reached the age at which I have to be careful about making such statements, and I am certainly not positing that there ever was a golden age, but I have been depressed in recent years by what seems to be a startling increase in the number of my first-year property students who do not seem to know who John Marshall was or who are unclear about the difference between John Marshall and Thurgood.

10. That phenomenon is also the product of the decline of language instruction in American high schools and colleges. Again, I don't want to pretend that there ever was a golden age, but the barriers to becoming a competent English or continental European legal historian are certainly lower if one starts off with a basic reading knowledge of Latin and French.

11. This story is largely derived from James S. Rogers, *The Early History of the Law of Bills and Notes* (Cambridge: Cambridge University Press, 1995). I will caution that it is the best explanation that we currently have, but economic historians have yet to come to grips with it.

12. Obviously, I am exaggerating here, but as a generalization, I think it holds true. This does not mean, of course, that such historians will not study the effect the legal system has on the society (even if the society determines what kind of legal system it is going to have).

13. Robert W. Gordon may have introduced this use of these terms. See, e.g., "J. Willard Hurst and the Common Law Tradition in American Legal Historiography," *Law and Society Review* 10 (1975): 11 and n. 5 (where, curiously, he derives the terms from Kuhn's study of the history of science rather than the French study of legal history); see also Gordon's "Critical Legal Histories," *Stanford Law Review* 36 (1984): 57, 60–61 and n. 11, 66, 88, 90, 101, 115, 123.

14. David Ibbetson, "Historical Research in Law," in *The Oxford Handbook of Legal Studies,* ed. Peter Cane and Mark Tushnet (Oxford: Oxford University Press, 2003), 870.

15. David Ibbetson, "What Is Legal History a History Of?" in *Law and History, Current Legal Issues 2003,* ed. Andrew Lewis and Michael Lobban (Oxford: Oxford University Press,

2004), 33–34. In fairness, Ibbetson argues that the history of institutions is not part of the history of law, which he seems to distinguish from legal history.

16. S. F. C. Milsom, *The Legal Framework of English Feudalism* (Cambridge: Cambridge University Press, 1976).

17. S. F. C. Milsom, "Trespass from Henry II to Edward III," *Law Quarterly Review* 74 (1958): 195–224, 407–36, 561–90, reprinted in Milsom, *Studies in the History of the Common Law* (London: Hambledon, 1985), 1–90. For a view of the same developments that emphasizes the social and political more than the institutional, see Robert Palmer, *English Law in the Age of the Black Death, 1348–1381* (Chapel Hill: University of North Carolina Press, 1993), 139–293.

18. Richard Chused, "Married Women's Property Law: 1800–1850," *Georgetown Law Journal* 71 (1983): 1398–99, argues, successfully in my view, that it was not the first, but I stick to the traditional date and place here because the circumstances of the passage of this statute have been particularly well explored. Elizabeth Gaspar Brown, "Husband and Wife: Memorandum on the Mississippi Woman's Law of 1839," *Michigan Law Review* 42 (1944): 1110–21.

19. A deft sketch may be found in Hendrik Hartog, *Man and Wife: A History* (Cambridge, Mass.: Harvard University Press, 2000), 287–308, but that book is largely devoted to antebellum developments.

20. E.g., Oval A. Phipps, "Tenancy by Entireties," *Temple Law Quarterly* 25 (1951): 24–57. The general story of married women's property acts, with particular emphasis on the period up to 1850, is well told in four articles by Richard Chused: "Married Women's Property and Inheritance by Widows in Massachusetts: A Study of Wills Probated between 1800 and 1850," *Berkeley Women's Law Journal* 2 (1986): 42–88; "Late Nineteenth Century Married Women's Property Law: Reception of the Early Married Women's Property Acts by Courts and Legislatures," *American Journal of Legal History* 29 (1985): 3–35; "The Oregon Donation Act of 1850 and Nineteenth Century Federal Married Women's Property Law," *Law and History Review* 2 (1984): 44–78; "Married Women's Property Law," 1359–425.

21. 30 N.J. 395, 153 A.2d 49 (1959). New Jersey's first Married Women's Property Act was passed in 1852.

22. *Ingoly c. Middleton, Easingwold and Wright*, York, Borthwick Institute, MS. CP.F.201 (1430). The case is discussed in Charles Donahue, "A Legal Historian Looks at the Case Method," *Northern Kentucky Law Journal* 19 (1991): 19–31, and is featured in my *Law, Marriage, and Society in the Later Middle Ages* (Cambridge: Cambridge University Press, 2007), 52–57, 60–61, 63, 69, 90, 126, 142, 201, 203, 264.

23. Donahue, "A Legal Historian," 25–27.

24. P. J. P. Goldberg, *Women, Work, and Life Cycle in a Medieval Economy: Women in York and Yorkshire c.1300–1520* (Oxford: Oxford University Press, 1992), 256–57.

25. An exception: Paul Brand, the scholar today who has the best command of the intricacies of thirteenth-century English law, was not trained as a lawyer.

26. Tom Green (personal communication) notes that it has long since been happening in American legal history. There certainly seem to be more people in American legal history who have formal training in both disciplines, and who make a serious effort to combine the two in their own work. To the extent, however, that I am right that it is very difficult to be equally up to speed in both disciplines, a call for collaboration, of which there seems to be very little, may be in order. The example of the hard sciences and some of the social sciences comes to mind.

16

The Moral Lives of Intellectual Properties

STEVEN WILF

NEW YORK'S SON OF SAM LAW IS A COPYRIGHT STATUTE. PASSED IN RE-sponse to attempts by David Berkowitz, the serial killer popularly known as the Son of Sam who terrorized New York City in 1972, to profit from his crimes, it could be invoked whenever accused or convicted violent criminals made a contractual agreement to speak or write about their crimes in exchange for remuneration. According to the statute, any profits from crime narratives would be placed in an escrow account. Victims may seek compensation by filing a civil action within five years of the signing of a media contract.[1]

If copyright's purpose is to create incentives for the creation and dissemination of expression, and if the Son of Sam law is, in part, intended to dissuade criminals by removing incentives, then Son of Sam is really part of intellectual property law's overarching system. The statute potentially barred profits from a wide range of speech acts (with respect to the enactment of such crime, by way of a movie, book, magazine article, tape recording, phonograph record, radio, or television presentation, live entertainment of any kind or from the expression of such accused or convicted person's thoughts, feelings, opinions, or emotions regarding such a crime."[2] Its stated purpose was to prevent a windfall from notoriety gained through a criminal act.[3]

In *Simon & Schuster Inc. v. Members of the N.Y. State Crime Victims Board*, the U.S. Supreme Court in 1991 struck down New York's Son of Sam law as unconstitutional.[4] Although the Court found a compelling state interest in limiting a criminal's profits from the fruits of the crime, the Son of Sam law was determined to be overly broadly defined and entailing content-based discrimination. What is striking is the collective amnesia—the almost psychological repression—concerning the idea that intellectual property laws might be used to distin-

I would like to thank Meredith McGill for her comments, and the Institute for Advanced Studies at Hebrew University in Jerusalem.

guish between moral and immoral writings. The Supreme Court framed its criticism of the Son of Sam law broadly under the umbrella of freedom of expression, never mentioning intellectual property issues. Seeking to surmount the constitutional objections leveled in the Supreme Court's *Simon & Schuster* opinion, New York in 1992 passed a new statute. It goes one step further in distancing the Son of Sam law from intellectual property concerns by embedding issues of expression in the overarching framework of criminal forfeiture.[5]

I do not wish to argue the legal implications of thinking about the Son of Sam law as a copyright statute—whether intellectual property itself allows for certain discrete limitations in freedom of expression, the importance of content nondiscrimination in various intellectual property regimes, or the possibility of copyright preemption barring the implementation of the state statute. What is striking to me is what *not* seeing this tells us about our legal culture. No one—not scholars, not judges, not practicing attorneys arguing cases before courts—has truly examined Son of Sam within its intellectual property skein.[6] No one has suggested that provisions stripping criminals of copyright protection should be incorporated into the 1976 copyright statute in a manner similar to the way additional protections were granted to artists as moral rights.[7] In a sense, we are looking at a repressed legal gaze—one that, in a Freudian sense, has led to an overlooking, a forgetting, a *mis(sed)*-classification, a lack of consciousness, that is noteworthy.

What is the source of this averted gaze? It has become a commonplace—I should say an unexamined commonplace—to claim that U.S. intellectual property law rests primarily upon utilitarian considerations.[8] Accordingly, the sole purpose of granting rights in intellectual property is to foster incentives for the creation and dissemination of the products of knowledge. As the Supreme Court has stated, "The framers intended copyright itself to be the engine of free expression. By establishing a marketable right to the use of one's expression, copyright supplies the economic incentive to create and disseminate ideas."[9]

Such an approach generally has looked for support in the language of the copyright and patent clause, often anachronistically referred to as the intellectual property clause,[10] of the U.S. Constitution: "The Congress shall have power . . . to promote the progress of science and the useful arts, by securing for limited times to authors and inventors the exclusive right to their respective writings and discoveries."[11] This is, I believe, the only place in the main body of the Constitution outside the Preamble where a goal is ascribed to a vested power. Such purposeful language of promoting the progress of science and the useful arts has been used to bolster claims of utilitarian objectives.

The dominance of this received narrative cannot be overestimated, and it has only been strengthened with the rise of law and economics.[12] In recent years, a turn toward literary history has sought to reconstruct the contingent cultural basis of authorship, suggesting that the myth of the author has been critically important in justifying rights in works of expression. However, the scholarship on authorship still focuses on markets—it is simply the myth of how the author shaped the literary market as opposed to the rational construction of a utilitarian system of incentives.[13] This essay takes a very different approach. It is an attempt to place the public at the very beginnings of U.S. copyright, and to show how the presence throughout the nineteenth century of notions of public virtue or public morality—what I call the moral lives of intellectual properties—brought to the fore issues of the public good. Such moral considerations often reflect counter-market issues of morality.

This essay has two parts. The first examines the U.S. Constitution's intellectual property clause, the copyright and patent clause, in the context of the political culture of the late eighteenth century, the aftermath of the American Revolution, and the establishment of the early Republic. A contextual reading of the clause suggests that it should be read as emerging within a republican framework. Since the Framers' recorded constitutional debates concerning intellectual property are remarkably thin, the evidence for a republican reading will come largely from context. As I will show, intellectual property, especially copyright, emerged as part of a larger Revolutionary project of constructing a public sphere predicated upon republican notions of virtue and the public good.

The second part will examine the nineteenth-century reworking of the idea of promoting progress as a moral venture with a focus on the public good. Here the moral lives of intellectual properties, and the purposes of the intellectual property clause, are read within the framework of nineteenth-century moral reform movements. Throughout the nineteenth century, copyright withdrew protection from obscene works, trademark developed a doctrine of barring registration of scandalous and immoral marks, and moral utility—the fact that an invention does not appear morally abhorrent to the public—became a prerequisite for patentability. How did these moral lives evolve over time? How were moral determinations made? And what does the fact that intellectual property has a moral life, as well as a utilitarian aspect, tell us about the role of the public good?

I realize that I am delving into odd, rather neglected corners of intellectual property doctrine. While the language of morals seems so alien to our thinking about knowledge and the protection of intangibles, it was for many in the late eighteenth and nineteenth centuries a way of expressing the core role of the public good as the centerpiece of intellectual property law. Yet from a methodological point of view, such shadowy traces, minor details, odd byways, and seemingly vestigial legal historical brushstrokes often tell us about how contemporaries viewed the *meaning*—the legal consciousness—behind norms. Early modern historian Carlo Ginzburg has famously argued that we need to adopt the methods of art historians, who look at the most minor aspects of a painting in order to determine its authenticity. Calling this the Morelli method, Ginzburg argues that marginal details are more important as clues than obvious facts.[14] But even the seemingly obscure aspects of doctrine have real significance. To unpack the meaning of earlier legal rules and justifications for past intellectual property law is to understand the contingent nature of this particular form of property—which ultimately allows us to reopen the question of alternative goals of intellectual property.

This essay ends with a discussion of the normative significance of the act of forgetting the republican beginnings of intellectual property and the moral doctrines of the nineteenth century. Morton Horwitz has taught us all the familiar narrative arc of the common law's "moral sense of community" being displaced by legal instrumentalism, which fosters the interests of existing organizations of economic and political power.[15] However, Horwitz and his many followers have often preferred to trace the rise of dominant legal discourses while ignoring those norms that have been superseded. I am offering here an alternative account about how past law is forgotten, misunderstood, rendered vestigial, and buried. When, toward the end of the twentieth century, American lawyers encountered European intellectual property public welfare provisions, they considered these notions, which were founded on natural law ideals, alien to U.S. law—but, I will argue, this is only because they failed to recall the biographical details of America's moral lives of intellectual properties.[16]

THE REPUBLICAN ORIGINS OF U.S. INTELLECTUAL PROPERTY

In 1774, the Continental Congress banned theatrical performances and public cockfights.[17] In 1783, when the military conflict was over, the Continental Congress passed a recommendation that states establish legislation to protect literary property. These two seemingly incongruous pieces of legislation were united by a concern with expression in the public sphere as the locus for creating an informed citizenry shaped by notions of republican virtue.[18]

Virtue was a core paradigm of Revolutionary America. Historians have traced the cultural inheritance of Renaissance virtue (*virtù*) from civic humanist sources through the American patriot trope of anti-corruption. Virtue had a different meaning for eighteenth-century Americans than it does for contemporaries. It reflected a bit of anti-modernism; a suspicion of patronage-related manipulations of power and of direct democracy at the same time; and, above all, self-sacrifice for the public good.[19] For American revolutionaries, history repeatedly showed that republics such as Rome and Venice might be destroyed by self-interest, ambition, and institutionalized corruption. England's society and politics stood as an exemplar of corruption as an antipode to the ideal of a future New World republic founded upon virtue.

To survive the constant threat from corruption, late eighteenth-century

Americans turned to public opinion as a tribunal. American Revolutionary politics were quintessentially what French historian Keith Baker has called a politics of contestation. Disputes about search and seizure, taxation, and the administrative organization of a transatlantic empire were argued in coffeehouses, through the printing of broadsides and political ballads, and in a rapidly growing number of newspapers. Protection of literary property was seen within the context of the emergence of the republican public sphere.[20]

The making of the first full-fledged American copyright law was really a two-step process. First, states created their own statutes securing copyright in the 1780s. For the most part, these statutes were passed as part of a Continental Congress proposal for states to promulgate legislation for the protection of literary property.[21] Second, with the ratification of the Constitution and the inclusion of the intellectual property clause, the federal Copyright Act of 1790 created for the first time protection under federal jurisdiction.[22] The state statutes have been largely ignored, and, as has been shown with the recovery of the earliest state constitutions, much is to be learned from their examination.

The beginnings of American copyright law in the new Republic looked much like contemporary movements to harmonize different national systems. States passed copyright statutes with some similarities, but also with significant differences in such matters as terms of protection, registration provisions, and affirmative defenses to infringement suits. This is not surprising. At the end of the eighteenth century, Americans still thought of the states as a confederation of republics. But from a contemporary point of view, it seems ironic that American intellectual property law, which through the nineteenth century resisted engaging in the project of international harmonization of statutes, truly began as international law.[23]

On May 2, 1783, the Continental Congress recommended that the newly formed states secure copyright for a term of fourteen years from the date of first publication for citizens of the United States who were authors.[24] Nothing was particularly remarkable about the term of protection, which directly followed the precedent of England's Statute of Anne (1710).[25] What was striking was the very act of protecting literary property. Copyright and patents were monarchical privileges. To claim the right to issue these was an assertion of sovereign rights on the part of the Continental Congress as much as executing felons, reconstructing treason law away from its monarchical roots, or striking coinage. Moreover, the Continental Congress's proposal must be understood in its eighteenth-century context as one of the signals of republican virtue, such as criminal law reform, an electoral process that sought to disfavor the influence of privileged interests, and democratically organized militias.

The Continental Congress proposed that states draft copyright statute in the midst of war. As it was debating how to protect fragile supply lines, establishing ad hoc mechanisms to deal with the collapse of the British administrative apparatus, and desperately raising funds to purchase arms, the Continental Congress certainly had more pressing concerns than authorial rights. Why, then, pass such a measure? The protection of literary property in the new Republic must be seen as pointing in two directions. On one hand, it was a simple statement of national aspirations. On the other hand, not only did copyright suggest the creation of an independent New World culture and the signaling of republican virtue, but it might also have been viewed as the basis of a new radical form of governance, where the democratic public sphere, the participation of an informed citizenry in an immediate and tangible fashion, might be accomplished. The construction of the public sphere as an autonomous locus of debates—coffeehouses, broadsides, and the rapid growth of political writing and street demonstrations—perhaps prompted a move toward making a legislative contribution to the public sphere through copyright statutes.

Indeed, this Janus-faced understanding of early copyright might be seen in the identities of the two founding fathers of American copyright law: Noah Webster, who untiringly traveled from state legislature to state legislature in the 1780s to lobby for the passage of state copyright statutes, and Joel Barlow, who prodded the Continental Congress in 1783 to recommend that states secure copyright protection for citizens. Yale classmates and fellow Connecticut authors, Webster and Barlow lived part of their lives within a few miles of each other. Nevertheless, they hailed from different ends of the political spectrum. Webster saw copyright as part of a national project to create a distinctive American language with its own grammar and spelling. A conservative at heart, Webster would become a Federalist.[26]

Barlow, one of the most radical members of the revolutionary generation, ultimately in his 1792 *Advice to the Privileged Orders* would serve as a cheerleader for the turning upside down of traditional hierarchies. While Webster abhorred revolutionary French politics in the 1790s, Barlow defended the French Revolution even during some of its excesses.[27] Yet the two men shared a mission to create a new American culture with a new language and a literature of its own. Webster did so through grammar, while Barlow composed *The Columbiad*—intended to be Revolutionary America's great epic.

Noah Webster completed his first books on the English language in the midst of the Revolutionary War. As he describes, school textbooks were difficult to obtain. In order to lobby for a law securing his rights to these manuscripts, he visited the legislatures of New Jersey, Pennsylvania, Connecticut, New York, and Massachusetts and Philadelphia and spoke with various well-connected individuals about passing a copyright statute. His success in enacting legislation was clearly dependent upon connections with literary figures. For example, Timothy Dwight, a poet who was at that time a member of the Massachusetts House of Representatives and later president of Yale University, was instrumental in passing the Massachusetts copyright statute. In May 1785, Webster took a tour through the middle and southern states with similar success.[28]

No doubt, Webster had pecuniary motives in promoting statutory protection for literary production. Enormously successful, Webster's *A Grammatical Institute* would be reprinted in 385 editions during his lifetime.[29] But Webster's attempt to bring the Revolutionary struggle to the field of language was very much part of a larger republican project. According to Webster, America must not slavishly import the literary taste of Europe but must sift through the wisdom of other nations, avoiding their corruption, and Webster's pivotal role in the creation of state copyright law is telling. As he wrote in the preface to one of his books, European "laws are perverted, manners are licentious, literature is declining, and human nature debased. . . . It is the business of America to select the wisdom of all nations."[30] In his petitions, Webster drew upon republican political commonplaces to lay claim to legislative protection. His work was useful because it would root out European linguistic corruption imported from England, and reform language to the establish American virtue.

While Webster took his model statute from state to state, Joel Barlow sought the establishment of copyright by directly lobbying the Continental Congress. We lack contemporary sources describing Barlow's rationale for advocating the establishment of copyright. Like Webster, Barlow was an author, and self-interest may certainly have been a motive. But Barlow was also an advocate of direct democracy. He urged the writing of laws free of legal terminology and easily accessible to the public at large. For Barlow, copyright might well have meant a strengthening of the public sphere. On January 10, 1783, Barlow wrote a letter to Elias Boudinot, a New Jersey delegate, suggesting that the Continental Congress should direct the states to pass statutes protecting literary property. A few months later, in March, a committee was appointed to determine the means for encouraging literature. On May 2, 1783, the Continental Congress recommended that the states secure the copyright for citizens of the United States who were authors for a term of fourteen years from the date of first publication.

During the next three years, only one of the original thirteen states, Delaware, failed to pass a copyright act.[31] The purpose of protecting literary property, as it was called, was not mentioned in the Continental Congress's resolution. However, various states set out reasons in their preambles. Connecticut, for example, called its statute "An Act for the Encouragement of Literature and Genius." Some preambles, such as New Jersey's, addressed issues of misappropriation and equity.[32] Maryland stated its statute was to prevent wrongful practices such as the reprinting of books without the consent of their authors.[33] Copyright, states the Georgia statute, flows from "the principles of equity and justice."[34] But many states, like Connecticut, trumpeted republican notions of service to the common good and securing profits so "men of learning and genius" would be encouraged to publish their writings and thereby "do honor to their country, and service to mankind."

The statutes of Massachusetts and Rhode Island spoke of the "progress of civilization" and the public good of the community.[35]

Britain's 1710 Statute of Anne provided a model for stating the purpose of copyright legislation. It was called "An Act for the Encouragement of Learning." The Statute of Anne pointed toward protecting both booksellers and authors. Describing the adverse impact of unauthorized copying on the families of authors, the Statute of Anne's preamble stated the need to encourage "learned men to compose and write useful books."[36] Nevertheless, most protections were directed toward publishers. In the American case, however, republican political notions formed the grounding for America's first copyright laws. On one hand, state laws underscored the role of copyright in creating the cultural fabric of the new Republic. On the other hand, certain state statutes such as those of Massachusetts and New Hampshire recognized the author's natural right to his or her intellectual products. As the Massachusetts statute states, "There is no property more peculiarly a man's own than that which is produced by the labor of his mind."[37]

These statutes protected books, pamphlets, maps, and charts published for the first time. South Carolina added a provision for inventors with similar privileges and terms.[38] Seven states—Connecticut, Maryland, New Jersey, Pennsylvania, South Carolina, Georgia, and New York—followed the Statute of Anne and granted a renewable fourteen-year term. Works therefore might be protected as in England for twenty-eight years. The remaining states chose to provide for a single term of protection. Massachusetts, Virginia, and Rhode Island, for example, granted a twenty-one-year term.[39] The duration of copyright was twenty years in New Hampshire, and in North Carolina half the length of time allowable under the recommendation of the Continental Congress, a single term of fourteen years.[40] The decision of states to depart from the recommendation of the Continental Congress to model copyright laws after the English Statute of Anne both speaks to the sense that states were acting as independent sovereign bodies and suggests a lingering concern that the monopoly granted literary property was too extensive. Each variation in copyright duration was a downward departure.

Registration was generally required. Massachusetts had a provision for the deposit of two copies at Harvard University.[41] Authors could accomplish this by registering either with the secretary of state or with a special office called a prothonotary, the clerk's office at the court of common pleas.[42] The very fact of registration suggested that copyright protection was vested as a privilege by the state, presumably in exchange for some benefit, and was not a natural right.[43] Registration also created formidable obstacles to protection, especially for non-locals. These statutes only provided rights for citizens or inhabitants of the United States, not for foreign authors. As one might expect in light of the fact that the original colonies still thought of themselves as distinct governing bodies, there was still a model of harmonization—the idea that different regimes would share common requirements—rather than a single overarching copyright regime.

The earliest U.S. intellectual property law, which existed prior to the ratification of the Constitution, included what might be considered international law provisions. The basis of copyright was territorial. Each state operated as a sovereign entity affording protection to authors of other states on a reciprocal basis. Authors from other states would only secure rights in Massachusetts or New York, for example, after those states granted their citizens similar exclusive rights.[44] Maryland's and Pennsylvania's statutory copyright protections would commence after statutes protecting literary property were passed in every state.[45] Although Delaware remained the only state without a functioning copyright statute, its failure to pass a law securing the rights of authors meant that the copyright laws of a certain number of other states never met their legal requirements to begin functioning. No state extended protection to authors who were not U.S. citizens.

Perhaps the most remarkable clause found in some of the state statutes is one meant to ensure that useful books would be available at reasonable prices. These would provide for public action whenever an author or publisher failed to furnish the public with a sufficient number of editions or overcharged for them. Taking into account labor, time, expense, and risk of sale, an author had a right to reasonable compensation, but not to set too high a price. After a legal complaint was lodged, a state court judge would summon the owner of the copyright to appear before him. A court might determine whether to order the author or publisher to print a certain number of additional copies at a set just price. If the owner of the copyright refused to comply, the court might assign to the person making the complaint a license to reprint copies. Connecticut, South Carolina, North Carolina, Virginia, Georgia, and New York all had this mechanism for making copyrighted material available even against the wishes of the copyright holder. This provision was a classic example of what historians have called the moral economy.[46] Just prices would be set for commodities by a regulatory institution. These prices reflected customary commercial mores, a sense of mutual obligation, and a balancing of the interests of producers and consumers. As has been shown, the moral economy—truly, a regulated economy—was a widespread form of political economy for participants in the American Revolution.[47]

Perhaps it was the very existence of state copyright protection that prompted the inclusion of an intellectual property clause in the U.S. Constitution.[48] The Framers had seen the difficulty of authors lobbying each state for protection. U.S. copyright really began as international copyright under the umbrella of a harmonization directive—the Continental Congress's 1783 motion. State citizens and non-citizens were often treated differently. The constitutional clause established a single, uniform national framework. In an address to the Constitutional Convention in April 1787, Madison spoke of the "want of uniformity in the law concerning naturalization and literary property."[49] As we have seen, it was easy to create a race for the bottom in terms of terms, to favor one's own citizens over others in the new Republic.

In the absence of recorded debates, we need to read the constitutional clause against the background of late eighteenth-century political culture and the establishment of earlier state protection of intellectual property in the aftermath of the American Revolution. Indeed, constitutionalization of a commitment to create a republican public sphere began at the state level. One section of the 1780 Massachusetts Constitution was entitled "The Encouragement of Literature, etc." It required the state legislature to "cherish the interests of literature and the sciences," since "wisdom and knowledge, as well as virtue, diffused generally among the body of the people . . . [are] necessary for the preservation of their rights and liberties." The connection between republican conceptions of virtue and the dissemination of knowledge is made explicit. Promoting literature and science will "inculcate the principles of humanity and general benevolence, public and private charity, industry and frugality, honesty and punctuality in their dealings; sincerity, good humor, and all social affections, and generous sentiments, among the people."[50]

In many ways, constitutionalizing intellectual property law is an unusual move. If the right to literary property, for example, were a common-law right, then it could enter U.S. law through reception statutes. If it was a property right, specific property regulations would be passed under the constitutional provisions dealing with legislative powers to regulate property in general. Why, then, is there a clause about the diffusion of knowledge in a state constitution? The example of Massachusetts provides structural evidence. Its section for "The Encouragement of Literature" is located in the section of the state constitution dealing with enumerated duties and responsibilities. The executive, legislature, and judiciary have their characteristics. The need for the people, this suggests, is to be an informed citizenry—a kind of fourth branch.

Nevertheless, the U.S. constitutional clause had three important aspects. First, the purpose "to promote the progress of science and the useful arts" clearly adopted the republican mission of those state statutes that saw copyright or patent as core to the Revolutionary experiment. "Securing for limited times," secondly, established limited terms for copyright and patent. It reflected concerns with monopoly. The intellectual property clause would not countenance perpetual protection—though this was promoted later by Webster, who pushed for a bill in 1830 to vest perpetual rights in literary property.[51] Those who grounded intellectual property on common-law norms also raised the specter of literary property protection without limited terms.[52]

Third, the copyright and patent clause was intended to restrict the power of Congress to provide rights to creators, not to "introducers of any new works or inventions."[53] As Doron Ben-Atar has shown, there was considerable emphasis in the eighteenth century on rewarding individuals who carried knowledge from one country to another—either through the transfer of written material or the appropriation of trade secrets of mechanical knowledge.[54] The Constitution decidedly chooses to link reward to the growing of local genius.

To be sure, we tend to think today of copyright as a default, a general utilitarian mechanism of diffusing knowledge. But in the context of the late eighteenth century, copyright was very much the exception, not the rule. A large number of works entered the United States through importation and were not afforded copyright. Formidable formality requirements in many of the state statutes and in the 1790 federal Copyright Act, and the recognition by many authors of the absence of a significant market, meant that publishers and authors rarely sought copyright protection. Although there are nearly fifteen thousand American imprints between 1790 and 1800, only 779 copyright registrations have been found for this period. Even accounting for failures in record keeping, this suggests that the vast majority of printed works were not protected.[55]

MORAL LIVES OF INTELLECTUAL PROPERTY

During the early nineteenth century, legal thinkers were divided about the grounding of literary property. Was copyright, for example, to be justified as common law as Joseph Story suggested, or through natural rights in property as Lysander Spooner claimed, or were these simply, in the words of Jacksonian proponent William Leggett, "artificial rights"?[56] This conceptual debate made a difference. Leggett celebrated cheap editions of books as a means to spread literature among all classes of society and sought to annul copyright since language is "the common property of all mankind."

This debate elicited a moral language about the equity of rights to intangible property.[57] But it was not until the nineteenth century, when post–Civil War reform movements reworked abolitionism into a broad pastiche of reform movements, that the moral lives of intellectual properties had their apotheosis. In the midst of this moral discourse, a collection of doctrines that set moral bars to intellectual property rights emerged. Copyright developed a doctrine of non-protection, which would provide a complete legal defense to infringement if the copied work were deemed obscene. Trademark doctrine would not allow the registration of scandalous or immoral marks. Patent developed the doctrine of moral utility, which made immorality a bar to patentability.

These three doctrines are today both fairly obscure and largely obsolete. Pornographic works currently receive the same copyright protection as great works of literature.[58] Gambling machines now can be patented. Only trademark law, with the scandalous-and-immoral-marks clause, section 2(a) of the 1948 Lanham Act, still has a functioning moral standard. Even in the case of trademark, as we shall see, the use of this clause has been curtailed. Nevertheless, a great deal can be learned from how courts drew upon and ultimately abandoned moral intellectual property doctrines.

Copyright Non-protection Doctrine

The United States inherited from England a long-standing doctrine that immoral works could not be protected under copyright.[59] To be copyright protected, a composition must be "free from illegality or immorality."[60] Indeed, an early case in 1720, *Burnett v. Chetwood,* extends nearly as far back as England's earliest statutory framework for copyright. This is not surprising. While we tend to think of copyright in terms of diffusion of knowledge, the granting of such monopolies in the early modern period often reflected the state's desire to *limit* expression. The very idea of registering copyright as required by the Statute of Anne brought works to the notice of the authorities and therefore might have well been part of a broader system of political control.[61]

English courts differed as to whether the author of an immoral work was ab initio not vested with property rights or whether the author simply could not collect damages.[62] In other words, is moral literary production a prerequisite for copyright—much like originality, expression, or having material fixed in a tangible medium of expression—or is it similar to an affirmative defense against unclean hands?[63]

In the American context this is a particularly interesting question, because perhaps the earliest U.S. copyright non-protection case in 1860 attributes this doctrine to the common law.[64] Courts also relied upon the language of the 1856 Copyright Act, which provided copyright for "compositions desired or suited for public representation" as establishing a statutory bar on protection of immoral works.[65] But within a decade, courts were again grappling with the basis for non-protection. In an 1867 case, *Martinetti v. Maguire,* for example, the court invalidated an infringement action for a play depicting a Mohammedan paradise, a harem of sorts, with scantily clad women in a variety of tableau poses, since—and here is the important part—as an immoral composition, it could not be said "to promote the progress of science and the useful arts."[66]

Does it matter whether the origins of copyright non-protection doctrine are common law, statutory, or constitutional? It did for courts. Common law contributed an element of flexibility, of change over time. In *Keene v. Kimball*, the early source for common-law roots, the court stated that "the particular application of this rule of the common law [which is] once made in conformity with the particular opinions, sentiments, or prejudices of one generation of men, will not control its application in a state of society when different views prevail."[67]

In other words, this is a flexible bar that shifts and is redefined according to varying community standards. The constitutional argument, with its claims of promoting public morals, took a similar approach. In *Simonton v. Gordon*, where a play was accused of infringing on a book describing the debauched life of the African tropics, the court declined to find the work immoral. According to its decision, since the principle of non-protection "rests in public policy, cases decided in one age are not a safe guide, on their facts, in subsequent times, and the present tendency, undoubtedly, is to allow much more latitude than formally to free speech."[68] The purpose of copyright, community standards, and other constitutional imperatives such as free expression must be balanced.

To see the doctrine of non-protection as relying upon the 1856 Copyright Act is to render it irrelevant, as some courts have done, as copyright's statutory language evolved.[69] Another approach was to raise the principle of nondiscrimination or content neutrality as a counterweight. In the well-known 1903 Supreme Court case of *Bleistein v. Donaldson Lithographing Co.*, Justice Oliver Wendell Holmes Jr. eschewed involvement in determining the value of popular art and therefore extended copyright to all forms of expression with categories of writing and art without regard to any evaluation of whether such works indeed promote the progress of science and the useful arts.[70] But if the source is common law—that is, if it is not statutory or constitutional in its origins—the limit of flexibility lies precisely in the common-law claim, which existed from the earliest U.S. discussions, that each generation must make its own decisions about morality.

Finding immoral tendencies was deeply contextual and placed courts in the awkward position of determining intent.[71] By the early twentieth century, one court resolved this conundrum by requiring a finding of criminal obscenity before invoking non-protection doctrine in order to deny recourse to damages or injunctive relief for copyright infringement.[72] Another shifted away from the classic definition of obscenity as set forth by the Hicklin test: a work that "depraves and corrupts those whose minds are open to such immoral influence and into whose hands a publication of this sort might fall" despite other redeeming features. Instead of Hicklin's imperative to focus simply upon immoral aspects, a California court borrowed a standard from postal regulations concerning obscene material and barred protection, which viewed corrupt tendencies only when the *work is considered as a whole*.[73]

Reluctance, cabining, placing legal rules within the framework of shifting social mores, and finding alternative tests, in the end, did not sufficiently shield courts from a doctrine believed to be increasingly at odds with modern notions of intellectual property. Two cases in the late 1970s and early 1980s finally extinguished the non-protection defense on the grounds that it was at odds with the language and intent of the 1976 Copyright Act.[74] No doubt, as common-law commentators would have pointed out, it was uncomfortable to extend non-protection to a broad array of writings that are seditious, obscene, immoral, blasphemous, or libelous. However, it is striking that the common-law and constitutional threads of this doctrine have disappeared—and, with them, a vestigial marking of copyright's interest in the public welfare.

Scandalous and Immoral Marks

While the copyright doctrine of non-protection faded away, the Trademark Office even to this day continues to grapple with the problem of determining whether a mark is scandalous or immoral, since under section 2(a) of the Lanham Act such marks should be refused registration.[75] The lack of federal registration does not mean that a mark deemed immoral cannot serve as a functioning trademark. It is simply stripped of the various procedural and substantive advantages of registration.[76] Nevertheless, the fact that similar bars against registration exist in almost all states underscores the prevalence of this doctrine.[77]

The origins of the scandalous-and-immoral-mark doctrine can be found in earlier common law.[78] However, it is only with the 1905 Trademark Act that it becomes fully embedded in an American legal framework, since such a doctrine requires a full-fledged registration system.[79] It seems that trademark law's statutory bar on scandalous and immoral marks emerged in the midst of copyright and patent's moral constraints. The first proposal for a statutory provision concerning immoral marks in 1892 echoed language that, as we shall see, derived from patent law's moral utility doctrine—the mark must not be "offensive to public sentiment or morals."[80] However, since this trademark doctrine has a clear and unambiguous statutory basis, it—unlike those in other regimes—has survived and has even been modified to meet shifting social mores.

Indeed, it has both expanded and contracted simultaneously. While the 1905 act only refers to marks that "consist of or comprise immoral or scandalous matter" (deceptive marks are dealt with elsewhere in the statute), the Lanham Act of 1948, the current operative trademark statute, bars registration of a much broader range of marks. It does not allow registration if a mark "consists of or comprises immoral, deceptive, or scandalous matter or matter which may disparage or falsely suggest a connection with persons living or dead, institutions, beliefs, or national symbols, or bring them into contempt or disrepute."[81]

Similar to the case with copyright, courts increasingly insisted that the scandalous-and-immoral-mark provision be interpreted in light of changing social mores. As one court noted, "what we considered scandalous as a trademark twenty, thirty, or fifty years ago may no longer be considered so, given the changes in societal attitudes."[82] Moreover, the determination of such a mark was to depend upon the particular goods upon which the trademark was affixed and its particular market. In a classic case where barring "Madonna" as a registered trademark for wine was upheld, a Pennsylvania court made reference to the distinctive nature of American culture, in which intoxicating beverages, as evidenced by Prohibition, are seen as morally troubling. As the dissent pointed out, the majority decision ignored the connection of wine with European culture, the elements of refinement, and even the miracle of Cannae, where at a wedding feast Jesus turned water into wine.[83]

Finally, in our own time, the Federal Circuit adopted a policy of favoring registration of a mark in ambiguous cases. For example, in the case of Bad Frog Beer, where the label depicts a frog "giving the finger," registration was permitted because the gesture does not have the bawdy meaning when made by an amphibian that it does when made by a human being. Although the use of scandalous and immoral marks has declined, section 2(a) of the Lanham Act's disparagement provisions has increasingly been used to address trademarks are perceived to be insulting to women and minorities. In contrast to copyright and patent, the moral lives of trademarks have had a new lease on life as a means to bring awareness of diversity to commercial morality.

Patent Moral Utility Doctrine

The third type of the intellectual property moral doctrine, moral utility, made moral issues a part of the general requirement that an invention had to possess utility in order to merit patent protection.[84] As early as 1827, Justice Joseph Story lay down the rule in *Lowell v. Lewis* that a device that is "frivolous or injurious to the well-being, good policy, or sound morals of society" does not fall within the ambit of patent law and cannot be infringed.[85] Justice Story provided examples such as inventions used to poison people, promote debauchery, and facilitate private assassination. But this per se list was expanded over the course of the nineteenth century to include gambling devices.[86] For Justice Story, morals and usefulness were inextricably connected. "By useful invention," in accordance with the 1793 Patent Act, he wrote, "is meant such a one as may be applied to some beneficial use in society, in contradistinction to an invention which is injurious to the morals, the health, or the good order of society. It is not necessary to establish, that the invention is of such general utility as to supersede all other inventions now in practice to accomplish the same purpose. It is sufficient that it may be applied to practical uses and that so far as it is applied it is salutary."[87] Indeed, the statutory meaning of utility in the 1793 Patent Act—which lacked any sort of examination system and granted patents when formalities were met—was limited to the requirement that inventions not be "hurtful, injurious, or pernicious."[88]

Clearly, not all devices that might be used in opposition to the "sound morals of society" fall under the moral doctrine. As is pointed out in one nineteenth-century treatise, a Colt revolver might be used for socially useful purposes such as self-defense or recreation, or alternatively, it may be a tool of private assassination.[89] Clearly, moral utility needed to be cabined. One approach was to shift the focus from a tendency to corrupt to an *absence* of a legitimate benefit for society—even one that could be imagined. For example, a device to detect counterfeit coins in a gambling machine was said to be able to do the same in other circumstances.[90] Finally, it seems that absent a direct legislative outlawing of a device, the Patent Office was increasingly unwilling to find a lack of moral utility.[91]

Nineteenth-century moral reform movements created the conceptual framework for moral utility. The focus shifted to discrete areas of life where moral battles were being waged over the utility not just of inventions, but of working-class and middle-class men. Gambling and saloons were seen as rendering men useless as breadwinners and productive members of society. Anti-gambling and anti-saloon organizations, promoted largely by reformist women, created a particularly gendered definition of moral corruption. Not surprisingly, moral utility appropriated this circumscribed moral focus. Connection to gambling, saloons, and, especially, the combination of the two suggested that an invention was not useful within the meaning of the Patent Act.[92] For example, a miniature automatic racecourse was seen as *contra boni mores* because wagers were placed in saloons.[93]

But it was difficult to know precisely what inventions were per se immoral and lacked any sort of redeeming social value. Gambling machines emerged in the 1870s as part of a general move toward mechanization. In the 1890s, Charles Fey, a German mechanic, created the modern version of the slot machine. The classic version of three fruits on the reel of the machine—cherries, oranges, and plums—suggested chewing gum flavors that one might win and therefore sidestepped patent limitations on gambling machines.[94] Even what looked like a clear-cut example of an invention that should be barred for reasons of moral utility might be allowed if an equally novel innocuous purpose could be invented.

As was the case with copyright's non-protection doctrine and trademark's scandalous and immoral marks, the move to cabin a troubling doctrine led to the eviscerating of moral intellectual property rules of any potential broader use. In a recent case, *Juicy Whip v. Orange Bang,* where an orange drink dispenser was intended to deceive customers as to how the drink was actually made, the court rejected the idea that the creation of false impressions for economic purposes was anything other than the usual course of business. The decision shed doubt upon whether there was any continued efficacy for the moral utility doctrine.[95]

CONCLUSION

Like the lives of cats, the moral lives of intellectual properties seem multiple. Although the received tradition of utilitarianism dominates intellectual property jurisprudence, we have recourse—whether we are aware or not—to broader concerns with the purpose of intellectual property and to moral doctrines simply because no other legal framework properly reflects the public good. As I pointed out at the beginning of this essay, the Son of Sam law is an example of copyright *non*-protection. A new crop of trademark litigation deals with the disparagement of women and minorities. Just a few months ago, Connecticut attorney general

Richard Blumenthal threatened the manufacturer of a high-caffeine soft drink labeled "Cocaine" with legal action if the product was not pulled off the shelves.[96] While the legal action dealt with deceptive trade practices, this was, of course, a classic example of the sort of cases addressed by the scandalous-and-immoral-mark doctrine. Patent debates over the bioethics of Harvard's oncomouse and the patenting of chimeras such as the sheep/goat clone (the "geep") are really a debates about patent moral utility.

I am not suggesting a return to the days when books were banned in Boston; Comstockery (to borrow the term coined by George Bernard Shaw); a return to a time when the invocation of the Madonna was limited to church services, and when seeking to patent a gambling device was itself a high-stakes risk.[97] But behind the trope of middlebrow moral prejudices, the moral lives of intellectual properties revealed a language of public welfare. This language has its origins in republican notions of virtue and nineteenth-century moral reform movements, and although this may seem an unlikely direction for contemporary legal reform, we might find ourselves in need of recovering a history of intellectual property's public good that goes beyond claims for public access to knowledge and points toward a more robust grounding for constructing a public welfare exception to ever-expanding intellectual property protection.

Jane Ginsburg has referred to "a tale of two copyrights"—the split between utilitarian American justifications for intellectual property and a continental European tradition that rests upon natural rights theories.[98] In light of the American concern with virtue and moral progress over the course of its history, it is ironic that the United States should have failed to develop public welfare exceptions to intellectual property rights while European countries have formulated these out of its natural rights tradition. European morality provisions have been the subject of a number of court decisions,[99] as well as academic analyses, though it is beyond the scope of this essay to discuss these here.[100] Even the United Kingdom patent act retains a moral utility provision.[101] What is remarkable in the American case is the act of *not* seeing. With a little digging into our own past, however, we may discover a public voice lurking behind our own moral language.

NOTES

1. *N.Y. Exec. Law* § 682a (McKinney 1982 and Supp. 1987).

2. Id. at 682a [1]. As far as I know, the earliest statute against publicizing a crime was the ban on mentioning the name of Herostratus, who in 356 B.C. burned down the Temple of Artemis at Ephesus solely to become famous.

3. A number of state statutes and a federal statute have been modeled on New York's Son of Sam law: *Ala. Code*

§ 41–9-80 (1991); *Alaska Stat.* § 12.61.020 (1990); *Ariz. Rev. Stat. Ann.* § 13–4202 (1989); *Ark. Code Ann.*

§ 16–90–308 (Michie 1987); *Cal. Civ. Code* § 2225 (West Supp. 1993); *Colo. Rev. Stat.* § 24–4.1–201 (1988 and Supp. 1994); *Conn. Gen. Stat. Ann.* § 54–218 (West 1985); *Del. Code Ann.* tit. 11, § 9103 (1987 & Supp. 1994); *Fla. Stat. Ann.* § 944.512 (West 1991); O.C.G.A. § 17–14–31 (1990); *Haw. Rev. Stat.* §§ 351–81 to -88 (1982 and Supp. 1991); *Idaho Code Ann.* § 19–5301 (1987); *Ind. Code* §§ 16–7-3.7–2 to -6 (1988); *Iowa Code Ann.* § 910.15 (West Supp. 1991); *Kan. Stat. Ann.* § 74–7301 (1988 and Supp. 1993); *Ky. Rev. Stat. Ann.* § 346.165 (Baldwin 1986); *La. Rev. Stat. Ann.* §§ 46:1831–39 (West 1992 and Supp. 1993); *Md. Ann. Code* art. 27, § 764 (1992 and Supp. 1994); *Mass. Gen. Laws. Ann.* ch. 258A, § 8 (West 1988 and Supp. 1994); *Mich. Comp. Laws Ann.* § 780.768 (West Supp. 1993); *Minn. Stat. Ann.* § 611A.68 (West 1987 and Supp. 1995); *Miss. Code Ann.* §§ 99–38–1 to -11 (1994); *Mo. Ann. Stat.* § 595.045 (Vernon 1986 and Supp. 1988); *Mont. Code Ann.* § 53–9-104(1)(d) (1991); *Neb. Rev. Stat.* §§ 81–1836–42 (1994); *Nev. Rev. Stat. Ann.* § 217.65 (Michie 1991); *N.J. Stat. Ann.* § 52:4B-28 (West 1986 and Supp. 1994); *N.M. Stat. Ann.* § 31–22–22 (Michie Supp. 1994); *N.Y. Exec. Law* § 632-a (McKinney 1982 and Supp. 1991); *Ohio Rev. Code Ann.* §§ 2969.01–.06 (Baldwin 1993); *Okla. Stat. Ann.* tit. 22, § 17 (West 1992); *Or. Rev. Stat.* § 147.275 (1991); *R.I. Gen. Laws* § 12–25.1–3 (1994); *S.C. Code Ann.* § 15–59–40 (Law. Co-op. Supp. 1993); *S.D. Codified Laws Ann.* § 23A-28A-1 (1988 and Supp. 1994); *Tenn. Code Ann.* § 29–13–202 (1980 and Supp. 1992); *Wash. Rev. Code Ann.* § 7.68200 (West 1992); *Wis. Stat. Ann.* § 949.165 (West Supp. 1994); 18 U.S.C. § 3681 (federal statute).

4. 502 U.S. 105 (1991).

5. In order to address the issue of content-based speech regulation raised by the Supreme Court in *Simon & Schuster Inc. v. Members of the N.Y. State Crime Victims Board,* courts have used a number of alternative strategies: (1) imposing large fines even where the criminal is indigent in order to have recourse to future profits, (2) ordering restitution upon notification of profits, and (3) prohibiting financial gain from criminal activity as a condition of parole. See Kathleen M. Timmons, "Note: Natural Born Writers: The Law's Continued Annoyance with Criminal Authors," *Georgia Law Review* 29 (1995): 1121–60.

6. Two brief comments indicating a possible relationship between Son of Sam legislation and copyright are "Note: The Son of Sam Laws: When the Lunatic, the Criminal, and the Poet Are of Imagination All Compact," *St. Louis University Law Journal* 27 (1983): 207–31; "Essay: First Amendment Limits on Copyright," *Vanderbilt Law Review* 55 (2002): 925.

7. *Visual Artists Rights Act of 1990,* 17 U.S.C. 106(a), was incorporated into the 1976 Copyright Act even though its provisions are seemingly at odds with traditional common-law notions of property.

8. See Paul Goldstein, *Copyright: Principles, Law, and Practice* (New York: Oxford University Press, 1989), sec. 1.1; Paul Edward Geller, "Must Copyright Be Forever Caught between Marketplace and Authorship Norms?" in *Of Authors and Origins: Essays on Copyright Law,* ed. Brad Sherman and Alain Strowel (New York: Oxford University Press, 1994), 159 ("Anglo-American copyright laws, in the usual course of affairs, rely on marketplace norms").

9. *Harper & Row Pub. v. Nation Enterprises,* 471 U.S. 558, 559 (1985).

10. The term "intellectual property," which first appeared in an 1845 federal appellate decision, *Davoll v. Brown,* 7 F. Cas. 197, 199 (C.C.D. Mass. 1845), was not used at the time of the Constitution's framing. Mark A. Lemley, "Property, Intellectual Property, and Free Riding," *Texas Law Review* 83 (2005): 1033 n. 4;Craig Joyce, "A Curious Chapter in the History of Judicature: *Wheaton v. Peters* and the Rest of the Story (of Copyright in the New Republic)," *Houston Law Rev*iew 42 (2005): 328 n. 3.

11. U.S. Const. art. 1, sec. 8, cl. 8. There is some question as to whether this is a mere "preambular statement of purpose," as suggested by the decision in *Eldred v. Ashcroft,* 537 U.S. 186, 193 (2003), or whether it creates substantive requirements for Congress. The dissent attributes more weight to the statement of purpose, claiming that "copyright statutes must serve public, not private ends." Id. at 247. See Judge Jerome Frank's dissent in *M. Witmark & Sons v. Fisher Music*, 125 F.2d (1942) 949, 960, where he asserts that a statement of purpose means that a pure grant of monopoly power would verge on unconstitutionality and urges, "We should keep a sharp eye on the Constitutional purpose of the clause."

12. See, for example, William M. Landes and Richard A. Posner, *The Economic Structure of Intellectual Property Law* (Cambridge, Mass.: Harvard University Press, 2003).

13. See Peter Jaszi, "Toward a Theory of Copyright: The Metamorphoses of 'Authorship,'" *Duke Law Journal* 41 (1991): 455–502; Peter Jaszi, "On the Author Effect: Contemporary Copyright and Collective Creativity," *Cardozo Arts & Entertainment Law Journal* 10 (1992): 293–420; Robert H. Rotstein, "Beyond Metaphor: Copyright Infringement and the Fiction of the Work," *Chicago-Kent Law Review* 68 (1993): 725–804; Keith Aoki, "Adrift in the Intertext: Authorship and Audience 'Recoding' Rights," *Chicago-Kent Law Review* 68 (1993): 805–39; Martha Woodmansee, "On the Author Effect: Recovering Collectivity," *Cardozo Arts & Entertainment Law Journal* 10 (1992): 279–92; James Boyle, "A Theory of Law and Information: Copyright, Spleen, Blackmail, and Insider Trading," *California Law Review* 80 (1992): 1413–540 (arguing that copyright protection is often predicated upon a distinction between public and private information informed by the archetype of the Romantic author). See also Brad Sherman and Alain Strowel, eds., *Of Authors and Origins: Essays on Copyright Law* (New York: Oxford University Press, 1994); and Martha Woodmansee and Peter Jaszi, eds., *The Construction of Authorship, Textual Appropriation in Law and Literature* (Durham, N.C.: Duke University Press, 1994). For a related philosophical inquiry, see Jeremy Waldron, "From Authors to Copiers: Individual Rights and Social Values in Intellectual Property," *Chicago-Kent Law Review* 68 (1993): 841–87 (noting that cultural assumptions about authorship inform how we think about the legal issues of copying). For an exploration of authorship in trademarks, see Steven Wilf, "Who Authors Trademarks?" *Cardozo Arts & Entertainment Law Journal* 17 (1999).: 1–6.

14. Carlo Ginzburg, "Morelli, Freud, and Sherlock Holmes: Clues and Scientific Method," *History Workshop* 9 (1980): 11.

15. Morton J. Horwitz, *The Transformation of American Law, 1780–1860* (Cambridge, Mass.: Harvard University Press, 1977), 253.

16. On the importance of the act of recovery of past lost legal doctrine, see Steven Wilf, *The Law before the Law* (Lanham, Md.: Lexington Books, 2008).

17. Ann Fairfax Withington, *Towards a More Perfect Union: Virtue and the Formation of American Republics* (Oxford: Oxford University Press, 1996), unpacks the Continental Congress's moral code.

18. The remarkable absence of scholarly attention to the link between intellectual property law, political communication, conceptions of republican politics, and the creation of a new American citizenry in the Revolutionary period and early Republic may be seen in the fact that copyright is never mentioned in Richard D. Brown, *Knowledge Is Power: The Diffusion of Information in Early America, 1700–1865* (Oxford: Oxford University Press, 1989).

19. J. G. A. Pocock, *The Machiavellian Moment: Florentine Political Thought and the Atlantic Republican Tradition* (Princeton, N.J.: Princeton University Press, 1975).

20. Keith Michael Baker, *Inventing the French Revolution* (Cambridge: Cambridge University Press, 1990), 167–202. **Error! Main Document Only.** On the significance of literary expression in the new Republic, see Jay Fliegelman, *Declaring Independence: Jefferson, Natural Language, and the Culture of Performance* (Stanford, Calif.: Stanford University Press, 1993); Michael Warner, *The Letters of the Republic: Publication and the Public Sphere in Eighteenth-Century America* (Cambridge, Mass.: Harvard University Press, 1990); Larzer Ziff, *Writing in the New Nation: Prose, Print, and Politics in the Early United States* (New Haven, Conn.: Yale University Press, 1991); Christopher Looby, *Voicing America: Language, Literary Form, and the Origins of the United States* (Chicago: University of Chicago Press, 1996); Sandra M. Gustafson, *Eloquence Is Power: Oratory and Performance in Early America* (Chapel Hill: University of North Carolina Press, 2000).

21. However, three of the state copyright statutes of the 1780s—those of Connecticut, Massachusetts, and Maryland—were enacted prior to the adoption of the Continental Congress's resolution.

22. 1 Stat. 124.

23. On the United States' response to join the international framework of the Berne Convention, see Catherine Seville, *The Internationalisation of Copyright Law: Books, Buccaneers, and the Black Flag in the Nineteenth Century* (Cambridge: Cambridge University Press, 2006), 146–252.

24. "Resolution Passed by the Continental Congress, Recommending the Several States to Secure to the Authors or Publishers of New Books the Copyright of Such Books," May 2, 1783.

25. 1710, 8 Anne c. 19. , Thorvald Solberg, ed., *The Copyright Law of the United States in Force July 15, 1908* (Washington, D.C.: Library of Congress, 1908), 1.

26. On Webster, see K. Alan Snyder, *Defining Noah Webster: Mind and Morals in the Early Republic* (Washington, D.C.: University Press of America, 2000).

27. Barlow's radicalism is described in William C. Dowling, *Poetry and Ideology in Revolutionary Connecticut* (Athens: University of Georgia Press, 1990); also, Robert F. Durden, "Joel Barlow in the French Revolution," *William and Mary Quarterly,* 3d ser., 8 (1951): 328–54.

28. Noah Webster, "Origin of the Copy-right Law in the United States," in *A Collection of Papers on Political, Literary, and Moral Subjects* (New York: Burt Franklin, 1843), 173–75.

29. Thomas Gustafson, *Representative Words: Politics, Literature, and the American Language, 1776–1865* (Cambridge: Cambridge University Press, 1992), 308–9.

30. Harry R. Warfel, *Noah Webster: Schoolmaster to America* (New York: Macmillan, 1936), 59–60.

31. These early state copyright statutes are reprinted in Thorvald Solberg, ed., *Copyright Enactments of the United States,* 2d rev. ed. (Washington, D.C.: Government Printing Office, 1906).

32. 1783 N.J. Laws 47.

33. 1783 Md. Laws ch. 34.

34. 1786 Ga. Laws. 323.

35. 1783 Mass. Acts 236; 1783 R.I. Pub. Laws 6.

36. 1710, 8 Anne c. 19.

37. 1783 Mass. Acts 236. The acts of New Hampshire (1783 N.H. Laws 161–62) and Rhode Island (1783 R.I. Pub. Laws 6–7) are nearly identical to that of Massachusetts.

38. 1784 S.C. Acts 49.

39. **Error! Main Document Only.** Seven states—Connecticut, Maryland, New Jersey, Pennsylvania, South Carolina, Georgia, and New York—followed the Statute of Anne and granted a renewable fourteen-year term. In Maryland (1783 Md. Laws, ch. 34) and New Jersey (1783 N.J. Laws 47), the copyright is renewable for an additional fourteen years. States with a twenty-one-year term are Massachusetts (1783 Mass. Acts 236), Virginia (1785 Va. Acts 8), and Rhode Island (1783 R.I. Pub. Laws 6). The reason behind the variable copyright terms is not clear. The Statute of Anne grandfathers already published books under a twenty-one-year term.

40. Craig Joyce and L. Ray Patterson, "Copyright in 1791: An Essay concerning the Founders' View of the Copyright Power Granted to Congress in Article I, Section 8, Clause 8 of the U.S. Constitution," *Emory Law Journal* 52 (2003): 934.

41. 1783 Mass. Acts 236.

42. Pennsylvania required filing with a notary; Virginia required filing with a clerk of council.

43. Compare the French approach, which was based on natural rights. Jane C. Ginsburg, "A Tale of Two Copyrights: Literary Property in Revolutionary France and America," *Tulane Law Review* 64 (1990): 991–1031.

44. 1783 Mass. Acts 236. New Hampshire had an almost identical provision (1783 N.H. Laws. 161–62).

45. 1783 Md. Laws, ch. 34

46. See the classic discussion by E. P. Thompson, "The Moral Economy of the English Crowd in the Eighteenth Century," in *Customs in Common* (New York: New Press, 1991), 185–258.

47. Gary Nash, *The Urban Crucible: The Northern Seaports and the Origins of the American Revolution* (Cambridge, Mass.: Harvard University Press, 1979).

48. As Akhil Amar points out, uniform intellectual property standards were part of a cluster of constitutional provisions reflecting an expansive vision of federal power, including uniform bankruptcy laws, standard weights and measures, federal post offices, and a single currency. Akhil Reed Amar, *America's Constitution: A Biography* (New York: Random House, 2005), 108.

49. James Madison, "Vices of the Political System of the United States," April 1787. See also "The Federalist No. 43" in Alexander Hamilton, James Madison, and John Jay, *The Federalist Papers* (New York: Penguin Press, 1987).

50. Mass. Const. 1780, ch. 5, sec. 2. A very similar provision is found in the New Hampshire Constitution, 1784, pt. 2.

51. Warfel, *Noah Webster,* 391–92.

52. The U.S. Supreme Court in *Eldred v. Ashcroft* found the phrase "To promote the Progress of Science and the Useful Arts" to be "introductory," and neither an authorizing grant nor a limitation. Craig W . Dallon, "Original Intent and the Copyright Clause: *Eldred v. Ashcroft* Gets It Right," *St. Louis Law Journal* 50 (2006): 307–59.

53. Joseph Story, *Commentaries of the Constitution of the United States* (Boston: Hilliard, Gray, 1833), 3:7.

54. Doron S. Ben-Atar, *Trade Secrets: Intellectual Property and the Origins of American Industrial Power* (New Haven, Conn.: Yale University Press, 2004), 8–9.

55. Elizabeth Carter Wills, ed., *Federal Copyright Records, 1790–1800* (Washington, D.C.: Library of Congress, 1987), ix.

56. Story, *Commentaries of the Constitution,* 3:46–51. Common-law protection for English works prior to publication was found in *Donaldson v. Beckett,* 2 Bro. P.C. 129. Lysander Spooner,

The Law of Intellectual Property; or, An Essay on the Right of Authors and Inventors to a Perpetual Property in Their Ideas (Boston: B. Marsh, 1855). Spooner argues that ideas are simply another form of wealth. Plain Dealer, Jan. 27, 1837. Reprinted in William Leggett, *Democratick Editorials: Essays in Jacksonian Political Economy*, ed. Lawrence H. White (Indianapolis, Ind.: Liberty Press, 1984), 391.

57. For a late enunciation of this idea, see Ernest Bruncken, "The Philosophy of Copyright," *Musical Quarterly* 2 (July 1916): 477–96. Authors "consider their 'copyright' as something to which as a matter of course they are entitled in morals; and if the law does not give it to them in full measure, they are inclined to say that the law falls behind what it should be in order to achieve its own ideal of justice."

58. *Mitchell Bros. Film Group v. Cinema Adult Theater,* 604 F.2d 852, 865 (5th Cir. 1979); *Jartech Inc. v. Clancy*, 666 F.2d 403 (9th Cir. 1982).

59. *Burnett v. Chetwood* (1720), 2 Mer. 441 n. (questions whether strange notions of morality concealed in Latin are immoral and hence not protectable); *Walcot v. Walker* (1802), 7 Ves. 1; *Southey v. Sherwood* (1817), 2 Mer. 455 (denies right to sue for infringement of obscene liable since this is "calculated to do injury to the public"). On the English cases, see Jeremy Phillips, "Copyright in Obscene Works: Some British and American Problems," *Anglo-American Law Review* (1977): 138–71. On the English origins of the non-protection doctrine, see E. Drone, *The Law of Property in Intellectual Productions* (Boston: Little, Brown, 1879), 185–87.

60. *Hoffman v. Le Traunik*, 209 F. 375, 379 (N.D.N.Y. 1913).

61. On the relationship between the origins of copyright and censorship, see Ian Parsons, "Copyright and Society," in *Essays in the History of Publishing*, ed. Asa Briggs, 29–60 (London: Longmans, 1974).

62. Phillips, "Copyright in Obscene Works," 138; Ronald L. Green, "The Obscenity Defense to Copyright Revisited," *Kentucky Law Journal* 69 (1980–81): 161–84.

63. Edmund S. Rogers, "Copyright and Morals," *Michigan Law Review* 18 (1919–20): 390–404. The origin of this doctrine is an English rule that emerges in the early nineteenth century. English courts customarily denied relief to those claiming copyright infringement when the underlying works were deemed obscene. The court in *Stockdale v. Onwhyn,* 108 Eng. Rep. 65 (K.B. 1826), refused to grant damages for the copying of allegedly indecent passages from the life of a courtesan.

64. *Keene v. Kimball,* 16 Gray (82 Mass.) 545 (1860). It is notable that there does not appear to be case law on this subject prior to the 1860s. This is consistent with the absence of concern with obscenity before the Civil War. Rochelle Gurstein, *The Repeal of Reticence: A History of America's Cultural and Legal Struggle over Free Speech, Obscenity, Sexual Liberation, and Modern Art* (New York: Hill and Wang, 1996).

65. Act of Aug. 18, 1856, 1 Stat. 138.

66. 16 F. Cas. 920 (C.C. Cal. 1867). See also *Broder v. Zeno Mauvais Music Co.*, 88 F. 74 (C.C.N.D. Cal. 1898); also, *Cain v. Universal Pictures Co. Inc.,* 47 F. Supp. 101 (1942); *Hoffman v. Le Traunik*, 209 F. 375 (N.D.N.Y. 1913) (to be copyrightable, a work must be original, meritorious, and free from immorality). For an excellent understanding of the manifold mechanisms for regulating obscene materials, see Donna I. Dennis, "Obscenity Law and Its Consequences in Mid-Nineteenth-Century America," *Columbia Journal of Gender & Law* 16 (2007): 43–95.

67. 16 Gray (82 Mass.) 545 (1860).

68. 12 F.2d 116 (S.D.N.Y. 1925).

69. *Mitchell Bros. Film Group v. Cinema Adult Theater,* 604 F.2d 852, 858 (1979).

70. 188 U.S. 239 (1903).

71. See, for example, *Broder v. Zeno Mauvais Music Co.*, 88 F. 74, 77–79 (C.C.N.D. Cal. 1898) (use of the word "hottest" in song had a vulgar meaning and is not entitled to copyright protection).

72. *Simonton v. Gordon,* 12 F.2d 116 (1925)

73. *R. v. Hicklin* (1868), LR3 QB 360. *Cain v. Universal Pictures,* 47 F. Supp. 1013, 1018 (S.D. Cal. 1942) (despite an objectionable scene of a liaison in a church, this was not found immoral when this rule was applied to the whole).

74. *Mitchell Bros. Film Group v. Cinema Adult Theater,* 604 F.2d 852 (5th Cir. 1979) (lack of congressional intent to provide for non-protection doctrine, which conflicts with the Copyright Act's granting of protection to all original works and undermines the creation of a unitary system of copyright in the face of alternative community standards for obscenity); *Jartech Inc. v. Clancy,* 666 F.2d 403 (9th Cir. 1982). See also, *Devils Films Inc. v. Nectar Video,* 29 F. Supp. 2d 174, 176 (S.D.N.Y. 1998) ("It strains credulity that Congress intended the protection of copyright law to contraband" [i.e., pornographic films]) (dictum). Robert Spoo, "Note: Copyright Protectionism and Its Discontents: The Case of James Joyce's *Ulysses* in America," *Yale Law Journal* 108 (1983): 633–67.

75. Stephen R. Baird, "Moral Intervention in the Trademark Arena: Barring the Registration of Scandalous and Immoral Trademarks," *Trademark Reporter* 83 (1993): 661–704; Joseph Gibbons Llewellyn, "Semiotics of the Scandalous and the Immoral and the Disparaging: Section 2(A) Trademark Law after *Lawrence v. Texas,*" *Marquette Intellectual Property Law Review* 9 (2005): 187–248; Jasmine Abdel-Khalik, "To Live in In-'Fame'-Y: Receiving Scandalous Marks as Analogous to Famous Marks," *Cardozo Arts & Entertainment Law Journal* 25 (2007): 173–236.

76. Bars to intellectual property protection for immoral copyrighted material, trademarks, and inventions may not have implicated First Amendment rights because a refusal to grant protection does not prohibit the use of the intellectual property itself.

77. In addition to the Lanham Act's proscription, nearly all states (as well as Puerto Rico) similarly have banned the registration of trademarks consisting of or comprising "scandalous"or "immoral" matter. See *Ala. Code* § 8–12–7(a)(1) (Michie Supp. 1992); Alaska Stat. § 45.50.010(1) (Michie Supp. 1986); *Ariz. Rev. Stat. Ann.* § 44–1442.1 (West Supp. 1993); *Ark. Code Ann.* § 4–71–104(1) (Michie Supp. 1991); *Cal Bus. & Prof. Code Ann.* § 14220(a) (West 1992); *Colo. Rev. Stat. Ann.* § 7–70–108(a) (West 1990); *Conn. Gen. Stat. Ann.* § 35–11b(1) (West 1991); *Del. Code. Ann.,* ch. 6, § 3303(1) (Michie Supp. 1990); *Fla. Stat. Ann.* § 495.021(1)(a) (West Supp. 1992); *Ga. Off. Code Ann.* § 10–1-441(1) (Michie Supp. 1991); Ida Code § 48–502(b)(1) (Michie Supp. 1992); *Ill. Stat. Ann.,* ch. 140, P 9, § 2(a) (West Supp. 1992); *Ind. Code Ann.* § 24–2-1–3(a) (West 1991); *Ia. Code Ann.* § 548.1.a (West 1991); *Kan. Off. Stat. Ann.* § 81–112(a) (1989); *Ky. Rev. Stat.* § 365.575(1) (Michie Supp. 1987); *La. Rev. Stat. Ann.* § 51:212(1) (West 1992); *Md. Bus. Reg.* § 1–404 (Michie Supp. 1993); *Mass. Laws Ann.,* ch. 110B, § 3(a) (West Supp. 1992); *Mich. Comp. Laws Ann.* § 429.32.2(a) (West 1990); *Minn. Stat. Ann.* § 333.19(1) (West 1992); *Miss. Code Ann.* § 75–25–3(1)(a) (Law. Co-op 1972); *Mo. Rev. Stat.* § 417.011(1) (Vernon 1990); *Mont. Code Ann.* § 3013–303(a) (1991); *Neb. Rev. Stat.* § 87–112(1) (West 1987); *Nev. Rev. Stat. Ann.* § 600.330.1 (Michie Supp. 1985); *N.H. Rev. Stat. Ann.* § 350-A:2.I (Equity Supp. 1991); *N.J. Stat. Ann.* § 56:3–13.2(a) (West 1992); *N.Y. Gen. Bus. Laws Ann.* § 361(a) (McKinney 1992); N.C. Gen. Stat. § 80–2(1) (Michie Supp. 1991); *N.D. Cent. Code* § 47–22–02.1 (Michie Supp.

1991); *Ohio Rev. Code Ann.* §1329.55(A) (Page 1992); *Okla. Stat. Ann.* § 22(a) (West 1993); *Or. Rev. Stat.* § 647.035(1) (1989); *Pa. Cons. Stat. Ann.*, tit. 54, § 1111(1) (Purdon Supp. 1992); *Laws of P.R. Ann.* § 194(a) (1992); *R.I. Gen. Laws* § 62–3(1) (Michie Supp. 1991); *S.C. Code of Laws* § 39–15–120(1) (Lawyer's Co'op 1976); *S.D. Code of Laws* § 37–6-6 (Supp. 1986); *Tenn. Code Ann.* § 4725–502(1) (Michie Supp. 1992); *Tex. Bus. & Comm. Code Ann.* § 16.08(a)(1) (West 1992); *Utah Code Ann.* § 70–3-2(1)(a) (Michie Supp. 1993); *Vt. Stat. Ann.*, ch. 71, § 2527(a) (1992); *Va. Code Ann.*, ch. 6, § 59.1–79(a) (Michie Supp. 1993); *Wash. Rev. Code Ann.* § 19.77.020(1) (West 1992); and *Wyo. Stat.* § 401–102(a)(1) (Michie Supp. 1993). Five states lack express prohibitions against registration of scandalous and immoral trademarks. See *Haw. Rev. Stat.* § 482–3 (1990); *Me. Rev. Stat. Ann.*, tit. 10, § 1522(1) (West 1991); *N.M. Stat. Ann.* § 57–3-1 (Michie Supp. 1991); *W.Va. Code* § 47–2 (Michie Supp. 1986); and *Wis. Stat. Ann.* §132.01 (1991).

78. "Notes and Comment: Scandalous Matter in a Trade-mark," *U.S. Law Review* 72 (1938): 421–25.

79. Act of Feb. 20, 1905, ch. 592, 33 Stat. 724. The first case of barring a trademark from protection was under the 1905 act: *Ex parte Martha Maid Mfg.*, 37 U.S.P.Q. (BNA) 156 (1938) (barring use of Queen Mary's name for underwear).

80. H.R. Rep. No. 52–1860, at 3 (1892) . Abdel-Khalik, "To Live in In-'Fame'-Y," 184–85.

81. 15 U.S.C. 1052(a) (2006).

82. *In re Old Glory Condom,* U.S.P.Q. 2d 1216, 1219 (TTAB 1993).

83. *In re Riverbank Canning Co*., 95 F.2d 327 (C.C.P.A. 1938).

84. On moral utility, see Andrew R. Smith, "Note and Comment: Monsters at the Patent Office: The Inconsistent Conclusions of Moral Utility and the Controversy of Human Cloning," *DePaul Law Review* 53 (2003): 159–203; Benjamin D. Enerson, "Note: Protecting Society from Patently Offensive Inventions: The Risk of Reviving the Moral Utility Doctrine," *Cornell Law Review* 89 (2004): 685–720; Dana Visser, "Note: Who's Going to Stop Me from Patenting My Six-Legged Chicken? An Analysis of the Moral Utility Doctrine in the United States," *Wayne Law Review* 46 (2000): 2067–87.

85. 15 F. Cas. 1018 (No. 8568) (C.C.D. Mass. 1817).

86. *Reliance Novelty v. Dworzek*, 80 F. 902 (C.C.N.D. Cal. 1897).

87. *Bedford v. Hunt*, 1 Mason 302, 3 F. Cas. 37 (C.C.D. Mass. 1817). Willard Phillips, *The Law of Patents for Inventions* (Boston: American Stationers' Company, 1897), 138.

88. Ruggles, Senate Report Accompanying Senate Bill 239, 24th Cong., 1st sess. (Apr. 28, 1836).

89. Albert H. Walker, *Lipscomb's Walker on Patents,* 3d ed. (New York: Voorhis, 1895), sec. 82.

90. *Fuller v. Berger* 120 F. 274 (7th Cir. 1903).

91. *Whistler Corp. v. Autotronics Inc.,* 14 U.S.P.Q. 2d (BNA 1885, 1886) (N.D. Tex. 1988) (absent statute outlawing automobile radar detection devices used to circumvent speed limits, there is no suggestion of congressional view that this is an immoral device).

92. T. E. Bell, "Patentability of Gambling Machines," *Journal of the Patent Office Society* 9 (1926–27): 104–11.

93. *National Automotive Device v. Lloyd,* 40 F. 89 (N.D. Ill. 1889) (court found only use of car-racing device in saloons does not receive patent protection).

94. David G. Schwartz, *Role the Bones: The History of Gambling* (New York: Gotham Books,

2006), 330–31. John P. Quinn, *Gambling and Gambling Devices* (Canton, Ohio: J. P. Quinn, 1912).

95. 185 F.3d 1364 (Fed. Cir. 1999) (a juice machine intended to deceive customers into believing there is only one liquid being mixed is found to be compatible with market needs and therefore has utility). Compare this case to *Scott & Williams v. Aristo Hosiery Co.*, 7 F.2d 1003 (Fed. Cir. 2003) (lines placed on hosiery to look like seems are intended to deceive customers and therefore violate moral utility).

96. "Blumenthal Talks 'Cocaine' on TV," *Legal News Line*, May 8, 2007.

97. A number of recent articles have warned against the reemergence of moral evaluations of intellectual property: Enerson, "Protecting Society from Patently Offensive Inventions" (patent); Gibbons, "Semiotics of the Scandalous, the Immoral, and the Disparaging" (trademark); Sonia K. Katyal, "Performance, Property, and the Slashing of Gender in Fan Fiction," *American University Journal of Gender, Social Policy and the Law* 14 (2006): 461–518.

98. Ginsburg, "A Tale of Two Copyrights," 1991.

99. *Oncomouse/Harvard* [1989] O.J. E.P.O. 451, [1990] 12 O.J. E.P.O. 476 [1992] 10 O.J. E.P.O. 588; *Lubrizol Genetics Inc.* (Lubrizol II) ([1992] EP-B1–122–791 (Opposition Division) unreported.

100. See D. Beyleveld and R. Brownsword, *Mice Morality and Patents* (London: Common Law Institute of Intellectual Property, 1993); E. Armitage and I. Davis, *Patents and Morality in Perspective* (London: Common Law Institute of Intellectual Property, 1994); R. Moufang, "Patenting of Human Genes, Cells and Parts of the Body? The Ethical Dimensions of Patent Law," *International Review of Industrial Property and Copyright Law* 25, no. 4 (1994): 487; Ulrich Straus, "Patenting Human Genes in Europe: Past Developments and Prospects for the Future," *International Review of Industrial Property and Copyright Law* 26, no. 6 (1995): 922; Schatz, "Patents and Morality," in *Biotechnology, Patents and Morality*, ed. S. Sterck (Brookfield, Vt.: Ashgate, 1997).

101. *Patents Act,* 1977, c. 37, § 1(3) (Eng.) as amended by the Patent Regulations 2000 (S.I. 2000/2037) ("a patent shall not be granted for an invention the commercial exploitation of which would be contrary to public policy or morality"). Section 130(7) of the UK Patents Act states that the "morality" provision must be interpreted in conformity with the European Patent Convention 1973 (as amended), which bars the granting of European patents for "inventions the publication or exploitation of which would be contrary to 'ordre public' or morality, provided that the exploitation shall not be deemed to be so contrary merely because it is prohibited by law or regulation in some or all of the Contracting States . . . . It is apparent that the purpose of this provision is to allow that, where commerciality would essentially be precluded because the product/process is regarded by the public as immoral, patent protection will not attach."

17

Geniuses and Owners: The Construction of Inventors and the Emergence of American Intellectual Property

OREN BRACHA

IN HIS FOUNDATIONAL DISCUSSION OF THE LATE NINETEENTH-CENTURY transformation of the conception of property, Morton Horwitz observed that during this time a "physcalist" definition of property was abandoned in favor of a more abstract understanding. The new conception of property could accommodate "new, abstract, and intangible forms of wealth such as business goodwill or copyright and patent rights."[1] Thus what we call today "intellectual property" was one of the major engines behind the transformation of property. How can one reconcile this with the fact that by the mid-nineteenth century, patents, copyrights, and goodwill had been in existence for centuries both as economic practices and legal institutions? The answer is that the construction of these legal fields as involving ownership of intangible objects of property was itself a relatively new phenomenon. Intellectual property as a conceptual category was as much the result of the nineteenth-century transformation of property as it was its cause.

The term "intellectual property" appears in the American law reports for the first time in an 1845 patent case. In *Davoll v. Brown,* Justice Levi Woodbury wrote about the need to protect "intellectual property, the labors of the mind, productions and interests as much a man's own, and as much the fruit of his honest industry, as the wheat he cultivates, or the flocks he rears."[2] The image of the inventor who creates and owns intellectual products juxtaposed against that of the farmer who owns his crops and flocks is a striking one. How did Americans, jurists and others, come to speak and think this way about inventors and inventions?

Much has been written about the appearance of a new concept of the author in the seventeenth and eighteenth centuries and its entanglement with the economic struggles of publishers and writers and with the development of modern copyright law.[3] It is often assumed that this account applies to inventors and patents, but actual descriptions of the rise of the image of the genius inventor in the context of patent law are sparse. Despite the parallels to the construction of the literary author, the invention of the technological inventor has its own distinct and unique history, a history that is still to be told.[4]

This essay's focus is on a transformative moment in America during the late eighteenth and early nineteenth centuries. During this time a new ideological synthesis was consciously developed and employed within public discourse about technological innovation and the societal treatment of its apostles. The inventor, whose public representation was previously bundled indistinguishably with that of the entrepreneur or the craftsman, was recast in a new image. An inventor came to be represented as an intellectual genius who creates novel technological ideas. Just as important, the inventor was constructed as a property owner who is entitled to own an intangible object of property: the ideas he created through his mental labor. The rise of the inventor as a genius-owner did not occur in a detached intellectual realm. It was, rather, developed as part of a struggle for recognition, status, and tangible benefits by agents of change—a newly self-conscious group of individuals working on the borderline between technological innovation and entrepreneurship. The new ideology of inventorship was constructed in the public debates surrounding patent law and policy instigated by these agents of change.

Several ideological elements that emerged within this process and became integral parts of modern patent and inventorship discourse are worth highlighting. The first is the rise of technological innovation as a discrete and significant category. At the end of the eighteenth century, technological innovation gradually moved to the fore of public consciousness and consolidated as a conceptually distinct sphere seen as crucial to national prosperity. The concept of inventorship was linked to this new category of technological innovation, and the two came to define each other. Second, technological innovation was increasingly constructed in informational terms. In contrast to earlier times, the basic concepts and concerns of the field came to be defined through abstract categories of knowledge and information. This trend was reflected in the focus of the image of the inventor on mental capacities and output. Inventors were increasingly described as geniuses, defined by their exercise of the intellect and the creation of new ideas. The combination of these two themes—the emphasis on the social value of technology coupled with the focus on intellectual production—opened up a new conceptual space between the traditional artisan or mechanic and the speculative scientist or natural philosopher, a space that came to be occupied by the new figure of the inventor. Third, technological innovators and innovation were conceptualized in increasingly individualist terms. The dominant image of invention became one of a solipsistic mental act of creation. In its extreme form it depicted the inventor as an individual who creates new ideas ex nihilo by the sheer power of his intellectual labor. The cumulative and cooperative character of technological invention was overshadowed by a "heroic theory of invention" that attributed discrete technological breakthroughs to single genius individuals.[5] Fourth, intertwined with the other conceptual elements there appeared a powerful set of images of inventors as owners and an elaborate concept of "mental property." The latter was understood as rights of ownership of informational objects known as inventions by those who created them through their mental labor, namely, inventors.

Taken together, these four themes are the unique expression in the field of technological innovation of what C. B. MacPherson called "possessive individualism": a worldview that regards human beings as atomistic individuals whose freedom is defined by the ownership of their person and capacities as well as their product.[6] Just as the modern image of the author is the embodiment of possessive individualism in the field of aesthetic creation, so is the modern image of the inventor in the realm of technology.

INNOVATION, PATENTS, AND INVENTORS IN COLONIAL AMERICA

In 1792 Joseph Barnes published a pamphlet entitled *Treatise on the Justice, Policy and Utility of Establishing an Effectual System for Promoting the Progress of Useful Arts by Assuring Property in the Products of Genius*.[7] Barnes was the son-in-law of the inventor James Rumsey, his close aide in his steamboat enterprise and often his mouthpiece.[8] Barnes's pamphlet wove together, in an unprecedented way, the themes of private property, the individual genius inventor, and national progress through technological innovation. His main claim was that "inventors are *equally* entitled to have property secured in the products of their genius . . . as in the product of industry."[9] This was part of a new emerging public consciousness in the late eighteenth-century United States. Just how novel was that consciousness is revealed when one contrasts it with the colonial public construction of technological innovation during the preceding century and a half. Notions of technological innovation were, of course, not unfamiliar in the colonies despite their predominantly agrarian character and their remoteness from the metropolis. However, roughly until the American Revolution, technological innovation, in and of itself, was not strongly associated with community welfare, national prowess, or progress.[10] Inventors and inventions did not occupy their later heroic status. To the extent they caught the public eye, it was usually as instances of the curious or the bizarre.[11]

The colonial image of technological innovation and innovators was most apparent in the context of their treatment by public institutions. Innovators were usually not completely ignored. Although their use was irregular and at some periods sporadic, some of the colonies and later the states used ad hoc legislative privilege grants to encourage activities beneficial to the public good. Colonial and state "patent" grants—a local version of their English ancestors—awarded limited-time exclusive privileges for the production, use, or sale of certain "manufactures."[12] The concepts embedded in the grant practice, however, constructed innovators and their proper relationship to the community in a way fundamentally different from the image that would be cultivated by Barnes by the end of the eighteenth century. To begin with, inventors were not seen as having rights, much less property rights. Patents were ad hoc privileges. They were granted on a discretionary basis as specific "bargains" between the government and certain individuals and were not subject to general principles or laws.

Second, colonial patents neither assumed nor created a distinct category of technological innovation. Colonial patents were manufacture privileges that often had little to do with invention in the modern sense. The defining trait of the patentee was that he offered an economic benefit to the public. For most of the period, contemporaries did not draw a sharp distinction between an entrepreneur—the person who initiates and operates a socially beneficial enterprise, and an inventor—the creator of new technology. At least in the context of their public treatment, the two figures and their activities were bundled together indistinguishably. Sometimes privilege grants did involve technological innovations, usually imported, less frequently discovered. In such cases technology played at least some part in supporting the public worthiness of the relevant activity. Nevertheless, technological innovations were just an instance—one indistinguishable variation among many cases of publicly beneficial activities. Even in these cases the basis of the grant was not the mere technological advance but, rather, the economic initiative that was to be based on it. The 1641 grant to Samuel Winslow by the Massachusetts General Court for making salt[13] was not seen as categorically different from the 1648 grant of exclusivity to John Glover for operating a ferry "over Naponset Ryver, between Dorchestr & Braintree," to ameliorate the "great preiudice of townes that are in those parts."[14]

Third, within the grant discourse, technological innovation was not conceptualized in informational terms. Even when technological innovation was recognized, it was usually not thought of in terms of ideas or information. Instead, the tendency was to objectify invention—to associate it with its physical embodiment—or to personify it, to associate it with the technical skill of its proficient developer or operator. Inventions were not predominantly seen as informational entities, and inventors were not defined by their intellectual capacities or activities. Instead the image of the inventor was conveniently conflated with that of the artisan or the mechanic. Skilled craftsmen were an important resource in the colonies—a resource that was in both demand and shortage. The colonial companies and later colonial authorities often tried to entice such skilled artisans by offering various boons.[15] Patent grants were a direct extension of this tendency. The grants neither required nor emphasized invention in the modern sense of discovering or developing a new idea. Often, the important element, alongside an economic initiative, was the offer of the grantee's skill. Thus Joseph Jenks, an English craftsman, emphasized in his 1646 Massachusetts petition his "knowledge in Making and Erecting of Engines of Mills." He was, in effect, offering his services as a skilled artisan. His patent was granted for the "liberty to make experience of his abillityes & inventions" in the field.[16] Almost a century later in 1753, Connecticut granted a patent to Jabez Hamlin and Elihu Chauncey. The two claimed "that there is a new-invented water-machine for dressing of lax lately brought into use in Scotland and Ireland" and promised "that upon proper incouragement they would set up and bring into use [the] said machine." Their fifteen-year grant was stipulated upon their ability to "make and set up one such machine at least in some convenient place" within eighteenth months, and it did not extend to any town where they failed within five years to "erect and set up one such machine" "or "suffer[ed] the same to be out of repair and unfit for dressing flax."[17] In short, the colonial grants were based not on new ideas or information, but rather on mechanical personal skill put into action.

THE COMING OF THE GENIUS INVENTOR

By the time Barnes was writing his pamphlet in 1792, the traditional public image of technological innovation and its apostles was undergoing a process of transformation. In the second half of the eighteenth century, technology gradually captured the American mind and came to be seen as the key for national prosperity and progress.[18] The conflict over technology transfer with Britain[19] and the appearance of various manufacturing and useful arts societies[20] fueled this process. Within patent discourse, technological innovation gradually moved to the fore and consolidated as a distinct category. Although the term "technology" would come into general usage only toward the mid-nineteenth century,[21] technological innovation became the defining essence of the increasingly differentiated category of inventorship. Colonial and state patent grants, in turn, came to emphasize inventors as technological innovators. A 1785 Pennsylvania grant declaring that "it is consistent with the honor of this state to reward the inventors of useful machines and the most rational and just mode of such reward is and ought to be the exclusive advantage resulting from the invention"[22] is typical of this new pattern. In 1784 South Carolina went further in distinguishing technological innovation by legislating what was, at least in the books if not in practice, the first general American patent statute, promising to "the inventors of useful machines" a fourteen-year exclusivity in making and vending their machines.[23]

The 1790 federal Patent Act and the 1789 constitutional clause that empowered Congress to legislate it sealed the differentiation of patents and inventors, based on the element of technological innovation. The Constitution demarcated the category of promoting "science and the useful arts," and limited Congress's power to securing the rights of "authors and inventors."[24] The 1790 Patent Act and its 1793 successor were both called "An Act to Promote the Progress of Useful Arts." They applied, with some variation of details, only to the person who invented any "useful art," "manufacture," "engine," "machine," "device," or "composition of matter."[25] Patents were now the exclusive and unique domain of inventors defined as technological innovators.

Invention and patents were also reconceptualized in informational terms. To invent increasingly meant an intellectual activity of creating new ideas. The inventor was gradually distinguished from the artisan and recast in the image of an intellectual genius: an individual who creates new ideas through his intellectual capacities. Benjamin Franklin, though a transitional figure, was probably the best-known early prototype of this new image of the genius inventor.[26] This process was part of a broader move to abstract technological know-how—to distinguish it from the people who practiced it and the machines that embodied it—that was in its infancy at the beginning of the nineteenth century.[27] A 1788 episode in Pennsylvania demonstrates nicely the state of flux during this period. In that year the Pennsylvania Society for the Encouragement of Manufacture and the Useful Arts hailed the state legislature for issuing a monetary prize to Joseph Hague. Hague, breaking British technology-transfer restrictions, managed to smuggle a cotton carding machine into the state. The society referred to Hague as "the ingenious Artizan, who counterfeited the Carding and Spinning Machine, though not the original inventor (being only the introducer)."[28] Thus the "artizan" or the "introducer" was already relegated to a lower status than the "original inventor." Yet "counterfeiting" associated with the former was still seen as both laudable and worthy of reward.

Some state patents showed an increasing concern about originality by beginning to condition their grants upon the grantee being "the true and original" inventor.[29] The 1790 federal regime limited protection to developers of new technology and despite recurring demands rejected importation patents, at least formally.[30] Similarly, the concept of invention as information was embedded in the specification practice—the requirement of depositing a written description of the invention. The specification appeared sporadically in late state grants,[31] and under the 1790 act it replaced introduction in practice as the "consideration" given by the patentee in exchange for the patent grant. A patentee was now not the craftsman who practices his skill, but the intellectual inventor who creates and discloses information.

Accompanying the new image of the inventor as the creator of technological ideas, there emerged a standard set of justifications for his government-protected entitlements. These justifications consisted of an uneasy mix of labor-desert and utilitarian arguments. Early colonial grants were usually justified on the basis of the grantee's expected contribution to the public good, sometimes accompanied by references to his effort and expense. In the late eighteenth century, two typical strands of arguments consolidated to support both individual grants and the general patent regime. One depicted the patent as a governmental grant of privilege, based on the social utility of encouraging inventors. The other appealed to the natural right of inventors to control and enjoy the fruits of their intellectual labor. Often the two arguments were combined, as in the case of a 1788 South Carolina grant that appealed simultaneously to "the principles of natural equity" and to the claim that securing rights "may encourage men of learning and genius to publish and put in practice such writings and discoveries as may do honor to their country and service to mankind."[32] At other times positions were more polarized. Whether at odds or in harmony, both the natural rights and the utilitarian tropes were based on the same underlying concept of inventors as individuals who create new technological innovation through their intellectual capacity.

The rise of a new image of inventors could be explained by a host of social forces both ideological and material. Interestingly, it could also be explained by the internal dynamics of the patent practice and the emerging patent law.[33] Those forces, however, were mediated through the agency of individuals: a new self-conscious class of technological innovators and their allies, who actively worked to cultivate the image of the genius inventor. Joseph Barnes was one of those agents of change. Barnes worked closely with his father-in-law, James Rumsey, and represented his interest in a range of venues such as public writing, arguments in priority proceedings before the federal patent board established by the 1790 act, and lobbying before Congress.[34] Rumsey, a millwright with some experience in building gristmills and iron mills, had been tinkering with the idea of building a steamboat since the early 1780s.[35] Following a common pattern, Rumsey sought public patronage for his project in any avenue he and his business partners could think of: petitioning Congress for a land grant, procuring the support of influential public figures such as Washington, advocating publicly in pamphlets, obtaining state legislative privileges, and later applying for a federal patent.[36] It was through the written and oral public arguments of men like Rumsey and Barnes and their fierce competitor—John Fitch—seeking to promote their interests and attain state patronage that the new image of the inventor developed and spread.

Benjamin Dearborn was another agent of change in this field. Like many of his contemporaries, Dearborn—of Portsmouth, New Hampshire, and later Boston—was a jack-of-all-trades. He apprenticed and briefly worked as a printer and then became a schoolmaster, a shopkeeper, a singing master, the author of several books, and for a time the owner of an "Intelligence Office," where he arranged the exchange of everything from horses to servants.[37] Dearborn also had strong technical inclinations. He was a member of the American Academy of Arts and

Sciences, the American Philosophical Society, and the American Military Philosophical Society, where he would sometimes present his various inventions. In the early 1800s Dearborn turned his craft and inventive skills into a more permanent occupation: he moved to Boston, where he owned a successful scale manufactory that produced, among other things, his self-invented "vibrating steelyard."[38] Like Rumsey and Barnes, Dearborn had experience with both the state and federal patent systems. He received several legislative grants from New Hampshire and Massachusetts and was denied others.[39] He also held one federal patent—and possibly more.[40]

Dearborn's advocacy of his own interests and of the class of inventors he saw himself as representing was similar to that undertaken by others. He, however, created an organizational framework for that advocacy. In 1806 Dearborn founded in Boston the New England Association of Inventors and Patrons of Useful Arts. Membership was open to anyone being an "inventor, patentee or author of some useful invention . . . or a proprietor of a patent-right," to persons who "possess extraordinary practical skill in some useful art or science," and to those who "have shewn a disposition to patronize the useful arts."[41] The association's constitution lists among its purposes a "liberal disposition to protect and patronize the production of genius," including providing advice and financial support to a member "for defending his rights"; drawing from obscurity "useful talents" by "medals, premiums and honorary notice"; and building a national network of inventors and societies.[42] For a brief time the association would publish a magazine called the *Useful Cabinet,* which contained miscellaneous essays ranging from technical news to quasi-historical narratives of great inventions of the past. It appears to have been mainly the mouthpiece of its editor and copyright owner and the association's president: Benjamin Dearborn.

What were people like Barnes and Dearborn seeking to obtain through their public advocacy and writing in which the image of the genius inventor came into being? The obvious and explicit goal was the promotion of specific interests of the writers and of the newly self-conscious class of inventors with which they associated themselves: the attainment of state support, the extension of the patent term, other modifications to the patent laws and procedures, and so on. Entangled with these, however, was another purpose: the glorification and cultivation of both the self and public image of inventors. After the Revolution, technological innovators acquired growing social recognition.[43] This was combined, however, with a lingering sense of insecurity, unwarranted inferiority, and maltreatment. Franklin captured this sentiment in 1755 when he wrote that one would not wish a friend or a child to be an inventor since "his attempts to benefit mankind . . . however well imagined, if they do not succeed, expose him, though very unjustly, to general ridicule and contempt; and if they do succeed, to envy robbery and abuse."[44] Almost every public writing by an inventor in the first decades of the nation reflected a similar mentality. Rumsey wrote of the woes of the inventor, who had "to endure the smarting shafts of wit . . . to bear up against the heavy abuse and bitter scoffs of ill-natured ignorance. . . . Happy for him if he escapes with so gentle an appellative as that of a madman."[45] In 1814 Oliver Evans, whose endless battles in Congress and the courts for obtaining and defending his patent rights[46] made him the quintessential bearer of victim mentality of the early patent system, expressed similar sentiments. He wrote of the common fate of the inventor: to be "insulted, abused, and robbed, by the very persons that he shall benefit . . . for envy and malice are universally excited against the inventor."[47] Against this backdrop the early image of the genius inventor was wrought both as an internal device for creating self-image and group identity and as an external means of legitimation.

One striking aspect of this process was the "discovery" and redemption of past heroic inventors, often accompanied by lamentations of the disregard that had been their share throughout history. In stark contrast to earlier periods, early nineteenth-century publications appealing to the emerging technological community are full of stories of heroic inventors from the ancient Egyptians to Da Vinci. Barnes digressed midway through his pamphlet on an *Effectual System for Promoting the Progress of Useful Arts* to a long discussion of Archimedes and his services to the king of Syracuse.[48] In the introduction of the first crude American patent treatise published in 1810, Thomas Fessenden spent many pages describing the technological achievements and the heroic inventors of past cultures from ancient Egypt to the Medicis.[49] The *Useful Cabinet* featured a lengthy series of pseudo-historical essays entitled "Origin of Arts." The series supplied "a brief chronological history of the various inventions and discoveries in the sciences and mechanic arts, to which mankind are indebted for civilization, and all the valuable enjoyments of wealth, power, equal laws, and civil governments."[50] The writer (most probably Dearborn) was very explicit about the purposes of the series. The first was to redeem the neglected inventors of the past: "we are struck with astonishment at the genius and labor the historian has exhibited, in raising monuments of lasting fame to the memory of ambitious adventurers, whose lives were spent in the destruction of their fellow creatures, while scarcely any mention is made of those benefactors, who by their inventions and discoveries have conferred upon mankind real and permanent benefit."[51] The second purpose explicitly connected the image-redeeming project to the more interest-oriented one. Acknowledging the contributions of inventors, one of the essays explained, would serve "to create a sense of gratitude toward those, who have multiplied the blessings of life, and a spirit of patronage."[52]

PROPERTY: INVENTORS AS OWNERS

The construction of the image of the heroic inventor past and present quickly gave rise to a shift from an old-style "spirit of patronage" to a novel vision of inventors as owners of property rights. Again the *Useful Cabinet* supplies a striking example. The cover page of the first issue of the magazine contained the seal of the New England Association (figure 1).[53] The following page described the seal as follows: "A TREE, richly laden with Fruit, is encircled by a Wall; within enclosure is TIME, who, having thrown his Scythe into the back ground is watering the root of the Tree." The seal bore the motto "IN ITS OWN SOIL PROTECT AND NOURISH."

For those who missed the less-than-subtle metaphor, an explanation was provided: "The Fruitful Tree represents the Benefits which Society may derive from the Labours of the Inventor, if properly secured by a Wall of Protection. The nourishment received from the hand of TIME, is emblematical of the long and arduous attention necessary for bringing to maturity a Useful Improvement."[54]

As shown by Mark Rose, the trope of property rights and especially property in cultivated land played a crucial role in the construction of the image of authors in eighteenth-century England. Recasting authors in the shape of owners and their intellectual product as their property served to create a new understanding of authorship, redefine copyright, and justify a bold set of claims for legal protection made upon the state.[55] The similarity between the strategies of eighteenth-century English booksellers seeking to extend their copyright protection and early nineteenth-century Americans agitating for state protection of technological innovation is striking. How did these Americans use the claimed parallel between real property rights and legal protection of invention, and how did they try to establish it?

One of the most eloquent examples of this discursive maneuver, and probably the earliest one, is Joseph Barnes's 1792 pamphlet.[56] The pamphlet was not simply a collection of abstract philosophical meditations. It was, rather, a targeted attack on the existing 1790 Patent Act and on a pending bill of what would become the 1793 Patent Act. It also contained a long list of specific defects identified by Barnes

Figure 1 The Seal of the New England Association of Inventors and Patrons of Useful Arts

in the proposed law, suggestions for change, and a complete outline of legislation more to his liking. It was in the service of this lobbying that Barnes wove together an image of the inventor as an intellectual genius and the trope of private property. Both were leveraged to justify the particular reforms promoted by Barnes and, presumably, his father-in-law.

The core of Barnes's argument was a defense of what he called "mental property." His strategy was based on a complete equivalence that he conjured up between the revered institution of property in tangibles and patents—now presented as property in intangibles. The starting point of the argument was the well-established dominant status of property. "The *security* of property and the protection of person," Barnes wrote, "are essential to national prosperity, and therefore are, in fact, the sole and primary objects of" the existence of the state.[57] Next came the crucial question: "In what does property consist?" Barnes's response was a new classificatory system: "Of property there are two species viz. local and mental. By the former is understood personal and real property. . . . By the latter is understood the *products* of *genius,* which consists in discoveries in science, and in the useful arts."[58]

Once this identification between the two was established, all the merits associated with property could be transferred to patents. Thus, the supposed self-evident justice of property rights was extended to patents: "since *equity* is the great *standard rule* of right, inventors are *equally* entitled to have property secured in the product of their genius."[59] The case was even stronger when it came to "utility" or "policy." From the point of view of national interest, Barnes explained, "mental property" in inventions is the key for enhancing the value of "local property": "Since therefore, the improvements in the arts are so necessary in the chain, and so *essentially,* not only enhance the value, but increase the net product of the sum-total of the local property, 'tis therefore the interest of the nation, that both should be equally secured."[60] Barnes supported this conclusion with a quick arithmetical exercise. Suppose, he said, that a person invents an improvement that enables one to double the product of a plot of land. The outcome would be doubling the net product of all such property. By contrast, a man who locates and cultivates an uncultivated farm adds to the existing net product in the United States only one five-hundred thousandth of its former value.[61] Any additional objections to patents Barnes refuted by the same method of extending the undisputed virtues of traditional property:

> It will be said that all discoveries ought to be free—Pray, why more free than local property? Was not the fertile soil, or land in which we live, previous to society, common property?
>
> . . . Again says popular prejudice, genius is the gift of the Deity, therefore its product ought to be common right—So is equally land.[62]

The moment inventions became property, the rest followed.

But how did Barnes make inventions property? How was the identification between the farm owner and the developer of a new machine achieved? The strategy was to construct inventors as Lockean individuals who through their labor bring into existence new intellectual products. "Discoveries," Barnes wrote, "have their origin, and *exist* but in the minds, and, consequently, are *exclusively* the property of those who have conceived them."[63] Barnes's was an individualist image of invention as a solipsistic process. The inventor's intellect was presented as the sole and ultimate source of inventions: discoveries emanated in his mind and remained locked there as part of the individual's person until the moment of disclosure. The image was also an informational one: to invent meant a mental process of creating ideas, and the invention possessed by the inventor's mind was an ideal object. Barnes, however, despite his use of the term "discovery," did not describe invention as a momentary flash of genius. He observed that "the most important discoveries are brought into existence and matured only by a series of experiments, in making of which, not only some years, but several thousand dollars are expended."[64] Years of working on the steamboat with Rumsey, no doubt, taught him that lesson.

From this individualist and ideal image of invention followed a theory of the inventor's natural rights and of his relationship with the state. For Barnes the creation of invention through a laborious mental process and its exclusive possession in the inventor's mind established a "natural and equal right which inventors have to *claim* of society to have property secured in the *products* of their *genius*."[65] The natural right, however, was supplemented by a positive right based on a social contract between inventors and the state: "a system for securing property in the products of genius, is a *mutual* contract between the *inventor* and the *public*, in which the *inventor* agrees on *proviso* that the public will secure to him his property in, and the exclusive use of his discovery for a limited time, he will at the expiration of such time cede his right in the same to the public: thenceforth the discovery is a common right, being the compensation required by the public."[66] Here were all the components of a Lockean property story: individuals producing new objects by exerting the powers of their personal capacities, exclusive possession of those objects, natural rights, a social contract in which individuals surrender some of their natural rights in return for the state securing and enforcing their rights, and a political organization whose raison d'être is the protection of property rights.

The one conspicuous difference between Barnes's justification of patents and general natural right accounts of property—the fact that in the political state rights in invention were limited in time—points to an interesting relationship with copyright discourse. Barnes's arguments are almost identical to those developed by the British pamphleteers and jurists who decades earlier during the "literary property" debate tried to justify the notion of copyright as a perpetual property right under the common law.[67] However, while some justifications of patents as natural rights would appear in Britain too,[68] the dynamics during the literary property debate were quite different. Critics of literary property were eager to point to the parallel between patents and copyright, while advocates desperately tried to devise techniques for distinguishing the two.[69] In that context, associating copyright with patents seemed a foolproof recipe for debunking the property argument. For centuries patents were seen as state-created monopolies. A dominant Whig narrative celebrated the curbing of the abusive royal power to grant "odious monopolies" by the Statute of Monopolies and the common law.[70] In mid-eighteenth-century Britain this was too heavy a burden to overcome. While patents could be justified as beneficial exceptions to the rule against monopolies, an argument that patents were perpetual property rights was unlikely. Anything that was identified with patents would have been tainted by association. This led proponents of literary property to reject any parallel between authors and inventors, copyrights and patents. Barnes, writing decades later in the American context, employed a different strategy. In his picture patents became the complete equivalents of traditional property rights and thus enjoyed the full justificatory aurora of property. At the same time, Barnes stopped short of claiming common-law or perpetual patent protection. Instead, he described the limited term of patents as part of the inventor's social contract with the state and casually counted this as one of the relative advantages of patent rights over other property rights, from the standpoint of social "utility."[71] He never bothered to explain the reason or the source of this crucial difference between patents and property rights. Unlike the field of copyright, where the United States would experience its own literary property debate in the 1830s,[72] there never appeared a full-fledged common-law patent claim in the mainstream of American patent discourse. The equivalence to property was, rather, strategically deployed. Barnes and later others could appropriate the full justificatory power of property while never making the unattainable demand that was its logical extension. The claim of patents as property rights and the limited statutory regime, thus, were uneasily combined.

Although the social utility of inventions was still very much emphasized by Barnes, his claim upon the state in the name of inventors was no longer the traditional appeal for patronage. It was rather based on a new story about natural property rights and a social contract. Idealization and propertization went hand in hand in this story. The new concept of invention as an informational object and of the process of inventing as an intellectual activity merged with the property claim. Inventions now could be seen as emanating from and being direct extensions of a discrete individual's mental essence. The idealized invention also supplied an "object" that could be seen as exclusively possessed by the inventor and could function as the object of ownership of the claimed property right. Ideas and ownership were two complementary parts in the new image of invention.

Sixteen years after Barnes's pamphlet, the New England Association published *Remarks on the Rights of Inventors and the Influence of Their Studies in Promoting the Enjoyments of Life and Public Prosperity.*[73] The pamphlet, which was probably written by Benjamin Dearborn, was again part of a lobbying campaign. The association had been trying to get Congress to extend the duration of patent protection,[74] and the pamphlet was written in the service of that goal. It nicely demonstrates how the new image of the inventor was created as a carefully cultivated self-perception of a rather precarious and fragile new interest group trying to assert itself in public discourse. The pamphlet begins with a lament of "the scale of reason [that] is inverted by the tyranny of custom."[75] The source of the complaint quickly becomes apparent: "the inventor is not only degraded the lowest, but is the only being from whom . . . society wrests his property without his consent."[76] The pamphlet's author goes on to construct the inventor and his claim upon society by comparison to three other figures: the scientist, the farmer, and the artisan.

As for the scientist, the pamphlet compares the person who "by his indefatigable exertions . . . had rendered essential and lasting service to mankind" and reaps only public contempt and the person who "is raised to honours above any which nobility can confer, because he had elevated his telescope for the stars, until he had espied one, so distant, that mankind have no prospect of ever beholding the light of its rays, or enjoying the smallest benefit from the discovery."[77] Thus, public utility becomes the yardstick that determines the proper, rather than the perverse, hierarchy between the inventor and the scientist: "What benefits could the mariner derive from astronomy, if the inventor's genius had not first furnished the vessel and her appendages?"[78] The half-apologetic, half-condescending subjection of the scientist to the inventor is characteristic of the period's defense of the "utilitarian" inclination of American scientific interest,[79] along the lines of the *Useful Cabinet*'s caveat to its readers not to expect "refined philosophical speculations" in its pages.[80]

Once the distinction from the speculative scientist is established, the pamphlet continues to contrast the inventor with two other archetypal types—the farmer and the mechanic:

> In making a rational estimate of the value of different professions according to their real importance in life, the first thought would naturally suggest agriculture, as the occupation that produces the means of our subsistence; and consequently that would claim the first rank, until, by a second reflection, we are reminded, that the farmer cannot progress a step in his labour, until the inventor has provided him with the means. The single consideration, that it is to the inventor's genius we are indebted for transmitting particles of earth into iron is sufficient to place *him* highest in the scale of useful beings. Next to him rank the farmer and mechanic, and to this trio are the world indebted for all artificial enjoyments.[81]

The creation of a clear hierarchy of professions at whose apex one finds the inventor is a bold, even brazen, ideological move. At the same time, it is, quite obviously, a defensive tactic pursued from a position of insecurity.

This stance of confident superiority covering up insecurity is most apparent in regard to the farmer. Some strands of republican ideology were quite suspicious of technological development and industrialization. In republican thought the survival of the republic was dependent on the public virtue of its citizens. Corruption—the degradation of virtue—was connected to luxuries and excesses and often to exploitation and dependence that were associated with commercial and industrialized European societies.[82] For influential figures like Jefferson, the hope of the American republic was agrarianism: the yeoman landowner, who has a stake in the public affairs of the republic and who, unlike the urban mobs of industrialized Europe, is independent.[83] "Those who labour in the earth are the chosen people of God," Jefferson wrote, "whose breasts he had made his peculiar deposit of substantial and genuine virtue. . . . Let us never wish to see our citizens occupied at a work-bench. . . . Let our workshops remain in Europe."[84] By 1807 things were more ambivalent. By then there already appeared vociferous and influential voices asserting that "home manufactures" constituted the key for national prosperity and progress, and that a robust local technological sphere was essential for achieving greatness or, indeed, ensuring the survival of the republic. There were also attempts to work these claims into the dominant republican ideology of the day.[85] Even Jefferson had moderated his views.[86] Nevertheless, the emerging worship of technological development and its apostles was far from being the unchallenged consensus. Against this backdrop, subordinating the farmer to the inventor was a bold attempt to reshape republican ideology and transform its traditional suspicion and disdain into a source of support.

Just as important was the sharp distinction between the inventor and the "mechanic," a distinction that was implicit in Barnes's pamphlet and that became explicit here. Traditionally the inventor was associated with the artisan. Even when technological development was praised, it was objectified and personified. Its agents were seen as those who had a high level of skill in the relevant "arts." The pamphlet represents an important break with this traditional approach. It constructs the inventor through opposition to the mechanic or the artisan. Although the pamphlet simply states the opposition without elaborating on it, its basis appears obvious from the depiction of the "inventive genius"[87] throughout the text. The defining trait of the inventor becomes not skill or the exercise of an art, but an intellectual capacity—"inventive talents"[88]—that results in innovative ideas. To be sure, Dearborn, Barnes, and many of those in whose name they saw themselves as speaking were not all that different from the traditional "mechanic." During the first half of the nineteenth century, many technological innovators were skilled machinists engaged in tinkering in small workshops.[89] Sharply distinguishing the inventor from the mechanic on the basis of his mental capacity and output was, thus, predominantly an ideological move.

Juxtaposing the inventor, the scientist, and the mechanic opened up a new semantic space between speculative-theoretical science and practical craft. The inventor was constructed as possessing the positive qualities of both of these spheres: the original, discovery-driven, and intellectual character of science, and the social usefulness of craft. By transcending both the merely theoretical and the completely practical, the inventor ends up being superior to both the scientist and the artisan. It is this duality that the pamphlet repeatedly uses in order to place the inventor above all the other archetypes with which he is contrasted. The outcome is identification between the inventor as the creator of technologically innovative ideas and social progress.

Like Barnes, the author of *Remarks on the Rights of Inventors* used the new image of the inventor as the individual creator of new ideas to conjure up the tropes of property and ownership, although in a somewhat more superficial manner. The pamphlet's strategy here was based on the establishment of a parallel between patents as ownership of inventions and traditional property, followed by appropriation of the justificatory power of the latter. The text asks the reader to consider the following case: "a clock-maker spends a month in his profession, and receives a bank-bill for his labour; this bill he deposits in his private drawer."[90] Next, the identification between the owner and the inventor is created through the hypothesis that the same clock maker "devotes the next month to the invention of a machine, by which he will be enabled to make two clocks in the time he had before required to make one. He conceals the description of the machine in the same private drawer."[91] At this point, the conclusion concocted by the juxtaposition of the two stories is assumed to be so obvious that it is simply stated: the invention "is the product of his labour, and it is as assuredly his property as the bill."[92] This was far from a deep or foolproof argument, but it was an effective legitimation tactic. Once the identification with traditional property rights was established, the pamphlet could simply frame all objections to patents as suggesting the "seiz[ure of] the inventor's property without his consent."[93] It then could reject such objections by using the powerful identification with property and appealing to the specter of a society in which "every man's estate is liable for confiscation."[94]

Again, when it came to translating the bold abstract claims of property and ownership to concrete practical terms, discontinuities surfaced. Presenting patents as identical to other property rights strongly implied perpetual duration. Yet such a demand was extremely unrealistic. Thus, even the author of the New England Association's pamphlet had to moderate the practical claims it made in the name of the inventor-owner. The pamphlet dealt with the gap between the ideal and reality with an admission that was framed as both noble and bitter. "As the practice of confiscating the inventor's discovery at some given period, has received the sanction of ancient usage," the pamphlet declared, the inventor "must expect no redress unless he can obtain an extension of the time, wherein he shall be indulged in the enjoyment of his right."[95] An 1806 petition submitted to Congress—"Address of the Advocate of the Patentees . . . in Defence of Mental Property—refined this technique of settling for less than what inventor-owners deserved by right.[96] The content and structure of the arguments suggest that this pamphlet was another product of the New-England Association's lobbying efforts. It repeated the claim that "mental property . . . is as justly and bona fide the property of those who thus acquire it as any real or personal property can be."[97] From the parallel with the tangible property owner followed the conclusion that the inventor, like "he who discovers a piece of vacant land[,] . . . is esteemed the right owner; it is secured to him, his heirs and assigns forever."[98] Returning to the harsh realties of Realpolitik, the pamphlet goes on to concede that "if this cannot be done, some good reasons would tend to convince the aggrieved, and might make them satisfied with less, say for and during the life of the inventor, and his heirs and assigns, to the third generation; or for fifty years certain."[99] "Any thing less," it stated, "would be to say—We want your property, and you must deliver it to us."[100]

PROPERTY IN IDEAS AND AMERICAN INTELLECTUAL PROPERTY DISCOURSE

By the early nineteenth century, people like Barnes and Dearborn had developed, as part of the political debates around state support for technological innovation, a peculiar new ideological construct of inventors as property owners. In this new construct, inventors became sharply distinct from the figures with whom they were indistinguishably associated in the past: the entrepreneur and the artisan. The new defining trait of the inventor was his individual intellectual abilities to create original and new ideas constituting technological innovation. This image supported, in turn, arguments about both moral desert and the social utility of inventors' property rights. All these elements combined to form a compelling ideological vision of inventors as individual owners of property rights in the intangible entities they created.

Did this ideological construct have a lasting effect beyond the local lobbying efforts of people like Barnes or organizations like the New England Association? The claim that inventors have a natural property right to their inventions, despite its growing popularity,[101] never achieved a consensus in the United States. The division between a positivist state privilege and natural right conceptions of patents (as well as the blurring of the two) persisted. The inventors-as-owners vision, however, became a powerful tool in public debates over the existence, scope, and strength of patent protection. Whenever the need arose, it was drawn out of the arsenal and deployed with at least some effectiveness, whether in justification of judicial "liberality" in the treatment of patents, in support of legislative amendments, or in pursuit of a lax approach by the Patent Office. In future times, when American society and economy changed, those who used such arguments were no longer exclusively individual inventors or their representatives. More often it was corporations whose innovation settings were far removed from the idealized image of the individual genius inventor-owner. The rhetorical strategy used in such cases usually followed that of Barnes and the New England Association: sweeping assertions about the broad and absolute nature of inventors' property, accompanied by more modest concrete claims.

The inventors-as-owners framework had another lasting effect—more subtle, but not less significant. Much of its basic assumptions were incorporated as part of the new understanding of intellectual property. Here the dominance of the new framework was more general. Its basic assumptions came to underlie the entire discourse of patents and invention. The field was now understood, whether from a natural rights or a utilitarian perspective, in terms of genius individuals creating new ideas and their ownership as a form of control over an informational object. Despite the general acceptance of this intellectual property paradigm in the early nineteenth century, later patent discourse was neither static nor predetermined. The basic framework, while defining the outline of patent debates and supplying their fundamental building blocks, left much room for maneuvering and could be concretized in multiple ways. Who exactly qualifies as an "inventor"? What exactly is the informational object of property? What does it mean to own or control such an object? All these questions could be answered in many, sometimes conflicting, ways. As changing economic, social, and ideological forces mediated by individual agency acted upon it, intellectual property discourse was filled with specific content, reworked, and reshaped. In later days, during the rise of corporate America, the specific content of patent discourse was often ironic or surprising, when looked upon from the vantage point of those who first developed the inventors-as-owners framework.

In these two senses—a specific natural rights argument and the comprehensive intellectual framework of the field—the intellectual property ideology created around 1800 is still with us. The dead hand of Joseph Barnes and Benjamin Dearborn, who invented the inventor-owner two centuries ago, still shapes our thinking about technological innovation, the people who create it, and their regulation by the state.

NOTES

1. Morton J. Horwitz, *The Transformation of American Law, 1870–1960: The Crisis of Legal Orthodoxy* (New York: Oxford University Press, 1992), 145.

2. 7 F. Cas. 197, 199 (C.C.D. Mass. 1845).

3. See, e.g., Martha Woodmansee and Peter Jaszi, eds., *The Construction of Authorship: Textual Appropriation in Law and Literature* (Durham, N.C.: Duke University Press, 1994), 16; Martha Woodmansee, "The Genius and the Copyright: Economic and Legal Conditions of the Emergence of the 'Author,'" *Eighteenth-Century Studies* 17 (1984): 425–48; Peter Jaszi,

"Toward a Theory of Copyright: The Metamorphosis of 'Authorship,'" *Duke Law Journal* 455 (1991): 455–502.

4. For a recent example of history writing in this vein, see Christine MacLeod, *Heroes of Invention: Technology, Liberalism and British Identity: 1750–1914* (New York: Cambridge University Press, 2007).

5. Louis C. Hunter, "The Heroic Theory of Invention," in *Technology and Social Change in America,* ed. Edwin T. Layton Jr., 25–46 (New York: Harper & Row, 1973).

6. C. B. MacPherson, *The Political Theory of Possessive Individualism: Hobbes to Locke* (Oxford: Clarendon Press, 1962).

7. Joseph Barnes, *Treatise on the Justice, Policy and Utility of Establishing an Effectual System for Promoting the Progress of Useful Arts by Assuring Property in the Products of Genius* (Philadelphia: Printed by Francis Bailey, 1792).

8. See Andrea Sutcliffe, *Steam: The Untold Story of America's First Great Invention* (New York: Palgrave Macmillan, 2004).

9. Barnes, *Treatise,* 5.

10. Neil Longley York, *Mechanical Metamorphosis: Technological Change in Revolutionary America* (Westport, Conn.: Greenwood Press, 1985), 6; Hugo A. Meier, "American Technology and the Nineteenth-Century World," *American Quarterly* 10 (1958): 117.

11. York, *Mechanical Metamorphosis*, 44–46.

12. See, e.g., Bruce W. Bugbee, *Genesis of American Patent and Copyright Law* (Washington, D.C.: Public Affairs Press, 1967); P. J. Federico, "Colonial Monopolies and Patents," *Journal of the Patent Office Society* 11 (1929): 358–65; E. B. Inlow, "The Patent Grant," *John Hopkins University Studies in Political Science* 67, no. 2 (1949): 36–43.

13. Nathaniel Shurtleff, ed., *Records of the Governor and Company of Massachusetts Bay in New England* (Boston: W. White, Printer to the Commonwealth, 1853–54), 1:331.

14. Ibid., 2:244.

15. Doron S. Ben-Atar, *Trade Secrets: Intellectual Piracy and the Origins of American Industrial Power* (New Haven, Conn.: Yale University Press, 2004), 23.

16. Shurtleff, *Records of the Governor,* 3:65.

17. James H. Trumbull and Hodlay Charles, eds., *The Public Records of the Colony of Connecticut, 1636–1776* (Hartford, Conn.: Press of the Case, Lockwood & Brainard Company, 1850–90), 231.

18. Meier, "American Technology," 117; John F. Kasson, *Civilizing the Machine: Technology and Republican Values in America, 1776–1900* (New York: Grossman, 1976), 1–21; Jennifer Clark, "The American Image of Technology from the Revolution to 1840," *American Quarterly* 39 (1987): 431–49.

19. Ben-Atar, *Trade Secrets,* 34–43; Kasson, *Civilizing the Machine,* 8–11.

20. Ben-Atar, *Trade Secrets,* 93–103; York, *Mechanical Metamorphosis*, 163–71.

21. The publication of Joseph Bigelow's *Elements of Technology* in 1829 is usually seen as the moment when the term "technology" started to diffuse into general usage. See Hugo A. Meier, "The Ideology of Technology," in Layton, *Technology and Social Change,* 80.

22. James T. Mitchell and Henry Flanders, eds., *The Statutes at Large of Pennsylvania from 1682 to 1801* (1896–1911), 9:412–15.

23. The patent statute was in fact a provision in the newly enacted copyright statute of the state. Thomas Cooper and David J. McCord, eds., *The Statutes at Large of South Carolina; Edited, under Authority of the Legislature* (Columbia, S.C.: A. S. Johnston, 1840), 6:618–20.

24. U.S. Const. art. 1, sec. 8, cl. 8.

25. Act of Apr. 10, 1790, ch. 7, 1 Stat. 109; Act of Feb. 21, 1793, ch. 11, 1 Stat. 318.

26. Ben-Atar, *Trade Secrets,* 44–77.

27. Eugene S. Ferguson, "Technology as Knowledge," in Layton, *Technology and Social Change,* 9.

28. Quoted in Ben-Atar, *Trade Secrets,* 79–80.

29. See, for example, Pennsylvania's 1789 grant to Robert Leslie, in Mitchell and Flanders, *The Statutes at Large of Pennsylvania,* 12:309–12; Maryland's 1787 patent to Robert Lemmon, session of November 6, 1786, through January 20, 1787, in *The Laws of Maryland,* ed. William Kilty, vol. 2 (Annapolis, Md., 1799–1800).

30. Edward C. Walterscheid, *To Promote the Progress of Useful Arts: American Patent Law and Administration, 1798–1836* (Littleton, Colo.: F. B. Rothman, 1998), 372–82.

31. See Oren Bracha, "Owning Ideas: A History of Anglo American Intellectual Property" (SJD diss., Harvard University, 2005), 114–15.

32. Cooper and McCord, *The Statutes at Large of South Carolina,* 5:71.

33. See Mario Biagioli, "Patent Republic: Representing Inventions, Constructing Rights and Authors," *Social Research* 73, no. 4 (2006).

34. See, e.g., Joseph Barnes, *Remarks on Mr. John Fitch's Reply to Mr. James Rumsey's Pamphlet* (1788). See also Sutcliffe, *Steam,* 113–14; Walterscheid, *To Promote the Progress,* 186–89.

35. Sutcliffe, *Steam,* 5–7.

36. Ibid., 7–9.

37. Margaret E. Lippencott, "Dearborn's Musical Scheme," *New York Historical Society Quarterly Bulletin* 25 (1941): 137–38; Emma Forbes Waite, "Benjamin Dearborn, Teacher, Inventor, Philanthropist," *Old Time New England* 42 (1951): 44–45.

38. Lippencott, "Dearborn's Musical Scheme," 140; Waite, "Benjamin Dearborn," 46.

39. Lippencott, "Dearborn's Musical Scheme," 139–40; Waite, "Benjamin Dearborn," 46; "Commissioner of Patents' Report: Concluding Remarks," *Scientific American* 6 (1850): 93.

40. "Miscellaneous Articles of Literary and Philosophical Intelligence," *Monthly Magazine and American Review* 2 (1799–1800): 156.

41. *Rules and Regulations Adopted October 22nd, 1807 by the Association of Inventors and Patrons of Useful Arts* (1807), sec. 1.

42. Ibid., sec. 15.

43. York, *Mechanical Metamorphosis,* 183–206; Kasson, *Civilizing the Machine,* 14–36.

44. Benjamin Franklin to John Lining, Mar. 8, 1755, in *The Papers of Benjamin Franklin,* ed. Leonard W. Labaree (New Haven, Conn.: Yale University Press, 1962), 5:526–27.

45. James Rumsey, *A Short Treatise on the Application of Steam: Whereby is clearly shewn, from actual experiments, that steam may be applied to propel boats or vessels of any burthen against rapid currents with great velocity* (1788).

46. P. J. Federico, "The Patent Trials of Oliver Evans," *Journal of the Patent Office Society* 27 (1945): 590; Walterscheid, *To Promote the Progress,* 406–9; Eugene S. Ferguson, *Oliver Evans: Inventive Genius of the American Industrial Revolution* (Greenville, Del.: Hagley Museum, 1980).

47. Oliver Evans, *A Trip Made by a Small Man in a Wrestle with a Very Great Man* (1814), 3.

48. Barnes, *Treatise,* 6–7.

49. Thomas G. Fessenden, *An Essay on the Law of Patents for New Inventions* (Boston: D. Mallory, 1810).

50. "Origin of Arts," *Useful Cabinet* 1 (Jan. 1808): 21.

51. Ibid., 21–22.

52. Ibid., 22.

53. *Useful Cabinet* 1 (Jan. 1808): 1.

54. Ibid., 3.

55. See Mark Rose, *Authors and Owners: The Invention of Copyright* (Cambridge, Mass.: Harvard University Press, 1993).

56. Barnes, *Treatise,* 6.

57. Ibid., 4.

58. Ibid.

59. Ibid., 5.

60. Ibid., 4.

61. Ibid., 12–13.

62. Ibid., 4–5.

63. Ibid., 12.

64. Ibid., 5.

65. Ibid., 16.

66. Ibid., 25.

67. See Rose, *Authors and Owners,* 54.

68. For the different views in Britain during the nineteenth-century debates, see H. I. Dutton, *The Patent System and Inventive Activity during the Industrial Revolution, 1750–1852* (Dover, N.H.: Manchester University Press, 1984), 17–33.

69. See Bracha, "Owning Ideas," 235–240.

70. See Oren Bracha, "The Commodification of Patents 1600–1836: How Patents Became Rights and Why We Should Care," *Loyola of Los Angeles Law Review* 38 (2004): 192–200.

71. Barnes, *Treatise,* 12.

72. *Wheaton v. Peters,* 33 U.S. 591 (1834).

73. *Remarks on the Rights of Inventors and the Influence of Their Studies in Promoting the Enjoyments of Life and Public Prosperity* (1807).

74. See *Journal of the House of Representatives of the United States* 6 (Jan. 30, 1808): 151.

75. *Remarks on the Rights of Inventors,* 1.

76. Ibid., 8.

77. Ibid., 4.

78. Ibid.

79. See Meier, "American Technology," 81–83; Meier, "The Ideology of Technology," 124–25.

80. "Introduction," *Useful Cabinet* 1 (Jan. 1808): 3.

81. *Remarks on the Rights of Inventors,* 8.

82. Gordon S. Wood, *The Creation of the American Republic, 1776–1787* (Chapel Hill: Published for the Institute of Early American History and Culture at Williamsburg by the University of North Carolina Press, 1969), 32–35, 65–70, 107–14.

83. Drew E. McCoy, *The Elusive Republic: Political Economy in Jeffersonian America* (Chapel Hill: Published for the Institute of Early American History and Culture at Williamsburg by the University of North Carolina Press, 1980), 48–69, 107–19.

84. Thomas Jefferson, "Notes on the State of Virginia," in *The Portable Thomas Jefferson,* ed. Merill D. Peterson New York: Viking Press, 1975), 217. See Ben-Atar, *Trade Secrets,* 119–21.

85. Kasson, *Civilizing the Machine,* 14.

86. See Ben-Atar, *Trade Secrets,* 119–21; Clark, "The American Image of Technology," 438–39.

87. *Remarks on the Rights of Inventors,* 10.

88. Ibid., 7.

89. See, e.g., Paul Israel, *From Machine Shop to Industrial Laboratory: Telegraphy and the Changing Context of American Invention, 1830–1920* (Baltimore, Md.: Johns Hopkins University Press, 1992), 18; Nathan Rosenberg, "Technological Change in the Machine Tool Industry, 1840–1910," *Journal of Economic History* 23 (1963): 414–43.

90. *Remarks on the Rights of Inventors,* 8.

91. Ibid.

92. Ibid.

93. Ibid., 9.

94. Ibid.

95. Ibid., 11.

96. *Address of the Advocate of the Patentees Inventors of Useful Improvements in the Arts and Sciences* (1806).

97. Ibid., 11.

98. Ibid.

99. Ibid., 10.

100. Ibid.

101. See Adam Mossoff, "Who Cares What Thomas Jefferson Thought about Patents? Reevaluating the Patent 'Privilege' in Historical Context," *Cornell Law Review* 92 (2007): 953–1012.

18

Morton Horwitz and the Teaching of American Legal History

DANIEL W. HAMILTON

DESPITE AN INCREASE IN SEMINARS AND SOME MOVES TOWARD SMALLER classes, the traditional model for successful law teaching remains, for the most part, a distinguished professor teaching great big classes, a powerful figure who is impressive, imposing, at times inspiring, yet still distant and even remote. Mort Horwitz is certainly a famous teacher of torts to first-year students at Harvard Law School, and he does fit within this traditional model. Yet he also has brought the PhD model for training new scholars into the law school and in doing so has helped shape a field over three decades and more.

In humanities departments inside universities, PhD students are linked to their faculty advisors like apprentices to masters in a medieval guild. We meet in small groups and then meet one-on-one with our advisors, discussing books and reading our chapters as they slowly emerge. It is a relationship that often lasts several years, culminating in a PhD dissertation, and in the process we generally tie our professional development to a small circle of advisors, with one faculty member usually taking the lead. To stay with the medieval analogy, PhD advising is, as Mort Horwitz told me in our first meeting, a remnant of feudalism that is alive and well in academe.

The drawbacks of this system are legion and well known. Will our advisor make time for us to talk over books and to read and discuss our work? Will we be treated as budding scholars or as a mostly anonymous cog in the machine? Will our advisor help launch us out into the profession, or will we fend for ourselves making the transition from student to professor?

Still, the benefits of this system are quite compelling, and when it works, it works well, which may be why it has lasted so long. Nothing is as enriching for a graduate student as talking seriously over time about ideas and scholarship and, ultimately, talking over the kind of work we want to do with someone who has made his or her mark. Attentive advisors can in ways large and small, over the course of years, continually open up new ways of understanding scholarly questions, help us challenge conventional wisdom, and most of all train us to do so without them.

Mort Horwitz is one of the few and certainly one of the best law professors to bring this PhD model into the law school. Students at Harvard, in the history department and in the History of American Civilization Program, often came to Harvard to work with him. This is itself rare. While law professors frequently serve on PhD committees, it is still exceptional for a student in a humanities program to go to a university in order to work with a law professor as a primary advisor. There are of course exceptions, but Mort is at the head of a short list. The question is, why did we seek him out, and why did he seek us out?

Part of the answer is that time spent working with Mort represents the best in PhD training and advising. At Harvard, Mort figured out how to get a magic number in the course catalog in history and in American civilization, and we graduate students could then fill out the necessary forms to take a field with him in preparation for our general exams and also add him to our PhD committees. From then on, he found students, and students found him. Soon, those not enrolled in PhD programs also began to seek Mort out, whether as a formal advisor for a third-year law school paper or simply to talk legal history. Over the years, Mort advised PhD students at Brandeis, and also students who came to work with him in the Harvard SJD program from Israel. In recent years he has helped train budding historians, as undergraduates taking his courses at Harvard College have also sought him out in Pound Hall.

All of us, together, are Horwitz students, and he has trained us, whatever our institutional relationship, as legal historians. He has been instrumental in helping shape several dozen PhD dissertations, many of which have become important books, including those by contributors to this volume. He has talked for countless hours with nervous grad students preparing for generals, sharing his insight and listening to endless questions posed to him about history, or how to frame a dissertation, or how to give a job talk. He has read still more chapters, papers, dissertation drafts, and law review articles. Perhaps most important, he has instilled confidence, challenged us to do our best work, and spent time dedicating himself to shaping students into scholars and teachers. He has, in short, acted over the course of decades as a model advisor. For someone widely known as one of the top scholars in his field, it is remarkable that he is equally well known as a teacher, not only for his classroom instruction, but also for helping to continually produce professors in law schools and history departments.

He has done all this inside a law school, a place where great teaching is valued, but where substantive conversation with students is often limited to office hours. For more than thirty years, Mort has taught a full load of law school courses, even as we students took up his afternoons talking over the reading list he provided. We asked, sometimes more than once, if he had read our most recent chapter yet, and then if he had read our dissertation, and could we talk it over and if he could write us a letter of recommendation, and maybe also make a call on our behalf. He did this for students across departments, and inside the law school, for students at Harvard and elsewhere. It's a wonder he wrote any scholarships at all, let alone books and articles that are of course landmarks within the field.

The result of such dedication to teaching is that there are so many of us who call ourselves Horwitz students. We do not share a party line, and Mort has never asked us—in fact, has actively resisted any attempts—to emulate his own work too closely. Equally impressive, as this volume makes clear, Howitz students teach and write across eras and across countries. His work is so varied and so original that we students have many choices. There is important Horwitz work on the colonial and antebellum eras in American legal history, on the Gilded Age and the New Deal, and on the Warren Court, all of which has drawn students in these fields. There is also methodological variety, and just as Horwitz's earlier work examines the relationship between law and the market and his more recent work explores American legal thought, so his students have gone to him and produced important work that reflects each methodology. His role as a teacher has international implications too, as several distinguished Israeli legal historians have sought Mort out as an advisor.

By now, there is a whole cadre of professors at law schools and history departments across the country and even across the world who call themselves Horwitz students. In fact, it may be that Morton Horwitz's biggest contribution to the field of American legal history is as a teacher. From the books we assign to the books we write, to the lectures we give, to the way we ourselves advise PhD students, our work bears the imprint of Professor Horwitz and affects those who have never read either volume of *The Transformation of American Law*. We steal his jokes, appropriate his "framing devices," crib from his reading lists, and ask our students the questions he once asked us. More than that, Mort has trained by now more than a generation of his students never to accept the easy answer, to press for original insights, to challenge claims of neutrality by judges and other scholars, and to treat our students as our advisor treated us.

It is rare that a festschrift is produced for a law professor by his own students. That this book exists is testimony to one of the chief accomplishments of Mort Horwitz's career—training a generation of legal historians. Within the field of American legal history he has brought the model of graduate advising into one of the world's best law schools, and students across the world, and across Harvard Yard, have sought him out at Harvard Law School. It was there, in his office, over the course of hours and years talking legal history, and everything else under the sun, including national politics, faculty politics, wine, Broadway musicals, literature, and Renaissance art, that so many of us first took our place as members of this profession and as teachers ourselves. As in so much of his work, in bringing the best of graduate training inside the law school, Mort was innovative and influential. In a career marked by groundbreaking scholarship, it is extraordinary that Mort Horwitz has had equal, perhaps greater, impact on the field as a teacher of American legal history.

About the Contributors

MARY SARAH BILDER is professor of law and a Law School Fund Scholar at Boston College. She is the author of *The Transatlantic Constitution: Colonial Legal Culture and the Empire* and is currently writing a book on James Madison's notes of the Constitutional Convention titled "Madison's Hand."

ELIZABETH BLACKMAR is professor of history at Columbia University. She the author of *Manhattan for Rent, 1785–1850* and co-author with Roy Rosenzweig of *The Park and People: A History of Central Park*. Her most recent articles have been on the history of REITs and on the ideological discourse of the "tragedy of commons."

OREN BRACHA is assistant professor of law at the University of Texas School of Law. Bracha is a legal historian and an intellectual property law scholar. His forthcoming book *Owning Ideas* is an intellectual history of American intellectual property law in the nineteenth century.

ALFRED L. BROPHY is the Reef C. Ivey II professor of law at the University of North Carolina. He is the author of *Reconstructing the Dreamland: The Tulsa Riot of 1921—Race, Reparations, Reconciliation* and *Reparations Pro and Con*, and he is completing a study of jurisprudence in the old South, tentatively titled "University, Court, and Slave."

CHARLES DONAHUE JR. is the Paul A. Freund Professor of Law at Harvard Law School. He is the immediate past president of the American Society for Legal History, and the author of a number of works in the field, most recently *Law, Marriage, and Society in the Later Middle Ages: Arguments about Marriage in Five Courts*. He is currently working on the fourteenth-century volume of the *Oxford History of the Laws of England.*

LEWIS A. GROSSMAN is professor of law at American University's Washington College of Law. He is the author of "James Coolidge Carter and Mugwump Jurisprudence," *Law and History Review*; "Langdell Upside-Down: James Coolidge Carter and the Anticlassical Jurisprudence of Anticodification," *Yale Journal of Law & the Humanities*; and "Food, Drugs, and Droods: A Historical Consideration of Definitions and Categories in American Food and Drug Law," *Cornell Law Review*.

He won the 2005 George Washington Egleston Prize for the best dissertation in the field of American history at Yale University.

SALLY E. HADDEN is an associate professor of history and law at Florida State University. She is the author of *Slave Patrols: Law and Violence in Virginia and the Carolinas*, and a contributor to the *Cambridge History of Law in America*. Her current research focuses upon law in three eighteenth-century cities: Boston, Philadelphia, and Charleston.

DANIEL W. HAMILTON is professor of law at the University of Illinois College of Law, and co-director of the Illinois Legal History Program. He is the author of *The Limits of Sovereignty: Property Confiscation in the Union and the Confederacy in the Civil War.* His work examines property ideology and constitutional history in the era of the Civil War and Reconstruction.

DANIEL J. HULSEBOSCH is professor of law and history at New York University School of Law. He is the author of *Constituting Empire: New York and the Transformation of Constitutionalism in the Atlantic World, 1664–1830* and is writing another book tentatively titled "Crafting Authority: Chancellor Kent and the Development of American Law." Throughout his work he explores the relationships between migration, territorial expansion, and the development of legal institutions and doctrines.

ELENA KAGAN, the Charles Hamilton Houston Professor of Law, is the 11th Dean of Harvard Law School. Kagan joined the faculty of Harvard Law School in 2001. While on the faculty, Kagan has taught administrative law, constitutional law, civil procedure, and a seminar on the law surrounding the presidency. During her tenure as dean, she has focused her energies on a wide range of priorities, including expanding the faculty, improving the quality of student life, renovating the campus, updating the curriculum, and deepening the school's commitment to public service.

ALISON L. LACROIX is assistant professor of law at the University of Chicago Law School. She is currently completing a study of federal ideas in the United States between 1754 and 1801, tentatively titled "A Well-Constructed Union: An Intellectual History of American Federalism."

ASSAF LIKHOVSKI is the director of the Cegla Center for Interdisciplinary Research of the Law and an associate professor at Tel Aviv University Faculty of Law. He has published articles and books on legal history, comparative law, taxation and the sociology of law, including *Law and Identity in Mandate Palestine*, which received the 2007 Shapiro book award for best book in Israel studies.

GREGORY MARK is a professor of law and the Justice Nathan Jacobs Scholar at the Rutgers Law School, Newark, where he also serves as associate dean for institutional planning and affairs and is a member of the university's Graduate Faculty in History. His work is in the history of the law and the political economy, especially the legal history of the business corporation.

DALIA TSUK MITCHELL is an associate professor of law at George Washington University. She is the author of *Architect of Justice: Felix S. Cohen and the Founding of American Legal Pluralism,* winner of the American Historical Association's Littleton-Griswold Award. She is currently working on a book tentatively titled "Corporate Law and the American Reform Tradition." It focuses on the interdependence between the history of corporate law and theory and the development of the modern American state.

POLLY J. PRICE is professor of law and associate dean of faculty at Emory University School of Law, and an associated faculty member of Emory's Department of History. In addition to numerous articles on legal history topics, she is the author of *Property Rights,* and a forthcoming biography of federal judge Richard S. Arnold, to be published in 2009.

CHRISTOPHER W. SCHMIDT is a visiting scholar at the American Bar Foundation and a visiting associate professor at Chicago-Kent College of Law. He received his PhD in the history of American civilization from Harvard University in 2004 and his JD from Harvard Law School in 2007. He is the author of several articles on civil rights law and legal history and is currently at work on a book manuscript, titled "Creating *Brown v. Board of Education*: Ideology and Constitutional Change, 1945–1960."

STEPHEN A. SIEGEL is the associate dean for research, scholarship, and faculty development, and Distinguished Research Professor of Law, at the DePaul University College of Law. His writing focuses on the history of common-law thought and nineteenth- and twentieth-century constitutional development.

WILLIAM MICHAEL TREANOR is dean and Paul Fuller Professor of Law at Fordham Law School. His academic work has focused on the original understanding of the Constitution.

STEVEN WILF is professor of law at the University of Connecticut. He is the author of *The Law before the Law*, which examines the meaning of law that exists prior to a law.

Index